PERIPHERY AND CENTRE

STUDIES IN ORISSAN SOCIETY, CULTURE AND HISTORY

Editors: HERMANN KULKE and BURKHARD SCHNEPEL

Vol. 1: Jagannath Revisited: Studying Society, Religion and the State in Orissa, edited by Hermann Kulke and Burkhard Schnepel

Vol. 2: The Jungle Kings: Ethnohistorical Aspects of Politics and Ritual in Orissa, by Burkhard Schnepel

Vol. 3: Text and Context in the History, Literature and Religion of Orissa, edited by Angelika Malinar, Johannes Beltz and Heiko Frese

Vol. 4: Altar of Power: The Temple and the State in the Land of Jagannatha, by Yaaminey Mubayi

Vol. 5: The Aghria: A Peasant Caste on a Tribal Frontier, by Uwe Skoda

Vol. 6: Time in India: Concepts and Practices, edited by Angelika Malinar

Vol. 7: Periphery and Centre: Studies in Orissan History, Religion and Anthropology, edited by Georg Pfeffer

PERIPHERY AND CENTRE

Studies in Orissan History, Religion and Anthropology

Edited by

GEORG PFEFFER

MANOHAR
2007

First published 2007

ISBN 81-7304-691-3

Published by
Ajay Kumar Jain for
Manohar Publishers & Distributors
4753/23, Ansari Road, Daryaganj
New Delhi 110 002

Printed at
Lordson Publishers Pvt. Ltd
Delhi 110 007

Distributed in South Asia by
FOUNDATION BOOKS
4381/4, Ansari Road
Daryaganj, New Delhi 110 002
and its branches at Mumbai, Hyderabad,
Bangalore, Chennai, Kolkata

Contents

Contributors

RAVI AHUJA is at the Department of History, South Asia Institute, Heidelberg; Centre for Modern Oriental Studies, Berlin.

N.J. ALLEN is Chair, Anthropology of South Asia, Oxford University.

SUSMITA ARP is at the Department of History, University of Kiel.

JOHANNES BELTZ is with Museum Rietberg, Zurich; Department of Religious Studies, University of Zurich.

PETER BERGER is at the Department of Anthropology, Free University of Berlin.

GEORG BERKEMER is at the Department of History, South Asia Institute, Heidelberg.

MARTIN BRANDTNER is at the Department of History, University of Kiel.

LIDIA J. GUZY is at the Institute for Academic Studies of Religions, Free University of Berlin.

ROLAND HARDENBERG is at the Department of Anthropology, Free University of Berlin.

BEATRIX HAUSER is at the Research Centre on Aesthetic Experience, Free University of Berlin.

BARBARA LOTZ is at the Department of Indology, University of Wuerzburg.

ANGELIKA MALINAR is at the Department of Indology, School of Oriental and African Studies, London.

CORNELIA MALLEBREIN is at the Department of Indology and Religious Studies, University of Tuebingen.

BABA MISHRA is at the Government College, Bhavanipatna, Orissa.

PRADEEP MOHANTY is at the Department of Archaeology and Ancient Indian History, Deccan College, Pune.

CHANDI PRASAD NANDA is at the Academic Staff College, Utkal University, Bhubaneswar.

TINA OTTEN is at the Department of Anthropology, Free University of Berlin; South Asia Institute, Heidelberg.

BISWAMOY PATI is at the Department of History, Venkatesvara College, University of Delhi.

GEORG PFEFFER is at the Department of Anthropology, Free University of Berlin.

UWE SKODA is at the Department of Anthropology, Free University of Berlin; Department of Political Science, University of Rostock.

CHRISTIAN STRÜMPELL is at the Department of Anthropology, Free University of Berlin.

PAUL YULE is at the Department of Languages and Cultures of the Near East, University of Heidelberg.

1

Introduction

Georg Pfeffer

The eastern Indian province of Orissa is not a very prominent region. To this day most inhabitants of the subcontinent, just like academic specialists on India all over the world, associate the land on the river Mahanadi with a rather limited thematic spectrum such as the natural calamities that seem to cause havoc regularly in the form of droughts, floods, cyclones, or tornados. In a more positive context, the ancient temples of Puri, Konarak and Bhubaneswar, or, older still, Asoka's rock inscription of the third century BC, the landmark initiating the long epoch of Buddhist history before the renaissance of Brahminism, serve as witnesses of happier events.

Indians, i.e. Orissans themselves as well as others, like to, with grave concern, debate the 'backwardness' of the province. Such a perspective, confined to the political economy, is shared by Westerners who otherwise might direct their interest towards Orissa's mineral wealth or the beauty of the natural resorts. Given such a superficial general mood, an Indo-German interdisciplinary research project of the human sciences endeavoured, in the early 1970s, to proceed beyond the clichés by a study of what appeared to be the cultural centre of Orissa: the sacred complex of Jagannath, the Lord of the World, i.e. the medieval royal temple in the coastal town of Puri, visited by millions of pilgrims every year. Numerous publications (see Eschmann et al. 1978) were the outcome of our combined indological, historical, and anthropological efforts and, after initial complications,[1] our results received a positive response even in the academic circles in the capital complex of Bhubaneswar and Cuttack. Moreover, the religiously engaged scholar honoured as the 'King of Puri' by the temple and numerous believers went so far as to suggest to me that, in case of a reprint, the title of our key publication should be changed from *The Cult*... to *The Culture of Jagannath*.

---

[1] Hopefully, we will never forget how Dr. R.K. Nayak, then Secretary to the Government of Orissa, helped us to overcome severe misunderstandings in that formative phase.

However, over the years, we began to question our initial hypothesis, doubtlessly born out of ignorance, proposing the existence of a neat, centrally administrated religious, economic, and political system which, during the course of a millennium, had been organized in the delta of the Mahanadi. A certain feeling, not altogether uncommon among ethnographers all over the world, indicated that our 'centre' had achieved such a status simply because we had engaged ourselves on a rather conspicuous spot without much information of the world beyond, thus projecting our own conventional religious, administrative and economic criteria of a system upon an unknown socio-cultural entity or mode of integration. Several members of the original research team had indeed subsequently intensified their research efforts and, after a widening of horizons in several directions, had entered into exciting new fields of popular movements and convictions or of non-centralized social systems that had remained unnoticed by news media or the academic world. As a result, Dash, Kulke, Pfeffer, von Stietencron, and Tripathi of the first project agreed to join hands with many younger colleagues in a new interdisciplinary team, as is represented in this volume, to engage in investigations beyond the geographical and social impact of the ancient and modern capital or the other religious or commercial agglomerations of the delta.

The second Orissa Research Project that started in the last year of the old century conceived several centres in the province, none of which was, as such, uncontested, just as not a single set of ritual conventions or an exclusive system of status allocation was taken for granted, leave alone overall political cohesiveness. Of the state's some 40 million inhabitants, about half live in the fertile lowlands on the Bay of Bengal and the Great River, with the other half spreading over the vast hilly and mountainous hinterland in the west. Neither in the whole province nor within each of these two major ecological zones could we agree on a pervasive homogeneous cult or a unified account of values.

The villages in the circle around Puri and the grand Jagannath temple are, for example, mainly inhabited both by Vedic Brahmins who conceive themselves as immigrant orthodox intellectuals from the Gangetic plain, and by Bauri coconut pluckers, at times named Savara ('tribals'), who cultivate the Brahmin land. While the 'untouchable' Bauri may remain unmentioned or unmentionable in public discourse, they are yet a major segment of the local population. Because they remain formally unnoticed, the sacred centre is assumed to adhere to a unified, i.e. Brahminical, system of conduct, while such an observation is certainly relativized once the subaltern segment is also taken into consideration. The partial view, however, seems to be the exclusive one. Within the cloak of a Brahminical religious and economic order, rather different socio-cultural values maintain a less conspicuous existence. The second Orissa Project (1999-2005) aimed to investigate these less obvious cultural traits and social contexts in the province, just as it was to engage in research efforts of several disciplines that had been left aside so far.

Initially, for example, the archaeologists M. Brandtner, B. Misra, P. Mohanty, and P. Yule show that *all* of western Orissa remains, to a large extent, archaeologically a *terra incognita*, though these scholars are presently engaged in altering this condition. Their inquiry is concerned with the interface between the so-called Iron Age (of south and central India) and the early historic period, i.e. the second half of the first millennium BC. The main archaeological feature of this age, the megaliths, is underrepresented in Orissa, but this may simply be due to the lack of research efforts, or to the fact that old megalithic constructions are frequently taken apart on being recycled at new settings, since, as I have personally witnessed, megaliths are erected to this day during the grand death ceremonies of several tribal communities. One archaeological priority endeavours to reconstruct the ancient funerary practices to define this temporal horizon of the Iron Age locally, while a second priority investigates the early historic fort horizon, incipient urbanization, and state formation along thc Tcl and Mahanadi valleys, i.e. in a part of western Orissa that reveals contacts with the coastal strip *and* with the Gangetic plains since the Mauryan period of the fourth and third centuries BC. The interface of the prehistoric megalithic culture with early historic urbanism may have included the transition from tribal to early state structures, a process which, quite amazingly, has, to the present day, not been concluded in Orissa.

The continued and vital presence of tribal features is undoubtedly the most exciting aspect of the contesting socio-religious contexts in Orissa, but these features have to be noted with care. Apart from an insignificant Muslim and Christian minority, all Orissans are counted as Hindus by the decennial Census operations and understand themselves as Hindus in common parlance. The category 'Hindu' does not exclude 'tribal' people, though caste and other Brahminical concepts may be absent in a tribal village. My inclusive concept of 'Hinduism' may best be illustrated by Angelika Malinar's contribution to this volume, the research among the followers of Sri Caitanya and their institutions, i.e. *matha* and *asrama*. This saint of the 15th and 16th century was, and is to the present day, forcefully rejected by the Vedic Brahmins of Puri while, at the same time, his monastic order and his lay support are strongly represented in the holy city and in many other towns. Very little has so far been published on Hindu monasteries, and Dr. Malinar's innovative field research can show that these institutions, though recognizing Puri as their centre, do not follow particular administrative directives. Caitanya's teachings has been preserved through different 'teacher-disciple-lineages', ordered by 'spiritual genealogies' so that, in analogy to the segmentary spreading of descent systems, spiritual connections within the movement could have numerous and contestant sub-centres that might or might not recognize one another. Diversification at the middle and lower levels is the method of the movement's expansion.

The grand monuments of orthodoxy in the delta region are the interlinked temple complexes of Jajpur, Bhubaneswar, Puri, and Konarak, and of these, popular narrative as well as academic consensus point to Viraja of Jajpur as the most ancient site. This emphasis on seniority is a major attribute of the Goddess' sacredness. However, after a thorough examination of a considerable corpus of Sanskrit manuscripts, Susmita Arp shows in this volume that, compared to the others, the Jajpur temple must be attributed to a much later period. She is also suggesting that the Goddess may have achieved her elevated rank due to a dominant trend to endow the coastal region with all the major Hindu deities, *after* royal followers had constructed the splendid temples of Siva and Vishnu at Bhubaneswar and Puri in the first centuries of the second millennium AD.

It follows that the major Brahminical sacred complexes of Orissa were diversified from an early age onwards, with the deities of the major temples being mutually related and positioned as spouses, siblings or affines, and their respective entourage of priestly servants being permanently engaged in domestic routine and life-cycle rituals, both on a divine or macroscopic level and on their own ordinarily micro-level with kin and affines in human households. The subsequent medieval *bhakti* movement of Sri Caitanya was averse to Brahmins and priestly institutions, and was rather conceptualized in 'spiritual genealogies' of 'teacher-disciple lineages' that represent the segmentary order, as shown above. Furthermore, Johannes Beltz provides an example of yet another ascetic movement, propagated by rural and lower castes during the colonial period, that arose in protest against 'idol worship' as such and was also, very soon after its inception, diversified into numerous contesting factions. Dr. Beltz narrates how Mukund Das, the founder of this Mahima Dharma movement, experimented in several different cults at a number of sacred sites before establishing his own ascetic religion which was once again marked by 'extraordinary and often contradictory diversity of local configurations'. Beltz tries to demonstrate how the movement intended to undermine the 'hegemony' of Puri and 'decentralize' or 'democratize the sacred power' in Orissa to the extent of even questioning the authority of its own newly established headquarters at Joranda in the inland Dhenkanal district. The figure of Mukund Das' disciple Bhima Bhoi is presently employed by the political proponents of a contemporary western Orissan separatist movement, just as the current leaders of this trend tend to shift their loyalties regularly from one branch of Mahima Dharma to another.

The three examples of a grand, orthodox and Brahmin-dominated temple complex in the delta, of the monastic institutions spread over the whole province and run by the devotional Caitanya movement, and of the ascetic rural and low caste inland-based Mahima Dharma religion born in colonial times all share the 'kinship' concepts in communal organization, i.e. the inability or unwillingness to cope with legalistic manifestations while preferring a kind of association that includes *both* patronage and symmetric exchanges, *both* unquestioned authority and fraternal loyalties or rivalries as long as *both*, submission and protest, commonality and segmentation, are expressed in highly emotional or 'genuine' and familistic gestures, proclamations and classification. Our European tradition may induce us to look for clarity in either institutional stability, or in reform, or even revolt, but I think familistic proximity and diversification, authority and rivalry as simultaneous and ongoing processes should be regarded as a durable organizational mode.

If millennia have seen tribal society as an ongoing process of segmentation (along lines of marriage and descent), the medieval Hindu kingdom, a mode of integration depending upon universalist ritual submission and maternalistic or paternalistic authority, may very well be defined by ongoing processes of cohesion and dissent, as is commonly experienced in the joint family, i.e. a system simultaneously and inevitably stressing and questioning kinship values, the members' common basis that is bound to disintegrate. A central authority may thus claim to exclude external ties while, at the same time, it may use the language of such patterns as a link to other divine authorities, devotional centres or reformist movements. Colonial and post-colonial times have also given way to socio-religious protest and innovation that were able to adapt, and could be adapted into, such fissiparous and combinatory processes rendering constant instability as the stable factor of their existence and diversification as the unifying trend.

Such a general pattern of Orissan institutionalised religion is slightly modified by the perspective of the tribal area. Lidia Guzy, like Johannes Beltz in another subregion, initially studied the Mahima Dharma religion in the central Dhenkanal district and, beyond the work on literature, engaged in ethnographic style, i.e. by long-term 'participant observation' in the company of male migratory ascetics. For reasons of comparison she then changed to a second site, a village of the tribal Rona in the distant south-western Koraput district of the hills, in order to understand the impact of the Mahima Dharma mission upon the 'people of the wilderness'. Here, professional and migratory ascetics are only secondary actors, whereas the new religion, called *Alekh* ('no-writing') in the hills, is represented and upheld by the indigenous female position of a *gurumai* who, in trance, is able to enter the world beyond to draw upon a rich body of poetry and oral traditions and to offer therapeutic as well as prophetic support to any visitor. These female ascetics, in obvious contrast to their tribal co-villagers, fast and abstain from meat and alcohol, just as they refuse participation in blood sacrifices for the village shrine, while their conspicuous performance, their divination and ecstasy, must be seen within the traditional tribal forms of possession and worship. They are also 'married' to a particular God and, in a manner comparable to the shamanism of the tribal Sora as described by Vitebsky (1993), they meet their lovers in the world beyond. The new asceticism, a dramatic inversion of tribal devotional intoxication, demonstrates how the opposed behavioural extreme can lead to very similar results in performance, while these traditional ritual expressions have very little in common with the Mahima Dharma religion as practiced in the environment of Dhenkanal caste society. Thus the missionary activities, as directed by the headquarters in that district, have neither spread a standard set of beliefs nor a definitive liturgical conformity, while such deviant thought and worship, adapted to tribal forms of ecstasy, have nowhere been a cause of concern. Consequently, it may be time to reconsider the concept of 'mission' far beyond the given case.

An explicit critique of, perhaps outdated, Western attempts to contain several manifestations of Hinduism within a number of mutually exclusive definitions of the Brahminical, the folk and the tribal kind is offered in the contribution of Beatrix Hauser. She presents three ethnographic examples of Goddess worship in the Berhampur region of coastal Orissa, i.e. initially that of unmarried girls to find 'a good husband'; secondly the annual fire walking ceremonies amidst, *horribile dictu*, women camping on the main cremation ground to watch blood sacrifices and the consumption of alcohol in a spectacular reversal of the standard behavioural norms; and, finally, the three-week-long worship of Berhampur's tutelary Goddess conducted in familistic style and attracting hundreds of thousands of pilgrims. By introducing these examples, Dr. Hauser intends to reject a concept of Hinduism in general and of the Goddess in particular that is viewed within a kind of evolutionary sequence ranging from a uniconic bloodthirsty tribal deity via a pan-Indian warrior Goddess to a pacified and homely Brahminical object of veneration. The author refutes the (perhaps German) tradition of tracing 'influences' and historical transformations in order to 'explain' diversity or opposition. In fact, she detects 'conflicting knowledge systems which are based not only on textual but on oral or even embodied communication' and pleads for context-bound research emphasizing, besides the components of the ritual, the mode of communication for a particular audience.

Any observer would probably agree with Dr. Hauser, since for example the 'ludic element' of Hinduism is obviously omnipresent at the annual Holi festival, and even in the most orthodox circles, tantric practices may go together with regular moderation, as may be exemplified by the swift procedure of sacrificing some 60 goats and sheep that I witnessed at the village temple of orthodox Vedic Brahmins. The concept of 'encompassing the contrary' (Dumont 1980, 240) has clarified such a relational worldview that cannot be defined by certain isolated and fixed criteria of behaviour or material form, just as Dumont's extended fieldwork among notorious 'robbers' (1986) presented Hindus of the rather explicitly non-Brahminical kind. In other words, formal manifestations of purity and pollution, e.g. vegetarianism and cremation grounds, may stand for the priority of certain value-ideas at one level, only to be reversed at another level of social classification. Roland Hardenberg's article is devoted to such methodological issues, i.e. Dumont's idea of 'context' and 'level', to overcome a trendy anthropological particularism, resting on subjectivity and situation, though Dr. Hardenberg has no intention of falling into the opposite extreme of imposing an analytical straightjacket for social analysis. In fact, he is pleading for the 'old fashioned' approach—when compared to postmodern proposals—of structuralism as represented by the work of E.E. Evans-Pritchard in the worldwide study of systems of ideas and values in their cultural application. This approach has certainly been applied in the Orissa Project's research conducted in tribal societies.

Officially, only about a quarter of the Orissan population is counted among the Scheduled Tribes, but the few anthropologists who have actually conducted long-term fieldwork in the vast tribal areas were quite unable to find relevant cultural differences between ST and the indigenous Other Backward Classes of western Orissa, such as the Rona, who were shifted from one administrative label to the other in the course of their recent history and, in a neighbouring province, are administrated as ST. Tina Otten shows how the Rona use this governmental ranking system for their own elaborate social concepts of status in the face of neighbouring indigenous communities of Koraput. Primarily, however, Dr. Otten introduces the classification of illness and healing among these Rona, offering an inclusive system that indicates marked contrasts when compared to Western biomedical or common sense principles, and that corresponds to the general tribal concept of hierarchy, i.e. the ranking according to relative seniority. Again, such conspicuous forms of healing make sense only if indigenous concepts are conceived within a general system of value-ideas, i.e.

if they are taken seriously, rather than being relegated to the status of an arbitrary situational performance.

Peter Berger's two years of intensive fieldwork among the tribal Gadaba, the neighbours of the Rona in the Koraput hills, has yielded such a system of meaning that, by its spectacular elaboration, encompasses the entire social thought and ritual action. Dr. Berger introduces Gadaba concepts of food and feeding as being instrumental for the creation of the Gadaba person. All annual and life-cycle rituals involve meaningful acts of nutrition, just as the intra- and the inter-village community, or the community linking Gods and humans, is based upon commensality of degrees. For example, an unmarried man cannot join those eating the head-meat of the sacrificial animal of the village shrine. Similarly, the sacrifices in the different seasons involve different meanings and consequently different species of animals, or, in the secondary funeral, the dead return in the shape of buffaloes, to be exchanged for megaliths and removed from the village before being slaughtered and eaten by external agnates. The boundaries of the Gadaba tribe are not marked by any 'essentializing' criteria, since a limited number of clan categories and intra-village descent groups are unified by specific concepts of affinity and territoriality, all sanctified by the alimentary code, i.e. ritual concepts quite different from, though intelligible to, those of other tribes of the neighbourhood.

Set in the northwest, i.e. at the other end of the province, Aghria death rituals are introduced in Uwe Skoda's contribution to this volume. The hosts of his lengthy field research belong to a peasant community that, during the 19th century, were called (from central India) by the petty king to the Sambalpur region in order to clear the forest, introduce plough cultivation, and transform the tribal population into rent paying subjects. The death rituals, however, also indicate the Aghria proximity to the tribal social order, since numerous ceremonies highlight the complimentary roles of the sister's son and the mother's brother as being essential for the transformation of the social person and the passage into the world beyond. Along with agnatic local lines and the identification of alternating generations, these enduring affinal ties constitute the basic features of the kinship universe for Aghria as well as tribal peoples in their neighbourhood. Thus marriage, generation, and descent systems of the tribes remain relevant lines of order once the economy has been transformed into the 'feudal' type. My own contribution is, in fact, the suggestion to examine these 'kinship' features among the Kondh not in terms of their political and economic functions but rather in the light of Nick Allen's tetradic theory on the classificatory potential of these simple oppositions. This Oxford scholar, as a guest of the Orissa Project, offers the gift of an article on Indo-European cultural comparativism with particular reference to Dumézil's 'trifunctional' interpretation of the *varna* scheme, thus demonstrating the close association of the Oxford anthropological tradition with the French sociological school and, against many German critics, the analytical work on an epoch in the distant past that is far from useless for the present, especially if we consider the potential within the intricate and complex classificatory schemes of present day Orissa.

Since the anthropologists, lacking relevant data on social history in western Orissa, are bound to exert their analytical potential within the wide range and intricate variations of ritual and kinship classification that include the order of work and property, the historian's competence is indispensable in the study of basic issues of the political economy with reference to the newly found data of colonial times. Ravi Ahuja contributes such an historical essay on the construction of a road through the wilderness of Orissa in the early colonial days of the 1840s, highlighting labour relations of the Raj as well as the reactions to the intrusion on behalf of the indigenous 'jungle kings' and the pious or progressive rhetoric covering the vested interests of the colonizers and the colonial power. 'Early colonial administrators were not so much interested in making a way *into* Orissa than in *getting past it* without hindrance', i.e. connecting the three Presidencies through the malaria-infested hills. In view of the many casualties, the strikingly callous attitude of the 'empire builders' is exposed by Dr. Ahuja, as well as the highly ambivalent attitude of those adventurers who had established little spheres of influence in the forest and were frequently far from eager to be linked to the centres of imperial power and reform.

Labour relations of a different era are the theme of Christian Strümpell's article, based on long-term anthropological fieldwork in an isolated hydro-electric power project right in the middle of the Koraput tribal area. This is genuinely innovative research, since, amazingly, culture and possible culture changes in the industrial complex of India have, with few exceptions, been excluded from the anthropological agenda as if India were a non-industrialized country. In fact, Dr. Strümpell is able to catch the pioneer spirit of sacrifice and patriotism, as is manifest, for example, in the form of poetry. Nehru's 'New India' at the time of Independence saw industrial plants as the 'temples of the new age' representing the inevitable progress of secularism and socialism and the equality of man in the liberated nation. To this day, most members of the industrial project (except perhaps the latrine cleaners) remain encompassed by this spirit of equality and brotherhood, even if the tribal people of the neighbourhood belong to an inferior world. What Strümpell (following Frank Heidemann) calls 'conviviality', implies regular commensality irrespective of caste, class and religion at the frequent feasts, as well as close neighbourly interaction qualified by functional differences only. But then the project is viewed as something like a grand (sometimes life-long) excursion, a time-out from the regular religious convictions, while caste distinctions and religious barriers are recalled in the 'home' villages of the workers where they also conduct the major life-cycle ceremonies. Independence and changes in the political economy have not altered the basic value-ideas.

Historical research on the Independence movement similarly presents an ambivalent picture of the leading figures in the province. Thus Georg Berkemer's contribution on the role of Maharaja Krushna Chandra Gajapati Narain Deo (1892-1974) of Parlakimedi during the formation of the province of Orissa, one of the celebrated luminaries of 'Oriya nationalism', shows that this 'little' king at the southern fringes of the state was willing to split his domain and sacrifice his petty royalty in order to become, at least for a short while, the modern ruler of the whole of Orissa. Adopting the approach of the *long durée*, Dr. Berkemer explains this by the centuries-old rivalry between this ruler, who is genealogically linked to the ancient Ganga dynasty (the builders of the Jagannath temple), and the 'upstart' Khurda king who had been the 'first servant' of Jagannath since the early 17th century. Ignoring the Congress electorate and the constitution of the new state, the Maharaja temporarily fulfilled the old ambition of his house by ruling from the centre for once.

From the field of modern literature, Babara Lotz then introduces a similarly ambivalent figure by interpreting Fakirmohan Senapati's fiction and autobiographical texts relating to the late 19th century. This civil servant conveyed a wide spectrum of policies and moral inclinations, ranging from the newly introduced Western liberalism and humanism, for which lip service was the general trend in the outgoing century, to tough authoritarian measures when the unlimited rule of the British-kept 'kings' was actually challenged by the people. Senapati's career as a minister in charge of several micro-states was based on his ability to negotiate the interests of royals and tribal spokesmen, British political agents and the Oriya administrative staff, a feat which demanded a considerable recourse to humanist rhetoric patching up the regular experience of exploitation, high-handedness and brutal measures of control. In a particular example, Senapati refers to his crushing the Bhuiyan *meli*, or revolt, in 1890/1, one of the many tribal risings, this time in Keonjhar, after the British had provided the 'jungle kings' with an unprecedented basis of support, allowing the latter to entrench their formerly precarious position. Rather than straightforward historiography, Dr. Lotz offers a piece of literary criticism, indicating new ways of applying a comparable analysis to more recent memoirs and recollections of leading actors in the multifaceted political dramas.

If Georg Berkemer introduced a petty 'king' during the late colonial period and Barbara Lotz a top administrator of such a 'kingdom', Chandi Prasad Nanda, also drawing on biographical and autobiographical sources, offers a contribution on two Gandhian leaders in the northern 'kingdom' of Mayurbhanj during the struggle of Independence. Significantly these Kudmi Mahanta are associated with a 'low caste' background since, on the one hand, they represent the indigenous population as opposed to the ruling or immigrant Oriya, while on the other hand they do not belong to the tribal owner-cultivators but rather to the category of petty traders and craftsmen, omnipresent in the tribal areas, and traditionally subservient but flexible in adapting to changing politico-economic fortunes. In times of devastating famines not infrequent in the colonial epoch, these traders were also prone to be attacked by the starving tribesmen, though both sides might also combine in their resistance against the atrocities of the rulers. Dr. Nanda's paper offers glimpses of the tribal freedom movement which is generally ignored by historiography and introduces two Mahanta leaders who publically criticize the Brahminical ideology and yet betray the movement in their efforts to be co-opted by the same hegemonic order which they had earlier denounced.

Both tribal and 'low caste' people of the tribal areas have been associated with efforts of foreign missionaries to convert the subaltern Indian categories to Christianity. This is the topic of Biswamoy Pati's article on the apparently paradox statement that nobody can convert to the Hindu faith though many members of other religious communities can *re*-convert. Dr. Pati is critical of the media coverage and the populist movements that spread all sorts of conspiracy theories, and rather draws attention to the relatively late introduction of the caste system into western Orissa which, in the pre-colonial process of feudalization and the colonial intervention, was instrumental in sharpening the class and caste conflicts and in drawing the indigenous population into the caste order. Successful landowners *became* Oriya and member of the warrior caste, thus losing their tribal status, as can be demonstrated by the amazing growth and decline of the relevant figures in the decennial Census of India, while the author sees tribal rebellions as resistance against such forms of conversion, and the given cases of Christianisation as marginal processes in which contradictions to tribal identity and cultural heritage were camouflaged. Tribal Christians may have been a major force within the Independence movement, though after this had been achieved, some tribal Kondh are said to have converted to Christianity as a form of protest against intrusion of outsiders that was then initiated. Since 1980, the author sees the 'homogenizing forces' of the Hindu nationalist movement at work: 'Communalized perceptions cloud the real world of poverty, hunger, and unemployment in a state where more than 55 per cent of the people and 89 per cent of the families live below the poverty line'.

A similarly sensitive issue is discussed in the final contribution of the volume, Cornelia Mallebrein's examination of recent tendencies and laws to prohibit animal sacrifice in any context. Thus the same 'homogenizing forces' are at work, restricting an ideology of 'encompassing the contrary'. Dr. Mallebrein carefully explicates the arguments of both sides, also involving the forces of globalization, i.e. the internet as the forum of international animal protection activities, as well as local examples of state intervention against the rituals of the Maliah Kondh of the Phulbani district. She elaborates on the historical and religious background of the case in

Orissa, as well as the combination of 'conservative' and 'progressive' forces favouring the prohibition of blood sacrifice. She has, in fact, toured most parts of the province and has also discussed the issue at length with those who fear the sanctions of the Goddess due to their neglect by decree in recent times. Her conclusion points to the fact that both the institution of animal sacrifice and the movement against such rituals have been very much a part of India's and Orissa's religious history ever since the earliest times.

The recognition of such an intricate, and yet rather intelligible, structure of opposed values as manifested in this diachronic feature of the regional and the subcontinental culture is yet another example, and one of plausibility, of the complex oppositions formulating Indian ideology. To confuse these with situational opportunities and subjective inclinations of the involved actors may satisfy a recent Western trend, but scholars of Indian history, religion, and anthropology have noticed such oppositional concepts, e.g. that of the Brahmin and the king or that of *kshetra* and *vana,* long before arbitrary and individual inclinations were proposed as guidelines of humanity, and such a structure of value-ideas is likely to survive subsequent trends.

References

Dumont, Louis 1980. *Homo Hierarchicus. The Caste System and Its Implications*. Complete Revised English Edition, Chicago: Chicago University Press.

Dumont, Louis 1986. *A South Indian Subcaste. Social Organization and Religion of the Pramalai Kallar*, Delhi: Oxford University Press.

Eschmann, Anncharlotte, Hermann Kulke and Gaya Charan Tripathi (eds.) 1978. *The Cult of Jagannath and the Regional Tradition of Orissa,* Delhi: Manohar.

Vitebsky, Piers 1993. *Dialogues with the Dead. The Discussion of Mortality Among the Sora of Eastern India,* Cambridge: Cambridge University Press.

2

Survey in Western Orissa: Preliminary Report*

M. Brandtner, B. Misra, P. Mohanty and P. Yule

Even into the 1980s, few usable publications existed for the archaeology of the region between coastal Orissa and Vidarbha.[1] More particularly, numerous repetitively published site lists provide little real information, and all of western Orissa and the newly founded Chhattisgarh state (some 250,000 sq.km) remain, to a large extent, archaeologically terra incognita. This includes the area known as Dakṣiṇa Kosala in antiquity as well as the adjacent land in northern Andhra Pradesh, that is, all of eastern central India. For prehistoric and protohistoric artefactual parallels here one must turn to other parts of India, especially looking toward the west, where vastly more research has been carried out.

The main archaeological feature of peninsular Iron-Age India, the megaliths, is little represented in Orissa[2] ('megalithic' simply means large stones, and includes many monuments in practice undated). The south and central Indian Iron Age, roughly covering the whole first millennium BC, manifests itself in western Orissa in its pottery, but less so in terms of burial structures. In the second half of the first millennium BC, more and more sites in our area display features of the early historic period, particularly proto-urban traits. The interface of the so-called Iron Age and the early historic period in western Orissa forms the basis of our inquiry.

---

* This report covers the period November-December 2000. We should like to thank H. Kulke as one of the initiators of the Orissa Research Project for sponsoring our work, and the DFG for funding it. In Orissa our special thanks go to K.K. Basa and B.K. Rath for their support in Bhubaneswar. This note is written up essentially as the brief talk upon which it is based, and thus cannot solve the problems which it registers. If not otherwise noted, P. Yule is credited with the text-figures.

[1] Recent substantive work dealing with the archaeology of Orissa includes, for example: Yule/Hauptmann/Hughes 1989 [1992], 193-275; Brandtner 1994 and 2001; Mohanty/Tripathy 1997-98; Basa/P. Mohanty 2000; Behera 2000-01.

[2] Cf. Thapar 1985, map on 105.

Two geographic areas must be highlighted at the outset: first, western Orissa contains a broad spectrum of monuments dating from prehistoric to medieval times, which have only recently been discovered.[3] In neighbouring Chhattisgarh, a new study reveals—not unexpectedly—a concentration of Iron Age megalithic structures immediately adjacent to our working area.[4] The same applies to the Godavari area of Andhra Pradesh, bordering western Orissa in the south.[5] Archaeologists working in the interior of Orissa have to rely almost exclusively on surface finds the chronology of which rests on external comparisons. This also holds for the continued efforts of J.P. Singh Deo *(yuvarāja* of Khariar) and his antiquarian-interested colleagues, who in fact do obtain interesting strayfinds, although little is known about the archaeological context. Often the range of the method in interpreting such surface and other stray finds is overestimated for lack of good excavated ones. On the other hand, an anthology, published by K.K. Basa and P. Mohanty in the year 2000, contains several substantial articles which bring the archaeology of Orissa a good step ahead, away from one of essentially local interest. In particular, one new contribution on the archaeology of Baudh (interior Orissa) district contains hitherto unknown sites of different periods and is relevant to our work.[6] It also updates our knowledge of the pottery of the region.

Second, coastal Orissa shows some progress with regard to a sequence of the protohistoric pottery, although their publication does little more than highlight attractive finds until now. Besides, newly discovered sites contribute to our knowledge about the interrelation between coastal sites and those situated in the interior. It is, therefore, significant that south of Lake Chilka some sites have yielded fragments of early historic fine black and red ware.[7] While the coastal variety is coarse, that of the interior is fine.[8]

Since the archaeology of Orissa still rests almost exclusively on surface finds and those excavated without documentation, it

---

[3] See, for example, Mohanty/Mishra 2001.

[4] Sharma 2000.

[5] Murthy 2000.

[6] Tripathy 2000, 392-417.

[7] Mohanty/Mishra/Basa/Badam 1999, 77-8.

[8] For Black-and-Red Ware from Nehena (in the interior): Brandtner 1994, 107-12, Figs. 8.4, 8.5

supports only the most superficial archaeological interpretation. Site plans are either not published or are published in such a way that they are of little use regarding the size, date, or importance of a given place. Often one experiences unreflected adherence to obsolete chronological notions and regional patriotic beliefs, such as N.K. Sahu's interpretation of the fortified site of Narla/Asurgarh (see below) as the Aṭavi ('forest') stronghold against Aśoka and, 600 years later, the fort of Vyāghrarāja, one of the opponents of the Gupta ruler Samudragupta.[9]

The central aim of the Kiel work group is to elucidate the polycentric nature of subregional and hegemonial identities of Orissa in historical perspective. Not only do we try to define the specifics of proto- and early historic cultures of western Orissa, but we also challenge the widespread modernocentric perception of interior Orissa as peripheral in contradistinction to the coastal area.

In November/December 2000 we concentrated our research resources in the field on eight sites which illuminate the proto- and early historic culture of western Orissa. In addition, we surveyed for unknown sites. The following sites commanded our attention (Fig.1):

Khariar/Sandohel (Dist. Nuaparha, 20°15'01"N; 82°47'03"E)[10]

In 1990 students from Khariar college excavated a site that had in the 1980s been identified as an Iron Age 'megalithic' grave.[11] Apart from a short unpublished report by J.P. Singh Deo, there is no documentation of this excavation. The finds preserved in the college are a mixture of Iron Age pottery and iron finds, among them a large iron spear. The stone circle around the grave is *c.* 7 m in diameter.

---

[9] Sahu 1982, 6-7.

[10] The coordinate readings which are cited at the beginning of each of the sites listed below were made without the selective availability distortion, use the map datum 'wgs 84' and conform with the maps of the Survey of India.

[11] Brandtner 1994, 102f., Fig. 8.1b; Singh Deo 2000, 421.

Manmunda/Karmapadar (Dist. Baudh, 20°49'44"N; 83°58'10"E)[12]

This is an interesting object for excavation. In close proximity lie mounds, a possible destroyed dolmen, and several stone circles of uncertain date (Fig. 2). Karmapadar (Kurumpadar) lies on the south bank of the Tel/Mahanadi and east of present-day Sonepur. Visible remains spread over 3 or 4 ha. The surface finds are largely chalcolithic and Iron Age potteries. Of special interest are fragments of a four-legged vessel and white-painted Black-and-Red Ware sherds, as they show parallels to some of the finds from the early chalcolithic period at the recently excavated site of Khameswaripali[13]

Bhuampada/Kharligarh (Dist. Balangir, 20°27'37"N; 83°33'38"E)[14]

One of the key sites for our line of inquiry is the early historic Kharligarh at the confluence of the Rahul and the Tel, owing to its large size (17 ha. *intra muros*). Lying above the steep banks of the Rahul, it is easy to defend and, by its position at the confluence of the two rivers, strategically important as well. For trade this site is favourably located, offering the prerequisites for an urban settlement. Possible landscaping, perhaps the remains of a boat pier, exist. Architectural remains are visible on the surface, especially baked bricks and dressed stone.

Manmunda/Asurgarh (Dist. Baudh, 20°50'00"N; 83°56'02"E)[15]

This badly eroded settlement (Fig. 3) appeared to others, and initially to us, as an interesting future excavation, owing to the chronologically diverse and qualitatively good surface finds. It

---

[12] Pradhan 1987-88, 18-9.

[13] Behera 2000-01, 21, Figs. 3 and 4.

[14] *Indian Archaeology—A Review* 1968-69, 68 no. 41; R.P. Mohapatra 1986, 221-2.

[15] S. Behera 1982; *Indian Archaeology—A Review* 1989-90, 80-6. Mohanty/Tripathy 1997-98, 90; P.K. Chhotray 2000.

offers a broad spectrum from the neolithic/chalcolithic to at least the early medieval period—thus spanning more than 2000 years. Possibly only the south wall of a fortification still exists, the other three evidently having been eroded by the Tel. This explains the lack of structures in the excavations at this site (although several seasons of excavation were conducted here by colleagues from Sambalpur University, the results remain practically unpublished). The site proved smaller than originally reported: it is, perhaps partly due to the effects of erosion, only 340 m and not the projected 1200 m long.

Among the finds of importance are painted sherds, some of them handmade and painted after firing, others wheel-thrown and painted pre-firing Black-and-Red sherds. A large variety of graffiti is also encountered. Knobbed Ware indicates the presence of Buddhist monks who used such vessels.

Ramapur/Budhigarh (Dist. Kalahandi, 20°18'29"N; 83°32'09"E)[16]

Some 10 ha. in size, this site attracted the attention of B. Misra and P. Mohanty, owing to a scatter of early historic pottery sherds (Fig. 4). Building remains are understandably difficult to confirm without excavation.

Notable is that at this site **for the first time in Orissa**, Northern Black Polished Ware in its different colour shades (Fig. 5, 3-5) is clearly identifiable, imported from the Gangetic Valley. This excellently made luxury pottery, a *leitfossil* for the early historic period in northern India and dated *c*.500 to 100 BC, derives from the so-called western Orissa 'periphery' and not from the coastal strip. Again, Knobbed Ware (Fig. 5, 1, 2) bearing owners' marks points to the presence of Buddhist monks (as also at Manmunda/Asurgarh). Other luxury goods are in evidence: for instance, fragments of an ivory comb, seals fashioned from jasper (one of them bearing the 'tree in railing' motive of Mauryan and post-Mauryan Punch-Marked Coins), another jasper seal with a problematic inscription, a jasper earring, one half of a double shell mould for casting metal beads or rivets. Aside from this, numerous beads fashioned of semiprecious stones derive from this site, as

---

[16] Mohanty/Joglekar/Misra 1998-99, 121-2.

well as from Narla/Asurgarh especially, which is the site we shall turn to now.

Narla/Asurgarh (Dist. Kalahandi, 19°54'32"N; 83°21'02"E)[17]

30 km north-east of Bhawanipatna, near Narla, a rectangular fortification measuring 700 x 580 m with a gate on each side, encloses settlement remains now under protection by the ASI (Fig. 6). The ramparts measure up to 11 m in height. Until now, neither epigraphic nor literary sources have yielded the ancient name of this fort. N.K. Sahu's suggestion that it in fact is the fort of Vyāghrarāja, the king of Mahākāntāra mentioned in the Allahabad inscription of Samudragupta, cannot be verified. Nor can his assumptions be confirmed that this is an Aṭavi stronghold that fought against Aśoka, that the Kaliṅgan army, which the Mauryan emperor trounced, were recruited from this area and that after battle they retreated here.

In 1958, a hoard of 539 pre-Mauryan, Mauryan and post-Mauryan silver Punch-Marked Coins accidentally came to light here.[18] Excavation by Sambalpur University followed in 1973. The pottery discovered in this excavation (most of which is lost now) is not recorded stratigraphically, and therefore eludes stratigraphic analysis. Aside from ceramics, to judge from the quantity and quality of the finds, an active bead industry is in evidence.

Lokapada hoard of Punch-Marked Coins (Dist. Balangir, 20°49'40")[19]

Near the village Lokapada, a hoard of silver Punch-Marked Coins was discovered on the banks of the Suktel in 1991. Although the police confiscated about 970 g of these coins, a considerable part of them are said to have been melted down by the villagers on their discovery.

---

[17] Sahu 1982; D. Mitra in: A. Ghosh, 2, 1989, 25; Mohanty/Joglekar/Misra 1998-99, 90.

[18] Deo 1966.

[19] Personal communication, S.N. Agrawal in Menda (Dist. Sonepur). Brandtner photographed some of these coins.

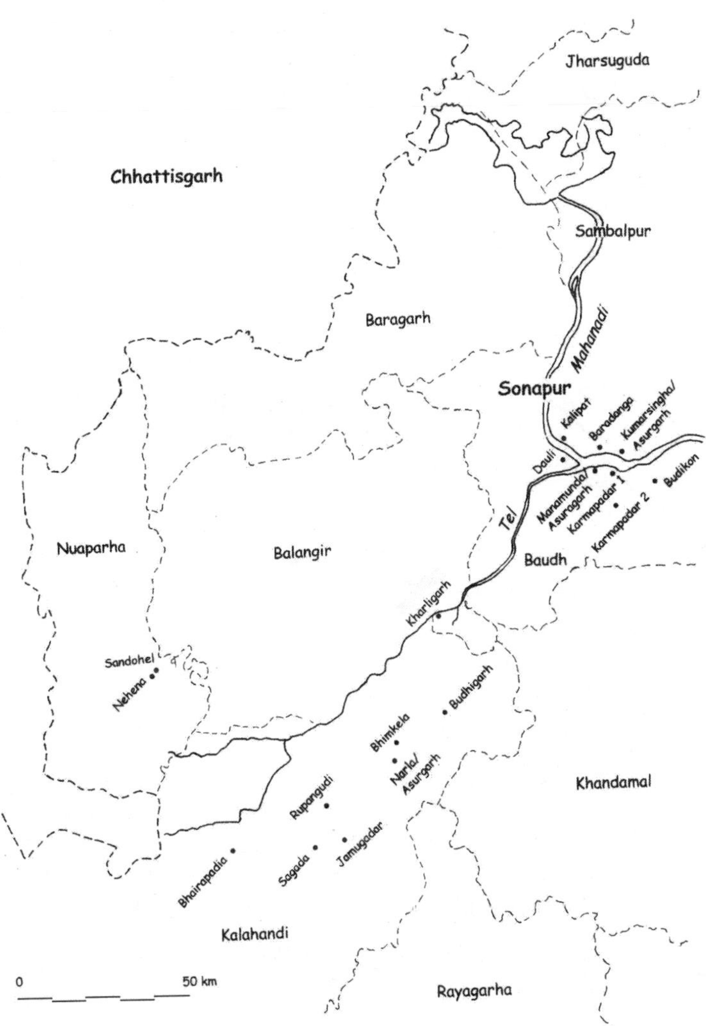

Fig. 1: Sites referred to in western Orissa.

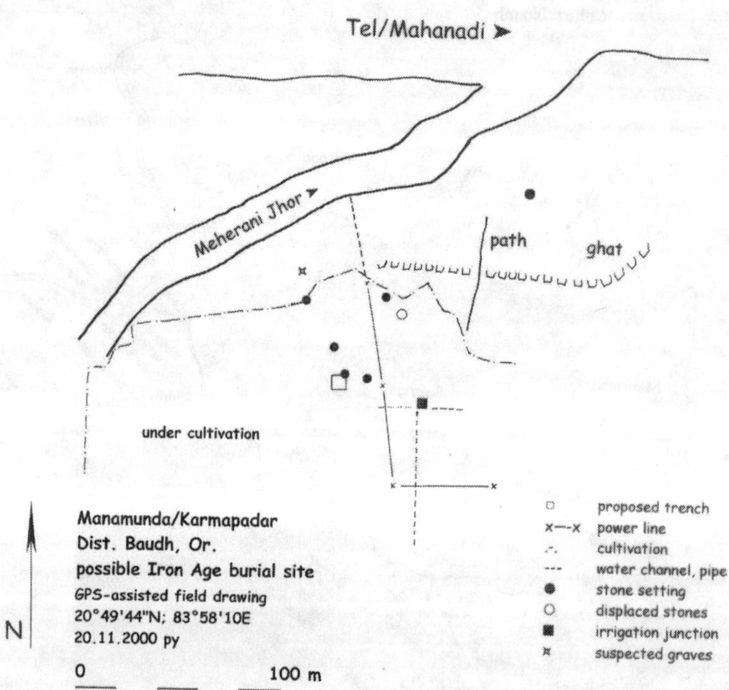

Fig. 2: Plan Manmunda/Karmapadar.

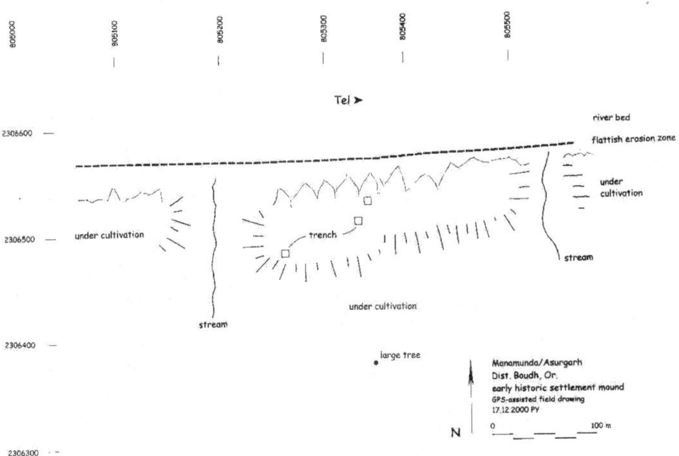

Fig. 3: Plan Manmunda/Asurgarh.

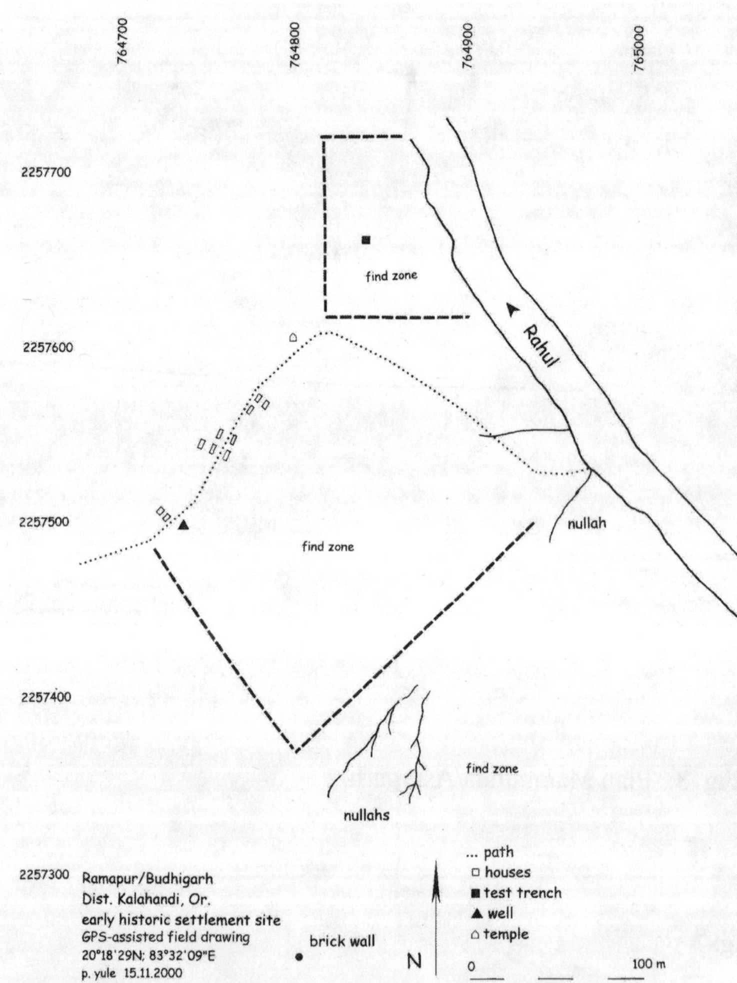

Fig. 4: Plan Ramapur/Budhigarh.

Fig. 5: Knobbed Ware (1, 2) and Northern Black Polished Ware (3-5) from Ramapur/Budhigarh.

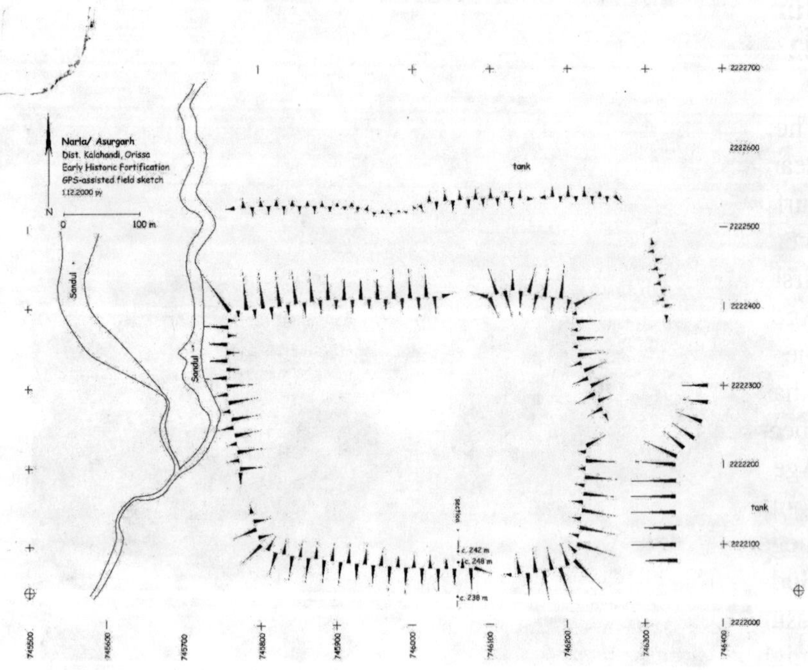

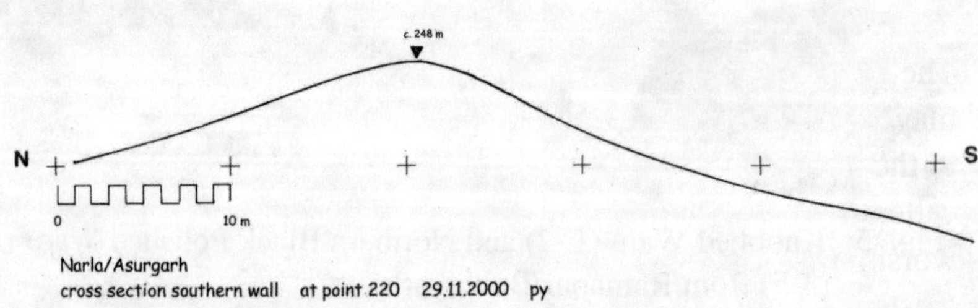

Fig. 6: Plan and profile Narla/Asurgarh.

This hoard has not been studied, but at least a part of the coins are certainly Mauryan in date.

Junagarh/Bhairapadia (Dist. Kalahandi, 19°52'11"N; 82°56'05"E)

The isolated presumed Iron Age 'megalithic' tomb lies in a copse near the town of Bhairapadia. Small finds are not visible on the surface. Nonetheless, this is one of the clearest examples of an early megalithic circle in western Orissa. Since the time we wrote the first grant proposal for this project, the evidence regarding the Iron Age here has mounted. That Iron Age 'megalithic' tombs exist in the area is confirmed by this tomb and a second one at Khariar/Sandohel, mentioned above. Until now, one could only speculate that stone enclosures and similar relics were of the Iron Age and not the products of tribal megalithic practices still continuing in this area. The above-quoted publications of megalithic stone alignments in nearby Chhattisgarh as well as in the Godavari region of Andhra Pradesh strengthen the reasonable assumption that megalithic structures were also present in neighbouring Orissa—although they are conspicuously absent from the coastal area.

Problems and Perspectives

The rarity of Iron Age megalithic graves in Orissa's back country may be due to the ubiquitous destruction of such structures and/or to the weak state of research. To complicate matters, to this day so-called menhirs and stone circles are still erected, reused and worshipped. We can do little more than acknowledge their existence without being able to establish their age. A main goal is to investigate Iron Age burial practices, preferably in a cemetery, in order to define this temporal horizon locally. The correlation of settlement and burial finds with each other would also serve the purpose of putting the chronology on a firmer footing.

A second project-emphasis is to investigate the early historic fort horizon, incipient urbanization, and state formation along the Tel and the middle Mahanadi valleys.

Whereas in earlier times the material culture of western Orissa had little in common with that of the coastal belt, from the Mauryan period onwards, i.e. from the fourth/third centuries BC, several sites reveal finds that show contact with this area as well as with the Gangetic plains. Over time, a gradual acculturation takes place in the early historic settlements in our research area. Sites bearing witness to this development include those just discussed: Budhigarh, Kharligarh, Narla/Asurgarh, as well as others which we surveyed. The contexts and their finds show characteristic signs of urbanization. These are, among others, a large settlement area, elaborate fortifications, baked brick architecture, coinage, seals with script, imported luxury ware and, with it, evidence for trade, not to forget indications of Buddhist enclaves which at this time are generally related to urban and mercantile settlements.

In addition to the large settlements, small ones exist in river ghats revealed by erosion. Herewith, the first elements of a settlement hierarchy come to light, which we hope to explore as far as time and methods allow it. The finds and contexts within the area selected for investigation are examples of an early process of urbanization which, in these dimensions, does not present itself on the coast. Today Orissa's back country is considered to be the poorest and most backward in all of India. In the light of the present-day economic wealth of coastal Orissa as compared to the poverty of the west, this interior urbanization comes as an initial surprise. But consider that, in the early Sanskrit literature (for example the *Kauṭilīya Arthaśāstra*), the economic importance and, in particular, the richness of the mineral resources of eastern central India are repeatedly mentioned. Moreover, the infrastructural situation is fostered in that this area is linked by important routes to the rest of ancient India. In this respect the coast is less fortunate. Thus seen, interior Orissa's early prosperity in fact is not at all surprising.

In the light of these preliminary findings, one may also review the question of Aśoka's motives and military options, since his conquests were limited to the coast and he left the Aṭavi land untroubled. A question occasionally raised is whether he was preoccupied with the control of the sea route along the eastern coast of India and the protection of the port of Tāmraliptī in the Ganges delta from competitors to the south, and not so interested in territorial gains. In any case, in Orissa's back country, Mauryan influence there may have been, but Mauryan presence is a different matter yet. Moreover, military action in the interior would simply have overtaxed Aśoka's resources, as his adversaries obviously possessed not only considerable economic but also military strength.

Gupta influence seems equally marginal. Samudragupta (*c.* 335-75 AD) marched through western Orissa on his great campaign to the south around 360 or 370 AD and conquered several rulers whose names he has left us. These are not mere petty chieftains, but rather princes who already used the legitimatizing power of northern Sanskrit culture: Mahendra from Kosala, Vyāghrarāja from Mahākāntāra, and Maṇṭarāja from Kurāḷa. Although the identification of the rulers named in the Allahabad inscription with the sites discovered would be premature, one can rest assured that the fortified proto-urban settlements mentioned here, with their early relations with north India, link with the military opponents of Samudragupta.

The interface of the prehistoric village megalithic culture with early historic urban culture, which includes the transition from tribal to early state structures, the continuities and discontinuities in the economic-social development, as well as the cultural orientation of the time between 1000 BC and 500 AD are the subject of our efforts. These are essential aspects of the 'change of socioeconomic identities' which lies at the core of the umbrella project proposal to the DFG.

References

Basa, K.K. and P. Mohanty (eds.). 2000. *Archaeology of Orissa*, Delhi.

Behera, P.K. 2000-1. 'Excavations at Khameswaripali—A Proto Historic Settlement in the Middle Mahanadi Valley, Orissa: A Preliminary Report', in *Prāgdhārā: Journal of the U. P. State Archaeology Department* 11, 13-34.

Behera, S.C. 1982. 'Manamunda', in S.C. Behera (ed.), 1982, 16-22.

Behera, S.C. (ed.). 1982. *Interim Excavation Reports,* Sambalpur.

Brandtner, M. 1994. 'Archaeology of Western Orissa: Finds from Nehena', in *South Asian Archaeology 1993.* A. Parpola and P. Koskikallio, eds., Helsinki: (Annales Academiae Scientiarum Fennicae, Ser.B, Vol. 271), Vol. I, 101-14.

— 2001. *Kaliṅga und seine Hauptstadt in frühgeschichtlicher Zeit: Zum Bedeutungswandel einer ethnischen und geographischen Bezeichnung,* Hamburg (Studien zur Geschichtsforschung des Altertums Band 7).

Chhotray, P.K. 2000. 'Asurgarh, the Mysterious Mound in Mahanadi Valley', in *Orissa Review,* October 2000, 24-6.

Deo, P.K. 1966. 'Forgotten Forts of Kalahandi (Part I): Asurgarh Fort and a Hoard of Punch Marked Coins', in *Orissa Historical Research Journal,* XIV, 25-61.

Ghosh, A. 1989. *Encyclopedia of Indian Archaeology.* 2 vols, Delhi.

Mohanty, P., P. Joglekar and B. Misra. 1998-9. 'Early Historic Investigations in Kalahandi District, Orissa: A Preliminary Report', in *Purātattva,* 29, 120-31.

Mohanty, P. and B. Misra. 2001. 'Early Historic Kalahandi', in *Orissa Revisited. Marg Special Monograph Issue,* Mumbai, 17-26.

Mohanty, P., J. Mishra, K.K. Basa and G.L. Badam. 1999. 'Archaeological Investigation on the Coast of Cilikā Lake, Orissa', in *Orissan History, Culture and Archaeology. In Felicitation of Prof. P.K. Mishra.* Ed. by S. Pradhan, New Delhi, 75-82.

Mohanty, P. and B. Tripathy. 1997-8. 'The Prehistoric, the Protohistoric and the Early Historic Cultures of Orissa', in *Prāgdhārāra: Journal of the U. P. State Archaeology Department,* 8, 70-98.

Mohapatra, R.P. 1986. *Archaeology of Orissa,* Delhi.

Pradhan, S. 1987-8. 'Megalithic Remains in the Upper Mahanadi Valley of Orissa', in *Journal of Ancient Indian History,* vol. 17, 1-2, 16-22.

Ramachandra Murthy, P. 2000. *Megalithic Culture of the Godavari Basi,* Delhi.

Sahu, N.K. 1982. 'Asurgarh', in S.C. Behera (ed.) 1982, *Interim Excavation Reports,* Sambalpur, 1-8.

Sharma, A.K. 2000. *Archaeo-Anthropology of Chhattisgarh,* Delhi.

Singh Deo, J.P. 2000. 'Archaeology of Kalahandi and Nuapada Districts, Orissa', in K.K. Basa and P. Mohanty (eds.) 2000, *Archaeology of Orissa,* Delhi, 418-30.

Thapar, B.K. 1985. *Recent Archaeological Discoveries in India,* Paris.

Tripathy, B. 2000. 'Archaeology of Boudh, Central Orissa', in K.K. Basa and P. Mohanty (eds.) 2000, in *Archaeology of Orissa*, Delhi, 392-417.

Yule, P., A. Hauptmann and M. Hughes 1989 [1992]. 'The Copper Hoards of the Indian Subcontinent: Preliminaries for an Interpretation', in *Jahrbuch des Römisch-Germanischen Zentralmuseums Mainz*, 36, 193-275.

3

Genealogies and Centres: Communities of the Caitanya Tradition in Orissa*

Angelika Malinar

As in other Hindu religious traditions *(sampradāya)* the followers of Caitanya (1486-1533) are localized and organized in networks of religious institutions (*maṭhas*, *āśramas*). These institutions are places of interaction between the religious specialists, the *gurus* or renouncers (*bābājī*), and the lay followers of the community. The latter support the religious specialists residing in the *maṭhas* and demand their ritual and spiritual services. The majority of these communities are organized in various networks of monastic institutions. These networks do not form a unified whole since they are not subordinated to any single commonly accepted head or spiritual leader. Indeed, one of the characteristics of the Caitanya tradition is the absence of a singular sacred and administrative centre, such as a 'head monastery' that represents the centre of the tradition and to which the other institutions are connected as its 'branches'. One reason for this decentralized structure is the fact that the members of the community regard three places as their main sacred centres (*dhāman*), namely Vrindavan (UP), Navadvipa (W. Bengal) and Puri (Orissa). All three are connected with the earthly sojourn of the god Kṛṣṇa and with Caitanya's sacred biography. They are unanimously accepted as 'sacred' and function as a common focus for a highly diversified tradition.

Another reason for the decentralized structure of organization lies in the very diversification of the transmission of Caitanya's

* The article is based on an analysis of literary sources as well as on field-work conducted during several stays in Orissa. I am grateful to the German Research Council for the research grant that made this research possible. I am very much indebted to all the representatives and members of the *maṭhas* who kindly offered me their cooperation, interest and hospitality, and who gave me their time for the interviews. I owe special thanks to Prabin Kumar Tripathy for his assistance and support during my fieldwork, and to Helene Basu for important comments and suggestions.

teaching in different teacher-disciple lineages (*guru-paramparā*).[1] The founders of these lineages are regarded either as the companions and direct disciples of Caitanya or as their disciples. The lineages or 'spiritual genealogies' signify and define spiritual kinship and descent. One consequence of this segmentation of the religious tradition into lineages is the establishment of different institutional networks.[2] Many of these networks create their own sacred centres which, in contrast to the three main centres mentioned above, may not be accepted as sacred by members of other networks and lineages. Yet, the different groups also seek to establish themselves in at least one, if not in all three of the main sacred centres. With each new foundation of a *maṭha* or *āśrama* the centrality of *dhāman* is enhanced and recreated.

In the following, the dissemination of the Caitanya tradition in Orissa will be discussed with regard to (1) the pattern of genealogical diversification and the creation of individual sacred centres according to affiliation with a certain genealogy; (2) the presence of certain spiritual lineages in Puri, one of the main sacred centres; (3) the emergence of networks that were created by two important *guru*s and reformers of the Caitanya tradition in the nineteenth and twentieth centuries.

Categories of classification and the genealogical model

The segmentary structure of transmission can be delineated by drawing on the categories used by the members of the institutions in order to place themselves within the tradition as a whole. These categories are of analytical importance as they serve to describe the traditional patterns of transmission, that is, the genealogical diversification of the tradition. The categories mirror not only the organizational structures of these communities, but also their patterns of dissemination. Thus the relationship between spiritual genealogies (*guru-paramparā*) and centres can be considered with the help of these categories of classification. The following

---

[1] For 'decentralization' as a characteristic feature of the Caitanya tradition, see also O'Connell 1999. The history of this diversification is detailed in Cakravarti 1985.

[2] For similar structures within the Rāmanandi tradition, see Burghardt 1978. On the relationship between segmentation and expansion, see Sahlins 1961.

categories are used by residents of the *maṭha*s in defining their position on the following levels: (1) *vis-à-vis* other religious traditions; (2) within the larger Caitanyaite community; and (3) in the context of their local or regional affiliation. These categories establish a referential framework that also points to different levels of the localization of tradition, that is, the pan-Indian, regional, and local level.

1. *Sampradāya (a community that transmits a religious tradition)*

The term *sampradāya* is used by many Hindu religious communities as a general term of classification. This term[3] is used to subsume different teaching traditions and religious institutions under a common designation, thus allowing it to be claimed that the different groups are part of a single religious tradition. The followers of Caitanya call their *sampradāya* Gauḍīya- or Madhva-Gaureśvara-Sampradāya.[4] This specification relates the group to other Hindu communities in two ways. First, it connects the Caitanya community to other Vaiṣṇava *sampradāyas* which have come to be grouped together as so-called 'four' *sampradāyas (catuḥ-sampradāya).* Secondly, it implies a distinction from non-Vaiṣṇava communities like the Śaiva Daśanāmin orders or tantric Śāktas. The category of *sampradāya* encompasses the different religious institutions because it refers to those markers of religious identity which are shared by all, including, *inter alia*, the following elements: that Caitanya is the founder of the tradition; that Rādhā and Kṛṣṇa are the highest godheads; that Vrindavan, Puri and Navadvipa are the three main sacred centres; that the *Bhāgavatapurāṇa* is a canonical text, and that membership in the *sampradāya* requires the initiation in the so-called *mahāmantra*. However, the *sampradāya* is not represented by a single powerful sacred. Rather, the unity of the *sampradāya* it is established by the interconnection of those very elements. They constitute the

---

[3] Another term used by religious groups is *panth*; cf. McLeod 1978.

[4] The first and more common designation 'Gauḍīya' stresses the fact that Caitanya was born in 'Gauḍadeśa', in Bengal. The second refers to his being '*gaura*', which means 'of light complexion'. This difference was explained to me during several interviews. For the historical problems connected with the inclusion of Madhva in the *paramparā*, cf. Deadwhyler 1992, Kapoor 1997.

sampradāya as a level of reference which is used and created by all followers through both their spiritual and their spatial activities (pilgrimages, establishment of shrines etc.). The category *sampradāya* thus signifies and circumscribes the Caitanya tradition as a whole. In its encompassing function it is like 'the mantle of our lady of mercy [that] shelters sinners of every kind in its voluminous folds' to quote one of Louis Dumont's metaphors of hierarchical encompassment.[5] This overarching category is only put in more concrete terms and made localized on the next level of classification:

2. *Parivāra (family, spiritual lineage)*

This category is used when the members of a *maṭha* identify themselves as belonging to a specific 'teacher-disciple lineage' or 'spiritual genealogy' (*guru paramparā*) founded by a companion or by a disciple of a companion of Caitanya. The individual lineages are named after their founder, for example, the Nityānanda-, Vakreśvara-, or Gadādhara-*parivāra*. The lineages mirror the historical diversification of the transmission of Caitanya's teachings. On this level the *sampradāya* materializes itself in monasteries, private hermitages, shrines and temples. Here, the religious affiliation of the individual follower becomes visible through those distinctive marks (*liṅga*) that were conferred on him through initiation, for example cloth, a necklace, and body-painting (*tilaka*). Initiation into the *sampradāya* is thus always an initiation into the spiritual genealogy of the respective teacher-disciple lineage. According to tradition, there once existed 64 *parivāra*s. During my field-work in Orissa I was able to trace and document *maṭha*s belonging to the following 'traditional' *parivāra*s: Nityānanda, Vakreśvara, Gadādhara, Śyāmānanda, Advaita and Jīva Gosvāmin. The term 'traditional' is used here for the *parivāra*s which trace themselves back to companions or direct disciples of Caitanya and which accept the unbroken teacher-disciple tradition as the sole authority.[6] In contrast to the *sampradāya*, an individual

[5] Cf. Dumont 1980, 78.

[6] The status of the different lineages of the so-called Orīya-Vaiṣṇavas, the followers of the 'five companions' (*pañca-sakhā*), is controversial, as is the process of classifying the followers of

parivāra is sometimes represented by one main centre. Mostly, however, it is not. Whether or not there is a main monastery, the *parivāra* is often subdivided into different teacher-disciple affiliations and thus again characterized by segmentation. This segmentary structure results in a proliferation of religious institutions because disciples often establish their own *maṭha*s. Within the *parivāra*, another level of segmentation is admitted, for which the term *gaṇa* is used. This category serves to accommodate a charismatic teacher who has come to be accepted as the founder of a 'sub-family' or 'group' (*gaṇa*).

3. *Gaṇa ('sub-family', 'group')*

By founding new monasteries and by propagating new teachings a charismatic teacher may gain the status of the founder of a group or sub-family within a *parivāra*. On this level, the tendency to establish a singular sacred and/or administrative centre seems quite strong. The opportunities for a place to acquire the status of a sacred centre of the *gaṇa* increase when the teacher has stayed there during a relevant period of his life. After his passing away a poly-centric structure may re-emerge if the succession is not regulated properly, or if there is a conflict among the followers and disciples. Thus, although the disciples of the respective *guru* often regard each other as *guru-bhāī* (spiritual brothers), this does not necessarily result in a common administrative or economic organization. Often this economic organization is nowadays established through the foundation and official registration of a Trust.

4. *Trusts*

In contrast to the other categories of reference, the Western term and institution of the 'trust' refers to a legally defined form of organization involving economic and administrative representation. Traditionally, the economic organization of a *maṭha* was embedded in structures of royal patronage, which enabled the establishment of large monastic institutions, as the case of Puri testifies. In addition to this, a number of institutions were also sponsored by rich traders,

Bhaktisiddhānta Sarasvatī, one of the great reformers of Caitanya faith in the nineteenth and twentieth centuries, *vide infra* 3.2.

businessmen and zamindars. However, nowadays the traditional system of royal patronage has changed and, to a great extent, vanished; especially since the Orissa Hindu Religious Endowments Act was passed in 1953. Many older monasteries were regarded as falling under this act and were placed under the control of the Hindu Religious Endowments Commission. The regulations of the Act bring the property and finances of the *maṭha* under the control of the District Commissioner. He is also entitled to appoint an executive trustee when the succession to the head of a *maṭha* has not been properly regulated or has become the subject of litigation.

On the other hand, newly founded or even re-established older *maṭha*s are often managed by independent and newly established trusts. These function as the owner of the *maṭha* and are often not controlled by the Endowments Commission. With its official registration and a functioning executive platform, the trust board, a trust does not come within the legal framework of the Hindu Religious Endowment Act. The trust allows the *maṭha* a degree of independence with regard to the disposal of its property, appointment of managers (*pracālaka*), succession of the heads of the institution etc. Thus a *maṭha* is not primarily controlled by representatives of the Endowments Commission, but rather by the trust board, which may consist either of monks alone or of both monks and lay followers. In any case, as the trust board is a place of interaction between the supporting lay followers and the monastic institutions, the influence of the lay followers may become quite strong on this level. The trust thus joins together specific monasteries of a *gaṇa* or a *parivāra* in the economic and administrative senses. However, it is not just economics that binds the *maṭha*s of one trust together. The trust board not only decides on questions of the succession, but also decides who is allowed to bestow initiation and thus continue the *guru-paramparā*. In this respect, the trust often has a centralized structure in the form of a head office and a president, who may also be the initiating *guru*. Thus, while the higher levels of classification take shape in rather decentralized structures of segmentation, the individual segments appear as centrally organized units.

These different categories signify different degrees of inclusion or encompassment that vary according to the different forms of organization. When used by followers in order to identify their position within of the Caitanya tradition, these categories are defined in relationship to each other. Their impact may vary according to their relevance in the respective context. Often the 'lowest' and the least encompassing level, that is a *gaṇa* or a trust, may be the most important one, as when the residence of the founder of a *gaṇa* becomes a sacred centres for his followers. This poly-valence of the categories also applies if one enquires what makes an institution a 'centre'. As indicated above, one finds centres on all levels. While a centre placed on the level of the *sampradāya*, for example Puri, is relevant for all followers, each segment and thus each level of organization allows and even calls for the creation of 'sacred centre'. Thus the centrality of a place does not only depend on its position within the categorical framework, but also on the particular regional and local context.

Conversely, the centrality of a place in the context of a *parivāra* or a *gaṇa* does not necessarily correspond to its sacredness with regard to the *sampradāya*. In any case, a sacred centre is not 'just there' as a fixed object or a quasi-substantial point of reference, rather its existence depends on the activities of those who regard, claim and use it as such. In this connection, socio-geographic approaches to the concept of centrality prove to be helpful. In an analysis of factors that make, for example, a city a 'central place' within its surrounding, Heinritz concludes that the centrality of a place depends on two conditions: first, on its capacity to produce meaning (its 'Bedeutungspotential'), and secondly, on a surplus of meaning ('Bedeutungsüberschuß') that draws people to visit the place, to settle there etc.[7]

Following the seminal act of investing a place with a specific meaning other factors become necessary in order for it to retain its significance. The most important of these is that the place is in demand: its persistent centrality results from processes of interaction. Basically, this also holds true for sacred centres. However, one has to keep in mind that meaning here is defined in relation to specific dimensions of time. On the one hand, a sacred place is often vested with a (hi)story of the once 'actual' presence of the divine and is therefore related to the memory of a unique event. On the other hand, this very meaning, the presence of the divine, is seen as timeless and as untouched by the units of historical time-reckoning. However, this timelessness does not

---

[7] Heinritz 1979, 16ff.

necessarily imply a permanency, but rather a 'potentiality' of this presence of the divine. The sacred centre exists in the prospect that this presence can be realized and experienced again and anew by devotees. In this perspective, the sacredness of the place seems to acquire a certain substantial quality, because the presence of the divine will never really vanish from it, however hidden, lost or unnoticed it may have become. Thus 'sacred centres' also require a process of interaction: its potential of meaning has to be required and used by devotees. How devotees relate to these centres depends on the traditions and practices that are part of the religious communities they belong to. Some contexts of these interactions and of the creation of centres have been pointed out with regard to the categories of classification. I shall now deal with the interplay between place and community, between genealogy and locality that is constitutive in making an institution central. This interplay between sacred centres and spiritual genealogies will be considered with regard to monastic institutions *at* a sacred centre, Puri, and with regard to monastic institutions *as* sacred centres.

Monastic institutions and the sacred centre of Puri

As already indicated, the category '*sampradāya*' refers to those elements of tradition that are accepted by all members of the different spiritual lineages *(parivāras*). Amongst these elements are canonical works like the *Bhāgavatapurāṇa* as well as certain places which are regarded as sacred. They are sacred because they are considered to be the *dhāman* of the god Kṛṣṇa, that is, the place of his appearance or residence, or the *līlāsthāna* the Kṛṣṇa and then of Caitanya Mahāprabhu, the founder of the *sampradāya. Līlāsthāna* literally means 'play-ground' or 'place of appearance'. In the context of the Caitanya tradition, this implies the manifestation of a god in the form of a human. In the case of Kṛṣṇa, this manifestation has no other purpose than to 'play' or to 'amuse' himself and to arouse the desire of human beings to be forever in his presence. Vrindavan is regarded as a *dhāman* and is thus venerated as the stage on which the god Kṛṣṇa appeared in the form of a charming young man in order to taste the joys and sorrows of earthly love together with Rādhā, his beloved *alter ego*.[8] The two other centres, Navadvipa and Puri, are associated rather with the life of Caitanya, who has come to be regarded as the incarnation of the divine couple, of both Rādhā and Kṛṣṇa.[9] His appearance is said to have been motivated by *kaliyuga*, the age of decay that is dominated by greed, crime, and disregard for laws and social boundaries. Yet, the *kaliyuga* is also considered to be extremely advantageous for gaining salvation on the path of *bhakti*. No complicated rituals, no torturing and time-consuming asceticism are requested; only the chanting of the name of God (*nāmasaṃkīrtana*) is needed to reach the divine sphere. This sphere is called the 'eternal play-ground' (*nityalīlāsthāna*), the unchanging stage on which the love-drama between Rādhā and Kṛṣṇa is continuously performed. This is the message that Caitanya both propagated and incorporated during his stays in Navadvipa and Puri and while being on a pilgrimage through South and, allegedly, also North India. Navadvipa is venerated as Caitanya's birth-place and Puri as the place where he lived for eighteen years until he finally 'disappeared' from there in 1536.

For the followers of Caitanya, Puri is not only the 'sacred compound' (*kṣetra*) of the god Jagannātha, the Puruṣottama-*kṣetra*, but above all the *līlāsthāna* of Kṛṣṇa Caitanya Mahāprabhu. Jagannātha is venerated by the followers of Caitanya as the Lord of Puri, but even more so because he was worshipped by Caitanya as Kṛṣṇa. The importance of Jagannātha for Caitanya not only becomes manifest in the fact that he stayed in the god's vicinity for eighteen years, it is also described in the hagiographies, in some of which it is related that Caitanya's earthly sojourn ended with his vanishing into the *mūrti* of Jagannātha. On the basis of these traditions, quite a number of places in Puri are connected with Caitanya's *līlā* and are thus regarded as places of veneration which should be included in a pilgrimage-tour (*parikrama*) through Puri. Most of these places have become 'institutions', that is, *maṭha*s or *mandira*s. Some of the *līlāsthāna*s were turned into monasteries that are now amongst the oldest in Puri. Their foundation goes back to the time of Caitanya and of the then ruling king of Puri,

---

[8] On Vrindavan see the detailed study by Entwistle 1987. On the 'ontology of the sacred places' that has been developed in the Caitanya tradition, cf. 71ff.

[9] For a study of this process in the hagiographies, see Stewart 1985.

Pratāparudra Deva, who is said to have been sympathetic to the young movement.[10]

Some of these older institutions are also nowadays widely renowned sacred centres on the local, regional and even pan-Indian levels. Their relevance also varies according to the referential framework of categories outlined above. Several factors contribute to establishing the sacred centrality of a monastic institution in the context of the Puri-*kṣetra*. The Rādhākānta Maṭha[11] can serve as an example of this process. This *maṭha* was founded during Caitanya's lifetime or shortly after his disappearance. In terms of the referential categories, the Rādhākānta Maṭha belongs to the spiritual lineage (*parivāra*) started by Vakreśvara Paṇḍita, one of Caitanya's companions. The centrality of the *maṭha* for the *sampradāya* results from the fact that its founding story is connected with certain events in the life of Caitanya. What has become the Rādhākānta Maṭha was formerly the house of the Brahmin Kāśi Miśra, the family priest of King Pratāparudra Deva. Kāśī Miśra gave Caitanya a room in his house, in which he stayed for several years. This room is called *gambhīrā* (lit. a hidden treasure room) and it is one of the principal pilgrimage sites in Puri for the followers of Caitanya. The importance of this room becomes apparent in that the *maṭha* is often addressed as 'Gambhīrā'. Nowadays, the practice of 'continuous chanting of the name of God' (*akhaṇḍanāma-kīrtana*) is practised in front of this room. Later, Vakreśvara Paṇḍita was put in charge of the worship of the *mūrti* of Rādhākānta.[12] In this way, a monastic institution was created[13] that until today has remained in the hands of the members of the Vakreśvara *parivāra*. Today, the *maṭha* also houses a 'museum', the 'Caitanya kuñja' (Caitanya-grove) where the life of Caitanya is staged in several tableaux. All this points to a

---

[10] Cf. Mukherjee 1940, 130ff.; on the controversy over the consequences of the king's alleged devotion to Caitanya, see ibid., 170-8.

[11] I am especially indebted to Śrī Dhyānacandra Dās, invested *mahanta* of the Rādhākānta Maṭha, who welcomed me and patiently answered my questions during several interviews.

[12] The idol, which is worshipped in the shrine of the *maṭha*, often plays a prominent part in many stories about the establishment of the *maṭha*. It is not unusual for the worship of an idol (*mūrti, vigraha*) of Kṛṣṇa or of both Rādhā and Kṛṣṇa to initiate the foundation of the *maṭha*.

[13] This story is told in a booklet published by the *maṭha* under the title *Śrī Gambhīrā*, cf. 7ff.

certain convergence between sacredness and centrality in the case of this *maṭha*, because it is relevant on the levels of both *sampradāya* and *parivāra*. This also seems to be connected with the persistence of older structures of organization which are, although transitional, still working.

One of these structures is the system of so-called *gaddi*s, the 'thrones' of the *ācārya*, the main representative of the spiritual lineage. Thus the Rādhākānta Maṭha is not only regarded as a *līlāsthāna* of Caitanya, but also as an *ācārya gaddi*, that is, the 'throne' of the *ācārya*. The position of an *ācārya* is the most powerful and encompassing position in the hierarchy of spiritual ranks. In order to achieve this position one must be born a Brahmin. Only then it is possible to acquire all the ritual rights (*adhikāra*) that are included in this position. This exceptional status of the *mahanta* is also indicated by the special ritual of investiture called *śāṛhī-bandha*, the 'binding of the *śāṛhī*.[14] In this ritual a piece of newly silken cloth is wrapped around the head of the future *mahanta* by a *mahanta* .who has also been invested through this ritual. Moreover, the ritual must to be conducted in the presence of other *mahanta*s holding the same position. Conversely, it is the *mahanta* of the Rādhākānta Maṭha who is called when the ritual of investiture has to be conducted in other *maṭha*s.[15]

Thus the head (*mahanta*) of the Rādhākānta Maṭha is *per officium* also the *ācārya* of the Vakreśvara *parivāra*. He is the one who confers not only the first initiation, the *mantra-dikṣā*, but also the final initiation, the *bheka-dīkṣā*, thus providing the adept with his true spiritual identity. This initiation implies the renunciation of social life and a permanent residence in a *maṭha*. The unbroken tradition of initiation and teaching (*guru-paramparā*) according to Vakreśvara Paṇḍita rests and persists in the *mahanta* of the Rādhākānta *maṭha*. The rules of succession are also evidence of this, since the next *mahanta* should be a disciple of the former

---

[14] This is not done in other *maṭha*s of the Caitanya tradition, especially those where the title of *mahanta* is no longer given to the monk who is the 'manager-administrator' (*pracālaka*) or the so-called 'executive trustee' of the *maṭha*.

[15] For example, when, some years ago, the ritual of investiture was conducted for the new *mahanta* of the Gaṅgāmātā Maṭha in Puri (belonging to Gadādhara *parivāra* of the Caitanya tradition), the actual binding was done by the *mahanta* of the Rādhākānta Maṭha.

mahanta. Thus, in the case of the Rādhākānta Maṭha, the *mahanta*-lineage (*mahanta-paramparā*) is also the *guru*-lineage (*guru-paramparā*). Ideally, the holder of the *gaddi* should unite ritual authority with spiritual power and scholarly erudition. All this makes him an *ācārya*. The head of the Rādhākānta Maṭha is widely renowned in Orissa for his position. All over Orissa one finds monks or lay followers who are in charge of a shrine or a small *maṭha* and have taken their initiation from the *mahanta* of the Rādhākānta Maṭha. However, this does not imply that all the representatives or members of institutions regard themselves as its branch (*śākhā*). Nevertheless, they take the *dīkṣā* preferably from the *mahanta* of the Rādhākānta Maṭha since he represents the highest spiritual and ritual authority. Seen from this perspective, the Rādhākānta Maṭha and its *mahanta* are the central institution within the Vakreśvara *parivāra*.

The eminent and long-established position of the *mahanta* of the Rādhākānta Maṭha as the holder of an *ācārya-gaddi* is also seen in his right to perform a *sevā* in the Jagannātha temple.[16] This right is also conferred on the *mahanta* through the ritual of investiture, the *sāṛi-bandha*.[17] This is a precondition for being allowed to perform rituals in the Jagannātha temple as a *mahānayaka mahanta*, that is, as a *mahanta* who has been approved by the Mahārājā of Puri.[18] The traditional and hereditary right of a *maṭha* to have a *sevā* in the Jagannātha temple testifies to the connection of the older *maṭha*s to the former structures of royal patronage. Another indication of this is the fact that most of the older *maṭha*s are located in close proximity to the Jagannātha temple. Still another sign of the importance of the *maṭha* is its size. The Rādhākānta Maṭha is a huge, palace-like compound which houses a quite impressive shrine and allows a large number of monks to be accommodated. Thus the older *maṭha*s were once related to the development of a type of urban infrastructure, which was started when the Jagannātha temple

---

[16] A list of the *maṭha*s who do such *sevā* is provided in Miśra 1998, 8-12. On the relationship between this *sevā* and the property of the *maṭha*s, especially the land-grants, see Rösel 1980, 90-7, Patnaik 2000, 173-91 (though this account lacks any reference to sources).

[17] The ritual of investiture for a *sevā* in the Jagannātha temple also consists of the 'binding of the silken cloth' (*śāṛhī-bandha*); cf. Patnaik 1994, 252-4, Rösel 1980, 67-9.

[18] See Patnaik 2000, 166ff.

was built.[19] The oldest *maṭhas* of Puri played an important part in the establishment of the Jagannātha cult as a royal or even state cult.[20] Because of this historical background, the oldest *maṭhas* of the Caitanya tradition and their *mahantas* are still accorded a certain prestige and authority within the internal infrastructure of the *maṭhas* of Puri. However, the impact and authority of the older system has been considerably restricted, because the Rādhākānta Maṭha is nowadays under the administration of the Hindu Religious Endowments Commission (HREC). Thus, for example, the performance of *śāṛhī-bandha* and the approval of the Mahārājā no longer guarantee *mahanta*-ship to one who has undergone these ceremonies. They are not legally binding and do not have to be accepted by the HREC, which alone decides on the legitimacy of succession. Thus the present *mahanta* of the Rādhākānta Maṭha has so far only been approved ritually, not legally, because a conflict over the succession is currently going through the courts.

Nevertheless, in the case of the Rādhākānta Maṭha several factors converge that contribute to its centrality in Puri and in the context of the Caitanya *sampradāya*. First of all, it is a *līlāsthāna* of the Caitanya within the *kṣetra* of Puri; therefore, it is important for the *sampradāya* as a whole. Secondly, it belongs to those *maṭhas* which once enjoyed royal patronage and were provided with the right *cum* duty (*adhikāra*) to perform a *sevā* in the Jagannātha temple. As a corollary, the accession to the position of *mahanta* was accompanied by the bestowal of this *adhikāra* through the 'binding of *śāṛhī*'. This implied that only Brahmans could become *mahantas* in this *maṭha*. Thirdly, on the level of the *parivāra*, the *maṭha* is regarded by the members of the Vakreśvara *parivāra* as the *ācārya gaddi*, that is, the seat of the *ācārya* who confers the final initiation and who is called upon by the other *maṭhas* to perform certain rituals. This position is also valid for those members of the *parivāra* who stay in institutions that are independent of the Rādhākānta Maṭha economically and/or administratively. Last, but not least, it is the largest *maṭha* of the Caitanya tradition in Puri, testifying to the extent of royal patronage that the *maṭha* once enjoyed. As has already been pointed out, the interplay of these factors and their impact on the institution are nowadays dependent on the legal and

---

[19] See Patnaik 1994, 61ff.

[20] On this process, see Kulke 1979, Patnaik 1994, 65ff., Miśra 1998, 1-3.

administrative framework established by the Hindu Religious Endowments Act.[21]

The existence of the framework seems to be one of the reasons why many *maṭha*s are nowadays part of a registered trust. This holds especially true for those who have been founded recently. As was pointed out above (sect. 1), these trusts can be integrated into the categorical and organizational framework provided by tradition. They can be regarded as the segments of a spiritual lineage. Among the impacts of this segmentation are the accommodation of different *guru*s and the proliferation of religious institutions. The different trusts often do not only create an administrative 'head office', but also new sacred centres that are connected with the life of the charismatic teacher. The impact of the 'trust' as the referential framework in which genealogies and centres have become embedded in modern times will be analyzed in the following. In doing so, we are shifting our focus from centres on the upper levels of the *sampradāya* and the *parivāra* to the more localized and regionalized level of the *gaṇa* and the trust.

Modern Groups: Rādhāramaṇa Caraṇa Das and Bhaktisiddhānta Sarasvatī

The centrality and sacredness of some of the religious institutions that belong to the Caitanya tradition in Orissa today are in many cases not based on their having been a *līlāsthāna* of Caitanya or of one of the founders of a 'family' (*parivāra*). Rather, they bear witness to the efforts to reform and revitalize the Caitanya tradition from the nineteenth century onwards. Two reformers gained special importance in Orissa since they both managed to establish new networks of monastic institutions and to attract many followers. One is Rādhāramaṇa Caraṇa Dās (1853-1905) who is quite renowned in West-Bengal and Orissa, but has until now remained almost unnoticed by scholars.[22] The other is the by now quite famous Bhaktisiddhānta Sarasvatī (1874-1936) who founded the Gauḍīya Mission and purposefully tried to spread his interpretation of the teachings of Caitanya not only all over India but also in

---

[21] The framework and its effects will be dealt with in a future publication. For some general orientation, see Derrett 1966.

[22] He is briefly mentioned by Mukherjee 1979, 108 and Chakravarti 1985, 299f.

South-East Asia, Europe and the USA. Both teachers contributed to a kind of renaissance of the Gauḍīya-tradition in the nineteenth and twentieth centuries by introducing new teachings and new practices as well as by reinterpreting certain terms and teachings. Thus institutions that are today regarded as central are often connected to the life of these two *gurus*. As will be shown, in spite of the changing patterns of organization and sponsoring, the segmentary structure, which the genealogical model of transmission implies, has become an element of continuity. In the following, I shall discuss these two reformers and the networks of institutions associated with them.

Rādhāramaṇa Caraṇa Dās and the revival of the Nityānanda parivāra *in Orissa*

Raicaraṇa Ghosh[23] was born in 1853 in Mahiṣkola (Jessore District, West Bengal) as the son of one of the richer zamindars. After losing his father and his three brothers, he married relatively early. Following the custom of the *kulīna kāyasthas* he practised polygamy, and he seems to have become a successful zamindar himself. But faced with a peasant rebellion, he left his job and his family and turned toward a religious life. Śaṅkarāraṇya Purī, who at that time was living near Ayodhyā, became his *mantra-guru.* After his initiation into the Nityānanda *parivāra* of the Caitanya-tradition Rādhāramaṇa went on a pilgrimage and visited Navadvipa, the birth-place of Caitanya, and Puri, where Caitanya had spend the last eighteen years of his life. Rādhāramaṇa stayed in Puri for quite a long time and he became, like Caitanya, famous for his ecstatic *kīrtana* performances especially during the car festival in Puri. He acquired a lot of support in Puri and was able to make his disciples the heads of two of the oldest *maṭhas* connected with the Caitanya tradition in Puri. He and his disciples also established themselves in other places in northern Orissa, mainly in Bhubaneswar, Cuttack and Kendrapara. He taught the doctrine of Nityānanda, who, being regarded as an incarnation of Balarāma (the brother of Kṛṣṇa), is renowned in the Caitanya tradition for his 'brotherly mood' towards the god Kṛṣṇa (*sakhya-bhāva*). Around 1885 he inaugurated a new

[23] The following sketch is based on information given in the *maṭhas*, in Kapoor 1993 and in Caritā-Sudhā 1996. The latter is a hagiographical account of Rādhāramaṇa; cf. Malinar 2002.

mantra-text, which was adopted by his followers and stresses the necessity to take refuge in Nityānanda in order to gain salvation. This new *mantra* was and still is a matter of controversy,[24] as is the acceptance of a practice, often denounced but never totally suppressed within the Caitanya tradition, of male devotees dressing up as a woman,[25] that is, as the maid-servant of the Goddess Rādhā. One of Rādhāramaṇa's closest disciples followed this practice. After several pilgrimages to Vrindavan and extended stays in Puri Rādhāramaṇa settled in Navadvipa in the newly founded Samājbādi Āśrama, where he died in 1905 and has his place of burial *(samādhi-pīṭha)*. In consequence, the Samājbādi Āśrama is now one of the sacred centres of the monastic institutions of that group within the Nityānanda *parivāra* which is called Rādhāramaṇa *gaṇa*. One of the closest disciples was Rāmdās Bābāji who became very influential and strengthened the position of the sub-family in Puri and in other parts of northern Orissa. Although the innovations introduced by Rādhāramaṇa Caraṇa Dās, like the new *mantra* text, are by no means not entirely accepted by other members of Nityānanda *parivāra* the institutions themselves are widely respected.

Rāmdās Bābājī had also been one of the key figures in a dispute that resulted in a split within the Rādhāramaṇa *gaṇa*. This relates to an argument over the spiritual status of Rādhāramaṇa Caraṇa Dās, which started in the Rāsabihārī Maṭha in Cuttack, where Rādhāramaṇa and some of his followers were staying. When one of them became infected with a deadly disease, Rādhāramaṇa started to recite a *mantra* and resuscitated the young man. As a result, some of his followers started to worship Rādhāramaṇa as a god (*deva*) and henceforth addressed him as 'Rādhāramaṇa Caraṇa Deva'. Although Rādhāramaṇa did not claim divinity for himself and seems to have been reluctant to encourage any open display of his veneration as a god, some of his followers continued with the practice. This was unacceptable to Rāmdās Bābājī, who left the Rāsabihārī Maṭha and established himself in the so-called Bengali Sahi of Cuttack in the compound of a family shrine for the Goddess Durgā, where he was taken care of by the priest in charge. The latter became deeply attached to Rāmdās Bābāji and it was decided to establish a *maṭha* on the compound. As a result, the Nitai-

[24] Cf. Malinar 2004.

[25] On this debate, cf. Haberman 1988.

Gaurāṅga Maṭha was established in this part of Cuttack. Today, it is better known as the Bengali Sahi Maṭha and it still belongs to the trust that was established by Rāmdās Bābājī.

The Rāsabihārī Maṭha, however, is not included in this trust, although it belongs to the Rādhāramaṇa *gaṇa*. Rather, it is regarded as the sacred centre in Orissa for the worship of Rādhāramaṇa Caraṇa Deva as a god. In the *maṭha* there a shrine with a golden statue of the *guru* standing on a *padmāsana*. Devotees can also be found in the districts of Cuttack and Kendrapara. A branch of the *maṭha* is located in Puri near Svargadvāra. However, this *maṭha*, which is also called Rāsabihārī, serves mainly as a *dharamśala*, a hostel for the devotees of Rādhāramaṇa Deva. Although the Rāsavihārī Maṭha in Cuttack belongs to the Rādhāramaṇa *gaṇa* and its head is related to the other members of the *gaṇa* through a common spiritual genealogy, their conflict with regard to the theological interpretation of their *guru* has also led to the existence of different sacred centres for the different groups.

Rāmdās Babajī seems to have been a charismatic teacher in his own right, and he was especially renowned as a singer. He succeeded in spreading the teachings of Rādhāramaṇa and assured that two of the older *maṭha*s of the Caitanya tradition in Puri, which had been re-established by Rādhāramaṇa, remained in charge of his disciples. These two *maṭha*s are the Jhāñjapitā Maṭha and Haridās Ṭhākura Maṭha. Still other disciples of Rāmdās Bābājī succeeded in establishing their own networks of religious institutions with corresponding sacred centres. The segmentation that is implied in the genealogical model thus again resulted in a proliferation of institutions. However, the members of the different segments regard themselves as *guru-bhāī*, or spiritual brothers. When Rāmdās Bābājī died in 1953, the following disciples of his (who were all related to each other as *'guru-bhāī')* were either in charge of important monasteries in Orissa or about to become charismatic *guru*s with *maṭha*s of their own:

1. Nitai Pada Dās: head of Haridās Ṭhākur Maṭha, Puri.
2. Paramānanda Dās: head of Jhāñjapitā Maṭha, Puri.
3. Śacīnanda Dās (also known as Bāyā Bābā): head of Nṛsimha Tikiri Maṭha in Kendrapara Town.
4. Chakradhara Paṇḍita: founder of Śyāmasundara Maṭha in Cuttack.

5. Mahānandana Dās (also known as Nanda Bābā): founder of Pañcatikiri Bāsudevapur Maṭha in Bhadrak District.

However, the fact that these monasteries are, on a conceptual level, related through spiritual kinship (*guru-bhāī*) does not mean that they form an economic or administrative unit. Rather, individual economic and administrative units have been created in the form of registered trusts managed by trust boards and head offices. Only the first two *maṭha*s on the list now belong to the same trust. Śacīnanda Dās and his two *guru-bhāī*s created their own trusts and became initiating *guru*s. Thus the trust is an important, if not the most important, level of organization. The trust board is often the arena of financial and administrative interaction between the monastic community and the lay followers and it also settles the procedure of initiation by choosing the initiating *guru*. I shall detail this structure with regard to the following two trusts:

The Nitai-Gaurāṅga Trust

This trust was founded by Rāmdās Bābājī, with its head office and head monastery in Calcutta. It is the Pathbādi Āśrama where Rāmdās Bābājī had resided until the end of his life and where his *samādhi-pīṭha* is now located. The trust board consists only of representatives of the more important *maṭha*s, who decide matters of property, the appointment of managers to the individual *maṭha*s etc. However, the individual *maṭha*s are also managed independently by their own local trust boards, though it is the head of the Pathbādi Āśrama in Calcutta who confers the final initiation (*bheka-dīkṣā*).

As already indicated, two of the oldest *maṭha*s of the Caitanya tradition in Puri have been re-established thanks to the efforts of Rādhāramaṇa and his disciple Rāmdās Bābājī. Thus the Haridās Ṭhākura Maṭha and the Jhāñjapitā Maṭha, two of the oldest *maṭha*s of the Caitanya tradition in Puri now belong by 'spiritual descent' to the Rādhāramaṇa *gaṇa*. Moreover, they are also related to each other organizationally by belonging to the Nitai-Gaurāṅga Trust. Rāmdās Bābājī made provisions for these *maṭha*s to remain in the *maṭha*-network he had created. The heads of both monasteries in Puri are members of the trust board and can thus exert an influence over affairs. Although not the most central institution of the trust or the *gaṇa*, the Haridās Thākura Maṭha is a sacred centre on the level of the *sampradāya*. It houses the burial place (*samādhi-pīṭha)* of Haridās Ṭhākura, the beloved companion of Caitanya. Haridās was a Muslim who had been converted to Vaiṣṇava *bhakti* by Caitanya. According to tradition, the *samādhi-pīṭha* was established by Caitanya himself. Haridās is venerated as the successful and unmatched master of *nāma-japa*, the continuous recitation of the name of god. In later times, the *maṭha* seems to have encountered problems since it had to be freed from mortgage (*bandha*). Also the Jhāñjapitā Maṭha is claimed to have been founded by a renowned teacher of the *samprādāya*, Narottama Dās. However, it is now primarily a sacred place for the followers of Rādhāramaṇa Caraṇa Dās, who not only re-established the centre, but also stayed there for several years. The room in which he lived has become a place of veneration. Presently, both *maṭhas* seem to be doing well. In recent years a huge gate has been constructed at the Haridās Ṭhākura Maṭha announcing that this is the burial place of Haridās. In the Jhāñjapitā Maṭha a remarkable crowd of about two hundred devotees gathers every evening in order to listen to the recitation and explanation of the *Bhāgavatapurāṇa* and other canonical texts by Śrī Sacīnanda Dās, the charismatic head of the *maṭha*.

Apart from these two *maṭhas* in Puri, the Bengali Sahi Maṭha in Cuttack, already-mentioned, also belongs to the trust. Furthermore, the trust also includes the Samājbādi Āśrama in Navadvipa, a *maṭha* at the birth place of Nityānanda and one in Vrindavan. Thus the trust, and with it the *gaṇa,* is institutionally present in all of the three main sacred centres of the *sampradāya*. It is an indication of the importance of the lesser organizational levels of *gaṇa* and trust that the trust has turned the *samādhi* site of its founder into the central and largest institution of its monastic network. This place is, however, central only for those who belong to this spiritual genealogy.

The Śrī Kalpataru Śacīnanda Sevā Trust

The other important network of monastic institutions in Orissa is the Kalpataru Śacīnanda Sevā Trust, which has spread over northern Orissa. Like the Nitai-Gaurāṅga Trust it belongs to the Rādhārāmaṇa *gaṇa* of the Nityānanda *parivāra*. The Kalpataru Śacīnanda Sevā Trust comprises fourteen *maṭhas*, of which only one is located outside Orissa.[26] The trust was founded by a disciple of Rāmdās Bābājī, Śacīnanda Dās (1898-1981), better known as Nāmācārya Bāyā Bābā, a charismatic *guru* with a remarkable following in the urban areas of Orissa.[27] The trust is managed by a trust board, about whose constitution particulars vary. According to some it consists of seven members, while others said that there are eleven or more. Apparently the original members of the Board had been personally selected and appointed by Nāmācārya Bāyā Bābā. Both monks and lay followers are members of the trust board. The trust legally owns the *maṭha*s and is thus in charge of the finances. It also decides who is to be appointed as the manager of a *maṭha*. In addition, each *maṭha* has a local executive committee. The influence of the lay followers is obvious in their presence in the decision-making bodies of the trust and in the individual *maṭha*s. Another sign of their influence is that the two largest and most resourceful *maṭha*s are now located in the two commercial and administrative urban centres of northern Orissa, Bhubaneswar and Cuttack.[28] Both *maṭha*s were founded by Nāmācārya Bāyā Bābā himself. Bhubaneswar houses the largest temple-complex of all the Bāyā Bābā Maṭhas and is a well-know place in this part of the city.[29] However, the *samādhi-pīṭha* of Bāyā Bābā is located in Cuttack and therefore this *maṭha* is one of the major sacred centres for the followers. In addition, the head of this *maṭha* is authorized to perform all initiations.[30] His followers consider Nāmācārya Bāyā Bābā to be a *guru* from Orissa, who came back from Vrindavan in order to continue with his spiritual- and healing activities in the region of his birth. Thus representatives of the *maṭha*s and lay followers regard it as their duty not only to preserve the memory of their *guru* but also to continue with his efforts to spread the

---

[26] This is the Akhaṇḍa Kīrtana Bhavan in Ramanareti, Vrindavan.

[27] For further details see Malinar 2004.

[28] Earlier, the most important *maṭha* was located in Kendrapara Town. This *maṭha* was given to Bāyā Bābā by his *guru* Rāmdās Babāji through his will. Bāyā Bābā resided there for almost twenty years and succeeded in making it a rather large compound. However, it now seems to be in a more difficult situation, especially since the devastation caused by the 'super-cyclone' in 1999 and the flood of 2001.

[29] On this *maṭha*, see Malinar 2004.

[30] Only the head of *maṭha* in Vrindvan, the only *maṭha* of this network outside Orissa, is also authorized to confer initiation.

chanting of the name of god in Orissa (and beyond, if possible).[31] However, many members of the *maṭha*s and lay devotees also seem to be attached to the Paṭhbādi Āśrama in Calcutta, the *maṭha* founded by Bāyā Bābā's *guru* Rāmdās Bābājī (see 3.1.1). They do not regard themselves as being separate from their institutions in West Bengal. In spite of the separate organization into different trusts, spiritual kinship binds together the different *maṭha*s and their members.

The Kalpataru Seva Trust also runs one *maṭha* in Puri, the Akhaṇḍa Nāma Maṇḍapa, founded by Bāyā Bābā in 1968. In contrast to the importance of the Puri *maṭha*s of the Nitai-Gaurāṅga Trust, this *maṭha* plays only a marginal role within the Kalpataru Trust and also in Puri itself. Nevertheless, its existence shows that it is important for this network too to be present in Puri. The significance of its presence is also indicated by the fact that the prestigious and costly practice of *akhaṇḍanāma-kīrtana*, the uninterrupted chanting of the name of god, is maintained in this *maṭha*.[32] Nevertheless, in the context of the Kalpataru network, the *maṭha* in Puri is less important than the main centres in Cuttack or Bhubaneswar . One reason for this is that Puri has never been a main residence of the *guru*. Another can be seen in the fact that the *maṭha* is not so much used by followers who visit Puri since many of them make the 'Puri trip' within one day, or else stay with relatives or friends. However, the *maṭha* is visited in order to pay homage to the seat, the bed and the chappals of the *guru*, which are exhibited in one of the rooms. If one compares the position of the Puri *maṭha*s in the context of these two trusts they differ in regard to their centrality. This, in turn, shows that the networks differ with regard to the social context in which lay followers support and use the respective institutions.

As already indicated, the Jhāñjapitā and the Haridās Ṭhākura Maṭha of the Nitai-Gaurāṅga Trust have strong connections with West Bengal and especially with some wealthy lay followers in Calcutta. For Bengali devotees, Puri is a very important pilgrimage centre and the *maṭha*s provide certain facilities such as teaching,

[31] Another aspect of these efforts is the large number of publications by the trust which deal with the life and teaching of Bāyā Bābā and give instructions to his devotees, for example a guide to the pilgrimage sites connected with the *guru*. Cf. Śrī Kalpataru Bera Parikrama 1989.

[32] On this practice, see Malinar 2004.

pūjā, the organization of festivals and sometimes also accommodation. In contrast to this, the dissemination of the *maṭhas* belonging to the Kalpataru Trust points to Orissa being the domain of their founder *guru*. Therefore, the *samādhī-pīṭha* in Cuttack is much more important for the followers of Nāmācārya Bāyā Bābā than the *maṭha* in Puri. This difference between the two networks shows that the trust indeed provides an interface between the monastic community and its lay followers, a place where the influence and the requirements of the latter become manifest. Yet another pattern of dissemination, which reflects major reforms concerning the tradition as a whole, is discernible in the network of *maṭhas* that has been created by Bhaktisiddhānta Sarasvatī and his followers.

Bhaktisiddhānta Sarasvatī and his followers in Orissa

The networks of the Rādhāramaṇa-*gaṇa* by and large mirror the genealogical model of transmission and of *guru affiliation* and show corresponding levels of segmentation. Since the teachings of Rādhāramaṇa did not result in a breach with the traditional lineage system, his followers are regarded as belonging to the Nityānanda *parivāra* as one its segments. In contrast to this, the aim of Bhaktisiddhānta Sarasvatī was to establish a more centralized organization which could function as the basis for co-ordinated missionary activities all over India and in other countries.

Bhaktisiddhānta Sarasvatī[33] was born in 1874 in Puri as Vimala Prasāda Datta, the son of Kedarnātha Datta, better known as Bhaktivinoda Ṭhākura, the important reformer of the Caitanya tradition in the nineteenth century.[34] He studied at the Serampore Missionary School and already at that time, around 1885, had received the *mantra* initiation from his father. Later, he received a thorough education in the various branches of Sanskrit literature. He was especially versatile in traditional astronomy (*jyotiṣa*). Later he was employed by the Rājā of Tripura as a chronicler. However, he decided to dedicate his life to the propagation of Caitanya's teachings and chose the life of a celibate. Consequently, from 1898

[33] This brief account is based on data collected in the *maṭhas*, the Advent Centenary Souvenir and Śrī Śrīla Sarasvatī Ṭhākura, 1973.

[34] On the life and teachings of Bhaktivinoda Ṭhākura, see R. Dasa 1989 and S. Dasa 1999.

onwards he accompanied his father on his pilgrimages and preaching tours throughout India. After his father's death in 1914, Bhaktisiddhānta intensified his activities. He became the president of the Viśva Vaiṣṇava Rāj Sabhā, which had been founded or rather re-established by Bhakti Vinoda Ṭhākura in 1886.[35] Another task, in which he followed his father, was that he became the editor of the influential Vaiṣṇava monthly *Sajjanatoṣanī*. In 1918 he took *saṃnyāsa*-initiation and renounced worldly life completely.[36] In the same year he founded the Caitanya Maṭha at Mayapur, which is regarded by his followers as Caitanya's real birthplace. The establishment of this *maṭha* was followed by the foundation of the Gauḍīya Maṭha in Calcutta in the same year, and many more *maṭha*s were established in the following years all over India (e.g. in Madras, Delhi, Bombay, Varanasi, Mathura, and Vrindavan). In 1931 the Puruṣottama Gauḍīya Maṭha in Puri was established, followed by other *maṭha*s in Cuttack, Bhubaneswar and Alarnath. In his attempt to enlarge the catchment area of his mission he also sent his disciples to Europe (in 1933, a preaching centre in London was founded) and to the USA. A huge network had been created when he died in 1937. However, since he had failed to determine succession, this network fell apart and became segmented.

Like his father, Bhaktisiddhānta Sarasvatī had tried to combine the Caitanya tradition with modernity. This involved him fighting against all the interpretations and practices that he thought to be against the 'true spirit' of Caitanya's teachings. He reinterpreted the concept of brahmanhood[37] and criticized the traditional view that only those who had been born as Brahmins could conduct rituals in the temple and confer initiation. Therefore he proclaimed that, at a certain stage, initiation into to the *sampradāya* turns any male[38] adept into a Brahmin, irrespective of his original caste. This is

---

[35] This assembly is traced back to the time of Jīva Gosvāmin.

[36] Consequently, the followers of Bhaktisiddhānta Sarasvatī regard themselves as *saṃnyāsī* after having taking the final *dīkṣā*; in contrast to this, the monks belonging to the 'traditional' *parivāras* call themselves '*bābājī*'. The difference is also indicated by the colour of their garments. While the *samnyāsī* wear saffron, the *bābājī* wear white.

[37] This had been exposed in his treatise *Brāhmaṇa and Vaiṣṇava*; cf. Sarasvatī Ṭhākura 1999.

[38] Female adepts are excluded from this procedure due to what is seen as their 'impurity', consequently, they cannot become *saṃnyāsinīs*.

symbolized by providing the adept with the sacred thread and allowing him to perform *pūjā*. Moreover, Sarasvatī argued that spiritual descent and kinship established by the 'tradition of teaching' (*śikṣā-paramparā*) is of greater importance than the traditional genealogical model of uninterrupted transmission from teacher to disciple. Consequently, the spiritual pedigree should not automatically consist of hereditary lineages of teachers, but only of those who have contributed to the development of theological doctrine or spiritual practice. In consequence, he created a new 'line of transmission of important teaching *gurus*', a *śikṣā-guruparamparā.*[39] Thus he claimed spiritual descent from instruction *gurus* (*śikṣā-gurus*), whom he grouped together on the basis of their scholarly or poetic achievements alone, without considering their traditional *guru-paramparā*. As a result, the application of the referential categories (see section 1) to the followers of Bhaktisiddhānta is more ambiguous since this *paramparā* implies a breach with the traditional genealogical model. His *śikṣā-paramparā* cannot easily be inserted into these pedigrees. Thus the categories of *parivāra*, *gaṇa* and even *sampradāya* do not easily apply. This difficulty is reflected in the divergent statements of my interview partners. Some claimed to belong to the Sarasvatī *parivāra*, some to the Nityānanda *parivāra*, others to the Narottama Dāsa *parivāra* etc., while yet others (and often those who are not followers of Sarasvatī) spoke of a Sarasvatī *sampradāya* and regarded the Caitanya tradition as divided. Time and again, tensions between the older *parivāras* and the followers of Sarasvatī become manifest, especially in the three main sacred centres (*dhāman*) of the *sampradāya* where they co-exist. In the case of Puri, this seems to go back to the time, around 1900, when both Rādhāramaṇa Caraṇa Dās and Bhaktisiddhānta Sarasvatī stayed in Puri and propagated their respective faiths.[40]

As pointed out above, during his life time Sarasvatī succeeded in establishing a centralized structure of organization which connected the single institution with one centre and head office and thus created a unified representation of the mission. The establishment

---

[39] For further details, see Brzezinski 1996.

[40] This the pointed out in Kapoor 1993, 473ff., Caritā-Sudhā V, 241-5 (hagiography of Rādhāramaṇa Caraṇa Dās) and Advent Centenary Souvenir, 4. The doctrinal aspects of this debate cannot be dealt with in this article.

of the so-called Gauḍīya- and Caitanya Maṭhas was a consequence of purposeful missionary activities. Correspondingly, the dissemination of the *maṭha*s shows certain characteristic features. First, it reflects Sarasvatī's efforts with regard to renew the *sampradāya.* Most spectacular perhaps was the establishment of the village of Mayapur (West Bengal) as the 'real' birth-place of Caitanya and as a new main sacred centre of the Caitanya tradition. In this he followed Bhaktivinoda Ṭhākura's 'discovery'[41] of the site. The acceptance or non-acceptance of this new place provoked a first division within the *sampradāya.* In Orissa these efforts materialized in the establishment of *maṭha*s in two important *līlāsthāna*s of Caitanya. One is located in Remuna (Baleshvar District) where, according to tradition, the deity's garland fell on Caitanya while he was worshipping the *mūrti* of Gopinātha; the other is in Alarnath (Puri District). Secondly, this points to the social groups which supported his activities. These were mainly the newly emerging upper-middle classes, rich families of traders, lawyers, politicians and bureaucrats. Later, followers from Europe and the USA also became sponsors. Thus only a few *maṭha*s of Sarasvatī's group are to be found in small towns or villages if they are not also regarded as *līlāsthāna.* Rather, the capitals of the provinces (before Independence) and the centres of commercial and administrative life were the preferred places for establishing *maṭha*s. Thus there exist *maṭha*s not only in Calcutta, but also in Delhi, Bombay, and Madras etc. Accordingly, in Orissa they can be found in Cuttack, Bhubaneswar, Puri and Berhampur.

However, as indicated above, the centralized structure that Sarasvatī created seems to have been anchored in him. Nowadays, his followers are divided into segments and are organized into different networks and trusts. After his death in 1937 two disciples claimed the position of successor since Sarasvatī did not appoint one. The quarrel about the succession resulted in litigation which kept the Calcutta High Court busy for more than ten years. The outcome was that the *maṭha*s were divided among the disciples. The two oldest *maṭha*s of the Sarasvatī network became the headquarters of the two separate trusts: The Gauḍīya Mission Trust kept its headquarters in Calcutta in the Śrī Gauḍīya Maṭha, while the Śrī Caitanya Maṭha Trust established the Caitanya Maṭha in

---

[41] Cf. R. Dasa 1989,162-9; S. Dasa 1999,102ff.

Mayapur as its head office. Both trusts run *maṭhas* in Orissa and both are represented in Puri. In the aftermath of the litigation and the tensions it created, other disciples created their own networks and trusts. All together there are seven Trusts in Puri that follow Bhaktisiddhānta Sarasvatī's line of teaching, each running a *maṭha* in Puri.[42] Numerically, is has a rather strong presence, which is also enhanced by the often impressive seize of the institutions. This demonstrates that the centrality of Puri as a main sacred centre of the tradition is also acknowledged by the followers of Bhaktisiddhānta Sarasvatī again testifying to the fact that the segmentation of the transmission of teachings results in the proliferation of institutions and thus in an expansion of the religious community. In this regard, the followers of Bhaktisiddhānta Sarasvatī also reflect the traditional patterns of dissemination in a modern setting.

These individual *maṭha*s are mainly connected with the activities of their respective trust, whose head offices are in all cases located outside Orissa, such as in Mayapur, Calcutta or Vrindavan. Most of them offer accommodation to their followers and sometimes also to other people. This testifies to their function as a base for pilgrimage in and around Puri. It also indicates that there are marked differences with regard to the lay followers and to the anchorage of the movement in regional and pan-Indian contexts. Thus these institutions seem to be rather disconnected from the internal infrastructure of the other *maṭha*s of the Caitanya tradition in Puri.

---

[42] The Gauḍīya Mission owns the Puruṣottāma Maṭha in Puri, which was founded by Bhaktisiddhānta Sarasvatī in 1931. The *maṭha* is located near the Ṭoṭa Gopinātha Temple; other *maṭha*s of the Trust in Orissa are in Cuttack, Alarnath, and Remuna. The Caitanya Maṭha Trust runs the Puruṣottama Gauḍīya Maṭha located next to the Haridās Ṭhākura Maṭha. Also close by is the Sarasvata Gauḍīya Āsana and Mission, which houses an impressive temple run by the Gauḍīya Sevait Sangha in Caluctta. Newly established in this area is the Caitanya Sarasvata Maṭha, which is included in a Trust of the same name. Near the Jagannātha Temple is the Gauḍīya Maṭha, which is run by the Caitanya Gauḍīya Maṭha Trust. The *maṭha* is claimed to be the birth place of Bhaktisiddhānta Sarasvatī and is the only *maṭha* of the Trust in Orissa within a huge network that spreads all over India. Then, there is the Caitanya Chandra Āśrama (Aiṭoṭa) near the Guṇḍīca Mandir. This belongs to the Śrī Kṛṣṇa-Caitanya Mission which has seventeen branches, the majority of them located in Andhra Pradesh and two more in Orissa (in Bhubaneswar and Berhampur).

This is not only asserted by members of the 'traditional' *parivāras*, it is also manifest, for example, in the fact that the *maṭhas* belonging to the Bhaktisiddhānta Sarasvatī tradition are not listed as belonging to the organization of the *sampradāya* in Puri, the 'Śrī Mādhvagaureśvara Vaiṣṇava Saṅgha Purī'.[43] The difficulties indicated above in integrating the followers of Sarasvatī into the genealogical model as one of its segment again become manifest. Nevertheless, the group shows patterns of segmentation that again result in a decentralized structure of what may be termed the Sarasvatī *parivāra* or even the Sarasvatī *sampradāya.*

Conclusion

The dissemination of Caitanyaite communities in Orissa has been analyzed (1) with regard to a set of categories of classification that is used by most communities, (2) by considering different networks and centres in contemporary Orissa with a special emphasis on Puri, one of the main sacred centres of the whole tradition. The transmission of Caitanya's teachings through different spiritual lineages has resulted in the segmentation of the religious community (*sampradāya*) and in a proliferation of centres and institutions. Differences in interpretation and practice with relation to the religious doctrine have not led to repeated schisms, but seem to have been accommodated within the genealogical model. This structure is also reflected in the referential categories that are used in defining the position of the individual segments within the tradition as a whole. The segments and the categories are defined in relation to each other, something that also applies to the central institutions and the sacred centres which one finds on the different levels. While the level of *sampradāya* (the category that refers to the religious tradition as a whole) is not represented by one central institution, its unity is nevertheless based, *inter alia*, on the acceptance of three main sacred centres. The case of Puri, the main sacred centre of the *sampradāya* in Orissa, has shown that the different groups, networks, and trusts are all represented there. In these ways, the centrality of the sacred centre is, on the one hand, acknowledged and enhanced, while on the other hand, it testifies to

---

[43] In the *pañjikās* published by the *saṅgha* 69 *maṭhas* and *kuṭīs* belonging to different *parivāras* and *gaṇas* are listed, but none of the Sarasvatī *maṭhas*, cf. *Vaiṣṇava bratotsava pañjikā*, 12ff.

the proliferation of institutions and centres as the effect of segmentation. The diversification of transmission on the middle and lower levels of organization can thus be seen as a method of expansion.[44] The *sampradāya* spreads and is disseminated, even though this results time and again in the fragmentation and isolation of institutions. The definitional scope of what is referred to as *sampradāya* cannot, however, be fundamentally changed or enlarged. The scope of this category seems rather to be limited, although this effect is not represented or administered by a singular central institution. Still, the quest for a common denominator in the face of an accepted refraction of the tradition has been and still is a decisive factor in the shaping of this tradition.[45]

Examples for these processes are the new networks that were established by Rādhāramaṇa Caraṇa Dās and Bhaktisiddhānta Sarasvatī respectively. Although the former created a new *mantra* etc., he made no attempt to alter the value structure implied by the category of *sampradāya*. Because the new group, the so-called Rādhāramaṇa Gaṇa, accepts its status within the genealogical model it can be positioned and identified as a specific segment of the *sampradāya*. This contrasts with Bhaktisiddhānta Sarasvatī's position. In his attempt to unify and to unite the *sampradāya* he changed one element of its definition, the genealogical model. He established a new line of transmission claiming to represent the most important teachers of the Caitanya tradition irrespective of the genealogical model. The other members felt and still feel this to be highly problematic, and the categories of classification and, along with them, the unity of the community are at stake. In consequence, the interaction between the 'traditional' *parivāra*s and the followers of Bhaktisiddhānta Sarasvatī shows certain patterns of exclusion and inclusion on both sides. Indicative of this are the difficulties and uncertainties in placing the followers of Bhaktisiddhānta Sarasvatī within the referential framework created by the categories of *sampradāya*, *parivāra,* and *gaṇa*. This indicates that here the question is which elements make up the *sampradāya* and how they are to be represented and transmitted. It has to be seen whether the genealogical model will accommodate the fission between those

[44] Following what Sahlins, in his study of segmentary lineages, calls 'predatory expansion' this could be called 'spiritual expansion'; cf. Sahlins 1961, 330.

[45] Cf. Haberman 1988 and Cakravarti 1985, passim.

who follow the line of teaching initialized by Bhaktisiddhānta Sarasvatī and the other 'families'. How this situation will be dealt with in the future is an open question. The debates continue, indicating that categories like *sampradāya* or *parivāra* are not just labels, but, rather, categories of reference whose interplay constitutes an important framework for the definition and the self-perception of the religious community. Decentralization and segmentation appear to be structures of the transmission, expansion and revitalization of tradition that continue to persist in the changing contexts of modernity.

References

Advent Centenary Souvenir of Shri Shrila Prabhupad 1874-1974. Edited by Tridandiswami Shrimad Bhakti Shrirup Bhagabat Maharaj, Calcutta: Gaudiya Math.

Brzezinski, J. 1996-97. 'The Paramparā Institution in Gauḍīya Vaiṣṇavism', in *Journal of Vaiṣṇava Studies* 5,1:151-82.

Burghart, Richard 1978. 'The Founding of the Ramanandi Sect', in *Ethnohistory* 25,2:121-39.

Caitanyacaritāmṛta. Caitanya Caritāmṛta of Kṛṣṇadāsa Kavirāja. A Translation and Commentary by Edward C. Dimock, Jr. With an Introduction by Edward C. Dimock, Jr. and Tony K. Stewart. Edited by Tony K. Stewart, Cambridge (Mass.), London: Harvard University Press.

Carita Sudhā 1996. *Carita Sudhā, patitapavana śrī śrī rādhāramaṇa devaṅka puṇya līilācarita,* Khaṇḍa 1-6, Cuttack: Rasabihārī Maṭha.

Chakravarti, R. 1985. Vaiṣṇavism in Bengal: A Historical Study, 1486-1900, Calcutta: Sanskrit Pustak Bhandar.

Dasa, Rupavilasa 1989. *The Seventh Goswami: A Biography of His Divine Grace Śrīlā Saccidānanda Bhaktivinoda Ṭhakurā (1838-1914)*, Manning: New Jaipur Press.

Dasa, Shukavak N. 1999. *Hindu Encounter with Modernity: Kedarnath Datta Bhaktivinoda. Vaiṣṇava Theologian,* Los Angeles: Sri.

Deadwhyler, W. 1992. 'The Sampradāya of Śrī Caitanya', in Steven J. Rosen (ed.), *Vaiṣṇavism: Contemporary Scholars discuss the Gauḍīya Tradition,* New York: Folk Books, 127-40.

Derrett, J. Duncan M. 1966. The Reform of Hindu Religious Endowments, in Donald E. Smith (ed.), *South Asian Politics and Religion*, Princeton: Princeton University Press, 311-36.

Dimock, E.C. 1966. 'Doctrine and Practice Among the Vaiṣṇavas of Bengal', in M. Singer (ed.), *Krishna: Myths, Rites, and Attitudes*, Chicago, London: University of Chicago Press, 41-63.

Dumont, L. 1980. *Homo Hierarchicus: The Caste System and Its Implications,* Chicago: University of Chicago Press.

Entwistle, A.W. 1987. *Braj: Centre of Krishna Pilgrimage,* Groningen: Forsten.

Haberman, D. 1988. *Acting as a Way to Salvation: A Study of Rāgānugā Bhakti Sādhana,* New York: Oxford University Press.

Heinritz, G. 1979. *Zentralität und Zentrale Orte. Eine Einführung*, Stuttgart: Teubner.

Kapoor, O.B.L. 1993. *The Life of Love. Biography of Sri Srimat Radharamana Charana Das Deva the Veritable Embodiment of Sri Caitanya Mahaprabhu's Universal Religion of Love,* Vrindavan: Sarasvati Jayasri Classics.

— 1997. 'Śrī Caitanya and the Mādhava Sampradāya', in *Journal of Vaiṣṇava Studies* 5,3:35-54.

Kulke, H. 1979. *Jagannātha-Kult und Gajapati-Königtum. Ein Beitrag zur Geschichte religiöser Legitimation hinduistischer Herrscher*, Wiesbaden: Steiner (Schriftenreihe des Süasien-Instituts der Universität Heidelberg, Band 23).

Malinar, A. 2002. 'Rādhāramaṇa Caraṇa Das und die Caitanya-Nachfolge in Orissa: Zur Textualisierung von Charisma', in D. Lönne (ed.), *Toḥfa-e-Dil. Festschrift für Helmuth Nespital,* Reinbek: Wezler, 295-313.

— 2004. 'Mantra-Performance as a Religious Institution: Śrī Kalpataru Sevā Āśrama in Bhubaneshwar', in A. Malinar, J. Beltz, and H. Frese (eds.), *Text and Context in the History, Literature, and Religion of Orissa*, Heidelberg, Delhi: Manohar, 175-202.

McLeod, W.H. 1978. 'On the Word *panth*: A Problem of Terminlogy and Definition', in *Contributions to Indian Sociology*, N.S. 12, 2:287-95

Miśra, Bhāskara 1998. *Pūrire maṭha saṃskṛti*, Purī: Sadgranth Niketan.

Mukherjee, P. 1940. *The History of Medieval Vaishnavism in Orissa*, Calcutta: Prabasi Press.

— 1979. *History of the Chaitanya Faith in Orissa*, Delhi: Manohar.

O'Connell, J.T. 1999. 'Chaitanya Vaishnava Movement: Symbolic Means of Institutionalization', in J. T. O'Connell (ed.), *Organizational and Institutional Aspects of Indian Religious Movements*, Shimla: Indian Institute of Advanced Studies, 215-39.

Patnaik, Himanshu S. 1994. *Lord Jagannath: His Temple, Cult and Festivals,* New Delhi: Aryan Books International.

Patnaik, N. 2000. *Sacred Complex in Orissa (Study of Three Major Aspects of the Sacred Complex),* New Delhi: Gyan Publishing House.

Rösel, J. 1980. *Der Palast des Herrn der Welt. Entstehungsgeschichte und Organisation der Indischen Tempel- und Pilgerstadt Puri*, München: Weltforum Verlag.

Rosen, Steven J. (ed.) 1992. *Vaiṣṇavism: Contemporary Scholars Discuss the Gauḍīya Tradition,* New York: Folk Books.

Sahlins, Marshall D. 1961. 'The Segmentary Lineage: An Organization of Predatory Expansion, in *American Anthropologist* 63,1:322-45.

Śrī Gambhīrā. *Yāṃ nivasita sadā śrīla gaurāṅga candraḥ. Paṇḍita Śrī Hemāṅga Prasāda Dāsaṅka dvāra sampādita,* Brahmapur: Brahmapur Siddhānta Presa, n.d.

Śrī Śrī Kalpataru beṛā parikramā 1989, Kendrapara: Kalpataru Presa Nṛsiṃha Ṭīkiri Maṭha.

Śrī-Śrīla Sarasvatī Ṭhākur; saṃkṣipt caritāmṛt 1973, Kalkattā: Śrīcaitanya Gauḍīya Maṭh.

Śrīla Bhaktisiddhānta Sarasvatī Ṭhākura 1999. *Brāhmaṇa and Vaiṣṇava: The Conclusive Comparison between Brāhmaṇas and Vaiṣṇavas*, Delhi: Vrajraj Press.

Stewart, Tony Kevin 1985. 'The Biographical Images of Kṛṣṇa-Caitanya: A Study in the Perception of Divinity', Chicago (unpublished Ph.D. thesis).

Vaiṣṇava Vratotsava Pañjikā 2001-2002, Puri: Prakāśika Śrīmadhvagaureśvara Vaiṣṇava Saṅgha, n.d.

4

In Search of Goddess Virajā*

Susmita Arp

Jajpur, Bhubaneswar, and Puri are generally seen as a triad of holy sites, uniting three great all-Indian gods: Śiva residing in Bhubaneswar, Viṣṇu in Puri, and Durgā in Jajpur. Of these, goddess Virajā of Jajpur is usually considered the most ancient. K.N. Mahapatra is thus expressing the common view when he says, 'the deity of Virajā attained great fame and prominence in Orissa long before Jagannāth and Lingarāja came into picture.'[1] In a recent book, Brighenti describes Virajā as 'the earliest known Śākta deity of Orissa' and her image as the 'oldest extant Mahiṣamardinī icon of Orissa'.[2]

Many scholars see Durgā as the presiding deity of Jajpur from at least the Gupta period onwards. They stress the great antiquity of the cult image in the present Virajā temple and, following R.P. Chanda, contend that it is a two-armed Mahiṣāsuramardiṇī in Gupta style.[3] Chanda's *Memoirs of the Archaeological Survey of India* reveal, however, that he only saw the icon wrapped in cloth, and that he based his notes mainly on what local priests told him.[4] The

---

* I would like to thank Professor Thomas Oberlies for several valuable hints during the preparation of this article.

[1] Mahapatra 1962, 26.

[2] Brighenti 2001, 6 and 219. See also Schneider 1984, 153.

[3] For the arguments and the continuous reference to Chanda, see Brighenti 2001, 72; Parida 1999, 44; Pradhan 1997, 23 and 62-3; Das 1985, 95 and Dhal 1984, 8-9. Even Panigrahi, who earlier had critized Chanda, seems to follow him in his *History of Orissa* without giving reasons. Compare Panigrahi 1961, 73 and Panigrahi 1981, 331.

[4] Chanda 1930, 4: 'The image of Virajā enshrined in the temple is hidden by clothes; consequently no other part of her body than the bejewelled head is visible. From the *dhyāna* or description of the image recited by the priests and from their account we learn that Virajā is a form of Durgā engaged in killing the buffalo demon.... Whatever may be the age of the present image of Virajā, the two-armed type of Mahishamardinī carries us back to an early period, probably to pre-Gupta period.'

age and iconographical features of the Virajā image still await proper study and are beyond the scope of this article. I am concerned with the other main argument adduced to prove the great antiquity of the Virajā cult, the references to it in Sanskrit literature. K.C. Panigrahi, considering the *Mahābhārata* and later texts, concludes that '[t]he Sakta shrine of Viraja at Jajpur existed in the pre-Christian era'.[5] U.N. Dhal, editing the *Virajakṣetramāhātmya*, collected many relevant text passages in his introduction, which show that the textual evidence on goddess Virajā is very weak.[6] Yet, he also is of the same opinion: 'It may be taken for granted that originally goddess Virajā was worshipped in the Kṣetra during the Gupta age.'[7] The Sanskrit texts, however, presents a different picture: I found only very few sources that suggested that Virajā is a goddess of the late medieval kind.

Beginning with the inscriptions, I could not find any epigraphical evidence about Virajā or any other goddess in Jajpur. As shown by S.N. Rajaguru[8] inscriptions of the Bhaumakara period only mention a city named Viraja. Most of them were not found in Jajpur but somewhere else. They contain little information on Viraja, depicting the place as a political and cultural centre where kings reside, land grants are issued, and scribes or famous physicians have their origin. One of the two inscriptions found in Jajpur itself records that a temple for Bhava (i.e. Śiva) named Mādhaveśvara was erected by a Bhaumakara queen. The other inscription consists of only two words inscribed on a Cāmuṇḍa figure, and, according to Sircar, probably presents the name of an early Bhaumakara queen who donated the image.[9]

---

[5] Panigrahi 1981, 330.

[6] Dhal 1984. For a study of puranic text passages, see also Dhal 1993.

[7] Dhal 1984, 57. It seems that his main argument, again, is the date of the Virajā image. See ibid., 8-9.

[8] Rajaguru 1980.

[9] See Sircar 1949 for the two inscriptions found in Jajpur.

The *Tīrthayātrāparvan* of the *Mahābhārata*[10] mentions the river Vaitaraṇī as a place of pilgrimage and calls it *virajam tīrtham* that purifies the visitor and his family, making him 'shine like the moon' (*virājati yathā śaśī*). It seems that with these words the text tries to devise a Sanskrit etymology for *viraja*, which might suggest that the name originally derives from some indigenous word. Another passage in the *Tīrthayātrāparvan*[11] describes the place as suitable for sacrifices and reports that the Pāṇḍavas took a bath in the river Vaitaraṇī and performed ancestral rites here. Neither passage mentions that any gods were worshipped here; Viraja only appears as the name of a place. No evidence suggests that the *Mahābhārata* 'certifies the existence of the shrine of Virajā on the river Vaitaraṇī in the first centuries of the Christian era'.[12]

Some Purāṇas know the river Vaitaraṇī or Virajā as a place of pilgrimage—here Virajā is the name of a locality, a city or a river. This is the case with a passage in a *Skandapurāṇa*, which is presently being edited by Bakker and others on the basis of some early manuscripts, one being dated AD 818. The passage praises Ekāmra (Bhubaneswar) and Virajā as two places where Śiva is

---

[10] *Mahābhārata* 3.83.6-7:
tato vaitaraṇīm gatvā nadīṃ pāpapramocanīm|
virajam tīrtham āsādya virājati yathā śaśī||6
prabhavec ca kule puṇye sarvapāpam vyapohati|
gosahasraphalaṃ labdhvā punāti ca kulam naraḥ||7

[11] *Mahābhārata* 3.114.4 6 and 13:
ete kaliṅgāḥ kaunteya yatra vaitaraṇī nadī|
yatrāyajata dharmo 'pi devāñ śaraṇam etya vai||4
ṛṣibhiḥ samupāyuktaṃ yajñiyaṃ giriśobhitam|
uttaraṃ tīram etaddhi satataṃ dvijasevitam||5
samena devayānena pathā svargam upeyuṣaḥ|
atra vai ṛṣayo 'nye 'pi purā kratubhir ījire||6 ...
tato vaitaraṇīṃ sarve pāṇḍavā draupadī tathā|
avatīrya mahābhāgā tarpayān cakrire pitṝn|| 13

The passage between 6 and 13 narrates how Rudra once seized the sacrificial animal and finally was appeased by the gods who decided that in future the best share of the sacrifice should be reserved for Rudra. Whoever recites this story and touches the water here will follow the path of the gods and his eyes shine forth, so the text promises.

[12] Brighenti 2001, 68-9.

worshipped.[13] Several other texts mention Virajā as a holy site but do not say anything about gods that are worshipped there. The *Brahmāṇḍapurāṇa* lists Virajā, and in another verse names Viraja (with a short 'a'), among the suitable places for the performance of ancestral rites (*śrāddha*).[14] The *Vāmanapurāṇa* names Virajā together with Prayāga, Gayāśiras, Puṣkara and Samantapañcaka as the five *vedi*s of Brahmā, Virajā being the southern one.[15] The *Garuḍapurāṇa* and the *Gayāmāhātmya* of the *Vāyupurāṇa* teach that tonsure and fasting are prescribed for all *tīrtha*s except Kurukṣetra, Viśālā, Virajā and Gayā.[16] In another section the *Garuḍapurāṇa* includes Virajas and Puruṣottama in a list of sacred places.[17] The *Padmapurāṇa* reproduces one of the *tīrtha* lists from the *Mahābhārata* with slight variations, including two verses on the Virajatīrtha.[18]

Of special interest is a passage in the *Kūrmapurāṇa* praising Nārāyaṇa-Puruṣottama of Puri which refers only to a river Virajā in Jajpur.[19] As it is difficult to give reliable dates for puranic texts a

---

[13] This passage was brought to my attention by H. Bakker. *Skandapurāṇa* 167.184:

ekāmre ca vibhoḥ sthānaṃ dṛṣṭvā svargam avāpnuyāt|
virajāyāṃ haraṃ dṛṣṭvā vājimedham avāpnuyāt||

[14] *Brahmāṇḍapurāṇa* II.3.13.57c (*virajāyāṃ tathā puṇyam*) and 84-5 (*viraje tv akṣayam śrāddhaṃ ...*). It is not certain that Virajā in Orissa is meant. The same uncertainty also exists concerning the three passages mentioned in the following.

[15] *Vāmanapurāṇa* 23.17-20 (19cd: *virajā dakṣinā vedir anantaphaladāyinī).* For the five *vedis*, see also Rai 1980.

[16] *Garuḍapurāṇa* 84.4 and *Gayāmāhātmya* 1.20:

muṇḍanaṃ copavāsaś ca sarvatīrtheṣv ayaṃ vidhiḥ|
varjayitvā kurukṣetraṃ viśālāṃ virajāṃ gayām||4

[17] *Garuḍapurāṇa* I.81.17ab (*virajas tu mahātīrthaṃ tīrthaṃ śrīpuruṣottamam*). Probably the same place is mentioned again in verse 20c (*virajaṃ sarvadaṃ tīrthaṃ).*

[18] *Padmapurāṇa* I.39.6-7. Compare *Mahābhārata* 3.83-6-7 quoted above. For the relation between the lists in the *Mahābhārata* and the *Padmapurāṇa,* see Vaidya 1941.

[19] *Kūrmapurāṇa* 2.34.26-28:

anyā ca virajā nāma nadī trailokyaviśrutā|
tasyāṃ snātvā naro viprā brahmaloke mahīyate||26
tīrthaṃ nārāyaṇasyānyannāmnā tu puruṣottamam|
tatra nārāyaṇaḥ śrīmān āste paramapuruṣaḥ||27
pūjayitvā paraṃ viṣṇuṃ snātvā tatra dvijottamaḥ|

similar passage from the *Vāmanapurāṇa* quoted in the twelfth century by the author of the *Kalpataru* is of importance. The passage advises baths in the river Virajā and the offering of rice-balls (*piṇḍa*) to the manes there, and in the following verses the text extols the sight of Puruṣottama.[20] Evidently, these texts know Puri with its supreme deity, Puruṣottama, as an important place of pilgrimage while the only thing they know or consider worth mentioning in Jajpur is the river. As Puruṣottama in Puri rose to more than just local prominence only in the tenth or eleventh century,[21] these passages were presumably not composed before this time.

A mention of goddess Virajā is found in the *Gayāmāhātmya,* which is part of the *Vāyupurāṇa.* Gayāsura, who frightened the gods because of the strength he gained from being an ascetic, agreed to offer himself as a sacrifice and laid down his huge body, covering the vast area from Gayā to the Mahendra. According to one verse, the mountain Virajā (or Viraja) pressed into his belly, evidently forming his navel, next to which goddess Virajā resides and where one should offer *piṇḍas.*[22] However, the *Gayāmāhātmya* is generally considered to be a late addition to the *Vāyupurāṇa.* Jacques, in his study on the *Gayāmāhātmya,* presumes that the legend about the Gayāsura was established at the beginning of the twelfth century. According to Jacques, the version from the *Vāyupurāṇa* mentioning goddess Virajā is a late one. It 'probably was not yet very ancient' when it was first quoted in a dated work,

---

brahmaṇan pūjayitvā tu viṣṇulokam avāpnuyāt||*28*

[20] *Kalpataru*, ch. 23 (nānātīrthamāhātmya), p. 235:
vāmanapurāṇe ...
upoṣya rajanīm ekāṃ virajāṃ sa nadīṃ yayau|
snātvā virajase tīrthe dattvā piṇḍaṃ pitus tathā||
darśanārthaṃ yayau śrīmān ajitaṃ puruṣottamam|
taṃ dṛṣṭvā puṇḍarīkākṣam akṣaraṃ paramaṃ śuciḥ||
upoṣya ṣaḍdināny eṣa mahendraṃ dakṣiṇām yayau| ...

Compare *Vāmanapurāṇa* 57.8cd-10. Here one finds *virajāṃ nagarīṃ* instead of *virajāṃ sa nadīṃ.*

[21] Stietencron 1978, 19 and Kulke 1978, 199-200.

[22] *Gayāmāhātmya* 2.75 (= 106.85 in the Ānandāśrama edition):
ākrāntaṃ daityajaṭharaṃ dharmena virajādriṇā|
nābhikūpasamīpe tu devī yā virajā sthitā|
tatra piṇḍādikaṃ kṛtvā trisaptakulam uddharet||

namely in the *Tīrthacintāmaṇi*, in the second half of the fifteenth century.[23]

Let us now turn to that puranic literature which is especially devoted to the holy places of Orissa. The *Puruṣottamamāhātmya* ascribed to the *Skandapurāṇa* has two short remarks on Viraja: Puruṣottamakṣetra is situated on the shore of the southern ocean extending over an area of 10 *yojana*s up to Virajamaṇḍala,[24] and Virajamaṇḍala washes off *rajas*—another common etymology for the name.[25]

A text of great importance is the *Brahmapurāṇa* which, in its present form, includes 45 chapters devoted exclusively to the greatness of Utkal. While there are 6 chapters about Konarak, 8 about Ekāmra, and 28 about Puruṣottama in Puri, the text has only 10 verses on Virajakṣetra, in which one finds two verses on the goddess Virajā.[26] She is designated 'mother' and Brahmāṇī, and—like the river Vaitaraṇī[27]—brings salvation to the ancestors and to lead the worshipper to Brahmā's world. The next verse glorifies 'the other mothers of the world' (*anya-lokamātaraḥ*), apparently

---

[23] Jaques 1979-80, 51. For the age of the Gayāsura legend, see also pp. 27 and 46-7.

[24] *Skandapurāṇa* 2.2.12.73cd-74. The same expression (*yāvad virajamaṇḍalam*) is also found in *Brahmapurāṇa* 28.1-2 and *Nāradapurāṇa* 52.8 where Oḍḍradeśa and Utkala respectively are said to extent up to Virajamaṇḍala. It is this context one would expect in connection with the term *maṇḍala,* which is usually used for political or administrative units rather than for sacred spaces as seems to be the case in the *Skandapurāṇa*.

[25] *Skandapurāṇa* 2.2.12.88cd (*rajaḥ prakṣālanaṃ śreyaḥ khyātaṃ virajamaṇḍalam*). The word *rajas* here probably means 'impurity' as well as one of the three qualities (*guṇa*), as the other two qualities are also mentioned in this passage. For the other common etymology given for the name Viraja see *Mahābhārata* 3.83.6 quoted above.

[26] The passage about Virajakṣetra is found in *Brahmapurāṇa* 42.1-10. Verses 1-2 are concerned with the goddess: *brahmovāca*
viraje virajā mātā brahmāṇī sampratiṣṭhitā
yasyāḥ saṃdarśanān martyaḥ punāty āsaptamaṃ kulam||
sakṛd dṛṣṭvā tu tāṃ devīṃ bhaktyāpūjya praṇamya ca
naraḥ svavaṃśam uddhṛtya mama lokaṃ sa gacchati||2

[27] *Brahmapurāṇa* 42.4:
āste vaitaraṇī tatra sarvapāpaharā nadī|
yasyāṃ snātvā naraśreṣṭhaḥ sarvapāpaiḥ pramucyate||4

connecting Virajā with the Saptamātṛkas. This description in the *Brahmapurāṇa* evidently does not portray the goddess as Mahiṣāsuramardiṇī. The remaining verses on Virajakṣetra praise Hari in the shape of a boar, eight smaller *tīrtha*s, and refer to the offering of *piṇḍa*s there.

It would of course be of great help to know the age of these verses. Although it is tempting to accept the approximate date given by a scholar and draw conclusions therefrom, the very nature of puranic literature makes such an exercise invalid, as has been explained by Rocher.[28] Even if we did accept, say, the thirteenth century as the time of the redaction of the *Brahmapurāṇa* as has been suggested by some,[29] we could not rule out the possibility hat the verses about Virajā had for centuries circulated in oral tradition before they were taken up by a puranic redactor, or, equally, that the verses entered the text in the course of some later reworking.

A *terminus ad quem*, however, may be fixed. From 1400 onwards several Nibandha authors cite the *Brahmapurāṇa* passage on Virajakṣetra, usually in a long section on Puri in which they also summarily deal with Bhubaneswar, Konarak, and Jajpur. Vācaspatimiśra of Mithila, who probably worked in the second half

---

[28] Rocher points out that material was transmitted orally by individual storytellers, who used to treat their stories with great freedom. What is found in our editions is nothing but a small part of this tradition. First, many stories or versions of stories were never written down. Second, the editions are usually not based on all surviving sources but rather on a few, sometimes on just one manuscript. Rocher presumes 'that the term *purāṇa* originally applied, not to groups of stories, legends, etc., but to each story, legend, etc., separately' and that the 'mini-purāṇas', as he calls these individual stories, 'are more basic than their conglomerations into large purāṇas' (Rocher 1986, 96 and 98). He further points out 'that a particular written version of a mini-purāṇa is not necessarily based on any other written version', which causes serious obstacles to the preparation of critical editions (ibid., 98-9). Finally, on the date of the Purāṇas, Rocher writes: 'In view of what has been said earlier in this volume, both on the transmission of materials and on the role of the "mini-purāṇas", I submit that it is not possible to set a specific date for any purāṇa as a whole ... even for the better established and more coherent purāṇas ... opinions, ... continue to vary widely and endlessly' (Ibid., 103).

[29] Rocher 1986, 155. See also pp. XXV-XXVII in vol. II of the *Brahmapurāṇa* edition by Söhnen and Schreiner.

of the fifteenth century,[30] has a long section on Orissa in his *Tīrthacintāmaṇi*, including two short passages on Virajakṣetra. He quotes the verses from the *Brahmapurāṇa* and, a little later, explains the mode of worship and the merit to be gained; evidently repeating in his own words the extant information from the *Brahmapurāṇa*.[31] In the first half of the seventeenth century Mitramiśra quotes the *Brahmapurāṇa* verses on Virajakṣetra in his *Vīramitrodaya* (*Tīrthaprakāśa*).[32] While in these two Nibandhas the verses on goddess Virajā are exactly like in the *Brahmapurāṇa* as quoted above, the *Puruṣottamatattva* of Raghunandana has an interesting difference. Here goddess Virajā is not the spouse of Brahmā (*viraje virajā nāma brahmaṇī saṃpratiṣṭhitā*) but 'installed by Brahmā' (.... *brahmaṇā saṃpratiṣṭhitā*).[33] It is difficult to say whether this reflects a different tradition, or whether it was an error that came to influence the development of a new idea found in the *Virajakṣetramāhātmya*. According to this text, which is probably younger than the *Brahmapurāṇa*, goddess Virajā was installed in the *kṣetra* in the course of a sacrifice performed by Brahmā.[34]

Another Māhātmya on Utkal, containing a description of Jajpur, is the *Kapilasaṃhitā*. Like the *Brahmapurāṇa* it has a section on the Sun Temple in Konarak (about 1250). Mainly for this reason and because puranic literature generally received the patronage of Anaṅgabhīma and other Gaṅga kings, both texts are usually believed to date to the Gaṅga period. But—as has been said—this does not necessarily lead to a definite date for every part of the text. The textual history of the *Kapilasaṃhitā* requires further study. Several details suggest that the text may have been originally a Śaiva one focussing on Bhubaneswar, later undergoing revision by

---

[30] Kane 1975, 844-54 and Lingat 1973, 116.

[31] *Tīrthacintāmaṇi*, 183 and 188.

[32] *Vīramitrodaya* (*Tīrthaprakāśa*), 598. Earlier the above-mentioned *Vāmanapurāṇa* passage from the *Kalpataru* is also quoted. The *Vīramitrodaya* was written at the request of Vīrasiṃha, king of Orccha (Bundelkhand). See Lingat 1973, 118 and Kane 1975, 941-53.

[33] *Smṛtitattva* (*Puruṣottamatattva*), p. 564. Raghunandana also quotes the *Vāmanapurāṇa* from the *Kalpataru* (561). On Raghunandana, the famous sixteenth century Bengali author, see Lingat 1973, 119-20 and Kane 1975, 890-902. Another text which quotes some of the *Brahmapurāṇa* verses is Narasiṃha Vājapeyin's *Nityācārapradīpa* from the sixteenth century. See Dhal 1984, 11.

[34] *Virajakṣetramāhātmya*, ch. 1-2.

a Vaiṣṇava hand. Apart from several rivers, the text deals with Puri, Konarak, Jajpur, the Kapilāsa hill, and Bhubaneswar, the last taking up more than half the work. According to the framework plot, Puṣkar was once questioned by the sages about the holy places of Utkal, and in one of the last chapters the sages finally set off for this holy land. Via Vārānasī and Gayā they reach Virajamaṇḍala where they take a bath in the Vaitaraṇī, visit Viṣṇu in the shape of a boar as well as goddess Virajā and three Śiva shrines (Mukteśvara, Akhaṇḍaleśvara and Trilocana),[35] and then proceed to the rivers Brāhmaṇī, Mahānadī, and Ekāmra, where apparently their pilgrimage ends.

Chapters 7 and 8 of the *Kapilasaṃhitā* are devoted to Parvatīkṣetra (Jajpur). As in the *Brahmapurāṇa,* goddess Virajā is the first topic dealt with and therefore seemingly enjoys a very prominent position. However, there are only 5 verses about her altogether. After an introductory remark saying that the *kṣetra* has been created by Brahmā, Bharadvāja tells the ṛṣis that the sight of Virajā frees a person from *rajas*. She, who was installed in the *kali* age for the benefit of her devotees, bestows prosperity and liberation (*bhuktimuktipradāyinī*)—a quality also attributed to the river Vaitaraṇī (7.19ab: *vaitaraṇī ... bhuktidā muktidā*). The merit acquired by the worship of Śiva (in another *kṣetra*?) is here achieved by the mere sight of Virajā.[36] Another two verses at the end of the section assure the reader that the recitation of mantras in front of her will be successful. Even worshipped at a distance of 1000 *yojanas*, Virajā grants all wishes.[37] The rest of the two

---

[35] *Kapilasaṃhitā* 19.34-5:
tato bahudine te ca prāpur virajamaṇḍalam|
snātvā vaitaraṇītoye dadṛśuḥ koparūpiṇam||34 k[roḍ]arūpiṇam?
tatas te virajāṃ devīṃ devaṃ mukteśvaraṃ haram|
akhaṇḍaleśvarañ caiva trilocanamaheśvaram||35

[36] *Kapilasaṃhitā* 7.2-5:
kathayāmi mahāpuṇyaṃ virajākhyaṃ sunirmalam
yat kṣetraṃ sṛṣṭirakṣārthaṃ brahmaṇā ca kṛtaṃ purā||2
tasmin kṣetre dvijaśreṣṭhā virajā virajapradā
virajāmukham ālokya rajaḥprakṣālanaṃ bhavet||3
yatra śrīvirajādevī bhuktimuktipradāyinī
sādhakānāṃ hitārthāya virajā sā kalau sthitā||4
daśavarṣasahasrāṇi yo vā pūjayate haram
tatphalaṃ samavāpn[o]ti virajālokane naraḥ||5

[37] *Kapilasaṃhitā* 8.16 and 21:

chapters on Jajpur praises Viṣṇu as Varāha, the river Vaitaraṇī and several smaller *tīrtha*s already mentioned in the *Brahmapurāṇa*. What is new in comparison to the *Brahmapurāṇa* are several *liṅga*s and a place called Gayānābhi where pilgrims perform ancestral rites.

A text in which one might expect more information about goddess Virajā is the *Virajakṣetramāhātmya*, devoted to the glory of Jajpur.[38] This text, however, turns out to be Śaiva, praising numerous *liṅga*s in the *kṣetra* which is called Avimuktakṣetra and therefore equated with Benares. As in the *Brahmapurāṇa,* Jajpur is termed Brahmakṣetra. According to the text it was in the course of some sacrifice performed by Brahmā that first Śiva, then Pārvatī and later on also Viṣṇu, appeared here.[39] The second chapter relates how Pārvatī emerged from the sacrificial fire and was praised by Brahmā, who requested her to stay in the *kṣetra* as Śiva's wife.

---

tatra śrīvirajāgre ca yaḥ paṭhen mantram uttamam|
sa mantraḥ siddhidaḥ tasya satyaṃ satyaṃ dvijottamāḥ||16 ...
sahasrayojanānte ca yo japed virajāṃ śubhaḥ|
tasyepsitam asau devī dadāti kila tatparā||21

[38] For the Māhātmya see Dhal 1984. In his introduction (p. 14) he writes about the date of the text: '... one can take it for certain that the text took its present shape between the fifteenth and sixteenth centuries A.D. at the latest'. His main arguments are that the text mentions the Varāha temple, which is said to have been built under Pratāparudra Deva (149-153). This argument is also found in an article by Mahapatra (1962, 27). Further, Dhal explains that the *Virajakṣetramāhātmya* is much more elaborate than the descriptions of Virajakṣetra found in the *Brahmapurāṇa* and the *Kapilasaṃhitā* and therefore must be later than these text, which is a rather weak argument. In a later article (1995, 82), Dhal calls the *Virajakṣetramāhātmya* 'a work of the c. fourteenth century' but does not give proof for this view. Chakravarti (1897, 333-4) much earlier opined that the text cannot be older than the thirteenth century because certain shrines are metioned, and that the text must be older than the *Kapilasaṃhitā* because the latter seemed to be a compilation of the *Virajakṣetramāhātmya* and other works.

[39] An interesting aspect which requires further study is the special importance attached to Brahmā. He is said to be worshipped as Gaṇeśa in Jajpur (21.137). According to another story, Brahmā once was cursed to become a female deity and manifested himself in Puri as Subhadrā, the female element in the Jagannātha trinity (19.96 and 20.6).

Worshipping Pārvatī purifies and leads to the fulfilment of one's wishes.[40]

Some other chapters also contain a few verses on Virajā. Chapter 21 calls her the mother of the world or of the three worlds (*jaganmātṛ, trailokyajananī*) and—at last—Mahiṣāsuramardiṇī. However, the text does not narrate how she slew the Mahiṣa, or any other myth of the Devī. It simply describes her appearance, among other things, as dark-coloured and two-armed and assures that she bestows prosperity and liberation.[41] Chapter 17 has two verses which correspond to *Brahmapurāṇa* 42.1-2.[42]

The *Virajakṣetramāhātmya* calls the goddess by the name Virajā several times, but in most cases simply uses the term Devī, Mother, or Pārvatī. Here the name of the goddess is evidently derived from *vi-rajas* ('free from dust, pure'), *virajā(s)* being the nominative. In Chapter 2 the Devī asks Brahmā to call her by the name Virajas.[43] Also the *kṣetra* is designated (2.21) *vairajase kṣetre*. In another context one finds *virājitam kṣetram* (1.40), which seems to connect the name with *vi-rāj* ('shine forth')? Both explanations of the name 'Virajakṣetra' are also found in other texts, as has been shown above.

---

[40] *Virajakṣetramāhātmya* 2.33:
dṛṣṭvā virajasaṃ devīṃ stutvā stotreṇa vedhasaḥ|
praṇamya pātakān muktaḥ sarvān kāmān avāpnuyāt||33

[41] *Virajakṣetramāhātmya* 21.175-181:
dṛṣṭvā trailokyajananīṃ mahiṣāsuramardinīm
śyāmāṅgīṃ siṃham ārūḍhāṃ dvibhujāṃ śūladhāriṇīm||*175*
bibhratīṃ vāmahastena mahiṣāsurapucchakam
surāsurair vandyamānāṃ trinetrām induśekharām|*176*
sarvābharaṇasampannāṃ lokānugrahakāriṇīm
evaṃ rūpāṃ paraṃ devīṃ bhuktimuktipradāyinīm||*177*
bhaktyā saṃpūjya vidhivat stutvā natvā samāhitaḥ
anena vidhinā yas tu jaganmātaram ambikām||*178*
samīkṣate suraśreṣtha! vāñchitāṃ gatim āpnuyāt
kiṃ bravīmi ca māhātmyaṃ jaganmātuḥ svadraṣṭari||*179*
api nīcakule jātā mahāpātakino yadā
devyāḥ sandarśanenaiva vaṃśān uddhṛtya sapta ca||*180*

[42] As in the *Puruṣottamatattva* we find *brahmaṇā saṃpratiṣṭhitā* instead of *brahmaṇī saṃpratiṣṭhitā*.

[43] *Virajkṣetraamāhātmya* 2.18ab: *tvaṃ māṃ virajasaṃ nāmnā manyasva kamalodbhava.*

Jajpur is sometimes described as the *kṣetra* of Brahmā or of Śiva, but only once, in the *Kapilasaṃhitā* as *Pārvatīkṣetra*. It seems that *Virajakṣetra*—usually written with a short 'a'—is not named after the goddess, but rather derived from the name of the place.[44] The literature presented so far shows that many texts, including early inscriptions, know Viraja (sometimes also Virajas or Virajā) as the name of a *tīrtha*, a city or a river, while the goddess of that name is found only in later puranic literature on Utkal.

Another text of interest is the *Puruṣottamamāhātmya,* ascribed to the *Viṣṇurahasya*.[45] Here Virajakṣetra is presented as part of the pilgrimage route leading to Puruṣottama. Starting from Jajpur the soil gradually becomes holier until the highest abode of Viṣṇu is reached. This text, edited by Schneider, contains three descriptions of the route.[46] It is the third and—according to Schneider—latest version that entrusts Virajā with a special duty. After they die, she sends the worthy pilgrims to enjoy pleasures (*bhogān bhoktum*) in various heavens; they finally undertake a pilgrimage from Jajpur to Puri, where they attain salvation. In Jajpur the pilgrims are advised ablutions in the Vaitaraṇī and a darshan of the goddess.[47]

---

[44] The designation Virajākṣetra—with long ā—is found in a few later texts. The *Tīrthacintāmaṇi,* e.g., introduces one section with *atha virajakṣetram* and another with *atha virajākṣetraprayogaḥ* (pp. 183 and 188). In an all-Indian list of *tīrtha*s, which varies considerably in different editions, the *Brahmapurāṇa* (25.78) has *virajātīrtham*, while in the section on Jajpur presented above it calls the place Viraja.

[45] Schneider suspects the authors to be some tantric brahmins of Jajpur because Virajā and several tantric elements especially figured in the late text layers. According to him, the Māhātmya was written between 1500 and 1568. Schneider's main arguments, which seem rather weak, are firstly that the text was not yet quoted in the *Muktacintāmaṇi* (end of the fifteenth century), and secondly that Virajā occupied a prominent position in the text which would be unlikely if the text had been written after 1568 when Muslim invaders caused severe destructions in Jajpur. Even if one presumes that all leading brahmins fled and that the Virajā temple was totally destroyed, this does not rule out Virajā and her *kṣetra* being praised in a later text. On the contrary, it is a peculiar feature of Sanskrit literature that it often seems to ignore the discontinuities caused by Muslim invasions or other events.

[46] *Puruṣottamamāhātmya* 3.63-153, 4.8-72, 8.1-145.

[47] Ibid., 8.127-39. The verses about the pilgrimage to Jajpur read as follows:

Virajā is also called Maheśvarī (8.134) and Ambikā (8.128) in this passage. Ambikā, the mother of the world, is described as standing to the left of Jagannātha (3.5). Whether this refers to Virajā is uncertain. Another relation needing further study is that between Virajā and Puri's Vimalā: the names display a striking similarity. Schneider thinks that Vimalā, not playing a prominent role in this *Puruṣottamamāhātmya*, is mainly a representative of Virajā in Puri.[48] Even if Vimalā is identified with Virajā by some, it is unlikely that Vimalā was introduced in the *kṣetra* for this purpose. As von Stietencron has shown, there are reasons for regarding Vimalā as one of the ancient deities of Puri.[49]

Last, I would like to mention the lists of tantric *pīṭha*s. The antiquity of the Virajā cult is often advocated by reference to these texts that enumerate the seats of the goddess. First of all it has to be emphasized that there is no fixed tradition concerning these *pīṭha*s. As Sircar's study on *The Śākta Pīṭhas* shows, the texts differ widely, reflecting, among other things, the regional bias of their authors. Some works indeed include Viraja or Virajā in their *pīṭha* lists.[50] Whether these refer to the name of a place or of a goddess is,

---

virajāṃ te punaḥ prāpya dṛṣṭvā vaitaraṇīṃ nadīm
snātvā tasyāṃ vidhānena dṛṣṭvā devīṃ tadā narāḥ||137
virajaskā bhavanty eva sattvodriktāḥ sunirmalāḥ
tatas tu sāttvik īṃ bhūmiṃ te paśyanti sunirmalām||138

In the descriptions of the pilgrimage route from Jajpur to Puri the text divides this area into three or four bhūmis and partly connects them with the absence or presence of certain guṇas. For a study of the number and the names of these bhūmis, see Schneider 1984, 100-2.

[48] Schneider 1984, 152: 'Vimalā ist im wesentlichen bloß eine Virajā-Stellvertreter-Figur. Auch im Jagannātha-Tempel findet sich nämlich die "Stellvertreter-Idee" ... Der Tempel hat die Neigung, in seine Mauern zu holen, was immer an bedeutsamen, mit ihm konkurrierenden Kulten anzutreffen ist.... So wird begreiflich, daß Virajā unter dem, zur Not auch die Identität verbergenden, Synonym Vimalā in den Jagannātha-Tempel einzog...'.

[49] Stietencron 1978, 26-8.

[50] See the list of 42 *pīṭha*s from the *Kubjikātantra,* which has names of goddesses as well as of places (e.g. Ayodhyā and Kurukṣetra), Sircar 1973, 19 n.2. See also the list of 50 *pīṭha*s from the *Jñānārṇava-tantra* (quoted by the author of the *Tantrasāra* in the seventeenth century), the *Tantracūḍamaṇi,* the *Śāktānandataraṅgiṇī* and the

however, uncertain. Besides, the lists are hardly datable. Sircar considers some of them to be rather late creations.[51] Interestingly, a list of 108 *pīṭhas* found in several Purāṇas mentions Bhubaneswar (*ekāmrake kīrttimatī*) and Puri (*vimalā puruṣottame*), but not Virajā.[52]

Only a few late texts from eastern India explicitly mention a goddess Virajā. Sircar refers to a work called *Aṣṭādaśapīṭha* that mentions Virajā as Devī of Utkal.[53] A list of 108 *pīṭhas* from the *Prāṇatoṣaṇītantra*, written in Bengal in 1820, places Vimalā in Puruṣottama and Virajā in Yāgapurī.[54] The *Pīṭhanirṇaya*, according to Sircar written between 1690 and 1720 in eastern India, contains an interesting verse.[55] It says that in Utkal one finds the land of (Satī's) navel, called Virajākṣetra, where Vimalā and Jagannātha reside.[56] Sircar thinks that this verse underwent later modifications and originally had Virajā and Jaya as Devī and her male counterpart.[57] In some manuscripts of Mukundarāma's *Caṇḍimaṅgala*, there is a list of 9 *pīṭhas*, all situated in eastern

---

Bṛhannīlatantra, ibid., 20-2. Apart from Viraja, this list has, also Ekāmra and Mahendra.

[51] For his opinion on the age of the passages from the *Kubjikātantra* and the *Bṛhannīlatantra* (which has 6 different lists of *pīṭhas*), see ibid., 20 n., 22 n, 25 n.

[52] Sircar 1973, 23-8 and app. II (verses 4 and 9). Ekāmra also appears in a Buddhist text from the twelfth century which lists 24 places and its goddesses. See Wayman 1995.

[53] Ibid.18-19. The manuscript used by Sircar was written in 1806, dictated by an Utkal brahmin from Jahājapura (= Jajpur).

[54] Ibid., 25 n. and 28 n.

[55] Ibid., 24.

[56] Ibid., 45:
utkale nābhideśaś ca virajākṣetram ucyate|
vimalā sā mahādevī jagannāthas tu bhairavaḥ||13

[57] A manuscript from the second quarter of the eighteenth century has *virajā cotkale khyātā nābhir me mama [jaya?] bhairavaḥ.* And a Bengali version of the list found in the *Annadāmaṅgala,* composed in 1752, says that the navel fell down in Utkal, where Vijayā and Jaya are present. On the basis of these two sources, Sircar reconstructs the original Sanskrit text as: *virajā cotkale khyātā nābhir me jayabhairavaḥ.* Ibid., 45 n. and 59, verse 11.

India. One verse says that Satī's right foot fell down in Yājapur, and calls it Virajā.[58]

I now sum up the picture that emerges of Jajpur from the Sanskrit literature. The inscriptions and Sanskrit works examined here do not confirm the common view that from earliest times onwards a form of Durgā called Virajā had been the presiding deity of Jajpur. Goddess Virajā appears for the first time in late texts on the holy places of Orissa, probably compiled in the Gaṅga period.[59]

A striking feature of the literature on Virajakṣetra is that even where the goddess is mentioned, great parts of the text are devoted to other *tīrtha*s in Jajpur such as the river Vaitaraṇī, various Śiva shrines, and Viṣṇu as Varāha. Further, it has to be noted that apart from just two verses in the *Virajakṣetramāhātmya*, the texts do not present the goddess as Mahiṣāsuramardinī.

Interestingly, some passages praise Puruṣottama in Puri, but only know a holy river in Jajpur, one text being quoted in the twelfth century. This might indicate that at a time when Jagannātha had already acquired widespread fame—presumably not until the tenth century—Jajpur was known only for its river and the performance of ancestral rites—at least to the all-Indian puranic tradition. Jajpur was, no more or not yet, known for its goddess.

Snigdha Tripathy made similar observations concerning another myth of Jajpur. According to a well-known legend, the famous king Yayātikeśarī invited 10,000 brahmins from Kanauj and performed 10 *aśvamedha*s in Jajpur. About this story Tripathy writes: 'Curiously enough, the above tradition and the legend of ten horse sacrifices do not find place in the epic, nor in the literature like the *Brahma-Purāṇa* ... In fact, we have not come across so far any recorded evidence of the so-called Yayāti-tradition, though it is now believed to have been handed over to us orally since the remote past.'[60]

The material presented here, of course, only shows how Jajpur is depicted in Sanskrit literature. In view of the fact that we know very

---

[58] Ibid., 33. It is not clear, whether Virajā is the name of a goddess here. Most editions do not contain this text passage and Sircar considers it an interpolated one. Mukundarāma's *Caṇḍimaṅgala* was written around 1600.

[59] These observations might have to be modfied by further research on different kinds of sources, especially Oriya literature.

[60] Tripathy 1998, 41.

little about the date and the background of most texts, we must be rather careful with any definite conclusions. It is very well possible that goddess Virajā has been worshipped in Jajpur at a very early stage, but for some reason did not receive much attention in the brahmanical literature.

At he same time we could also consider the possibility that a goddess called Virajā, identified with Durgā, did not become the principal deity of Jajpur until late. This is not to say that the worship of female deities had not been prominent earlier. Archaeological finds including old images of the Matṛkās, Cāmuṇḍā, and Mahiṣāsuramardiṇī point to the contrary. What makes me doubtful about Virajā-Durgā as the ancient patron deity of the place is that the later Sanskrit literature about her does not seem to draw on a rich tradition. The goddess lacks a distinctive image, and there are few myths about her. Although Virajā occupies an important position in later texts, she is nowhere presented as the all-surpassing highest deity and final destination of every pilgrimage as is the case with Jagannātha in Puri.[61]

In view of these observations, the question arises why Jajpur is regarded as the Orissan seat of the Devī par excellence. Perhaps this is due to the concept mentioned in the very beginning, namely the idea that coastal Orissa is endowed with a special sanctity because of the joint presence of Viṣṇu, Śiva, and Durgā. Added to Puri, Bhubaneswar, and Jajpur one often finds Konarak, the abode of Sūrya, and sometimes also a fifth place.

Panigrahi, for example, calls 'Puri, Bhubaneswar, Konarka, Mahavinayaka and Viraja or Jajpur the traditional five pithas representing five distinct cults'.[62] This idea of five *kṣetra*s, including Mahavinayaka as the seat of Gaṇeśa, evidently follows the example of the *pañcāyatanapūjā*. While it is a common thesis in modern literature on the religious history of Orissa that the country is divided into these five *kṣetra*s, this does not seem to be a very old

---

[61] In the 1970s the 'All India Vaitarani Tirtha and Nabhi Gaya Committee' was founded to increase the popularity of Jajpur as a place of pilgrimage. The name of the committee, as well as their booklets, bearing titles like *Glorious Teerth Vaitarani*, show that for them, too, Virajā does not seem to be the main attraction of Jajpur but one among several.

[62] Panigrahi 1981, 340. Other examples are Acharya 1969, 358 and Dash 1963, 273.

idea. Medieval sources document instead a concept of three or four *kṣetras*.

Coḍagaṅga and several of his successors pursued what has been termed 'policy of religious inclusiveness'. [63] In the first half of the thirteenth century, for example, Anaṅgabhīma calls himself 'son of Puruṣottama, Śiva, and Durgā'. His son Narasiṃha built the famous Sūrya temple in Konarak where several sculptures show a king worshipping a *liṅga*, Puruṣottama, and a goddess together. The three gods plus Sūrya are also presented as a unity[64] in several Sanskrit texts, e.g. the *Brahmapurāṇa* and, presumably following it, several Nibandhas. Equally, the *Virajakṣetramāhātmya* (I.44-7) in its introduction speaks of four *kṣetras*. The *Kapilasaṃhitā* apart from several rivers describes five great *tīrthas*. The fifth, however, is not Mahavinayaka, but the Kapilāsa hill with its Śikhareśvara temple.

Presumably the purpose of this religious policy was to depict the king as patron of all major religious traditions of the region. On the other hand, the great all-Indian gods were shown to reside in Orissa united. One might say that Orissa was imagined as the new centre of the Hindu world. This attitude also found expression in the idea to call Cuttack Abhinava-Varanasi, 'New Benares'.[65]

Coming back to the Virajā cult, I think it is quite conceivable that in the course of these developments in the Gaṅga period, Jajpur was integrated into the concept as the seat of Durgā, the great Indian goddess. Jajpur was one of the ancient centres known for the worship of female deities, though the cult of Virajā-Durgā had not been the dominant tradition, as suggested by the material presented here. Possibly a goddess who until then had only been loosely connected with Durgā, and had only been one among several gods and goddesses in Jajpur, in this way she became the presiding deity of the locality.

---

[63] See Kulke 1978, 200f., Stietencron 1978, 22-5 and Kulke 1979, 49ff.

[64] In Sanskrit literature as well as in royal policy one does not only observe tendencies to place these gods side by side, but often al are subordinate to Jagannātha.

[65] Kulke 1979, 53-4.

References

Acharya, P. 1969. *Studies in Orissan History, Archaeology and Archives*, Baripada.

Brahmāṇḍapurāṇa, ed. K.V. Sarma, (Krishnadasa Sanskrit Series 41), Varanasi, 1983.

Brahmapurāṇa. ed. R. Söhnen and P. Schreiner, 2 vols. (Purāṇa Research Publications, vol. 1-2), Wiesbaden, 1987/1989.

Brighenti, F. 2001. *Śakti Cult in Orissa*, Delhi.

Chakravarti, M.M. 1897. 'Language and Literature of Orissa', *Journal of the Asiatic Society of Bengal*, vol. LXVI, 317-48.

Chanda, R.P. 1930. *Exploration in Orissa. Memoirs of the Archaeological Survey of India No. 44,* Calcutta: ASI.

Das, H.C. 1985. *Cultural Development in Orissa*, Calcutta.

Dash, M.P. 1963. 'Interrelation between Vaiśṇavism and Śaktism in Orissa', *Orissa Historical Research Journal* IX.4, 273-81.

Dhal, U.N. 1984. *The Glory that was Virajaksetra, Virajaksetramāhātmya*, Delhi.

— 1993. 'Virajakṣetra in Purāṇic Tradition', *Journal of the Ganganatha Jha Kendriya Sanskrita Vidyapeetha,* vol. XLV, Allahabad.

— 1995. 'Sacred Performances at Jājpur', in D.P. Dubey (ed.), *Pilgrimage Studies: Sacred Places, Sacred Traditions.* Allahabad, 81-7.

[*Garudapurāṇa*:] *Garuda Mahāpurāṇa,* Delhi: Nag Publishers, 1984. [reprint of the Veṅkaṭeśvara Press edn.]

Gayāmāhātmya, Édition critique, traduction française et introduction, par C. Jaques (Publications de l'Institut Français d'Indologie No. 20), Pondichery, 1962.

Jacques, C. 'Gayā Māhātmya, Introduction', *Purāṇa* 21.2-22.1, app. (being an English translation of the French introduction to his edition of the *Gayāmāhātmya*).

Kane, P.V. 1975. *History of Dharmaśāstra*, vol. 1, part II, revd. and enl. edn., Poona.

[*Kapilasaṃhitā*:] *Kapilapurāṇa*, ed. Shrikrishnamani Tripathy (Chaukhamba Surbharati Granthamala 57), Varanasi, 1981.

(Kṛtya)kalpataru, of Bhaṭṭa Lakṣmīdhara, ed. K.V. Rangaswami Aiyangar, 12 vols. (Gaekwad Oriental Series), Baroda, 1948.

Kūrmapurāṇa, critical ed. A.S. Gupta, Varanasi, 1971.

Kulke, H. 1978. 'Jagannātha as the State Deity under the Gajapatis of Orissa', in A. Eschmann, H. Kulke; G.C. Tripathi (eds.), *The*

Cult of Jagannath and the Regional Tradition of Orissa, Delhi, 199-208.
— 1979. *Jagannātha-Kult und Gajapati-Königtum*, Wiesbaden.
Lingat, R. 1973. *The Classical Law of India,* transl. from the French with additions by J.D.M. Derrett, Berkeley, etc.
Mahapatra, K.N. 1962. 'Purānic Literature of Orissa', *Orissa Historical Research Journal* XI.1, 21-31.
[*Nāradapurāṇa:*] *Nāradīyamahāpurāṇa*, Delhi: Nag Publishers, 1984. [reprint of the Veṅkaṭeśvara Press edn.]
Panigrahi, K.C. 1961. *Archaeological Remains at Bhubaneswar,* Calcutta.
— 1981. *History of Orissa (Hindu Period),* Cuttack.
Parida, A.N. 1999. *Early Temples of Orissa,* Delhi.
Pradhan, B.Ch. 1997. *The Origin and Development of Saktism*, Calcutta.
Puruṣottamamāhātmya, assigned to *Viṣṇurahasya*, see Schneider, 1984.
Rai, G.S. 1980. 'The Five Vedī-s of Brahmā', *Purāṇa* 22.2.
Rajaguru, S.N. 1980. 'A Historical Account of Viraja-Kshetra from Inscriptions', in *Orissa Historical Research Journal* XXIV-XXVI, 193-8.
Rocher, L. 1986. *The Purāṇas* (A History of Indian Literature, vol. II, fasc. 3), Wiesbaden.
Schneider, U. 1984. *Der Holzgott und die Brahmanen* (Freiburger Beiträge zur Indologie, Band 16), Band. 1: Interpretation eines bislang nicht bekannten Puruṣottama-Māhātmya, Band 2: Textausgabe, Wiesbaden.
Sircar, D.C. 1949. 'Two Inscriptions from Jajpur', *Epigraphia Indica* 28, 179-85.
— 1973. *The Śākta Pīṭhas*, 2nd revd. edn., Delhi.
Skandapurāṇa. Delhi: Nag Publishers, 1982.
Smṛtitattva, by Raghunandana, ed. by Jivananda Vidyasagara, 2 vols., Calcutta, 1895.
Stietencron, H. v. 1978. 'The Advent of Viṣṇuism in Orissa: An Outline of its History according to Archaeological and Epigraphical Sources from the Gupta Period up to 1135 A. D.', in A. Eschmann, H. Kulke, G.C. Tripathi (eds.), *The Cult of Jagannath and the Regional Tradition of Orissa,* Delhi, 1-30.
Tīrthacintāmaṇi, ed. Kamala Krishna Smritirtha, Calcutta (Asiatic Society) 1919.

Tripathy, S. 1998. 'The Unique Neulpur Charter of Śubhākara II of the Bhauma-Kara Dynasty and a local Tradition of Virajā-Kshetra', in *Orissa Historical Research Journal* XLII, 35-46.
Vāmanapurāṇa, critical ed. by A.S. Gupta, Varanasi, 1967.
Vaidya, M.V. 1941. 'Tīrtha-yātrā in the Āraṇyakaparvan and the Padma-Purāṇa', in S.M. Katre, P.K. Gode (eds.), *A Volume of Studies in Indology presented to Prof. P V. Kane*, Poona, 530-7.
Virajakṣetramāhātmya, see Dhal, 1984.
Vīramitrodaya, Tīrthaprakāśa, by Mitramiśra, ed. Vishnu Prasad, (Chowkhamba Sanskrit Series 241), Benares, 1918.
Wayman, A. 1995. 'Twenty-Four Tantric Places in 12th Century Indian Geography', *Dhīḥ (Journal of Rare Buddhist Texts Research Project)* 19, 135-62.

5

Contested Authorities, Disputed Centres, and Rejected Norms: Situating Mahimā Dharma in its Regional Diversity

Johannes Beltz

Mahimā Dharma functions as a marker of regional, religious and social difference and specificity.* According to the news reports of the nineteenth century, Mukund Das is its legendary founder. Mahimā Svāmī or Mahimā Gosain, as he was later named by his followers, is said to have appeared for the first time in 1826 in Puri. Dissatisfied with being a Vaiṣṇava, and criticizing the ritualized idol worship of Lord Jagannath, he left Puri and travelled to the Kapilas hills near Dhenkanal via Bhubaneswar and Cuttack. There he became a Śaiva before engaging in severe yogic practices. In 1862 he attained *siddhi* and descended from the hills in order to preach a new *dharma*. He is said to have attained *samādhi* in 1876. Under his first disciples, Govinda Bābā and Bhīma Bhoi, the movement shifted away from the coastal region towards the central and western part of Orissa. Spreading also to other states (MP, AP, West Bengal, Assam), people from different regions and socio-cultural backgrounds joined as followers. Since then, several currents have emerged and various regional centres have been established. My paper will analyse the extraordinary and often contradictory diversity of local configurations of Mahimā Dharma in Orissa.

---

* This research was done in the context of the German Orissa Research Project. The data are based on fieldwork effectuated in western Orissa from 2000 to 2002. My research could not have been done without the help of my many friends and colleagues from Sonepur; I am especially grateful to Kedar Mishra and Sanjeeb Kumar Nayak for their assistance with transliteration and translation.

Lord Jagannath: Mahimā Gosain's First Disciple

The first incident that demonstrates how Mahimā Dharma functioned as a mark of religious as well social contest is the famous attack on the Jagannath temple in Puri. In 1881 the *Utkal Dīpika* reported that 'half-naked' men and women came into the *mandira* carrying cooked rice in a pot, shouting *Alekha*. They were reported to have attempted to pollute the sanctum and to burn the idols of Jagannath, Balabhadra, and Subhadra. Subsequently a violent struggle between the attackers and the priests ensued, during which one person was killed.

Although the archive material is now ready for publication, questions and contradictions remain.[1] I do not intend to enter into the debate on the background of the attackers, their motivation, or religious affiliation.[2] Whether the reports are true or not, the issue remains important because for the first time public media focused upon Mahimā Dharma. The incident was seen as a scandal, the Mahimā Dharma movement appearing as a dangerous revolt threatening the established order. Puri's religious hegemony over Orissa and the predominance of Jagannath were radically questioned. Ishita Banerjee-Dube rightly points out that the attack signifies 'a statement against the exclusiveness, domination and power with which Jagannath had become to be associated, a

---

[1] For further details see the articles by Eschmann 1978, Nepak 1997, Deo 1999, D. Das 1997, and Banerjee-Dube 2001.

[2] A controversy exists about the attackers, their origin and their intentions. Anncharlott Eschmann (1978, 384) thought that they came from Bhīma Bhoi's group. Bhagarathi Nepak (1997, 68) rigorously rejects any involvement of Bhīma Bhoi and accuses 'some impetuous and irresponsible' Mahimā Dharmīs for the attack. Biswamoy Pati (2001, 144) recently claimed that the news in the reports as well as the gazetteers are based on misunderstandings and misconceptions maintained by colonial administrators and upper caste officials. He argued that it was not an aggression but an attempt of a few Mahimā Dharmīs 'to go in the "presence of the Lord" who had been "stolen" by the Brahmans and the rajas'. Ishita Banerjee-Dube (2001, 174) in her detailed study on the making of Mahimā Dharma rejects Pati's conclusion emphasizing the attack as a challenge to the authority of Raja and Brahmins, caste society and Hindu pantheon. In her view, it was an attempt to clear the way for the spreading of the new dharma, impossible as long as the lifeless idol was worshipped in Puri.

debunking of the myth about the universality of the *bara thakur*, the great lord of Orissa'.[3]

Apparently, this movement never questioned the existence of Lord Jagannath. What was vehemently criticized was the worship of an idol and the pseudo-universal claims associated with such worship. In fact, Jagannath figures in Mahimā Dharma mythology as the first disciple of Mahimā Gosain. In other words, Orissa's *rāṣṭra devatā* is clearly subordinate to the ultimate authority of the founder of Mahimā Dharma. Shiba Charan Dhala of Balasingha near Baudh, a Mahimā Dharmī aged 70 years, likes to narrate the following:

> The first enlightened *sādhaka* of Mahimā Svāmī was Govinda Bābā. He was Lord Jagannath himself. By the command of Lord Mahimā, Sri Jagannath became incarnated as Govinda Bābā in order to propagate Mahimā Dharma. We worship the *jaṭa samādhi*[4] of Govinda Bābā existing in our village as a form of Lord Jagannath. Many patients are cured after obtaining the dust and the holy ashes of this place. Many issueless parents have been blessed by children by the grace of Govinda Bābā.

Initially I found this statement extraordinary. As my research progressed, however, I discovered the dissemination of the story beyond the individual narrator. Jagannath as Govinda Bābā has been canonized by the religious memory of the Mahimā Dharmīs and has become part and parcel of their living mythology. Let us quote Chaitanya Mahapatra from Sonepur on how Jagannath came to Balasingha:

> As the Kaliyuga began to reign over the world, people became more irreligious and the sin (*pāpā*) increased day by day.[5] As a result, the weight of the earth increased. The situation became unbearable for Bāsukī who had the earth on his head. Observing Bāsukī's pain, Surabhi, his wife, prayed to Paramabrahma to

[3] Banerjee-Dube 2001, 173.

[4] The *jaṭa samādhi* signifies the temple in Balasingha where the matted hair of Govinda Bābā was buried and which is today covered with a big ant-hill.

[5] In Hindu cosmology, time is conceptualised as cyclic. Anncharlott Eschmann (1978, 391) rightly points out that the present age terminates in the end of Viṣṇu's ninth *avatāra* as Buddha or Jagannath. According to this time table, Jagannath's reincarnation as well as Mahimā Dharma represent the beginning of a new cycle.

> remove the burden. Paramabrahma, pleased by the prayer of Surabhi, assured the latter that he would descend upon the earth along with Jagannath and sixty-four *siddha*s in order to remove the sin and to help Bāsukī. When Paramabrahma asked Surabhi who would supply them with food, she promised that she would herself fill their bowls. Thus Paramabrahma appeared before Jagannath and told him, 'you are luxuriating here, eating tons of sacrificial food, while the world is perishing. As the burden of sin is increasing, Bāsukī feels unable to bear the earth. Give up luxury and come with me! Go to Balasingha, I shall get there after you. Wait there and incarnate as a *brahmacārī* with matted hair and beard.' After this, Paramabrahma ordered the gods of the heaven and the saints of the Himalaya to descend with him upon the earth.

The legend continues with Jagannath's initiation into the Mahimā Dharma by Mahimā Gosain. He also received a new name, Govinda Bābā. It is recounted that, one day, devotees came to see him in Balasingha asking him about Puri. Was it not strange that the Jagannath cult continued in Puri after he had left the place? They asked who was taking the *bhoga* in his name, and how he could be in Balasingha and accept offerings in Puri at the same time. Govinda Bābā answered that *betalas* (demi-gods) took the donations in his place. This myth clearly questions Puri's exclusivism as well as the expensive rituals, and the priesthood as such.

The tradition recounted above may help to explain why so little emphasis is put on the Puri attack in the collective memory of the Mahimā Dharmīs. Probably the attack was initiated by a militant branch of the Mahimā movement from Sambalpur. Personally, I believe Dasaram and the attackers to have been untouchable Gaṇḍa-Paṇas by caste.[6] Keeping in mind that they were officially excluded from the entry into the Jagannath temple, the incident has yet another signification. The attack is not only a protest against idol

[6] In the news reports it was suggested that they were Santhal, i.e. tribal people. Others argued that they looked like Kelās (snake charmers) or low castes. I would like to stress here that the very fact of carrying a *bhāta hāṇḍi* (an earthen pot with cooked rice) is typical for the Gaṇḍa-Paṇas. I have to add that the 'untouchable' Gaṇḍa-Paṇas, not being allowed to use metallic utensils, were derogatorily called *hāṇḍikhiā* (who eats in an earthen pot). It is further stated that Dasaram, the main actor who died in the incident, came from Sambalpur, where most of the Mahimā Dharmīs belong to the Gaṇḍa-Paṇa caste.

worship and Brahmin priesthood, but also the expression of an emerging social protest of the downtrodden communities. Although the intention of the attackers was to burn the idol, not worship it, and the act of entering the temple should be seen in the context of other temple entry movements.

However, the attack remains mysterious because the event is—as Biswamoy Pati confirms[7]—forgotten by the Mahimā Dharmīs today. Irrespective of the issue whether it is a colonial myth for the attackers to belong to a dissident Mahimā Dharma group, the fact remains that the Mahimā Dharmīs narrate the relationship of Jagannath and Mahimā Svāmī in a mythological framework of domination and submission. To quote Anncharlott Eschmann, Mahimā Dharma 'regards itself as a counter as well as succession movement'.[8] Not Jagannath but Mahimā Gosain is the king of the world. He is *Pra*-Buddha and mightier than Jagannath. Consequentially, the Jagannath *tīrtha* in Puri with its sacred meaning is annihilated and new centres, holier and more important, are established.

Mahimā Svāmī's Contested Legacy: Balkaladhārīs *versus* Kaupīnadhārīs

It is well known that, when the founder of a religious movement disappears, conflicts arise. His legal successors, wielding the right to initiate new members and to lead the community, must be elected. In the present case, today's Mahimā Dharma community consists—apart from the laity—of two rival ascetic orders: the Balkaladhārīs and the Kaupīnadhārīs. The former are called Balkaladhārīs because they wear nothing but a *balkalabāna*, a piece of bark from the Kumbhi tree. The latter are also named for their clothing, which consists of a *kaupīnabāna* or a loin cloth. The split between the two groups goes back to history as transmitted orally as well as by news reports. It should be recalled that Mahimā Gosain himself initiated Govinda Bābā in Balasingha by supplying the latter with a piece of *balkala* to be worn instead of clothes. After this event, Govinda Bābā initiated the legendary sixty-four *siddhas* by giving them *balkalabāna* as well. The obvious question arising

[7] Pati 2001, 144.

[8] Eschmann 1978, 376.

from this tradition would be after the reason of this selection: why should the sixty-four be privileged? Could the piece of bark be bestowed upon other disciples as well? The fission of the two orders, however, does not simply relate to the question of who would be entitled to *balkalabāna* and who not. Rivalries and struggles over influence and power already existed during the lifetime of Mahimā Gosain, but they had never turned into open conflict. In the mid-seventies, for instance, Nrusingha Bābā was disqualified and degraded.[9] The decisive break, however, took place in 1876, after the death of Mahimā Gosain. In 1877, Bhīma Bhoi founded his own *āśrama* in Khaliapali, while in 1896, Nanda Bābā, in charge of the Dadhisingha *āśrama*, is said to have presented *balkalabāna* to 56 ascetics. This bestowal was performed against the resistance of the *kaupīna*-wearers under the guidance of Krupasindhu Bābā. In 1912, the latter officially founded the Kaupīnadhārī *samāja*.

It goes without saying that the Balkaladhārīs consider themselves at the top of the sacred hierarchy. Wearing *balkala* is considered as a symbol of *siddhi*. However, the Kaupīnadhārīs deny that *balkala* should be given to any ascetic and, obviously, refuse to accept an inferior status. After the separation, both sects founded their own *tungīs*[10] throughout Orissa and in some neighbouring states, such as Assam and AP as well. Did both groups cover the same regions or did they choose different areas for their mission? How many *tungīs* did they establish? It is extremely difficult to answer these obvious questions. In both Dhenkanal and Angul in central Orissa, the Balkaladhārīs are probably more prominent just as the Kaupīnadhārīs are in the western region of the province. To express these differences in terms of numbers is next to impossible. However, Anncharlott Eschmann did offer some figures.[11] Apart from the fact that these data are more than 20 years old, I doubt the accuracy of the original figures. The author herself admits that the

---

[9] A feast was organised in Malbiharpur where thousands of people joined crying for food. It is narrated that a terrible bloodshed took place and that Nrusingha Bābā was arrested by the British government. It is further reported that Mahimā Svāmī commanded Nrusingha Bābā to wear silk because his *balkalabānā* had become polluted. He is said to have commanded: 'Leave bark (*paṭa*) and wear silk (*pāṭa*)!'

[10] A *tungī* is a place of worship, see Eschmann 1978, 402.

[11] Eschmann 1975, 14.

data were supplied by Biswanath Bābā himself. Did he give a correct picture? Considering the likelihood of the inaccuracy of his account, the small number of Kaupīnadhārī *āśrama*s is debatable.

During my interviews and interactions with both groups, I noticed a significant difference in behaviour, discursive practice, accent, body language, physical statue and general outlook. On discussing this point with colleagues and assistants, we concluded that the senior Balkaladhārī monks are mostly recruited from higher castes, in contrast to the Kaupīnadhārī ascetics who seem to come largely from lower or even untouchable castes. This observation is highly speculative. It is extremely difficult to verify the social background of any ascetic. Generally a Bābā strongly refuses to respond to this question at all. He might resent it as obscene and offensive because he has symbolically died with regard to his original social identity.[12]

However, my suggestion seems to be supported by the fact that the Balkaladhārīs are strong in numbers all over central Orissa, whereas in western Orissa the Kaupīnadhārī section is predominant. The different centres of gravity could be related to the largely accepted fact that members of Mahimā Dharma in western Orissa are former untouchables. The data of the Tribal Research Institute of Bhubaneswar support my theory.[13] Still, this is certainly a point that deserves further investigation. Mahimā Dharma ascetics, I suppose, follow a pattern similar to other ascetic sects and subdivisions who, according to Robert Lewis Gross, recruit their members along caste affiliations.[14]

---

[12] In his book on Indian *sādhu*s, Robert Lewis Gross (1992, 144) confirms that information regarding the caste background of contemporary *sādhus* and specific caste recruitment practices are extremely difficult to elicit.

[13] In 1969, the Tribal Research Institute published an article which mentions the different caste backgrounds of converts. According to the given sample the majority of converts in Puri district belong to the Saora-Khond tribe. In Cuttack converts come mostly from the Teli caste. In Sambalpur area the Gaṇḍas form the absolute majority.

[14] Gross (1992, 145) mentions that the Dandi *samnyāsins* are comprised solely of former Brahmins and that the Naga Akharas primarily recruit members from Rajput and from Sat-Śudra *jātis*.

Joranda: The Emergence of a New Sacred Centre in Central Orissa

Once a religious tradition divides into groups, specific centres are created. In the case of Mahimā Dharma, the Balkaladhārī-section of the monks is commonly taken as that of the authentic followers, Joranda being the uncontested centre. The place has a history, and it is worth while going back to understand how the centre came into being. Mahimā Gosain himself is said to have founded several *tungīs* in order to perform *dhuni.*[15] Interestingly, he is supposed to have destroyed them after having used them. Mahimā Gosain and his male and female disciples were wandering ascetics. They never stayed for long in one place. By contrast, the monastery in Joranda was founded only a few years after the death of Mahimā Gosain. Although it is claimed that the guru's *samādhipiṭha* is Joranda, he probably did not die there. Such issues did not seem to trouble the founders of the tradition when they created their hero. As Ishita Banerjee-Dube has observed, Mahimā Gosain was progressively deified.[16] The notion of 'the making of Mahimā Gosain' must be stressed here, since Mukund Das, as he was called in the news reports of the time, never pretended to have a divine nature.[17] Even the intention to create a new sacred centre in Joranda may have been alien to Mahimā Gosain, because it would contradict his claim to worship the Formless everywhere.

The construction of the Mahimā Gaddī at Joranda is thus the result of an ongoing divinization of Mahimā Gosain and the progressive institutionalization of the movement. Today, the temple compound undoubtedly represents the biggest and the richest Mahimā Dharma monastery in Orissa, impressing the visitor by its splendour and magnificence. The huge complex contains many temples. A few monks, mostly the aged, reside there permanently, while the younger generation wanders through the country. The managing monk is elected once a year. In fact the actual outlook and observed practices are similar to the functioning of typical

[15] *Dhuni* means fire ritual. For further information on the use and significance of fire rituals in ascetic practices see Gross 1992, 357-68.

[16] Banerjee-Dube 2001, 152.

[17] Mahimā Svāmī has been canonized as *ayonisambhūta* by his followers, that means he was 'born not out of a women's womb', see Dash 1998, 5 and Nath 1990, 32.

Hindu *maṭhas*. The daily ritual routine in Joranda is performed by the Bābās and several restrictions are maintained, regarding the accessibility of the *mandiras*. Only the Balkaladhārī Bābās are allowed to enter the holy shrines, the Kaupīnadhārīs have to stay outside. Once a year, around Magha Dasamī[18] a *mela* is organized to honour Mahimā Svāmī. This tradition is said to go back to as early as 1874.

Women, it should be noted, are not allowed to stay in the temple complex. No women have been accepted as *samnyāsinis*, since they are considered to be of inferior status. Women are supposed to be dependent upon and subordinate to their father during their childhood, their husband after marriage, and their sons in their old age. These discriminating features demand an explication, since Mahimā himself, when still alive, accepted women as disciples and even commanded them to stay in this *āśrama*. Nowadays, however, the official discourse justifies this fact by regarding them as *devī*s or goddesses.

The presence or absence of women, however, is not the most significant difference with regard to the fission of Mahimā Dharma. The most important characteristic of the Balkaladhārī-branch is its progressive Sanskritization and saffronization. This trend goes back to Biswanath Bābā, ordained in 1925, who later became the head of the Balkaladhārī order in Joranda. He was the first to attempt a systematization of the Dharma. While Bhīma Bhoi's poetry was composed in a style similar to medieval *bhakti* literature, Biswanath introduced a new form of writing.[19] His numerous essays are sophisticated and scholastic speculations.[20] Rather than leaning upon Bhīma Bhoi's Oriya texts, he quoted from the Brahmanical Sanskrit tradition. He also introduced a rigid monastic discipline and contributed to the exclusion of the Kaupīnadhārīs as *apara* 'imperfect' ascetics, a development I shall discuss below. Not only did he recognize other 'orthodox' Hindu scriptures such as the *Manusmṛti* as equally important, he also argued that the philosophy of Mahimā Dharma is in full accordance with the Vedas, the Purāṇas, and the *Bhāgavadgīta*. According to him Mahimā Dharma is nothing else but true Vedānta.

---

[18] *Magha Paurṇimā* is the full moon night of the Magha month.

[19] Eschmann 1978, 368.

[20] Biswanath Bābā 1954, 1987, and 1991.

Biswanath Bābā's attempt to transform Mahimā Dharma into a coherent doctrine was successful. Among the Balkaladhārī monks, he is considered to be the unquestionable authority. His theological stands and interpretations are seen as the true essence of the Dharma. As a consequence, Bhīma Bhoi's revolutionary and challenging positions are neutralized and annihilated. The peculiarity of Mahimā Dharma as a protest movement and the extraordinary poetic creativity of Bhīma Bhoi become less visible. The contesting appeal of the Mahimā Dharma movement, which allowed some people to conclude that Mahimā Dharma was a new religion, is thus misguided. On the contrary, Mahimā Dharma conforms as the true *Sanātana Dharma*, the fulfilment of Hinduism.

Joranda, in public opinion, figures as the centre of Mahimā Dharma. This perception is manifest in most of the recent academic publications and repeated by the public discourse, as spread by print media as well as by the *All India Radio*. Most Mahimā Dharma literature, texts written by actual followers and reflecting as such the inside view, are distributed by Dharmagrantha Store in Cuttack. Vidyadhara Sahu, the owner, has himself been a devotee of the late Biswanath Bābā, head of the Joranda *āśrama* for a long time. In fact, it is the degree of institutionalization, the monopol of knowledge and the concentration of sacred power which contribute to the exclusive status of the Balkaladhārī order rather than the different social background of the two religious orders. Accepting that Joranda as Mahimā Dharma's most influential and important centre, one has to keep in mind that its hegemony has always been—and still is—a matter of discord and contest.

Mahulpada: An Abandoned Kaupīnadhārī Centre

Let us return to the so-called Malbiharpur riots. What happened after Mahimā Gosain commanded Nrusingha Bābā to leave *balkala*? It is commonly believed that he was ordered to found his own *āśrama* in Mahulpada. Although he is not remembered as the founder of the Kaupīnadhārī *samāja* (officially it was Krupasindha Bābā), one could consider his *āśrama* as the first institutionalized division of the ascetic order. It was commemorated as the centre of the Kaupīnadhārīs. In 1883, Samodar Patnaik, a writer from Cuttack and the editor of *Sangeet Sagar*, explains that the followers of Mahimā Dharma are divided into two groups, the Kumbhipatias[21] whose *āśrama* is in Joranda, and the Kanāpatias of Mahulpada.[22] Interestingly, he finds the first place not as 'enjoyable' as the latter. Let us quote from his rather romanticized description:

> The followers of the second group are Kanāpatias, meaning they wear cloths smeared with red ochre. Their monastery is in the solitary forest near the village Mahulpada. ... Their monastery reminded me of the *āśramas* as they are described in the past. Seeing it, all thoughts left my mind and wonderful divine feelings arose. Through the entrance of the monastery flows a clear fountain that caters the need of animals and beasts. There is a high altar at a distance. There are many small houses for the disciples. There is a *śūnya gṛha* built with bricks, a stone house and a fire house. There fire house has four doors on its four sides. Small trees of mango, jack fruit and banana bending down, being fruit-laden, express the glory of the place. The inhabitants of the *āśrama* never eat fruits from their trees. Only other people eat them. There is a trench around each tree at the bottom, from which birds drink water.... The smooth terraces, the mind-stealing twitter of the birds, the sweet buzz of bees, those holy sacrifices in the fire-house, the slow-blowing fragrant breeze, the peace-of-mind-giving and enchanting clay altar under the Kadamba trees are adding to the beauty of the *āśrama* and filling the minds of the visitors with ripples of bliss.[23]

It should be emphasized that even as early as 1883 it was a well established fact that the Balkaladhārīs and the Kaupīnadhārīs were two distinct groups with their distinctive *āśramas*. It seems also that the Balkaladhārīs were largely recognized as supreme leaders because they are always mentioned first in the official reports.

I decided to visit Mahulpada and the *āśrama*. Surprisingly nothing is left except the *samādhipiṭha* of Nrusingh Bābā. The place completely is abandoned. How did this happen? Why did this *āśrama* disappear without a trace? Similar stories about the origin of the *āśrama* are given by the present villagers. Banamali Parida, 70 years old and a Khandayat by caste, remembers that Lord Mahimā deprived Nrusingha Bābā of his *balkalabāna* and commanded him to establish an *āśrama*. Apparently, he was

---

[21] Kumbhipatia means 'who wears the bark of the Kumbhi tree' and is just another name for Balkaladhārī.

[22] Kanāpatia (wearer of *kanā*) is another name for Kaupīnadhārī. *Kanā* signifies an old cloth, a rag.

[23] See *Utkal Dīpika*, 17 March 1883, quoted in Dash 1997, 142-3.

excluded from Joranda and forced to create his own *āśrama* in Mahulpada. What happened after that? Why was this *āśrama* deserted? The question remains unanswered. Asked about the actual, rather pitiful condition of the place and the causes of such a development, Banamali Parida replied: 'Nrusingha Bābā himself had foretold that a road would run through the *āśrama*. Ultimately a train line was constructed. Therefore this *āśrama* has been completely abandoned.'

In fact, the village is close to a road, but the latter's influence upon the *āśrama* is unclear. Another—more interesting—hint is given in an accusation against the Joranda community, supposed to have contributed to the decline of the *āśrama*. Could we imagine a boycott or a stigmatization to have kept people from going to Mahulpada? I'm told that formerly the *āśrama* was on the route to Joranda and a regular stop for all pilgrims. A new road, however, not touching the village, was constructed from Dhenkanal to Joranda. Be it because of Joranda's decision to boycott Nrusingha Bābā, or because of the changed infrastructure, the *āśrama* of Mahulpada was abandoned.

The different organizations of the Kaupīnadhārī centres are primarily based on the observation that they exist side by side and are not closely interconnected. Anncharlott Eschmann, for example, mentions another *āśrama* at Baunsudi in the district of Keonjhar.[24] The temple complex is said to contain several temples, being a perfect pendant of Joranda. By contrast, Eschmann underlines its institutional independence; the present managers, father and son, celebrate the festivals under their own management and avoid donations. The same observation could be made regarding Bhīma Bhoi's *āśrama* in Khaliapali. Although it is somehow linked with the Kaupīnadhārī *samāja*, it is, institutionally speaking, independent.

Contested Authorities and Legal Debates

The quarrels between the two groups continue until the present day. Although the Kaupīnadhārīs fight for equal recognition, the Balkaladhārīs retain absolute authority in Joranda. Madan Das

---

[24] Eschmann 1978, 403.

Bābā, 80 years old and member of the *Kaupīnadhārī Mahimā Society*, Joranda, reports in an interview:

> The Kaupīnadhārī sect is the real upholder of Mahimā Dharma. The Balkaladhārīs do not have the right to claim to be chiefs. Mahimā presented *balkalabāna* to the sixty-four enlightened *sādhus* only, and *kaupīna* to all the rest. As the Balkaladhārīs do wear *balkala* and disobey the command of the Lord, we do not have any relationship with them. Mahimā Dharma has no existence without Bhīma Bhoi. He wrote down in verse the sayings of God. Devotees initiated as Kaupīnadhārīs can never wear *balkala.* This is the command of Lord Mahimā. We are not going to their temples or *āśramas*. Our principle, however, is one and the same. Balkaladhārīs are proud and haughty.

Let me add here that this discourse is not a mere question of control. It is a very important struggle concerning the temple management, a lot of property, money, influence, authority and domination. The Kaupīnadhārīs argue that they have equal rights and say that Mahimā Gosain did not create the Balkaladhārī *samāja.* According to the Balkaladhārīs, there is no difference between these two groups, since there is only one *samāja.* Both opinions can be considered rhetoric, of course. The Kaupīnadhārīs are not allowed to worship in the main temples and can only work as servants for the Balkaladhārīs; they are clearly inferior. Behind the scene it is also argued that Kaupīnadhārīs are somehow against the Mahimā Dharma religion by not recognizing the Balkaladhārī's superiority. Dibakar Das Bābā, a Balkaladhārī *sādhu* from Joranda, explains:

> Kaupīnadhārīs and Balkaladhārīs are not two separate sects. There is only one community of Mahimā Dharmīs. The corrupt and apostates have organised a separate sect. They (i.e. the Kaupīnadhārīs) do not have any right over the *samādhi* of Mahimā or this *āśrama.* Mahimā religion is nothing but pure Hinduism. In order to save Hinduism from corruption and degeneration and to lead it along the sacred path, Mahimā Dharma was founded. No worship is being performed in Mahimā's temple. The *gurupiṭha* is only being purified; there is no idol worship in Mahimā Dharma. Only Balkaladhārī *samnyasīs* can enter into the *samādhi* temple of Mahimā. We do not believe in sectarianism.

This statement is self-contradictory. It reveals polemics as well as justifications. On the one hand it is claimed that there is no sectarianism in Mahimā Dharma and that there is only one community of Mahimā Dharmīs. On the other hand, the Kaupīnadhārīs are accused of separatism and any share in the *āśrama* is denied to them. The ritual practices are justified by the excuse that they are not seen as an expression of a worship of the guru but only as purification.

Legal debates and decisions are at the base of the claim that Kaupīnadhārīs have no rights in Joranda. Although the conflict is much older, let us quote an order published in 1970 by the Orissa Hindu Religious Endowment Office at Bhubaneswar aiming to settle the matter of the Shrī Mahimā Gaddī at Joranda. First, it was recalled that the previous orders passed by the commission in 1965 and 1967 had not solved the existing conflict between the two groups. A common board had been proposed—composed of four Balkaladhārī members, two Kaupīnadhārīs and one *gṛhastha* (lay member). Thereafter, two separate boards were created. The order was challenged immediately because the existence of two boards could not be permitted. The report reveals that the ongoing competition of these two groups had led, once again, to legal debates, so that a final decision had become necessary.

Interestingly, the reports take the side of the Balkaladhārī group. It was acknowledged that a Mahimā Dharmī was to become a *tyāgī* (novice) and a Kaupīnadhārī first, before being ordained as a Balkaladhārī. The efforts of the Kaupīnadhārīs to reaffirm their equal status were judged as an attempt to revolt. It was further stated that the chief of the Kaupīnadhārīs, Bābā Kasinatha Das, was inciting mischief. Unfortunately, we are not informed about the substance of the accusation. It was concluded, however, that the Kaupīnadhārī group should no longer be accepted as part of the Mahimā Dharma. It was reaffirmed that the Kaupīnadhārī had no right to the temple complex in Joranda. They were allowed to form a separate religion, but prohibited the use of the name Alekha Dharma or a stay in the Mahimā Gaddī. In fact, they were denied all rights to the land. Consequently, the Balkaladhārīs were granted the right to evict the rival group from the properties belonging to Mahimā Gaddī.[25]

---

[25] See the document 'Shri Mahimagadi at Joranda, District Dhenkanal', signed by B.K. Misra, Comissioner of Endowments, dated 6 April 1970, and kept in the Orissa Hindu Religious Endwoments Office, Bhubaneswar. A typed copy of the document is kept in the Orissa Archive of the South Asia Institute in Heidelberg (MSS 175).

This decision had important consequences. As mentioned above, the Balkaladhārīs are now officially recognized as the legitimate representatives of the Mahimā Dharma religion. Their institution is considered to be the centre of the movement. They are officially recognized as the sole leading and most authoritative group. The Kaupīnadhārīs have to stay outside the Balkaladhārī territory. After being defeated in court and deprived of the right to perform worship within the main temple complex, they bought some land nearby in order to establish their own *āśrama* and *mandira.*

Finally, I may add that the conflict between these two ascetic groups is quite significant for the identity construction and the institutional affiliation of the Bābās. This, however, is less intelligible to the common laymen, however. I often met Mahimā Dharmīs unable to explain the difference between the two groups. For most followers, the Balkaladhārīs are clearly the supreme authority. They do not, however, bother much about the institutional quarrel.

Bhīma Bhoi: Saint-Poet and Dissident of Khaliapali

Ishita Banerjee-Dube has pointed out that after the death of Mahimā Gosain 'Sambalpur emerged as the new centre of the faith'.[26] This remark requires further comments, since I would rather apply a perspective recognizing the existence of several parallel centres competing with one another. Accordingly, the question arises whether Bhīma Bhoi intended to challenge the ascetic order of Joranda.

In order to develop my arguments, let me briefly recall some events in the life of Bhīma Bhoi, transmitted by oral tradition and some newspaper reports. Born somewhere between the districts of Sambalpur and Sonepur, Bhīma Bhoi grew up in great poverty. He was most probably an orphan, cared for by a tribal couple. Losing his father early, he was forced to tend cattle. It is said that he composed beautiful songs, although he was completely illiterate. Later he became a disciple of Mahimā Gosain, to whom he devoted all his poetry. It is generally accepted that after the death of Mahimā Gosain, Bhīma Bhoi went to Joranda where he discovered

---

[26] Banerjee-Dube 2001, 169.

an institutionalized 'Mahantism'.[27] Disgusted by what he had witnessed, he returned to Redhakhol and Binka. Under the patronage of Raja Niladhar Singh Deo of Sonepur, he then founded his own *āśrama* at Khaliapali in 1877. It is there that Bhīma Bhoi composed not only the major but also the most beautiful and original part of Mahimā Dharma literature.[28]

Evidently Bhīma Bhoi contested Joranda's authority. In his famous poem *Stuticintāmaṇi,* he advocated the *gṛhastha dharma,* and in his still unpublished *Mahimā Vinod*, he openly criticized Joranda. Bhīma Bhoi's protest did not remain restricted to poetry. In his *āśrama* he started a rival celebration of the Magha Mela. He further accepted some popular Hindu ritual practices such as the use of the *amba toraṇa* (mango leaf gate), which was thought to be superstitious, and was therefore disregarded by the Balkaladhārī ascetics. The most important expression of his dissidence was his initiation of women, ignoring possible sanctions and even giving an equal status to Annapurna, his spiritual companion.

Joranda monks, not surprisingly, reacted vehemently. It is reported that one of the dissident's first *āśrama*s, established prior to 1877, was burnt down by some Balkaladhārī monks because Bhīma Bhoi had been accused of abducting women. This kind of ongoing confrontation finds its expression in a story told by an old man from Khaliapali. He told me that one day, four holy men came from Joranda to meet Bhīma Bhoi:

> These *sādhu*s were very proud of themselves and arrogant. They disregarded and underestimated him. They thought: 'How can a tribal and a blind fellow preach such a great religion?' This was their idea of him. Bhīma Bhoi knew the inner thoughts of other people. He could already foresee their coming and he ordered Basu Panda[29] to get ready to welcome four *bhakta*s. Then the *sādhu*s arrived in Khaliapali. The first saw Bhīma Bhoi as Viṣṇu with his conch, wheel, club and lotus, and touched his feet.[30] The second *sādhu* saw Bhīma Bhoi as an old man and accused the first *sādhu*. The third *sādhu* saw Bhīma Bhoi in form of the most beautiful

---

[27] A *mahanta* is the head of a religious place. 'Mahantism' designates an autocratic and hierarchical monastic institution.

[28] Nepak 1999 and 2001.

[29] Hari Panda and Basu Panda were Bhīma Bhoi's scribes.

[30] *Śaṅkha*, *sudarśana*, *gadā*, and *padma* are the four iconographic characteristics of Viṣṇu.

> Rādha and asked her why she came from the Baikuntha heaven down to the earth. The fourth *sādhu* saw a child in Bhīma Bhoi. All four saw Bhīma simultaneously in four different forms. Finally, they could see the real Bhīma Bhoi and concluded that he and Mahimā Svāmī were equal. They asked Bhīma Bhoi to excuse their arrogance and false pride.

The characteristic arrogance of the Bābās from Joranda is striking. Furthermore, the divinization of Bhīma Bhoi receives a new quality here. He appears as a divine incarnation, linked to Viṣṇu. The relationship between Mahimā Dharma and Vaiṣṇava *bhakti* should not be underestimated. Bhīma Bhoi is also identified as Mahimā Gosain; teacher and disciple are but one. Such stories prove that Bhīma Bhoi is remembered as one of the most outstanding and charismatic preachers of Mahimā Dharma in western Orissa. Chittaranjan Das rightly pointed out that 'although Mahimā Gosain was the founder of Mahimā Dharma, it was really the works of Bhīma Bhoi, the blind poet, that brought home to all people the essence and excellence of the new doctrine. He shines with such prominence in the history of this particular religious movement that more than one critic has taken him to be the actual founder.' [31]

This statement is not exaggerated. Bhīma Bhoi spread Mahimā Dharma through his poetry. Indeed, the most important Mahimā Dharma texts we possess today are attributed to him. It is often claimed that after the death of Lord Mahimā, Bhīma Bhoi had taken up the lead to propagate and establish the Mahimā cult.[32] The Balkaladhārīs contest his leading role. According to them Bhīma Bhoi remains 'only' a disciple of the guru. He should not be compared to him. In an interview with a Balkaladhārī monk from Joranda, I was told:

> Bhīma Bhoi was a *bhakta* (devotee). He was not a *samnyāsī*, but a poet and a *gṛhastha* (householder). Hari Panda and Basu Panda and others wrote his poems. He was married and had progeny. Khaliapali is Bhīma Bhoi's *āśrama*. Joranda is Mahimā Svāmī's holy place. We like Bhīma Bhoi's writings, because his words are inspired by Mahimā Svāmī. He was a tribal and illiterate. He wrote what Mahimā Svāmī had told him.

---

[31] Das 1951, 160.

[32] S.P. Sharma (1942, 35) for example also thought that Bhīma Bhoi was the next leader after Mahimā Svāmī.

In the same interview I was told that Bhīma Bhoi never came to Joranda. It is denied that he ever put so much as a foot on the ground of the sacred centre: 'Bhīma Bhoi has never been to Joranda. Mahimā Svāmī himself denied Bhīma to come. This was the *āśrama* of the guru. He visited only Malbiharpur, Mahimā Svāmī's previous *āśrama*.'

This contest is interesting and important for our study, and we will return to it. Clearly Bhīma Bhoi is considered a disciple of Mahimā Gosain, and has no significance as an independent authority being a nobody without his guru. Interestingly, he is regularly considered to be blind, but many who are closely associated with the *āśrama* in Khaliapali contradict this statement. According to Biswanath Bābā, Bhīma Bhoi even refused to accept the gift of vision when it was offered to him by Mahimā Svāmī.[33] His blindness becomes a religious topic of spirituality, total submission and devotion. Khaliapali is disregarded as an *āśrama* for *bhakta*s and *gṛhastha*s. It should be added here that with Biswanath Bābā, the particularity of Mahimā Dharma which was due to the challenging positions and the extraordinary creativity of Bhīma Bhoi becomes less and less visible. Even polemics are uttered against Khaliapali. Seminars were organized and books published to strengthen Biswanath Bābā's position. It is interesting that these claims have influenced the perception of leading intellectuals like Chittaranjan Das and Satrughna Nath.[34] A certain innocence with regard to this issue also characterizes Anncharlott Eschmann's interpretations; even Ishita Banerjee-Dube mentions Bhīma Bhoi only once in her recent paper.[35] In fact, in discussions on Mahimā Dharma in Orissa, Bhīma Bhoi's particularity is deliberately neglected.

Another point should be highlighted here: The present *āśrama* in Khaliapali is not run by the monastic community. The reconstruction of the *maṭha* as well as its management is in the hands of a trust not immediately connected with the ascetics. A former Collector of Sonepur mobilized important financial resources to prevent the site from erosion and destruction. One could see this as a form of patronage. The new administration unfortunately contributed to a devaluation of Khaliapali as an

[33] Biswanath Bābā 1991, 53-6.

[34] Nath 1990, C. Das 1951.

[35] Eschmann 1978, 382-3 and Banerjee-Dube 2001, 169.

independent religious centre and it has become a kind of secularized place of pilgrimage and a tourist site. The community of Kaupīnadhārī Bābās, residing in the temple compound, lacks financial and logistic strength and independence. Although criticism is expressed from time to time by the Bābās, they are deliberately kept in a subordinate position regarding the management and administration of the *gaddī*. Nonetheless, the creation of the trust contributed to a positive revaluation of the poet and reformer Bhīma Bhoi, and as such represents a necessary move to counter Joranda's 'propaganda'.

Autonomy or Separatism? Satya Svādhin Mahimā Dharma in Kardula

The debate about the authority of Bhīma Bhoi is only one of the many open fields of discussion. In this ongoing process of interpretation, adaptation, and re-appropriation, the Satya Svādhin Mahimā Dharmīs of the Kardula village probably represent the most exciting agent.[36] The place is situated near Chiplima, Sambalpur, and the movement traces its origin to Bābā Satya Nārāyaṇa, born an 'untouchable' Gaṇḍa in the Talpadar village. Let us quote Durbadala Das, the son of Bābā Satya Narayanan, who today continues his father's mission and is an eloquent representative of his group:

> Sri Guru Satya Narayan Das' parents were poor. When he was a boy he used to collect wood from the jungle every day. By selling this he maintained his family. One day while he was cutting wood in the forest he saw Mahimā, the eternal, in the form of a seven-hooded cobra. The guru initiated him there. This place is called Ratnadham and is the most important place in the world.

It is further said that after his *darśana* of Mahimā Gosain, Satya Nārāyana obtained his blessings. For some days he wandered from place to place as an ascetic. After eight years he returned home and was ordained as a Balkaladhārī *samnyāsī* in Joranda. Later he left the order and founded his own independent branch. Personally, I have doubts about this claim, which seems to be a rhetorical

---

[36] I would like to express my gratitude to Rambhakta Mishra, Lecturer in History at Sonepur College, who suggested that I conduct research on this particular 'sect'.

argument in order to strengthen the authority as well as the rebellious character of Satya Nārāyaṇa Bābā. The affiliation with Joranda was, however, repeatedly reaffirmed by his family; he and his disciples were wearing *balkala.*

The Mahimā Dharmīs of Kardula, as is usual in western Orissa, mostly belong to one and the same caste, the Gaṇḍa-Paṇas. N. Patnaik and S.C. Mohanty confirm that the majority of converts to Mahimā Dharma in western Orissa come from this specific caste.[37] I identified in Sonepur more than 99 per cent of all Mahimā Dharmīs as belonging to this particular social group. In an interview Dasharathi Bābā, a Kaupīnadhārī ascetic from Julunda, states that in western Orissa Mahimā Dharma is therefore called 'Gaṇḍa Dharma'. In contrast, in eastern Orissa, people from so-called 'higher' castes have found shelter in this religion. In Dhenkanal, Chāsas or cultivating castes form the major part of the Mahimā Dharmīs. In southern Orissa the Desi tribes are representatives of an extraordinary social diversity within the movement.[38]

The claim that people from other castes such as Brahmins, Chāsas, and Dumals take *dikṣā* and join the Satya Svādin Mahimā Dharma group is highly doubtful and has yet to be proved. I do have, however, evidence that this particular branch is not restricted to the locality of Kardula. Near Sonepur I met Gaṇḍas who had visited Kardula and who also belonged to this group. Regarding the claim that many Satya Svādhin Mahimā Dharmīs reside outside of Orissa, the usual lack of quantitative data must be observed.

How do we interpret the fact that Mahimā Dharma is characteristic to the Gaṇḍa-Paṇas? One could argue that right from the beginning, the Gaṇḍas saw in Mahimā Dharma a possibility of affirming a new socio-religious identity. Excluded from the right to enter not only local temples but also the Jagannath *mandir* of Puri, one could easily understand this argument. The new religious trend, however, was relevant in western Orissa and not in the coastal belt. One could argue that this fact was a direct result of Bhīma Bhoi's uprising against social discrimination and orthodox Brahmanism. In fact Bhīma Bhoi was well known in western Orissa for his radical opposition to caste and social inequality. Does Bhīma Bhoi's

---

[37] Patnaik and Mohanty 1988, 174.

[38] See Lidia Guzy's (2001) fieldwork among the Desi tribes in Koraput.

charisma and influence explain the important impact of Mahimā Dharma on the Gaṇḍas?

Such a conclusion appears to be justified.[39] The independent Mahimā Dharmīs reject any kind of asceticism, even asking their Bābās to get married before they are ordained. It is said that because Bhīma Bhoi was a *gṛhastha*, they have to be *gṛhastha*s also. In other words, Mahimā Dharma is seen as a lay religion. Jyanendri Das, widow of Satya Nārāyaṇa Bābā, explained that she only initiates those devotees who lead a family life. According to her, the one who lives with his family is the real *samnyāsī*. To quote Dhurbadala Das once more: 'Mahimā Dharma is the religion of the mother. So we initiate the women first. Ours is primarily a *gṛhastha dharma*. We don't believe in *samnyāsa*. Bhīma Bhoi has taught us this. *Samnyāsa karma*s can be performed staying at home. We have learnt it from Bhīma Bhoi.'

The Svādhin Mahimā Dharmīs legitimate their difference by arguing that they alone are the true followers of Bhīma Bhoi. Satya Nārāyaṇa Bābā is considered as an incarnation of Bhīma Bhoi and Jyanendri Das, his wife, presents herself as the incarnation of Annapurna. She said:

> Satya Nārāyaṇa Bābā was in his previous life Bhīma Bhoi himself. He was blind and a Khond in the form of Bhīma Bhoi. He is dead for the people, but he still survives in me. In this life, choosing to be born in the *Śāsani kula*,[40] he has taught the Satya Svādhin Mahimā Dharma. I was his consort in the form of Annapurna, the arch-mother. In our previous life we have founded the *āśrama*s of Joranda and Khaliapali.

Satya Nārāyaṇa Bābā is seen as an incarnation of God. It is said that he continued the mission of Bhīma Bhoi after he left this world. He completed the unfinished work, initiating a large number of followers and disciples into Mahimā Dharma. In other words, what Bhīma Bhoi had written as a poet, Satya Nārāyaṇa translated into action. Furthermore, one has to note that Ratnadham is seen as more important than Joranda. Dhurbadala Das used to go to Joranda

---

[39] The Gaṇḍa's mass conversion to Christianity can be seen as a similar attempt of rebellion against orthodox Hinduism (cf. Behera 1989).

[40] *Śāsani kula* means 'dynasty of rulers' and refers probably to the Brahmin villages in coastal Orissa. As a caste designation, it is used by the Gaṇḍa-Paṇas to claim a higher social status.

in order to argue with the monks. According to him, they oppose him out of jealousy and do not understand the concepts expounded by Satya Nārāyana Das.

In fact, this section of the Mahimā Dharmīs illuminates clearly the demotic aspect of the Orissa Research Project. If one looks exclusively at Joranda, one might find it difficult to see Mahimā Dharma as a subaltern movement. The untouchable Gaṇḍa-Paṇas, however, took Bhīma Bhoi as a symbol of their own, being a poor, marginalized, and low caste man. He is their prophet and affirms their desire for social recognition. Through him, a universal brotherhood is formulated. The underprivileged Gaṇḍa-Paṇas are also Hindus. Even better, they are the authentic Hindus, practising real Hinduism because they know the hidden meaning of the Veda, the theory of the void.

Let us refer to Joranda in order to illustrate the diverse settings and shapes of Mahimā Dharma in Orissa. Joranda's monastery does not question existing power structures. On the contrary, Lidia Guzy pointed out that Mahimā Dharma continued to function under the traditional patronage system.[41] Such a conclusion cannot be applied to the Kardula case. In fact, this particular branch of Mahimā Dharma questions caste hierarchies and traditional power structures. Mahimā Dharma can therefore, at least in this particular context, be analysed in the framework of social movements. It is an expression of the fight for difference and social recognition, to use Martin Fuchs' term.[42]

Finally, Kardula is another, often ignored, expression of Mahimā Dharma's doctrinal and organizational diversity. Anncharlott Eschmann, for instance, visited Kardula during her field work as can be seen from her slides and field notes in the archives of Heidelberg's South Asia Institute. Surprisingly, she did not notice the striking differences. Perhaps her visit was short or without her interpreter. It is, nonetheless, astonishing that she overlooked the particularity of the site.

---

[41] Guzy 2000, 326-7.

[42] Fuchs 1999, 219-72.

Conclusion

Going into the history of Mahimā Dharma, one discovers several centres emerging at different times. During the lifetime of Mahimā Svāmī, Malbiharpur, Joranda and Mahulpada were established. After his death, Bhīma Bhoi spread the religion in western Orissa and shifted its centre from Joranda to Khaliapali. Again under the leadership of Biswanath Bābā the centre of attention and authority shifted to Joranda. It was the intention of this paper to explain why these changes took place.

I have adopted a regionalist perspective. If the coastal belt of Orissa with Puri and Lord Jagannath is considered its centre, one may find it strange that Mahimā Dharma abandons it. The eminent historian Chittaranjan Das illustrates this point of view. In his overview of Oriya literature, published by Orissa's Sahitya Akademi and representing as such a kind of officially sanctioned discourse, he found it 'very strange ... that the centre of the movement was not the coastal districts of the state' and observes that the seat of Mahimā Dharma continues to be in the district of Dhenkanal in central Orissa.[43]

I think this observation is misguided. It seems evident Mahimā Svāmī's intention was to question the hegemony of Puri and to democratize and decentralize sacred power in Orissa. We should further shift our attention not only away from Puri but also away from Joranda, from the central to the frontier Orissa. I have to add here that Bhīma Bhoi is currently easily integrated into the separatist discourse demanding an independent Koshal Pradesh. More and more intellectuals reclaim him for their sake, demanding that his writings must be republished in the original language, Sambalpuri. It is not only that Bhīma Bhoi was a son of the soil, he was also a critic of the Jagannath cult, the coastal hegemony, and the Puri Brahmins.

Mahimā Dharma has been, and still is, a decentralized religious movement. I have argued that despite Joranda's claim to exclusiveness and domination, many other parallel 'centres' existed and continue to exist. Even if they do recognize Joranda as Mahimā Gosain's *āśrama*, they are—institutionally speaking—independent. In other words, Khaliapali and Kardula are not peripheral

[43] Das 1982, 157.

dependants of Joranda. The reality is more complex and overlapping. The actors may shift from one branch of the movement to another, or they may belong to many 'centres' at the same time. I suggest, therefore, that Mahimā Dharma in Orissa has to be understood as a polycentric, highly diversified and multi-faceted movement.

References

Banerjee-Dube, Ishita. 1999. 'Taming Traditions: Legalities and Histories in Twentieth-Century Orissa', in G. Bhadra, G. Prakash and S. Tharu (eds.), *Subaltern Studies X, Writings on South Asian History and Society*, New Delhi: Oxford University Press, 98-125.

— 2001. 'Issues of Faith, Enactment of Contest: The Founding of Mahima Dharma in Nineteenth-Century Orissa', in H. Kulke and B. Schnepel (eds.), *Jagannath Revisited*, New Delhi: Manohar, 149-77.

Behera, Deepak Kumar. 1989. *Ethnicity and Christianity: Christians Divided by Caste and Tribe in Western Orissa*, Delhi: Indian Society for the Promotion of Christian Knowledge.

Behera, Subhakanta. 1997. 'Jagannath and Alekh', *Economic and Political Weekly*, 16-23 August 2006-7.

Biswanath Bābā, Abadhuta. 1954. *An Exposition of Satya Mahima Religion*, Cuttack: L. N. Press.

— 1987. *Philosophy of Mahima Dharma (Philosophy of Unalloyed Non-Dual Supreme Being)*, Cuttack: Mahima Dharmalochana Samiti.

— 1991 [1935]. *Mahimā Dharma Itihāsa* (Oriya), Dhenkanal: Mahimadharma Granthakosa Samiti.

Das, Chittaranjan. 1951. 'Studies in Medieval Religion and Literature of Orissa', *Vishva Bharati Annals*, 3, 107-94.

— 1982. *A Glimpse into Oriya Literature*, Bhubaneswar: Orissa Sahitya Akademi.

Das, Sidharth. 1997. *Mahima Dharma: A Cultural Dissent*, Cuttack: Arya Prakashan.

Dash, Debendra Kumar. 1997. 'Bhīma Bhoi o Mahimā Dharma' (Oriya), *Eshana*, 34, 120-52.

Dash, Achutananda. 1998. *Ayoni Sambhūta Mahimāswāmī in Śastric Perspective*, Dhenkanal: Mahima Gaddi, Mahima Philosophy and Literature Research Centre.

Deo, Fanindam. 1999. 'Institutional and Organisational Aspects of Mahima Dharma', in Joseph T. O'Connell (ed.), *Organisational and Institutional Aspects of Indian Religious Movements*, New Delhi: Manohar, 137-51.

Eschmann, Anncharlott. 1975. 'Spread, Organization and Cult of Mahima Dharma', in Nilamani Senapati (ed.), *Mahima Dharma*, Cuttack: Dharmagrantha Store, 9-22.

— 1978. 'Mahimā Dharma: An Autochtonous Hindu Reform Movement', in A. Eschmann, H. Kulke and G.C. Tripathi (eds.), *The Cult of Jagannath and the Regional Tradition of Orissa*, New Delhi: Manohar, 375-410.

Fuchs, Martin. 1999. *Kampf um Differenz, Repräsentation, Subjektivität und soziale Bewegungen. Das Beispiel Indien*, Frankfurt a. M: Suhrkamp Verlag.

Gross, Robert Lewis. 1992. *The Sadhus of India*, New Delhi: Rawat Publications.

Guzy, Lidia. 2000. '"On the Road with the Babas": Some Insights into Local Features of Mahima Dharma', *Journal of Social Sciences* 4 (4), 323-30.

— 2001. 'Voices of Gods. Ecstatic Alekhs and Local Configurations of Mahima Dharma', paper presented at the ORP-conference 'Centre and Periphery' at Salzau, May 2001.

Mahapatra, Sitakant. 1983. *Bhima Bhoi*, New Delhi: Sahitya Akademi (Makers of Indian Literature Series).

Mishra, Bibhuti Bhusan. 1998. *Religious Reform Movements in Orissa*, Jaipur: Publication Scheme.

Nath, Satrughna. 1977. *Biswanath Baba: A Saint, Self-Realised in the Mahima Faith*, Cuttack: Dharmagrantha Store.

— 1990. *Mahima Dharmadhara*, Bhubaneshwar: Hemalata Nath.

Nepak, Bhagirathi. 1987. *Bhima Bhoi: The Adivasi Poet Philosopher*, Bhubaneswar: Bhagiratha Prakashan.

— 1999. *Bhima Bhoi*, Bhubaneswar: Bhagiratha Prakashan.

Nepak, Bhagirathi (ed.). 2001. *Bhima Bhoi: The Greatest Adivasi Poet Prophet*, Bhubaneswar: Bhagiratha Prakashan.

Panigrahi, S.C. 1998. *Bhima Bhoi and Mahima Dharma*, Bhubaneswar: Utkal University, Department of Special Assistance in Philosophy (Utkal Studies in Philosophy, 2).

Pati, Biswamoy. 2001. *Situating Social History, Orissa (1800-1997)*, New Delhi: Orient Longman.

Patnaik, Nityananda and Sarat Chandra Mohanty. 1988. *The Ganda, A Scheduled Caste Weaver Community of Western Orissa*, Bhubaneswar: Tribal and Harijan Research cum Training Institute.

Sharma, S.P. 1942. *Three Years in Orissa*, Calcutta: Thacker Spink & Co.

Swain, S. 1999. *Mahima Concept of Salvation*, Dhenkanal: Mahima Philosophy and Literature Research Centre.

(The) Tribal Research cum Training Institute (Bhubaneswar). 1968-69. 'Impact of Satya Mahima Dharma on Scheduled Castes and Scheduled Tribes in Orissa', *Adibasi*, 10 (1), 41-76.

6

'Negative Ecstasy or the Singers of the Divine': Voices from the Periphery of Mahima Dharma

Lidia J. Guzy

'Who knows God?
Who knows the creator?
Who knows how all this
Came into existence?
Your fate and mine.
God will bring them together.
Don't cry, don't cry !
Oh, You!
The large and the length of earth!
I will hold you
And purify—
With the dust of the earth.'
Alekh *gurumai*, October 2000

My paper concentrates on local patterns of Mahima Dharma, a new ascetic religion in Orissa which recently proselytised in the Koraput region. It presents extracts of on-going research* based on twelve months of comparative fieldwork conducted among ascetics and devotees in the district of Dhenkanal (September 1999-February 2000) and Koraput (October 2000-March 2001). In Koraput the percentage of the Mahima Dharma adherents can be assessed to 10 per cent of the local (*Desya*)[1] population.

---

* My research project on Mahima Dharma is part of the Orissa Research Programme (ORP) funded by the German Research Council (DFG/Deutsche Forschungsgesellschaft). I thank the DFG for the generous grants without which the research could not have been conducted.

[1] *Desya* is a local term shared by those who live in the hills of the hinterland of Koraput. Literally it means 'locals', but at the administrative level it is associated with formal categories such as Scheduled Tribes (ST), Other Backward Classes (OBC) and Scheduled Castes (SC). For more details cf. Pfeffer 1997; Otten 2000; Berger 2001.

The spread of the new ascetic religion in Koraput—where a high percentage of the total population are of indigenous[2] origin[3]—might exemplify processes of social and religious change relevant for the whole of indigenous India. My paper, therefore, is intended to approach issues of cultural change and the structure of conversion.

With reference to selected records of ecstatic song compositions, the article will also illustrate some new selective data from an 'ethnography of song'. During six months of my stay in Koraput I witnessed over a hundred ecstatic song séances of Alekh *gurumai*, the ritual specialists of the new religion. I collected and recorded more than one hundred of them and my Indian colleague, Sunita Dolhei, translated them from Desya-Oriya[4] into English. The presentation of some extracts of this work is intended to illustrate the oral creativity of local cultures.

Mahima Dharma

Mahima Dharma, literally 'the glorious *dharma*' is professed by monks and laymen. The monastic organization is represented by two brotherhoods of monks, the Balkaldhari and Kaupindhari, mostly dispersed throughout central Orissa (Dhenkanal). These two ascetic groups are organized around a network of local centres[5] with the institutional axis in the holy city of Joranda (Dhenkanal). The lay followers mainly stem from the rural and, only recently, also

---

[2] My paper—in its limited character—cannot offer an adequate presentation of the terminological problem and academic discussions with regard to the term 'tribal' spanning decades. Therefore, I use a less academically challenged term for my presentation. For looking at the definitions cf. Fortes and Evans-Pritchard (eds.) 1940 and Sahlins 1968; for discussion see Helm (ed.) 1971 (1968); Kuper 1988; for comparative discussion cf. Pfeffer 2004.

[3] See Senapati and Kuanr 1971, 19.

[4] The local language of the Desya of Koraput.

[5] At least five 'official' centres (*tirtha)* exist: (1) Joranda, (2) Kamakhianagar, (3) Angarabanda, (4) Jaka, (5) Barambur. Beside these, Khaliapalli as the holy place of Bhima Bhoi (the popular blind poet) is of greatest importance; Topo Bono also represents a centre of pilgrimage. Cf. also Beltz 2001: 'Disputed Centres, Rejected Norms and Contested Authorities: Situating Mahima Dharma in its Regional Diversity', paper presented during the Annual DFG-Salzau-Conference May 2001, and Beltz' article in this volume.

from the indigenous population of Orissa.[6] There are no official statistics concerning the number of monks and devotees. According to informal accounts,[7] approximately 100 ascetics live permanently in Joranda; another 900 move from one holy centre to another. Around 10.000 registered devotees in Joranda are responsible for the livelihood of the ascetics and the finance of the various monastic centres.[8] We can assume that less then 1per cent of the total population of Orissa[9] sees itself as belonging to Mahima Dharma.

The main features of the new religion are asceticism, a vegetarian diet, a denial of caste, and a conception of god that lies between heno- and monotheism.[10] Mahima Dharmis worship Mahima Alekh as the highest, unwritten *(a-lekh),*[11] indescribable, and only God. Mahima Alekh is conceived as *śunya*—the void—all and nothing. This God can only be approached by meditation, an ascetic lifestyle and ritual practices, and is thus opposed to idol worship. The concepts and values go back to the founder of the religion, Mahima Gosvami, who lived at the beginning of the nineteenth century. His origin is unknown, but of his devotees, Mahima Gosvami is considered to be the incarnation of Mahima Alekh. According to legend, Mahima Gosvami came from the Himalaya and appeared in Puri in 1826, from where he began his religious mission over Orissa. For the next 24 years, Mahima Gosvami is said to have meditated in the Kapilas Hills of

---

[6] Cf. Eschmann 1975, 9-22; ibid 1986 (1978), 386-7 ; T.R.B. 1968-9.52.

My own observations during my fieldwork in the Koraput district confirm this statement.

[7] Derived from conversations with several ascetics who confidentially told me about the numbers. The access to internal information about the monastic organization are reserved only for monks.

[8] Informal information from several ascetics.

[9] Total population of Orissa estimated in 1994 is 33.795.000, In: *Microsoft WorldAtlas 2001.*

[10] In reference to the neologism of Friedrich Max Müller, henotheism means the belief-system in one highest god to whom the devotee is mostly emotionally attached. It implies the existence of other inferior gods. Monotheism means the belief in one, and only one, god.

[11] *A-lekha* being explained to me as 'not to write/unwritten' refers to the everyday usage. The term itself means 'without writing', 'illiterate', in Sanscrit indicating a pejorative meaning.

Dhenkanal. There he lived for the first 12 years on fruits and roots of the forest delivered to him daily by a Savara[12] Chief. During the following 12 years Raja Bhagirati Mahindra Bahadur, the king of Dhenkanal, used to supply Mahima Gosvami with a daily ration of milk. After a long period of meditative preparation he is said to have started his religious teachings in the Feudatory States of Orissa.[13] The legends further tell that Bhima Bhoi, a blind poet of Khond origin, became the first enthusiastic propagator of this religion.[14]

Eschmann[15] thought that Mahima Dharma must be seen as 'an autochthonous Hindu reform movement'[16] which derives 'its criticism of the Hindu tradition directly from the tradition itself'.[17] Eschmann's main work concerns the dynamics of indigenous regional traditions in correspondence with pan-South Asian forms and ideas. Dube later investigated the historical development of Mahima Dharma as a sect, contesting the dominant structures in the nineteenth century[18] and undergoing changes within the processes of institutionalization.[19] Dube found that Mahima Dharma was a 'transformation of a subaltern religiosity' into 'an institutionalized religious order'.[20]

My own research is a comparative socio-anthropological analysis of the diverse religious features of Mahima Dharma in Orissa. I attempt to grasp the emerging new religion in terms of social change and structure.

---

[12] Savara—also referred to as Soara/ Saura or Sahara—is the name of a Scheduled Tribe in Orissa. Cf. Senapti and Tripathy (eds.) 1972, 104. In Dhenkanal, the Savara people live in the neighbourhood of the Malaygiri Hill (ibid., 48). Dhenkanal city, the capital of the district, is said to owe its name to the Savara Chief called Dhenkanal (ibid., 427).

[13] For further information on the places of Mahima Gosvamis' travels in Orissa cf. Senapati 1972, 443-8.

[14] Today, Bhima Bhoi is the key poet of the Mahima Dharma religion whose (orally composed) verses and songs became the literary basis of this religion. For details, cf. Beltz in this volume or Mohapatra 1983.

[15] Eschmann 1986 (1978), 374-410.

[16] Ibid., 375.

[17] Ibid., 375.

[18] Dube 2001, 149-78.

[19] For this topic see also: Deo 1999, 137-51.

[20] Dube 1999, 98; 125.

Brief Comparison of Socio-religious Contexts of Mahima Dharma

A brief regional comparison of Mahima Dharma in Dhenkanal, the region of the origin and main spread of the ascetic tradition, and Koraput can be understood as an introduction into the topic:

Dhenkanal	Koraput
Predominant is the monastic, polycentric structure. The monastic organization is always connected with local ruling elites who provide for the ascetics (*babas*). Asceticism of Mahima Dharma reflects the patronage system between local leaders and *babas*. The local tradition of otherworldly asceticism in rural Dhenkanal can only be seen in relation to local patrons. By sponsoring the holy men, rituals, and religious places, worldly patrons gain religious merits[21]	Professional ascetics are very rare. They appear only once a year in order to initiate new devotees (*dikhya*). Instead of *babas*, local ritual specialists, the Alekh *gurumai,* themselves perform all religious rituals that concern ecstatic[22] singers. Borrowing from Kakar[23], Vitebsky[24], Vargyas[25] and Atkinson[26], I will call these local religious specialists 'Alekh-shamans'. Apart from the *dikhya* ceremony, Alekh shamans are totally self-sufficient. In their therapeutic, ecstatic and prophetic functions they communicate a rich body of oral culture and poetry.

---

[21] For more details cf. Guzy 2000, 326-7.

[22] The term 'ecstasy' derives from the Greek origin *ekstasis*, which can be translated as an alienation from the external reality. In reference to psychoanalytical and sociological approaches, Zinser gives in his article an introduction to the various definitions of ecstasy as 'abnormal' or 'altered state of consciousness' (Zinser 1988, 274-84). In using 'ecstatic' or 'ecstasy', I refer to an altered state of consciousness as meant by Lewis. Cf. footnote 40.

[23] Kakar 1984 [1982], 92-121. In reference to the crucial work of Lévi-Strauss on 'the effectiveness of symbols', Kakar classifies local Indian healing specialists as shamans. They, in terms of Lévi-Strauss, give a symbolic language to their suffering clients. Kakar's descriptions of the

The two different regions and social contexts depict two facets of asceticism. On the one hand, we are confronted with the Hindu version of institutionalized world renunciation in Dhenkanal which is closely tied to local rulers. The alliance between local leaders and ascetics is a well-known model of Indian kingship[27] as described, for instance, by Bouillier[28] and extensively discussed by Quigley.[29] In this vein, the asceticism of Mahima Dharma in Dhenkanal seems to represent patterns of Indian kingship at a very local level. Male *babas* ritually interact with various worldly patrons who were tied historically to 'Little Kings' of Orissa and who exercise a local political influence to this day.[30] The monastic asceticism of Mahima Dharma may also be comparable to Buddhist structures of monasticism where kings were closely allied with ascetics.[31]

Koraput seems to be of a completely different character: asceticism results in ecstasy, but is featured by its permanent

---

therapeutic and ritual specialists of the Oraon tribe (ibid., 95-111) correspond with my own ethnographic observations within the Alekhs of the Koraput.

[24] Vitebsky 1993, 1995. Vitebsky (1993) deals with Sora shamanism. He describes Sora cosmological concepts, the Sora personality and the specific ideas of continuity always structured around dialogues between the dead and the living. In his analysis, the oral polyphonic character plays a crucial role during shamanic sessions. Later (1995) he establishes a general description of different features of the unsystematized shamanic religion.

[25] Vargyas 1993, 120-27; ibid 1994, 123-75. Vargyas` studies in South-East Asia emphasizes the oral literary character of shamanic phenomena.

[26] Atkinson 1992, 307-30. In her review article, Atkinson refers to the different topics within the scholarly constructed models of 'shamanism'. Aware of the criticism concerning the Western category, she postulates its exchange with its plural form 'shamanisms', 'in favour of close scrutiny of local practices embedded in particular historical, cultural, and social contexts' (321). In order to cultivate interdisciplinary dialogues apart from local ethnographic results, Atkinson argues for preserving studies on shamanisms.

[27] Cf. Cohn 1990 (1962), Dirks 1979, Galey 1989, Schnepel 1997.

[28] Bouillier 1997.

[29] Quigley, 1999.

[30] For details cf. Guzy 2001/2.

[31] Tambiah, 1976.

individual 'negative rules' [32] of life conduct which I therefore label 'negative ecstasy'. Ecstasy can be thus attained through ascetic techniques of fasting, a vegetarian diet and abstinence from alcohol. This ascetic ethic is popularized by female and male shamans in Koraput. In contrast to male *babas* of the religious centres in Dhenkanal, ecstatic female and male *gurumai* become the religious specialists in the monastic periphery of Koraput. The structural feature of the new religion in Koraput lies not in an institutionalized set of values and ideas, but in the non-systemic expression of ecstatic singing. For my analysis I decided to use the sometimes problematic and romanticizing terms shamanism/ shaman[33] since I do not think that avoiding them would lead to 'more conceptual precision', as Thomas and Humphrey put it.[34] Shamanism as a religious phenomenon—contrary to its 'ism'—does not indicate any institutionalized structures of literary, canonized religions;[35] rather, it should be understood as culturally diversified 'forms of inspirational religious practice'[36] found in societies without centralized socio-political powers. As such, Alekh shamanism seems to me an operational term for describing the unsystematized structures of ecstasy within a new religious tradition.

Alekh Dharma or Alekh Shamanism in Koraput

Mahima Dharma in Koraput is known as Alekh dharma and its followers as 'Alekhs'. Alekhs wear *gerua*-coloured clothes; worship Mahima Alekh and the earth goddess Basmati or Basudha. Alekhs use a symbolic code in their dress. The colour of their clothes (*gerua*) is the same as the colour of the red anthills, local

---

[32] With the term 'negative rules ...' I am referring to the classical Durkheimian definition of ritual practices. Durkheim differentiates between the 'negative cult' and the 'positive cult'. The 'negative character' of a cult is represented by a system of restrictions, especially visible in ascetic rituals. He considers the 'positive character' of a cult to be a sacrifice, connected with ceremonies. I use Durkheim`s terminology for describing the 'negative'—ascetic—practice of Alekhs. Durkheim 1912, III, Chaps. 1-3, 405-96.

[33] For discussion cf. Kuper (ed.) 1991.

[34] Thomas and Humphrey (eds.) 1994, 3.

[35] Vitebsky 1995, 11.

[36] Thomas and Humphrey 1994, 1.

manifestations of the earth goddess. A symbolic identification with the goddess makes Alekhs as holy as the earth. Specialized Alekhs become ecstatic Alekh *gurumai* and, as such, are capable of communicating with the divine. As oracles, as husbands or wives of the earth goddess or other male and female Hindu deities, Alekh *gurumai* become virtuoso singers of the Divine.

Spread of Mahima Dharma

In the last decade, proselytizing ascetics from Dhenkanal spread the religion among the population of Koraput. The statistics compiled by the Tribal Research Bureau in 1968-9[37] indicate the existence of the religion since the 1950s in areas of Orissa predominantly populated by indigenous people. Through several interviews with ascetics of Mahima Dharma during my field research in Dhenkanal (1999/2000), proselytizing activities of the *babas* in Koraput could be confirmed during the *tyagi*-wandering-period of every ascetic.[38] According to my recent observations in Koraput, similar activities of *babas* from Dhenkanal could only be observed during the annual initiation time (*dikhya*) in February/March (*falguno*). (Temporal) proselytizing activities can thus be assumed for the last fifty years in this region. The initiations performed by *babas* from Dhenkanal take place in local places of worship where locally popular Alekh *gurumai* (shamans) have established their own local centres frequented by their own circles of devotees for local pilgrimages. The recent adherents are statistically registered as belonging to the Mahima Dharma community: new devotees receive an identity card[39] after they have paid the necessary fees to the *babas*.[40]

---

[37] T.R.B. 1968/69, 43-76. The statistics were compiled in indigenous areas of the Puri, Cuttack, Sambalpur, and Kalahandi district.

[38] The *tyagi* period is the 15-year long period of learning and wandering before taking the final decision to remain an itinerant for one's whole life.

[39] Original term.

[40] The issues of religious identity, local places of pilgrimage and the bureaucratic structures of an indigenous religion in the process of being institutionalized will be discussed in a separate paper and therefore will not be approached at the moment.

According to my observations, two generations of converts to Mahima Dharma can be found in Koraput. They mostly represent aged persons (50-60 years) whose adult (20-35) children took the initiation during the last ten years. The annual initiation ritual involves approximately 2000-3000 new adherents, with a rising tendency every year.

Conversion to the Alekh Religion

Conversion is conceptualized in terms of initiation into the new religion. The initiation contains a generalized and a specialized complex and thus establishes two categories of devotees: the common Alekhs and the specialized Alekh *gurumai.*

1. In order to become an Alekh one has to undergo the initiation (*dikhya neba*) either with a *baba* from Dhenkanal or with an 'elder brother' (*boro bhai*) of the local Alekh centres. This *boro bhai* is authorized by monks from Joranda to perform rituals. The initiation involves receiving sacred clothes/colours (*ranga neba*) from *babas* or from *boro bhai,* and taking an oath to God to adhere strictly to the religious rules (*niyam*) of Mahima Dharma. Alekhs define themselves by adherence to a strict ascetic ethic. They abstain from meat and alcohol and refuse to participate actively in the traditional blood sacrifices. As such, they are a new ascetic group within the *Desya,* who generally are known for their 'pleasure complex',[41] (a variety of ceremonies, general intoxication, and a preference for meat).

2. The new religious specialists of Alekhs are the Alekh *gurumai.* They perform séances of ecstatic singing for the purpose of divination, here labelled shamanic (*gurumai*) practices. The Alekh *gurumai*—female or male, but mostly female—communicate with the Divine while singing with the one-stringed instrument *dudunga.*[42] They go on a spiritual journey while in trance (*baya*) and cure patients by consulting the supernatural. To become an Alekh *gurumai* it is necessary to convince the community that he or she had no choice but to

---

[41] Orans, 1965.

[42] Apart from the ritual context of the Alekhs, the instrument is also used by the Joria, an indigenous group of Koraput. Here, the instrument is called *jorunga* (personal communication, P. Berger).

undergo the Alekh *dikhya.* Alekh *gurumai* often tell of their long-suffering, destructive, dreams and attacks of madness/craziness (*baya*) before having undergone the *dikhya.* Had they not done so they would have died, they insist. Only by receiving the *gerua* clothes were they able to be cured. In this way, their destructive madness was transformed into a capacity to heal and communicate with the supernatural, which Alekh shamans described as 'good' (*bolo*) *baya.*

The next step in becoming a socially respected and sought after religious and therapeutic specialist consists of a symbolic marriage—the *alekh biba*—with a favoured god or goddess. After an elaborate and costly marriage ceremony, the worldly Alekh bride or bridegroom—comparable with Vitebsky's description of the Sora—will meet her or his lover while going '*baya*'. The altered state of consciousness[43] is preceded by a long fast and will finally culminate in a dialogue with the divine spouse. Thereafter, the Alekh *gurumai*'s utterances and singing will heal individual and collective ailments. Accompanied by the sound of the *dudunga*, the new shaman will utter prophecies and give advice to suffering clients.

In contrast to the worldly human marriage practices of the *Desya*, where divorce is accepted, the Alekh *biba* is irreversible. Once an Alekh has followed her or his vocation of spiritual marriage, it is no longer reversible. Only through the marriage idiom does the Alekh become an Alekh-shaman, the female or male 'Alekh-*gurumai*'. *Gurumai* literally means 'the bride (*mai*[44]) of her husband (*guru*)'. Either male or female, both Alekh bride and bridegroom are classified as brides of the chosen deity. Whether male or female, all *gurumai* form the female part of the Alekh-*biba*; however, in *baya* trances the *gurumai* can transform their gender into male and female roles visible in different forms of ritual speeches. A similar phenomenon is known in the devotional religious traditions, of Sufism[45] and *bhakti.* The marriage idiom of

---

[43] Common meta-term for ecstatic states derived from the works of Lewis 1971 and Bourguignon 1973.

[44] The Desya word '*mai*' is a polysemic term meaning 'mother', 'wife', 'bride' and 'woman' simultaneously.

[45] Cf. Schimmel, 1975. The *sufi* mystic lives a love relationship with God. It is said that he performs the feminine role, serving, devotion, and emotion.

the Alekh *biba* represents the crucial social values of worldly marriage. Here the bride stands for alliances and systems of exchange between affinal groups demonstrating the *fait social total*[46] of marriage. The spiritual marriage of the Alekhs is the basis of communication between the sphere of the gods and that of humans. After the Alekh-*biba*, Alekh shamans will heal with their words and voices and as such the Alekh-shamanism is deeply inscribed in the *gurumai* and *dissari*[47] tradition[48] of the *Desya.*

Contexts and Reasons for Initiation (Dikhya)

The general motivation for taking *dikhya* to the Alekh dharma is closely connected with the sociological principle of seniority within the patrilineal clan-system of the *Desya* in Koraput.[49] Relationships among the *Desya* are largely determined by whether one is junior or senior; this is the most frequent source of quarrels and rivalries. I observed that it was mostly junior brothers or phratries who were initiated into the Alekh religion. In *Desya* society senior brothers are responsible for performing rituals for the earth goddess. In a case of ritual neglect, misfortune or illness could befall the family and the clan. Compared with the seniors thus occupied, juniors are of lower social status, but are also freer to experiment with new cults. Seniors, on the other hand had no need to try out new religious orientations since their traditional ritual obligation guaranteed them the highest respect within the community. In the case of general initiation into the Alekh dharma, social juniors find the opportunity to modify their traditional status. By differentiating themselves from others through a permanent ascetic life-conduct, they gain a new religious seniority and therefore a higher self-esteem. Conversion therefore seems to be implemented in the specific social features of local hierarchies.

General initiation into Alekh dharma means also testifying the powers of the new god. If a family suffers the death of a child, misfortune or disease after having taken *dikhya*, the new adherents might soon return to their traditional beliefs, or turn to new

---

[46] Mauss 1923-4.

[47] *Dissari* is a term for another traditional healing expert which might be translated as 'astrologer'.

[48] For more details cf. Otten 2000, 347-56.

[49] On the principle of seniority see Pfeffer 1997, 13-14.

Christian sects. The expectations and hopes connected with the new god Mahima Alekh were not fulfilled.

Looking at the structure of conversion in Alekh dharma one can draw some preliminary conclusions. We have seen two phases of *dikhya*: the general one in terms of Alekhs and the specific in terms of the Alekh *gurumai*. The first is reversible for general adherents; the other one irreversible for the specialists. This feature leads to the conclusion that the issue of 'conversion' should be approached in terms of initiation. This allows conceptualizing conversion in a culturally specific context: either as a temporal, reversible way of religious pragmatics or as a characteristic of ritual specialization within a traditional system of knowledge.

Cultural Change and the 'Negative' Ecstasy of Alekhs

Alekhs permanently practise negative rules of behaviour. This new life conduct changes the traditional short-term form of ascetic custom in Desya society. Traditionally, ritual specialists (*gurumai, dissari*) exercise a phase of temporary renunciation before performing ritual activities, such as animal sacrifice or divination. Via fasting or other personally modified negative rules of everyday diet, traditional *gurumai* and *dissari* prepare for communication with the holy sphere. The common temporal ascetic preparation finally leads to ecstasy during specific ritual séances. In this context, the altered state of consciousness is accompanied by the use of alcohol.[50]

For Alekhs, the temporary renunciation in terms of a preparation for ritual ecstasy transforms into a permanent religious ethic of restriction. The restrictive code of behaviour represents an inverted set of traditional ideas and values. Traditionally, everyone eats meat; Alekhs do not. Traditionally, ritual ecstasy demands intoxication; Alekhs are abstinent. Traditionally, rituals require blood sacrifice; Alekhs, however, refuse to conduct these. On the one hand, the formal morphology of religious practice of Alekhs is a negation of the common meaning. On the other hand, the perpetuation of negative rules of behaviour represents a continuity of the traditional ritual formalism. In the Alekh religion, traditional temporality is transformed into a permanent new life conduct (ethic). Neither the form nor the function changes, only the old

[50] Concerning this topic cf. Pfeffer 2000, 342-3.

meaning of rituals. The ritual séances remain ecstatic (the form), they still fulfil the purpose of healing (the function), but they change in character to abstinence (new meaning). In this manner, the traditional structure of ecstasy is recomposed through a perpetuated asceticism. In the Alekh religion we discover a transformation from reversibility, and temporality of traditional forms of renunciation (ritual fasting) into a permanent form of life conduct. This new ethic is systematized by negative rules of behaviour. Alekhs consider themselves new voices of the Divine and, as such, constitute a new religious identity depicting recent processes of internal change (possibly comparable with processes of Max Weber's analysis[51] on asceticism in Christian societies). Weber argues that ascetic processes are responsible for internal change in society and its fundamental ethics. In this vein, the new tradition of Alekh asceticism, in terms of its 'negative' or abstinent ecstasy, is an indicator for cultural change.

The Ethnography of Song

The Ritual Language of Alekh *Gurumai*

When night falls in the Desya villages, you can hear the sound of Alekh *gurumai*s' voices. Accompanied by their one-stringed *dudunga*—made of the head of a melon and the skin of a snake—they sing. An Alekh *gurumai* sits on the ground with loose hair, the instrument in her[52] hands, her eyes closed. She sings for herself and also for those who suffer. Those who are sleepless or those who 'carry some pain (*dukho*) in their heart'[53] gather to listen to the voices of gods. 'The *gurumai* is *baya*' , people explain. It is 'good (*bolo*) *baya*', a good 'craziness', which is divine.

Spontaneous songs and narrations of the Alekh *gurumai* composed during her altered state of consciousness represent *khelo*, the divine play. *Baya* and *khelo* are expressions of a 'religious

[51] Weber, 1988 (1920).

[52] Since there are empirically more female Alekh *gurumai* than male, I have used the female form for description. Males are included in the generalization.

[53] Free translation of an often used expression.

language'[54] often characterized by a polyglot shift between several languages,[55] through glossolalia, invocations, and poetic fragments. This code used in divine communication expresses the holy Otherness. Dialogues with the supernatural are expressed by incomprehensibility. The regular monotone, one-stringed music of the *dudunga* indicates the rhythm of the holy sphere into which the Alekh *gurumai* loses herself. While playing the *dudunga*, Alekh *gurumai* transforms herself into the voices of gods. Séances of ecstatic, non-systemic singing lasts two to three hours. After regaining consciousness, the Alekh *gurumai* will not remember a word she had uttered during her trance.

The language of ecstasy consists of three elements: systematic preparation via the negative rules of the Alekh life conduct; entering into an altered state of consciousness; and the ritual temporality of the séance.

The ritual grammar of *baya* and *khelo* is based on the music of the *dudunga*: repetitive and monotonous in its rhythm. One-stringed music induces an altered state of consciousness; it accompanies the divine singing and finally and ends in *baya* and *khelo*. *Baya* and *khelo* are thus attributes of a sacred temporality, which only endures during ritual ecstasy. The time of trance is considered holy and is expressed by a vocal 'play' which will last during the song compositions. A sacred 'play' is characterized by its finality, its pauses. Divine appearance is that which ends. The holy time has its spaces marked by the sound of the *dudunga,* which is temporal in character. *Baya* and *khelo* indicate an interwovenness between music, song compositions and the sphere of the conceptualized Divine.[56] For the Alekhs, the Divine is the 'crazy' (*baya*) 'play' (*khelo*) of voices, words and meanings. The sacred language of the Alekh *gurumai* is expressed by unsystematic song compositions, poetic epic fragments and hymnal sequences. The narration seems always impulsive, spontaneous and dependent on the situation and the specific mood of the Alekh *gurumai*. The songs of the Alekh *gurumai* can be regarded as fragments of 'inspirational religious practices' illustrating the creativity of the rich local oral culture of Koraput.

---

[54] Cf. Keane 1997, 47-71.

[55] As for instance Desya, Orya , Kui, Gutop.

[56] On the interwovenness of music, social structure and academic terminologies cf. Lévi-Strauss 1964.

An exemplary transcription of one *baya* and *khelo* composed by an Alekh *gurumai* shall textualize the structure of the divine speech. The language of the *baya* is Desya-Oriya, the local version of the *Desya.*[57] This *baya* was induced by the sound of the *dudunga* when a worried mother whose child suffered from a sudden illness, consulted the Alekh *gurumai*. It lasted two hours. Some fragments of the *baya* are presented below. After the end of the *baya*, the Alekh *gurumai* sacrificed a coconut brought by the troubled mother to Mahima Alekh and the earth goddess Basmati.

Transcription of a *baya*, 9 October 2000

'Oh, mother!
Oh, father!
Dhenkanal, Joranda !

'My father is Mahima Guru!
I will give food for my
Guru Brahma,
for my Guru Mahima!

'Hey Guru, Mahima Guru, Invisible Guru!
Mahima Alekha!
Forehead of the invisible God!

'We will not tell you any lies!
We will not pretend anything!

'Bhima Bhoi and Gondas Baba!
My door is open for you!

'Bhima Bhoi, give me an order
I will give a message, oh Bhima Bhoi!

---

[57] There are many other different languages also known by the Desya-Oriya speaker. Specific indigenous groups within the Desya population all have their own languages such as Gutop, Kui, Gadaba. The common language for communication between the different groups is Desya-Oriya.

'Oh, truthful Narayana,
I will give you a true message!

'Oh, Goddess Lamunda,
Oh Goddess Chamunda,
Oh Lamunda temple!

'In Lamra, there is a Chamunda temple and there was an invisible God!

'God and sunya [nothingness], *oh invisible God, oh Nirakara.*

'In the temple of sunya you cure diseases and sorrow!

'Oh invisible One, save me and him!

'Thirty-two thrones!
Your foot is like a lotus blossom!
I serve you!

'Who knows, oh mother?
Who knows, oh father?

'Have Mercy, oh Bhima Bhoi!

(Unknown language/polyglot glossolalia
in dialogical structure; mixture of some Oriya words with incomprehensible utterances.)

'My master, my father Mahima !
Who knows how I should worship you?
How should I do my fasting for you?

'Oh, Josudha Doimoti!
The Goddess of seven sisters of the palace!

'Oh God mother, oh my God father!
Oh holy mother, oh holy father!
Goddess Basudha, holy Earth!

'I have never seen your shape.
Your heart is big I pray to you,
Inexplicable Basmati!
You have no shape, you have no figure!

'Go away! 33 Millions of Gods!
I give you the order: away!

'Holy Narayana,
Great God!
You see the entire Universe!
Oh Holy Mahima!

'As the God of the winds goes all over the world, I speak to you:
Never worry, for what, about what?

'Oh three times Indescribable One!
God, you save the mother!
Oh Mother, you serve God in heaven!

'Twelve years I remembered the name of God! Twelve years I meditated!

'Oh holy Goddess of chastity!
Oh my Earth, hear my words
Goddesses Maybati, Chayabatti!
Save us from the destruction!

'I take rest in your feet!
Oh mother, oh father!

'All over the world I spread this message!
Rama Lakshmana, first mother!
Puri Jagannatha, enter into my heart and speak to me!

'Lamunda, Chamunda was born here.
I need this type of temple which was built there

'Do I tell lies or do I tell truth?
I am telling you only the truth, I promise!

'I give an order, without cheating!
You know it!

'You hear my words, oh God, oh God.

'I am wearing the type of clothes of the ascetics.

'Oh Mayabati, Chayabati, Ishwara, Parvati!
Oh, invisible Nirakara!
I am holding the stick in my hands and the whole world in it!

'Oh, sacred place Kotinmala ! [(place in A.P.]
A temple is built there for you!

'Millions of fruits and flowers people give me for you

'I will give you this time an order:

(Glossolalia in dialogical structure.)
(Incomprehensible language.)

'I serve in your feet!

'I am not usual, I am the Earth

'I have no chastity and I am no Goddess like you !

'Who knows the mother?
Who knows the father?
Who knows the Earth?

'When the war began, I saw it.
I was there.
My name is Adi Mata, the first mother!
I am the Universal Beauty!
The Beauty of the Universe!
My name is Basudha, the Earth!

'I am also your mother, your father!
I have no shape!

'How many brave men, leader and heroes were there! There was a big war but it did not destroy me!

'I give you this order!
I am telling you the truth!
I do not tell any lies!

'Oh, Ayodya, Puri, Cuttack, Baleshwar, Bhubaneshwar! Cabinet and the Minister!
I will give you the type of government of the time when Indira Gandhi was the Prime Minister!

'I am now in heaven!
I am telling the truth!

'Do not tell me any lies, go away!

'You are searching everywhere and you visit all places, also the places of the white people and of the Muslims!

'This type of government I will give you!

'When the earth will be destroyed,
Oh, Mother, I will see all the Gods and Goddesses!

' I am the Earth Medini
I am telling you only the truth!

'Indira, Chandra, Nakulo, Saha Devo, Bhima Bhoi, Gondas Baba!

'I am always telling the truth!
What are you worried about?

(Glossolalia in dialogues.)

'What are you worried about it?
I give you my promise, oh Guru Mahima!

'Guru Brahma Mahima Alekh, you the temple of the nothingness!

'I give order to the Earth.

'Millions of invisible Gods and Goddess told: go away! Go with fire!

'I have eaten only fruits
and meditated 12 years

'Do not worry about it, I promise you. How many times have I served you?

'Oh, Mahima Brahma Guru Brahma Guru!
Vishnu, Jeipori, Basmati, the first mother, Seven hundred Snake Goddesses!
Oh Tula Batti, Phulmati, Komla, Bhimla Radhika!

'Go away!

' I will give you all! What are you worried about?

'Go away, I give you the order!

'Nirakara, You Invisible, Indescribable, God of sunya [nothingness]*!*

The transcription reveals the dialogical structure of the ecstatic song composition. The songs of the Alekh *gurumai* have a hymnal psalm character and can be compared with a prayer. Several invocations of the different names of God and holy places show that the conceptualized sacred is always combined with a locality. Holiness is thus local. Moreover, the fact that God is sometimes approached as the earth goddess Basudha or Basmati, but also as Jagannath, Shiva, Narayana, or Mahima Alekh, illustrates that different categories and concepts coexist in a plurality of ideas about the sacred. God is female and male, but also nothing and the whole creation. The invocations of the various names of God also brings to mind adjuration and its exorcizing quality.

'*My speech* (*basa*) *has power* (*shakti*)', explained the Alekh *gurumai* after her séance. For her and her listeners the sound of her voice, the rhythms and words expressed during her singing séance, are the power, voice and speech of the Divine. Incomprehensible passages indicate the speech of the supernatural, for what is not understandable for humans is regarded as having divine character. In this context, frequent shifts from understandable to incomprehensible passages show the temporal appearance of the sacred. The music of the *dudunga* and the polyglot glossolalia do not last forever and as such are an expression of the divine time of the séance.

The transcription as well indicates a ritual transformation from the ritual subject (Alekh *gurumai*) into the ritual object (God). In the beginning, the Alekh *gurumai* approaches the conceptualized Divine by using the second person 'you'. Later, she herself transforms into Divinity and expresses it by using the first person 'I'. For the transformative character of the solo séance, the play of the *dudunga* is of greatest importance. Only the sound of it opens her ecstatic singing and changes her ritual personality during the ritual 'play'. The music transforms the Alekh *gurumai* into a singing goddess.

Conclusion

The new ascetic tradition in tribal Koraput has a twofold profile. On the one hand, it consists of Alekhs, the common converts representing a new systematized abstinence and vegetarian life conduct. On the other hand, it is characterized by Alekh *gurumai,* the virtuoso singers of the Divine demonstrating the non-systematized value of religious ecstasy. In this sense, Alekhs are new indigenous moralists, rejecting the common ritual values of the *Desya* whereas Alekh *gurumai* represent vocal artists perpetuating the traditional value of ecstasy. The specific feature of the Alekh dharma is the new life conduct; it transforms the traditional temporality of ritual preparation into the permanency of the everyday ethic. The new religious tradition thus combines processes of systematization with structures of cultural virtuosity and creativity. This twofold process of cultural change I labelled 'negative ecstasy'.

Especially for socially junior categories of the *Desya,* the new permanent practice of negative rules of life conduct presents an option for changing their own social status. Conversion to Alekh dharma means therefore an agency and mobility within the traditional structure of status.

I suggest interpreting the cultural dynamics of the Alekh tradition in terms of a cultural *bricolage.*[58] A bricolage is the creative making of tradition by recomposing common elements in order to work on something new. The creativity of local culture implies new protagonists who create new cultural compositions. Those cultural artists are the Alekh *gurumai* who create new songs and other oral expressions during their solo séances. The presented extracts of recorded ecstatic songs of the new religious specialists show instances of artistic recompositions of cultural elements, i.e. the concept of God is a cacophonic plurality. In this sense, song compositions of Alekh shamans can join the broad palette of the creativity of oral cultures in South Asia.[59]

References

Atkinson, J.M. 1992. 'Shamanisms Today', *Annual Review of Anthropology 21,* 307-30.

Beltz, J. 2001. 'Disputed Centres, Rejected Norms and Contested Authorities. Situating Mahima Dharma in its Regional Diversity', paper presented at the Annual DFG-Salzau-Conference May 2001 (unpublished).

— (in this volume). 'Contested Authorites, Disputed Centres and Rejected Norms: Situating Mahima Dharma in its Regional Diversity', in G. Pfeffer (ed.), *Periphery and Centre: Groups, Categories and Values,* Delhi: Manohar.

Bouillier, V. 1997. *Ascète et Roi. Un monastère de Kanphata Yogis au Népal,* Paris: CNRS Éditions.

Berger, P. 2002. 'The Gadaba and the "non-ST" Desia of Koraput, Orissa. Some Observations on their Interrelations', in D.K. Behera and G. Pfeffer (eds), *Contemporary Society: Tribal Studies,* Vol. 5, New Delhi: Concept Publishing Company; 57-90.

---

[58] Lévi-Strauss 1962, Chap. I.

[59] Cf. Champion (ed.), 1996.

Biardeau, M. 1994. *Études de Mythologie Hindoue II. Bhakti et Avatara.* Podichéry: Publication de l'École Française d'Extrème-Orient.

Bourguignon, E. (ed.) 1973. *Religion. Altered States-of-Consciousness and Social Change*, Ohio: Columbus.

Cohn, B.S. 1990 (1962). 'Political Systems in Eighteenth-Century India: The Benares Region', in B.S. Cohn, *An Anthropologist among the Historians and Other Essays,* New York: Oxford University Press, 483-99.

Champion, C. (ed.) 1996. *Tradition Orales Dans le Monde Indien.* Collection Purusartha 18, Paris: Édition de l'École des Hautes Études en Sciences Sociales.

Deo, F. 1999. 'Institutional and Organizational Aspects of Mahima Dharma', in J.T. O'Connell, *Organisational and Institutionalisational Aspects of Indian Religious Movements,* Delhi: Manohar, 137-51.

Dirks, N. 1979. 'The Structure and Meaning of Political Relations in South Indian Little Kingdom', *Contributions to Indian Sociology,* 13 (2), 169-206.

Dube, I.B. 1999. 'Taming Traditions: Legalities and Histories in Twentieth-Century Orissa', in G. Bhadra, G. Prakash and S. Tharu (eds.), *Subaltern Studies X: Writings on South Asian History and Society,* New Delhi: Oxford University Press, 98-125.

— 2001. 'Issues of Faith, Enactments of Contest: The Founding of Mahima Dharma in Nineteenth-Century Orissa', in H. Kulke and B. Schnepel (eds.), *Jagannath Revisited. Studying Society, Religion and the State in Orissa,* Delhi: Manohar, 149-78.

Durkheim, É. 1912. *Die Elementaren Formen des Religiösen Lebens.* (Elementary Forms of Religious Life), Frankfurt: Suhrkamp.

Eschmann, A 1975. 'Spread, Organisation and Cult of Mahima Dharma', in Shri N. Senapati, *Satya Mahima Dharma,* Cuttack: Dharma Grantha Store, 9-22.

— 1986 (1978). 'Mahima Dharma: An Autochthonous Hindu Reform Movement', in A. Eschmann, H. Kulke, G.C. Tripathi (eds.). *The Cult of Jagannath and the Regional Tradition of Orissa,* Delhi: Manohar, 374-410.

Fortes, M. and E.E. Evans-Pritchard (eds.). 1940. *African Political Systems,* London: Oxford University Press.

Galey, J.-C. 1989. 'Reconsidering Kingship in India: An Ethnological Perspective', in J.-C. Galey (ed.), *Kingship and the Kings: History and Anthropology,* Vol. 4, London/Paris/New York: Harwood Academic Publishers, 123-87.

Gonda, J. 1977. *Medieval Religious Literature in Sanskrit,* Wiesbaden: Otto Harrassowitz.

Guzy, L. 2000. '"On the Road with Babas" Some Insights into Local Features of Mahima Dharma', *Journal of Social Sciences,* Nr 4 (4.), 323-30.

— 2003. 'Mahima Dharma Ascetics: A Case Study on Popular Asceticism and its Patronage Structure in Rural Orissa', in A. Copley (ed.). Hinduism in Public and Private. Reform Hindutva Gender Sampradasay. New Delhi: Oxford University Press, 211-229.

Helm, J. (ed.) 1971 (1968). *Essays on the Problem of Tribe. Proceedings of the 1967 Annual Spring Meeting of the American Ethnological Society, Washington:* University of Washington Press.

Kakar, S. 1984 (1982). *Schamanen, Heilige und Ärzte* (Eng. *Shamans, Mystics and Doctors),* München: Biederstein.

Keane, W. 1997. 'Religious Language', *Annual Review of Anthropology* 26, 47-71.

Kuper, A. 1988. *The Invention of Primitive Society: Transformations of an Illusion,* London: Routledge.

Kuper, M. (ed.) 1991. *Hungrige Geister und Rastlose Seelen. Texte zur Schamanismusforschung*, Berlin: Dietrich Reimer Verlag.

Lévi-Strauss, C. 1962. *La Pensée Sauvage (The savage mind),* Paris: Librairie Plon.

— 1964. *Mythologiques. Le Cru et le Cuit,* Paris: Librairie Plon.

Lewis, I.M. 1971. *Ecstatic Religion,* Harmonworth: Penguin Books.

Lund, S. 2001. 'Bequeathing and quest. Processing personal identification papers in bureaucratic spaces (Cuzco, Peru)', *Social Anthropology,* 2001, 3-24.

Mauss, M. 1923-4. 'Essai sur le don. Forme et raison de l'échange dans les sociétés archaïques', *L'Année Sociologique*, Paris: Seconde Série.

Mohapatra, S. 1983. *Bhima Bhoi: Makers of Indian Literature,* Delhi: Sahitya Akademi.

O'Flaherty, W.D, J. Duncan and M. Derrett (eds.). 1987. *The Concept of Duty in South Asia*, SOAS: Vikas Publishing House Pvt Ltd.

Orans, M. 1965. *The Santals—A Tribe in Search of Great Tradition.* Detroit: Wayne State University Press.

Otten, T. 2000. 'In a Remote Area: Categories of the Person and Illness among the Desia of Koraput, Orissa', in *Journal of Social Sciences,* Nr 4 (4), 347-56.

Pfeffer, G. 1997. 'The Scheduled Tribes of Middle India as a Unit: Problems of Internal and External Comparison', in G. Pfeffer and D.K. Behera, *Contemporary Society: Tribal Studies,* Vol. I: *Structure and Process,* New Delhi: Concept Publishing Company, 3-27.

— 2000. 'Tribal Ideas', *Journal of Social Sciences,* Vol. 4 (4), 331-46.

— 2004. 'Tribal Society of Highland Orissa, Highland Burma, and Elsewhere', in A. Malinar, J. Beltz and H. Frese (eds.), *Text and Context,* Delhi: Manohar.

Sahlins, M. 1968. *Tribesmen,* New Jersey: Prentice-Hall.

Schimmel, A. 1975. *Mystical Dimensions of Islam,* Chapel Hill: North Carolina Press.

Schnepel, B. 1997. *Die Dschungelkönige. Ethnohistorische Aspekte von Politik und Ritual in Orissa,* Stuttgart: Franz Steiner Verlag.

Senapati, S. and D.Ch. Kuanr. 1971. *Gazetteer of India: Orissa State. Supplement Koraput District Gazetteer,* Cuttack: Revenue Department Government of Orissa.

Senapati, N. and P. Tripathy (eds). 1972. *Orissa District Gazetteers: Dhenkanal*, Cuttack: Orissa Government Press.

Senapati, N. 1972. 'Appendix. Mahima Dharma', in N. Senapti, P. Tripathy (eds), *Orissa District Gazetteers*: *Dhenkanal*, Cuttack: Orissa Government Press, 443-8.

Tambiah, S.J. 1976. *World Conqueror and World Renouncer: A Study of Buddhism and Polity in Thailand Against a Historical Background,* Cambridge: Cambridge University Press.

Tribal Research Bureau (T.R.B.) 1968/9. 'Impact of Satya Mahima Dharma on Scheduled Castes & Scheduled Tribes in Orissa', *Adibasi,* Vol X, No. 1, 43-76.

Thomas, N. and C. Humphrey (eds.). 1994. *Shamanism, History, and the State.* Ann Arbor:The University of Michigan Press.

Quigley, D. 1999 (1993). *The Interpretation of Castes,* New Delhi: Oxford University Press.

Vargyas, G. 1993. 'The Structure of Bru Shamanic Ceremonies', in M. Hóppal and K.D. Howard (eds.), *Shamans and Cultures.* Budapest: Istor Books, Akademia Kiadó/International Society for Trans-Oceanic Research, 120-7.

Vargyas, G 1994. 'Parole de Chamanes—Paroles d'Esprits', in *Cahiers de Littérature Orale No. 35, Inalco* (Paris), 123-75.

Vitebsky, P. 1993. *Dialogues with the Dead,* Delhi: Cambridge University Press.

— 1995. *The Shaman,* London: Duncan Baird Publishers.

Weber, Max 1988 (1920). *Gesammelte Aufsätze zur Religionssoziologie I,* Tübingen: J-C.B. Mohr (Paul Siebeck).

Zinser, H. 1988. 'Ekstase und Entfremdung', in H. Zinser, *Religionswissenschaft. Eine Einführung,* Berlin: Dietrich Reimer Verlag, 274-84.

7

Tribal or Tantric? Reflections on the Classification of Goddesses in Southern Orissa

Beatrix Hauser

The scholarly discourse on goddess worship in Orissa is characterized by an emphasis on development and change. Since Anncharlott Eschmann in 1978, scholars have concentrated on the transformation of tribal goddesses into Hindu deities,[1] on their royal patronage as a strategy to gain regional power,[2] and on recent developments of an urban goddess temple.[3] These studies are certainly of great importance because they highlight the capacity of Hinduism to integrate and alter religious practices. With respect to the phenomenon of goddess worship or Śāktism in Orissa, however, they evoke a rather partial view. The scholarly emphasis seems to recognize the specific features of this religious strand only in terms of another previous and supposedly 'non-Hindu' form of worship. Scholars implicitely suggest an evolutionist hierarchy that begins with an uniconic bloodthirsty tribal goddess who, in course of time, is identified with the pan-Indian warrior-goddess Durgā in order to be pacified and—finally—worshipped by Brahmin priests. Besides, scholars do not get tired to draw the contrast between folk/popular practices and brahminical ones. This often leads to the stigmatization of ludic and transgressive forms of worship (such as ritual masquerade or animal sacrifice) as well as female votive rites,

---

[1] Eschmann 1978a, b, Kulke (1984) 1993, Mallebrein 1999, Rath 1987, Schnepel 1997, Chapter 5, Stietencron 1983.

[2] Kulke (1984) 1993, Rösel 1994, Schnepel 1997, Chapter 6.

[3] Preston 1980. Recently, Brighenti has given an all-encompassing study on Orissan Śāktism from an ethno-historical perspective. Based on secondary sources, it touches the empiric practice of goddess worship only briefly, a limitation the author has pointed out himself (Brighenti 2001, 418).

which tend to be relegated to the margins of Hinduism 'proper', if not discussed in terms of folklore.[4]

This essay focuses on the worship of goddesses (*ṭhākurāṇī*) in coastal southern Orissa where this is the most popular form of religious practice. Drawing on three examples from my fieldwork, I discuss contrasting features of goddess worship and reflect on their possible links with other religious traditions.[5] The examples are (1) the votive rite of Jahni Oṣā, where unmarried girls pray to goddess Bṛndābatī for a good husband; (2) the firewalking ceremony of male ritual specialists who cross-dress in order to become possessed by the goddess; and (3) the festival of Berhampur's patron goddess Buṛhī Ṭhākurāṇī that attracts hundreds of thousands of visitors. The evaluation of these examples leads to a criticism of the parameters generally used to distinguish tribal from 'Hinduized' modes of worship. I argue that many ritual features hint at other religious expressions beyond this dichotomy. I shall not try to be exhaustive by invoking the theories of Sanskritization (Srinivas), little and great tradition (Redfield), or inclusivism (Hacker). The aim of this essay is rather to focus on the problem of classification itself and its heuristic value. Accordingly, I propose a context-sensitive approach that might lead to a better understanding of the significance and power of goddess worship in South Asia. This approach should incorporate and reflect on the different, and partly competing, interpretations and knowledge systems involved in the discourse on the goddess.

I intend neither to criticize Eschmann's initial emphasis on the process and dynamics of 'Hinduization,' nor the difficult work of reconstructing the metamorphosis of tribal goddesses under the influence of acculturation. Although the idea of a development from a tribal to a 'Hinduized' religious tradition helps for the understanding of certain socio-religious phenomena, when *any* mode of goddess worship is considered on this assumption, it serves as a simplification and corruption of complex realities. After all, Eschmann had warned that the village goddess 'might have

---

[4] For instance, Michaels (1998) deals neither with possession nor with 'domestic worship.'

[5] My argument is based on ethnographic fieldwork in Ganjam District, where I spent altogether fourteen month in the years 1999, 2000 and 2001. This research was part of a larger study on women's cultural performances.

originally been a tribal goddess. Might but not must: every village, regardless of its present or past connection with tribal cults, has a *grāma devī' (*village goddess).[6]

Jahni Oṣā

For the whole month of *Āśvina* (September-October), young, unmarried Hindu girls observe the votive rite of Jahni Oṣā. They do so by following a certain diet and by gathering every evening to worship Bṛndābatī in the shape of a *tuḷasī* plant. The ritual helps to overcome health problems and, moreover, to obtain a 'good husband'. Therefore, in almost every neighbourhood, about five to fifteen girls join to celebrate the daily *pūjā.* Every participant has to 'install' (*sthāpana*) the goddess in a sacred pot. These pots are arranged around the *tuḷasī* and the altar is decorated with *jahni* flowers, vermillion, earthen lamps and auspicious drawings from rice powder. The girls praise the goddess with songs and perform the *pūjā.* While doing so, it may happen that one of them is possessed by the goddess, and in this form answers questions or gives advice.

Jahni Oṣā is one of those votive rites (*oṣā-brata*) followed by Hindu women for the wellbeing of their husbands or sons.[7] They all include some kind of fasting (*oṣā*, Skt.: *upavāsa*) and possibly a vow (*brata*, Skt.: *vrata*).[8] Many of them are done yearly, at a specific stage in life, or for a fixed period (for instance, sixteen consecutive Mondays). In addition to the daily domestic worship, they constitute a significant part of women's religious practice in Hinduism.[9] Most of these rituals are transmitted orally, the only written source being small booklets telling the legend (*kathā*) of the respective deity. Besides, many votive rites address goddesses who

---

[6] Eschmann 1978a, 84.

[7] See also Dash 1991, 114, Tokita-Tanabe 1999, 35-7.

[8] These fasts rarely restrict the consumption of any food (and sometimes water); more often it is a prohibition against certain kinds of food. In case of Jahni Oṣā, the girls are not allowed to eat meat, oil, garlic, onions and — most important — *jahni* (ridge gourd). During this votive rite it is also forbidden to cut this vegetable and to pluck its flowers.

[9] With reference to Orissa, Miśra (1994) mentions altogether 83 different types of *oṣā-brata*. For women's votive rites in other parts of India see Gupta 1999, McGee 1989, 1991, Tewari 1991.

are rarely served in temples (like Maṅgaḷā or Ṣaṣṭhī). There is also no need for a Brahmin priest to worship them. It is the women themselves who, according to their needs, perform the *pūjā* collectively. Pots, plants, kitchen utensils etc. represent the deity; the divine power can be realized through possession.

If we try to understand and classify goddess worship as practiced during Jahni Oṣā, we are confronted with seemingly contradictory elements. On the one hand, the ritual is 'typically Hindu' in many respects: (1) women all over India worship *tuḷasī*, (2) fasts and other forms of austerities (*tapasyā*) are common means in Hinduism to obtain divine power, and (3) in many regions we find female votive rites for a good husband. On the other hand, Jahni Oṣā includes—like many other *oṣā-brata* rites—certain elements that have been used to distinguish tribal cults (or rather a tribal background) from Hindu practices. Most prominent among these are the use of an aniconic representation of the goddess, the fairly irregular procedure of the *pūjā* in comparison to the orthodox 'sixteen services' (Skt. *upacāra*) observed in temples, the collective performance of the ritual and, finally, the phenomenon of possession. Those familiar with ritual practices in rural India could well remark that these features also describe folk religion in general. But so long as we stress singular parameters to categorize goddesses and cults, be it only for the analytic purpose of constructing ideal types,[10] we omit the entire field of (Hindu) women's religious practices as a whole. Discussing Jahni Oṣā, it seems almost absurd to classify this votive rite as tribal or somehow 'pre-Hindu'. So let us watch the religious practice closely and analyse the oral and performative references given by the devotees themselves.

During one evening of Jahni Oṣā, a young woman in her early twenties was possessed by three different goddesses: by Bāṭa Maṅgaḷā, by Jāṛī Mā and finally by Bṛndābatī. In the latter possession, the goddess appeared benevolent, gave advice, and explained why the marriage negotiations of another participant were delayed. Even though none of the girls was aware of Bṛndābatī's mythology,[11] it is this modest and caring appearance

---

[10] Like for instance Eschmann 1978, 80-1, or Schnepel 1997, Chapter 5.

[11] Goddess *Bṛndābatī* is usually associated with *Bisṇu* (Skt. *Viṣṇu*); her mythology is given in the Oriya *Kārttika Purāṇa* as well as in the

that they associate with the goddess. In the second possession the deity appeared in her form as Jāṛī Mā, lit. 'Dumb Mother', and the participants could identity her by her gestures and stammering. However, since the goddess' uttering was not audible, it was not of much help to the girls. Like Jāṛī Mā, there are many other divine 'Mothers' who are simply named and recognized by their performative features. All of them originate in a purely local context, possibly in the spirit of a deceased female ancestor. For the purpose of categorizing goddesses, the first possession is the most interesting one: the divine spirit appeared to be rather aggressive and as such was identified as Bāṭa Maṅgaḷā (Wayside Maṅgaḷā), complaining about the shortcomings in the performance of the *pūjā*. Goddess Maṅgaḷā (lit. Bestower of Wellbeing) is famous all over Orissa and belongs to a varied group of eight goddesses ('mothers' or Śaktīs), worshipped in and around the Mahanadi delta as forms of Caṇḍī. Apart from Maṅgaḷā (in Kakatpur), this group usually includes Birajā (Jajpur), Bimaḷā (Puri), Carchikā (Banki), Śāraḷā (Jhankada), Hiṅguḷā (near Talcher), Samaḷāi (Sambalpur) and Bhagabatī (Banpur).[12] According to Brighenti, these eight Śākta centres of Orissa were established to attain the goddess' blessings for the welfare of the people, to protect the state from its enemies and to serve various other functions. Some of these goddesses are mentioned in puranic accounts, some are known for animal sacrifices, firewalking ordeals, or shamanistic practices.[13] All these sites are famous in Orissa from ancient times and draw large numbers of followers. Even though Brighenti (with reference to secondary sources) is convinced of the tribal background of some of these goddesses and their temples, to me the worship at the Śākta centres rather resembles the Caṇḍī cult of rural Bengal. In Bengal, goddess Caṇḍī is one of the most popular divinities and adored as

---

Kārttika Māhātmya. For an oral version from Puri see Rösel (1980, 263), Babb (1975, 107) provides one from central India.

[12] Most of these eight *Śākta pīṭha* are not connected to the mythology of *Satī*. However, the list of its names varies. Brighenti (2001, 207) adds *Bhubaneśvarī* (Bhubaneshwar), according to Kulke ([1984] 1993, 126) people include the tutelary deities *Bhaṭṭārikā* (Baramba) and Maṇināgeśvarī (Ranpur). Marglin ([1985]1989, 331) cites a hymn that also mentions the goddesses *Rāmacaṇḍī* (near Konarak) and *Bāliharacaṇḍī* (near Puri).

[13] Brighenti 2001, 171.

household and village deity, as goddess of disease and as tutelary deity of the traders.[14] Her worship appears equally multifaceted as the Śākta tradition of Orissa, incorporating indigenous, folk and brahminical elements. Even Maṅgaḷā is worshipped and identified with Caṇḍī. Considering these parallels, Fuller assumes that the Caṇḍī cult in Orissa was heavily influenced by Bengal, more specifically by Bengali Tantrism.[15] In any case, a one-sided influence and development is not only unlikely, but also hard to prove. I agree with Manna, who in his study on the Bengali Caṇḍī cult explicitly states that one should not assume the history or origin of the different Śākta deities to be the same.[16] However, in conclusion we may say that there is a geographically and socially widespread continuum of Śakti worship dispersed over Bengal and Orissa (and further).

In spite of these parallels, the observance of Jahni Oṣā is limited to southern Orissa. Both men and women identify this votive rite with 'their country' (*deśa*) and view it as typical for Ganjam District with its mixture of Oriya and Telugu people. Hence, even though the Jahni Oṣā-songs are in Oriya, girls of both mother tongues join in the ritual. However, on the performative level, the participants link goddess Bṛndābatī and her worship with the Oriya tradition of Śakti worship. They can easily do so since there is no historical evidence (or rather authority) on Jahni Oṣā and its relation to Bṛndābatī.[17]

---

[14] Manna 1993.

[15] Fuller 1992, 86.

[16] Manna 1993, 99.

[17] One of the first scholars who mentioned Jahni Oṣā was Ś. Rājaguru from Parlakimedi in a collection on 'Feasts and Fasts of the Uriyas' by the end of the nineteenth century (reprinted in 1992), i.e. approximately at the same time when it became fashionable all over India to print cheap booklets containing religious legends, prayers and songs. It is very likely that even the booklet on Jahni Oṣā was first published at that time and henceforth reprinted. It contains different prayers, songs and stories illustrating the benefit of observing Jahni Oṣā, but neither the myth of goddess Bṛndābatī nor the origin of her worship.

Jhāmi Yātrā

Another facet of goddess worship reveals itself at the Jhāmi Yātrā, an ordeal where pious Hindus walk over glowing charcoal. This ritual takes place in slightly modified versions all over Orissa in honour of Maṅgaḷā, Hiṅgulā, Śāraḷā, Carchikā and other goddesses.[18] The Jhāmi Yātrā in the commercial town of Berhampur is celebrated in the name of Jhāmi Ṭhākurāṇī (Oriya: Our Lady Fire) alias Ellāmmā (Telugu: Mother of the Boundary). It takes place once a year outside her temple, which is attached to the main cremation ground of the city. In this temple the goddess manifests herself in a termite hill; priests of the Tuḷābuni caste perform her *pūjā*.[19] The devotees belong mainly to subaltern strata, they are frequently female, and more often speak Telugu than Oriya. The basic elements of the Jhāmi Yātrā are (1) the firewalking ceremony, which displays and celebrates the goddess' protective powers through a cross-dressed male ritual specialist remaining unhurt by the heat of the charcoals,[20] and (2) the sacrifice of animals, alcohol and sweets on the cremation ground itself. Close by, there are a number of small vendors who sell ice cream, snacks, toys, and souvenirs. Since hundreds of people gather for this *yātrā,* at first sight it looks like a huge picnic covering the whole cremation ground, irrespective of the corpses that have just been burnt. In short: we find the total reversal of the Hindu ideal of purity: mostly women—who are not supposed to enter cremation grounds at all—choose an impure place to do such a pure thing as cooking, moreover, they prepare non-vegetarian food.

It is hardly possible to understand the significance of Hindu goddesses like Jhāmi Ṭhākurāṇī (alias Ellāmmā) and her worship through an analysis of individual features of her cult, for example, the kind of sacrifice (animal or alcohol), divine manifestation (snakes), realization of divine power (possession) or the priest's

---

[18] Brighenti 2001, 348-50, Freeman 1981, Eschmann 1978b, 277, Mahapatra, 1981/2, 37-8, Marglin/Mishra 1991.

[19] The hereditary occupation of this Oriya caste is the procession of cotton wool. In the outskirts of Berhampur, this priestly service is performed by the Telugu farmer caste (Reddi).

[20] Due to a lawsuit concerning the territory of the firewalking ceremony, the actual crossing of glowing charcoal was stopped a few years ago. Yet it is common at the Jhāmi Yātrā at the outskirts of the town.

caste (Śūdra). As will become clear, the interpretation of individual values, categories, and groups, be it even for an analytic purpose, shows nothing but the extent to which such an interpretation is subject to the perspective of the observer. Let us assume that a member of the rising urban middle class or a traditional Sanskrit scholar learns about the Jhāmi Yātrā in Berhampur. He will immediately realize that this ritual does not follow the orthodox brahminical paradigm. Possibly motivated by the idea of Hinduism as a 'cultivated' religion or socio-cosmic order, he might classify the firewalking festival as 'primitive', 'archaic' or somehow 'pre-Hindu'. Indeed, *some* features of the cult are common among the tribal population in the hinterland of Orissa, for instance, the worship of snakes.[21] An animal sacrifice and also the offering of liquor are well known to satisfy a tribal goddess. Moreover, among many tribes we find shamans, usually dressed as females, who act as intermediaries between humans and the supernatural world. Self-torture acts are frequent to prove that they are truly possessed by some divinity.[22] However, these features do not occur in tribal contexts only, they may also belong to the worship of village deities (*grāma debatā*) or to tantric ritual practices.

Let us first consider the worship of village deities, who are mostly female.[23] Usually there are specific reasons why a devotee chooses to worship a *grāma debī* instead of a male god like Kṛṣṇa or Jagannātha. She is believed to be specifically able to deal with family, health or material problems, rather than what we may think of as spiritual goals. The best and most adequate way to please her is certainly the animal sacrifice. In Orissa it goes without saying that goddess temples are run by priests of various lower, i.e. Śūdra castes, for instance by a Bhaṇḍārī (barber) or Māḷī (gardener), and only rarely by Brahmins. The image of the goddess is usually limited to her head, which is painted in orange (or vermilion) and decorated with a silver tongue, silver eyes and ornaments. It is equally common that this idol is attached to a termite hill, from which the goddess is believed to have risen. Apart from her priests, there is often another type of ritual specialist who, in case of epidemics or other calamities, assumes a sacred function in order to

---

[21] For the worship of snakes in Orissa see Brighenti 2001, 35-44.

[22] Brighenti (2001, 350), with reference to the Saora, Gond, Bondo, Kondh and Munda tribes.

[23] See also Kinsley 1986, Chapter 13, Flood 1996, 193-6.

deal with the *grāma debī*.[24] These ritual specialists display their 'blessings' by the goddess in ordeals, which take place during the annual village goddess festival.[25] The devotees of Jhāmi Ṭhākurāṇī identify themselves with this context of *grāma debatā* worship. Naturally, they do not perceive themselves and their ritual practices as 'Hinduized' but as truly Hindu. The Oriya priest explicitly refers to the Telugu origin of Ellāmmā and her festival, which became popular in Ganjam in the nineteenth century after a wave of migration from the south. Indeed, we find references to firewalking in many studies on south India.[26] It is this geographic background of the goddess with which devotees of both mother tongues identify.

Let us also include the tantric framework of goddess worship and consider the openly displayed transgression incorporated in the ritual, i.e. the complete reversal of the Hindu paradigm of purity. According to tantric belief, a cremation ground, being a liminal place of transformation suitable to communicate with ghosts and demons, serves as a particularly apt *pūjā* site to liberate the practitioner's consciousness through the gruesome experience he has to undergo.[27] To share the goddess' supreme female energy (*śakti*) he will try to be absorbed in a total identification with her (possession). Therefore, a male adept may even transform his body in dress and appearance into a female one. As a further spiritual exercise, he may also offer otherwise forbidden substances, i.e. liquor, meat or specific kinds of sweets, which may be interpreted as three (*madya, māṁsa, muā*) of the five items to appease a tantric goddess (the so-called 'five Ms').[28] However, it is not only these features that hint at this esoteric tradition. The priest himself

---

[24] Brighenti 2001, 53; Dash 1903, 84.

[25] In academic discourse their altered state of consciousness is usually classified as 'possession' while their tribal counterparts rank as 'shamans', a distinction which ignores the continuities between the two phenomena.

[26] See Hiltebeitel (1982, 1991) for firewalking in the *Draupadī* cult, for examples from Andhra Pradesh see Rama Raju ([1978] 1997) and Knipe (1989).

[27] Flood 1996, 186, Kinsley 1998, 233–52.

[28] According to Flood (1996, 189) these five offerings are wine (*madya*), meat (*māṁsa*), fish (*matsya*), parched grain (*mudrā*) and sexual union (*maithuna*). Here, the *muā* sweets might serve as a substitute of the parched grain, in any case, they are offered to goddesses only. See also Fuller 1992, 87.

confirms this idea: 'Yes, in earlier times a lot of tantric adepts (*sādhana*) used to come from Bengal; however, when their rituals were prohibited they stopped coming.' With the term 'tantric' we have reached another diffuse category. In academic literature on South Asia this term communicates basically three overlapping ideas: (1) it refers to rituals which imply the complete inversion of the Hindu ideal of purity to reach salvation;[29] (2) it signifies a particular sectarian strand of Hinduism, which is aware of the esoteric meaning hidden in the *tāntra*-scriptures;[30] and (3) similar to the term 'Śāktism', it characterizes popular unorthodox ritual practices to worship a goddess as supreme divinity.[31] There are many further connotations. In Orissa, tantric magico-esoteric rituals became particularly widespread during the Bhaumakara dynasty in the eighth century and continued to flourish all through medieval times.[32] According to Brighenti, Tantrism became the dominant religious trend in Orissa and continued to influence (not only) Śāktism but also Śaivism, Buddhism, and even Jainism.[33] From the thirteenth century onwards and due to various influences, like the penetration of the ideals of Vaiṣṇavism, the tantric tradition watered down to simplified devotional practices which can hardly be recognized as tantric anymore.[34] In contrast to these academic attempts to clarify the term, people in Ganjam consider someone who, as a result of sincere worship of the goddess, is gifted with magic powers to be used for good or bad, as *tāntrika*. As such, he may know the art of manipulation as well as the art of exorcism.[35]

---

[29] Biardeau (1981) 1994, 149, Kinsley 1998, 51, Fuller 1992, 86-7. Strictly speaking, it is the 'left-handed' strand of Tantrism that follows transgressive practices.

[30] Michaels 1998, 238.

[31] Biardeau (1981) 1994, Kinsley 1998, 50.

[32] There are different theories about the origin of Tantrism. While some scholars attribute it to Himalayan Vajrayana Buddhism or shamanistic cults from central Asia, others view its roots in Kashmir or south India (see Biardeau [1981] 1994, 153, Flood 1996, 184-93). As a matter of fact it developed particularly well in eastern India, where we still find the most famous tantric pilgrim centres. Brighenti (2001, 57) adds that the popularity of Tantrism in Orissa was due to an incorporation of many indigenous rites by giving them a new religious significance.

[33] Brighenti 2001, 67.

[34] Ibid., 210.

[35] See Kinsley 1998, 56.

In short, he is believed to be a kind of sorcerer. In any case, the performance of most tantric rituals is rather unobtrusive. Biardeau and Kinsley have pointed out that tantric rituals resemble those of the *bhakti* tradition to a large extent, and also many temples serve as a meeting place for both strands of Hinduism.[36] Yet, not every temple visitor may be aware of this. To identify a ritual as tantric is rather a matter of perception. According to Biardeau, a tantric adept can be distinguished only by his initiation. By contrast, mainstream Hindus who worship the goddess often have only a vague notion of the meaning of ritual and their own devotional practice. They would never dream of taking initiation into a tantric sect.[37]

It should be clear by now that it is not possible to grasp the significance of either Jhāmi Ṭhākurāṇī or her *yātrā* by classifying the latter's features as tribal, village Hindu or tantric. Through the historic development of Orissa, there has been an amalgamation of ritual traditions instead. Here, tantric ritual practices do not only serve to promote 'Hinduization', as Stietencron assumes,[38] but constitute a religious strand in its own right. Moreover, it remains a matter of perspective and perception whether certain features are considered tantric, tribal or mainstream Hindu, i.e. which meaning is emphasized or else considered peripheral. Conflicting opinions may exist at the same time. Thus, firewalking in honour of goddess Maṅgaḷā is denied by her priests in Kakatpur while it is common practice at her annual festival.[39]

Ṭhākurāṇī Yātrā

Let us consider the third example of goddess worship, the biennial festival in honour of Buṛhī Ṭhākurāṇī (Old Ṭhākurāṇī), the tutelary deity of Berhampur. It lasts for about three weeks during March and April, includes an elaborate ritual sequence as well as entertainment, and attracts hundreds of thousands of pilgrims and visitors. According to legend, the festival signifies Buṛhī Ṭhākurāṇī's visit to her natal home.[40] Thus she is transferred from

[36] Biardeau (1981) 1994, 153, 156-157, Kinsley 1998, 50-1.

[37] Biardeau (1981) 1994, 151-3.

[38] Stietencron 1983, 139.

[39] Marglin/Mishra 1991, 210, 228.

[40] For a summary of the legend see Fischer/Pathy (1996, 220-1) and Pātra (1997, 9-12).

her temple to a temporary shrine where she is worshipped by the Telugu weaver caste (Ḍerā), whose leader, the Desibeherā, is believed to be her father. On ordinary days, her 'in-laws' from the Oriya barber caste (Bhaṇḍārī) perform the temple service. In the temporary shrine, earthen pots represent Buṛhī Ṭhākurāṇī as well as her eight 'sisters' or 'daughters'.[41] Every evening, nine selected Ḍerā women carry these pots in a procession around different streets of old Berhampur. In each neighbourhood women come to worship these pots. During the last night of the festival, Buṛhī Ṭhākurāṇī returns with pomp and presents to her in-laws' place. In this final procession, about 10,000 female devotees escort her, each carrying a holy pot.

Buṛhī Ṭhākurāṇī of Berhampur is one of the most popular goddesses of southern Orissa. Like Jhāmi Ṭhākurāṇī, she is a specified and personalized manifestation of those ambiguous and independent (i.e. without a male consort) female deities, who are feared for their anger, which may cause disease or calamities, and who are appeased with animal sacrifices in order to ensure their protective power as well as to obtain a boon. In Orissa, this kind of goddess is classified by the generic term *ṭhākurāṇī* (our lady, great mistress) and worshipped in uncountable shrines and temples all over the country.[42] Hindu scholars would consider them *grāma devatā*; from the local perspective, however, the eight Śākta goddesses mentioned in the previous section are also summed up under this term. Since both low-caste Hindus as well as tribal strata of the Oriya population worship and address goddesses as *ṭhākurāṇī*, scholars assume that their origin was tribal. Since Dalton in 1872 and Das in 1903, who viewed the 'blood-thirsty tutelary goddess' as a connecting link between the 'fetishism of the aborigines' and the 'more refined Śakti worship of the upper classes',[43] many scholars have come to this conclusion, taking into account nothing but blood sacrifice and the low caste of the

---

[41] The—again not unvarying—list of the eight 'sisters'/'daughters' shows the local priorities in the goddess pantheon. According to Pātra (1997, 20f.) it includes *Haracaṇḍī*, *Maṅgaḷā*, *Carchikā*, *Bhaṭarikā*, *Tāriṇī*, *Bhagabatī*, *Rāmacaṇḍī* and *Mahākāḷī*.

[42] See Das 1903, Eschmann 1978a, Fischer/Pathy 1997, 32-8, Hauser (2004), Rath 1987, 101-12, Schnepel 1997, 205-27.

[43] Das (1903, 81) with reference to Cuttack, Dalton draws his conclusion on the basis of Keonjhar district.

priests.[44] Likewise, Khambheśvarī (Stambheśvarī), Maṇikeśvarī, Tārātāriṇī, Byāghradebī, Mahurī Kāluā and other goddesses are considered 'Hinduized', and originally worshipped by the Kondh or the Saora.[45] Actually, no *ṭhākurāṇī* has ever entered the scholarly discussion without being attributed a tribal or at least 'Hinduized' background, and one might wonder where all the indigenous Hindu deities have disappeared! Since there is hardly any systematic research on the *ṭhākurāṇī,* scholars also presume a tribal origin of Buṛhī Ṭhākurāṇī of Berhampur.[46] For her devotees, at any rate, she is one, if not the main deity, of the pantheon. Buṛhī Ṭhākurāṇī serves not only as tutelary goddess of the town but also as the personal goddess (*iṣṭadebatā*) of many Oriya and Telugu families. Yet she is adored and feared. While she is worshipped and 'installed' in many household shrines, there are occasions on which she is believed to wander around in the night and has to be 'tied up' like other evil spirits.[47] On the institutionalized level of religion, Buṛhī Ṭhākurāṇī is identified with the tantric group of the ten *mahābidyā*, i.e. Kāḷī, Tārā, Ṣoṛasī, Bhubaneśvarī, Bhairabī, Chinnamastā, Dhūmābatī, Bagaḷeśvarī, Mātaṅgī and Kamaḷā.[48] As a pan-Indian model, this group reflects the common idea that the innumerable female deities of the local traditions are regarded as manifestations of goddesses legitimized in the written tradition (in this case the *Caṇḍī pāṭha*). Yet the arrangement of their anthropomorphic representations in the Buṛhī Ṭhākurāṇī temple shows that from a local perspective, the ten *mahābidyā* are considered subordinate to the power of Buṛhī Ṭhākurāṇī.

The cultural context of the Ṭhākurāṇī Yātrā and its links to other traditions are equally diverse. While the goddess can be worshipped in the form of an earthen pot (as in many rituals), in the Desibeherā's house her seat (*pīṭha*) consists of a deliberately empty

---

[44] For example, Eschmann (1978a, 91) interprets the animal sacrifice in honour of goddess *Tārātāriṇī* as 'aboriginal element' and neglects the possibility of either a local village or a tantric ritual context.

[45] Eschmann 1978a, Rath 1987, 80-9,101-12, Rösel 1994, 123-6, Schnepel 1997, 207.

[46] Rath 1987, 110, Schnepel 1997, 211-12.

[47] On the relation of goddesses and evil spirits see also Brighenti 2001, 28, Das 1903, 82-3.

[48] For the Ten *Mahāvidyā* (Skt.) see Kinsley (1986, 161-77, 1998), who translates their name as 'Ten Great Revelations' or 'Manifestations'.

room without an idol.[49] Besides, at the beginning of the festival, people erect a sacred pole. Both features are reminiscent of tribal goddesses manifest in this 'shape'[50]. Conversely, Buṛhī Ṭhākurāṇī receives vegetarian offerings during the whole *yātrā* and only a rather insignificant animal sacrifice at the very end. Possession occurs to a very limited extent. Although the goddess may overpower ordinary women who carry a sacred pot on their head, there is no opportunity for possession during the regular nightly processions of Ḍerā women. This is explained with the latter women's association with the Desibeherā and his family. Although Buṛhī Ṭhākurāṇī may enter the bodies of her 'children' (i.e. her devotees), she will never inhabit her 'parents'. In general, Ṭhākurāṇī Yātrā resembles a communal pot festival, in a manner that is particularly associated with southern India.[51] These festivals take place during the hot season. They last for several days with regular and elaborate pot processions, and hence constitute the main ritual event of a village or town. They centre on the temple of a mostly female tutelary deity and celebrate her links with the people as well as the territory she protects and rules over. This is symbolized by a division of ritual labour between the different castes of the settlement. In case of Berhampur, there are the (Oriya) Bhaṇḍārī as regular priests of the goddess, the (Telugu) Ḍerā as hosts of the festival, the (Oriya) Dāmaḷā as a specific class of priests, the (Oriya) Baurī as musicians, and the (Telugu) Kumuṭi businessmen as donors. Moreover, the costs of the festival are shared among the community. There is no local chief who acts as patron, yet the descendant of the Mahurī Rājā is treated attentively. Last but not least, the festival includes different entertainments like, for instance, tiger dance (*bāgha nāca*) and dramatic performance.[52] Therefore, some authors claim that Ṭhākurāṇī Yātrā was established

---

[49] For other empty shrines see Eschmann 1978a, 81.

[50] For the worship of pole-goddesses see Brighenti 2001, 58, Eschmann 1978b, 275, Rath 1987, 80-9.

[51] For pot festivals in Andhra Pradesh see Rama Raju ([1978] 1997, 126) or Tapper (1979, 11-12), for examples from central India compare Babb 1975. Scc Fuller (1992, Chapter 6) for a typology of north and south Indian village festivals.

[52] The tiger dance is a famous attraction of Andhra Pradesh (Rama Raju [1978] 1997, 132).

by Telugu migrants from Andhra Pradesh.[53] However, pot processions are not only popular in south India—the earthen pot serves as a matrix of all forms of life and as such symbolizes the goddess across the entire Indian subcontinent.

To conclude the discussion on these case studies, I should like to point out that we find not only a considerable plurality of goddesses (and gods) but also an amount of variation in the style of their worship. Many of these goddesses are related to each other or perceived in groups, and one might certainly recognize some continuities, interrelations and common themes. Culture contact between northern and southern varieties of Hinduism (be it the tantric ideology or the tradition of mostly female *grāma debatā*) appears to be much more influential than a linear development on the tribal-Hindu axis. In other words, tribal heritage as well as royal patronage—the two prominent topics in the academic discourse on Orissan goddesses—seem to be secondary issues and do not meet the empirical variety of goddess worship (at least) in southern Orissa. There is definitely an amalgamation of tribal, village Hindu, and tantric rituals, which is worth further investigation. Moreover, we may also examine the influence of commercialization on goddess worship. In the last quarter of the twentieth century, for instance, goddess Durgā, who in comparison to the strong and diverse *ṭhākurāṇī* worship in Ganjam had remained rather inferior, gained popularity due to the spread of glamorous Durgā Pūjā celebrations in the Bengali fashion.[54]

Let me draw some conclusions from those data presented which go beyond the remote Ganjam District, keeping the different viewpoints of centre and periphery in the regional and social respects in mind.

1. Many parameters that distinguish tribal worship from 'Hinduized' modes of worship are highly ambiguous. Features like animal sacrifice, non-Brahmin priests, the absence of an anthropomorph idol, a deity speaking through possession, irregular ritual procedures instead of the prescribed 'sixteen services', and the lack of an actual temple building are

---

[53] D. and P. Behera 1997, Candra 1998, 24-5. Compare Manna (1993: 157-9) for a similar event in Bengal.

[54] Preston 1980, on the limitations of Durgā worship in Ganjam see also Fischer/Pathy 1996, 14-15.

prominent in many of those religious practices which usually come under Śāktism, popular or 'folk' tradition. If we do not wish to exclude large strands of devotees, we must accept that these features are basics of Hindu religiosity, even though rarely appreciated by orthodox Brahmins or the urban 'educated' classes. Besides, we should ask whether we gain anything by excluding those seemingly 'awkward' facets of ritual practice from studies on Hinduism. Do we, for instance, characterize female or subaltern forms of devotion as 'Hinduized,' meaning not really Hindu yet, or still undergoing a process of transformation? Unwillingly we may support the present Hindu-nationalist discourse with its tendency to eliminate intracultural diversities for an authentic 'Indian' monoculturalism, as Bharucha recently pointed out.[55]

2. Furthermore, we should discuss the very dichotomy of 'tribal' versus 'Hinduized' deities and traditions. Even though it is tempting to presume such a dichotomy in a region where statistically every fourth person is registered as a member of a 'Scheduled Tribe',[56] in many cases this leads to oversimplification and misrepresentation of religious practice. After all, the majority of devotees in Orissa (and elsewhere) are neither tribal nor Brahmin (the other reference point of the tribal–Hindu spectrum). Most of them belong to a variety of lower castes, categorized either as Śūdra or as lower middle and lower classes, i.e. artisans, farmers, vegetable vendors, petty businessmen, drivers, and so on. The basis of their religious practices and identity is to be found in their locality where religious traditions have been mutually influencing each other for centuries and where there is no such thing as a clearly separate tradition. In nineteenth-century Ganjam the population density was low, and it is likely that most Hindus did not have access to the main temples of the region. Moreover, their lives were probably not very different from those of the neighbouring Kondh or Saora.[57] My suggestion is that instead of emphasizing the contrast between 'pre-Hindu' elements and other ritual

---

[55] Barucha 2001, 15.

[56] This may also be a very helpful analytic tool in those areas, where the majority of the inhabitants belong to that category.

[57] Fischer/Pathy 1996, 210.

practices any further, we should consider Sontheimer's definition of Hinduism as a *composition* of (1) the work and teachings of Brahmins, (2) asceticism and renunciation, and also (3) tribal religion, (4) folk religion, and (5) *bhakti* devotion (being overlapping categories).[58]

3. The subject of 'Hinduization' is not only a problem of terminology but also one of perspective. If, for example, a particular form of worship became Hinduized in medieval times, in a study of present-day India I would consider it a Hindu practice. Let me explain why I stress this point: it is still common to link 'Hinduized', 'Sanskritized', or 'Aryanized' forms of goddess worship to so-called 'tribal', 'Dravidian' or 'autochthonous' forms of religious expression. Yet this kind of statement often does not result from historical analysis, but rather indicates the presumptions and the worldview of the scholar.[59] Conversely, in each and every Hindu tradition, we may sooner or later discover some kind of archaic or pre-Hindu roots. Thus in the case of the Jagannātha cult in Puri, scholars have traced the absorption of tribal features in ancient and medieval Orissa,[60] all the same the temple serves as one of the main Hindu pilgrimage sites, and there is no controversy on its importance. This shows how it actually is a question of perspective and power whether a ritual or a form of worship is recognized as Hindu practice. I do not deny that in many cases there certainly is a linear development; however, it should be made explicit that analysing levels of 'Hinduization' represents a centre-defined process.

4. Finally, let me address the problem of varying viewpoints and contesting interpretations. In my opinion, it is not enough to search for even more refined groups, categories, and values to distinguish tribal, 'Hinduized', and Hindu practices. We could

---

[58] Sontheimer 1989.

[59] Like for instance Rath (1987, 101-12). Similarly, in his study on the 'Cultural History of Orissa' Sahu (1997, 67) describes the votive rite of Jahni Oṣā in the period between 1435 to 1751 as resembling present day practice! Yet, there is no historical evidence that Jahni Oṣā was observed at all more than five hundred years ago.

[60] See for example Dash 1998, 43-4.

certainly try to do so and ask, in the case of blood sacrifices for example, *how* the animal was slaughtered, and we may certainly find some new points to reconsider our categories.[61] However, to gain further insights we need to look for other approaches. Let me start from another angle. The problem classification and conceptualization does not (only) result from the difference of scholarly and local perspective. With reference to every religious tradition there are varying standpoints and also competing explanations, not as a contestation of this practice, but as a part of it. Moreover, people tend to attribute meaning to their rituals, and these meanings sometimes change according to context. Culturally transmitted ideas and categories do also reflect those personal, partly inconsistent and partly overlapping interpretations, which relate to each other directly or indirectly. Naturally, the Telugu women cooking Ellāmmā's non-vegetarian food offerings on the cremation ground will view their custom in a different light than the medium walking on glowing charcoal or a tantric adept from Bengal—all of them joining the same Jhāmi Yātrā. In other words, every participant will perceive, grasp and essentialize the event according to her or his own understanding, and all the interpretations have to be viewed in their own right. Certainly there is mutual influence between those ideas, but this does not necessarily mean that one community borrows or exploits a ritual sequence from another group, even though this often happens. Moreover, we should consider that not every group or institution contributes to the religious discourse with an equal voice. There may be conflicting knowledge systems which are based not only on textual but on oral or even embodied communication. This, however, says nothing about the value of the knowledge system.[62] It is a peculiarity of Indian religion that there is no privileged point of view from which to look at things, as many scholars have pointed out.[63] One can be a good Hindu without believing in the Veda. The important point is not only which component is emphasized and which may be subordinated or

[61] While a Hindu ritual specialist usually snips through the neck of the animal in one stroke, the Kondh jointly cut it into pieces.

[62] Marglin/Mishra 1991, 229.

[63] Sontheimer 1989, 197, Marglin (1985) 1989, 289.

peripheral,[64] but also how it is communicated to a specific audience, for instance, to the participants of a ritual, a Hindu scholar, or an anthropologist. It is the range of interpretations and its circumstances that I consider to be the challenge.

References

Babb, L.A. 1975. *The Divine Hierarchy: Popular Hinduism in Central India*, New York: Columbia University Press.

Behera, D. and P. Behera. 1997. 'Thakurani yatra of Brahmapur', in *Sun Times*, 11 May 1997.

Bharucha, R. 2001. *The Politics of Cultural Practice: Thinking Through Theatre in an Age of Globalization*, New Delhi: Oxford University Press.

Biardeau, M. 1994. *Hinduism: The Anthropology of a Civilization*, New Delhi: Oxford University Press.

Brighenti, F. 2001. *Śakti Cult in Orissa*, New Delhi: D.K. Printworld.

Chandra, S. 1998. *Oṛisāra Śaktipīṭha*, Berhampur: Sarasvati Publications.

Dalton, E.T. 1872. *Descriptive Ethnology of Bengal*, Calcutta.

Das, J.M. 1903. 'Note on the Grām Devatī or Tutelary Village Deity in Orissa', in *Journal of the Asiatic Society of Bengal* LXXII (III), 81-5.

Dash, G.N. 1998. *Hindus and Tribals: Quest for a Co-Existence (Social Dynamics in Medieval Orissa)*, New Delhi: Decent Books.

Dash, K.B. 1991. *Folklore of Orissa*, Bhubaneswar: Orissa Sahitya Akademi.

Eschmann, A. 1978a. 'Hinduization of Tribal Deities in Orissa: The Śākta and Śaiva Typology', in A. Eschmann, H. Kulke and G.C. Tripathi (eds.), *The Cult of Jagannath and the Regional Tradition of Orissa*, Delhi: Manohar, 79-97.

— 1978b. 'Prototypes of the Navakalevara Ritual and their Relation to the Jagannātha Cult', in A. Eschmann, H. Kulke and G.C. Tripathi (eds.), *The Cult of Jagannath and the Regional Tradition of Orissa*, Delhi: Manohar, 265-83.

[64] Sontheimer 1989, 198.

Fischer, E. and D. Pathy 1996. *Murals for Goddesses and Gods: The Tradition of Oṣākoṭhi Ritual Painting in Orissa,* Delhi: Indira Gandhi National Centre for the Arts.

Flood, G. 1996. *An Introduction into Hinduism,* Cambridge: Cambridge University Press.

Freeman, J.M. 1981: 'A Firewalking Ceremony That Failed', in G.R. Gupta (ed.), *The Social and Cultural Context of Medicine in India*, Delhi: Vikas, 308-36.

Fuller, C.J. 1992. *The Camphor Flame: Popular Hinduism and Society in India*, Princeton: Princeton University Press.

Gupta, S. 1999. 'Hindu Woman, the Ritualist', in H. Tambs-Lyche (ed.), *The Feminine Sacred in South Asia*, Delhi: Manohar, 88-99.

Hauser, B. 1990. 'Göttinnenverehrung im modernen Indien. Eine Bestandsaufnahme (Teil 1)', in *Mitteilungen aus dem Museum für Völkerkunde Hamburg*, Neue Folge, Bd. 20, 65-108.

— 1991. 'Göttinnenverehrung im modernen Indien. Eine Bestandsaufnahme (Teil 2)', in *Mitteilungen aus dem Museum für Völkerkunde Hamburg*, Neue Folge, Bd. 21, 75-118.

— 2004. 'Creating Performative Texts: The Introduction of Maṅgaḷā pūjā in Southern Orissa', in A. Malinar, J. Beltz and H. Freese (eds.), *Text and Context*, Delhi: Manohar, 203-38.

Hawley, J.S. and D.M. Wulff (eds.) 1996. *Devī: Goddesses of India*, Berkeley: University of California Press.

Hiltebeitel, A. 1982. 'Sexuality and Sacrifice: Convergent Subcurrents in the Firewalking Cult of Draupadī', in F.W. Clothey (ed.), *Images of Man: Religion and Historical Process in South Asia*, Madras: New Era Publication, 72-111.

— 1991. *The Cult of Draupadi II: On Hindu Ritual and the Goddess,* Chicago: Chicago University Press.

— 1986. *Hindu Goddesses: Visions of the Divine Feminine*, Berkeley: University of California Press.

Kinsley, D. 1998. *Tantric Visions of the Divine Feminine: The Ten Mahāvidyās*, Delhi: Motilal Banarsidass.

Knipe, D.M. 1989. 'Night of the Growing Death: A Cult of Vīrabhadra in Coastal Andhra', in A. Hiltebeitel (ed.), *Criminal Gods and Demon Devotees: Essays on the Guardians of Popular Hinduism*, Albany: State University of New York, 123-56.

Kulke, H. (1984) 1993. 'Tribal Deities at Princely Courts: The Feudatory Rājās of Central Orissa and Their Tutelary Deities (iṣṭadevatā)', in *Kings and Cults: State Formation and Legitimation in India and Southeast Asia,* Delhi: Manohar, 114-36.

Mahapatra, L.K. (ed.). 1981/82. *Man in Society. Bulletin of the Department of Anthropology, Utkal University* 2, Bhubaneswar: Department of Anthropology, Utkal University.

Mallebrein, C. 1999. 'Tribal and Local Deities—Assimilations and Transformations', in V. Dehejia (ed.), *Devī: The Great Goddess. Female Divinity in South Asian Art*, Munich: Prestel, 137-55.

Manna, S. 1993. *Mother Goddess Caṇḍī: Its Socio Ritual Impact on the Folk Life*, Calcutta: Punthi Pustak.

Marglin, F.A. 1989. *Wives of the God-King. The Rituals of the Devadasis of Puri*, Delhi: Oxford University Press.

— and P.C. Mishra. 1991. 'Death and Regeneration: Brahmin and Non-Brahmin Narratives', in D. Eck and F. Mallison (eds.), *Devotion Divine: Bhakti Traditions from Regions of India. Studies in Honour of Charlotte Vaudeville*, Groningen/Paris: Egbert Forsten, 209-30.

McGee, M. 1989. *Feasting and Fasting: The Vrata Tradition and Its Significance for Hindu Women*, Ann Arbor, Michigan: University Microfilms.

— 1991. 'Desired Fruits: Motive and Intention in the Votive Rites of Hindu Women', in J. Leslie (ed.), *Roles and Rituals for Hindu Women*, London: Printer Publishers, 71-88.

Michaels, A. 1998. *Der Hinduismus: Geschichte und Gegenwart*, München: C.H. Beck.

Misra, N. 1994. *Oṣā brata gapa*, Brahmapura: Taratarini Pustakalaya.

Pātra, S. 1997. *Pāramparika Ṭhākurāṇī yātrā o mā'ṅka mahīmā*, Berhampur: Siddhabhira Publication.

Preston, J.J. 1980. *Cult of the Goddess: Social and Religious Change in a Hindu Temple*, Delhi: Vikas.

Rajaguru, S. (n.d.) 1992, 'The Feasts and Fasts of the Uriyas', in *Abhinaba Bhañjabhāratī* 4-9, i-xx.

Rama Raju, B. 1997. *Folklore of Andhra Pradesh*, Delhi: National Book Trust (revised edition).

Rath, A.K. 1987. *Studies on Some Aspects of the History and Culture of Orissa*, Calcutta: Punthi Pustak.

Rösel, J. 1980. *Der Palast des Herrn der Welt: Entstehungsgeschichte und Organisation der indischen Tempel- und Pilgerstadt Puri*, München: Weltforum Verlag.

— 1994. 'Göttinnen, Krieger und Brahmanen: Volksreligiosität und Herrschaftsbildung im Hinterland von Orissa', in W.J.G. Moehlig and T. von Trotta (eds.), *Legitimation von Herrschaft und Recht*, Köln: Koeppe, 113-28.

Sahu, Bh. 1997. *Cultural History of Orissa (1435-1751)*, Delhi: Anmol Publications.

Schnepel, B. 1997. *Die Dschungelkönige: Ethnohistorische Aspekte von Politik und Ritual in Südorissa, Indien*, Beiträge zur Südasienforschung 177, Stuttgart: Franz Steiner Verlag.

Sontheimer, G.D. 1989. 'Hinduism: The Five Components and their Interaction', in G.D. Sontheimer and H. Kulke (eds.), *Hinduism Reconsidered*, Delhi: Manohar, 197-212.

Stietencron, H. v. 1983. 'Die Göttin Durgā Mahisāṣuramardinī. Mythos, Darstellung und geschichtliche Rolle bei der Hinduisierung Indiens', in *Visible Religion,* Vol. II: *Representations of Gods,* Leiden, 118-66.

Tapper, B.E. 1979. 'Widows and Goddesses: Female Roles in Deity Symbolism in a South Indian Village', in *Contributions to Indian Sociology* 13 (1), 1-31.

Tewari, L.G. 1991. *A Splendor of Worship: Women's Fasts, Rituals, Stories and Art*, Delhi: Manohar.

Tokita-Tanabe, Y. 1999. 'Body, Self and Agency of Women in Contemporary Orissa, India', Tokyo: University of Tokyo (unpublished Ph.D. thesis).

8

Context and Values: A Discussion of Concepts

Roland Hardenberg

This paper deals with two questions. First, how can social anthropologists compare their ethnographic findings and the abstractions based upon them? Second, what is the use of the notion of 'context' for social anthropology? At first sight, both questions seem to be unrelated. My point is that both questions depend on our idea of culture (and society). I here suggest adapting the culturalism described by Sahlins in one of his latest contributions (1999a) and the concept of context as employed by Needham and Dumont. These notions of culture, society, structure, and context may help us overcome a widespread anthropological particularism without imposing a rigid frame of analysis on everybody. They may also provide a way to bridge the gap between anthropological concreteness and abstraction.

This paper consists of five sections. First, I contrast Sahlins' notion of culture (and society) as a system of meaningful structures with the notions of agency, text and discourse of writers partly influenced by debates about the so-called postmodernism. Next, I show how 'context' has become a major catchword in any critique of structuralism and discuss to what extent this critique is justified. In the third part, I ask how representatives of the French and British schools of anthropological structuralism employed the notion of context in their writings, and attempt a synthesis of both schools by arguing for a combination of analytical levels (Needham) and levels of value (Dumont) in the study of 'contexts'. The fourth section will deal with the question of anthropological projects as tools to partly overcome particularism in our branch of scholarship. I will first mention the experimental ethnography of Marcus that in my opinion will lead to an extreme diverseness of facts and raises the question of how we can relate the different settings and contexts we experience in the field. Marcus, in a typical postmodern fashion, is sceptical about grand theories and thus provides no general conceptual schemes that might help overcome the problem. I contrast this postmodern approach with a project designed by Evans-Pritchard. He developed a model for interpreting diverse ethnographic data belonging to different contexts in a comparative framework. His approach, however old-fashioned it may appear to many, is discussed here because of its usefulness in providing a frame of analysis for different research results in the field of anthropology. In the final part of this paper the study of contexts and their values systems as suggested by Dumont, which closely resembles the approach of Evans-Pritchard, will be proposed as an additional research programme for the Orissa Research Project (ORP). I would like to point out that I am not suggesting a single programme for the entire project, but attempting to hint at ways to overcome the isolation some scholars experience when it comes to analysing and discussing field results.

Culture and Text

For many decades the binary opposition of culture and society divided our discipline. Both were seen as distinct categories and as belonging to different disciplines: American cultural versus British social anthropology. This dualism continues to exist, but it has been challenged for many years. One of the latest attempts to unite the allegedly different phenomena is Sahlins' 'culturalism'. Since social and cultural phenomena are both symbolically instituted, Sahlins does not bother to distinguish them or build different theories around them. What unites these phenomena is a meaningful order consisting of structures. Sahlins defines structure as 'the organization of conscious experience that is not itself consciously created' (1999a: 413). The majority of anthropologists, many of whom have been influenced by 'postmodernism', do certainly not share Sahlins' definition of culturalism. This trend started in architecture, where it was made popular by Charles Jencks' *The Language of Post-Modern Architecture* (1975), but it was Jean-Francois Lyotard who became the most important advocate of postmodernism in philosophy and cultural theory (1979). What Lyotard and others like Baudrillard and Derrida postulate is both a rejection of any 'grand narrative' like Marxism and structuralism, and advocate a sceptical attitude towards any form of authority, received wisdom, or cultural and political forms.[1]

---

[1] For differences between the above mentioned authors see A. Easthope 2001, 15-27.

Critique on structuralism termed 'poststructuralism' was most powerfully expressed by Derrida in his deconstructionism. As Sim puts it, 'Deconstructionism was directed against the system-building sidc of structuralism, and took issue with the idea that all phenomena were reducible to the operations of systems. What Derrida was concerned to demonstrate was the instability of language, and indeed systems in general' (2001: 5). A similar deconstructionism has been applied to the structural notion of culture (and society) in sociology and social anthropology. Clifford (1988) substituted culture by discourse (discourse analysis being associated mainly with the work of the philosopher H.P. Grice) in order to point out that norms and institutions are not given but negotiated and in a continuous flow. In a further move, attempts were made to classify such discourses, as in Baumann's (1997) writings, by distinguishing dominant from subaltern and demotic discourses. Within anthropology, structural notions of culture were particularly criticized by Geertz, who postulated a 'thick description' that provides us with a better interpretation of culture than the structural outlines of objective features. Instead of seeing culture as a unified phenomenon or 'thing' he prefers to see culture as a series of texts whose semantics have to be analysed in order to understand how meaning is produced. His *The Interpretation of Cultures* (1973) can thus be seen as part of the general postmodern deconstructionism. The same can be said of Giddens' writings (1984), particularly his emphasis on 'agency' of the individual, or of Hobsbawn's and Ranger's (1983) thesis that traditions are not given but purposefully invented. There is no space here to deal with the various differences between the above-mentioned authors. Rather, I would like to point out what they may have in common apart from a deconstructive method. My concern is that the individual and his/her actions, his/her role as originator of social relations and of social constructs may be lost—a concern which may be deeply rooted in the Western ideology of the individual (see Dumont 1986). This is not the place to discuss the role of ideology in anthropological theories, but it seems to me a worthwhile effort to compare the place given to the individual in different societies (see, for example, Alvi, 2001). The question that concerns me now is whether postmodern deconstructionism correctly represents structuralist approaches to culture (and society). I will deal with this question by showing how structuralists deal with 'context', a notion often used against structuralism.

Context in Question

Partly as a reaction to structuralism, several kinds of 'post-theories'[2] have emerged, rejecting the alleged anti-historical stance of structuralist theory, its failure to recognise agency and its reification of culture. Roy Dilley gives the following example for such a critique: 'Lévi-Strauss's work on myth ... can be seen as removing the processes of retelling of such oral accounts from their performative contexts, from the way in which recitation is embedded within a broader set of interactive processes' (1999: 20-1). Context and social action became catchwords of the 'new' trend.[3] The importance given to contexts and situations can easily be explained with the above mentioned anti-structuralist critique. To overcome the alleged anti-historicism of structuralism one must consider each phenomenon and its change in a historical framework and in its embeddedness in concrete relations of power. To re-introduce agency, one has to focus on individual decision-making in particular situations. And in order to question the alleged reification of culture, one has to show how identities are negotiated in certain contexts. 'Context' or 'situation' seems to guard us against the evils of structuralism. Invoking 'context' has become an instrument for questioning any formal principle (Dilley 1999: 6-7).

Focussing on particular situations, however, does not mean that we have to abandon the idea of latent structures or meaningful orders. As Sahlins says: 'Although in theory structure is supposed to be a concept antithetical to history and agency, in practice, it is what gives historical substance to a people's culture and independent grounds to their action' (1999a: 412). Sahlins himself gives a good example for this statement in his analysis of change in Hawaii (1994). However, the question remains whether we are

[2] Collectively called 'afterology' by Sahlins (1999a), a term coined by Jacqueline Mraz.

[3] In a critique on Durkheim, Radcliffe-Brown points out that rules of behaviour cannot be defined without social interaction: 'Social usages ... are both in the behavior of the given individual, and outside that individual in the behaviour of other individuals and in the relationship between these behaviours' (1948, 57).

allowed to analyse abstracted features of the cultural system without recourse to particular situations or praxis.

Modern kinship studies answer this question positively. One of the first to distinguish three levels of social life was Rodney Needham (1973a). According to him, it is useful for analytical purposes to make a distinction between behaviour, rule, and categories (ibid., 171). For several reasons, he pays particular attention to classification, but 'we need be under no inclination to ignore or to underrate the associated rules and modes of behaviour'. Indeed, this approach actually brings out more clearly the fact that categories, rules and behaviour are independent variables (ibid., 174). Following Needham, Anthony Good (1981) applied this distinction successfully in his analysis of kinship in south India and, since his joint publication with Alan Barnard (1984), it has become standard knowledge in kinship studies. It is high time these insights were applied to other branches of our discipline, particularly when dealing with holistic societies, where distinctions between politics, economy, religion, etc., are not really useful.[4] This is in accordance with Needham who applied his distinction of three levels to 'the study of social life' and 'aspects of collective conduct and representation' (1973a: 171), and not to any specialized field called kinship. Such an approach would also solve what Dilley calls the 'dilemma of social anthropology between the Scylla of contextual relativism and the Charybdis of "extreme sameness and objectivity"' (1999: 9), because both approaches may be combined. On the one hand, behaviour can be analysed from a relativistic point of view, i.e. in relation to the particular cultural rules, which are again seen in connection with specific categories. On the other hand, the formal aspects of systems of classification may be compared on a universal basis. This is possible because these structures have a double nature—they are realizations of a limited number of principles and they are attached to various kinds of rules and actions. This is only feasible because these three levels of social life are partly independent, i.e. they do not determine the specific form of one another.[5]

---

[4] See the debate between Lang (1989) and Pfeffer (1992) about the 'realm' of kinship.

[5] A similar distinction, also based on the study of kinship, was made by Firth in somewhat different terms: 'People often do what rules lay down, but these rules alone are an incomplete account of their organized

The general criticism against structural theory is, of course, informed by the bias toward praxis and the alleged structuralist denial of agency. Studying specific contexts may be considered as an advance, because this method allows us to see why a particular person acts in a specific way, why he or she breaks the rule or actively resists forms of oppression. This is very plausible and it might help if social anthropologist learnt from psychology in order to be better equipped when dealing with inner motivations, as demanded by Firth almost half a century ago (Firth 1954, 11-12). But to separate culture as a meaningful order from individual motivations, as structuralists often do, does not mean to deprive the individual of his or her agency. Sahlins brings it to the point when he compares culture and language: 'Just because what is done is culturally logical does not mean the logic determined that it be done—let alone by whom, when or why—any more than just because what I say is grammatical, grammar caused me to say it' (1999a: 409).

A major point of postmodern criticism is the alleged structuralist essentialization, homogenization, and reification of culture and community by structural theory. An alternative, as suggested by Baumann, is to render '"culture" and "community" into terms of active negotiation and debate, the social processes that underlie the forging of multi-ethnic "communities of action" out of reified "communities" of "culture"' (1997: 209-10). Studying local processes of cultural change by negotiation and invention of traditions is presented by him as novel and antithetical to former concepts of culture. But former notions of culture were not at all rigid and /or based on the idea of homogeneity. As exemplified in the studies of Boas and his students, cultures are necessarily heterogeneous in origin. Various processes contribute to a unique combination of cultural phenomena in a particular locality. However, this hodgepodge does not remain chaotic, but is constantly ordered by existing categories into indigenous systems of meaning. Again, Sahlins presents the argument with his usual conciseness: 'cultures are generally foreign in origin and local in pattern' (1999b: xi).

---

activities. Again, this ordering of social action may coincide and support the structural features of the society, the major principles on which its form depends. But it may vary from the structural principles, and even bear against them in some particulars' (Firth 1958, 10).

Roy Dilley has summarized the problems connected with a persistent contextualization and a lack of recognition of structures. The main point of critique is that such a method may lead to an extreme relativism since, if applied radically, 'everything becomes the context of everything else' (1999: 7). He quotes Scharfstein in this respect, who reminds us that if we consistently attach things to their contexts, in the end everything must become utterly unique and individualistic. One may indeed wonder how such an approach is compatible with a science concerned with collective phenomena. But since this contextualizing approach emphasizes the uniqueness of the individual, it is no wonder that it is particularly attractive to members of a society whose highest value is the individual.

If structuralist theory is not completely ignorant of contexts, in what ways are contexts treated and conceptualized in structural theories? There is no unity, as a discussion between two of the leading figures of structural theory in the 1970s may demonstrate.

Contexts in Structural Analysis

There is a tendency in the field of anthropology to differentiate contexts without reference to values. Emphasis is placed on contexts regardless of their relation to the overall mentality. This has given rise to a debate between Rodney Needham and Louis Dumont, who represent the British and French schools of structuralism respectively. While Needham deals with contexts in an egalitarian manner, Dumont proposes to understand each context in relation to a given hierarchy of values. In other words, contexts according to Dumont are not situations demarcated by the anthropologist who selects certain events in a particular period of time as his/her frame of analysis, but are sets of relations marked by the value system under study. Contextualization in Dumont's sense is no longer a strategy to bring order to the data, but a way to understand the culturally given order.

A good example for the treatment of contexts in the tradition of the British school of structuralism is *Right and Left: Essays on Dual Symbolic Classification* edited in 1973 by Rodney Needham in honour of Robert Hertz. The papers in the volume deal with various systems of ideas and the relations between cultural elements in different contexts. Needham illustrates his method by reference to the Vedic symbolism of Mitra and Varuna (Needham 1973b: xxvi-

xxvii). Mitra produced the day, Varuna the night. Therefore, the day and the sun belong to Mitra, while the night and the moon are aspects of Varuna. This does not mean, however, that all qualities ascribed to the moon are automatically part of Varuna's identity. Thus, while the moon is associated with magic and female power, Varuna must not necessarily be related to these ideas. The association of Varuna with the night and the moon exists only in a particular context, in the opposition to Mitra during the process of creation. Neither is the moon a feature exclusively related to Varuna. If, for example, the texts focus on the difference between the waning and the waxing moon, these two lunar phases are also related to the opposition between Mitra and Varuna.

Needham and others summarize these binary oppositions in two-column tables. They do not, however, treat these two columns as monolithic blocks. For Needham, the elements of one column are not related with each other through homology. The table only serves the purpose of summarizing the dualistic structures found in various contexts. If, for example, the data are presented in two columns under the heading 'right' and 'left', this does not mean that 'right' and 'left' are exclusive domains. The same elements can be found on both sides depending on the aspect by which they are contrasted. This can best be illustrated by Needham's interpretation of the relation between Mitra and Varuna. Depending on the context, Mitra is associated with either the right or the left side, because each side has more than one quality of which one may be related to Mitra, the other to Varuna. According to Needham, the connection between all of these binary oppositions should not be sought in the elements but—by analogy—in the relations between the elements.

While Needham's analysis is in agreement with most methodological considerations found in the work of Dumont, he differs from the latter in his contextual relativism. For Needham, there is no fixed hierarchy of values, only ranking according to context. His example is the status of the Mugwe, a religious dignitary of the Meru in Kenya (ibid., xxvii-xxviii, 109-27). This figure aroused Needham's curiosity because he blesses and exercises his religious power with the left hand. Thus, in this society the left hand seems to represent the sacred. This contradicts the writings of Hertz, who collected a great amount of data proving the universal pre-eminence of the right hand (Hertz 1973 [1909]).

For Needham the issue is not whether either of the two hands is ultimately of higher value. For him the question of pre-eminence depends on the context. The Mugwe's status exceeds that of the elders in the ritual context, while he is subordinate to them in the political context. The hierarchy of values governing these two contexts is secondary to Needham. What counts is the complementarity of ideas (1973b: 117).

Although Needham's emphasis on relations and systems of ideas is in agreement with many tenets of French structuralism, the strongest reaction to his writings came from Louis Dumont. In two articles[6] Dumont expressed his critique of *Right and Left*, prompting Needham to write a sharp and polemical answer in *Counterpoints* (102-45). Needham feels that Dumont's critique is unjustified, particularly when Dumont writes that 'what is curious ... is that Evans-Pritchard's distinction of situations should have been neglected' (Dumont 1986: 225) and that 'it is clear that in the two-column presentation of the table, all contexts are confused and elided' (ibid., 226). At first view this criticism seems indeed unjustified because all authors in *Right and Left* explicitly distinguish between various contexts in their contributions. Dumont's statements, however, make sense if we consider the holism implied in his critique. He is concerned with ideologies or 'mentalities', in which values and ideas form a systematic whole. To Dumont, situations or contexts are valued by reference to an ideological whole. What Dumont means when criticizing Needham and others is that they treat all contexts in the same manner and that they analyse cultural representations independently of social entities and values. He explains this approach with reference to the egalitarian ideology that dominates our own society and thinking. According to Dumont, we tend to separate between fact and value (ibid., 227).

How does one recognize ideological holism? According to Dumont, 'value-ideas' share three features (ibid., 252-3). First, values are ranked. Higher values are distinguished from lower values. The relation between these values is described by Dumont as the 'encompassment of the contrary'. Second, value systems entail reversals, which produce meaningful changes, because the values involved are in an asymmetrical relationship. This must be

[6] 'The Anthropological Community and Ideology', and 'On Value, Modern and Nonmodern', reprinted in Dumont 1986.

distinguished from symmetrical oppositions, because reversals of the latter do not produce anything new. Third, values are segmented in their application. The same values are applied in a variety of situations. This creates a complex system of interrelated features without strict boundaries.

The difference between both approaches manifests itself in the word 'level' (or 'niveau') frequently used by Dumont in his later writings. In *Counterpoints* Needham expresses his failure to understand Dumont's use of the word 'level' (Needham 1987, 135-9). The Frenchman is accused of neither defining nor illustrating what he means by this term. In two passages, however, Dumont explains his understanding of 'levels'. In 'The Anthropological Community and Ideology' he suggests that the reversal of an asymmetrical opposition creates a change of levels. As an example he refers to Bourdieu's study of the Kabyle house. In this passage he speaks of a change of the 'level of life' (Dumont 1986, 230), meaning that basic ideas, values and conceptions of the concerned social entities are affected by the reversal. For Dumont, these levels are not independent of each other, but hierarchized in accordance with the values existing in the particular society. One level represents the whole and encompasses the lower level.

In 'On Value, Modern and Nonmodern', Dumont elaborates these considerations. To him, values are ranked, and each value foresees, inscribes, or implies certain contexts. The sum of situations and relations defined by a common value are called 'level' by Dumont. The relation between two levels always entails a reversal of the situations belonging to it. This reversal may be acknowledged in the ideology itself, or it may come into existence through the confrontation between the ideological and the empirical level. Thus Dumont has shown the caste system to contain two types of situations, value situations and power situations, the latter manifesting themselves only on the empirical level.[7]

---

[7] According to Dumont, contexts are ordered along with their entities. This means that in India not only Brahmin and king stand in a hierarchical relationship, but also the situations that arise out of the exercise of their respective functions. Applying these considerations to Needham's two-column table, Dumont argues that every context should not be dealt with in isolation, but as part of the 'mentality as a whole' (Dumont 1986: 226). To him, we have to consider whether the ideology in question equates or distinguishes certain contexts. Are all situations of the

In general, I suggest we distinguish different understandings and methodological applications of the term 'context'. In one sense, 'context' may be understood as a particular setting. History produces new situations in which the elements are permanently re-arranged. The complex interplay of individual motivations, personal decisions, property relations, cultural restrictions and geographical boundaries, for example, may be responsible. The meaning of an element is derived from its function or efficacy in this particular setting: 'Context as "setting" can be seen in the work of the linguist J.L. Austin, who shifted his focus away from the analysis of words and sentences to conceive of language as a mode of action' (Dilley 1999, 18). Tambiah has applied this method to the study of rituals in his 'performative approach' (1985 [1979]). The performance is seen as linked to a specific social, religious, political etc. framework and to concrete relations of power. In a performance agents actively order ('index') their social relations and legitimize them via cosmological notions (ibid., 144). This idea of a setting or situation can be distinguished from the use of the word 'context' in structural linguistics and structural anthropology. Each phenomenon is analysed within 'closed-system contexts' (ibid., 21). Meaning is not exclusively sought in the relations between one domain of phenomena and the 'external context', but within 'internal contexts': 'a connection is made not with things outside of the object of inquiry, but internal to it' (ibid., 12). In these systems, meaning can be derived from syntagmatic relations, i.e. the relation between the elements in praesentia, as well as from paradigmatic relations, relations between elements in absentia. One question remains: can we analyse these different contexts independently of each other? i.e. how do we demarcate a particular set of relations or 'context'?

I answer this question positively, because it seems possible to distinguish different levels of life as suggested by Needham. Acts of speech or actual marriages are different from rules and categories. They may coincide—an asymmetric terminology often coexists with asymmetric marriage rules—but they do not have to. The logic of paradigmatic relations between words in a certain

---

same kind or do they belong to different levels? Reversals help us decide the matter since they indicate a change of level. A good example is the reversal of time described in my book about the renewal of the wooden deities in the Jagannatha temple of Puri (Hardenberg 1999, 334-42).

language or of kintypes in a specific kinship terminology can be studied independently from the act of speech or the concrete behaviour between relatives. The structure of a sentence or the ideal sequence of a ritual can be analysed regardless of the situation in which the sentence is spoken or the ritual performed. I agree with Tambiah (and with Evans-Pritchard) that social action should be seen in relation to ideas. However, studying categories or ideas separately allows us to understand specific features of the systems of which they are a part. This will guard us against assumptions derived from common sense, in particular the idea that categories, rules and behaviour determine each other in a simple and direct way. Whether this will provide us with 'full understanding' (Tambiah) is an altogether different question. Why should we restrict ourselves to finding only one type of meaning in our data? For example, when studying a ritual, we may find its meaning in the place it has in the ritual system, and in the way the elements are arranged in a ritual sequence, as well as in the relations of the ritual symbols in a system of classification and its sociological efficacy in a given setting. This mechanical approach will provide us with insights we will never gain when we mingle all analytical levels with undue haste. But can we leave it there?

I think no, at least not if we attempt to understand different mentalities. In addition to analysing the three levels of social life, I suggest we follow Dumont's holistic method of seeing situations in relation to a particular mentality. That way, contextualization is no longer a 'strategy or practice of an agent who seeks to structure material in a particular way' (Dilley 1999, 10) but rather a part of our attempt to understand the viewpoint of others. According to this approach, a social unit and all situations (or contexts) related to it are marked by the values of the particular culture (or society) under study and not by the anthropologist. Contextualization becomes a way to understand how others order their own reality in accordance with their hierarchy of values.

Anthropological Projects

By introducing the idea of a hierarchy of values and of context in the structural sense we have moved far away from a postmodern interpretation of culture. The basic difference seems to be the premise of structural anthropologists that cultural forms—like our language—are based on a system of ideas and values. Accepting this idea does not mean moving away from reality, since cultural performances are to the anthropologist what speech is to the linguist. Due to postmodern deconstructionism, cultures (and societies) have sometimes been dissolved in favour of individual subjects negotiating the rules of their social games. Because of this trend, our own society becomes the focus of anthropological studies. Unconcealed sociocentrism[8] has been 'negotiated' in the following postmodern project: 'For example, moving from a study of Italian villagers to the multinational European parliament, from the Amazon jungles to pain centres in Boston, from a study of a Japanese factory to the international fashion industry, from the study of ancestor worship in village Taiwan to medical versus American female discourses about the body, from Transylvanian villagers to Romanian intellectuals, from the study of Sherpas in Nepal to one's own high school class, and many more shifts of careers like these involves testing the limits of the ethnographic paradigm (Marcus 1994, 52). Such a project blurs the distinction between observer and observed and deprives us of one of our most powerful tools of understanding. Moreover, I do not see how we will ever be able to stitch together the various shreds and patches

[8] The word 'sociocentrism' is used by Dumont to point out the universalism members of a holistic society claim for its collectively shared ideas and values (Dumont 1986: 207). In a holistic society, where man is absolutely subordinated to society, sociocentrism expresses itself in the idea that only the members of this society are really man while every outsider is being devalued. In modern society, sociocentrism is according to Dumont 'mediatized' (ibid.). It is not absolutely clear what Dumont means. As I understand him, our ideology does not subordinate the individual to society, but gives highest value to the individual. Our sociocentrism consist in the universalism we attach to our individualistic ideology. Our society is made universal, while other forms of society are being devalued. Dumont probably calls the sociocentrism of a holistic ideology 'absolute', because it is centred on a particular society. Our sociocentrism is 'mediatized', because it is centred on the individual, which however encompasses a particular notion of society. Mediated (as I rephrase Dumont's expression) by the value we attach to the individual, our form of society is turned into a model of the proper order of the world. The Human Rights are in this sense an expression of the basic values of Western sociocentrism. Since this is not a matter of ethnic features but of social ideologies, Dumont avoids the word 'ethnocentrism' (ibid., 206).

produced by such projects if we do not have a certain degree of unity in our concepts, or at least certain notions beyond the joint denominator of common sense. An alternative to this 'experimentation' are research programmes based on clearly defined notions of structure and culture (or society) that are designed to combine the results of different researches. An example of such a programme may be found in the writings of Evans-Pritchard's (1962), whose major contents will now be summarized because it may help to overcome the particularism of ethnographic research.

In his Marett lecture (Oxford 1950), Evans-Pritchard argues that social relationships form moral, not natural systems and that the human being is not an automaton responding to universal laws. Sceptical about the discovery of any such laws, he expresses his doubts on the prospects of anthropologists creating the best of all worlds. Instead, he advocates the idea that social anthropology is part of the humanities and basically similar in method to historiography. Evans-Pritchard does not reject the idea of a system when arguing against the naive comparison of society and the biological organism, but suggests one of the most comprehensive theoretical approaches to social phenomena by distinguishing three levels of abstraction.

Ethnographic data, either derived from participant observation or from various kinds of documents, stand at the base of all anthropological research. Evans-Pritchard is fully aware that this description is itself an abstraction. Today, following Geertz, one would say we are producing texts. This text, however, must not necessarily be a report about certain individuals and their actions and motivations. When comparing social anthropology with historical science, the ideal is not a historical chronology but a history of institutions. Evans-Pritchard does not want to explain individual behaviour. Rather he intends to show how actions make sense in a given system of ideas and institutions. On this level of abstraction he focuses more on concepts expressed in words and actions than on individual behaviour. The individual is not absent, but is generalized in relation to collective representations. This approach can be seen as a reaction to dominant theories of his time. At the time Evans-Pritchard started studying social anthropology, the question 'How Natives Think' dominated the debate. As Mary Douglas shows, Evans-Pritchard's sociological theory of knowledge as exemplified in his book *Witchcraft, Oracles and Magic among the Azande* should have stopped analysing thought without paying attention to social action (Douglas 1980, 54), but perhaps his book was not read by many, although it is frequently cited (ibid., 59).

Evans-Pritchard's second level of abstraction goes a step further. After writing a descriptive account of various institutions in relation to ideas and actions, he wants us to construct a model.[9] This model is based on empirical data, but challenges the imagination. Starting from the same facts, different models can be constructed, and none of them is 'real' in the sense of a natural system. What he has in mind is perhaps similar to what Lévi-Strauss called a mechanical model that relates social morphology to norms and ideas, but Evans-Pritchard calls it a latent structure and avoids the expression 'unconscious'. An example of such a model is the segmentary lineage model of the Nuer or Louis Dumont's model of the relation between the caste organization and the values of purity and impurity. On this second level of abstraction, Evans-Pritchard aims to understand how the system works, while at the first level he intends to establish the relations that make up the system. This second level is thus structuralist in the sense that it deals with the relations between relations.

The third level of abstraction can only be achieved after a model of a particular society has been constructed as part of the second level of analysis. This final step consists of comparing the models derived from the study of different societies. Here we meet one of the most treasured and enduring aims of anthropology, the aim to study humanity as a whole. The method suggested is neither prejudiced, like the comparative method of the evolutionists, nor simple and substantialist like Murdock's *Human Relation Area Files*.[10]

It requires the combined efforts of anthropologists working in various regions in the world who are all aware that at all levels of analysis we are only dealing with abstractions of reality and not with truths. Like the models we construct and the similarities we establish, texts are products of our imaginative faculty. This faculty

---

[9] For an early discussion of the problems involved in creating models see Firth 1954, 6-8.

[10] Since Murdock's first overview (Murdock 1949), completing the files has been an ongoing process.

does not imply our liberation from the data at hand. It implies the very opposite. All abstraction depends upon data. But when presenting and analysing it, we produce our own orders, some of which are more intelligible than others, being better equipped to establish the connections between the facts than others. We use our mental capacities to understand systems that have been produced by human beings living in specific societies, not by nature.

This extended reference to a text produced half a century ago, appears to be necessary when we ask ourselves how many anthropologists have indeed adapted Evans-Pritchard's methodological suggestions. In fact, many of us either put too much emphasis on the concrete or hurry to establish the universal with undue haste. The reason is obvious: Evans-Pritchard's programme is too big for a single person or even a small group of scientists. It requires a worldwide cooperation and a unitary anthropological project—one that just does not exist due to a general 'anthropological particularism'. A major obstacle is the ongoing notion of anthropology being a science because of its recourse to quantitative methods. Quantification is mystified, resulting in the researchers' obsession with individual actions and events. The latter are considered 'real' because they are what the anthropologist really experiences in the field: people in flesh and blood as well as observable action based on accessible motivations. This empiricism is the basis of our trade, but, as Evans-Pritchard has shown, it is largely relevant for only the first level of analysis. Our descriptions of observed facts will and should always be abstractions. We ought to make sure they are good generalizations by establishing links between the details, and not by accumulating more and more details. Judging by Evans-Pritchard's programme, progress in our branch of scholarship may consist of a combined effort to relate our ethnographies and abstractions in order to build upon them and achieve a better understanding of meaningful orders in the past and the present.

Studying Value-Ideas: A Few Examples

Instead of a conclusion, the following is to exemplify the above-mentioned comparative approaches as well as the manner in which the Orissa Research Programme, the current endeavour of many authors of this volume, might employ these. The scientific project deriving from Evans-Pritchard's and Dumont's analytical approaches is the worldwide study of systems of ideas and of values in their cultural application. Dumont himself made the beginning with his study of the caste system in India which he later compared with Western ideology (1986), in particular that of Germany. Later authors have continued his approach by studying other societies. Their results have been published in *Context and Levels* (1985), in *Ethnos* (1990), in *Cosmos and Society in Oceania* (1995) and in different anthropological journals. Three examples are to illustrate this project, which may be useful to the ORP.

Dominique Casajus deals with the question why the Tuareg veil their faces. She argues that male veiling refers to two value levels existing in Tuareg culture. Depending on the context, the veil either signifies the superior relationship between men on the one hand and god and the saints on the other, or it reminds the Tuareg of the close and inferior relationship they entertain with the '*kol asuf*', malevolent spirits of the dead (Casajus 1985, 76). Saints and spirits are associated with different situations, and together they are ordered by a system of higher and lower values.

Cécile Barraud, after doing fieldwork on the Kei Islands, published a similar study of a value system. She comes to the conclusion that in this society rituals create a relation between a soul principle (*inya*) deriving from God and a body principle (*itumun*) originating in the ancestors and transmitted by spirits (Barraud, 1990, 222). The bodily aspect of the person is relevant at the level of the house and its relations. The soul principle becomes important when the relations between the islands are concerned, invoked during the annual millet ritual when the life of the whole community has to be brought in from the outside. The soul principle refers to the whole and represents the higher value, of which the body and the houses are a lower part (ibid., 228).

Like Barraud, another French anthropologist, André Iteanu, studied a value system and related it to the culturally derived concept of the person. He did his fieldwork amongst the Orokaiva of Papua New Guinea, whose central values are called *pure* and *jo*. Iteanu describes the domain of *pure* as that of ritual, of the repetition of prescribed actions and of the totality of traditions that form the collective identity of the Orokaiva (Iteanu 1990, 42). In contrast to *pure*, *jo* refers to an inner condition that has to be concealed and is at the origin of society and action. During rituals, *jo* appears twice, once as the source or immediate cause of the rite, another time as a phase of non-differentiation. *Pure* orders relations belonging to the level of the whole society, while *jo* is part of a lower level of relations characterized by non-differentiation.

These three studies illustrate the variability of social morphology in relation to particular ideas. They are based on long-term ethnographic work and present an impressive amount of concrete data. However, the universal aspect of our subject is not lost sight of, because the analysis is carried out along similar lines and aims at establishing latent structures and the composition of society as a whole. These wholes can be compared without neglecting their specific features. In this comparability lies the advantage of the closely related approaches of Evans-Pritchard and Dumont, here proposed for the Orissa Research Programme. Several of our sub-projects deal with tribal groups in remote areas of Orissa. These researches will produce, and have already produced, new ethnographic data. Analysing these data the members of the project will be dealing with different questions. Additionally, however, an attempt could be made to compare the latent structures of cultures and societies in question. The models established in this way can be compared not only across Orissa, but alsc on a universal basis.

References

Alvi, Anjum. 2001. 'The Category of the Person in Rural Punjab', in *Social Anthropology,* 9/1, 45-64.

Barnard, Alan and Anthony Good. 1984. *Research Practices in the Study of Kinship*, London: Academic Press.

Barraud, Cécile. 1990. 'Kei Society and the Person: An Approach through Childbirth and Funerary Rites', in *Ethnos*, 55/III-IV, 214-31.

Barth, Fredrik. 1994. 'A Personal View of Present Task and Priorities in Cultural and Social Anthropology', in R. Borofsky (ed.), *Assessing Cultural Anthropology,* New York: McGraw-Hill, 349-61.

Baumann, Gerd. 1997. 'Dominant and Demotic Discourses of Culture: Their Relevance to Multi-Ethnic Alliances', in P. Werbner and T. Modood (eds.), *Debating Cultural Hypbridity,* London: Zed Books, 209-25.

Casajus, Dominique. 1985. 'Why do Tuareg veil their faces?', in R. H. Barnes, Daniel de Coppet and R. J. Parkin (eds.), *Context and Levels: Anthropological Essays on Hierarchy,* Jaso, Oxford, 68-77.

Dilley, Roy. 1999. 'Introduction: The Problem of Context', in R. Dilley (ed.), *The Problem of Context,* New York: Berghahn Books, 1-46.

Douglas, Mary. 1980. *Evans-Pritchard,* Glasgow: Fontana Paperbacks.

Dumont, Louis. 1986. *Essays on Individualism: Modern Ideology in Anthropological Perspective*, Chicago and London: The University of Chicago Press.

Easthope, Antony. 2001. 'Postmodernism and Critical and Cultural Theory', in S. Sim (ed.), *The Routledge Companion to Postmodernism,* London and New York: Routledge, 15-27.

Evans-Pritchard, E.E. 1962. 'Social Anthropology: Past and Present', in E.E. Evans-Pritchard, *Essays in Social Anthropology,* London: Faber and Faber, 13-28.

Firth, Raymond. 1954. 'Social Organization and Social Change', in *The Journal of the Royal Anthropological Institute of Great Britain and Ireland*, 84/1: 1-20.

Geertz, Clifford. 1975 [1973]. *The Interpretation of Cultures*, London: Hutchinson & Co.

Giddens, Anthony. 1984. *The Constitution of Society: Outline of a Theory of Structuration,* Berkeley: University of California Press.

Good, Anthony. 1981. 'Prescription, Preference and Practice: Marriage Patterns among the Kondaiyankottai Maravar of South India', in *Man*, 16: 108-29.

Hardenberg, Roland. 1999. *Die Wiedergeburt der Götter: Ritual und Gesellschaft in Orissa.* Hamburg: Verlag Dr Kovac.

Hertz, Robert. 1973 [1909]. 'The Pre-eminence of the Right Hand: A Study in Religious Polarity', in R. Needham (ed.), *Right and Left: Essays in Dual Symbolic Classification,* Chicago and London: The University of Chicago Press, 3-31.

Hobsbawm, Eric and Terence Ranger (eds.). 1983. *The Invention of Tradition.* Cambridge: Cambridge University Press.

Holy, Ladislav. 1999. 'Contextualisation and Paradigm Shifts', in R. Dilley (ed.), *The Problem of Context,* New York: Berghahn Books, 47-60.

Iteanu, André. 1990. 'The Concept of the Person and the Ritual System: An Orokaiva View', in *Man* (ns), 25: 399-418.

Jencks, Charles. 1975. *The Language of Post-Modern Architecture.* Revd. Edn. (1984), London: Academy Editions.

Lang, H. 1989. 'Was ist der Gegenstand der Verwandtschafts-ethnologie?', in *Zeitschrift für Ethnologie,* 114: 39-54.

Lyotard, Jean-Francois. 1979. *The Postmodern Condition: A Report on Knowledge,* Manchester: Manchester University Press.

Marcus, G. 1994. 'After the Critique of Ethnography: Faith, Hope, and Charity, but the Greatest of These is Charity', in R. Borofsky (ed.), *Assessing Cultural Anthropology,* New York: McGraw-Hill, 40-52.

Murdock, George P. 1949. *Social Structure,* New York: Macmillan.

Needham, Rodney (ed.). 1973b. *Right and Left: Essays on Dual Symbolic Classification,* Chicago and London: The University of Chicago Press.

— 1973a. 'Prescription', in *Oceania,* 42: 166-81.

Needham, Rodney. 1987. *Counterpoints,* University of California Press, Berkeley.

Pfeffer, Georg. 1992. 'Zur Verwandtschaftsethnologie', in *Zeitschrift für Ethnologie*, 117: 41-54.

Sahlins, Marshall. 1994. 'Goodbbye to Tristes Tropes: Ethnography in the Context of Modern World History', in R. Borofsky (ed.), *Assessing Cultural Anthropology,* New York: McGraw-Hill, 377-94.

— 1999a. 'Two or Three Things I Know About Culture', in *Journal of the Royal Anthropological Institute*, 5/3: 399-421.

— 1999b. 'What is Anthropological Enlightenment? Some Lessons of the Twentieth Century', in *Annual Review of Anthropology,* 28: i-xxiii.

Sim, Stuart. 2001. 'Postmodernism and Philosophy', in S. Sim (ed.), *The Routledge Companion to Postmodernism,* London and New York: Routledge, 3-14.

Tambiah, Stanley J. 1985 [1979]. 'A Performative Approach to Ritual', in S.J. Tambiah, *Culture, Thought and Social Action,* Cambridge: Harvard University Press, 123-66.

9

'Given by God' and 'Come by Itself': Concepts of Illness Among the Rona

Tina Otten

Research on tribal medicine is not very popular in India. Other Indian medical systems like the Ayurveda, Unani, and Siddha are better known and are practised in other countries as well.[1] By contrast, tribal medicine—in all its variations—is practised in secluded hill areas like the Koraput district[2] in the Eastern Ghats by Desya[3] society.

In this paper I offer first insights[4] into a medical system of knowledge[5] practised in rural Koraput. My material has been collected among a section of the Desya, the Rona,[6] and I intend to show that their social structure in general and their medical system

---

[1] There are quite a few works that cannot be discussed here. See, e.g. Daniel and Pugh (1984), Leslie and Young (1992).

[2] Koraput district is a highly fascinating area, condensing in a small district people of different tribes and classes. These groups speak languages which have their roots in three different families, in Munda, Dravidian and Indo-European. The *lingua franca* in the district is Desya.

[3] From the Sanskrit word *deśa* (land) *deśya* (Skt.) means 'belonging to the land', i.e. 'indigenous people'.

[4] The paper is part of an ongoing research project and some of the results presented here are still tentative and need to be strengthened by more field data.

[5] There is virtually no documentation on the Rona. Some works deal with tribal medicine or related topics in Orissa (Bailey 1997; Behura 1997; Boal 1982; Carrin 1980, 1986, 1991, 1999; Pati 1998; SCSTTI 1997a, 1997b; Vitebsky 1993), but none of them investigates the Koraput district in regard to the medical knowledge and practices of its inhabitants. Elwin's compendium (1954) contains some myths about illnesses, but the stories are collected from people who call themselves adivasi and not from the entire Desya society. The Rona are seen as strangers in the myths.

[6] The title 'Rona' refers to the royal Rajput title of 'Rana' applied to the noblemen of western India (Pfeffer 2001a). Most probably people in the service of the king of Jeypore adopted the title Rona in the course of Rajputization of Orissa in the eighteenth century (Banerjee 1928).

in particular corroborate the thesis that in all parts of society the whole is visible.[7] My main focus is the question of how parts of this indigenous knowledge are influenced by social structure. I will also see if and how these categories can be translated into Western terms.

Certain categories, structures, and symbols form the realms of health, illness, and the body. They mirror those values that constitute society. Values are often unconscious determinants of social behaviour of a given society, while people are aware of categories derived from these values. By investigating social categories about the body, the anthropologist thus concerns her/himself with concepts related society as a whole. This idea was forwarded by Mary Douglas (1973) under the influence of a paper on body techniques by Marcel Mauss.[8]

In this paper I aim to contribute to this field of research by investigating the social organization of healing specialists and the concepts of illness among the Rona. I strive to demonstrate connections to structural concepts of the tribal kind. I also hope to open up a new chapter of research; to this date, no study has been published on the Rona. Not being of the Scheduled Tribes category, they have been altogether overlooked in social anthropology.

The term 'Rona' carries two meanings. It alludes to a high social status within Desya society and it implies the occupation of Paiks,[9] the local militia. Of all Desya, the Rona are associated with service to the king. The importance of the royal function can be seen in the fact that even in 2001 the Rona have referred to the old realm of Nandapur as the 'real kingdom', even though the royal government

---

[7] This thesis of the *Année sociologique* was put forward in the analysis of healing rituals by Platenkamp (1996).

[8] 'Techniques of the Body' (1979) was presented by M. Mauss 1934 as a lecture to the Société de Psychologie in Paris. His main thesis is that body techniques are learned in different societies in different ways. He claims that body techniques and body concepts are not to be considered the same in every society. Therefore, what is considered 'natural' is in fact a highly complex and unconscious part of ideas that structure the worldview of a society. As Douglas puts it: 'The social body constrains the way the physical body is perceived. The physical experience of the body, always modified by the social categories through which it is known, sustains a particular view of society' (1973: 93).

[9] *Paiks* (Skt. *paadaka*) are the traditional peasant militia of the little kings of Orissa.

there ended around 1480. Later dynasties resided at Jeypore, some 40 km. away.[10] The former king of Nandapur appears as a mythical figure waiting to come back to his seat. The kings of Jeypore and the modern Indian government are given only temporary significance.

The word Desya can also be somewhat misleading, because it has two meanings as well. One refers to the 'Desya' as the indigenous people of Koraput as distinguished from those of the coastal plains. Secondly, the Rona distinguish between the 'Desya' on the one hand (those who, like the Rona, Mali, Sundi, Gouda and Kamar, do not eat beef and pork) and the 'Adivasi'[11] and 'Harijans' on the other (i.e. Gadaba, Kondh, Porja and Bondo (Adivasi) or musicians and basket weavers (Harijan)).

Desya		
Desya	**Adivasi**	**Harijan**
Rona, Mali, Gouda, Sundi, Kamar, etc.	Gadaba, Kondh, Joria Porja, Bhumia, etc.	Musicians, Weavers
Non-beef-eating	**Beef-eating**	

There is virtually no literature available on those people who do not consider themselves Adivasi, i.e. those who relate legends of their migration into the Koraput district in the service of the king. Such stories have been collected from among the Rona,[12] Mali[13] and Gouda.[14] In Koraput they can hardly be distinguished from the 'adivasi'-population, even though they wear the sacred thread to

[10] See Deo (1939), Chapter 1.

[11] In India we find the distinction between the first inhabitants of a place and the people who live there now. *Adi-* (Skt.) means 'first', *vaasin* (Skt.) means 'one who dwells'.

[12] See Choudhury (1963: 51-6) and Thurston (1987, 257-9).

[13] The name refers to the first occupations of the Mali: they make garlands and provide flowers for the service in Hindu temples. The Mali say that their ancestors lived originally at Kasi (Benares) whence they emigrated to serve under the Raja of Jeypore. Nowadays, most Mali are kitchen gardeners. Their vernacular is Oriya (Thurston 1987, 441).

[14] According to Thurston (1987, 273) the Gouda are the great pastoral caste among the Ganjam Oriyas and have been descendants of the Yadava tribe in which Krishna was born.

raise themselves symbolically above the tribal communities. In the present context, I will not speculate whether the Rona are 'actually' a tribe or a caste that was tribalized. For the present analysis it is more important that the Rona share a set of ideas with the 'adivasi': principle of seniority, intra-village relationships, and to exogamous totemic clans. The structural characteristics of the Rona community, just like those of other indigenous people, come close to the general sociological pattern of tribal societies.[15]

As a basic idea of tribal societies in Middle India, the principle of seniority is reflected in the ideas and values of hierarchy and affinity and in other values as well (Pfeffer 1982, 1997, 2000). Closely interwoven with the idea of seniority is the principle of equating alternate generations (McDougal 1963, Pfeffer 1994). The reflection of these basic ideas is the background of my article, in which I explore the realm of illness and its connection to hierarchy and affinity.

The Principle of Seniority and the Healing Specialists

The Desya society of Koraput is quite distinct from the Hindu society of the plains.[16] Of the diverging characteristics, the principle of seniority is the first to be mentioned. It divides the whole world of the Rona, and of Desya society in general, into a senior and a junior status segment. The terms are *boro* (senior) and *sano* (junior). This opposition does not signify older or younger in terms of biological age, but works as a structural principle. *Boro* indicates the values 'sacred, old, big, senior, and higher status' in comparison to others whereas *sano* indicates 'secular, young, small, junior, and lower status' in comparison to others. This basic distinction can be observed in many different aspects of society. The binary principle is generally applied without exception. Thus the healing specialists like all other village dignitaries are categorized according to the principle of seniority.

Healing is a specialized occupation, requiring an apprenticeship under a recognized practitioner and the ability to communicate with the deities. In the field of tribal medicine different fields of

---

[15] For more information about the structural pattern of tribal society see McDougal (1963), Pfeffer (1994). For general information see Pfeffer (2001b) and Sahlins (1968).

[16] See Pfeffer (2000).

knowledge are assigned to a variety of specialists. When they practise their skills, the rewards add to their daily income, even though nobody is an absolute professional. Most healers own fields and cultivate paddy or grow vegetables to make a living. They lack a formal education. Knowledge on health and illness is transferred orally or in visions and dreams. Only astrologers (*dissari*) know how to read and write and are able to use almanacs, calendars, and local puranas for their predictions and for arranging important rituals.

Some exceptional positions in the village are hereditary and accorded only to males. Among the ritual specialists, astrologers and sacrificers (*pujari*) belong to this category. Their positions go to their (classificatory) sons. Others can be obtained by merit only, like the post of a spirit medium (*gurumai*)[17] or that of midwife (*dhai*). At times, the relatives of a common local line perform the same task within alternate generations. This may imply that a *gurumai* will transmit her abilities to her (classificatory) granddaughter rather than to her daughter.

In some cases the *gurumai*'s mother as well as her daughter may be a *dhai*, while her granddaughter will again become a *gurumai*.[18] The observation is a reminder of a general tendency to equate alternating generations in all spheres of life. This relational pattern, observed long ago by Radcliffe-Brown (1952) in many societies of the globe, has been described elsewhere in central India by reference to affinal relationships and death rituals.[19]

Every ritual position is conceived in pairs. On the village level, a senior astrologer (*boro dissari*) opposes a junior one (*sano dissari*), and the same holds true for a senior medium (*boro gurumai*) and a

---

[17] Spirit mediumship is here understood as an active process of ritual specialists to act as a medium for gods and spirits in contrast to shamanism. Following Eliade's definition (1964), 'shamanism' includes a shamanic journey to the underworld and the heaven, the climbing of the world tree. The soul of a spirit medium does not travel. Instead it awaits the gods and spirits in her or his environment. Further discussion of the terms 'spirit possession', 'spirit mediumship' and 'shamanisms' will be be the subject of another paper, including the discussions raised in the works of Aitkinson (1992) and Boddy (1994).

[18] If there should be a general structure it has to be verified with more field data.

[19] Classificatory grandparents call their classificatory grandchildren 'husband' or 'wife'. See also Pfeffer (1994).

junior one (*sano gurumai*), a senior sacrificer (*boro pujari*) and a junior one (*sano pujari*). Not every village is necessarily endowed, however, with such a pair of specialists. Sometimes a village has no *dissari*, sometimes many. The importance of bifurcation comes to light in the performance of important annual rituals. Here we may perceive the principle called 'dual sovereignty' by Needham (1980) and applied to Middle Indian Society by Pfeffer (1982: 6).

The senior *dissari* has an important role in the affairs of the entire village, like festivals, while the junior ritual specialist will be called for minor occasions only. In the case of spirit mediumship (*gurumai*), the twofold division is even encountered twice: first there is the distinction between the junior singing and dancing *gurumai* and the higher valued divining *gurumai*. Furthermore, within these categories the distinction between *boro* (higher status) and *sano* (lower status) medium can be observed at the annual rituals. The same principle is responsible for the ranking of the ritual specialists in the area. The Rona seem to consider a particular *dissari* and a certain *gurumai* of the Lamtaput Block as the senior-most among the others, even though this spatial concept is not viewed in meticulous administrative terms.

Categories of Illness and their Social Implications

In the Koraput region, no overall doctrine of medical, religious, or social knowledge is accepted. Even though I spoke to many ritual specialists, all had slightly different explanations. Certain general 'prototypes' of medical knowledge may, however, be discovered.

The particular situation of research must be taken into account. For me as a Western visitor, local categories at times appeared to be blurred, insofar as the explanation for some illness listed several different causes.[20] Consequently I was bound to ask myself how 'sure' and 'safe' the categories to be presented were. Having discussed the issues at length with several specialists and laypersons, eight major categories finally emerged.[21] The Rona do

[20] Allen (1976) describes this situation for the Thulung in Nepal.

[21] The material for this article was collected in many lengthy discussions and tape recordings with a traditional midwife (*dhai*), two prominent and accepted astrologers (*dissari*), the most famous medium (*gurumai*) in the district, and the women and men of the neighbourhood of

not explicitly name them as the *eight* categories causing illness, but they are seen as *the* 'reasons' of illness. There may be more such categories, but since the number eight plays a prominent role in the structure of socio-cultural categories in Hindu and tribal society, I suggest that it is applicable to the present case as well,[22] in the same way as the eightfold system of totemic clans is applicable among the Rona.[23]

The eight causes of illness imply different values. Accordingly I would like to suggest a ranking in an order reminiscent of the hierarchical pattern of seniority. The senior-most cause of illness is related to a person's fate and is named *bhagyo onusare*[24] or 'according to one's fortune'. The fortune is given to a person by the gods. Illnesses of this category have a wide social relevance because they are seen as predetermined for the person according to his or her actions in former lives. In contrast, the cause of illness ranked junior-most is called *tar monke heba ro*[25] or 'of its own accord' and refers to illnesses that have developed in the physical, 'natural' body without a predetermined cause.[26] Illnesses of the—

Rona village where Sunita and I lived. The recordings were translated by Sunita Suna and her brother Sunny David Suna.

[22] The number 'eight' occurs in many different contexts, for instance the eight cardinal points, the eight totems and the eight main categories of souls of the deceased (*duma*). In 1926, Mark Collins put forward a curious hypothesis of a tribal origin of the dominant number eight in India. He believed that the octal system and its multiples are of Dravidian origin and were originally developed by 'primitive Dravidians of northern India who preceded the Aryans as settlers along the Indus and the Ganges' (Collins 1974: 193). The 'eight half-hooves of the buffalo' are supposed to have given them the idea of the octal system.

[23] The eight subdivisions or totems among the Rona are: 1. Sun (*kora*), 2. Cobra (*nag*), 3. Tiger (*bagh*), 4. Bird (*chorei*), 5. Fish (*macho*), 6. Bear (*balu,*) 7. Cow (*goru*) and 8. Monkey (*hanuman*). Sun is ranked senior-most.

[24] *Bhagyo onusare* is: *onusare* – according to; *bhagyo* – fortune, luck, destiny.

[25] '*tar monke heba rog*' means in direct translation: *tar* – its, her, his; *mon* – 1. the mind, will, seat of emotions; 2. liking, desire, longing; *heba* – to be, to come; *rog* - illness.

[26] As we are concerned with concepts of the body and their reflection of social ideas, it should also be understood that the concept of a 'natural' body is always culture-bound (see Lock 1993).

physical—body are by no means less serious and may also cause much suffering or death, as is the case with puerperal fever or malaria which are endemic in the district. These illnesses, however, have little social relevance, because no other agents of the Desya world, such as gods or the souls of the deceased, are involved. Thus such illnesses are of lower status.

Contrasting the senior-most category with the junior-most, the idea of the person, his/her agency in the community and the physical body are distinguished clearly. Following Douglas (1973), the concept of the social or socialized body on one hand, and that of the physical body on the other, must be kept apart. Most illnesses relate to agency. They are said to be caused by agents related to the afflicted. Issues of social life coincide with the outbreak of an illness.[27]

Diagnosis of the illness may vary according to its development. In a case of worsening, the healing specialist may revise his initial diagnosis or come to the conclusion that other agents are at work. Other experts may diagnose different causes for the same illness. Such variations are not seen as mutually contradictory, but as simply coexistent, a feature frequently observed in Indian reasoning (Eichinger Ferro Luzzi 1989).

Categories of Illness

In describing the causes of illness, I shall concentrate on the categories as such, rather than on all the numerous maladies included in a specific category. A few examples of illnesses will have to suffice.

---

[27] Primary Health Care programmes have created an awareness that some illnesses can be cured by 'modern medicine'. The impact of modern medicine will be the subject of another paper.

Eight Categories of Illness

Category in Desya	English Translation	Ranking
Bhagyo onusare	according to one's fortune	high
Mapuru jor	fever given by gods	
Depta jor	fever given by (lower) gods	
Pangan	sorcery	
Daini kaiba	witchcraft	
Duma	spirits of the deceased	
Disti	evil eye	
Tar monke heba rog	it comes of its own accord	low

Tar monke heba rog (Illness coming of its own accord)

In the junior-most category, illnesses are caused by a condition of the physical body.[28] exposure to rough weather in the hills, unhealthy conditions in the mud huts, insufficient, wrong or poisoned food, and exhaustion due to overwork.

Obviously some illnesses which are ranked in this category occur predominantly in certain months of the year, while others, at other times of the year, are linked to socially relevant categories. The common cold, for example, is a seasonal illness appearing 'of its own accord', while cholera, a typical disease of the rainy season, is sent by certain divine agents.

The highest-ranking illness within this category is puerperal fever (*pokti molu*). I was most astonished to hear that the explanation for this fever was 'of its own accord' because birth and death are closely related to the socially relevant ideas of incarnation as well as the quality of a person's relationships to the souls of the deceased. Apparently, however, the Rona do not see a direct relation between a child's birth and the mother's death. Instead,

---

[28] Consequently, concepts of the body differ from concepts found in biomedical view (Hahn and Kleinman 1983). In this paper I refer to the Desya concept of the body. One of the most important notions about the Desya concept of the body is the vulnerability and permeability to influences from outside which enter the body.

they explain the demise as the total exhaustion of the body after labour.

Other illnesses, ranked junior in relation to puerperal fever, are specific forms of malaria (*malia jor*). Our biomedical concept of malaria is unified, i.e. it derives from a single cause, whereas the Rona attribute the illness to several causes, depending on the circumstances of diagnosis. *Malia jor,* related to bodily causes only, is distinguished from fevers caused by gods or the malevolent souls of the deceased. These fevers of the second category, which a biomedical eye would also diagnose as a form of malaria, are caused by an agent requiring pacification in ritual. All this may be explained by the fact that the biomedical concept of malaria was unknown to my hosts until recently.[29] In 1991, or only ten years earlier, the doctors of the new hospital in the neighbourhood began to explain the concept of malaria to the local people.[30] Thereafter the Rona incorporated the concept *malia jor* into their causes of illness under the category of natural causes with little social relevance.

This example may show how the Rona chose to deal with new concepts and social change. Generally I would suggest that they (just like other Desya) put new concepts in the category *sano*. The fact that everything new is *sano* also helps to explain why hierarchically junior sections of their society may be allowed to experiment in new religions, in the system of formal schooling, and in other modern innovations.[31]

Other illnesses coming 'of their own accord' are headache (*mund duka*), fevers in the hot season when the patient vomits due to the overheating of his body (*tati tikan jor*), fever appearing on alternate days and various versions of the common cold (*losom dabok*, *sitlijor*). The logic behind the common colds of infants is also attributed to this category: if infants have a cold (*sitlijor*), it is said to have been caused by mothers who consumed 'cold' substances. Due to this belief the grandmother of a child would

---

[29] This fact was astonishing indeed because Primary Health Centres have been active in the area since the nineteen-sixties.

[30] There are other programmes against illnesses as well, such as those against leprosy and tuberculosis which are endemic in the district. The impact of biomedical concepts upon the perception of these illnesses will be discussed in another paper.

[31] See Guzy (2001) and Otten (2001).

forbid the mother to drink water in the first weeks after delivery. At that time mothers are supposed to eat and drink edibles that warm up the body with meat, bamboo shoots, and mild country liquor. Against illnesses of the lowest category, herbs or other oral medicine are taken. No rituals are required in such cases.

Disti (Evil eye)

As opposed to the category discussed above, this has social implications. It is called *disti*, the evil eye, and is connected with sentiments of envy.[32] The Rona distinguish between *disti* of envious neighbours, often kinsmen, and an illness called *graham disti*, which is caused by the gods of the planets.[33] For *graha disti*, ranked senior, one has to pacify the gods of the planets with offerings. For normal *disti*, ranked junior, a ritual is needed to eliminate it or to return it to its source. The ritual lasts a few minutes and may be performed at any time of day, preferably in the house.

The normal remedy for symptoms of *disti* is a belly-massage with castor oil. On completion the healer blows away the evil with his breath and sweeps it away with a broom. Since the *disti* ritual is of minor status, any healing specialist can perform it. *Disti* is often diagnosed in people with stomach problems. This is connected with the ingestion of food upon which the eyes of another person have been cast. Presumably the latter act is instrumental in removing the life sustaining ingredients of the food, which are mentally devoured before the victim eats the 'mental' leftover. This leftover would, of course, belong to the category of impure and polluting intake. Such an interpretation is supported by the fact that the purity of food is generally most important. People of high esteem are supposed to stop eating if they hear an invective.

Innumerable stories deal with people envious of a person's food, wishing to consume it themselves. Such envy is the cause of illness. In many cases, the tale concludes with the punishment of the 'thief'.

---

[32] *Disti* (Skt. *drsthi*) means look. This concept of illness is known in nearly all cultures throughout the world, but apart from the term the meaning varies considerably (Eichinger Ferro Luzzi 1989).

[33] In Rona community, *graha disti* is usually caused by Saturn (Sani). In Hindu astrology Sani is also a very important god. The planet god Saturn is endowed with such terrible power in the gaze of his eyes that even the planets and gods take ill and continue to suffer (Svoboda 2000).

For example, in one story a person wants to eat another's pumpkin; consequently, his head transforms into something like a pumpkin,[34] indicating the danger for both persons involved. Stories about pregnant women are even more serious. When a baby is born, the food that the mother had formerly desired to take from a third person will be visible on the baby's body. Such stories are told to explain the deformations of some babies.[35]

Duma ('Spirits' of the deceased)

The second-highest category of illness is caused by beings from the realm of the dead. When a person dies his/her soul turns into a *duma*, acting according to her or his own will The *duma* dwell in cremation grounds and are associated with ashes and dust, the sole remains of a person's body. They can be observed in the form of a dust devil, but usually, they lack a physical shape. The *duma* enter the realm of the living at dusk with the homecoming cattle, visiting their live relatives at night. *Duma* of important men whose memorial stones have been planted at a meeting place of the men of the village (*sadar*) will assemble there at night. They interact with people through dreams and possessions, forcing the living to fulfil their desires, if necessary by resorting to special powers.

Among the many different communities of the Koraput District, the concept of *duma* varies considerably. The manner in which the different communities and tribes envisage the realm of the dead and care for the departed souls is one of the crucial points of distinction between Scheduled Tribes, Other Backward Classes and Scheduled Castes. Some, for instance, invite the *duma* in order to pacify them with conciliatory rituals. The Rona, however, try to keep them out of the villages in order to avoid any type of interaction.

Common to all Koraput communities is the belief in *duma* as such, as well as the idea of a transitory stage, which is associated with the *duma*. Among the Rona, the transition is that from junior

---

[34] A similar story is told about Rübezahl, a spirit in German fairy tales, who takes revenge on a greedy inn-keeper by forcing him to lay two dozen eggs which the inn-keeper had eaten from the dish ordered by one of his guests.

[35] As a general rule however, a pregnant women will be fed with all food items and when and wherever she desires to have them.

to senior *duma*. People who die initially become *sano duma*. They are very dangerous for the living agnates of their respective local lines. The *duma* are known by their names and often possess family members in order to demand new clothes and the food they loved most when still alive. Later they become *boro duma*, no longer known by name. *Boro duma* rarely come to possess their family members but, if unfed, pose a danger during ritual.

When a person dies, his or her *duma* will belong to one of various categories of spirits. Those are often described in eight varieties, but never explicitly accounted for as such.[36] The way in which a person dies determines the resultant *duma*. Often the tiger spirit (*baghduma*) is named first. Vitebsky describes this category as a place in which all the spirits of those people gather who were killed by wild animals. The Rona do not have a similar spatial concept, but know of this kind of collective spirit category as well.

In the river spirit (*gadduma*) the remains of all victims of drowning are assembled. Women who have died during pregnancy or childbirth will be in the 'lady in labour' spirit (*chulguniduma*). The children who die before they can speak, and who are therefore not cremated but buried, enter the *mirchiduma*. People who die from *bor jor* (small pox) go to the *nindgoladuma* and those who are killed by cholera go to the *mordiduma*. Victims of trees they have felled or burnt down for slash and burn cultivation have been attacked by the forest spirit (*bonduma*) because they had 'mistreated the wilderness'. The only benevolent category among the *duma* is the house spirit (*ghorduma*), but sometimes even this category of spirit brings fever. It arrives after 3 o'clock during the day[37] and departs around midnight. Except for those of the house

---

[36] Piers Vitebsky (1993), in his work on the memories or souls of the dead (*sonum*) in Saora Society has listed seven main categories of *sonum* and one miscellaneous *sonum* category. His main *sonum* are: 1. Sun *sonum*, 2. Convulsion, epilepsy, spasm *sonum*; 3. Earth *sonum*, 4. Leopard *sonum*, 5. Ra`tud *sonum* (untranslatable) 6. Ruga-boj (smallpox woman) 7. Sorcery *sonum*; 8. Miscellaneous *sonums*. The concept of *sonum* has similarities with the concept of *duma* in Desya society; even though the *duma* concept does not have the significance for the community as the *sonum* in Saora society.

[37] This is the time when the cows and buffaloes come back to the village from the fields. In tribal communities, cows and buffaloes play a crucial role in connection with the death ceremonies. Sometimes, an

spirit (*ghorduma*) and the spirit of small children (*mirchiduma*), all other categories of *duma* stand for a sudden and often violent death and are feared as more harmful than the other two.

Daini kaiba ('Witch' is eating)

In a community structured on the principles of kinship and affinity, and adhering to preferential cross-cousin marriage of the bilateral type, the realm of illness and health is also influenced by the overall structuring principle of marriage alliance. When a Rona falls ill, a healing specialist from among his agnates in the village, the local line or *kuda*, initially inquires about the cause of the illness. If his treatment is not effective other healing specialists will be called. They may be either Rona of other villages and kin groups or specialists from various tribes. In the latter case, specialists with a high reputation are preferably invited. Accusations of witchcraft[38] (*daini kaiba*) and sorcery (*pangan*) are often seen as the source of illness. They are associated with suspects of the agnatic line as well, since close relatives are known to be the fiercest enemies. The following two categories of illness will further illustrate these social implications.

People are extremely afraid of witchcraft. The indigenous term, *daini kaiba* [39] denotes a witch (*daini*) in the process of eating (*kaiba*). People carry the notion that neighbours are capable of making themselves invisible at night. These witches fly naked to the houses of their victims, sit on the roof and—by the aid of an invisible reed used like an ordinary straw—suck the blood out of the sleepers' bodies. Other witches are said to prey on the liver (*koloj*), the most important organ of the body and closely related to life-energy (*jibon*).

After an attack from a *daini,* a victim notices bruises on his or her body the following morning. The witches prefer to devour the blood (*rokto*) and *koloj* of their relatives. I've seen many a woman

---

animal acts as the body who carries the soul of a deceased. For further details see Berger (2001a) in this volume.

[38] I hesitate to translate the concept as 'witchcraft' because witchcraft has other connotations in the English language.

[39] In other parts of India the word *dahini* denotes a woman who has died in labour (Kakar 1992).

in despair, convinced that a close relative was killing her baby in this manner.

There are special rituals to catch witches. A mother with a new born baby is never left alone at night. Another woman, knowledgeable in the evil designs of witches, sleeps next to her in order to sense any disturbance on the roof.

Informants mentioned that any witch, while sucking blood, could be made visible by a spell from an experienced witch-hunter. This spell also glues the witch to the roof whence she can be taken down and punished. People wear amulets to ward off the witches and other malevolent influences. Infants wear necklaces of garlic and other materials around their necks and waists for this purpose.

Widows who live alone in single households are often accused of being witches who devour the organs of other people's bodies. They like the liver of relatives who are junior (*sano*) to them, and prey especially upon newly born babies. In one case, I could observe people telling each other behind the back of an old lady that she was the witch who ate the liver of a baby girl. The old lady was the girl's father's mother's sister (classificatory FM). She lived in a state of poverty alone in a very small hut and had to beg for food every day. During my inquiries I came to know that all women after menopause who lived alone as widows had been thrown out of the houses of their sons and had thereafter been accused of witchcraft.

A common feature of Koraput and other tribal societies is the antagonism between adjacent generations, especially the aggression directed by the younger towards the older generation (Pfeffer 2000). This antagonism is regularly known to lead to quarrels between son and parents, and even lead parricide at times. Similarly, strong antagonisms between brothers are a common feature and often lead to accusations of sorcery (*pangan*).

Pangan (Sorcery)

Fraternal strife regularly leads to rumours. Brothers are said to have killed each other by *pangan* in order to 'eat' the other's share of landed property. The act is carried out by a *gunia*. The latter generally has the ambiguous role of causing as well as healing illness. Moreover, the *gunia* identified as the culprit later on is often called to set things right again unless, of course, the victim has died.

People say that some of the *gunia* are also able to command certain *duma* (spirit of the deceased) to carry out their deadly work.

Gunia can conjure materials such as fish-bones, glass, wood, or frogs into the body of the victim. Such materials weaken or kill a person. The body of the person bloats and the victim, in pain and lacking appetite, loses his or her life energy. The rituals performed in order to cure the illness aim to return the evil energies to the sender. For this, an effigy of the suspect is formed out of mud and destroyed at the peak of the ritual. This act is often accompanied by the ritual killing of a crayfish.

Other symptoms, not leading to immediate death but known to be caused by *pangan,* are a woman's infertility, certain fevers, and nightmares. As far as the responsibility for these effects is concerned, the *gunia,* by performing a rite, is believed to have put items on a path somewhere outside the village. The first to step over the –sometimes invisible—objects on the path draws the illness into her or his body. Often people believe that affines from neighbouring villages order a *gunia* to carry out these rituals near their own village. Other sufferings caused by *pangan* are *cerang bat* (rheumatism) and blindness in old age. All illnesses in this category are connected with social relationships.

Depta jor (Fever brought by gods)

We have seen that the above categories are closely related to concepts of kinship. The next is related to the realm of the deities. Illnesses in this category are fevers caused by gods (*depta*).

Among the *depta jor* the number eight features again when the subcategories of fever are counted. Seven different types of Saturn fever (*sani jor*) oppose one type of Rahu[40] fever (*rahu jor*). The significance and importance of Saturn in the Koraput district is immense. Many healing ceremonies I have seen involved Saturn, and most of the fevers (*jor*) are diagnosed as being effected by him. Moreover, the healing specialist only begins to treat a patient after the gods have indicated that they refuse to take the ill person on the occasion.

Saturn and Rahu seem to be the rulers of time: Saturn is the lord of the week, for every day of the week has a different Saturn—and

[40] In Hindu astrology, Rahu is the north node of the moon.

therefore a different type of fever—Rahu is the ruler of dawn. The time of Rahu is twilight, just before the rays of the sun touch the earth. This is a crucial time for the beginning or ending of important rituals. Rahu is also connected with wind and with disorder.

Epilepsy would also be included in the category of *depta jor* as *upriya jor* and *murcha jor*. Depending on the time of occurrence, the Rona distinguish at least these two types of epilepsy.

Mapuru jor (Fever brought by gods)

Like the previous category, the second -highest category of illnesses refers to fevers 'given by gods' (*mapuru jor*). The distinction between the category '*depta*' and the category '*mapuru*' again refers to gods or deities of higher (*mapuru*) and lower status (*depta*).

The gods, most of all the goddess Thakurani in all her local variations, want to 'eat' the body of the affected person and therefore manifest themselves within the particular body. The category of *mapuru jor, boro jor* is ranked highest. The direct translation of *boro jor* is 'senior fever', known in English as smallpox. Cholera (*mordi*) is also part of the category of *mapuru jor*. Another type of fever is called *mojha lok* (middle people) and is most probably the same as chickenpox in English. Yet another type is named *gundimatra*, which is most probably measles. Among several other fevers these are the main varieties.

People who die from illnesses of the *mapuru jor* category are considered to be 'sleeping' (*nin ailani*) rather than 'dead' (*mori gola*). The patient remains between the worlds and enters into a special group of *duma*. Normal death rites will be avoided. His or her body is not carried to the cremation ground and burned there, but at some other place. Accordingly, the most important distinction between *mapuru jor* and *depta jor* is that people who die from *depta jor* are buried with the normal funeral rites.

Bhagyo onusare (According to one's fortune)

The senior-most category of illnesses is called *bhagyo onusare* ('according to one's fortune or destiny'). The important point is that the illnesses in this category are predetermined before a person's birth and can be caused during his or her lifetime, while the illnesses in the other categories are only caused during a lifetime. The former therefore have the biggest influence on the entire existence of the person, both in the physical and in the social sense. Fortune depends upon two features: as in the Hindu karmic existence, deeds in the former life determine the present one; but Fortune also depends upon luck. The gods whom a person meets before being born on his or her way to the earth (*monchpur*) are decisive. They determine the burden of one's life according to their sympathy. The individual burden is closely related to the social person: it depends upon the social position he or she is born into, as well as on his or her agency. Often but not always, this concept is explained by the effect of the nine planet gods *nanograha*[41] upon the life of a person. Frequently, however, it is related to the difficulties faced by a spirit when trying to find its way to earth or back to human existence and encountering deities in that course.

The effects of illnesses of the senior-most category have serious consequences for the whole agnatic line: in the case of the outstanding disease, leprosy (*kusto rog*), the agnates will face considerable difficulties in arranging the marriages of their children. Moreover, their lives will be rather isolated. By implication the future of the whole line is in danger.

These senior-most illnesses are rarely called by their real name. Leprosy is referred to as senior disease (*boro rog*) and the slightly junior ranked *gond* is described by its features, but not by name.[42] People fear that even the naming of the illness will attract the attention of the deities responsible. Therefore at least the highest ranking category of illness has direct long-term effects upon society.

---

[41] This concept is widely known in Indian tradition and refers to the planet gods Sun (Surya), Moon (Chandra), Mars (Mangal), Mercury (Budha), Jupiter (Guru), Venus (Sukra), Saturn (Sani), Rahu and Ketu. However, healing rituals in the Koraput district concentrate on Sani, Rahu, the Moon and the Sun.

[42] Here is a structural similarity with concepts of illness in Ayurvedic medicine. There the illness which is ranked highest is called *rajrog* (the king of illnesses or the illness of the king). In biomedical terms *rajrog* is tuberculosis.

Example of an illness of the category *bhagyo onusare*: *gond*

The social relevance of illnesses that come 'according to one's fortune' will be demonstrated using the example *gond*, a word that cannot be translated into English.[43] There is no indication of any connection to the Gond tribe even though the name may suggest this. Junior only in relation to leprosy, *gond* is among the senior-most diseases. As we shall see, the concept of *gond* is closely related to the role of women in society.

Gond is the name of creatures said to be like insects growing and moving freely within the bodies of women. The concept of *gond* is wide-spread in Koraput, even Christians and Muslims believe in, or at least know of it. *Gond* is transmitted by women (and very rarely by men), but not every woman carries it. The insects in the body of a woman are believed to consume the woman's husband and her offspring up to the third child at least. In the end, they kill her. It is said that a child whose mother has had *gond* often has these insects in her or his body because *gond* may be transmitted through breastfeeding. In the latter case the insects turn the milk into blood. In drinking this blood-milk, the child takes ill and is soon close to death.

A *gond* in a boy often kills him, while a girl is more likely to survive. The manner by which a man may contract *gond* is sexual intercourse, but he is only affected if it is his destiny. A *gond* insect can reside inside a girl's body without harming her and become active only after she has reached maturity and has had sexual intercourse. If a *gond* is diagnosed in time, a healing specialist, a sorcerer called *gunia*, may be able to extract it.

My Rona hosts told me that the number of different insects (*gond*) is twelve, but they could name and describe only six, leaving open the question of ranking. Thus the following description implies no senior-junior relation. The six named categories are *idla gond* (three insects), *jogol gond* (two insects), *jalendri gond* (spider-in-a-web), *nag nari* (insect like a long stick, like the Milky Way), *bagh gond* (tiger insect) and *sap gond* (snake insect).

---

[43] In this article I can only give a first insight into the meaning of *gond*. The work is still in progress and may serve here as a first illustration of indigenous categories.

The number of insects in a body is often two as in *jogol gond*. When these two insects unite inside the body of a woman, they kill her. The more insects in a body, the higher the risk of uniting, i.e. if three insects are in a body as in *idla gond*. The insect called *jalendri gond* resides in the body of the affected person like a spider in a web. The exact location of this web, called *mahindra jal*, can be anywhere in a body from the forehead to the lower part of the belly. The metaphor of the web is also used to characterize fortune or destiny. Fortune as a web is woven by the nine planet gods (*nanograha*) for each single person. It is the materialized form of destiny inside a person's body.

The same concept can be found behind the imagery of *nag nari*. This insect looks like a stick and is located somewhere between the forehead and the anus. The name of the insect is also the indigenous name for the Milky Way. The Milky Way extends from one side of the night sky to the other, as does the insect in the body. A symbolic merger of body and cosmos may be detected in this image.

Additionally, the web of the planet gods and the Milky Way play a crucial role in almost all healing rituals. Of the remaining two insects, the Rona could name one which is said to be spotted like a tiger skin, while the other is supposed to have the shape of a snake. Interestingly, the names of the main affinal clans who intermarry are the 'snake' and the 'tiger'. This could also indicate the dangers involved in affinal relations.

Generally this category of illness, transmittable through women and often lethal for men, refers to crucial values of Rona society. It reflects the role of women and the concept of the body as a part of the cosmos, in which the whole is visible. The role of women in Rona society is related to affinity, to the female reproductive power, and to the impurity of women. All these concepts are closely related to socially determined time.

The impurity of girls and women is related to their reproductive power, to be tamed in two important life cycle rituals. One is carried out before maturity, another thereafter. Both rituals must be conducted at an auspicious time. The correct performance of life cycle rituals is crucial for a woman. Later, during her married life, diseases of her husband or her children are often explained as the result of a lifecycle ritual improperly carried out. If a woman reaches maturity at an inauspicious time of the year, she is often prohibited to marry at all. Her only option then is to elope with a suitor.

The concept of the illness *gond* reveals a conflict immanent in the organization of Rona socicty: from a male point of view, we could say that the need to give away the sister and to take women from outside into the village is an invitation to external danger for the patrilineal descent group. Such women come from a group of permanent affines who are not part of the village. The women themselves stress their alien character and remain strangers in their conjugal village. The relation to affinity is also apparent in rituals removing the *gond* that are carried out in a brook next to a wet rice field (*beda*). Berger (2001b) has recently observed the symbolic relation between wet rice fields and affines. Following this reasoning, the ritual of 'extracting *gond*' would symbolically 'extract the danger' affiliated with affinity.

The danger of *gond* and its relation to sexuality also links it to life in general: as a women gives life, she also sends it onto a path that inevitably ends in death. A woman's impurity is closely connected with her ability to reproduce. Women who become sexually active are the source of reproduction since they have all the inherent ambiguous powers.[44] This dangerous power is expressed in the idea that the female body can play host to dangerously devouring beings. Her powers enable her to survive where a male body would die. In other words, the body of a woman seems to be stronger in resisting the consuming forces, but her power entails the danger of transferring the deadly forces. In this case we find the distinction between power and status: women are related to the power of reproduction, but their status and purity is junior to that of men.

The concept of femaleness in general focuses on the power to 'create' and to 'destroy'. It is therefore closely related to worldly or polluting affairs. By contrast, the concept of maleness, lacking this ability, remains in a 'purer' state. This idea, roughly sketched, is a prototype of Hindu thought. Among the Rona, the concept of permanent female pollution is equally prominent. It may is manifest in the belief that women are, due to their 'polluted' state, unable to

---

[44] Here I can only refer to some works which illustrate this idea. They have been carried out in different regions of India and Nepal, most of them among high caste women: Bennett (1983), Fruzetti (1982), Hershman (1977), Tokita Tanabe (1999) and Thompson (1985).

consult the stars and determine auspicious or inauspicious times. In the eyes of a Rona, only he who is able to read the signs of the stars is able to announce the time for important rituals and activities which ascertain the continuation of the Rona community as such.

Conclusion

This paper was intended to put forth certain hypotheses on the interrelations between ideas of illness and the structure of society. As part of an ongoing research endeavour,[45] many more themes and questions remain unmentioned. I wanted to demonstrate how the principle of seniority and other socio-structural ideas similarly determine concepts of illness. The organization of healing specialists and Rona concepts of illness are constructed and valued by reference to their general worldview. The categories of illness reflect the structures constituting society, i.e. the totemic clan system; the equation of alternate, and the opposition of adjacent, generations, the concept of affinity with implications of hidden hostility, and the principle of seniority.

References

Aitkinson, J.M. 1992. 'Shamanisms Today', in *Annual Review of Anthropology* 21, 307-30.

Allen, N.J. 1976. 'Approaches to Illness in the Nepalese Hills', in J.B. Loudon (ed.), *Social Anthropology and Medicine*, London: Academic Press, 500-52.

Bailey, F.G. 1997. *A Witch-Hunt in an Indian Village or, the Triumph of Morality*, Delhi: Oxford University Press.

Banerjee, R.D. 1928. 'Rajput Origins in Orissa', in *Modern Review* 43, 285-91.

Behura, N.K. 1997. 'Cultural Dimensions of Diseases and Their Treatment: Case Studies from Tribal Societies of Orissa', in *Adivasi* 37 (2), 1-20.

---

[45] I take the opportunity to thank Sunita Suna for her collaboration and friendship in the field.

Bennett, L. 1983. *Dangerous Wives and Sacred Sisters : Social and Symbolic Roles of High-Caste Women in Nepal*, New York: Columbia University.

Berger, P. 2001a. 'Feeding the Dead: Rituals of Transformation among the Gadaba of Koraput', in *Adivasi* (in print).

— 2001b. 'Reis, Milch und Blut: Prozesse der Produktion und Reproduktion im Hochland Orissas', paper presented at ICAS 2001, Berlin.

Boal, B.M. 1982. *The Khonds: Human Sacrifice and Religious Change*, Warminster: Aris & Phillips.

Boddy, J. 1994. 'Spirit Possession Revisited: Beyond Instrumentality', in *Annual Review of Anthropology* 23, 407-34.

Carrin-Bouez, M. 1980. 'Des Maux et des Mots', in *L'Homme* XX (3), 85-107.

— 1986. *La Fleur et L'Os. Symbolisme et Rituel chez les Santal*, Cahiers de l'Homme, n.s. 16, Paris.

Carrin, M. (ed.) 1999. *Managing Distress: Possession and Therapeutic Cults in South Asia*, Delhi: Manohar.

Choudhury, B. 1963. 'Notes on the Ranas of Koraput', in *Adivasi*, 51-6.

Collins, M. 1974 (1926). 'On the Octaval System of Reckoning in India', in M. Collins (ed.), in *Dravidic Studies*, Madras: University of Madras, 169-211.

Daniel, V. and J.F. Pugh (eds.) 1984. 'South Asian Systems of Healing', in *Contributions to Asian Studies* 18, Leiden: E.J. Brill.

Douglas, M. 1973 (1970). *Natural Symbols. Explorations in Cosmology*, London: Barrie and Jenkins.

Eichinger Ferro-Luzzi, G. 1989. 'The Polythetic-Prototype Approach to Hinduism', in G.D. Sontheimer and H. Kulke (eds.), *Hinduism Reconsidered*, Delhi: Manohar, 187-95.

Eliade, M. 1964. *Shamanism: Archaic Techniques of Ecstasy*, Princeton: Princeton University Press.

Elwin, V. 1954. *Tribal Myths of Orissa*, Bombay: Oxford University Press.

Fruzetti, L.M. 1982. *The Gift of a Virgin: Women, Marriage, and Ritual in a Bengali Society*, New Brunswick, N.J: Rutgers University Press.

Guzy, L. 2001. 'Voices of Gods: Ecstatic Alekhs and Local Configurations of Mahima Dharma', in *Adivasi* (in print).

Hahn, R.A. and A. Kleinman. 1983. 'Biomedical Practice and Anthropological Theory: Frameworks and Directions', in *Annual Review of Anthropology* 12, 305-33.

Hershman, P. 1977. 'Virgin and Mother', in I. Lewis (ed.), *Symbols and Sentiments: Cross-Cultural Studies in Symbolism*, London: Academic Press, 269-92.

Kakar, S. 1992 (1982). *Shamans, Mystics and Doctors: A Psychological Inquiry into India and its Healing Traditions*, Delhi: Oxford University Press.

Leslie C. and A. Young (eds.). 1992. *Paths to Asian Medical Knowledge*, Berkeley, Los Angeles, Oxford: University of California Press.

Lock, M. 1993. 'The Anthropology of the Body', in *Annual Review of Anthropology* 22, 133-53.

McDougal, C.W. 1963. 'The Social Structure of the Hill Juang', unpublished Dissertation, The University of Mexico.

Mauss, M. 1979 (1935). 'Body Techniques', in *Sociology and Psychology*, 97-123.

Otten, T. 2000. 'In a Remote Area: Categories of the Person and Illness among the Desya of Koraput, Orissa', in *Journal of Social Sciences*, 4(4), 347-56.

— 2001. 'People of the Hills: How Rona Deal with Social Change', in M. Carrin (ed.), *People of the Jungle* (in print).

Pati, B. 1998. 'Siting the Body: Perspectives on Health and Medicine in Colonial Orissa', in *Social Scientist* 28, 3-26.

Pfeffer, G. 1982. *Status and Affinity in Middle India*, Wiesbaden: Steiner.

— 1994. 'The Dualistic Culture of the Juang', in G.C. Tripathi and H. Kulke (eds.), *Religion and Society in Eastern India*, Delhi: Manohar, 103-17.

— 1997. 'The Scheduled Tribes of Middle India as a Unit: Problems of Internal and External Comparison', in G. Pfeffer and D.K. Behera (eds.), *Contemporary Society: Tribal Studies*, Vol. 1, Delhi: Concept, 3-27.

— 2000. 'Tribal Ideas', in *Journal of Social Sciences* 4(4), 331-46.

— 2001. 'Sahlins' Tribesmen Reconsidered: Highland Orissa in Eastern India' (paper presented at the ICAS in Berlin 2001).

— 2002. 'The Structure of Middle Indian Tribal Society Compared', in G. Pfeffer and D.K. Behera (eds.), *Contemporary Society: Tribal Studies*, Vol. 5, Delhi: Concept, 208-29.

Platenkamp, J.D.M. 1996. 'The Healing Gift', in S. Howell (ed.), *For the Sake of the Future. Sacrificing in Eastern Indonesia.* Leiden: CNWS-Publications, 318-36.

Radcliffe-Brown, A.R. 1952. *Structure and Function in Primitive Society.* London: Routledge & Kegan Paul.

Sahlins, Marshall D. 1968. *Tribesmen.* Englewood Cliffs: Prentice Hall.

Singh Deo, K.B. 1939. *Nandapur: A Forgotten Kingdom*, Jaipur.

Svoboda, R.E. 2000 (1997). *The Greatness of Saturn: A Therapeutic Mythic*, Delhi: Rupa.

Thompson, C. 1985. 'The Power to Pollute and the Power to Preserve: Perceptions of Female Power in a Hindu Village', in *Social Science and Medicine* 21 (6), 701-11.

Thurston, E. and K. Rangachari. 1909/1987. *Castes and Tribes of Southern India*, Delhi and Madras: Asian Educational Services.

Tokita-Tanabe, Y. 1999. 'Women and Tradition in India: Construction of Subjectivity and Control of Female Sexuality in the Ritual of First Menstruation', in M. Tananka and M. Tachikawa (eds.), *Living with Śakti: Gender, Sexuality and Religion in South Asia*, Senri Ethnological Studies 50, Osaka: National Museum of Ethnology, 193-220.

Vitebsky, P. 1993. *Dialogues with the Dead: The Discussion of Mortality among the Sora of Eastern India*, Cambridge: Cambridge University Press.

10

Sacrificial Food, the Person and the Ritual System of the Gadaba*

Peter Berger

All concepts mentioned in the title of this paper are highly problematic, and it would probably not be very difficult to find social scientists who claim that one or other of the cited categories should be excluded from academic discourse. Although each of the terms is in danger of being deconstructed, or has already been questioned (e.g. Barraud and Friedberg 1996 on sacrifice), the present paper ventures to consider sacrificial food, the person, and the ritual system together—because the Gadaba of southern Orissa think of these domains as being very much interrelated. My aim is to trace these interrelations and describe the way in which Gadaba social personas are created and transformed within life-cycle rituals that focus on the preparation and consumption of different types of ritual or sacrificial food. Life-cycle rituals are connected with the wider framework of the ritual system, i.e. the collective sacrifices at village shrines during seasonal festivals. In the latter contexts, communion of sacrificial food between men and gods of the village are crucial for the maintenance of social relations and group identity on several levels, and for the permanence of society in general.

By ritual system I mean a set of interrelated and interdependent elements (ritual acts) integrated into a coherent and ordered whole. The entity or whole may consist of sub-systems or sub-wholes, which are ordered hierarchically. Thus life-cycle rituals are embedded in the cycle of the collective village rituals. The idea of a cyclical movement corresponds to the perception of time, since

---

* This paper is based on twenty-one months of field research between January 1999 and April 2001. Funding was provided by the FAZIT foundation and the German Research Foundation (DFG). My gratitude to my friends and colleagues Arlo Griffiths and Noel Smith, who made valuable comments and corrections on the manuscript. Finally my deepest gratitude goes to my Gadaba friends in Koraput who made me understand a little bit of their culture.

seasons, agricultural activities, rituals, and the flow of life are of a recurrent and alternating quality. By talking of life-cycle rituals or collective village rituals, I refer to an indigenous model: the Gadaba themselves have very much the idea that their rituals are ordered and interconnected. This becomes clear when, for example, they stress the correct sequence of rituals, or state that only a married man is eligible to participate in the communion of sacrificial food in village rituals. Nevertheless, the indigenous model can be a matter of negotiation and interpretation among the participants themselves. As such, in the hands of the anthropologist, it becomes an abstract model of analysis and comparison.

In the following I will first introduce some ideas on sacrifice and the concept of the person. Asserting that Robertson Smith's theory may still be of value for the study of sacrifice, I will highlight some of his arguments. The concept of the person is of more recent interest in anthropological theory. Although introduced to the discipline by Mauss as early as 1938, the topic only gained currency in the 1980s, particularly through the collection of essays edited by Carrithers and others.[1] For my considerations of the person I mainly rely on the ideas of André Iteanu[2] expressed in an article on the ritual system of the Orokaiva of Papua New Guinea. I will describe some features of the ethnographic context, especially the main social units relevant for understanding the rituals, before outlining the features of sacrificial and ritual food. I will then detail the different steps of the life-cycle rituals, focussing on the role of food in the process of creating the social relations which make up the social person. In conclusion, the position of Smith and Iteanu will be set up against the background of the Gadaba material, and the relatedness of the different sub-systems within the overall ritual structure will be emphasized, as the issue of sacrificial food and identity will be raised.

Sacrifice, Food and the Person

Sacrifice occupies an outstanding position in the *Lectures on the Religion of the Semites* of William Robertson Smith, first published in 1889. While his contribution to the subject is frequently

[1] Carrithers et al. 1985.

[2] Iteanu 1990.

subsumed under the aspect of sacrificial commensality and communion,[3] others concede a more general importance to Smith's work,[4] even regarding him as the 'founder of modern sociology of religion'.[5] For the present purpose I will indulge in neither a general debate of theories of sacrifice nor in a detailed critique of the *Lectures*.[6] I want instead to emphasize only three major aspects of Smith' work as relevant to the ethnographic material presented here: the relationship between society and religion; sacrifice or, more generally, ritual; and the social relevance of the 'natural' acts of preparing food and eating.

Although his book is mainly on the Semitic religion, Robertson argues that his findings are generally valid for all early, ancient and primitive peoples, be they Hebrew, Bedouin or others. In primitive societies, Smith says, the only type of community which is sacred and absolute is the kinship group. 'Primitive man' thinks of his world in two classes: kin or potential friends, and non-kin or potential enemies.[7] Kinship is therefore of absolute value, without differences of degree[8], and every individual grows up in a web of rights and obligations, which are self-understood and unquestioned. Kinship in primitive societies is not limited to humans: it includes the gods as part of its 'natural' state. Religion is part of the social organization. That relations to humans and relations to gods are just two sides of the same social system or lifestyle, Smith goes on, is taken literally by primitive man. Collective action is directed towards gods and men, and there is no separation between religion and 'ordinary life',[9] Since this form of religion is based on kinship, kinship and the sacred are one and the same.[10]

In his evolutionist conception of society, Smith is in accordance with the spirit of his time. However, as far as the relationship of

---

[3] For example, Bourdillon 1980.

[4] Evans-Pritchard 1981, Beidelman 1974.

[5] Beidelman 1974, 68.

[6] For example, I do not deal here with Smith's theory of development of different sacrificial forms, his considerations on matriarchate or the totemistic aspect of sacrifice. Beidelman (1974) has discussed these issues in detail.

[7] Smith 1997, 254.

[8] Ibid., 255.

[9] Ibid., 30f.

[10] Ibid., 271.

myth and ritual is concerned, he does not assume a mainstream position. Against the 'intellectualists' like Tylor, Müller and Frazer, who were mainly interested in early religions as an expression of 'primitive philosophy', Smith proposes the priority of ritual over myth. Although myths might be seen to take their place, Smith says, it is secondary to ritual action, which is the central part of primitive religion. Ritual, especially sacrifice, is prior and primary to myth, which has only an explanatory function. Belief and myth are subject to change and are not obligatory while sacred action, according to tradition, expresses the basic ideas and represents the persistent and binding core of religion.[11]

The ultimate expression of kinship between men and gods is the sacrificial meal that periodically declares and renews the sacred relationship. The ties created by a common meal, Smith states, are as such stable. Religion just confirms and supports this 'natural' act.[12] Further, kinship is understood as a shared substance. After an infant is weaned from its mother's milk, it is the community itself which nurtures its members jointly with the communal meal and thus constitutes and confirms kinship ties as physical relations.[13]

While the Iteanu's paper[14] on the person is separated by more than hundred years from the *Lectures* of Smith it is nevertheless located in the same sociological tradition. Via the links of Dumont, Mauss and Durkheim, Smith can be regarded as Iteanu's distant academic ancestor. Following Iteanu, the Orokaiva conceive of the person in a way quite different from the way 'Western' societies normally do. While the latter see persons as discrete and autonomous essences that imply a strong and one-dimensional subject-object distinction, Orokaiva society has a pronounced relational perspective on the person in which the subject-object signification depends on the ritual context. All elements, whether gods, animals, things or humans, are only defined in relation to the superior and all-encompassing ritual system. If any such two elements occupy a similar position in relation to the ritual system, they are seen as identical. 'Thus subjects do not possess ontological identity in the Western sense; their identity is instead defined as a

---

[11] Ibid., 19f.

[12] Ibid., 207.

[13] Ibid., 253ff

[14] Iteanu 1990.

conjunction of ritually created social relations'.[15] From birth to death, '...a social person continues to "grow" by accumulating relations each time he participates in a ritual. After his death, the process is reversed. The funeral ritual extinguishes one by one each of the relations that had a part in the constitution of the social person, and the deceased is thus transformed into an image (*ahihi*).[16]

Essential in the constitution of social persons are exchanges of raw pork which are distributed in the final phase of each ritual. The giver does 'ritual work'[17] on the social person of the receiver, a favour which has to be reciprocated at a later date. Only after death, through the social person's participation in his own death rituals—the point of his actual dissolution or transformation into an 'image'—does he combine the full compliment of his social relations. Hence, a social person, while alive, is never complete,[18] a difference to the Gadaba conceptions as will be seen. For the Orokaiva, every form of existence is in flux depending on rituals, which as Iteanu strongly reminds us, are no separate institutions, 'but rather constitute a totality co-extensive with the realm of relations, that is, with the entire social universe'.[19] This would indicate that there are no relations outside the configuration which he would, for comparative purposes, call 'ritual system'.

The Orokaiva case as described by Iteanu is an extreme example, where the individual is completely subsumed within the holistic ritual framework. Maurice Bloch, too, stresses the contrast between 'our' concept of the 'bounded individual',[20] where social relations are conceived only as external and the 'unbounded person' in many other cultures. 'For us different people are linked *merely* by "social" or "emotional" or "moral" relationships, but these relationships are not for us as real as those which exist between the component parts which make up the individual'.[21] However, Bloch criticizes the theoretical position that radically polarizes holism and individualism and thereby ignores the possible shades in between.

---

[15] Ibid., 38.

[16] Ibid., 40.

[17] Ibid., 44.

[18] Ibid., 40.

[19] Ibid., 50.

[20] Bloch 1988, 15.

[21] Ibid., 16, emphasis in original.

Ethnographic Setting

The Gutob speaking Gadaba or Boro Gadaba are part of the indigenous Desia population that inhabits the hills of the Eastern Ghats in southern Orissa, namely the Koraput District. Every individual grows up with the Desia dialect of Oriya as a second mother tongue and, in almost all villages, Gutob speakers live side by side with other groups that speak only Desia.[22] According to administrative criteria, the Desia are classified into Scheduled Tribes (ST), Scheduled Castes (SC) and Other Backward Classes (OBC) by the government.

Before I describe the categories of ritual food and the life-cycle rituals specific to the Gadaba, it is necessary to provide a few words about the social structure of which they are a part.[23] In social, ritual and economic respects the village (*gl, ungom**) is a most relevant entity. According to the general pattern, every village is dominated by one of the ST categories,[24] the people referring to themselves also as Adivasi. They are regarded as the spiritual and economic landowners or *roit* and are said to be the first settlers or *matia* ('earth-people'). All other village inhabitants, whether Adivasi or non-Adivasi, are distinguished as *upria*, those who came 'later'.

In a typical village, the Gadaba would all belong to the same patrilineal clan (*bōso*). Among the Boro Gadaba we find four different clans (Cobra, Tiger, Sun and Monkey) and according to our ideal type there would be several villages made up only of Cobra, Sun, Tiger or Monkey. The Gadaba of each village have a different name and may therefore be regarded as a type of 'subclan'. Each of these villages is in turn divided into four local lines[25] or *kuda*-groups holding one of the following titles: Sisa,

---

[22] Throughout the text Gutob words are marked with '*', all other words are Desia.

[23] Cf. Pfeffer 1997, 2001; Berger 2000, 2001a.

[24] From among the ST or Adivasi categories the Boro or senior Gadaba have the Ollar or junior Gadaba, Joria, Kond, Parenga, Bonda, and Didaye among their neighbours.

[25] Leach (1961) introduced this term in the context of affinal exchange and it has been revived by Pfeffer (e.g. 2000). In Leach's context 'local line' refers to diagrammatic representations of 'local decent groups' (ibid., 56f). The important difference with the notion of 'lineage' is that 'local descent groups' or 'local lines' depend on descent *and*

Kirsani, Munduli, and Boronaik. These groups again segment into several smaller units, which are also called *kuda* and generally consist of a group of 'real' brothers. The smallest social unit is the house (*gor*, *dien**).

Unlike in the classical 'African' cases, descent is not the only important feature in the Desia social structure. Ancestors do not play any important role as a genealogical focus and pedigrees are not remembered. Generally, clan-members conceive of themselves as 'brothers', in opposition to all others, deemed marriageable non-brothers. Genealogical reckoning is irrelevant. Although the names of *kuda* categories span the village boundaries, *kuda* groups, as units of social action, are only significant in intra-village contexts. In contrast, clan membership defines intra- and inter-village relations.

As Weber[26] shows, we rarely encounter such ideal types in reality and they merely serve as analytical tools for the sociologist. In many Gadaba villages we find only two or three of the four title groups and in some we find additional *kuda*-categories. Also, most big villages include members of different Gadaba clans and villages as internal affines of the indigenous dominant clan. Generally they do not own land and have a ritually inferior position in relation to the native clan. Thus the situation gets more complicated. Every village is related to all other villages of a different clan as affines. In addition, villages or sometimes *kuda*-groups of different villages are linked in terms of 'brotherhood'. Three such collective and diachronic relationships are distinguished: *tsorubai*, *panjabai* and *moitr*. I want to introduce them briefly here because they will become relevant in the context of the life-cycle rituals.

Tsorubai are the most relevant of these relations for the purpose of this paper. When two groups are related as *tsorubai* or *tsoru*-'brothers' they have reciprocal ritual duties on specific occasions, especially life-cycle rituals, but also in the case of excommunication. Their main function is to prepare and often to feed the sacrificial food called *tsoru* to their *tsorubai*. *Panjabai* are much more rarely needed but they are nonetheless indispensable. It

---

locality. In systems where the genealogical bias of the 'African' lineage is lacking 'local lines', detached from Leach's diagrammatic context, may be a useful tool. Among the Desia *kuda* refers to such an agnatic group with common residence (*vide* Pfeffer 1997, 2000; Berger 2000, 2001a).

[26] Weber 1947, 109f.

is their task to finally free each other from the 'spirits' of the deceased (*duma*). This point will be discussed below. Different from *tsorubai* and *panjabai*, groups linked by the *moitr* relationship may be of different clans. Despite this, it is 'taboo' (*dos*, *umrang**) to exchange brides between them and they are therefore conceived as 'brothers'. When we look for the 'function' of the *moitr* relationship we are apt to be disappointed. Although they are always invited on important ritual occasions, they do not perform such obvious services as ritual cooking. They are just present, never demand anything from their hosts, but accept gifts humbly. The *moitr* relationship is considered sacred and, because it is highly formalized, in day to day life *moitr* avoid visiting each other.

The social entities of village, local line, and house are relevant not only for political and economic activities, they are also units of ritual action. In most rituals the Gadaba perform animals are killed as offerings (*bog*) to the gods (*maphru*), malevolent 'demons' (*soni* and *rau*) or the spirits of the dead (*duma*). Words for 'ritual' including sacrificial killing are *puja*, *biru* or *gelgel**. Before humans consume the meat of the animals, some of it is cooked and, along with rice, given to gods, demons, or spirits. To make an offering is called *betisong* or *lenobong**.

The ritual unity of a village is demonstrated during all seasonal festivals, most lucidly during the month of April (C*hait*), when the village is closed to outsiders and trespassers have to pay a toll (*pajor*). On all occasions of collective village sacrifices led by the Sisa group of the dominant clan, the village displays unity as well as its internal hierarchy. Two of the major places of sacrificial worship are the shrine of the village goddess (*hundi*) in the centre, and the shrine of the 'big' or 'senior house' (*boro gor*, *moro dien**) outside the village boundaries. Members of the dominant clan have an agnatic (*bai*) relation to the village gods, since they initiated the relationship when they settled. Accordingly, internal affines say that their relation to the village gods is of an affinal nature (*bondu*). This status difference is articulated through the commensal rules which regulate the consumption of *tsoru*, which is cooked as part of all collective sacrifices. Without question all Desia of the village participate in each collective sacrificial ritual, but to a very different degree.[27]

---

[27] Cf. Berger 2001a.

Tsoru and 'Ritual Rice'

Tsoru contains boiled rice and the meat of a sacrificed animal. Cows, buffaloes, pigs, goats, sheep and chickens are sacrificed on different occasions, the gods being distinguished by what they eat. *Tsoru* is made from the victim's head, except when chicken are sacrificed, when the whole animal enters the *tsoru*. The rules prescribe *tsoru* be cooked in a new earthen pot (*handi*) near the place of sacrifice or shrine. Those who cook, as well as those who consume *tsoru,* should have fasted on the day of the sacrifice. Who should cook and who is eligible to eat depends on the context. There are three interrelated domains in which *tsoru* is cooked and consumed.

First, as already mentioned, *tsoru* is prepared for all collective rituals at seasonal village festivals. In these contexts, the village priest (*pujari*) performs the sacrifice[28] while the ritual cook (*randari*) prepares the *tsoru*. The two always work together for the village as a whole and the Randari explained to me that they are like husband and wife, he himself occupying the female and junior position in relation to the Pujari. Whereas the collective sacrifices are taken care of by this 'ritual couple' at village festivals, every man performs sacrifices for his own house-god (*doron deli*)—the central wooden pillar of the house—and his wife cooks *tsoru*, which all household members consume jointly. Second, *tsoru* is cooked, served and sometimes directly fed to individuals at different life-cycle rituals. Pujari and Randari play no part in these contexts, but the sacrifice and cooking is done either by a ritual expert (*dissari*) or by the agnatic and affinal kin of the person. Finally, the sacrifice of a cow or pig is required in cases of *jati,* i.e. excommunication from the tribe *jati*. The temporarily excluded then have to be fed with *tsoru* by their *tsorubai* in order to rejoin the community.

Life-cycle rituals also include the consumption of a different type of cooked rice (*bat*) which is not considered as *tsoru*. Although part of a ritual process, this food (referred to with various names depending on the ritual context) is not part of a sacrifice and the regulations concerning *tsoru*—such as fasting and using a new

---

[28] The actual killing is mostly done by a young man from the local line of the *pujari*, i.e. the Sisa *kuda*.

earthen pot – do not apply. This food, consisting of cooked rice, fish and bamboo-sprouts, does not figure in collective rituals on village level but only during rites of passage. In the following I will refer to it as 'ritual rice' or 'ritual food' in contrast to 'sacrificial food' or *tsoru*.

Life-Cycle Rituals

The Gadaba Person

Three aspects of a person may be distinguished: the human body (*deho*, *neri**), an impersonal life-force or 'breath' (*jibon* or *punda*) and a social quality.[29] During the transformations of a person in the course of the life-cycle rituals these parts have a different fate. At birth, the individual has a body and a life-force but not yet a social quality, which has to be constructed through ritual action. All three aspects make up the complete living person (*lok*). After death the complete person disintegrates. The body is quickly cremated and the social quality of the deceased is referred to as *duma*. For some time after death the *duma* is thought of as possessing life-force and in this condition the *duma* is dangerous to the living. After about a month the life-force attaches itself to the body of a woman, to be reborn later. Then only the social quality remains. It is possible that two *jibon* are reincarnated in a single body. Such children are said to cry more, because the different *jibon* fight for the mother's milk. As far as life-cycle rituals are concerned, most ritual activity is focussed on the social quality and only little on the life-essence or the body. Hence I will concentrate on the transformations and changes of social status the life-cycle rituals bring about, especially through the consumption of ritual rice and *tsoru*.

Steps Towards Personhood

The birth (*jonom*) of a child in general takes place at home, at the same spot where people ideally should die. As soon as the woman

---

[29] I am referring here to the indigenous classification. However, no Gadaba would be able to spontaneously describe such a scheme, which I have deduced from conversations as well as from observations of rituals. This holds especially for the social quality of a person. During a lifetime this aspect is included in the general word for 'human', 'man' or 'people' (*lok*); after death it is more specifically described as *duma* (*vide* Berger 2002).

is in labour, the midwife (*bandki dokri*) is called to deliver the child. Later, the umbilical cord and afterbirth are buried near the house and a flat stone is put on top, but no ritual (*biru*) is performed in the sense that no sacrifice takes place. While there is no *tsoru*, ritual rice is prepared. This *poti bat* is cooked by women of the neighbourhood, and jointly consumed by the midwife and all other people who had been present during delivery. The mother receives two plates, one for herself and another for the newborn child, who is thus thought of as participating in the food. Until the day the child receives its name, he or she is bathed by the mother twice a day at the place where the umbilical cord has been buried.

Name-giving

The name-giving ritual is performed on an odd-numbered day, the seventh or ninth day after birth. Should the infant die within this period (i.e. before name-giving), he or she would also be buried at the location of the umbilical cord and not cremated, as is the usual procedure for all individuals[30] after the name-giving ceremony. The names of the ritual (*sutok sorani* and *handi darani*) indicate that the period of impurity (*sutok*) is over and that the clay pot (*handi*), in which the bathing water for mother and child has been heated, is now thrown away.

The sacrificial ritual commences before sunrise at the 'burial place' of the umbilical cord. A ritual expert (*dissari*) performs the ritual in front of the stone, beside which the mother sits with her child. Although all gods are evoked the ritual is especially addressed to *soni* and *rau*, two principally malevolent spirits, who are a major source of illness and death. Domestic animals (chicken, and a pig or goat) and wild animals (catfish and/or dove) are sacrificed. Along with a few grains of rice, a tiny portion of every animal[31] is cooked in a leaf over a small fire and then offered to the gods and spirits at the place of sacrifice. While the midwife later cleans clothes and utensils and performs purification rites for all members of the house, the men of the local line cut up the animals. Heads and liver are cooked as *tsoru* separately from the animals' bodies. After the ritual expert has given a name to the child, he does

---

[30] People who died of smallpox or leprosy are an exception and are also buried.

[31] Often a piece of the gullet from the severed head.

betisong inside the house[32] and then feeds the mother with *tsoru* and puts some of it in the hand of the infant. Then ritual specialist, midwife, and senior members of the local line start eating *tsoru*, followed by the other men and women of the local line. Non-*tsoru* rice is distributed to all households of the village.

This ritual accomplishes several transformations. First, it finally disconnects the child from the umbilical cord and the place where it is buried. No further rituals are conducted at this spot and, should the infant die, she or he is not buried there, but cremated on the collective cremation ground. The ritual brings about the end of the pollution period, which has affected the houses of all village agnates and prevented affines and outsiders from eating in their houses. Moreover, the child may now be touched by others and has received a name, which is of social and ritual relevance. Only if an individual has a name can he or she become the target of witchcraft. Finally, through the commensality of *tsoru* the child is officially incorporated within the local line. The additional distribution of cooked non-*tsoru* rice to all households is a declaration and recognition of the new village member. Thus for the child *sutok sorani* represents his entrance into society. Lacking many other relations complete persons have, the infant is nevertheless attached to the basic social units of house and local line.

Birth Thread and First Haircut

However, the child's existence is not immune to attack from malevolent forces. Therefore, a week after *sutok sorani* and around two weeks after birth, the malevolent spirits of *soni* and *rau* are again invoked and the 'birth threads' (*jonom suta*) are tied around the infant's neck and hip along with 'medicine' (*oso, sindrong**) to protect him from evil influences. Prior to such protection, the child should not be moved beyond the realm of the house and village. A white chicken is presented and dedicated to *soni-rau* and then released. If *soni-rau* do not harm the child within the subsequent year and a half, the chicken will then be sacrificed for them. This promise (*manasik*) is fulfilled around the time the child begins to walk, in a ritual called *bal utrani* ('to lift the hair'). Outside the village, at a place where two footpaths cross, the animal is

---

[32] The offerings are placed on the threshold to the sacred room, at the fireplace, at the entrance to the house and in the yard—sometimes also near the sacred pillar of the house.

sacrificed by a ritual expert (*dissari*) and the child's hair is cut for the first time, either completely or partially, and left within the sacrificial area, together with the birth thread from the neck.[33] The meat of the chicken is not cooked in a new pot and the food is not referred to as *tsoru*. However, the ritual expert does *betisong* inside the house of the child, i.e. he offers cooked rice and meat to the gods and then feeds the child with the same rice.

At about six months after birth, in between these two interconnected ritual sequences of *jonom suta* and *bal utrani,* the child begins to eat rice. This step is not accompanied by any ritual action and it could be argued that the Gadaba do not think of this step as important, since the child has previously already eaten *tsoru*, although not in a material way. However, there is significance attached to the 'real' consumption of rice. When a baby is born, it is still associated with the realm of the dead (*duma*) and said to 'play' (*keliba*) in the 'community of the dead' (*duma kul*). That newborn children are smiling or laughing without an obvious cause and are unable to focus their eyes on somebody else is reported as proof of this fact. From every meal, a portion is put aside for the *duma* first, then the family members commence eating. This first rice is also referred to as *sig bat*. When a child starts to eat rice, everyday rice as well as sacrificial rice, it seems that the infant has loosened its ties with the world of the dead and is situated more firmly in the community of 'people' (*lok*).

Completing the Person

Following the cutting of hair (*bal utrani*), the next regular phase of the life-cycle is marriage. In the process of accumulating social relations, marriage is a decisive phase. In order to commence the marriage rituals, one should not be in debt to the extra-human sphere for promised sacrificial offerings. When a child is in danger of dying of fever, the parents consult a spirit medium and, on his advice, may promise to perform a *bato biba* (path-marriage) should the child recover. This promise may be redeemed only years after the infant has recovered but it has to happen before marriage. *Bato biba* is a very expensive and elaborate ritual which lasts for around three days and resembles the marriage procedure in many ways. It differs mainly in that it includes a whole night of dance and

[33] The thread around the waist is only removed on the day of cremation.

play of a multitude of gods, who are invoked and possess the body of a spiritual medium (*gurumai*). Several chickens and a black ram are sacrificed in front of the house of the child, and a white wether is sacrificed for *rau* before dawn outside the village. During the following day, the hair of the person in question is cut and the ritual expert feeds the whole family with *tsoru*. Although a more thorough analysis of the ritual is necessary, some basic features seem to be clear. The period between the promise of the ritual and its actual performance resembles the period between the 'birth-thread' (*jonom suta*) ritual and the first haircut (*bal utrani*). In both cases, a promise (*manasik*) has been made to *soni-rau* on behalf the child by its family. During this time, the person is in an extraordinary situation and subject to certain prohibitions. The person's hair may not be cut and he or she should not eat anywhere but in his or her own house. The *bato biba* disconnects the relationship between *soni-rau* and the person, and the debt is paid. Through the consumption of *tsoru*, the person re-enters the realm of the ordinary or profane and is set back on his or her path to complete the next step to personhood, the marriage (*biba*).

Before her actual wedding ceremony, a woman has to accomplish the passage leading her away from her house of birth into that of her future husband. She will therefore be served her final *tsoru* (*ji-tsoru*[34]) of her father's house. From that day onwards, she can no longer receive the *tsoru* of her father's house, nor enter the sacred room or the attic of the same. The groom is not the subject to such change. When the young woman is first brought to the groom's father's house, the future couple is mouth-fed with ritual-rice (*tikdar bat*) by the members of the groom's family. Bride and bridegroom are then also made to feed each other.

In marriage, as in death rituals, the *tsoru* complex is the most conspicuous (at least for those concerned) aspect of the proceedings, and in both cases the sacrifice of cattle is prescribed. On the actual marriage day, the couple is provided with four or five different types of *tsoru* in the groom's village. Unlike the previous occasions (e.g. name-giving), here the *tsoru* is not fed by the ritual specialist but by different social relations, who also perform the sacrificial killing of the animals (chickens and cows). In front of the

[34] The kinship term *ji* here means 'daughter', but it is also a term of address for ego's father's sister; i.e. signifies women of alternate generations leaving the village for marriage.

house, the couple is provided *tsoru* by the village-clan members of the groom. This *tsoru* (*atri tsoru*) is shared within the local line. Later, the couple is called and in turn served *tsoru* (*mamu tsoru*) by the two maternal uncles (*mamu*) of the couple and by the bride's father.[35] Finally, on the following day, the above mentioned *tsorubai* of the groom's local line prepare *tsoru* inside the sacred room of the house. This *tsoru* should only be eaten among the so-called *baro bai* (twelve brothers), which refers to clan members of twelve different villages who are said to have shared *tsoru* in mythical times.[36] No affine may attend this meal.

I have focussed on the consumption of *tsoru* in the marriage ritual because it is this aspect which is considered to be most effective and brings about the transformation of status. After a man is ritually married he is said to have a 'name' (*nl̲*). He can now participate in every group activity and the totality of his social relations is the equivalent of the complete social person. Bride and groom have previously eaten the *tsoru* of their respective houses in the context of seasonal festivals and at the rituals of name-giving and possibly *bato biba*. However, during the marriage they are fed for the first time by their maternal uncles and their *tsorubai*. Although we may see these relationships as existing collectively before the wedding, for the two newly married persons these links are ritually activated only from then onwards. This is expressed in their participation in exchanges. The new couple set up a household and a hearth of their own and participate in the exchange of rice (cooked, husked or paddy), beer, and liquor within the village and beyond. Furthermore, since others can only accept *tsoru* from a ritually married person, only a married man may act as *tsorubai*.

Similarly, the couple's relationship with the gods has been transformed. A passive beneficiary of the sacrifices before his marriage, a married man becomes the sacrificer for his own house, communicating directly with the divine,[37] the *tsoru* being prepared

---

[35] Unless the groom's wife's father (*satra*) and his mother's brother (*mamu*) are identical.

[36] The 'twelve brothers' are very important as a category but it hardly takes shape as a group, which is joined in social or ritual action.

[37] This does not mean however that unmarried boys and girls may do have a ritual status in some contexts. On the contrary as junior counterparts of the priest (*pujari*) his young son may perform a sacrifice

by the woman of his house. Husband and wife become a junior mirror image of the village priest and his ritual cook. On the village level, the new household contributes money for the sacrificial animals and rice (*potri caul*) for the preparation of *tsoru* at the shrines of the gods in and around the village. The *tsoru* cooked at these shrines can only be consumed by young boys or married men from the dominant clan, whereas all others are excluded.

Although ideally every man and woman should ritually marry and receive the different types of *tsoru*, some cannot afford the expenses and remain unmarried even though they have children. In fact, in the village where I lived, the priest's son had a wife and children without being ritually married. As a consequence, he cannot follow his father into office. Nobody accepts *tsoru* cooked by him or his wife and he is not eligible to share *tsoru* at the village shrines together with the other men of the dominant clan. Thus, even though an unmarried man suffers no disadvantages in everyday life, his ritual capacities are limited and his social person remains rudimentary, lacking the ritual relations that are established through the commensality of *tsoru*.

The Process Reversed: Removing the Dead

Tsoru and ritual food have the capacity not only to build up the relations a social person consists of and to integrate him or her into society, but also to transform the person into a status beyond the realm of the living. A series of death rituals[38] aim at removing the social person from society, to disconnect the previous established relations.

Following a death, the *tsorubai* and the mother's brother (*mamu*) of the deceased are immediately informed and if possible the corpse is cremated on the same day.[39] In this procedure the *tsorubai* perform most ritual tasks. They cut the first wood, build the pyre,

---

along with him. In different rituals unmarried boys and girls are required in diverse ritual roles.

[38] In a different paper I have dealt in some detail on the transformations the death rituals accomplish (Berger 2001b).

[39] *Mamu* is a classificatory category; if the genealogical mother's brother is already dead at his nephew's funeral, his son or grandson may be present in his stead. If for some reasons no representative of the mother's brother's local line is available, any senior affine may perform the tasks.

and take a tiny clay pot of cooked rice, as *tsoru*, to the cremation ground to feed the *duma*—all on the day of the death.

The feeding of the *duma* by the *tsorubai* is repeated on the third day after death, when the period of impurity (*sutok*) ends. In a small ritual the *tsorubai* and then all family members offer rice (*tsoru* and ritual rice) and liquor to the deceased on the cremation ground and at his or her house. Inside the house, the *tsorubai*, *mamu* and senior men of the local line assemble. The *mamu* offers liquor to the dead, who is addressed, told that everything has been provided for her or him, and asked not to harm or otherwise interfere with the living. Then the *tsorubai* offers *tsoru* to the *duma* from a special plate and distributes the remaining food equally on the plates of all others, who are thus effectively sharing one plate with the dead.

A more elaborate ritual for the dead called *bur* or *obdel** follows within ten days or in the month of *Pus* (January) and all large scale rituals of its kind fall in this month. The *bur*, lasting in the elaborate version for two or three days, includes exchanges of living cows and raw meat parts, and a big feast. The general structure, however, is basically the same as the one of the small ritual performed on the third day. A cow is sacrificed in the name of the dead and *tsorubai* and *mamu* separately cook *tsoru* for the *duma*, some of which—along with all sorts of paraphernalia, liquor and beer—is brought to the cremation ground. In case the *bur* is performed several months after a person's death, the *duma* has already lost the capacity to attack and possess people. Nevertheless she or he is again told to retreat and stay away from the living. On return from the cremation ground, the *duma* is again served with food and drink around and inside the house, like before. After the *bur,* concern for the *duma* dies down and he or she is not provided with any more offerings.

The Final Revival

Perhaps many years later, when the *duma* of a village or a local line have increased in numbers, the men decide to perform the *gotr* ritual in order to abandon all spirits of the dead simultaneously.[40] For this purpose all *duma* are collectively raised and later individually transformed into the bodies of buffaloes, one animal for each *duma*. On the main day, the revived *duma* in their buffalo forms are dressed up and led outside the village where they are tied

[40] Cf. Pfeffer 2001.

at a specific place. Several groups of clan members from other villages—foremost the above mentioned *panjabai*, but also the *tsorubai* of the hosts—then take the buffaloes to their villages and slaughter and eat them in the following weeks.

Again, food and feeding are decisive in this process. By feeding the buffaloes with *sig bat* (*tsoru* and/or ritual rice) the transformation is accomplished and the *duma* is revived in the buffalo body. It should be noticed that this food is called by the same name as the rice first put aside for the newborn baby (more specifically, for the *duma* still associated with the newborn baby). After the *duma* are thus brought back to life the buffaloes are feasted for one or more days by all villagers and guests. While the women weep and console their revived relatives, the *panjabai* behave in a frenzied fashion, dancing around their buffalo brothers and sharing their food and drink. All this happens in the host's village before the buffaloes are led away.

There may be several buffaloes for one deceased individual. Not only do sons provide a buffalo for a deceased father, but also a *mamu* may provide a buffalo for a deceased nephew. Therefore, the spirit of the deceased comes to life in two different villages simultaneously in the form of two different buffaloes. Both are fed with *tsoru* or ritual rice, by his affines in one village and by his agnates in another. On the main day of the ritual, the *mamu,* along with his own *panjabai,* takes his 'buffalo-nephew' to the *gotr* performing village to be slaughtered. Thereafter the other (agnatic) buffaloes are led away by the external agnatic groups, i.e. the sponsor's panjabai and tsorubai. Afterwards the *duma* are said to be gone without the possibility of return. They have left the social world and the system of exchange which constitutes it.

Conclusion

The concept of the person that emerges from these ritual actions clearly is of the unbounded and relational type as described by Iteanu and Bloch. Iteanu's phrase that the social person grows, '… by accumulating relations each time he participates in a ritual',[41] perfectly corresponds with the Gadaba material presented here. Life-cycle rituals compose the person in a process of gradual

[41] Iteanu 1990, 40.

additions and subtractions of social relations. In contrast to the Orokaiva however, the Gadaba person is considered to be complete after marriage, not after the death rituals have been performed. For the Gadaba, a person is of high social relevance directly after death because of the potential threat he or she represents for the village. However, the rituals up to the *bur* are aimed at removing the *duma* and to try to decrease his or her social capabilities. The relational and unbounded properties of the person perhaps become most obvious in the final phase of the death rituals. Far from being conceived as a unique essence, the social person of the dead can be revived in two different places, by two different relatives simultaneously. The person, representing a specific social relation rather than a fixed substance, becomes an object of exchange. In one case, it is exchanged along affinal lines between the maternal uncle's group and the group of his deceased nephew. In the other case, the same *duma* is given away to clan brothers by the sponsors of the ritual. For the participants, the multiple nature of the person poses no contradiction. A similar situation is faced when the life essence (*jibon*) of two deceased persons reincarnate into one womb and then are present in a single individual. However, it would probably be incorrect to describe the concept of the person as something wholly ephemeral. It is true that the life essence remains instable throughout the life and is put out of balance through instances of shock or fear. Likewise, social quality is not considered to be something that is necessarily attached to life. A newborn child has no social person and, through misconduct, an individual may loose his or her social quality. 'Socialness' in both cases is created and regained through ritual action. Nevertheless, to say the Gadaba conceive of their personality in day-to-day actions as fleeting would be overstressing the point.

In the Orokaiva case, 'ritual work' is done on social persons by means of meat exchange. The receiver of pork 'grows'[42] as a consequence of this exchange. Among the Gadaba, although exchange of living animals and meat parts is also obligatory in many rituals such as marriage, *bur* or *gotr*, the constitutive part of 'person building' is effected by the ingestion of ritual food and *tsoru*. That is, it is not the exchange of food but the actual eating of it which brings about the transformation.

---

[42] Ibid., 44.

The social production of the person through life-cycle rituals is not an end in itself. Rather this cycle is related to other levels of the ritual system. Supplied with *tsoru* and ritual food during life-cycle rituals, individuals maintain due relationships with the village gods. As Smith points out, alimentary communion is a central aspect of such relations. On several occasions through the year, the village gods receive sacrificial offerings. *Tsoru* is prepared in the immediate vicinity of the shrines and jointly consumed by men and gods. Although different gods are not attributed with clearly defined functions, the Gadaba stress that without proper relations to the gods (i.e. without sacrifice), life would be impossible. In these contexts, *tsoru* confirms more than it transforms, in that offerings and alimentary communion renew and perpetuate these essential relations. Smith's other thesis—on the kinship relation between god and worshippers—is also partly supported. For the founding clan of the village, the gods are like ancestors, i.e. they are agnates. This view is again based on a relational perspective, not on one of essence. Gods are different from humans and spirits of the dead[43] but the fact that they share *tsoru* indicates an agnatic relation. The relational logic of the clan system then defines all others as 'affines' of the gods. Relationships are made transparent in the sacrificial and the alimentary code, the division of the sacrificed animal and consumption of *tsoru*. Village agnates eat the head of the animal, their affines the neck, and all others may only consume the body of the animal.[44]

Smith's kinship hypothesis is only partly accepted because I do not share his evident materialism. He argues that in 'primitive society', kinship is of a 'natural' kind:[45] as gods are understood as being of the 'same stock' as their worshippers, they form a 'physical unity'[46] of shared substance, especially of blood. Through commensality this physical bond is strengthened, even constituted 'in a very real sense'.[47] I have already underlined the view that

---

[43] They are, for example, different in that they occupy different positions in the ritual exchange system.

[44] Cf. Berger 2001a.

[45] Smith 1997, 257.

[46] Ibid., 255.

[47] Ibid., 257. In the last paragraph of his book Smith writes, 'In primitive ritual this conception [the sacramental communion] is grasped in a merely physical and mechanical shape, as indeed, in primitive life, all

kinship is more a matter of relations than of essence. Blood, milk, bones and other material items which are thought to be shared as an essence are symbolic representations of these relations. By describing the way persons are 'constructed' through *tsoru* and arguing for the generative capacity of sacrifice, I am talking of the field of symbolic action and ideas. Nevertheless, it may be sensed what Smith points at when talking about the 'real sense' in which eating constitutes relationships. *Tsoru* is thought to be effective through the 'material' act of consumption, the actual eating. During the name-giving ceremony, the child is symbolically fed with *tsoru*, which is put on his cheek or into his hands, and this changes his social status. However, the child is only considered to have completely left the world of the spirits when he starts eating rice itself—*tsoru* and profane rice—and strangely enough this transformation is brought about without ritual, but as a gradual process. In conclusion, I stress that eating is always a cultural and hence a symbolic act, not only in ritual context. In every human society probably there is no such thing as merely 'natural eating', as Smith would have it. Among the Gadaba, as elsewhere, also everyday consumption is regulated in relation to time, place, and company. In alimentary as in sexual intercourse, two themes closely related in many cultures, the mental and the material are inseparable.

Further, food, eating and commensality are in many cultures, especially in India, a question of identity. This aspect has been latent through my paper. The consumption of *tsoru* assigns identity at different levels. It provides the individual with the social relations that make up his or her existence. Identity is bestowed on the level of the household and local line in rituals like the name-giving ceremony. For women it is a question of identity, when they change their *tsoru* sharing group with marriage. At a more inclusive level, the commensality of *tsoru* is a demonstration of the identity of the village, its gods, and the dominant clan. Finally, only through the feeding of *tsoru* to those who have been excommunicated can the status as Gadaba be regained.

---

spiritual and ethical ideas are still wrapped up in the husk of a material embodiment' (ibid., 418).

References

Barraud, C. and C. Friedberg. 1996. 'Life-Giving Relationships in Bunaq and Kei Societies', in S. Howell (ed.), *For the Sake of Our Future: Sacrificing in Eastern Indonesia*, Leiden: CNWS Publications, 351-98.

Beidelman, T.O. 1974. *W. Robertson Smith and the Sociological Study of Religion*, Chicago: University of Chicago Press.

Berger, P. 2000. 'Gesellschaft, Ritual und Ideologie. Eine relationale Betrachtung der Gadaba des Koraput Distriktes, Orissa', *Mitteilungen der Berliner Gesellschaft für Anthropologie, Ethnologie und Urgeschichte* (21), 15-28.

— 2001. 'Feeding the Dead. Rituals of Transformation Among the Gadaba of Koraput.' In preparation for *Adivasi* (41), 35-50.

— 2002. 'The Gadaba and the 'non-ST' Desia of Koraput', in G. Pfeffer and D.K. Behera (eds.), *Contemporary Society: Tribal Studies*, vol. 5, Delhi: Concept Publishing Company, 57-90.

Bloch, M. 1988. 'Introduction: Death and the Concept of Person', in S. Cederroth, C. Corlin and J. Lindström (eds.), *On the Meaning of Death*, Uppsala: Almquist & Wiksell International, 11-29.

Bourdillon, M.F.C. 1980. 'Introduction', in M.F.C. Bourdillon and Meyer Fortes (eds.), *Sacrifice*, London: Academic Press, 1-27.

Carrithers, M., M. Collins and S. Lukes (eds.). 1985. *The Category of the Person in Anthropology, Philosophy, History,* Cambridge: Cambridge University Press.

Evans-Pritchard, E.E. 1981. *A History of Anthropological Thought*, London: Faber & Faber.

Iteanu, A. 1990. 'The Concept of the Person and the Ritual System: An Orokaiva View', *Man* (25), 35-53.

Leach, E. 1961. *Rethinking Anthropology*, London: Athlone.

Pfeffer, G. 1997. 'The Scheduled Tribes of Middle India as a Unit: Problems of Internal and External Comparison', in D.K. Behera and G. Pfeffer (eds.), *Contemporary Society: Tribal Studies,* Vol 1: *Structure and Process,* Delhi: Concept Publishing Company, 3-27.

— 2000. 'Tribal Ideas', *Journal of Social Sciences*, Special Issue No. 4, 331-46.

— 2001. 'A Ritual of Revival Among the Gadaba of Koraput', in H. Kulke and B. Schnepel (eds.), *Jagannath Revisited: Studying*

Society, Religion and the State in Orissa, Delhi: Manohar, 99-124.

Smith, W. Robertson. 1997 (1889). *Lectures on the Religion of the Semites*, Vol. VI of *The Early Sociology of Religion*, ed. B.S. Turner, London: Routledge/Thoemmes Press.

Weber, M. 1964 (1922). *Social and Economic Organization*, New York: The Free Press.

11

Death Among the Aghria: Death and the Continuity of Life in a Peripheral Mixed Tribal and Caste Society*

Uwe Skoda

The Aghria[1] are a peasant caste in the north-western part of Orissa, an area predominantly populated by the so-called 'Scheduled Tribes'. At the time of thc princely states the Aghria probably migrated into the area from the north-west direction. In many cases they became wealthy landowners and village headmen collecting the revenue for the king. Today too, they enjoy many of their former privileges. Through immigration and the processes of acculturation, a mixed tribal and caste society developed in this rather peripheral region in which tribes and castes closely interact and in which they have influenced each other.

Accordingly, I shall argue on the one hand that in Aghria funeral rituals, one finds not only the usual north Indian elements, but also tribal features, a synthesis already found in their kinship system (Skoda 2000). On the other hand I shall highlight the role of the sister's son, which seems to be complimentary to the role of the mother's brother in life cycle rituals up to marriage. Both roles are essential for the formation and transformation of a social person or, to put it in a slightly different way, for guidance into the world and beyond. Apart from the continuity of the local line of the father and from a possibly ritually stressed continuity of alternating generations among the Aghria, the relation to the sister's son (mother's brother) marks an enduring affinal tie. But let me begin with a detailed account of the funeral rites.

---

* I thank Lidia Guzy, Tina Otten and Peter Berger for discussing an earlier draft of this paper.

[1] I am grateful to the family of Prasanna Kumar Patel, Pramod and Khirod Patel for their generous support during my on-going field research. Without them the article in its present form would not have been possible. In the same way I am obliged to the Deutsche Forschungsgemeinschaft (DFG)/German Research Council.

The Death Rituals

The first day

On the day of death, the body of the deceased is laid out in the courtyard on the floor, the feet pointing south. The body is then anointed with turmeric (*haldi*) by the daughters or daughters-in-law, who may also, with the turmeric, write 'Ram' and 'Krishna' on the legs and 'Om' on the forehead of the dead. Small coins, preferably of copper, are placed around the body and on the hands, and are wrapped in a part of its new clothes (*sari* for women, *lungi* for men). A small piece of the cloth is retained in order to throw it into the Ganga with the bones later on. A *tulsi* twig is put on top of the body, and the mouth is filled with some Ganga water and gold. Furthermore, the head is decorated with several flower garlands (*mala*). Relatives and neighbours come to the house to bid the dead farewell.

At the same time, the preparations for the cremation start. Firewood has to be arranged. If a family is not capable of providing the wood, burial is possible, but cremation is preferred. The rituals prior to the cremation or burial are the same. A bed turned upside down is prepared and its legs are decorated with banana leaves.

In the evening (or, if the death occurs in the evening, on the next morning), a procession starts from the house to the cremation ground (*masani pada*). The women of the house either bid farewell in an outer yard of the house or join the procession, but usually do not stay for the cremation. Sometimes a group of singers is arranged for the procession. The bed is carried by the eldest son, who is supported by other sons or relatives of the deceased like the son-in-law. Often, they do not wear shoes on the way. Preceeding the bed, a lamp is carried by a daughter's son. In the procession, husked rice is thrown and a gong and a shell are used to produce additional sounds. During the procession, the bed is put down on the ground seven times—six times on the way and a last time next to the pyre. Each time, relatives circle it seven times and put cotton, raw rice (*dhan*) and husked rice on all four corners of the bed during every round. Both cotton and raw rice are carried in a basket used for winnowing, which is also burned subsequently. The pot used to boil rice by the family of the deceased is carried during the procession by a *jati*, a member of a different clan (*bansa*), who destroys it near the pyre. A *jati* member who acts as a witness to almost all the ceremonies is imperative among the Aghria.

After the cremation ground is reached, the bed is carried anti-clockwise around the pyre seven times, and the body is put on top of it with its head towards the north and the feet to the south. Sometimes, relatives call the dead person one last time—as if they wanted to wake him or her up. Relatives and friends usually throw some pieces of sandalwood dipped in *ghee* on the pyre after all the knots in the clothes of the deceased have been opened, or the clothes themselves have been removed. Then the eldest son, standing with his back to the pyre, lights the fire using the lamp which was carried by the daughter's son. Usually, only very few relatives remain to observe the burning or to occasionally add salt to the fire in order to speed up the process. The bed is also burned after one leg has been broken off at the arrival at the cremation ground. At a later stage of the burning, the skull is broken by a relative.

The men participating in the burning are not allowed to enter the house before the corpse is burned to ashes. From the cremation ground, the men go to a pond or river in order to take a bath. There, a small plant, e.g. a mango, is set on the banks by the eldest son. The plant is watered then and on the following day. Before leaving, all the men stand in a row and the first man picks up a stone and hands it over his shoulder to the man behind him, who repeats the action, and so on, until the last man throws the stone into the water. Some Aghria believe that this procedure may cause death never to occur again. When entering the house, one has to wash one's feet and water is sprinkled over one's head.

After the cremation the family sits together, and rice is served. Certain restrictions have to be observed by the family from now on. Particularly no oil (*tel*) should be used (even for oil lamps). Milk, onions and garlic are forbidden, but not chili, salt or turmeric. The family, and to some extent the whole clan, is not allowed to attend any weddings or to visit any temple. No god may be worshipped inside the house either. Additionally, the eldest son should not sleep in a bed, but on the floor.

The following day, the eldest son, accompanied by other relatives, returns to the cremation ground and collects seven small bones which are kept to be stored in a tomb (*samadhi*), and later immersed into the Ganga near Allahabad. Water is sprinkled on the ashes, which are then immersed in a nearby river or pond. The participants have to take another bath, after which water is given to the recently set plant again.

The third day: *telghar/telkam*

In the morning, the barber comes to shave all the men except the sons who participated in the cremation and to cut the nails of the women. The washerman collects one cloth from every Aghria household, a ritual token, since the rest is washed by the Aghria family itself. Most of the restrictions regarding food are lifted on that day, and the family is allowed to use oil again. Some *jatis* offer a simple meal to all caste members in the village. However, the restrictions regarding oil, fish, meat or eggs remain for the eldest son (or sons), and the entire family is not yet allowed to eat non-vegetarian food. On the following days, invitations for the funeral are distributed and a tomb is built.

The ninth day: *naakiria/nabakriya*

On the ninth day, the funeral period called *kam ghar* that lasts till the eleventh or twelfth day begins. For the rituals of this period, the presence of a priest is required—usually one of the Aghria's own priests called Tihari. In a first *puja* in the evening, the priest lights the *akhanda dipa*—a continuous and inextinguishable light, which burns the whole night. Additionally, water—ideally a mixture of seven holy rivers, milk, curd, *jabdhan* (a kind of wheat), *kusa*-grass and flowers—is put into a special pot with holes so that drops of water run onto the ground the whole night.

The tenth day: *dasah*

The next morning, a little hut (*dasah ghar*) is erected near the pond. The *akhanda dipa* and the pot with holes from the evening before are placed near that hut (the pot is destroyed after the *puja*). Sitting under the hut, the Tihari is facing north while the son sits facing south. The priest, the eldest son (or sons) and a *jati* member have to be present. Next to the hut a fire is lit, and unbroken pulses (*mug*), half-boiled rice (*darsijha bhat*) and, in a smaller pot, *bara*—a cake made of pulses (*birhi*)—are cooked. From the rice and the pulses, ten balls (*pinda*) plus one for the ancestors (*pitru*), are formed. After the offering of these eleven rice balls to the ancestors, everything is put in a pot together with fruits and a cloth. The pot is then immersed into the pond by the eldest son toward the west. Afterwards the hut is burned down by the eldest son.

After that morning *puja*, the eldest son and the other male relatives are shaved by the barber, but only the sons have their heads shaved. Another bath follows, and again the plant near the pond is watered. The sons receive new, white clothes from their father-in-law or mother's brother. A set of clothes consists of a white *dhoti*, a white *ganji* and a towel. At the same time, the women of the family take their bath. Widows take off their jewellery and bangles and receive a white *sari* from their brothers.

Later, a small *ghar sanskar* takes place inside the house to purify it. It can be combined with the *asthi sanskar,* to purify the bones if the family wishes to keep the bones inside the house instead of the *samadhi.* After this *puja,* a procession to the *samadhi* takes place. It is led by the priest and the eldest son, who carries the seven bones. They are followed by other relatives. Again a gong and a shell are used in the procession. The *samadhi* erected previously is surrounded by four little trees, one in each corner. Between the trees, a line of mango leaves is placed. After a short *puja,* the eldest son places a red flag on top of the *samadhi* and circles around the *samadhi* seven times clockwise. Relatives, but not the priest, do likewise. Now the bones and some coins are placed inside the *samadhi,* which is subsequently closed with bricks.

The eleventh day: *kam ghar/antestikriya*

On the most important day of the funeral, the largest number of relatives, friends and neighbours is present. Outside, the participants offer a gift of money, and a member of the family carefully writes down who gives what.

In the morning, a more elaborate *puja* is performed inside the house. Here, the relatives bring gifts for the deceased such as all kinds of food (fruits, vegetables, rice, ghee, curd, etc.), cloths, household goods (oil lamp, torch, etc.), umbrellas, toilet articles (soap, hair oil, shampoo, etc.). A seat is offered to the deceased where, if possible, his photo is kept. First, the eldest son as main sacrificer (*kartta*) sits on the left side of the priest facing east. After the invocation of several gods, four leaf-plates are put in front of the priest. Next, the deceased is worshipped on his chair with the photo with flower-garlands. The eldest son changes his seat—now facing south. A mixture of boiled rice is brought by the eldest son's wife, and fruits and sweets are added. Three rice balls are formed from this mixture by the eldest son and are placed on one leaf-plate each. Later, another ball is prepared and placed in a short distance from the other three. The eldest son then adds Ganga-water mixed with rice, milk, and *duba-* and *kusa*-grass, for all the leaf-plates. Furthermore, a cloth (*dhoti*) is given by the eldest son and placed around the three rice balls. The rice balls (*pinda*) are worshipped by the eldest son by circling some incense and an oil-light (*dipa*) around them. All four rice balls are then put together in a bowl, and the eldest son holds the bowl for a few minutes on his right shoulder, promising to take the bones to the Ganga. The content of the bowl is later immersed in a nearby pond. A fire sacrifice (*homa*) follows, fed with *ghee* by the priest.

In the following sequence, ten leaf-bowls with rice (*arua chaul*) are given to the priest by the eldest son. These ten gifts called *dasa dan* symbolize 1. a cow (*go dan*); 2. land (*bhumi*); 3. gold (*hiranya*); 4. a cloth (*bastra*); 5. water (*jala*); 6. raw material for oil (*til*); 7. rice (*arua chaul*); 8. a mixture of milk and ghee (*prapanaka*); 9. a light (*dipa*); and 10. a bed (*sajja dan*). All these gifts must be equally distributed among all present priests or Brahmins, because in wealthier families other priests in addition to the family priest (*purohit*) may sometimes be invited. At the same time, near the fire of sacrifice, a new bed including bed cover, blanket, mosquito net as well as fruits and rice, is prepared. A junior Brahmin takes his seat on the bed, which is considered to be a gift of the 'bed of death' (*mrutya sajja dan*) or the 'bed of the ghost' (*preta sajja dan*). He has his feet massaged and is fed by the eldest son. Afterwards, the junior Brahmin has to leave the house immediately, taking the gifts with him.

After the *sajja dan,* the women of the family can present another gift symbolizing a cow (*go dan*), which is usually substituted by money. At the end, the priest distributes some *ghee* among the sons and other people present, the so-called *homa ghee,* which was also used for the fire ritual and is said to have a purifying effect when eaten and applied to one's head.

The *puja* is succeeded by the *bhanja dan*—a special gift for the sister's son (*bhanja*) of the deceased (or in case of a woman the sister's son of her husband). The *bhanja* is worshipped and fed by the family, e.g. the widow, and is usually given some money and clothes.

One or two meals are served to the relatives and guests on that day. The Aghria prefer to cook for themselves. A *jati* is engaged to cook for all caste members of the village while another Brahmin acts as cook for all guests including Aghria from other villages. Since it is practically impossible to invite the whole village and cook for all inhabitants on such an occasion, raw food for one meal is distributed. The eleventh day is the first day on which the family is allowed to eat non-vegetarian food again, and it is also served to the rest of the *jati*, the relatives and the guests.

Sometimes, in fact quite often, death occurs at a time favourable or auspicious for the deceased; but it is always very inauspicious for the family of the dead. This necessitates rituals to remove the danger or negative effect from the family. If such a ritual is performed, it is usually done on the night of the eleventh day at a time set by the priest or astrologer according to the stars. In a special *homa,* nine kinds of wood, which resemble the nine stars, are burned in the presence of the eldest son, the family priest (*purohit*) and a few family members. Afterwards, an earthen pot named *dan patro* is filled with rice, cloth, a little bit of gold, some money and two little iron nails symbolizing Yama, the god of death, and his brother Sama. The pot is given by the eldest son to a lower Brahmin, who is called upon for this ritual. Ideally, nobody should see this moment, and everyone should close his or her eyes while the pot is handed over. Immediately afterwards, the Brahmin has to leave the house—even if it is the middle of the night. Then the *homa* is completed. Water is sprinkled inside the house and cowshed by family members with the help of a mango-leaf.

The twelfth day/the ritual of six months: *chhamasi*

Traditionally this ritual should take place six months after the *kam ghar*. However nowadays it is usually performed on the twelfth day. The *puja* in the morning is almost identical with the *puja* on the eleventh day. Again, the eldest son appears in his white clothes. In front of the priest three leaf-plates are arranged once more, and the eldest son, facing south, puts a rice ball on each of them. Later he adds some water. However, only three rice balls instead of four are used on this day. The names of ancestors, as far as they are remembered, are called out by the eldest son and other relatives. In the end, the eldest son fills a bowl with rice again and puts it on his shoulder.

The recipient of the *sajja dan* is now the family priest. Now the bed is considered to be a 'happy bed' (*sukha sajja dan*) or the 'bed of the ancestors' (*pitru sajja dan*).

After the main *puja,* another ritual for the ancestors called *sraddha* is observed in the kitchen—this time conducted by the eldest son and his wife. One big leaf plate for the deceased is placed in the middle, some smaller (sometimes twelve) for other ancestors around it, and another small one for Vishma Deb is set out slightly apart. First rice, raw vegetables, pulses, etc., and clothes are given, and everyone leaves the room as the ancestors should not be disturbed while eating. In the second part of the *sraddha,* boiled rice (*bhat*) and cooked food (*dal*, curry, *kiri,* etc.) is offered by the eldest son. On the big leaf plate, six portions of food are served. Again, the room is vacated. Afterwards, the raw food is given to a Brahmin. The cooked food is eaten by the family members. Some Aghria argue that the food on the main leaf should be eaten by the daughter's sons of the deceased or by other grandchildren.

This *puja* is repeated exactly a year after the death and is then known as *barsika sraddha*. The procedure is identical, apart from a minor difference that twelve portions of food are offered to the deceased instead of six.

Analysis and Comparison

The Concept of Death

For the decision over life and death the God of Death, Yama, is responsible. Once the decision is made, Yama sends his assistants (Yamdut) to bring a person to his court. Sometimes, Aghria feel that the bed with the dead person that they carry in the procession to the cremation ground is much heavier than could be expected if only an old person were on it. They believe that the reason for this is that the Yamdut also sit on the bed. Yama's secretary, Chitra Gupta, keeps a huge book in which every person has his or her own page. According to the deeds listed there, a person is sent to heaven (*swarga*) or to hell (*narka*), which means that he or she will either get a place near the gods or will be punished, say by being thrown into boiling oil.

There is no unanimous opinion among the Aghria regarding the exact role of Yama. While some Aghria see him as a ruler over heaven and hell, others consider his kingdom to be hell alone. In my opinion, Yama's latter role as the ruler over dark and evil forces is expressed in the *puskara*-ritual on the eleventh day, to which I will return while dealing with inauspiciousness later.

Nevertheless, necessary steps or precautions can be taken by the family to secure a place in heaven for the soul (*atman*) of the deceased. In the procession to the cremation, a daughter's son should carry a light—it helps the deceased to find a place in heaven. Furthermore, the body is burned naked on the pyre, or at least all knots in its clothes are opened so that the soul can easily depart from the body. Another step is the giving away of all items the deceased had used in his life. On the eleventh and twelfth day in particular, all kinds of gifts are given according to the means of the family. These gifts are handed over to a priest because it is argued that the deceased will receive them through the priest. Particularly necessary is the *go dan*—the gift of a cow by the eldest sons. It is believed that the soul needs to hang on to the tail of the cow on the way to heaven in order to cross the river Baiterani.

Even if these precautions are taken, the soul still cannot find peace or a place in heaven if the sister's son (*bhanja*) is not fully satisfied. Accordingly, after the *bhanja* has been worshipped, a special gift (*bhanja dan*) has to be given to him on the eleventh day. On the role of the *bhanja* I will elaborate later.

The Transformation from *pret* (ghost) to *pitru* (ancestor)

Among the Aghria, there is no clear-cut distinction between the soul (*atman*) and the ghost (*pret*). Sometimes both are combined in the term *preta-atman*, which people use to describe the fate of the deceased. In contrast, the term *bhut-pret* is sometimes coined when people are attacked by evil forces. *Bhut* stands for evil spirits in general. It seems, therefore, that a main objective of the funeral is to turn the *pret*, who has a dangerous potential, into an ancestor or *pitru*, who is seen rather as a protective force, and whose blessings are sought for agricultural works, weddings, etc. Such a transformation is the theme of death rituals in India (Bennett 1983, Conzelmann 1996, Gaenszle 1999, Kaushik 1976, Parry 1994 et al.), and many of the rituals already described resemble a general north Indian Hindu pattern. In all these cases, the transformation is a gradual process aimed to pacify the *pret* and to fulfil its needs in order to facilitate the transition, and finally to merging with the ancestors.

Generally, among the Aghria as in 'Brahmanically influenced Hindu contexts the status or place of a departed person is not well defined' (Michaels 1999, 116). He or she is conceptualized as wandering around in complete darkness. Lights either carried by a daughter's son in the funeral procession or the continuous and inextinguishable light on the ninth day are therefore offered. Immediately after the cremation and a bath, a little mango-plant is set near a pond or river, which is said to offer shade for the *pret*. Next to it, some stones are placed to offer a temporary house or shelter, and a tomb is erected.

Furthermore, the *pret* is imagined as an extremely thirsty and hungry being. The mangoplant is watered regularly to ease his thirst. On the ninth day, a pot of water is placed inside the house which is not just considered to be a seat for the *pret*. Through holes in the pot, drops fall onto the ground. People either say that this is done to quench the thirst or they say that the *pret* leaves the house in the same way the drops fall to the ground.

On the tenth day the eldest son, guided by the family priest, prepares half-boiled rice and offers water and ten rice balls (*pinda*) to the *pret,* one for each day. The offering of the 10 *pinda* on the tenth day is common in north India where it is described as *pindadan* and 'seen as the symbolic recreation of the dead man's body' (Kaushik 1976, 274). Here the half-boiled rice obviously also symbolizes the liminal state of a *pret* who is still a 'passenger' and has not yet reached the state of a *pitru,* to whom fully boiled rice is offered later. The *pinda* is then immersed into the water, and the family priest claims that life will develop in the womb of the mother in the water in the tenth month. Similarly, the *pret* needs ten days to leave the house and leaves it by water.

On the eleventh day boiled rice mixed with fruit, etc., is offered by the eldest son to the ancestors in three *pinda* representing the last three generations. An extra *pinda* is given to the deceased. Finally, everything is mixed. This part shows similarities to rituals known as *sapindikarana* (Kaushik 1976, 279) or *sapinda sraddha* (Bennett 1983, 105) which are seen as decisive steps in the transformation to ancestorhood. Although the *puja* is repeated on the next day, only three rice balls for the last three generations are prepared and the *pret* seems to have been transformed into an ancestor by now.

However, in the case of the Aghria, the transition is marked in yet another way—by the offering of the gift of a bed or *sajja dan.* This custom again is quite common in north India, from Brahmins (Dumont 1998 [1966], 96) to the so-called Untouchables (Randeria 1999, 103-4), but while one *sajja dan* is usually given to a Brahmin,[2] here, two different kinds of *sajja dan* are found, *mrutya sajja dan* (the bed of death) or *preta sajja dan* (the bed of the ghost). They are given to a lower Brahmin, who represents the *pret* on this occasion. The eldest son says, as he hands over the gift: 'I give you, *pret*, this gift. Please accept it happily.' On the telfth day, the *puja* is repeated, but no 'bed of death' or 'bed of the ghost' is given. Instead a bed known as *sukha sajja dan* (happy bed) or *pitru sajja dan* (bed of the ancestor) is given, and now accepted by the family priest, who is then identified with the *pitru.* The necessity of giving two *sajja dan* is probably not only related to the transformation from *pret* to *pitru*, but also to the transformation from inauspiciousness to auspiciousness.

The Transformation from Inauspiciousness to Auspiciousness

Death is considered as inauspicious (*asubha*), but is accompanied by auspicious and inauspicious symbols. Often one finds elements regarded as highly inauspicious for the living but in a similar manner auspicious for the deceased, and life and death are symbolically inverted. A case in point is the position in which the deceased is laid in the house with the feet towards the south—nobody in the house would sleep in such an inauspicious direction. The bed turned upside-down for the procession is another similar example. Apart from these ambivalent symbols, cotton placed on all four corners of the bed is clearly seen as inauspicious. And contrary to that, banana leaves in the corners, the group singing devotional songs during the procession, or the witnessing of a cremation—all are unambiguously considered auspicious.

In any case, the family tries to secure auspiciousness by giving certain gifts. On the eleventh day, the giving of ten gifts, a ritual

---

[2] Sometimes the *sajja dan* is given to a high status Brahmin (Bennett 1983, 104), sometimes to a funeral Brahmin, lower in status (Conzelmann 1996, 367) and sometimes in case of Brahmins highest in status to a wife-taker (Dumont (1998 [1966], 96).

also common among Brahmin castes in north India (Kaushik 1976, 277), is considered auspicious for the giver as well as for the receiver, with the exception of the bed of death (*mrutya sajja dan*). It is also very auspicious to give and receive the *bhanja dan,* although in this case it is not quite clear if it is auspicious for the deceased himself or the actual giver, or (probably) both.

If, however, the death occurs at a certain time called *puskara,* it is explicitly auspicious for the deceased, but very inauspicious for his family. The *puskara* is determined by the day of the week (*bara*), e.g. every Tuesday, by the day within a fortnight (*tithi*), e.g. every second day, and by a certain constellation of stars (*nakhyatra*). In such a case, additional rituals are necessary.

In the case of *puskara,* a special ritual is usually performed during the night in which a *dan* is given to a lower Brahmin in the name of Yama and his brother Sama. Again this is auspicious for the giver, but highly inauspicious for the receiver, and the family *purohit* would not accept this *dan* (a pot full of raw rice in which every family member has thrown one handful so as to symbolically remove the inauspiciousness).

The Brahmin lower in status is sometimes called Danua Brahmin because of his obligation to accept certain *dan.* He is considered an appropriate receiver of the bed of death (*mrutya sajja dan*) and of the *puskara dan.* Two out of three Danua Brahmins I asked acknowledged the inauspiciousness they receive, and one told me that he would never sleep on a *mrutya sajja dan*, but would give it away.

Raheja, who did pioneering work on the relation between categories of gifts and *dan* in particular, as well as on the transfer of inauspiciousness as an ordering principle in a peasant caste of UP, concluded that 'the significance of dan ... was focused on the transfer of inauspiciousness from donor to recipient' (Raheja 1988, 31). Contrary to that, in the context of Aghria funeral customs, certain *dan,* e.g. the *puskara dan,* transfer inauspiciousness to a lower Brahmin to ensure auspiciousness for the family of the deceased, while other *dan,* such as the *bhanja dan* or *go dan,* which are given on the same occasion, are clearly auspicious for the donor as well as the receiver—here a *bhanja* and a higher Brahmin or *purohit.*

Generally, one finds that certain times such as *puskara*, certain spaces or directions, e.g. south, certain objects, e.g. banana leaves, or even certain persons such as a Danua Brahmin are considered either auspicious or inauspicious, as Madan (1985, 13) has pointed out. This seems to confirm what Apffel-Marglin (1985, 79) observed in the context of the devadasis of Puri: namely that the 'coexistence of both auspiciousness and inauspiciousness has the transformative effect of renewal'.

The Transformation from Impurity to Purity

The family of the deceased is considered to be impure (*asuddha*) after the death, and the pot used to boil rice has to be destroyed. Furthermore, the family is excluded from all marriages, and from worshipping gods in the house or in their temples. To some extent, as some Aghria explained, they are temporarily 'untouchable'. These restrictions should be observed not only by the nuclear or joint family, but also by the whole patrilineal clan, considered to be polluted. In addition, rituals for the village goddess (*gram sri*) cannot take place for eleven days after a death, because the whole village is regarded to be in a state of impurity.

Separated from the social realm, the family members, and the eldest son in particular, have to purify themselves according to their contamination. Apart from destroying polluted articles, a series of purifying baths and a strict diet especially until the *tel kam,* the barber, the washerman and the *purohit* facilitate the purification. Only on the eleventh day the family will be fully integrated into the caste again.

The Role of the *Bhanja,* Alternating Generations and the Continuity of Life

The role of the sister's son of the deceased is not pronounced among the north Indian castes. However, among the Aghria his presence is obligatory on the eleventh day. If there is no close *bhanja,* a distant, classificatory *bhanja* will replace him. A *bhanja* is held in particular high esteem among the Aghria: 'To feed a Brahmin is more valuable than feeding 100 cows. But to feed a *bhanja* is more valuable than feeding 100 Brahmins.' When asked about this prominent characteristic of an Aghria funeral, the informants gave vague responses.

The same custom of *bhanja dan* is also common among the Chosa, another peasant caste of the region structurally similar to the Aghria. Here, the *bhanja* not only receives his *bhanja dan*, but also has the right to demand his share of all gifts considered auspicious for a receiver. His share should be equal to that of the family priest.

Elwin (1945) mentions in his description of funerary rites in Bastar the necessary presence of a *bhanja* among the tribal Bison-horn Maria Gond. Apart from being a ritual specialist the sister's son is the 'chief actor' (Elwin 1945, 95). As part of his obligations he 'climbs up to the roof and makes a hole which is intended symbolically to allow the message of death to spread out through the world' (ibid.); he beats the drums and finally, and probably most importantly, 'he sits on the *uraskal* [the memorial menhir] while it is being carried to its hole; he makes the appointed offerings before the stone; he kills the sacrificial and festal cow' (ibid.). By bringing the menhir for the ultimate peace of the deceased, it is the sister's son 'who plays a leading part' (Elwin 1945, 113) because he 'touches the stone and addresses the dead man. 'In your name,' he says, 'we are bringing this stone ...' (ibid.).

Similar examples of a prominent role for a *bhanja* in funerary rites can be found among tribal groups in Nepal. Oppitz' (1991) research on the Magar in north-west Nepal is a case in point. Let me briefly summarize the *bhanja's* role according to Oppitz (1991, 413-35). The *bhanja* is to a large extent responsible for the transport of the corpse or, more explicitly, for ensuring the safe passage of the dead on his way by firing a gun at certain critical points of the procession. Thus, the role of the sister's son can be understood as that of a guide for the dead. Furthermore, the *bhanja* acts as a barber for the sons of the deceased who are of higher status. More importantly, it is the *bhanja* who guides the dead symbolically into the other world at a later stage by leading an ox through the village and by crossing the separating river together. Only by holding the tail of that ox is the deceased able to cross the river. This service of the *bhanja* is highly valued among the Magar; the agnates of the deceased present not only the ox to him, but also other valuable gifts such as copper dishes, gold, silver or clothes. The next day the *bhanja* once more escorts the deceased to the world beyond by guiding a sheep, a companion of the deceased on his way, out of the village. Apart from other tasks, e.g. during ritual feasts, it is also the sister's son's responsibility to erect the memorial stone where the deceased finds a permanent place and rest as ancestor. Again, the role of the *bhanja* is essential in transforming the deceased into an ancestor.

The role of the *bhanja* in death rituals of the tribal Mewahang Rai in East Nepal does not seem to differ considerably from the Magar. In his account, Gaenszle (1999, 49ff) also describes the sister's son or son-in-law as main actor of the ritual, who plays 'a significant role at all the important stages of the funeral' (Gaenszle 1999, 62), in particular in the procession—a 'journey to the beyond' (Gaenszle 1999, 56), in which the deceased is 'guided away' (ibid.). 'The procession is headed by men who fall into the category of *makcha* (CM. 'DH, yZH' [DH = daughter's husband/yZH = younger sister's husband) or—if none is available—a bhānij (N. 'ZS' [sister's son—US]) in relation to the deceased. These son-in-laws [...] open the way to the beyond ...' (Gaenszle 1999, 52).

Obviously the sister's son plays an important role in some death rituals in the hill region or hinterland of Middle India (Orissa/Chhattisgarh) and in parts of the Himalaya. He (or the son-in-law) guides and escorts the deceased into the world beyond. He ensures the safe passage into the next world. I want to argue that the role of the *bhanja* among the Aghria must be understood in the same way, because informants explained that the soul of the deceased cannot find peace as long as the *bhanja* is not satisfied. Other possible explanations for the *bhanja dan* such as a compensation of the mother's brother to the sister's son for not giving him his daughter as a bride as expected in a society with a traditional ideal of matrilateral cross cousin marriage, could neither be confirmed among the Aghria nor among the Chosa. In my opinion, it would also not fully explain the content of the rituals described above.

Furthermore the role of the *mama* in relation to the *bhanja* seems noteworthy. In Aghria-society the presence of a mother's brother is required during lifecycle rituals until the marriage of the sister's son (or daughter). Particularly during the name-giving ceremony and during marriage the *mama* is obliged to be present and to give certain gifts. Without his presence and before the arrival of his gifts, these life cycle rituals would be incomplete or could not even start. That, of course, means that the *mama* is deeply involved in the transformation of his newly born *bhanja* into a complete social person. However, his responsibility is terminated at the time of marriage. According to the *Brahmana*-literature (Pandey 1993

[1969], 153-4) as well as ethnography (Dumont 2000 [1957], 277), it is precisely at this stage that a man is considered to be complete, insofar as he is then able to perform rituals in which his wife is, by necessity, involved as well.

To summarize: obviously the *mama* guides the *bhanja* into the world and is to a large extent responsible for the formation of his *bhanja* as a social person. After marriage, however, it is the *bhanja's* responsibility to guide his *mama* into the world beyond. In some cases among the Aghria, the presence of a *bhanja* is already required before the death of his *mama*—at the time of the death of his *mami*. When someone's wife dies, the presence of the husband's *bhanja,* and not the wife's *bhanja,* is imperative. In other words, the role of a *bhanja* starts precisely when the *mama* begins to lose his full ritual status—without his wife, he is no longer able to perform certain rituals and is thus a ritually incomplete person.[3] I have tried to systemize the two opposite, or rather complimentary, ritual roles in Figure 1.

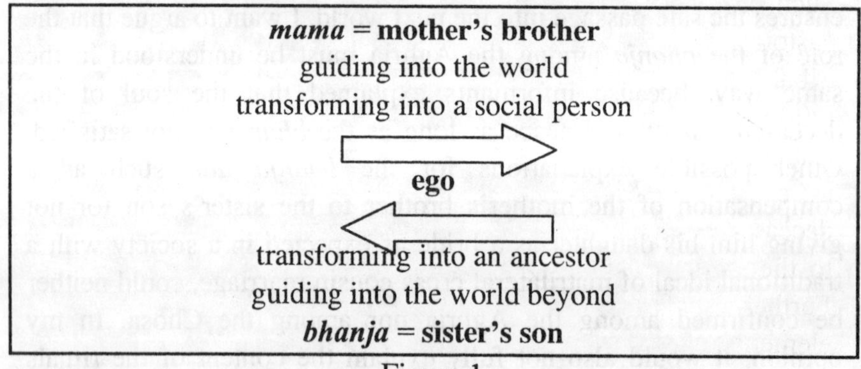

Figure 1

Figure 1 shows that the closest affine of a the older generation guides a person into the world, while the closest affinal relative in the younger generation, your son-in-law or sister's son (when cross-cousin marriage is practiced), escorts you to the other world. Additionally one has to take into consideration that to some extent *mama* and *bhanja* are terminologically equated among the Aghria and, possibly, among the Gond.[4] In terms of address you may call

[3] I have not considered cases of remarriage here.

[4] Among the Magar one does not find such an equation. Instead the categories *mama* and *bhanja* extent over three generations each, but

your *bhanja* '*mama'* and vice versa. In an ideal formula of bilateral cross-cousin marriage, *mama* and *bhanja* are related as FF and SS. That would simplify Figure 1, because then one has to deal with two generations only. To put it differently: the closest affinal relative of your adjacent generation forms the social person and transforms it –shown in Figure 2.

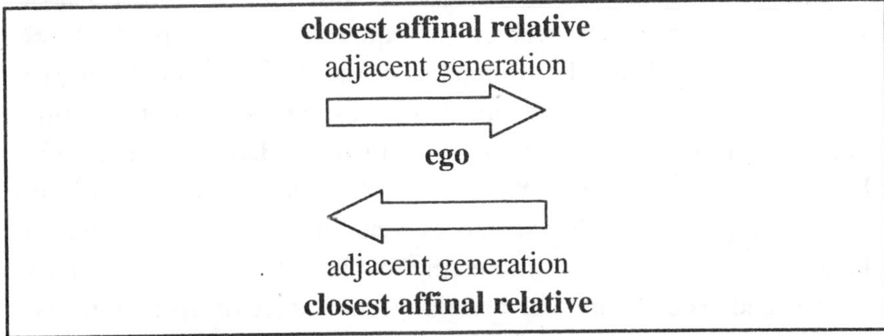

Figure 2

Such a formula would probably also accomodate the funeral customs of the tribal Gadaba of Koraput and, to some extent, the tribal Juang of Keonjhar. Among the Gadaba, according to Berger (2000/2001), one finds two main actors figuring prominently in rituals prior to the final *gotr*-ceremony: an agnate (*tsorubai*) acting as a funeral priest, and the mother's brother (*mamu*) of the deceased. Together with the *tsorubai* the *mamu* leads the procession to the cremation ground and offers drinks to his *bhanja* later on. Furthermore, he gives and receives gifts—just to mention a few elements. Naturally it is rather unlikely that the genealogical *mamu* will be present at the funeral of his sister's son or *bhanja* due to the age difference, and quite often the 'real' mother's brother is replaced by his son or even his son's son. Obviously the role of the *mamu* is stressed among the Gadaba. Contrary to the other cases cited, the *mamu* not only participates in forming the social person

---

nevertheless one has the important reciprocal set *mama/bhanja*, which as such is comparable to the Middle Indian cases. Furthermore also among the Magar it is the *mama* who plays an essential role during marriage, because ideally he gives his daughter to his sister's son and helps to complete the transformation of his *bhanja* into a full social person in a very direct way (the mother's brother being the wife's father according to the traditional Magar alliance system). See Oppitz 1991, 45ff, 76ff, 327ff.

due to his prominent role in marriage rituals, but also in transforming it. Here, as in Figure 2, the closest affinal relative of an adjacent generation fulfils both tasks: the bringing into the world and the guiding into another. Thus the *mamu* combines both functions directly, and the case seems not to contradict my general hypothesis.

The case of the Juang shows a similarity to the Gadaba. Although the mother's brother (or equivalent in his role) is not directly involved in the funeral, an unmarried man from the mother's brother's village must be responsible for the ritual purification of the deceased and his family (McDougal 1963, 131). Furthermore, although the mother's brother has no specific role in the marriage of his *bhanja* and is generally treated more like a father, there is still an interesting exchange between mother's brother and sister's son. The *bhanja* offers a share of his game meat to his *mama* in exchange for bow and arrows (ibid.). Thus, one might argue that the *mama* has to be involved in transforming his *bhanja* into a successful hunter in this world. Additionally, McDougal (1963, 155ff) shows that the principle of alternating generations is prominent among the Juang in particular in relation to marriage rules.

The rather abstract Figure 2 shows similarities to the formula of a tetradic society as developed by Allen (1986, 2000). This quadripartite model is represented in Figure 3 (left) as 'the simplest structuring of society' (Allen 2000, 82). It is based on the opposition between even and odd generations (horizontal line—dividing A and B from C and D) and between two moieties exchanging marriage partners. Or, to put it in a different way: agnates versus affines (vertical line—dividing A and C from B and D)—the distinction of the sexes taken for granted. A tetradic society would consist of four sections or categories only, a tetradic terminology of four terms respectively.[5] Both distinctions are implicit in Figure 2.

---

[5] Applied to Figure 3 (left) in a simplified way these categories include the following relations starting from an imaginary ego as D being identical with brother = father's father = son's son; A: mother's brother = wife's father = sister's son etc.; B: father = father's brother = son etc. and C: wife's brother = sister's husband = mother's father = daughter's son etc.

Obviously in lifecycle rituals of the Aghria, but probably also structurally similar cases the diagonal relation (mother's brother/sister's son) as shown in Figure 3 (middle) is of utmost importance. If one generalizes, for every ego it is the closest affine of the adjacent generation who guides him into the world and beyond—for A it would be D and vice versa.

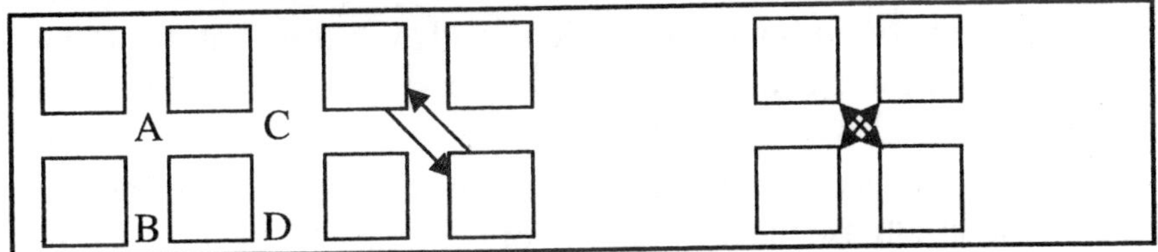

Figure 3 (left part as applied from Allen)

True, the Aghria rituals are not as simple as the model may suggest. Even if one may have found an explanation for the presence of the *bhanja* at the funeral, it is still more complicated to accommodate the ritual role of the daughter's son who not only carries a light in the death procession, but is also presumed to be the primary recipient of food offered first to the deceased at the time of the *sraddha* on the twelfth day as well as one year later,—a feature I have not found in any other description of north Indian *sraddha.* Following the principle of equation of alternating generations just illustrated and in fact common to the Middle Indian tribal society (Pfeffer 1983), the daughter's son is the younger brother of the deceased. But he is also an affinal relative, and he is the *bhanja* of the next generation, i.e. he is the *bhanja* of the son of the deceased or the sister's son of the chief mourner. Considering that the daughter's son may be replaced by any grandchild if there is no close daughter's son, one might argue that alternating generations share a special commensality[6] on certain occasions (*sraddha*), but further comparative research is necessary on this point.[7]

[6] Here a commensality shifted in time.

[7] One might also argue that the daughter's son of the deceased as *bhanja* of the son of the deceased helps his *mama* who is the chief mourner to attain his new status, namely, that of the head of the family after his father has passed away. Somehow similarly among the south Indian Pramalai Kallar (Dumont 2000 [1957], 275ff, 284-92) the mother's brother (or his son in the role of the mother's brother) of the chief mourner plays a leading part in the funeral. It is the mother's brother who ties a

It is noteworthy that a granddaughter plays a prominent role in the already mentioned funeral customs of the Bison-horn Gond (Elwin 1945, 95-7). The granddaughter (together with the wife of the funeral priest) is described as responsible for ensuring that the deceased, in case of rebirth, returns to his house. Furthermore, she offers water to the deceased and is involved in the preparation of food. All this may suggest a relation which symbolizes a continuity of the generation in both cases—Gond and Aghria—, but has to be confirmed by more data. In the Nepalese cases, however, there is no such evidence.

Additionally, a continuity of the local line is emphasized ritually, not only by the shouldering of the *pinda* by the eldest son, but also by building a tomb for the deceased on the land of the family, sometimes in a walled compound next to other patrilineal ancestors, where the bones of the deceased are kept until they are finally immersed into the Ganga. This may actually take decades. As Bloch and Parry (1982, 34) observed in relation to non-Hindu cases the tombs stand 'as a symbol of the property holding kinship group'.[8]

To summarize, there seem to be three essential relations pointing at a continuity of life during these death rituals. First, the

---

turban on the head of his sister's son symbolically reintegrating him into society. However such an explanation alone does not take into consideration that according to my informants the daughter's son helps his grandfather (mother's father) to reach heaven and he should eat specifically the grandfather's cooked food at the *sraddha*.

[8] In relation to Hinduism Bloch and Parry (1982, 37) rather speak of 'a total destruction of the physical body', but do not mention any tombs. However they mention the clear influence of ascetic ideals in funerary customs of Hindus, which might be applied to the *samadhis* as well. *Samadhi* in some yoga-traditions means ecstasy or a kind of trance in which the ascetic (*yogi*) does not realises anymore that he is meditating. Thus he becomes one with the object of his meditation and his individual consciousness becomes part of the cosmic self (Waterstone 1995, 87). But *samadhi* is for the *yogi* also a way of departure from this world by 'burying himself alive' (Sharma 1988, 82). On the one hand the building of *samadhis* known in the region only for the last decades and representing a rather recent change might by influenced by this ascetic ideal. On the other hand memorial stones are very common among tribal groups of the region, which however were already in a process of change at the time of Elwin's research (1945, 109) when he noted a 'Hinduization' of tombs.

aforementioned relation between father and son aims at a continuity of the local line. Secondly, the relation of the *bhanja* or sister's son/son-in-law with the mother's brother probably shows continuity in affinal relations,[9] but also a continuity in the lifecycle itself. Third, a possible ritual relation between an ego and the daughter's son (or grandchildren in a wider sense) may not only imply a continuity of the generations, but also has some affinal connotations because it is first and foremost the daughter's son. All three relations are genealogically represented in Figure 4. Coming back to the tetradic model, the three lines of continuity strikingly correspond in this quadripartite model with the three other sections apart from the ego's own, because according to the principles formulated earlier, A would include the sister's son equated with mother's brother; B the son again in terms of address equated with father among the Aghria and C the daughter's son (= wife's brother). All four sections are once more represented in Figure 5:

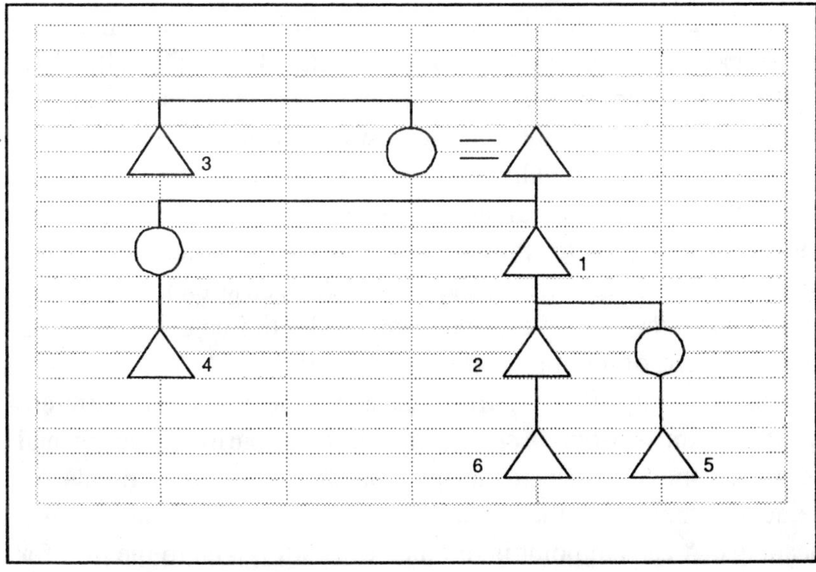

Figure 4: three lines of continuity presented in a genealogical manner—starting from ego (1) to a son (2) to a sister's son (4) or mother's brother (3) and to a daughter's son (5) or son's son (6)

[9] The presence of a *jati* member always a potential affine, may suggest the same idea.

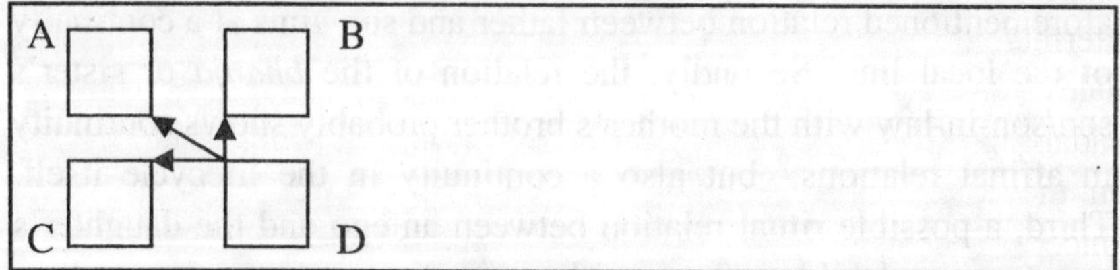

Figure 5: three lines of continuity presented in a tetradic way—starting from ego (D) to the son (B), to the sister's son or mother's brother (A) and to daughter's son (C).

Conclusion

After death, there is what Hertz (1960 [1907]) in his pioneering essay called an 'intermediary period' followed by a 'final ceremony'. After a first provisional burial, the mourners need time to come to terms with the death of a relative and the 'opposition between the persisting image of a familiar person who is like ourselves and the image of an ancestor, who is sometimes worshipped and always distant' (Hertz 1960 [1907]), 82). Furthermore death 'does not only confine itself to ending the visible bodily life of an individual; it also destroys the social being grafted upon the physical individual and to whom the collective consciousness attributed great dignity and importance' (Hertz 1960 [1907], 77). Therefore, the 'final ceremony has three objects: to give burial to the remains of the deceased, to ensure the soul peace and access to the land of the dead, and finally to free the living from the obligations of mourning' (Hertz 1960 [1907], 54).

Death among the Aghria consists essentially of different transformations—from *pret* to *pitru*, from impurity to purity and from inauspiciousness to auspiciousness. However, rituals or elements which mark these transitions overlap, and contain various meanings. A case in point is the 'bed of death' given to the *pret* for his peace, but also for the auspiciousness of the family.

The transformation of the *pret* into a *pitru,* for which two kinds of ritual specialists are engaged, as well as the necessary purification of the family after the death pollution, are well known from other north Indian Hindu cases, as reported by Bennett (1983), Parry (1994), Conzelmann (1996) et. al. However, no complete severance of the relations with the ancestors is intended, but rather a transition from one state to another. On the one hand, the transformation of the deceased into an ancestor with an intermediary period in which the deceased belongs to a potentially malevolent category, is also known from tribal cases like the Gadaba (Pfeffer 2001, 132) and is not unique to north India alone. On the other hand, the Aghria share a strong emphasis on the concept of auspiciousness with the Gujar, to which Madan (1985, 25) already attributed a 'basic importance at least in the scheme of values of upper castes'.

I have tried to highlight the role of the sister's son (*bhanja*) or potential son-in-law during the funerary rites among the Aghria because here they do not comply with a general north Indian pattern. However, I have shown that there are traditions comparable to those of the Aghria among the Gond of the region (Elwin 1945), where the *bhanja* rides on the dead man's memorial stone. Also, among the tribal Rai (Gaenszle (1999) and Magar (Oppitz 1991), the sister's son plays an important role comparable to that of the *bhanja* in Aghria society, guiding the deceased into the world beyond and transforming the mother's brother into an ancestor. The role of the *bhanja* in funerary rites seems to be complementary to the role of the mother's brother in helping his *bhanja* into the world, or to become a complete social person. Generalizing this result and combining it with the basic tetradic model suggested by Allen, the diagonal link within the four sections or the relation to the closest affinal of the adjacent generation may be of the utmost importance in other life cycle rituals, in particular in tribal ones. In this respect, the Aghria may have adapted a pattern found in their predominantly tribal surrounding. However, compared to the middle Indian tribal Sora described by Vitebsky (1993; for south Indian hunters and gatherers see also Demmer 1999), no verbal communication with the ancestors via shamans is possible.

The imperative presence of a sister's son in all these cases seems to be in contrast to cases cited by Parry and Bloch (1982) in which 'the avoidance of exchange constructs the image of permanence' (Bloch/Parry 1982, 32) and in which eternity seems to be symbolized by an 'end of affinity' (ibid., 27). Here the *bhanja* seems to hint at a continuity of kinship ties or affinal links beyond death, because it can be argued, as Elwin and Gaenszle also did, that his role is connected to cross-cousin marriage in which the sister's son is ideally also the daughter's husband and son-in-law.

Furthermore, the duty of the daughter's son (or a grandson) to carry a light in the procession and to receive boiled food offered first to the deceased as an ancestor is significant because the Aghria seem to deviate in this point from the well-known north Indian standard again. The principle of alternating generations, expressed explicitly among the Aghria in their wedding customs and in their kinship terminology which is, as Pfeffer (1983) has argued, typical for middle Indian tribes, is present here. In this regard, too, the Aghria may have been influenced by tribal groups of the

Apart from a continuity of affinal ties—probably highlighted in the role of the *bhanja*—and apart from a continuity of generation-sets most likely underlined in the role of grandchildren, a continuity of the local line is very prominent in the role of the eldest son as chief mourner. this is illustrated by the *samadhi* of the deceased which is built next to the other tombs of the family on their land symbolizing the descent group. The *samadhi* built separately for each ancestor stands in contrast to the postulated 'lack of individuality in Brahmanical conceptions of the after-life' (Michaels 1999, 127-8) or the destruction of the individual after death in Hinduism, 'where nothing of the individual is preserved which could provide a focal symbol of group continuity' (Bloch/Parry 1982, 36). By retaining an individual *samadhi,* the deceased may also keep a limited individuality comparable to that which we find in tribal groups where 'shape and size of the memory stones are selected according to certain calculations on the basis of male/female and social-status considerations' (Nayak 2001, 44). Thus the dead may keep individual aspects even after becoming ancestors.

References

Allen, N.J. 1986. 'Tetradic Theory: An Approach to Kinship', in *Journal of the Anthropological Society of Oxford*, vol.17, no. 2, 87-109.

— 2000. *Categories and Classifications: Maussian Reflections on the Social*, New York.

Apffel-Marglin, F. 1985. 'Types of Opposition in Hindu Culture', in J.B. Carman and F. Apffel-Marglin (eds.), *Purity and Auspiciousness in Indian Society*, Leiden.

Bennett, L. 1983. *Dangerous Wives and Sacred Sisters*, New York.

Berger, P. 2001, 2000/2001. 'Feeding the Dead: Rituals of Transformation among the Gadaba of Koraput', in *Adibasi* 44/45: 35-50.

Conzelmann, E. 1996. *Heirat, Gabe, Status. Kaste und Gesellschaft in Mandi*, Berlin.

Demmer, U. 1999. 'How to Make the Spirit of the Dead Happy: The Rhetoric of Words and Deeds in a Jenu Kurumba Death Ritual', in E. Schömbucher and C.P. Zoller, *Ways of Dying: Death and its Meanings in South Asia*, Delhi.

Dumont, L. 2000 [1957]. *A South Indian Subcaste: Social Organisation and Religion of the Pramalai Kallar*, Delhi.

— 1998 [1966]. 'North India in Relation to South India', in P. Uberoi (ed.), *Family, Kinship and Marriage in India*, Delhi, 91-111.

Elwin, V. 1945. 'Funerary Customs in Bastar State', in *Man in India*, vol. XXV, no. 2.

Hertz, R. 1960 [1907]. *Death and the Right Hand*, Aberdeen.

Gaenszle, M. 1999. 'The Making of Good Ancestors: Separation, Transformation and Exchange in Mewahang Rai Funerary Rites', in E. Schömbucher and C.P. Zoller, *Ways of Dying: Death and its Meanings in South Asia*, Delhi, 49-67.

Kaushik, M. 1976. 'The Symbolic Representation of Death', in *Contributions to Indian Sociology* (N.S.), vol. 10, no. 2.

McDougal, C.W. 1963. *The Social Structure of the Hill Juang*, Ph.D. thesis (Albuquerque, The University of New Mexico), Ann Arbor: University Micro Films.

Madan, T.N. 1985. 'Concerning the Categories Subha and Suddha in Hindu Culture: an Exploratory Essay', in J.B. Carman and F. Apffel Marglin (eds.), *Purity and Auspiciousness in Indian Society*, Leiden.

Michaels, A. 1999. 'Ancestors, Demons and the Ritual Impossibility of Death in Brahmanical Hinduism: Bala's Fourteenth in Deopatan (Nepal)', in E. Schömbucher and C.P. Zoller (eds.), *Ways of Dying: Death and its Meanings in South Asia*, Delhi, 112-34.

Nayak, P.K. 2001. 'Jagannath and the Adivasis: Reconsidering the Cult and its Traditions', in H. Kulke and B. Schnepel (eds.), *Jagannath Revisited. Studying Society, Religion and the State in Orissa*, Delhi, 25-48.

Oppitz, M. 1991. *Onkels Tochter, Keine Sonst. Heiratsbündnis und Denkweise in einer Lokalkultur des Himalaya*, Frankfurt/M.

Pandey, R. 1993 [1969]. *Hindu Samskaras: Socio-Religious Study of the Hindu Sacraments*, Delhi.

Parry, J. 1994. *Death in Benares*, Cambridge.

Pfeffer, G. 1983. 'Generation and Marriage in Middle India: the Evolutionary Potential of "Restricted Exchange"', in *Contributions to Indian Sociology* 17 (1).

— 2001. 'A Ritual of Revival among the Gadaba of Koraput', in H. Kulke and B. Schnepel (eds.), *Jagannath Revisited: Studying Society, Religion and the State in Orissa*, Delhi.

Raheja, G.G. 1988. *The Poison in the Gift. Ritual, Prestation, and the Dominant Caste in a North Indian Village*, Chicago

Randeria, S. 1999. 'Mourning, Mortuary Exchange and Memorialization: The Creation of Local Communities among Dalits in Gujarat', in E. Schömbucher and C.P. Zoller, *Ways of Dying: Death and its Meanings in South Asia*, Delhi.

Sharma, A. 1988. *Sati: Historical and Phenomenological Essays*, Delhi.

Skoda, U. 2000. 'The Kinship System of the Aghria', in *Journal of Social Sciences*, vol. 4, no. 4, Oct., special edition: '*Asian World Views: Context and Structure*', by R. Hardenberg.

Vitebsky, P. 1993. *Dialogues with the Dead*, Cambridge.

Waterstone, R. 1995. *Indien: Religion und Riten, Götter und Kosmos, Meditation und die Kunst des Yoga*, Gütersloh.

12

Bailey's Kondh Structure on the Tribal Frontier

Georg Pfeffer

If administrative classifications are ignored, about half the Orissan population can be assigned to 'tribal society'. Yet the structure of this society type is ignored by the dominant discourse. Among the very few professional tribal monographs, only Bailey's is quoted regularly (but discussed rarely). The present paper introduces Bailey's fine ethnography in the context of major theoretical controversies. As a member of the Manchester School, this author studied the forces of social change in the north-eastern Kondhmals: or the impact of the colonial administration and the lowland caste society upon the indigenous tribal and settler society. For him the three different 'structural forms' within the same field result not only in intra-systemic conflicts but also in inter-systemic contradictions of the actors involved. My paper re-examines Bailey's Kondh data to discard the structural-functionalist lineage theory and apply the structuralist alliance theory. The agnatic scheme of the Kondh is in fact ordered by the principle of fraternal seniority and the overall opposition of agnates and affines. Such a far-reaching and physically reified juxtaposition—combined with rules equating ego's generation with alternating ones (third, fifth, ninth)—are compared with N.J. Allen's tetradic model so that variations—seen as transformations in the evolutionary context—can be identified, even if such an exercise is far away from Bailey's theoretical aspirations.

Orissa is about the size of modern Italy. Almost a quarter of its population falls under the administrative category Scheduled Tribes, but 'tribalsociety' in the anthropological sense is represented by about half the population, inhabiting almost three quarters of the province.[1] Anthropologists speak of a tribe when they mean a people without central authority or clear-cut

[1] Recently (Pfeffer 2002) I have discussed tribal society in highland Orissa at length.

boundaries that is organized by affinity and descent, household and village communities rather than by functionally specialized institutions (Sahlins 1968). In tribal Orissa the sovereign centre does appear today in the guise of policemen and teachers, magistrates and land-revenue officers, bankers and postmen, but caste and bureaucracy have failed to drive out the tribal order.

To my knowledge, these proportions have remained unnoticed so far. They are mentioned here to underline the relevance of our general investigations into the socio-political periphery of the province, or the culture of the hill people, when compared to the well-known caste society that has been recorded in the lowlands over the last millennia. The tribal complex has been peripheral in the dominant discourse of Orissan studies and for those ruling from the urban centres in the Mahanadi delta.[2] I have noticed only a handful of professional anthropological monographs[3] on Orissan tribes.

Of these only Bailey's publication (1960) on a Kondh village in the old[4] Phulbani district has gained a certain popularity. The Kondh are one of the few tribes settled only in Orissa. With about a million members, they are also the biggest of the many tribes in the province. As the author of the standard work, Bailey is well-known and honoured in Orissa. In his later career, he published a number of books concerned with the local and regional political process. As such he is a prominent scholar in a field called 'political anthropology' by some.

In India however—particularly in Orissa—formal honours have not led to substantial discussions of his work. Orissan colleagues generally hesitate to debate each others findings. Frankly, I doubt whether many have read Bailey's books. Though much of his work is devoted to recent political history and the fluctuating relations between bigger and smaller former rulers of the hills, German academics have also—at least formally—relegated his work to a peripheral position. The first Orissa Research Project, for example,

---

[2] In 1999/2000 two successive short-term chief ministers of Orissa belonged to the Scheduled Tribes, but they had spent their respective lives in the Oriya context.

[3] Bailey 1960, McDougal 1964, P.K. Nayak 1989, Niggemeyer 1964, Vitebsky 1992).

[4] The present article will ignore the administrative reforms of 1995.

failed to recognize Bailey's years of fieldwork[5] and his ambitious theory. His name was mentioned, no doubt, in the list of references. But that was all.

Irrespective of my critical comments on Bailey's Kondh study, the present paper should be seen as a belated attempt to do justice to his ethnography, unsurpassed for half a century, and his attempt to come to terms with the complex relational pattern in the hills. I shall first introduce his theoretical frame of reference and his research methods even if the recent post-modern fashion flatly rejects any type of social theory and discards any attempt of social analysis—for fears of 'reification'—in favour of an amalgamation with the subjectivism of the situation. Though Bailey's theory and research method have been devised half a century ago, a number of prominent colleagues—many of them in Germany—are proud to follow these directions to the present day.

Theory and Method

F.G. Bailey, professor emeritus at the University of California, is a representative of the Manchester School. Social Anthropology was confined to a few outstanding individuals in the middle of the last century, when Bailey joined Max Gluckman's department at Manchester along with others who came from a wide variety of subjects and were to become prominent anthropologists in subsequent decades. Bailey's anthropology is always a study of political process under given economic constraints. It is conducted in the framework of a materialist philosophy.

Manchester theory, for Bailey, meant structural functionalism. Societies were seen as systems involving persons, i.e. timeless social positions and not mortal individuals complying with specific behavioural demands in relation to other persons. These relationships involved a third element of land or leadership or other material constraints. Gluckman's social analysis did not simply designate the working of Radcliffe-Brown's 'structural form' (1952, 192), but showed how society coped with deviations and variations regarding that third element in the sense of struggles for power and influence, survival or expansion.

[5] See also Bailey 1957)

Most of us know of Talcott Parsons' (1949) 'pattern maintenance'. Structural functionalism was concerned with the societal equilibrium—mostly of the fluctuating kind—to be maintained by certain prerequisites. Peace, for example, might be disturbed by murders, abductions, or betrayals, and recovered by certain sanctions of assemblies or rulers, or by segmentary retaliation, or perhaps simply by ignoring deviant behaviour.

So far Gluckman's school was in agreement with the then general trend of British Social Anthropology. But whereas many colleagues in Oxford, Cambridge, and London confined their efforts to what they called 'primitive societies', i.e. those of the closed type in remote rural areas, Gluckman and his students became famous for their work in the African copper belt among miners and other 'detribalized' inhabitants of modern cities. Manchester specialized in social change. While others studied structural variations *within* a social system, Gluckman's crew, the so-called 'Maxists', also worked on the contrast *between* different social systems.

In this intellectual milieu, Bailey—working in the eastern Kondhmals in the 1950s—discovered three distinct structures of political activity in a single field: the tribal order, the caste system, and state administration. In later books he also concerned himself with the electoral process in Orissa and the popular will in general. While others had studied the structural prerequisites of conflict and its resolution *within* a tribal framework, Bailey went beyond that level by focussing upon the crises arising out of confrontations *between* the tribal, the Oriya, and the state system, the subsequently contradictory aspirations of the actors involved, and thus the modifications of the structural forms.

In the Kondhmals tribal society had specific mechanisms for pattern maintenance. Moreover immigrant settlers led by the warrior caste had also been present in the hills for at least a thousand years. With the tribesmen they had found a mode of coexistence which at times implied the subordinate allegiance but not the submission of the Kondh, just as the 'hill chiefs' among the settlers knew how to react to the demands of the kings, residing in the adjoining lowlands. The colonial administration introduced a third type of political system in 1855. Then the language of the settlers privileged them in relation to the new authorities, just as new roads and the general impact of *pax britannica* brought many more and new types of settlers into the Orissan wild west, diminishing the influence of the warrior caste in favour of scribes and traders, such as the distiller caste from Baudh. The kings of the lowlands would try to use the new order to tighten their grip on the 'hill chiefs', just as, on the other hand, kings, chiefs and tribesmen joined to conspire against the British at times and the Kondh for their part rose against exploitative middlemen.

Most of the European administrators came to prefer the 'noble savage' to the 'cunning Hindu' collaborators on whose help they depended, and the sale and purchase of land was formally restricted to tribesmen. Furthermore empire builders quarrelled with empire builders. The so-called Meriah campaigns from 1832 to 1850 were led in turn by two rival Scotsmen, Campbell and Macpherson, who had each other arrested during different phases of their carriers. The two have been incorporated into Kondh religion, because during the *Meriah* sacrifice in present times, the shaman—communicating with the earth goddess—mentions their names in his efforts to excuse the non-human nature of the gifts for the 'hot' deity (Niggemeyer 1964, 195).

It should also be clear that the colonial administration had slender resources and limited political ambitions in the hills. As a result most British officers were withdrawn after pacification and Oriya administrators were given considerable leeway to fill their coffers and enhance their influence. Thus 'caste' policies combined with bureaucratic rule, just as members of the dominant warrior caste frequently acted within a code of solidarity intelligible to the tribesmen. Bailey's monographs—reconstructing colonial history with materials from the Baudh archives—thus not only introduce the political framework of a single social system but the mutual combinations and permutations, conflicts and contradictions observed in three different types of public order within a single field. Tribe, caste, and nation are seen as 'three forms of allocating scarce resources and of uniting to compete for those resources' (1960, 269). This competition became complex and harder by the mishmash of rights and duties, of institutions, and forces. Stressing 'agency' like the recent trends in social science, Bailey, writing 40 years ago in a structural functional frame of reference, confines his work to observed action executed by individuals who are not 'passive creatures exhibiting for our benefit regularities of behaviour, but ... actors who may not only choose between systems but may attempt to twist and amend these systems to their own advantage' (1960, 271).

Bailey's books are concerned with frequently contradictory demands of persons coexisting as Kondh, Oriya and Indians. Tribe, caste, and nation are the 'fixed points' (Bailey 1967, 416) in a first stage, to be followed by a deeper analysis which takes account of time and movement or direction of social change.

If Manchester functionalism introduced plurality and the interrelation of several structural forms, it also stands for a particular procedure of research, the 'extended case method'. Bailey and his peers arrive at generalizations and inter-subjectivity by reporting numerous cases of real life situations. Conflicting and contradictory action is presented in the context of ongoing controversies and subsequently interpreted on account of the ethnographer's detective work following up the tracks of each participant and his or her arguments, thus extending the given situation into longish case histories. Individuals deal with individuals in these confrontations. They are always testing social norms in one way or the other. The anthropologist indicates how the norm is enhanced or weakened, circumvented, abolished or changed. The ethnography gains substance and credibility through the extended case method. Mere impressions of the foreign observer are corrected by the nature of the relational knots tying together the actors on an ethnographic stage that is beyond his directions.

Kondh structure

My present paper will discuss the tribal structure of Bailey's three-tired concept of western Orissa. I use the monograph of 1960 as well as an article of 1957 which was incorporated into the most important textbook on comparative political systems (Cohen and Middleton 1967, 415-38) and has been frequently republished until the present day. Thus the analysis of the Kondh social structure has become standard literature of the discipline as such, but not, to my knowledge, of the regional experts in India or elsewhere. Specialists on Orissa should close this gap.

In the tradition of the 1950s, Bailey's book is a village study, but the author rightly points to a 'bond which is much stronger than that of neighbourhood' (1960, 20), the tie of agnation. He does mention the religious and ritual community of the villagers, closely connected to the agnatic principle, but devotes very little attention to these spheres. The formal framework of the village Baderi seems to be an agnatic genealogy. Minute statistics indicate that 70 per cent of the villagers are Kondh and of these again 79 per cent according to Bailey, 'can be shown on one agnatic genealogy' (1960, 21). Our author speaks of 'the Baderi lineage' and its 'four segments' of which 'the first three are descended through seven generations from three brothers' and the fourth is 'believed to be connected further back in the genealogy'. For the first three 'the genealogy can be shown complete' (ibid.).

In fact the author, normally meticulous in his reporting, does not present such a charter of ancestors. I think this very core of Bailey's argument entails certain weaknesses. In short, I also see the relevance of agnation, but additional forces come into play which can be discovered from Bailey's own excellent ethnography. The above passages have been quoted in detail because they lead to certain discrepancies with major consequences.

To begin with, many anthropologists of recent decades have differentiated genealogy and pedigree (Barnard and Good 1984, 21), the latter being the construct of the people concerned, while genealogies are based on objective criteria. In the present case, Bailey may have been depending upon pedigrees. At times he mentions the possibility of groups being 'written into a common genealogy' (Bailey 1960, 57). Perhaps such a remark refers to the fact that Kondh 'are calling on the names of ... ancestors' (ibid. 41) on marriages and other ritual occasions,[6] but such recounting call cannot be compared to a pedigree of an African, Polynesian or Biblical society.

In the course of his argument (1960, 22-7 and 40-5) we learn that three of his five Kondh 'lineages' in the village have a different ancestry, being either 'adopted' by or 'amalgamated' with the others in the course of history. Other villagers are not classified as agnates but as 'sister's sons' in Kondh terms, as 'in-laws' in Bailey's terms (1960, 29), and as affines, or marriageable people, in the jargon of most modern anthropologists. Affines have left their original village in historical times. These neighbours, however, share many rights and duties of the agnatic group by the fact of

[6] Among the Kuttia Kondh I have witnessed name-giving ceremonies that included such recitations.

their co-residence. 'People resident uxorilocally and avuncolocally have to act in many situations as if they were agnates' (1960, 37).

Beyond the village, the Kondh unit of reckoning is the 'localized agnatic clan' (1967, 419). The residents of the clan territory, like those of a village, again share 'the obligation of an agnatic kinsman towards the rest of the people living there' (1967, 420). The territorial clans, however, are *composite* clans. 'They are made up of lineages which frankly acknowledge that they are of different descent, but which treat one another as agnatic brothers' (ibid.). Again these territorial clans view each other by what Bailey calls 'institutionalized friendliness and hostility'.[7] Those clans who are friends are linked 'by agnation or fictions of agnation (blood-brotherhood[8] and adoption) and they do not intermarry' (ibid.).

Summing up, we notice how Bailey sometimes suggests genealogical data to prove the agnatic links between 'lineages' within his village, sometimes other mechanisms, and that fictional agnation is practised beyond the village within the territorial clan and the larger territory combining friendly clans. We have here not an anthropological obsession with kinship but the outline of a constitution for a territorial and social complex to the size of the German semi-province Holstein. The whole eastern Kondhmals consist of two such clan-territories which—from an ego's point of view—are either dominated by friendly agnates or by clans hostile to his or her people. Such an order, mapped out over a whole page (1960, 55), does not entirely make up the tribal structure of Bailey's account, but it serves as the core. Some additional patterns will be presented further below.

My own research in other Kondh regions and among a number of other Orissan tribes offers an important contrast to Bailey's findings. Nowhere have I found pedigrees, since none of the indigenous people of the highlands was ever interested in ancestors. In fact, grand tribal rituals, akin to the Kondh sacrifice, imply a cyclical rebirth of kinsmen (see Pfeffer 2001) which would exclude any concept of lineal time conveyed by pedigrees. But then the author—confining his ethnography to observed behaviour and functional explanations of resource management—has certainly not

[7] As far as I can see, this is Bailey's only reference to supra-individual value-ideas.

[8] This term refers to the type of ritualised or sacred agnation found all over tribal Orissa and called 'bond-friendship' by some authors.

invented these relations of descent. I think the apparent contradiction of our data can be dissolved, and we must, for a moment, return to anthropological theory in the 1950s.

Descent *versus* Alliance

In those days, so-called 'lineage theory' was highly influential in Britain and elsewhere. Evans-Pritchard of Oxford, and Fortes of Cambridge, had published detailed ethnographies on two large acephalous African tribes, and they had also included general findings in their standard work, *African Political Systems* (1940) which remains a textbook to this day. Much of 'lineage theory', as developed in these works, has been under heavy criticism throughout the last fifty years.

The African tribes called Nuer, Tallensi, or Tiv offered 'ordered anarchy' by the complementary opposition at each level of their inclusive agnatic lineages. A number of minimal units, hardly bigger than agnatically extended households, merged into relatively larger ones of the same type at successively higher levels of 'minor' and 'major segments', until they had become part of the all-inclusive 'maximal lineage' or agnatic clan that dominated a certain territory. Conflicts were resolved by sanctions of opposed segments at each level. This was Durkheim's segmentary society *in vivo* (Durkheim 1893/1933, 177). I will not dwell on this subject, but emphasize that most British departments were debating this type of 'ordered anarchy' in the 1950s. It was the dominant theme. Bailey, stationed within the acephalous political system of the agnatically organized Kondh, must have been influenced by these debates.

Some more history of anthropology may offer further understanding: in 1954 Leach brought out his *Political Systems of Highland Burma,* presenting the patrilineal Kachin without pedigrees or other descent concepts. Instead, local agnatic lines were related to one another *not* by relatively superior inclusive lineages of the same form, but by bonds of affinity, bride-givers (*mayu*) always being superior to bride-takers (*dama*) so that the latter were the political vassals, the economic clients, and the religious followers of the former in a multivalent social structure. Leach emphasized that ties of affinity, as independent variables, could provide the same amount of stability for an acephalous political system, as supplied by descent structures elsewhere.

Against the dominant opinion or Western common sense, marriage was not a secondary institution in the classification of the Kachin and numerous other peoples.

Leach and Gluckman were major enemies, however, since the former had frontally attacked and ridiculed the latter in 1953. Bailey, working in Gluckman's realm, is unlikely to have demonstrated more than formal recognition of the *mayu-dama* alternative offered by Leach. But again this is not all.

The idea of diachronic affinity, so much present in the Kachin concepts, had been worked out for India by Louis Dumont who, like Leach, was greatly influenced by Claude Lévi-Strauss (1949). In 1953 Dumont introduced *The Dravidian Kinship Terminology as an Expression of Marriage* followed by *Hierarchy and Marriage Alliance in South Indian Kinship* (1957).[9] Both contributions were at that time published in British anthropological media. The term 'alliance' thereafter stood for repetitive intermarriage as the foundation of social structure. 'Alliance theory' came to oppose 'descent theory' in heated debates of the subsequent decades.

Bailey, however, was hostile to Dumont, though their personal dealings were—to my knowledge—not marred by the type of insults Leach liked to distribute. Having shown very little sympathy for French mentalism, our author could hardly be expected to join the alliance camp. For Bailey Dumont's project of a 'sociology of India' was not concerned with sociology at all, but with 'a form of culturology' (Bailey 1959, 98-9), while Bailey saw himself as a comparative sociologist who was working on Society beyond the specific socio-cultural context. His contribution was *not* supposed to be confined to some 'Indian sociology'.[10] Directly opposing the Dumontian approach, particularly Dumont's anti-individualism, Bailey stated: 'A valid sociological understanding can be achieved ... by making abstractions from behaviour or from other non-verbal information, and by using only our own concepts and evading the ideas of the people (suppose they have any ideas, which is not always the case)' (1959, 90).[11]

For Dumont, we may remember, sociology was the study of value-ideas pervading a great society like that of India. A

---

[9] Both contributions are reprinted in Dumont 1983.

[10] He rejected 'Indian sociology', as he rejected 'Indian chemistry'.

[11] The basis of the controversy is, of course, a very different notion of 'society' in the USA compared to the European tradition.

'sociology of India' studied the formally articulated system of ideas, on which observable institutions and actions were based. Interpretation implied the crossing of the boundaries of our own categories, such as that of the priority of individual agency. Marriage alliance in India implied a concept of affinity beyond the familiar individual decisions and beyond the utilitarian ends of such action and thus beyond Manchester's programme.

I would like to argue that Bailey offered outstanding ethnographic findings for the working the 'alliance model' in the Kondhmals. His behaviourism, however, and his orientation within the framework of 'competition for scarce resources', excluded any approximation towards the structuralist models of Dumont and Leach. Bailey's is a contribution to 'powerism',[12] since the observed phenomena are seen and interpreted with our own concepts relating to struggles over land and leadership and the power to enforce or to break social norms. Kondh tribesmen appeared in constant struggles. Their clans and lineages were presented as kinds of super-individuals or corporations, like the familiar corporations of our own world, again involved in power-struggles. The Kondh worldview never appears in the book, as if such a consistent and distinct metaphysical system—articulated in the multivalent structures—had never existed. Other indigenous categories being obvious and therefore unavoidable, Bailey reports them but does not trace their meaning. The opportunity is missed.

Marriage in the Kondhmals

Much of the following will concern 'affinity as a value',[13] a category that arose as a fruit of Dumont's fieldwork in Tamil Nadu. South Indian marriage alliance can be explained to non-anthropologists by reference to the repeated intermarriages of cross cousins, or children of a sister and a brother, from one generation to the next.

Bailey too has discussed the behaviour of Kondh cross cousins in the context of affinal relations (1960, 29), but the possibility of their marriage is not mentioned. My own visits to the eastern

---

[12] The term has been coined by Sahlins 1999 and refers to approaches reducing social phenomena to competition for power.

[13] Dumont's later book (1983)—combining and correcting his former articles on marriage alliance—carries this title.

Kondhmals and to the agencies of Kuttia and Dangria Kondh revealed the strict prohibition of such unions, which are the norm further south among the Kondh of Koraput.

This is significant, since many cosmological concepts, e.g. settlement patterns, major sacrifices, or the order of the house display an amazing unity within the widespread Kondh complex, accompanied by clear-cut differences in view of the respective neighbours. If we avoid our own commonsense jargon, however, i.e. 'cross cousin-marriage', or the union of two individuals, and substitute it with the holistic concept of 'diachronic affinity', i.e. intermarriage as a principle of social order, the discrepancy between northern and southern Kondh will vanish.

After extended interrogations in the northern groups, I was told that a marriage was only renewed with the same local line only after an interval of seven generations. Roland Hardenberg will undoubtedly clarify this point during his ongoing fieldwork among the Dangria Kondh, but it should be clear that the prohibition of cross-cousin marriage in no way implies the 'caste'-complexity of affinal ties. The upper castes of coastal Orissa,[14] like those of northern India, follow a straightforward negative marriage rule without conceiving an agnatic block of 'brothers' opposed to permanently marriageable clans or collections of clans in the Kondh manner.

Since Bailey explicitly traced descent in his village through seven previous generations, I presume that these forefathers are remembered and recalled at the time of weddings, *because* their marriage links proscribe present affinal ties with the lines of their spouses while advocating such ties thereafter. Individual cross cousins, Bailey's ethnography implies, belong to groups of institutionalized affines, even if, as individuals, they are non-marriageable for the time being.

None of the Kondh I met operated with pedigrees in the African segmental fashion: ancestors did not provide names or the code for segmental solidarity of particular groups of descendants. I do not dare debate the Africanist work, but in Orissa the segmental calculus does not operate. Nowhere in tribal Middle India, I venture to say, can we find inclusive agnatic lineages of the African type. Everywhere the *composite* clan, as described by Bailey, is the

[14] In the southern Ganjam district the strong Telugu influence has modified the 'north Indian' attitudes.

standard, i.e. an agnatic category uniting local lines without a construct of a common forefather. Since the common patrilineal descent line of the clan—as known from African, Middle Eastern, Polynesian or even north Indian[15] conventions—is nowhere in sight in tribal Orissa, we are bound to inquire about the basis of agnation, the ordering principle of Kondh and other tribesmen.

If we look for the answer in Bailey's work, we find commonsensical historical speculations dealing with lineages involved in struggles for land, readjusting their surplus population in different clan territories so that migrants come to cultivate virgin forest, in case they do not physically exterminate or join the ranks of other local groups (1967, 421-2). Given these tendencies towards a 'repetitive equilibrium',[16] the *composite* clan, i.e. an agnatic category without a genealogical pyramid or a notion of common descent, could be the outcome. Our author does not explicitly offer such a materialist explanation, but the reader is led to the conclusions by Bailey's repeated excursions into the realm of conjectural history.

Personally I think a simpler solution lies at hand: the agnatic relationship between the members of Bailey's 'lineages', clans, and clan federations is based on their mutually non-marriageable status. Rather than marriage prohibition being a consequence of common descent, constructions of sibling categories are implied by the marriage prohibitions.

My argument indicates the rupture between Kondh categories and our own, the guideline of Bailey's argument. Nowhere in Middle India do we find the type of lineages as units of a 'sectoral morality' or as adversaries in the type of complementary opposition that enforces law among the Nuer or Tiv (see Sahlins 1968, 20).

---

[15] Helene Basu 2001, in a major contribution to the social anthropology of India, has recently presented her detailed study on the caste of genealogists in Kachh as a post-doctoral dissertation (Habilitation) at the Faculty of Political and Social sciences, Free University of Berlin. A good ethnographic example of widespread inclusive agnatic pedigrees is presented by Pradhan in *Political System of the Jats of Northern India*, 1966

[16] Bailey (1960, 245) has adopted this concept from Gluckman (1942, 244)

Middle Indian agnation, in my opinion, is a secondary aspect of affinity, not the other way around, as conceived in Europe.[17]

The anthropological notion of marriage alliance implies repetition of intermarriage from one generation to the next. In tribal Middle India, however, I have tried to show (Pfeffer 1982, 43-60) that such repetition operates at intervals. Positive marriage rules, frequently—but not always—implying cross-cousin marriage in the tribal south of Orissa, are applied for alternate generations in the second, the fourth or the eighth generation north of the old Koraput District. They are marked by proscription of immediate intermarriage.

The concept of 'dispersed alliance', floated by Lévi-Strauss (1966) in a different context and—under those circumstances—rightly rejected by R.H. Barnes (1976), should be applicable to an affinal system implying ordered dispersal of repetitive marriage links. Northern Kondh intermarriage is renewed after an interval of at least seven generations. Marriage ties of the agnatic ascendants in the previous seven generations must therefore be remembered, and the Dangria Kondh even have an unusual relationship terminology extending to eight generational levels. The long interval of intermarriage can be conceived in this manner, i.e. the interval between the renewal of individual marriages rejoining the lines of two mutually affinal collectives.

Bailey does not really discuss Kondh religion. Had he done so, he would—at least—have to mention Macpherson's data on sacrifice to the same extent as he discussed the empire builder's data on tribal warfare. The unavoidable conclusions would have to be similar to Boal's interpretations of the grand Meriah. Following Macpherson's early account (1865), this author describes and even maps out a repetitive or cyclical system of the obligation to conduct the human sacrifice connecting different localities (Boal 1997, 203). I speculate that such regularly dispersed ritual ties will be closely interrelated with the regularly dispersed affinal ties, but substantial information will have to wait for Hardenberg's publication. My point is that the specific schemes of agnation, intermarriage and sacrifice cannot be explained adequately by

[17] During my field excursions in the company of female anthropologists, my local hosts—after some time of silent observation—introduced us to others as 'siblings' or in a 'father:daughter' relationship, even though we had never mentioned any consanguinal links.

commonsensical or utilitarian reasoning and action concerned with individual ambitions—so-called agency—or by facts in the fields of economy, geography, biology, or psychology. Other things being equal, I see observed institutionalized behaviour as representation of a more general and cohesive socio-cultural logic. The frontiers of 'tribe', 'caste', and 'administration' are in fact frontiers between such socio-cultural logical schemes.

Reading Bailey, we do not find a hint of such differences. Humans universally appear as calculating individuals under given material constraints. The author does not, for example, go so far as to mention the Kondh kinship terminology. Had he examined the terms in the way suggested by his academic opponent Dumont, he would have been forced to recognize the *idea* of diachronic affinity expressed by the terminology irrespective of norms and practices. 'Idea' in this sense does not refer to the working of an individual brain, as implied by Bailey's witty remark (1959, 90), but to a system of ideas within a prescribed relational pattern of the societal whole providing the values for that whole. 'Idea' in this sense is a supra-individual document or a text composed beyond the level of motives or agency.

The Kondh vocabulary of kinship[18] can be presented in a highly symmetrical manner opposing agnates and affines. As such the relationship terminology would appear in absolute conformity with Bailey's observation of actual marriage behaviour[19] when a man takes a wife who is a sister of the man to whom the own sister has gone, even though these siblings are usually 'classificatory' ones in anthropological jargon (1960, 30). Needless to say, no such relations are permitted in the Oriya caste context, where hierarchy privileges bride-takers over bride-givers.[20] Thus although both Kondh and Oriya (like Europeans) do not practice cross cousin-marriage or offer examples of marital unions between agnatic or

---

[18] I was able to draw the traditional type of diagram of the terms collected for the book of P.K. Nayak (1989, 41). By a non-egocentric diagram—such as those presented by Dumont—the oppositional nature of the categories would become more obvious.

[19] Such conformity should not imply the vocabulary to be the 'reflection' of the behaviour or generally be a secondary aspect of action.

[20] Prasanna K. Nayak has rightly suggested these terms to substitute the standard jargon of 'wife-givers' and '-takers' which sounds very offensive to Indian ears.

other non-agnatic kin, the overall tribal order of affinity—equivalent to the tribal political, economic and religious order—is absolutely different from the caste constitution and has nothing to do with European genetic rationalizations. In fact tribe, caste, and nation dance to the tunes of different music-styles, even if some of these physical movements—be they folkloristic, classical, or modern—resemble one another or happen to be healthy exercises.

Bailey's excellent ethnography opposes *dada-koku* and *seri ahpa loku* at the village level (1960, 28). The first of these two holistic categories refers to a combination of grandfather/elder brother and father's younger brother/mother's younger sister's husband, or the Kondh version of 'agnatic kin' in Oriya terms[21] while the second category literally means 'bride-seizing folk'. The same opposition governs the relation between the localized clans (ibid. 53) and the opposition between the two great clan federations confronting each other in the north-eastern Kondhmals (see map 1960, 55). Like the people of highland New Guinea, the Kondh could proclaim, 'we marry the people we fight' (Meggitt 1977, 42). As has been elaborately described by Macpherson (1865) for the pre-colonial times and stressed by Bailey, affines are enemies. Similarly P.K. Nayak points out for the Dangria Kondh in present times:

> From the point of view of any particular clan, the clans of the society are divided into two clear-cut categories: brother clans (*tai bai*) and affinal clans (*samdin gota*[22]).
>
> The affinal clans are potential enemy clans with whom hostilities may crop up any time, anywhere, irrespective of the fact

---

[21] Indo-European terms are frequently intermingled with Dravidian or Munda terms in tribal kinship terminologies at the local level, so that the terms themselves tend to differ in different regions or villages—or even within the same village. What does not differ, however, is the structure, or the relational pattern of the terms, which is obviously very different from the Oriya terminology but similarly 'invariant' in tribal systems of Indo-European, Dravidian, or Munda languages. In P.K. Nayak's diagram of the Dangria Kondh, the terms for *kaka* (or *koku*) and *kaki* have been exchanged and these Indo-European terms on the maternal side are being substituted by equivalent Dravidian terms on the paternal side (1989, 41). Bailey's Kondh, being more exposed to Oriya influence than the Dangria, are likely to have adopted more Oriya words.

[22] Here 'father's father/brother' (i.e. agnates) are opposed to '*exchange-partner clans*'.

> that one has no other way of acquiring wives, except from potentially hostile clans. (1989, 53)

Furthermore he writes of 'structural brothers' and structural enemies' (ibid.). In other words: marriage alliance, or inherited affinity, a concept developed by Dumont, is nowhere in India *reified*, or translated into normative and physical reality, to such a universal extent as observed among the Kondh by Bailey (1960) and Friend-Pereira (1904)[23] in the northern Kondhmals, Niggemeyer (1964, 45-9) in the Belgarh region, and Nayak (1989) in the Niamgiri Hills. This overall and multivalent binary opposition of agnates and affines is reported by Bailey but ignored in his interpretation due to his 'powerism'.

Kondh Agnation Reconsidered

The time of Bailey's Kondh publication (1960) must be remembered when the issue of 'totemism' is discussed. Lévi-Strauss' seminal contributions[24] came out two years later and Bailey never bothered to change his witty remarks linking Kondh totems with an obsolete religious cult. The subject is too big for the present context, but it must be mentioned as an aspect of the agnatic order.

These remarks were supplied in the context of the Kondh 'lineages' which I prefer to call 'local lines' in order to avoid any confusion with the inclusive descent groups of 'lineage theory'. No descent concepts exist, except that of mythological origin. The earth-goddess is said to have given birth to the Kondh agnatic clans in a particular order of seniority. Thus the original paradox: patrilineal clans are linked by descent from the same mother.

For the present, Bailey's extended case method offers detailed information on the village but—typical for behaviourist approaches—only a very limited view of institutionalized ideas beyond. Thus the local lines are only seen in the village context. On many occasions (e.g. 1960, 40) Bailey mentions the honorific titles of villagers, i.e. 'Malik', or some similar term, and 'Kohoro' throughout the north-eastern Kondhmals. The translation, a reference to secular and to sacred leadership, is omitted by the ethnographer. In fact everywhere Kondh local lines referring to

---

[23] Quoted by O'Malley (1908, 73 f.)

[24] Lévi-Strauss, Claude 1962a, 1962b.

worldly leaders oppose those formally defined by priestly functions. The terms themselves are of foreign origin. In much of tribal middle India lowland languages are employed for the designations of leaders. Everywhere in the old provinces of Orissa, Bihar, and Madhya Pradesh all tribal members of the local lines carry titles opposing the sacred and the secular. The extended case method is unable to lead to such supra-individual oppositions of values.

One of the local lines has a *tone* relationship to another (1960, 40). This is called 'blood-brotherhood' by Bailey, but in fact has nothing to do with blood. The author, as usual, offers as translation what he considers to be the nearest English equivalent, even though 'blood-brotherhood' in the European context is an individual and temporal affair, whereas in tribal Orissa it is not only a time-bound tie between two men but also a timeless bond between two local lines proposing a sacred type of agnation, ritually superior to 'mere' physical brotherhood.

Such ritual brotherhood is relevant in all spheres of life. The senior value is openly expressed in the dealings between any two ritual brothers. Bailey, however, sees only the single case of his village and offers an explanation of the usual commonsensical kind: one local line, called BX, was the former owner of the earth, until the village was conquered by outsiders who now wield superior power. Rather than exterminating BX, the latter, as the true 'owners of the earth', were given special ritual privileges and offered 'some kind of seniority in this situation' (Bailey 1960, 43). In the argument the senior status was traded against the superior political power of the juniors, ending in equilibrium. Individual decision-making was responsible: 'the result is always short of perfect uniformity, because it is to someone's advantage to keep alive the differences' (ibid. 46). The author is quite unable to conceive ritual and senior status in non-utilitarian, non-individual terms.

All over tribal Middle India ritual agnation between local lines carries highest social value. Local lines of the Kondh appear, as described in the specific case, opposed by the principle of seniority. Agnatic lines or clans are never equals but always *seniors* or *juniors* of one another. This opposition is in fact the Orissan substitute for African genealogical oppositions. The same relativism, but without pedigrees, is at work.

Each so-called composite clan unites local lines by reference to another category of the kinship language, the aspect of agnatic siblingship. Fraternal concepts are uniting the territorial clan, and the latter again is a fraternal part of the local clan federation covering a vast territory. Nayak (1989, 54) has, in the Niamgiri Hills, fully confirmed Bailey's observation of the north-east.

It is significant that brothers at various levels of collectivity in all Orissan tribes refer to agnatic units, but *not* to a common father. The sky-god may be the husband of the earth-goddess, but he is far too remote to appear within a parental relationship. A male god or founding father is beyond approach, his wife being the universal provider. Mother earth is physically present and called at the time of Meriah. Her womb, a cave, is a known site in the landscape and certainly *taboo* for most Kondh who emerged out of her body at that site as 'brothers'.

Brothers are never equal. My former student Albert Götzelmann was able to collect the foundation myth of the Kuttia Kondh marking the relative seniority of the Nondruka clan. The Timaka, on the other hand, were the junior most. According to the myth the latter did *not* emerge out the womb, but somewhere else, near the river Godavari. Perhaps the relative pollution of the Timaka is related to the odd site of their mythological birth.[25] As usual, they are despised—and married—by the Nondruka. To the present day the Timaka offer the blood sacrifice for all other Kuttia Kondh clans at the site of the goddess' womb because it is not the site of their birth. The other clans will contribute to the sacrifice but avoid the sacred grove around the cave for obvious reasons.

Individual siblings, local lines, clans and clan federations, tribes and tribal federations are always differentiated by relative seniority and all tribal relationship terminologies oppose seniors and juniors within one generational level. What is the significance of this observation?

Tetradic Theory

Let me recall Nick Allen's (1986) approach to kinship in the Maussian tradition, called 'tetradic theory', an evolutionary design dealing not only with the familiar egocentric system but also, more importantly, with the sociocentric system or kinship relating to

---

[25] It is always ethnographically difficult to find out the details of an embarrassing natal process, or the very opposite to the well-known cultural construction of 'virgin birth' (see Leach 1966).

society as a whole. His tetradic model relates to 'a quadripartite society which handles the relations between the sexes and generations in such a way that the egocentric and sociocentric systems are co-extensive and isomorphic' (1986, 93). Four 'sections' imply inter-marrying, child-exchanging moieties subdivided by generational 'levels'. If I understand the author correctly, we are to relate attested socio-cultural patterns, such as Kondh social structure, to the tetradic model to approach historical transformations by such a comparison.

In the Kondh case, Bailey's empirical evidence points to an order not far away from the opposition of the prescribed 'sections'. The whole consists of two intermarrying clan federations. Those Kondh who are non-marriageable for one another are related through the value of seniority: agnates are relative seniors or juniors of one another at all sociocentric levels.

The first significant departure from Allen's model is the fact that—in Nayak's ethnography—the two intermarrying moieties appear as such not in an overall perspective but only in the view of any individual involved. Bailey is not clear in this aspect.

The more important difference concerns agnation as a reference to siblingship rather than to generational levels when the value of seniority is applied. Allen's alternating generational 'levels' are present among the Juang, as described by McDougal (1964, 141), but apparently in no other Orissan tribe. Among the Kondh a social norm does suggest a marriage-interval of seven generations, but this form of alternation refers to local lines only—not to greater collectives—and as such cannot be the basis of a second bi-partition of the whole.

All over tribal Middle India, alternating generations are equated egocentrically (Pfeffer 1982, 20) and in case we join the evolutionist argument, we could point to the structural similarity with regard to the sociocentric equations of the Juang. Tribal ritual in general is grossly underreported so we may hope for further examples of ritual equations[26] once empirical research of the McDougal quality can be achieved.

---

[26] The Gadaba *gotr* ritual, for example, sees to it that one generation of the dead is 'eaten' by agnates from other villages in the next generation who are in turn 'eaten' at their death by the first villagers. Thus alternate generations are equated (see Pfeffer 2001).

The third obvious transformation is the application of the standard of seniority even among mutually marriageable clans. If we want to ignore the examples of other tribes, like the Santal, and stay with the Kondh, we must resort to Götzelmann's ethnography, confirmed during my later visits among the Kuttia. On account of their prior birth the Nondruka clan is senior to the Timaka clan and yet the Timaka are the prescribed affines of the Nondruka.

What we seem to observe is the presence of Allen's concepts of a vertical and a horizontal partition of the whole, of which only one is implemented in practice. But experiments and some supra-individual 'play' with value-ideas otherwise lead to variations of a common theme, still visible. The most obvious of this 'play' follows the general trend of evolution from the sociocentric to the egocentric phenomena. If we want to study *anthropos*, we are well-advised to recognize the patterns and the trend.

Bailey has set different priorities. For him the political order of caste and the state or the working of electoral democracy are the themes. They are the forces that change Kondh society. This process may be obvious and physically visible at times, just as many forms of 'culturalism' (Sahlins 1999) show how Kondh use modern instruments to retain traditional values. And yet, I find it amazing that no tribal person with roots in a village has ever emerged as a political leader. Sobriety, planning and associationalism have yet to become tribal values whereas the supreme reference to specific transcendental forces—and as such to a devaluation of the here and now—remains. Culturalism is slow, when indigenous institutions remain untouched by European destruction. Kondh affinity and agnation as religious values are in force today wherever the tribal frontier has not been torn down physically.

References

Allen, N.J. 1986. 'Tetradic Theory: An Approach to Kinship', in *Journal of the Anthropological Society of Oxford*, XVII/2:87-109.

Bailey, F.G. 1957. *Caste and the Economic Frontier*. Manchester: University of Manchester Press.

— 1957/1967. 'Political Change in the Kondmals', in *Eastern Anthropologist* 11/2:88-106, reprinted in Ronald Cohen and

John Middleton (eds.) 1967, *Comparative Political Systems: Studies in the Politics of Pre-industrial Societies* Austin: University of Texas Press, pp. 415-38.

— 1960. *Tribe Caste, and Nation*, Manchester: University of Manchester Press.

— 1960. 'For a Sociology of India?', in *Contributions to Indian Sociology* 3:88-101.

Barnard, Alan and Anthony Good. 1984. *Research Practices in the Study of Kinship*, London: Academic Press.

Barnes, R.H. 1976. 'Dispersed Alliance and the Prohibition of Marriage: Reconsideration of McKinley's Explanation of Crow-Omaha Terminologies', in *Man* (n.s.) 11:384-99.

Basu, Helene. 2001. 'Die Göttin und die Charan—das Gedächtnis des Königtums, Verwandtschaft und Askese in Kacch (westl. Indien).' Unpublished thesis of Habilitation. Faculty of Political and Social Sciences: Free University of Berlin.

Boal, Barbara M. 1997. *Human Sacrifice and Religious Change: The Kondhs*, New Delhi: Inter-India Publications.

Dumont, Louis. 1983. *Affinity as a Value: Marriage Alliance in South India, with Comparative Essays on Australia,* Chicago: The University of Chicago Press.

Durkheim, Emile. 1893/1933. *The Division of Labor in Society*, New York: The Free Press of Glencoe.

Fortes, Meyer and E.E. Evans-Pritchard. 1940. *African Political Systems,* London: Oxford University Press.

Gluckman, Max. 1942. 'Some Processes of Social Change Illustrated from Zululand', in *African Studies,* vol. 1 (cited in Bailey 1960:245).

Leach, E.R. 1953. 'Correspondence on Bridewealth and the stability of marriage' in, *Man,* vol. 53, art 279, 179-80.

— 1954. *Political Systems of Highland Burma,* London: Athlone.

Leach, Edmund. 1966. 'Virgin Birth', in *Proceedings of the Royal Anthropological Institute* 1966, 39-49.

Lévi-Strauss, Claude. 1949. *Les Structures Élémentaires de la Parenté,* Paris: Presses Universitaires de France

— 1962a. *Le Totémisme Aujour'hui,* Paris: Presses Universitaires de France.

— 1962b. *Le Pensée sauvage,* Paris: Plon.

— 1966. 'The Future of Kinship Studies', in *Proceedings of the Royal Anthropological Society of Great Britain and Ireland for* 1965, 13-22.

McDougal, Charles. 1964. 'The Social Structure of the Hill Juang'. Unpublished Ph.D. thesis of the University of New Mexico, Albuquerque.

Macpherson, W. (ed.). 1865. *Memorials of the Service in India from the Correspondence of the Late Major Samuel Charles Macpherson C.B.*, London: John Murray.

Meggitt, Mervin. 1977. *Blood is Their Argument: Warfare Among the Mae Enga Tribesmen of the New Guinea Highlands,* Palo Alto: Mayfield.

Nayak, Prasanna K. 1989. *Blood, Women and Territory: An Analysis of Clan Disputes of Dongria Konds,* Delhi: Reliance.

Niggemeyer, Hermann. 1964. *Kuttia Kond: Dschungel-Bauern in Orissa*, München: Renner

O'Malley, L.S.S. 1908. *Angul. Bengal District Gazetteers*, Calcutta: Secretariat.

Parsons, Talcott. 1949. *Essays in Sociological Theory*, New York: The Free Press.

Pfeffer, Georg. 1982. *Status and Affinity in Middle India,* Wiesbaden: Steiner.

— 'Tribal Society of Highland Orissa, Highland Burma, and Elsewhere', in Johannes Belz, Heiko Frese und Angelika Malinar (eds.), *Text and Context*. Delhi: Manohar, 427-55.

— 'A Ritual of Revival Among the Gadaba of Koraput', in Hermann Kulke and Burkhard Schnepel (eds.), *Jagannath Revisited: Studying Society, Religion and the State in Orissa,* New Delhi: Manohar, 99-124.

Pradhan, N.C. 1966. *Political System of the Jats of Northern India,* London, Oxford: University Press.

Radcliffe-Brown, A.R. 1952. *Structure and Function in Primitive Society*, London: Routledge and Kegan Paul.

Sahlins, Marshall D. 1968. *Tribesmen*, Englewood Cliffs: Prentice Hall.

— 1999. 'Two or Three Things that I Know about Culture', in *Journal of the Royal Anthropological Institute* 5/3:399-421.

Vitebsky Pierce. 1992. *Dialogues with the Dead*, Cambridge: Cambridge University Press.

13

The Close and the Distant: A Long-Term Perspective

N.J. Allen

> *It is not always the phenomena that are closest in time that are the deep causes of the phenomena we see around us.*
>
> Mauss

My main research interest in recent years has been in Indo-European (IE) cultural comparativism, and although at first sight this field may seem remote from the interests of the Orissa Research Project, I shall try to show the links that can be made.

To an anthropologist IE cultural comparativism is of course just one instance of language-family based cultural comparativism. This method of research has been widely applied in different parts of the world, for instance by Robert Blust to the Austronesian speakers of the Pacific or by Chris Ehret in Africa. I was first drawn to it in my study of the kinship terminologies of Tibeto-Burman speakers (Allen 1975). However, as a method in its own right, it appears surprisingly seldom in introductory texts for anthropology students—or, I suspect, historians. Yet, until recent developments in genetics, it was the only method available to complement archaeology in studying the long-term history of preliterate cultures.

True, language and culture *need* not move in parallel. Moreover, extra-linguistic cultural change (to the point where convincing similarities cease to be demonstrable) may sometimes be faster than language change. But language families provide a framework within which, in favourable circumstances, cultural comparativism can sometimes reach unambiguous results regarding a prehistoric common origin, and the IE family probably offers a particularly favourable field of study because of its geographical distribution and abundant documentation. While the method can also be applied to the other language families of South Asia, application to IE will remain basic, if only because of the centrality of the Sanskritic tradition in the history of the subcontinent.

Let us recall Dumont's manifesto 'For a Sociology of India', which opened the journal *Contributions to Indian Sociology* in 1957. Adapted (with the aid of David Pocock) from his Inaugural Lecture at the École Pratique des Hautes Études, it starts: 'In our opinion, the first condition for a sound development of a Sociology of India is found in the establishment of the proper relation between it and classical Indology.' Dumont is using 'sociology' in the old Durkheimian sense which includes social anthropology, and he goes on to refer to a small band of scholars who have combined sociology and Indology to good effect. After mentioning Mauss, Bouglé and Paul Mus, he continues: 'The sociological spirit is much in evidence … in the work of Professor Dumézil, where it has brilliantly resuscitated the IE comparison. Dumézil's work on an epoch in the distant past is so far from being useless in helping us to understand the present that in fact his analysis of varna completes and corrects Hocart's views' [Hocart being the last in the list].

Dumont is right, I think, about the brilliance of Dumézil's work, its basis in the French sociological tradition and its relevance to recent India; but is he right either to limit this relevance to varnas or to endorse Dumézil's views on them? More widely, what is the standing of Dumézil's work? These questions orient my paper. Regarding the second (Allen 1993), extremely negative judgements can still be found. Summarizing a hundred pages of detailed critique, a learned philologist recently concluded: 'Das Endergebnis ist, daß es die *idéologie tripartie* nie gegeben hat'[1] (Schlerath 1996, 60): so Dumézil's central idea is baseless. Though I consider the verdict mistaken, some of the individual criticisms are serious ones; often Dumézil is only partly right.

Triads and Pentads in IE ideology

Dumézil's trifunctionalism goes back to his 1930 article on the prehistory of caste distinctions among the Indo-Iranians and, hackneyed though it is, we can start with the myth of origin of the varnas in the *Puruṣasūkta* (*RV* 10.90, 11-12):

---

[1] Transl.: The result is that the *idéologie tripartite* never existed.

> When they divided the Man [Puruṣa], into how many parts did they apportion him? What do they call his mouth, his two arms and thighs and feet?
>
> His mouth became the Brahman; his arms were made into the warrior [Rājanya, the later Kṣatriya], his thighs the people [Vaiśya], and from his feet the Servants [Śūdra] were born.
>
> (O'Flaherty 1981, 31)

At first this looks like a straightforward correlation of the four social categories with the four body parts of the cosmogonic/sociogonic primal man, the hierarchy of the varnas being expressed in the order of listing of the body parts and in their vertical position. The first stanza (*katidhā*, into how many parts?) may imply the total of four that is later emphasised by Manu (10.4: 'there is no fifth (varna))'; and as Mus saw (1962), the verb *ajāyata* ('was born'), applying to the Śūdra alone, foreshadows the three-plus-one structure that is seen in Manu's distinction of the twice-born from the once-born Śūdra. But if we recall Durkheim's idea that the category *par excellence* is the concept of totality (1912, 629), we see that there is more to the myth than the quaternities: there is also the pre-existing totality, the transcendent Puruṣa in his undivided body, who both gives rise to the varnas and provides their top-down order. Puruṣa, coupled with Prakṛti, remains fundamental in Sāṃkhya philosophy, but in cosmogonies, as is well known, he soon gives way to other figures, such as the Prajāpati of the Brāhmaṇas. In Manu's sociogony he is replaced by Brahmā—surely the commonest creator figure in classical Hinduism.

Looked at in this way the myth has *five* elements. First, a transcendent representative of totality; then a block of three ranked estates—priests, warriors and producers in descending order; then a final estate at the bottom of the hierarchy. Excluded from most Vedic ritual, the Śūdras' only positive duty is to serve the others obediently.

In focusing on the three central elements out of the five, Dumézil was following the common view of the Śūdra as descendants of the aboriginal inhabitants of India: earlier referred to as Dāsa or Dasyu, by the time of this late Rigvedic hymn they were purportedly sufficiently assimilated by the incoming Aryans to be incorporated in the sociogonic myth. In other words, he saw the Aryans as bringing with them a model of social tripartition and expanding it by adding the local people they subjected, thereby forming a fourth inferior category.

As for the top of the hierarchy, the transcendent starting point was easily overlooked. Creation myths need creators, but once their task is done they often fade out—neither Puruṣa nor Brahmā has been much worshipped. It is only in the cosmogonic context that these beings are linked to social structure.

However, many societies contain living individuals who represent the totality and transcend the divides within it—namely kings. So does the king correspond to Puruṣa/Brahmā? Certainly the texts seldom say anything so clear and simple, and usually present the king as a Kṣatriya. But I would argue that in some sense (either originally or essentially) the king is not just a warrior. The best arguments are probably comparative, but sufficient hints exist within the Sanskritic material (Allen 1999c, 247-50).

Thus in some contexts the king is clearly set apart from all four varnas. In the ideal fortified city described in the *Arthaśāstra*, the royal palace near the centre is surrounded by separate quarters at the cardinal points, one for each varna. In the anointing ritual (*abhiṣeka*) during the royal inauguration (*rājasūya*), the king on his throne is differentially anointed by members of the four varnas standing around him, one in each direction—a Vedic ritual still performed for Nepalese kings (Witzel 1987). In other contexts, the king is set apart from all ordinary mortals, independent of varna. His body is composed of particles of the eight Lokapāla gods who guard the eight directions, and even a boy king is no mere mortal (*manuṣya*): he is a great deity in the form of a man (Manu 5.96, 7.8).

In all these cases the cardinal point symbolism locates the king at the centre of space. This applies also to Brahmā, whose only significant temple is at the symbolic centre of India at Pushkara, and whose heavenly hall climaxes the description of the halls of the Lokapālas in *Mahābhārata* 2.7-11. Abstractly then, the king does correspond to Puruṣa/Brahmā.

As for Dumézil's understanding of the Śūdra, the question is not whether some or all of them descended from aboriginals, but whether the incoming Aryans brought with them a model of social structure that included a category inferior to the priests, warriors and producers. Any society will recognize the existence of outsiders, so the question becomes whether such outsiders were incorporated in Aryan ideology—whether in an economic role (e.g. as slaves) or a political or religious one. To point to the Śūdras' ritual role in the royal inauguration or in the *mahāvrata* rite marking the winter solstice (Eggeling 1885 II, 430n) is inconclusive since this could be historically secondary. We have to turn to comparison. If one looks for it, the Indo-Iranians do provide evidence for a five-element model of society—some of it mentioned by Dumézil himself (1971, 251 ff.).

Iranian sources usually give three occupational strata, but one Avestan list includes craftsmen at the bottom of the hierarchy, as does the corresponding list in the *Shahnama* (Ferdowsi 1996, 9-10).[2] Moreover one often finds lists of five peoples, or fivefold groupings of people or of the spaces they inhabit. Thus Yayāti, one of the 'first king' figures in the *Mahābhārata*, distributes the known world between his five sons, of whom the youngest stays with his father in the centre—cf. the Rigvedic concept of the five peoples or the five countries. In Iran the notion of seven cosmic regions probably derives from an earlier notion of five, linked with centre and cardinal points. Although the Pehlavi figure of Frētōn divides the world between his three sons whose specialities parallel the twice-born varnas, earlier Avestan forms of the same names occur in a list of *five* divisions (Allen 2000d, 285). Outside Iran, the mythic founder the Ossetes of the Caucasus, Os-bogatyr, had three sons with specialities much like Frētōn's, but in all he had *five* sons, for two of whom specialities are not recorded (Vaneev 1956, Dumézil 1983, 97 ff.). Before their Islamization in the 1890s the Nuristanis told an origin myth about their creator god Imra, his wife (a golden milk churn), a triad of daughters who go to populate different countries, and a fourth daughter who stands apart from the others. The triad is not differentiated, but the females show the characteristic 1 + 3 + 1 structure.[3]

Let us then suppose that the Aryans brought with them to India a picture of society as essentially fivefold, and see where the hypothesis leads. Starting from the triadic division of labour among the twice-born, Dumézil, as he surveyed the IE-speaking world, Dumézil found scores of parallel triads in a whole range of

---

[2] In these cases the 'creators' are humans and kings.

[3] Since the word *varṇa* means 'colour', it is worth noting the symbolic colours associated with them: white, red, yellow, black in descending order (Allen 1998c). The four varnas plus king were already compared with the five provinces of Irish sacred geography by Rees and Rees (1961).

contexts, not only in social structure but also in the pantheon, in myth, epic, and folklore, and in ritual and law. As he saw it, these reflected the survival among IE speakers of an ideology which in the proto-culture must have been extremely strong and pervasive. This basic concept is not affected if his triad is replaced by a pentad.

But what makes one triad 'parallel' with another? In the simplest and most typical case one triad paralleled another when both are wholes within which the first ranked element pertains to sacredness or wisdom, the second to physical force or war, and the third to a bundle of concepts including wealth, productivity, fecundity, sexuality, beauty, health, good nutrition. The ideas that were linked separately with the three positions came to be called 'functions' after the functions performed by the twice-born varnas, and they were labelled 'first', 'second' and 'third' (F1, F2, F3) according to their rank and typical order. Here the shift to a pentad necessitates naming and defining two new positions, one for the Śūdra and parallels, one for the king and parallels.

Too much work has used the Dumézilian paradigm for one to alter his numerical labels for the functions, so might one add a fourth function at the bottom of the hierarchy and a 'noughth' function at the top? The label 'nought' is altogether awkward. It is better to start from the fact that king and Śūdra have something in common. Not only do they together form the extremes of the hierarchy, but also, as seen by the twice-born, both are in different ways 'other, outside or beyond'. Thus both can be labeled 'fourth function', provided that one then distinguishes within the function a valued and a devalued *aspect* (F4+, F4-). The discordance between numerical label and rank (or list) order is a small price to pay, especially since in some contexts the extremes come together in opposition to the triad.

The advantages of a pentadic scheme over a triadic one are best shown by examining particular contexts, but without going into details from Rome and elsewhere, here are some general advantages.

(i.) A well defined fivefold structure is less likely to occur by chance than a triadic one, and provides a stronger argument (if one is needed) against those who dismiss Dumézil's comparisons as due to chance similarities.

(ii.) The 'ideology' of the proto-IEs becomes more like the 'primitive classi-fications' of the Zuñi and Chinese, as analysed by Durkheim and Mauss in 1903, and hence more common in anthropological experience (Allen 2000e, 39 ff.). For instance it can now fit easily with the widespread schema of centre plus cardinal points.

(iii.) What Dumézil called *le probleme du roi* is recast, if not resolved. The problem is that, if the first function tops the hierarchy, it has to cover sovereignty, which Dumézil regularly includes in his definitions of that function (even if elsewhere he sometimes refers to the king as 'transfunctional'). But then India becomes anomalous. The Indian king was usually regarded as a Kṣatriya (F2) and was emphatically not a Brahman (F1), and similarly Indra, king of the gods, appeared to rank as F2 relative to the F1 paired deities Mitra and Varuṇa—while comparable sovereign gods like Zeus and Jupiter were analysed as F1. So how and why did India diverge from the IE norm? If the king basically belongs in neither F1 nor F2 but in F4+, the problem becomes one of divergent secondary developments.

(iv.) One can eliminate an unsatisfactory complication in Dumézil's conception of the first function, within which he distinguished two aspects called after Varuṇa and Mitra.[4] Whatever one makes of these paired gods among the Indo-Iranians, Dumézil's projection of the split between them into the proto-ideology is problematic: it has no clear parallel in social structure, and the parallels claimed for it in other contexts (mainly narrative) are few and weak. In some cases at least (e.g. Romulus), the purported 'Varuṇa' figure is better analysed as F4+.[5]

Varna and Caste

Thus when Dumont (1979, 94, 351-3) cites Dumézil's account of the varnas, we need to be careful. Dumont starts by stating that

---

[4] It is from here that I take the idea of a *fourth* function having two aspects.

[5] My current hypothesis about Varuṇa is that he emerges within the first function in connection with the rise of that function relative to F4+, or with the correlated decline of F4+ relative to F1.

India knows two distinguishable hierarchies, that of castes and that of varnas. If caste is based on the pure/impure opposition, the varna hierarchy is based on a nested series of different oppositions, which he takes from Dumézil (1948, 76). Brahman versus Kṣatriya is as spiritual to temporal; the elite 'two forces' versus Vaiśya is as control of all creatures to control of domesticated animals; and the twice-born triad versus Śūdra is as initiated to uninitiated. But this particular 'Hegelian' understanding of the varnas is dropped in Dumézil's later writings, and he even attacked those who when faced with a system of three homogeneous terms wanted to reduce it to 'comfortable' binary oppositions (Allen 1985, 29): the homogeneity of the triad was more fundamental than the sporadic division into 2 + 1.

Dumont took the 1948 formulation as important partly because it was phrased in terms of dichotomies or binary oppositions, partly because it was essentially religious. This suited him for reasons both theoretical and empirical. His theory of *caste* hierarchy relied on a formally similar binary opposition, again religious, and the resulting similarity between caste and varna had facilitated the observable tendency of Indians to assimilate them. Moreover, in grouping together the two powers at the top of the hierarchy, the 1948 formula resolved what would otherwise be a problem for a theory of caste based on purity/impurity. A vegetarian diet is purer than a meat-eating one, but the vegetarian merchant castes are outranked by the meat-eating Rajputs (1979, 103-8). This is because the merchants as Vaiśya are outranked by the Rajputs as Kṣatriya. In the middle and less fundamental part of the system, purity gives way to power.

Thus I have two levels of criticism. First, Dumont does not use Dumézil's three functions as such, but only a rare and atypical formulation of one of their manifestations. Second, Dumézil himself is operating with a triadic framework that is too tight to fit the facts. So what are the implications of replacing Dumézil's triadic model with a pentadic one?

One effect is to approximate Dumont's two hierarchies, caste and varna. Although analytical clarity demands a distinction between the fixed four varnas of the texts and the variable and multiple castes of everyday life, the two already have much in common. Both present sharp divides between units (like Australian sections and like clans, but unlike social classes), and both tend to list units in descending hierarchical order. Both assume an ideal division of labour between units, and both put Brahmans at the top, followed by secular power holders (Kṣatriya or dominant castes). But we now have a clearer similarity at the bottom. The most salient partition among varnas separates the twice-born from the Śūdra, who are viewed comparatively as representing what is other, outside or beyond in a devalued direction. The most salient partition among castes usually separates 'clean' castes from 'Untouchables'—who are also devalued outsiders at the bottom of a hierarchy. In this sense the Śūdra in the textual hierarchy correspond to the Untouchable castes in society, and the Vaiśya correspond to the mid-ranking castes—those coming between dominant castes and Untouchables. Admittedly, these middle-rankers often include castes said to be Śūdra, but this is a matter of nomenclature, not of basic ideas—such 'Śūdra' are not nowadays devalued outsiders.

Dumont's emphasis is rather different: just as the Śūdra were added on to the original tripartite model, so, much later, the Untouchables were added on to the four-varna model (1979, 95, 98-9). While not denying the occurrence of historical change of various sorts, the formal/comparative view emphasizes rather the astonishing tenacity of Indian ideological structures. Whatever their name, and whether as model or reality, a category of devalued outsiders is always there; and this is still relevant. To put it concretely, current political struggles over reservations still express the ancient conceptual divide between F4- and the core functions (F1-3). How this may be played out in contemporary Orissa is for the regional specialists to say.

Caste and varna come together in another way too. For Dumont, caste is based on criteria of purity that are segmented in multiple ways, the varna scheme on different principles and less systematic ones (1979, 95). But his concept of purity abstracts from the lifestyle of the ideal Brahman, while impurity is related similarly to Untouchables. Now if the Brahman belongs as much to varna as to caste, and if Untouchable *castes* occupy the same ideological position as the Śūdra *varna*, then Dumont's pure-impure opposition derives by abstraction from the first and last varna. But we already know that the purity principle can be overruled in the middle ranges of caste (problem of the meat-eating Rajput), so the middle two varnas also affect its operation. Ultimately then, we do not need to envisage two hierarchies based on different principles, but rather a single hierarchical ideology with IE roots, which expresses itself both in the complex structuring of society as lived, and in the neat mythic model that dominates the literature.

This leads to a more general point: the principles involved need not be binary oppositions. Such thinking dominated the structuralism of the 1950s and 1960s, but there was never any good reason for confining the notion of structure to its minimal form. A structure is an abstract whole made up of elements between which there exist clear relationships that endure when the content of the elements changes (Allen 1990), and it makes no difference whether it has five elements or two.

The King

At the top end of the IE hierarchy, as we saw, India forces us to postulate a historical shift in the ideology: in many contexts, instead of transcending the varnas, the king was felt to belong to the second varna. This is what Dumont calls the secularization of kingship, and even if he exaggerates the completeness of the shift, he is certainly perceiving a real phenomenon. But this raises a further problem. For Dumont, the secularization of kingship was a precondition for the appearance of hierarchy in the full religious sense. It is because the king is secularized and demoted below the Brahman that purity and pollution can fix the extremities of the hierarchy and thereby provide its ideological foundation (1979, 100).

This argument would imply—paradoxically—that the original pentadic scheme was not truly hierarchical. Dumont defines hierarchy as 'the principle of ranking elements of a whole by reference to the whole, it being understood that in most societies it is religion that supplies the view of the whole and that the ranking will thus be of a religious nature' (ibid., 92). But the whole is of higher value than its parts and outranks them, so the king, representing totality, is perfectly qualified for the top position in a hierarchy. The difficulty lies, I think, not in the concept of kingship or hierarchy, but in our notion of religion, and more precisely in the way we link it to priesthood. Religion in this narrow 'priestly' sense needs to be distinguished from religion in a broader sense, which is better called 'cosmology' (Allen 2000e, Chap. 7[6]). Expressed in these terms, the pentadic scheme was a hierarchical cosmology within which religion (in the narrow sense) occupied the second position, and the secularization of kingship can be seen either as a 'decosmologization' of the royal role or as an expansion of the priestly role, tending towards its 'cosmologization'. These are proposed not as exclusive alternatives but as complementary aspects of a complex process unfolding at different rates and in different forms in different contexts. Although the state has now gone a good way towards replacing the kings, Orissa and its history surely provide copious material for studying the process.

Wider Issues

I have concentrated so far on caste and kingship, on social structure in one sense of that unfashionable expression, for several reasons. It was Dumézil's own starting point; it was mainly on this topic that he was used by Dumont; the topic, although less popular than it was, remains important, with major questions still controversial; and it illustrates IE comparativist discourse. Moreover, it is historically interesting that Dumont never followed up or commented on Dumézil's move from three varnas to three functions.[7] But social structure is only one direction among the many that need to be pursued, for relatively little has been done since Dumézil to apply the idea of functions to South Asian material. The nearest approach to a synthesis is by the trifunctionalist Hellenist/comparativist Bernard Sergent (1997); but the pentadic model both answers some of the objections raised against the triadic model and opens up new possibilities.

Logically one would expect the IE heritage to be clearest in the earliest sources, and to tail off as Vedism developed into classical Hinduism. This is true for language, but not for culture: Dumézil found more inherited material in the *Mahābhārata* than in the

---

[6] My argument is based partly on Mauss's classification of religious phenomena, partly on the contrast between the earthly pilgrimage of F1 Yudhiṣṭhira and the cosmic journey to heaven of F4+ Arjuṇa.

[7] Why was this? Did the Durkheimian, Hertzian and Lévi-Straussian habit of thinking in dualisms run too deep? Did he regard the theory as too controversial, or did he sense that in some way it was incomplete as it stood?

Vedas. Presumably it is a matter of genre—the fragmentary, allusive character of the hymns and the scholasticism of the ritual texts contrasting with the copiousness and range of the Great Epic; but whatever the reasons, the epic has proved a good focus for comparativism. Moreover, it is far more relevant to contemporary Hinduism than are the Vedas (Biardeau 1989).

The basic comparativist insight into the *Mahābhārata* (first made, not by Dumézil, but by the Swedish Indo-Iranianist Wikander) is that the Pāṇḍava brothers, the heroes, manifest the three functions. Yudhiṣṭhira, son of Dharma, represents the first function, the beefy Bhīma the second, and the humble half-brother twins, the third. The arguments are numerous, convergent and convincing, but four-function theory makes two further points (Allen 1999b, 1999c). First, there is one other half-brother (and only one), namely Karṇa, who fights for the Kaurava villains and represents the devalued aspect of the fourth function (F4-). Second, Arjuna, who often represents the Pāṇḍavas as a whole and thus transcends them, is best interpreted as representing F4+.[8] But it is not without reason that trifunctionalists see him as F2, so we meet in epic an exact analogy to the sociostructural secularization and demotion of the king—and the analogy extends to Arjuna's father, Indra, king of the gods, who in some contexts represents F2. The concordance between the phenomena in the different domains suggests a major ideological shift that may not be easy to conceptualize precisely; but selfish manipulation by Brahmans could hardly provide a satisfactory explanation.

Another four-functional pattern in the *Mahābhārata* proves to have wide ramifications. Consider the marital history of Arjuna (Allen 1996a, 1999d). His first and most salient wife is Draupadī, whom he wins at a *svayaṃvara* and shares with the other Pāṇḍava brothers, but soon afterwards he goes on a journey around the four quarters of India and acquires three further wives. Ulūpī in the north he acquires in a manner hinting at dowry, Subhadrā in the

[8] Arjuna and Karṇa, embodiments of Nara and Naraka respectively, are arch-enemies. If Arjuna actually represents F4+, Karṇa could have done so since, being older than Yudhiṣṭhira, he is offered the throne if he will change sides. This is one instance, among several, where two F4 entities appear as particularly close to each other, rather than maximally far apart. Note that just as Arjuna is third in birth order among the five Pāṇḍava, Karṇa is third in sequence among the five Kaurava generals.

west (I ignore the order of events) is acquired explicitly by capture, Citrāṅgadā in the east by *śulka*, bride-service or bride-price. It can be argued that these three modes of marriage are linked to the three core functions (Dumézil 1979) and to most of the eight modes listed in Manu (3.20-21). But in the south Arjuna has bodily contact with five females (temporarily metamorphosed into crocodiles). Given that the *svayaṃvara* is a royal mode (F4+), and that it here links a single female with five males, the 'bestial' contact of a single male with five females could well represent F4-. Is it not a mythical and bowdlerised form of the despised *paiśāca* union with which Manu ends his more or less hierarchical list.[9] One might look for parallels in the 'loathly hags' of recent folklore, but the analysis as a whole raises a topic of greater political significance: the massive prestige of the F1 dowry marriage, with all its contemporary abuses—now that *svayaṃvara* has disappeared (or been democratised into *gāndharva* 'love' marriages).

Another ramification is the comparison with Greece (Allen 1996a, 1996c, 2000a). Arjuna's dealings with females turn out to be cognate with those of Odysseus, Ulūpī corresponding to Circe, the crocodiles to Scylla and her associates, and so on. We need to envisage an IE oral proto-narrative lying behind the epics we now read. This, and the extension of the argument to the Irish hero Cūchulainn (Allen 2000b), may appear utterly remote from contemporary Orissa, but again appearances are deceptive. Historians tell us about the *local* origins of the celebrated Puri triad of Krishna, Subhadrā and Balabhadra (Eschmann, Kulke and Tripathi 1978), but the three characters are first brought together in the *Mahābhārata* in just the section of Book 1 that we have been discussing. When Arjuna arrives in the western quarter, Krishna encourages him to abduct Subhadrā by force, and when he does so, Balabhadra heads the opposition. The Homeric comparison forces us to recognize the following cognates (apart from Arjuna-Odysseus): Krishna-Laodamas, Subhadrā-Nausicaa, Balabhadra-Euryalus (Allen 2000f). But the three Greek figures are brought together in a scene where Odysseus displays his sporting prowess among the Phaeacians by a superlative throw of a discus, and the Puri triad is often accompanied by Sudarśana, the discus of

---

[9] The contrast between the two F4 plural unions and the three F1-3 single unions provides another instance of the phenomenon mentioned in note 7.

Krishna. Again, is the link between the triad and Narasiṃha the Man-Lion to explained purely in local terms? When Odysseus first emerges from his thicket to meet Nausicaa, an elaborate Homeric simile compares him with a lion advancing on its prey (*Od.* 6.130).

Here is another ramification. Correspondences need not be one-to-one, and it turns out that Odysseus's journey to Scheria is cognate not only with Arjuna's Book 1 journey to Dvārakā but also with his Book 3 journey to Indra's heaven. But this journey in turn is related to the classical yogin's progress to the condition of *kaivalya* (Allen 1998a), as well as to the Buddha's progress to Enlightenment (Allen 2000c). Moreover, among the Hindu *darśanas* or soteriological philosophies, yoga is linked with Sāṃkhya, and arguably the Sāṃkhya sequence of Puruṣa, then Prakṛti with her three *guṇas*, then (after *buddhi*) *ahaṃkāra*, is a manifestation of the IE sequence F4+, core functions, F4- (Allen 1998b). These brief references are intended only to suggest the range of contemporary topics to which IE comparativism can contribute—for the ancient doctrines live on in today's religious thinking.

More generally, as a method, IE cultural comparativism extends the history of Sanskritic culture backwards in time before the *Rigveda*—even before the Indus Civilization—and outside the soil of India (much as the cultural history of Britain extends outside its shores). Doubts have recently been raised as to the reality of the Aryan immigration (as distinct from an Aryan *invasion*, for which there is no good evidence), but they have been laid to rest by Witzel (2001), and the method need not be neglected because of political sensitivities (Allen 1999a). It has of course been familiar to historians of language for a couple of centuries, but the application to culture has in the past mostly been too speculative and controversial to have much impact either on Indology or on the wider public.

The method also bears on what one might call the social as distinct from the chronological depth of Sanskritic culture. Let us glance through the main items we have linked with the devalued fourth function: first Dāsas, Śūdras (with black as symbolic colour) and Untouchables, then in the epic Karṇa (adoptive son of an outcaste), the Kauravas supported by demons, and the man-eating female crocodiles apparently linked with abominable *paiśāca* unions. It is easy to 'feel' that all of these somehow belong together, and it is then a small step to the feeling that they are all somehow aboriginal and non-IE. But each case needs detailed attention, and it is the role of the comparativist to stress that representatives of F4- have been present ever since the proto-culture. If elements with this 'feel' about them have been incorporated into the Sanskritic tradition from outside, then they have replaced or complemented what was already there. It is all too easy to assume that what is ideologically other or outside comes from a different culture. Here are two examples, taken from the pantheon.

The nature of Rudra-Śiva is surely complicated, but in many senses he is an outsider deity—the bowman on the fringes of civilization, the god not invited to Dakṣa's sacrifice. Predictably, he has often been regarded as essentially non-Aryan, e.g. by Brockington (1981, 21). But in certain respects he is cognate with the trident-wielding Poseidon, who tends to be odd man out among the Olympians. As usual with such comparisons, the relationship need not be one-to-one, and others have been suggested (as Śiva ~Dionysus by Sergent 1997, 321-4); but at least some aspects of the Sanskritic deity are of IE origin.

Similarly it is often assumed that the Goddess—so inconspicuous in the Vedas, so prominent in Puranic and later Hinduism—is an import from aboriginal culture. Maybe so, in part. But we saw that ancient traditions often bypass the Vedas to surface in later texts, and the Book 4 intervention of Durgā relegated in the *Mahābhārata* Critical Edition) is paralleled by the intervention of Athena when Odysseus first arrives back in Ithaca (Allen 2001). IE cultural comparativism offers many such surprises.

References

Allen, N.J. 1975. 'Byansi Kinship Terminology: A Study in Symmetry', in *Man* 10, 80-94.

— 1985. 'Hierarchical Opposition and Some Other Types of Relation', in R.H. Barnes, D. de Coppet and R.J. Parkin (eds.), *Contexts and Levels: Anthropological Essays on Hierarchy*, Oxford: JASO, 21-32.

— 1990. 'On the Notion of Structure', *JASO* 2, 279-82.

— 1991. 'Some Gods of Pre-Islamic Nuristan', in *Revue de L'Histoire des Religions* 208, 141-68.

— 1993. 'Debating Dumézil: Recent Studies in Comparative Mythology', in *JASO* 24, 119-31.

— 1996a. 'The Hero's Five Relationships: a Proto-Indo-European Story', in J. Leslie (ed.), *Myth and Myth-making: Continuous Evolution in Indian Tradition*, London: Curzon, 1-20.

— 1996b. 'Romulus and the Fourth Function', in E.C. Polomé (ed.), *Indo-European Religion after Dumézil* (JIES Monograph Series 16), Washington: Institute for the Study of Man, 13-36.

— 1996c. 'Homer's Simile, Vyasa's Story', in *Journal of Mediterranean Studies* 6, 206-11.

— 1998a. 'The Indo-European Prehistory of Yoga', in *International Journal of Hindu Studies* 2, 1-20.

— 1998b. 'The Category of Substance: A Maussian Theme Revisited', in W. James and N.J. Allen (eds.), *Marcel Mauss: A Centenary Tribute*, Oxford: Berghahn, 171-91.

— 1998c. 'Varnas, Colours and Functions: Expanding Dumézil's Schema', in *Zeitschrift für Religions-wissenschaft* 6, 163-77.

— 1999a. 'Hinduism as Indo-European: Cultural Comparativism and Political Sensitivities', in J. Bronkhorst and M.M. Deshpande (eds.), *Aryan and Non-aryan in South Asia: Evidence, Interpretation and Ideology,* Cambridge, Mass.: Department of Sanskrit and Indian Studies, Harvard University, 19-32.

— 1999b. 'Arjuna and the Second Function: a Dumézilian Crux', in *J. Royal Asiatic Society,* Ser. *3,* 9, 403-18.

— 1999c. 'Hinduism, Structuralism and Dumézil', in E.C. Polomé (ed.), *Miscellanea Indo-Europea,* Washington: Institute for the Study of Man, 241-60.

— 1999d. 'Les Crocodiles Qui Se Transforment en Nymphes', in *Ollodagos* 13, 151-67.

— 2000a. 'Argos and Hanuman: Odysseus' Dog in the Light of the *Mahābhārata*', *Journal of Indo-European Studies* 28, 3-16.

— 2000b. 'Cūchulainn's Women and Some Indo-European Comparisons', in *Emania* 18, 57-64.

— 2000c. 'Scripture and Epic: a Comparativist Looks at the Biography of the Buddha', in *Visvabharati Quarterly,* N.S. 9, 51-62.

— 2000d. 'Imra, Pentads and Catastrophes', in *Ollodagos* 14, 278-308.

— 2000e. *Categories and Classifications: Maussian Reflections on the Social*, Oxford: Berghahn.

— 2000f. 'Review of *Balarāma im Mahābhārata* by A. Bigger', in *JRAS* 10(3), 411-13.

— 2001. 'Athena and Durgā: Warrior Goddesses in Greek and Sanskrit Epic', in S. Deacy and A. Villing (eds.), *Athena in the Classical World*, Leiden: Brill, 367-82.

Biardeau, M. 1989. *Hinduism: the Anthropology of a Civilization*, Delhi: Oxford University Press.

Brockington, J.L. 1981. The *Sacred Thread: Hinduism in its Continuity and Diversity*, Edinburgh: Edinburgh University Press.

Dumézil, G. 1930. 'La Préhistoire Indo-Iranienne des Castes', in *J. Asiatique* 216, 109-30.

— 1938. 'La Préhistoire des Flamines Majeurs', in *Revue de L'Histoire des Religions* 118, 188-200 (reprinted in idem 1969, *Idées Romaines*. Paris: Gallimard.

— 1948. *Mitra-Varuṇa*: *Essai sur Deux Représentations Indo-Europennes de la Souveraineté*, Paris: Gallimard.

— 1968-73. *Mythe et Épopée* (3 vols: I 1968, II 1971, III 1973), Paris: Gallimard.

— 1977. *Les Dieux Souverains des Indo-Européens,* Paris: Gallimard.

— 1979. *Mariages Indo-Européens*, Paris: Payot.

— 1983. *La Courtisane et les Seigneurs Colorés*, Paris: Gallimard.

Dumont, L. 1957. 'For a Sociology of India', reprinted in idem 1970, *Religion/Politics and History in India*, Paris: Mouton, 2-18.

— 1979. *Homo Hierarchicus,* édn Tel, Paris (trans. 1980, Chicago: University of Chicago Press).

Durkheim, E. 1912. *Les Formes Élémentaires de la Vie Religieuse: Le Systeme Totémique en Australie*. Paris: Alcan.

— and M. Mauss. 1903. 'De Quelques Formes Primitives de Classification', in *Année Sociologique* 6, 1-72.

Eggeling, J. 1882-1900. *The Śatapatha-Brāhmaṇa*, 5 vols, Oxford: Clarendon.

Eschmann, A., H. Kulke and G.C. Tripathi. 1978. *The Cult of Jagannath and the Regional Tradition of Orissa,* Delhi: Manohar.

Ferdowsi 1996. *The Epic of the Kings:* Shahnama, abridged, trans. R. Levy, Mazda: Costa Mesa.

Mauss, M. 1968. *Oeuvres*, vol. I, Paris: Minuit.

Mus, P. 1962. 'Du Nouveau sur Ṛgveda 10.90? Sociologie d'une Grammaire', in *Indological Studies in Honour of W. Norman Brown*, New Haven: American Oriental Society, 165-85.

— 1998. *Barabudur: Sketch of a History of Buddhism Based on Archaeological Criticism of the Texts*, New Delhi: Indira Gandhi National Centre for the Arts.

O'Flaherty, W.D. 1981. *The Rig Veda: an Anthology*, Harmondsworth: Penguin.

Rees, A. and B. Rees. 1961. *Celtic Heritage*, London: Thames and Hudson.

Schlerath, B. 1995-6. 'Georges Dumézil und die Rekonstruktion der Indo-Germanischen Kultur', in *Kratylos* 40, 1-48; 41,1-67.

Sergent, B. 1997. *Genese de l'Inde*, Paris: Payot.

Vaneev, Z.N. 1956. *Narodnoe Predanie o Proiskhozhdenii Osetin,* Stalinir: Gosizdat Yugo-Osetii.

Witzel, M. 1987. 'The Coronation Rituals of Nepal', in N. Gutschow and A. Michaels (eds.), *Heritage of the Kathmandu Valley*, Sankt Augustin: VGH Wissenschaftsverlag, 3-53.

— 2001. 'Autochthonous Aryans? The Evidence From Old Indian and Iranian Texts', in *Electronic Journal of Vedic Studies* 7 (3) (25 May).

14

'Captain Kittoe's Road': Early Colonialism and the Politics of Road Construction in Peripheral Orissa*

Ravi Ahuja

'...if the Sahib breaks through the old established usage, my dependents will rebel against my authority, and my country will be ruined.'

Jadunath Bhanja, Maharaja of Mayurbhanj, 1841

Early colonial administrators were not so much interested in making a way *into* Orissa than in *getting past it* without hindrance. From the mid-eighteenth century, when the East India Company emerged as an expansionist colonial power in Eastern India, up to the last third of the nineteenth century, Orissa's economic potential was only of secondary interest to the colonial government. Any opportunity to extract land revenue was, of course, appreciated, and Orissa's agriculture was subjected to particularly heavy tax demands in the early decades of British rule.[1] However, the considerations that led to the annexation of the coastal plains in 1803 were primarily strategic.[2] Even later, an 1815 report on the 'province of Cuttack' clearly stated that the 'importance of this Territory to the British Government consists chiefly in its geographical situation, the possession of which connects the two Presidencies of Fort William and Fort St. George[,] secures an uninterrupted intercourse between the two Governments of Bengal & Madras and places the whole range of Coast on this side of the

---

* Research for this paper was conducted as a contribution to the Orissa Research Programme of the German Research Council.

[1] Chaudhuri 1982, 90-1, 94-5.

[2] Clive enquired in 1766 whether the Marathas could not be persuaded to 'cede the province of Orissa, for an annual tribute, and thereby give a contiguity to the British dominions in India, which would strengthen them greatly': Motte 1952, 2. Wellesley planned Orissa's conquest in order to 'unite the Northern Circars by a continued line of sea coast with Bengal'; quoted in: Ray 1960, 106-7.

Bay under the immediate eye and control of the British Government.'[3]

In Orissa's mountainous periphery, the so-called 'Garjats', where powerful households ruled over numerous minor kingdoms, zamindaris and villages, colonial interest was even more restricted to strategic considerations, at least before the massive resources of timber and minerals began to attract colonial attention in the last decades of the nineteenth century. Indirect rule seemed to be the cheapest means to serve this strategic interest-*limited* (rather than *non-*) interference with the affairs of the so-called 'Tributary Mahals' was the official line of policy as long as local rulers accepted British overlordship, regularly paid tribute, granted passage, maintained a pathway, and supplied passing troops or official travellers with porters and victuals. Many colonial officials found it hard to accept that 'unreasonable and inimical petty rajahs' were tolerated and the 'rule of [British] law' was not being established. Yet revenue expectations were too low to justify the trouble and the expenses which would have followed a more aggressive policy of annexation. Moreover, during the 'Great Rebellion' of 1857 the 'Tributary Mahals' proved to be an efficient 'breakwater', a *cordon sanitaire* against the spread of insurgency towards the east despite some local insurrections, namely, in Sambalpur.[4] Prior to the last third of the nineteenth century, communications works were, therefore, very limited in extent in peripheral Orissa. Some were executed in areas like the 'Khond Mahals' to facilitate counter-insurgency operations.[5] More extensive and important measures were, however, implemented on two interregional lines of communication. The first of those was the road following the course of the Mahanadi from Sonepur via the crucial Baramul Pass to Cuttack, which connected coastal Orissa with central India. The second (on which the focus lies in this paper) connected Midnapur in Bengal with Raipur in Chhattisgarh

---

[3] OIOC: Board's Collection, F/4/505, 12139: John Richardson, 'Report on the conclusion of his Mission to the Province of Cuttack', 18 May 1815 (extracted from Bengal Revenue Consultations), 7.

[4] Cf.: Praharaj 1988, 53; Sahu 1993, 5-6.

[5] For relevant material concerning the 'Khond Mahals' from between 1837 and 1854 cf., for instance: *History of the Rise and Progress...* 1854, 16-17, 33-4, 37, 85, 93, 128.

passing through the 'Tributary Mahals' of Mayurbhanj, Kendujhar, Pal Lahera, Bonai, Bamra and Sambalpur.[6]

This route was a section of the main *dak* (mail) road between Calcutta and Bombay before 1853 when a new line was opened between Mirzapur and Jabalpur. Contracts with local rulers had been signed in the early decades of the nineteenth century concerning the right of way and the establishment of '*dak* stations'. By the 1820s a rough sort of military road had been made under British supervision.[7] At the end of the following decade it was decided to establish a more permanent, safe and fast line of communication, the so-called 'Raipur Mail Road': it was completed in 1846. It extended over a distance of about 1,000 kilometres, half of which ran through the territories of 'Tributary Mahals'. Almost five lakh rupees were spent on the project by the colonial regime, rendering it the second most important 'public work' undertaken in the entire Orissa region before the 1870s.[8] As for expenditure, only the 'new Jagannath Road' surpassed it, a partly realigned modernization of the old pilgrim route from Bengal to Puri along the coastal plains of Orissa.[9] The Raipur Mail Road was, however, a rather limited achievement. The Governor-General-in-Council kept expenditure low, as the main objective was to create a line of postal communication.[10] While the construction of a cartable trading road would have been rather expensive, an easier and safer track for '*dak* runners' and palanquin bearers could be provided with considerably less expense. Thus forest was cleared away on the sides for one to two hundred yards, the road raised in some sections and a few wooden bridges constructed. The actual pathway was only 6 to 10 ft wide, neither surfaced nor cartable and, therefore, of little

---

[6] I discuss these problems more systematically in a longer essay which is presently being prepared for publication.

[7] OIOC: Board's Collection, F/4/1196, 30905/29, 6-9 (Bengal Pol. Consultations, 15 July 1825: Lieut. Col. Gilbert, 'Agent to Governor-General in Sumbhulpore and South Behar', to Swinton, Secretary to GoB, 22 June 1825); ibid., 37-40 (Bengal Pol. Consultations, 17 August 1827: Gilbert to Swinton, 29 May 1827; OSA: BoRLR 18,167 Bd.Doc: (Superintendent of Tributary Mahals?) to H. Shakespear, Secretary to GoB, Judicial Department, 19 July 1830.

[8] OIOC: BPWP, 19 January 1860 (P/16/37), Communications, No. 14, 198-9.

[9] Cf. note 4 above.

[10] NAI: PMB, 26 February 1841, 10701-4.

commercial importance. Its alignment towards Midnapur (instead of Baleshwar) precluded any positive effect on Orissa's integration with the rest of the country. When the new '*dak* road' towards Jabalpur was opened in 1853, expenditure of the maintenance of the Raipur Mail Road was stopped so that it was soon overgrown and almost forgotten.[11]

However, this line of communication is of some interest for students of social history as its construction is documented in considerable detail. In 1840 and 1841, Captain Markham Kittoe who had also surveyed the line in the two preceding years supervised works on the 'Garjat' section of the 'Raipur Mail Road'. Kittoe is better known for his wide-ranging scholarly ambitions: being in his early thirties when setting out for peripheral Orissa, he had already published several reports on his archaeological and geological findings in the Orissa plains in the Journal of the Asiatic Society of Bengal.[12] He had also served as a curator and librarian to this institution of orientalist scholarship and was later appointed official archaeological surveyor of Bihar and Varanasi.[13] Yet Kittoe was as much a man of the whip as he was a man of letters. His survey diaries and construction reports show him as the typical embodiment of colonial progressivism—an aggressive mindset that blended an unconditional belief in the superiority of the European 'race', 'civilization', and science with a carefree brutality in dealing with those outside this 'civilization'. His diaries and reports, on which this paper is mainly based,[14] are unusually eloquent and give a detailed account of the various conflicts early colonial road construction projects triggered off in peripheral Orissa. Moreover, a

---

[11] OIOC: BPWP 19 January 1860 (P/16/37), Communications, No. 14: J. Beadle, Superintendent of Embankments and Superintending Engineer, 3rd Circle, Lower Provinces, to Officiating Chief Engineer, Lower Provinces, 19 October 1859, 197-8; ibid., G.F. Cockburn, Commissioner of Cuttack Division, to Superintending Engineer, 3rd Circle, Calcutta, 27 September 1859, 199; ibid., No. 15: Rivers Thompson, Jr. Secretary to GoB, to Officiating Chief Engineer, Lower Provinces, 13 January 1860, 200.

[12] Kittoe 1838a; Kittoe 1838b, Kittoe 1839a.

[13] Cf. Everest 1958, 452.

[14] The survey report was published as: Kittoe 1839b. The construction reports can be found, together with other relevant material, in: NAI: PMB 1840-42.

close reading of these sources enables us to distinguish the contradictions of colonial administration in this period.

For all its persistent rhetoric of 'opening up the country' towards 'civilization', 'commerce' and the 'rule of law' by improved means of communication, when it came to administrative practice, the British government often preferred to leave the country 'closed'. Samuel Macpherson, the officer in charge of the 'Meriah operations' in the 'Khond Mahals' in the 1830s, articulated this contradiction in his own terms. Though new roads were essential, he argued, for exerting those 'civilizing influences' which alone could 'remove barbarism', their first effect was to unsettle the local balance of power and create political problems. Macpherson specifically referred to one economic facet of this phenomenon, namely that a new road often meant that one local ruler received more revenues from his *chaukis* (toll stations), while his neighbour, across whose territory the earlier track had passed, received less.[15] The more general point is, however, that even the few measures for improving communications that were considered unavoidable for military reasons conflicted with the British policy of indirect rule in northern and western Orissa. For road construction affected the structures of local society deeply and in several ways: extensive road works implied heavy demands on local labour and produce, more often than not enforced by coercion; improved accessibility of a territory entailed reduced protection from military invasions; when the armed forces of an alien power guarded road works and *dak* stations or marched along a military road within the dominion of a local ruler, the latter's authority and legitimacy was dangerously undermined in his subjects' and rivals' eyes.[16] These unsettling effects were not merely disapproved of by villagers and ruling households in the 'Tributary Mahals' but also by Orissa's colonial administrators who sought to preserve the existent configuration of power in this region in order to maintain *pax Britannica*. In the case under discussion, this contradiction formed the background of persistent conflict between Captain Markham Kittoe on the one hand, whose main concern was to find cheap and efficient means to construct a road, and the Commissioner of Cuttack, A.J. Moffat Mills on the other, who was disinclined to tolerate any measure likely to cause unrest.

---

[15] Macpherson 1842, 93.

[16] Cf. note 4 above.

Before we look at these conflicts in greater detail, a few reflections on the nature of this paper may be in order. To some extent, it is a plain narrative, a straightforward historical account based on material from the 'colonial archive'. Textual material of this sort, it is well known, reflects no more than one of many conflicting historical perspectives. In the process of its production, information was digested and reorganized according to the dominant, colonial, ideological matrix. In our case, this is even reflected in the habit of naming roads that often followed the course of long-established pathways after the officers who had 'discovered' them or supervised their 'construction': it was 'Jackson's', 'Babington's' or 'Kittoe's Road' because these men were seen as pioneers of 'civilization' in a lonely struggle against the odds of an 'insalubrious climate' and a country which 'is one continuous wild', against the 'proverbial impudence and haughtiness', the 'malicious underhand practices' and even open resistance of 'semi-barbarian', 'indolent' and 'inimical' 'natives'.[17] It is for the same reason that Kittoe felt the necessity to explain why he was using the pronoun 'we' when writing about his 1838 journey though it was perfectly clear that he had commanded a survey party that included dozens of Indian bearers, *sepoys* and administrative staff: 'We' only included the two other British officers who accompanied him for a while; Indians, even those in his immediate service, could never be more than 'they'.[18] Similarly, individuality was, in these texts, a privilege of Europeans and the superior ranks of Indian society. Persons from subordinate classes are virtually always dealt with in the plural and in generic, mostly ethnic categories (*'dhangars'*, *'bildars'*, 'Oriyas', etc.). Hence, in reports on situations of intense conflict, when groups of migrant workers confronted the British official directly and generated leaders, it is obvious that Kittoe found it unseemly to refer to them as *persons* or in any greater detail. 'Ring leaders', i.e. those who had transgressed the boundary of anonymity, risked exemplary (corporal) punishment and were even then only referred to summarily and in

---

[17] Cf. e.g. Kittoe 1839b, 372 and NAI: PMB, 26 January 1841, 9502 (statement by Captain J.A. Crommelin, Offg. Superintending Engineer, South Eastern Province).

[18] Kittoe 1839b, 379.

impersonal terms.[19] Rendering the subordinated anonymous was a procedure integral to the prevalent mode of representing authority.

Such narrative qualities can be found in many colonial documents from widely different historical contexts. To add another *purely* discursive analysis to the 'postmodern archive' could not help to create what most of such contemporary textual productions create: a sense of repetition and intellectual claustrophobia. Kittoe's reports and diaries refer to the world 'out there' in a particular ideological vein but they *do* refer to a material world that exists outside 'text'. For our purposes, these texts from the 'colonial archive' can be used for an analysis of the specific historical repercussions of road development on structures of political and social power in early nineteenth-century peripheral Orissa. They permit a reconstruction of the contradictions of early colonial communications policy and the very material implications of this policy for the lives (and deaths) of people from various social and cultural groups.

In order to spell out these contradictions and implications it has been necessary to present the material systematically rather than chronologically. This paper is hence organized as follows. Section II deals with aspects of early colonial communications policy concerning the 'political system' of peripheral Orissa in a narrow sense. Here we discuss how road construction led to conflicts between colonial administrators and dominant households in zamindaris and kingdoms over geographical knowledge, military security and legitimacy. Such conflicts occurred as soon as a new road was planned and surveyed. The following section (III) also relates to problems of political power but focuses on conflicts over resources, mainly labour and agricultural surplus. Conflicts of this type arose when large numbers of labourers from Chota Nagpur, central India and coastal Orissa were brought to the 'Garjats' and when large survey and construction parties roamed the country for 'coolie labour' and supplies. Yet they continued when the road was taken into use and '*dak* stations' and 'bungalows' for official travellers were established and maintained. At the end of the paper we return to more general questions and a brief discussion of new developments that took off when the period under discussion drew to a close.

---

[19] NAI: PMB, 12 Februrary 1841, 10266.

Knowledge, Security and Legitimacy

'... for in verity, it appeared that the great desire to prevent the road passing through or near the gurh, was the great cause of all mischief which had arisen....'

Lieutenant Markham Kittoe, 1839

The interests of ruling households in peripheral Orissa were highly contradictory during the early colonial period in respect of communications development (as I have argued in greater detail elsewhere).[20] For some 'little kings', zamindars and village headmen, roads and river crossings were sources of revenue as various 'protection charges' could be imposed on pilgrims, merchants, Banjara traders and other travellers. Moreover, new lines of communication could also increase a ruler's sphere of influence and intensify his hold over outlying tracts of his domain. However, roads implied, at the same time, potential risks for 'Garjat' rulers—risks they were well aware of. Even in Maratha times their armed forces were inadequate for defence against serious military aggression. Their strongholds were usually simple 'mud forts' surrounded (like many villages) with a palisade which fended off arrows well enough but became ineffective when firearms were increasingly used. Inaccessibility, i.e. the absence of 'good communications', was thus the most effective protection for dominant households in peripheral Orissa. Strongholds were often surrounded by dense forest and care was taken to defend approach roads. Several rulers constructed fortified retreats in the most inaccessible parts of their dominions. When the Nagpur Bhonsles extended their influence to Orissa in the latter part of the eighteenth century and bands of Maratha horsemen pillaged the country, local rulers and village headmen ordered the obstruction of existing roads and discouraged their use.

The dominant households of peripheral Orissa apparently felt no more secure under British overlordship, and continued this practice of obstruction for decades. Kittoe reported that a tree felled across a road was the usual warning for travellers and their guides not to proceed further and to look for another path.[21] British officials who

[20] For the following paragraph cf. note 4 above.

[21] Kittoe 1839b, 379-80.

ignored such signs sometimes found themselves surrounded by armed and angry villagers.[22] There is also evidence that some inhabitants of peripheral Orissa intentionally left a strip of 'jungle' between their settlements and nearby roads to screen themselves off from passing-by troops. Mud forts and villages were protected by palisades and many strongholds and settlements immediately bordered on forests to which their inhabitants retreated as soon as foreigners were discovered in the vicinity: '[I]t is to facilitate their escape', wrote Kittoe, 'that the jungle is never entirely cleared near the villages; a narrow belt connected with the forest is usually to be found.'[23]

Hence rulers and subjects of the little kingdoms and zamindaris of peripheral Orissa often perceived new roads and improved communications as a serious threat to their security; they opposed them by all available means. This is the reason why Kittoe met with non-cooperation and muted resistance as soon as he reached peripheral Orissa on his survey journey for the new road in April 1838. The first difficulties occurred in an area formally part of the dominion of the Raja of Bamra but practically under the control of a 'Kund' (Khond?) chief whom Kittoe called 'Chundro Bearer'. A direct and easy route had been obstructed in many places; the British engineer felt that he was led along circuitous, even 'villainous' tracks; he believed that his guides feared retaliation by the local population and rulers, and, therefore, refrained from showing him a more direct route through the fertile and populated parts of the valley; he reported that a 'poor coolie was taken to task by one of the Kunds for offering to point out where drinking water could be found', and that he had been unable to prevent it because 'we were completely at their mercy, for they had taken us off the road'.[24] Geographical knowledge was dangerous knowledge, a closely watched and fiercely defended key to power. Kittoe pointed out 'the great reluctance which the natives of Orissa have to afford any information, and what is more, [...] their decided silence; it being (as I have always had occasion to remark) more than a life of an individual is worth were he to be detected by his chief in divulging the scanty resources of his country'.[25]

---

[22] Leckie 1954, 12.

[23] Kittoe 1839b, 607.

[24] Ibid., 380-2.

[25] Ibid., 367.

British officials regularly depicted this type of 'reluctance' as an expression of 'demi-civilized' irrationality and 'bigotry'.[26] Yet the experience with pre-colonial (especially Maratha) regimes as well as with their British successors had taught local rulers to resist improvements in communications. This was specifically true for the rajas through whose territories the new 'Raipur Mail Road' was to pass. Even the old *dak* road had impaired their authority, drained their resources and resulted in popular discontent. For the existence of a mail road implied the establishment of regular institutions (*dak* station) and the permanent presence of British armed forces (in this area the Ramgarh Light Infantry). In effect, additional foci of authority were created which supported themselves on the agricultural surplus of the surrounding country through 'plunder', 'requisition', or similar practices.[27] Moreover, the existence of such additional points of authority diminished a ruling household's hold over its subjects by creating an alternative and informal 'court of appeal'. Kittoe thus reported from Kendujhar that 'the villagers come freely to me this year and appeal to me on all occasions'.[28] New roads were, in this perspective, primarily channels through which a powerful overlord drained their political and economic resources. Hence non-cooperation on the part of ruling households as well as of their subjects was hard to overcome. Even after the construction of the road had started, an enervated Kittoe complained that on asking villagers in the kingdoms of Bamra and Pal Lahera about a more convenient alignment of the road he was regularly told 'the old ooreya story … of "what do I jungle manush know[,] I live far away[,] ask the Rajah's Mooktar [*mukhtar*, ruler's agent]"'.[29] In conversations with rajas and their officials, he noted, it was never possible to extract any useful geographical information about their own dominions though they were somewhat less secretive regarding the lands of neighbouring and rival chiefs.[30]

---

[26] For a typical formulation of such views cf.: OIOC: BPWP December 1862 (P/16/59), Communications, No. 95, 85 (T.W. Armstrong, Superintending Engineer, Cuttack Circle, to Officiating Chief Engineer, Bengal, 15 November 1862).

[27] Cf., for instance: Basu 1956, 167.

[28] NAI: PMB, 20 August 1841, 3825.

[29] Ibid.

[30] Ibid., 3829.

Yet non-cooperation had its limitations. Rajas could not risk an escalation of conflict with the British beyond a certain degree as the latter left no doubt that they were quite prepared to dethrone tributary rulers when they deemed it opportune. In the period under discussion, in 1839, the 'little kingdom' of Banki was annexed by the British—a measure which was evidently perceived as ominous by the other Garjat rulers. A few years later, the Commissioner of Cuttack stated thus with considerable satisfaction that this measure had 'introduced a better line of conduct' among the 'principal and most independent Rajahs' like those of Mayurbhanj and Kendujhar.[31] Under such conditions, negotiation was also important: if the construction of a road could not be prevented altogether, there was still the question *where* exactly these unpopular and dangerous channels of communication and rival power would be located. The point was to keep them as far away as possible from the ruler's residence, his 'garhs' or fortified strongholds, and from his main sources of revenue. Hence when the road was surveyed in 1839, Raja Tribhuban Deo of Bamra 'expressed great anxiety about the new road, and begged I would not bring it through Deogurh, as there were (of course) other much better paths, but that if I did so, that Lehragurh and Keunjurgurh must have the road through them likewise'. In Kittoe's view, the Raja's reason for the latter proposal was 'that if he were to have the nuisance imposed on him, he thought that the Lehra and Keunjur Raja should share it likewise'.[32] The Kendujhar Raja's diwan tried to cajole Kittoe into accepting a present for the promise that the road should not pass through Kendujhargarh and told him 'that if I would take it out of their district they would give even more'. Kittoe reported that he refused the bribe but found it advisable to keep a distance of about 8 miles between the road and the Raja's residence in order to avoid further 'mischief'.[33]

When the construction of the Raipur Mail Road was taken in hand, a section of the line that passed through the kingdom of Bonai had not yet been surveyed. Reaching the state on 15 May 1842, Kittoe attempted to close this gap, in total disregard of Raja Indra Deo's wishes. This triggered off a dramatic confrontation and the ten days in the course of which the situation escalated fill twenty

[31] Quoted from: Mukherjee 1964, 232; cf. also ibid., 229-31.

[32] Kittoe 1839b, 476-7.

[33] Ibid., 616-8.

pages of Kittoe's diary. Conflicts concerning early colonial public works are rarely documented in such detail, which may justify a closer scrutiny of this episode.[34] Kittoe reached the state bursting with confidence about his abilities to handle the 'natives' and their rulers and it was in this mood that he was received by the Raja's *mukhtars* (emissaries). Indra Deo's letter was, in Kittoe's view, 'replete with excuses and evasions' which is why he 'dismissed them with a reply to their master that I would listen to no excuse, that if he assisted me well and good, his services would be appreciated, if not he would only get into trouble.'[35] Apart from supplies and labour, Kittoe required assistance most urgently in respect of geographical information, but it was here that he met with open resistance. On surveying Bonai he

> was followed and watched every where by a couple of men who came out from the place where the old Rajah is encamped[,] could not get a soal [sic!] to come near me as the two men and others appeared to be instructing every person they met: they passed [close] to me once but stared at me and looked very fierce and bold in their own estimation, they lagged behind and questioned my bearers as to whether I was going to measure the Gurh ....[36]

Kittoe then moved away from the Raja's stronghold to the river bed to avoid direct confrontation as he had only few men in his company. The two 'spies' followed him yet and instructed curious villagers not to talk to the foreigner. Hence when he asked them to come near and tell him the name of the riverside settlement, the villagers refused, went off and, worst of all, laughed at the 'sahib' who now felt his authority at stake. He then 'ordered' the villagers to come down, sent out two of his peons who met with resistance and finally rode up himself and detained two men. These refused to answer his questions; he first suspected them to be 'Pooree Brahmins (who are notorious for their arrogance)'[37] but one of them finally admitted to living in the village. The 'sahib' had the men brought to his camp where they were further examined though without success. In his diary, Kittoe blamed his underlings that

---

[34] The following paragraphs are based on: NAI: PMB, 20 August 1841, 3836-55.

[35] Ibid., 3836.

[36] Ibid., 3840.

[37] Ibid., 3842.

force was then used against the 'spokesman' of the two detained persons: he was beaten with a cane. 'I am a Rajpoot and why do you strike me, what have I done',[38] the man protested. In reply he was further caned by a *chaprasi* in British service who ridiculed his claim to be a Rajput and called him a Chamar. It was at this point that it was found out that this detainee was an illegitimate son of the raja while the other captive was a Baniya. Kittoe was 'vexed and distressed by this disclosure', and sent 'all the respectable people of my Camp' to the Raja with his apologies insisting, at the same time, that the incident was no more than the result of the latter's 'obstinacy'.[39] The situation escalated further when the Raja's son poisoned himself a few days later, after settling his accounts and writing a will. Kittoe suspected that the suicide attempt was feigned to scare him away. He offered the assistance of his doctors, which was declined. The Raja advised Kittoe, instead, to leave his territory at once as he might find it difficult to muster 'coolies' and supplies from now on. The 'sahib' was still not impressed by that 'demi-civilized' ruler's wishes, and he stayed on. It was only when the Raja's son died the following day that Kittoe 'thought it better to clear of [*sic*!] the state where such an untoward event had come to pass'.[40]

Kittoe's superiors in Calcutta feared that this story was not yet concluded, and it would be interesting to know if another version of it has been preserved in the local memory of Bonai. Yet this is as much as we can find out presently about this incident and what we have to base our discussion on. The point that is highlighted by this episode is that colonial road construction *necessarily* implied that local structures of authority were called into question. Kittoe's aggressive contempt for the rulers and villagers of peripheral Orissa was possibly to some extent rooted in his personality but the dominant colonial ideology that claimed civilizational superiority of the British no doubt promoted such attitudes. In fact, they were helpful in achieving the goals of colonial communications policy, which relied, in the final analysis, on coercion. Kittoe was hence not removed from his position even though his superiors were not always happy with his single-handed actions. British officers who operated in peripheral Orissa had, of course, to negotiate with

[38] Ibid., 3843.
[39] Ibid., 3844-5.
[40] Ibid., 3851.

dominant local households: the military detachments under their immediate command were rather small while their supply lines to the centres of British power were long and weak. Yet the rajas were aware of the massive military power behind these undesired guests and were regularly reminded that punitive measures and even loss of their *gaddi* could be the consequence of non-compliance to their demands. Moreover, not only the threat but also the immediate availability of coercive means was required for the implementation of early colonial road projects. Hence, Kittoe insisted that the recruitment of a band of irregular *barkandazes* (*peons*, watchmen) for his construction party, which the Government of Bengal had ordered, was inadequate and that a detachment of a regular *sepoy* regiment was required instead. The colonial government obviously found Kittoe's arguments convincing.

> The Country is one continuous wild, there are no merchants or even petty shop keepers, therefore we are all at the mercy of the Chiefs and their dependents, who, if they will act as they do when we are supported by our guards, what must be the case when we are deprived of them? if supplies are cut off, as they are frequently, what must be the result? that my follow[er]s will be driven to help themselves by plunder and acts of violence, which may lead to something worse.[41]

Kittoe, like other colonial officers, feared that his subordinates would get out of hand and apply coercive means without his sanction for their own benefit. His concern was not the use of force as such but its *uncontrolled* use. Yet the presence of an outside armed force in the territory of a local ruler implied that his authority and legitimacy were seriously jeopardized no matter whether its actions were efficiently controlled by a hierarchic command structure or not. While a survey or construction party would by itself constitute only a temporary challenge, the improved road would in eventually be supplied with *dak* stations, bungalows for British travellers and even police *thanas*—an infrastructure that would render these inroads into the authority of local rulers permanent. Colonial officials were quite aware of this—Richardson in his report on the 'Province of Cuttack' had argued as early as in 1815 that every police *darogah* (officer) would transform himself

---

[41] Ibid., 19 February 1841, 10575.

into a 'petty tyrant' in these remote and 'uncivilized' regions.[42] The dominant households of peripheral Orissa, for their part, had much reason to resist such developments as long as possible.

What Kittoe chose to call an 'untoward event' in his report can possibly be understood as a crisis of legitimacy of the ruling household of Bonai, which was solved by the suicide of one of its members. Not only was the 'illegitimate son' (who was clearly a person of elevated social status) dishonoured, but so was, by implication, the entire royal household. It was, therefore, a situation that induced Indra Deo to take the risk of breaking off negotiations with the British and to assume a more openly non-co-operative attitude for some time in order to protect his local authority and his legitimacy as a ruler. This was also understood by Kittoe. He had no choice but to pack up camp and withdraw from Bonai without closing the gap of colonial geographical knowledge of 18 to 20 miles – a gap that had proved to be, most literally, 'more than the life of an individual is worth'.

Labour and Agricultural Surplus

... that Government will be no party to extortions, if a percentage on the price of the Coolies' labor be claimed on the plea of usage, the appropriation must be made with the free will and consent of the laborers and that [if] the work should be obstructed in consequence of any differences arising between the Rajah and the Coolies in regard to this point the Rajahs themselves will be held responsible for the consequences of such conduct which will undoubtedly bring on them the displeasure of Government.

A.J. Moffat Mills, Commissioner of Cuttack, 1841

The construction of a road interfered with local structures of power not merely on the level of knowledge and legitimacy but also by way of reallocation of resources. The globally canonized 'paradigm' that presently dominates the humanities could, of course, not be less concerned with the material side of human existence. However, any discussion that ignores the economic context of communications development would be founded on an abstract notion of social organization and would produce another

42 OIOC: Board's Collection (F/4/505) 12139, 61-4 (J. Richardson, 'Report ...', 18 May 1815).

elitist historiographical text. For if the lower strata of Indian society were affected by early colonial road construction, it was most immediately through additional demands on their resources. Local ruling households had, of course, appropriated shares of their harvests and labour power even earlier; yet the construction of a road meant that another structure of state power entered the stage, that competing claims on their agricultural surplus were asserted and, in most cases, that a greater proportion of it was drained off. The passing by of a survey party, the presence of external armed forces or of a large construction camp in the vicinity of a village, the establishment of post or police stations—all such measures necessarily implied increased demands for 'coolie' labour, provisions, and land. Since the acquisition of construction land appears to have been less problematic and contentious in sparsely populated peripheral Orissa than on the fertile plains, we will focus on the former two aspects labour and provisions.

Not all resources were drawn from the country through which the Raipur Mail Road ran. Kittoe's labour force, for instance, amounted to over one thousand men and boys, the large majority of which was recruited from outside peripheral Orissa. There were between 200 and 300 Bildars (specialized migrant earth workers) from central India, between 500 and 600 'Dhangars' ('hill men'), mainly from Chota Nagpur, about 100 skilled artisans (blacksmiths, masons, carpenters and sawyers), some of whom are identified as Muslims and some as having been recruited in Cuttack.[43] Moreover, 300 prisoners of Midnapur jail were employed for forced labour on the Raipur Mail Road, mainly on the section between that town and the kingdom of Mayurbhanj.[44] These groups constituted the permanent work force whereas the number of 'village coolies' who were recruited near the road in peripheral Orissa fluctuated strongly. Depending on the level of co-operation or non-co-operation of local rajas and zamindars, on some days not a single 'coolie' could be impressed while on others, up to 260 were entered in the pay roll.[45] In this section, we will first discuss 'labour

[43] Ibid., 12 January 1841, 8930-5; ibid., 9 February 1841, 10125; ibid., 5 March 1841, 11009; ibid., 26 March 1841, 12375; ibid., 25 May 1841, 732-3.

[44] Ibid., 18 December 1840, 8084; ibid., 5 February 1841, 9855; ibid., 9 February 1842, 10575.

[45] Ibid., 16 April 1841, 13037-52; ibid., 18 May 1841, 492;

imports' from outside peripheral Orissa and then turn to the acquisition of resources from within the region.

At this point, it may be asked why labourers had to be brought to peripheral Orissa at all. Here political and economic reasons seem to be interconnected. For one, the British had far less difficulties in recruiting labourers in areas under their direct control where they could determine the terms of labour relations more comprehensively. At the same time, 'free' or 'marketable' labour power was more easily available outside peripheral Orissa for various reasons:

- A specialized labour market for seasonally or permanently nomadic earth workers had already existed in several regions of pre-colonial South Asia, but not in western and northern Orissa. Such communities of earth workers were known as 'Wudders', 'Ottar' or 'Bildar' in different regions. They travelled from one construction site to the other where they worked for wages and it was from this source that the British recruited 'navvies' for their 'public works' in India—for roads in the beginning, then, in the latter half of the century, for railways and canals.[46] Kittoe mentions that the Bildars engaged on the Raipur Mail Road came from 'Nagpur', i.e. from central India, and it appears that this work was seasonal employment for them.[47]
- According to Kittoe's pay tables, 'Dhangars' amounted to more than half the total workforce on the Raipur Mail Road.[48] In colonial terminology, the generic term 'Dhangar' ('hill men') usually encompassed various ethnic communities from Chota Nagpur and the Santhal Parganas. These regions had been emerging as a major 'labour catchment areas' for colonial capitalism since the 1830s. Cheap labour for Calcutta's service sector, for Assam tea gardens, Bihar indigo, and overseas sugar plantations was often recruited in these areas where marginal peasants not only felt the pressure of an adverse colonial revenue policy, but found themselves also subjected to an extremely coercive impressment

---

[46] Cf.: Kerr 1997, 105-13. Cf. also: Ahuja 1999, 158-61.

[47] NAI: PMB, 25 June 1841, 1926.

[48] Ibid., 9 February 1841, 10125; ibid., 5 March 1841, 11009; ibid., 26 March 1841, 12375; ibid., 25 May 1841, 733.

system.[49] This combination of factors was not to be found in peripheral Orissa then. Therefore, many of the so-called 'Dhangar' labourers on the Raipur Mail Road seem to have been 'imported' from Chota Nagpur though some appear to have originated in the Sambalpur area.[50]

- Commodity production was apparently not developed enough in peripheral Orissa to give rise to a labour market for skilled artisans, who were, therefore, recruited in the towns of coastal Orissa and possibly also in urban areas of Bengal and Bihar.[51]

Construction workers for the Raipur Mail Road were thus predominantly recruited in regions were a rudimentary labour market had been created. Moreover, the colonial regime's practice to impose forced labour on prisoners in their districts provided another important source of construction labour. As on the 'Jagannath Road' in coastal Orissa[52] and on most other public works of the period,[53] convicts accounted for a considerable proportion of the workforce on Raipur Mail Road. A contemporary report enlightens us that convicts had '3 times the number of Clashees and Burkundauzes [watchmen] over them to make them work that Coolies have, that Fetters altho they prevent a man from *running* away do not prevent his digging earth or moving as fast on level ground as free labourers generally move.'[54]

---

[49] Ghosh 1999, 8-48.

[50] OIOC: BPWP 19 January 1860 (P/16/37), Communications, No. 14, 197 (J. Beadle, Superintending Engineer, 3rd Circle, Lower Provinces, to Officiating Chief Engineer, Lower Provinces, 19 October 1859); NAI: PMB, 25 June 1841, 1939; ibid., 6 April 1842, 12206.

[51] NAI: PMB, 12 January 1841, 8930-5.

[52] OSA: BoRLR 18,773 Bd.Doc (various letters on employment of prisoners on Cuttack-Ganjam Road, 1834); ibid., 18,905 Bd. Doc (various letters on employment of convicts on Jagannath Road, 1834).

[53] For interesting material on the economics of convict labour on roads in the Bengal Presidency cf. the voluminous proceeding of the Military Board in: NAI: PMB, 8 December 1840, 7585-661.

[54] Ibid., 8 December 1840, 7603 (Minute by Major A. Irvine, member of the Military Board).

Kittoe, like other colonial officers, repeatedly lamented the prisoners' low productivity.[55] Yet they continued to be employed since a cheaper source of labour could hardly be found, especially in a region to which labour had to be imported. Coercion ensured that they could be maintained below subsistence costs, though one implication was that mortality rates were, even in the view of colonial administrators, appallingly high. The Assistant Civil Surgeon of Midnapur District thus reported in 1841 that the *annual* mortality rate of the prison population shot up to 9 per cent after the able-bodied male prisoners had been sent to work on the Raipur Mail Road.[56]

In colonial accounts of the time, tribal labourers acquired, as Kaushik Ghosh has shown,[57] rather mythical qualities as exceptionally pliant workmen who 'have no caste', 'may be made to do any thing' and required very little remuneration for their subsistence.[58] Yet Kittoe's construction diaries create the impression of rather tense industrial relations on the road works where Dhangars and other workmen set certain limits to the control the 'sahib' and his five British 'Assistant Overseers' exerted over them. Kittoe reported conflicts over the length of the working day, the Bildars' and Dhangars' 'sulkiness' when he tried to extend the working season, and even mentioned that they struck work when not supplied with provisions.[59] Like most colonial labour relations, those on the Raipur Mail Road were not based on transactions between legally equal parties, but on a measure of coercion. I have already mentioned that Kittoe 'punished the ringleaders' when 'Dhangar coolies' remonstrated against overlong working hours, and these 'punishments' were in all likelihood corporal.[60] Coercion

---

[55] Ibid., 12 January 1841, 8930-5; ibid., 15 January 1841, 9121; ibid., 9 February 1841, 10124-5; ibid., 5 March 1841, 11008.

[56] Ibid., 23 April 1841, 13281-2 (J. Pagan, Civil Assistant Surgeon, to G.J. Shakespear, Magistrate of Midnapore, 12 March 1841).

[57] Ghosh 1999, 8-48.

[58] NAI: PMB, 12 February 1841, 10261 (J.A. Crommelin, Officiating Superintending Engineer, South Eastern Division, to Military Board, 22 January 1841). Cf. also: *Report by the Chief Engineer Bengal* 1861, 107-8.

[59] NAI: PMB, 12 February 1841, 10266; ibid., 5 March 1841, 11008; ibid., 16 April 1841, 13042; ibid., 25 June 1841, 1926; ibid., 20 August 1841, 3821.

[60] Ibid., 12 February 1841, 10266.

had, however, its limits as British engineers pointed out time and again—there was always the risk of the 'coolies' deserting the site collectively while the chance of apprehending and forcing them back was minute. 'I dare not punish them in any way lest they should desert' noted Kittoe in his diary.[61] On the occasion of cholera outbreaks the engineers were repeatedly confronted with the absconding of large parts of the work force. Rather than being treated in what the British officer called his 'hospital' the labourers would leave the camp in great numbers (which was probably the best they could do to save their lives).[62] Physical violence on the part of superiors was deeply resented. Hence Kittoe noted in his construction diary on 25 April 1841 that the 'coolies' were 'an independent race [who] shewed their spirit to day by an attempt to cut down my Jemadar [*Jamadar:* subaltern officer or policeman] who had imprudently given one a slight cut with a cane'.[63] He felt that it was difficult to get the 'Dhangars' and the 'Village Coolies to work to advantage; each man does as he pleases and several dialects being spoken it is difficult to make them understand; they are a strange race.'[64] 'Thó Strong the Chota Nagpoor Dangurs are very lazy and slow in their movements',[65] complained the sahib, while villagers were 'indolent workmen' at best.[66] Yet it was felt that the labourers had to be accommodated to some degree. In 1840, on Christmas day, the British officers gave a 'treat to the Dangurs who had a dance ... such treates having a salutary effect towards evening these strange people'.[67]

It is clear that the inhabitants of nearby villages did not appreciate the presence of large labour camps that implied invasions into the local 'order of things' and the enforcement of tribute in the form of labour or of kind. Hindu villagers resisted the use and ritual pollution of their wells by prisoners.[68] Provisions and labour power were usually only provided under the threat of military violence or, more effectively, when enforced by local

[61] Ibid., 5 March 1841, 11008.
[62] Ibid., 14 May 1841, 357; ibid, 5 March 1842, 11238.
[63] Ibid., 25 June 1841, 1922.
[64] Ibid., 1929.
[65] Ibid., 1939.
[66] Ibid., 26 March 1841, 12374.
[67] Ibid., 12 February 1841, 10271.
[68] Ibid., 23 April 1841, 13284

rulers and dominant households though some of the rural poor apparently came to appropriate road labour to their own ends: being a source of income external to local power relations, it was also a means to enhance one's bargaining power within these relations. However, 'village coolies' were, on the whole, hardly motivated workers and Kittoe insisted that 'all the inhabitants of the jungles are proverbially lazy'.[69] When the authorities of Kendujhar supplied him with hundreds of labourers in May 1841, Kittoe noted that he had also engaged one of the Raja's *paiks* (soldiers) for every twenty-five 'coolies'[70]—obviously to make them work and prevent their 'absconding'.

That road construction entailed an increased demand for labour and provisions created opportunities as well as risks for the rajas and dominant households of peripheral Orissa. As for the opportunities, the assumption of the role of an intermediary between the villagers and the British could yield handsome profits. Rajas and zamindars, therefore, insisted that supplies required for the maintenance of the labour camp were solely acquired through their agents for a previously fixed price. 'Village coolies' were correspondingly only to be recruited by way of their mediation. The raja or zamindar then imposed an irregular tax *(magan)* on the peasants of this area, which was collected in kind by his agents.[71] Labour was usually, too, acquired through a feudal levy: it was forced corvee *(begar/bethi)* which had to be contributed with little or no remuneration while the lion's share or even all of the wages that were received from the British officer went into the local ruler's coffers.[72] Attempts on the part of a British officer to bypass a local ruler in the acquisition of village resources were likely to give rise to various practices ranging from non-cooperation to open resistance. The above system, which utilized precapitalist tributary relationships through a subcontracting arrangement, yet also had its drawbacks. Supplies that had been collected as tribute were, for instance, often of inferior quality[73] while corvṛe labour was even more problematic. The exploitation of forced labour could create

---

[69] Ibid., 13 April 1841, 12859; cf. also: ibid., 26 March 1841, 12374; ibid., 25 June 1841, 192.

[70] Ibid., 18 May 1841, 492.

[71] Ibid., 16 April 1841, 12974-6, 12984-98.

[72] Ibid., 5 January 1841, 8559-63.

[73] Ibid., 16 April 1841, 12973, 12988.

political embarrassment for the colonial government in a period when Parliament abolished slavery in most British colonies and when the Charter of 1833 had required the Governor-General in Council to find 'means of extinguishing slavery' in India.[74] Such embarrassments could specially emerge from forms of coerced labour that were, unlike convict labour and indenture, not sanctioned by British law. Moreover, *begar* and *bethi* services were intensely unpopular with the villagers even in this period and were likely to entail low work discipline, mass desertions and resistance to recruitment. Kittoe was, accordingly, instructed by the Government of India through the Commissioner of Cuttack to act according to the following formula that was also communicated to the rulers of Mayurbhanj and Kendujhar:

> … that Government will be no party to extortions, if a percentage on the price of the Coolies' labor be claimed on the plea of usage, the appropriation must be made with the free will and consent of the laborers and that [if] the work should be obstructed in consequence of any differences arising between the Rajah and the Coolies in regard to this point the Rajahs themselves will be held responsible for the consequences of such conduct which will undoubtedly bring on them the displeasure of Government.[75]

When writing of the labourers' 'free will and consent', the colonial government obviously sought cover against potential abolitionist criticism from Britain. What the rulers of peripheral Orissa were to understand, however, was that their right to claim corvre from their subjects would not be called into question by their British overlords as long as they provided them with a sufficient supply of 'coolie' labour. This attitude is very clearly expressed in the official papers. A.J. Moffat Mills, the Commissioner of Cuttack, wrote, for instance that a 'Rajah of a Country like Mohurbunge exercising, as he does almost unlimited control of his subjects will not forego his right to a portion of the Coolies labour'–objectionable as the system is, it must be endured and Captain Kittoe would do well not to look into matters such as these, but to settle with the Rajah what is to be paid to each man, to see that they are paid, and to look to the Rajah only to supply them.'[76]

---

[74] Anderson 1993, 100.
[75] NAI: PMB, 5 January 1841, 8565.
[76] Ibid., 8562-3.

Kittoe, for his part, when reporting on the 'successful' recruitment of 'village coolies' in Kendujhar, admitted that 'the same bad practice of ill payment of labours prevails here, but I do not notice it, I consider it more politic to be silent as long as I have a supply of men & pay them myself'.[77]

However, I have also said that external demands on the country's resources implied some risk for local rulers. This is clearly borne out by a dispute in the early months of 1841 between Kittoe and Birbul Mohapatra, the zamindar or sarbarahkar of Jashipur, on the one hand, and Jadunath Bhanja, Maharaja of Mayurbhanj, and A.J. Moffat Mills on the other. Two years earlier, when surveying the line of the future road, Kittoe had found himself depending on the assistance of the zamindar of Jashipur in the Bamanghati region of Mayurbhanj as the Raja, in his opinion, 'either has no authority over his Zemindars or does not choose to exercise it'. The zamindar, however, did not prove cooperative then in regard of information and provisions.[78] Yet by the time Kittoe returned to supervise the construction of the road, an agreement had been signed between the Maharaja and the Commissioner of Cuttack according to which the mukhtars or agents of the former were to supply 'coolie labour' and provisions to the construction party. Kittoe found this arrangement very unsatisfactory feeling that the amount and quality of the supplied labour power and foodstuffs did not answer his requirements. He now came to terms with the Jashipur zamindar who offered to act as his intermediary in place of the Maharaja. Kittoe had his 'coolies' impressed by the zamindar from whom he also bought grain that his own *mudis* (shopkeepers) sold in the camp bazaar. The Maharaja forwarded his protest to the Commissioner, who supported his view. The conflict escalated when Kittoe arrested the *bewarta*, the Maharaja's district administrator, and a 'nizam', an Indian government official A.J. Moffat Mills had sent out to him.[79] Kittoe argued that these men had been obstructing his work and defended himself by painting the system that had prevailed earlier in the darkest colours. The mukhtars, he wrote,

---

[77] Ibid., 26 March 1841, 12374.

[78] OSA: BoRLR, 20,868 Bd.Doc: M. Kittoe to T. Prinsep, Secretary to GoB, General Department, 19 February 1839.

[79] NAI: PMB, 16 April 1841, 12957-13018.

> used to retail the goods themselves having first collected them by begging, bouncing and plundering, under the Cloak of the Raja's authority they made large sums of which they rendered but a flemish [sic] account to the Master, who verily I believe has lost extensively on this account; almost all of these worthies are of the Mahuntie or writer Caste and either directly related to the head functionaries of the Raja's Court or Caste brothers to whom they pay a share of their ill gotten gain... .[80]

These representations failed to make an impact on the administration in Calcutta—Kittoe was severely reprimanded and ordered to return to the earlier arrangement and to co-operate with the Maharaja's representatives.[81] The colonial government's priority was clearly not to create the most favourable conditions for the construction of the Mail Road (which was Kittoe's sole concern) but the maintenance of a precarious balance of power in the Bamanghati region which had repeatedly been in turmoil in the preceding decades.[82] The point was, once again, that communications development and changes in power relations were necessarily intertwined. Kittoe's measures did not merely reduce the revenues of Maharaja Jadunath Bhanja and his officials but also jeopardized their authority in an outlying but rather productive region of the Mayurbhanj raj. For the zamindar of Jashipur they created, at the same time, an opportunity to augment his income and to assert his independence. It was for this reason that the Maharaja wrote the sentence that has already been quoted at the beginning of this paper: '... if the Sahib breaks through the old established usage, my dependents will rebel against my authority, and my country will be ruined.'

Conclusion

In conclusion, some more general observations may be in order. The inconspicuous term 'public works' obscures that infrastructural measures like the construction of a road were then (as much as they are today) highly contentious measures that were necessarily related to questions of political and social power. Hence, in the periphery of early colonial Orissa, a 'good road' was not necessarily in the

---

[80] Ibid., 12985.
[81] Ibid., 13016-18.
[82] Cf.: Praharaj, 104-13.

interest of all social groups concerned. A social history of communications would have to reconstruct the conflicting interests and practices of the various historical agents that were generally far from 'irrational' and deserve to be saved from what has been called, in a different context, the 'enormous condescension of posterity'. I have tried to show that dominant households as well as dominated villagers of peripheral Orissa had good reason to resist a colonial mail road. There is evidence, moreover, that the specific form of indirect colonial rule in this area and the limited interest of the colonial regime even in the fertile Orissa plains did decisively contribute to the region's stagnation in terms of communication. Up to the mid-nineteenth century the absence of a means of swift communication afforded protection not only to villagers and the dominant households of the periphery but also (and most visibly during the 'Great Rebellion') to the colonial power itself. Despite all rhetoric, the early colonisers' interest in Orissa consisted not so much in 'opening it up' to 'civilization', the 'rule of law' and 'commerce' but in getting past it and securing control over this strategic region as cheaply as possible. In respect of the communications infrastructure, thus, a specific historical configuration of social forces emerged under British rule, the most powerful of which was the colonial administration itself. Most of these forces shared an indifference or even aversion to the development of communications infrastructure though for widely different reasons and interests.

This configuration did change considerably in the latter part of the nineteenth century when the colonial regime developed an appetite for the timber and mineral resources of the 'Garjats', when Indian mercantile capital from the plains took deeper roots in the 'Tributary States', and when local rulers, following the example of the Maharaja of Mayurbhanj, discovered that communications development did not merely improve their prestige and record with the British but also promoted the emergence of a kind of commercialized 'feudalism'. Improved transport enabled them to derive increased revenues from the accelerated exploitation of mineral and forest resources and growing exports of agricultural produce. New palaces and other 'public works', in turn, exhibited their growing prosperity and were celebrated in self-righteous colonial accounts. They were quoted as indicators of the civilizational advancement of modern, British-educated 'Garjat' rulers in comparison to their 'semi-barbaric' ancestors. However, *bethi* and other types of 'feudal' levy continued to play a role in the construction of roads and other 'public works' with the connivance of the colonial government up to the 1940s.[83]

References

1. *Archival Material*

National Archives of India, New Delhi (NAI)
 Department of Public Works, Proceedings of the Military Board (PMB)

Oriental and India Office Collections of the British Library, London (OIOC)
 Board's Collection
 Bengal Public Works Proceedings (BPWP)

Orissa State Archives, Bhubaneswar (OSA)
 Board of Revenue, Loose Records (BoRLR)

2. *Printed Sources*

History of the Rise and Progress of the Operations for the Suppression of Human Sacrifice and Female Infanticide in the Hill Tracts of Orissa, 1854 (= Selections from the Records of the Government of India [Home Department] no. V). Calcutta: F. Carberry, Bengal Military Orphan Press.

Kittoe, M. 1838a. 'Extracts from the Journal of Lieut. Markham Kittoe, submitted to the Asiatic Society at the Meeting of the 6th Oct. 1836' [*sic* 1837?], in *Journal of the Asiatic Society of Bengal* [hereafter: *JASB*] *VII*, 53-6, 200-6, 660-2.

— 1838b. 'Mr. Kittoe's Journal of his Tour in the Province of Orissa', in *JASB VII*, 679-85, 828-9, 1060-3.

— 1839a. 'Report on the Coal and Iron Mines of Tālcheer and Ungool …', *JASB VIII*, 137-44.

— 1839b. 'Account of a Journey from Calcutta via Cuttack and Pooree to Sumbulpr̃r, and from thence to Mednipr̃r through the Forests of Orissa', *JASB VIII*, 367-83, 474-80, 606-20, 671-81.

[83] Cf.: NAI: Orissa States Agency Files, CS-Branch, F.No. XXVI-35-CS/1941-2 (vols. I and II). These development will be discussed more extensively in another forthcoming article.

Leckie, G.F. 1954. 'Journal of a Route to Nagpore by the Way of Cuttac, Burrosumber, Dongur Ghur and the Southern Banjare Ghaut, in the Months of March, April, May, to the 3rd June, 1790', *Orissa Historical Research Journal* 2, 3-4, Appendix IV, 1-14.

Macpherson, S.C. 1842. *Report upon the Khonds of the Districts of Ganjam and Cuttack*, Calcutta: G.H. Huttmann, Bengal Military Orphan Press.

Motte, T. 1952. 'A Narrative of a Journey to the Diamond Mines at Sumbhulpoor' (reprint of a 1766 diary), *Orissa Historical Research Journal* 1 (3), Appendix, pp. 1-49.

Report by the Chief Engineer Bengal, on the Progress of Public Works for the Year 1861-62, Calcutta: Savielle & Cranenburgh, 1862.

3. *Secondary Material*

Ahuja, R. 1999. *Die Erzeugung kolonialer Staatlichkeit und das Problem der Arbeit. Eine Studie zur Sozialgeschichte der Stadt Madras zwischen 1750 und 1800*, Stuttgart: Franz Steiner.

Anderson, M.R. 1993. 'Work Construed: Ideological Origins of Labour Law in British India to 1918', in P. Robb (ed.), *Dalit Movements and the Meanings of Labour in India* (= SOAS Studies on South Asia), Delhi: Oxford University Press, 87-120.

Basa, K.K. 1956. 'Tour-Diary of J.R. Ouseley' [1840], *Orissa Historical Research Journal* 5 (3), 166-78.

Chaudhuri, B. 1982. 'Eastern India', in Dharma Kumar (ed.), *Cambridge Economic History of India*, vol. II, Cambridge: CUP, 86-177.

Everest, George. 1958. *Historical Records of the Survey of India* (collected and compiled by R.H. Phillimore), vol. IV, Dehra Dun.

Ghosh, K. 1999. 'A Market for Aboriginality: Primitivism and Race Qualification in the Indentured Labour Market of Colonial India', in G. Bhadra, G. Prakash and S. Tharu (eds.): *Subaltern Studies X. Writings on South Asian History and Society*, Delhi: Oxford University Press, 8-48.

Kerr, I. 1997. *Building the Railways of the Raj, 1850-1900*, Delhi: Oxford University Press.

Mukherjee, P. 1964. *History of Orissa in the 19th Century*, Cuttack: Utkal University.

Praharaj, D.M. 1988. *Tribal Movements and Political History in India—A Case Study from Orissa, 1803-1949*, Delhi: InterIndia Publications.

Ray, B.C. 1960. *Orissa under Marathas (1751-1803)*, Allahabad: Kitab Mahal.

Sahu, B. 1993. *Princely States of Orissa under the British Crown, 1858-1905*, Cuttack: Vidyapuri.

15

Chatamput—An Industrial 'Camp' in the Tribal Zone

Christian Strümpell

This paper discusses social relationships among settlers within a small industrial settlement in the middle of an Indian tribal area.* Ethnographies focusing on industrialization in India are scarce. The limited number of significant publications in this field has been discussed by Parry (1999a) in his introduction to the volume *The Worlds of Indian Industrial Labour*.

According to Parry, the study of industrial labour suffers from two basic deficits. On the one hand 'industrialization' is a much neglected topic among social anthropologists. The established sociology of India is mostly concerned with 'traditional' Indian society. The flagship journal of the anthropological elite, *Contributions to Indian Sociology*, has not published a single article in the last fifteen years on the structure or situation of India's industrial workforce. All the while, India was being transformed into one of the world's major industrial powers. This under-representation of topics focusing on industrialization has its roots in the conceptual manifesto of the journal where Dumont claimed 'that a sociology of India lies at the point of confluence between Sociology and Indology' (1957, 7). Such an approach was bound to lead to a preference for the 'book view' of Indian society over the 'field view' (Parry 1999a, xi), a critique stated by Béteille (1991, 6) in similar terms. Social relationships of industrial workmen or migrant labourers, however, cannot be treated as secondary when compared to such topics as north and south Indian kinship systems or similar issues, if a broader understanding of contemporary South Asian society is to be achieved.

---

* This paper is based upon ongoing fieldwork in the Koraput district of Orissa, financed by the German Research Foundation (DFG). By now I have completed two periods of fieldwork (March-June 2000 and September 2000-March 2001), with two more periods to follow in the near future.

The neglect of India's industrial labour force by anthropology is only one side of the problem; the other is the disjunction between sociology on the one hand and the economic and political sciences on the other. Just as the sociology of India neglects the topic of industrial labour, Indian labour studies tend to neglect culture as a result of the particular academic division of labour. When culture is invoked in these studies,

> it is generally as a *deus ex machina* to explain India's apparent failure to conform to the evolutionary teleology supposedly revealed by the industrialization of the West. Why is the workforce less 'committed' than both its bosses and the outside analyst suppose it ought to be, and than it supposedly is in the 'developed' world? In a word, 'culture', according to the analytical tradition of Moore and Feldman (1960). Why is it less solidary and class-conscious than Marxian theory supposes it ought to be? In a word, 'culture', according to Chakrabarty (1989). But though its icon is there on the desktop, its actual content is safely tucked out of sight. So what Ram Singh Yadav from Saran actually thinks about the machine he handles in the jute mill, how he negotiates his relationship with the Chamar from Champaran on the next machine, and whether he flirts with the Telugu women in the same shop, is left largely unexplored. (Parry 1999a, xii)

The tendency to exclude cultural topics is also present in the few qualitatively high standing recent publications on industrial workers in India. Breman's study of Maharashtrian migrant labourers in the sugarcane fields of Gujarat, for example, focuses on the interrelation between capital and labour (1994). Following Parry one must ask why Breman's study does not take into account kinship patterns along which the mobilization of migrant labour takes place and in what ways the sugarcane fields are a 'disenchanted' world for them (ibid., xiii). According to the evolutionary teleology of the above cited passage, industrialization has the intrinsic power to shape all societies in the same way, irrespective of their cultural particularities. Thus, when concerned with the process of industrialization, the particularities of a given society can be regarded as peripheral (ibid., xiv).

Such an emphasis on the intrinsic power of industrialization, along with the neglect of cultural particularities, was debated several decades ago. It underscored Gluckman's statement that 'an African townsman is a townsman, an African miner is a miner' (quoted in Parry 1999a, xv). Gluckman, he founder of the materialistic Manchester School of social anthropology was, however, sharply opposed by Pocock, one of the founders of *Contributions*. For the latter 'the Indian city, old or modern, is Indian just as an American city is American' (1960, 67).

In view of this controversy, the aim of my article is to question the effect such evolutionary teleology assigns to the process of industrialization. I will give a 'field view' of an industrial settlement, I (following Pocock) perceive as Indian. I do so because I am convinced that indigenous conceptualization of society can be understood only by reference to value-ideas, irrespective of whether these social relationships occur in 'traditional' villages or in 'modern' industrial neighbourhoods. The priority of systems of value-ideas was first postulated by Dumont (1980). I will deal first with the abolition of caste hierarchy within a particular venture of industrialization. At the end this context will be viewed in relation to others and the very different ways of evaluating these other contexts.

The Concept of Conviviality

Before turning to the industrial settlement, I would like to introduce the concept of conviviality as developed by Heidemann. In a lecture at the Berlin Institute of Ethnology in 2000, he examined two distinct spheres or enclaves of Indian society which allowed status distinctions to vanish and relationships of equality to emerge. One of these enclaves is based on the well-known concept of commensality and the other on the less familiar concept of conviviality. The standard formula of commensality, ubiquitous phenomenon, implies that eating is communication and eating together places the participants in social proximity.

As demonstrated in numerous publications, the rules concerning commensality in India are expressions of a ritual hierarchy. Indian commensal groups are, for example, family members sharing daily meals, affinal groups eating together in the course of rites of passage, or the agnatic group of villagers receiving *prasad* during their temple feasts. The ritual order is at the foundation of these groups. Those united by commensality are regarded as equals in terms of ritual status.

Convivial groups stand in a stark contrast to commensal ones. They are based on a breach of the traditional commensal rules, being negatively derived from the ritual order. Furthermore, conviviality conceptually unites individuals of different ritual status, i.e. those of different castes. Although Heidemann emphasizes that conviviality should not be treated as a recent phenomenon of Indian society, relationships based on conviviality regularly emerge in modern contexts, in educational and political associations, sport clubs, and trade unions. A major issue for the constitution of such groups is not simply joint action, but rather joint celebration, as observed regularly after sport events, university examinations, election campaigns or labour disputes. Heidemann calls those involved in such celebrations convivial groups. They are defined by a deliberate breaking of the commensal rules of caste, one of the expressions of hierarchy in India.

Whereas commensality is an expression of the given, the religious, the eternal order of caste, conviviality establishes an order conceived by the actors as being created, as secular and temporary. Convivial relationships refer to inter-caste issues as opposed to commensal rules that refer to intra-caste relationships. Conviviality relates to matters of the political economy which—according to the influential view of Dumont (1980)—in India should be regarded as being encompassed by the religious order or *dharma*.

The obvious contradictions resulting from the co-existence of commensality and conviviality are suppressed by temporal seclusion. Commensal groups meet indoors or at temple feasts which are clearly marked events in time and space. Similarly, convivial gatherings withdraw from public view while transgressing the proclaimed rules of respect and commensality, and while indulging in other deviant behaviour such as the consumption of liquor and meat.

According to Heidemann, the two concepts contain a common feature. Both are based upon the idea of equals sharing equal experiences and goods. This kind of equality, however, is basically different from the European status concept among individuals. Furthermore, it also differs from the kind of equality Béteille (1991) has discovered in India since Independence. In his critique of Dumont's analysis of Indian society, Béteille puts to the fore Gandhi's and Ambedkar's concepts of equality, as well as the constitutional principle of equality. For Heidemann, however, the existence and the growing importance of conviviality in India does not support Béteille's argument, however, since ideas of equality unexceptionally relate to the normative level, whereas they do not touch the ontological inequality at the ideological level. Thus the superficial equality within convivial groups may be regarded as a temporary avoidance of norms and behaviour only expressing the ontological inequality between them. The convivial groups are well aware of their deviant behaviour. Breaking the norms, in fact, is an expression of support for the very same demands in another context.

Even if the standard ritual regulations are broken on occasion, this should not imply a lack of norms. The consumption of liquor must take place in seclusion and never in front of women or inside a *puja* room. In addition, brothers cannot join the same convivial group, because no doubts should arise about their asymmetrical relationship.

Conviviality among the First Settlers

Let me now introduce the electric power plant at Chatamput, situated in the Machkund Valley on the Orissan border with Andhra Pradesh. From the mid-1940s to the mid-1950s, the construction of the plant and its three attached settlements lasted for about ten years. Until today, it is not exactly known how many workers were settled in and left the area, but intelligent guesses mention 15 to 20,000 individuals.

Formerly, the Desia alone, the 'natives' or tribal people of the Koraput District, populated the Machkund Valley.[3] Before construction work begun the Indian Government requisitioned the required land, offering either money or land as compensation to the displaced population. The new land was situated some 80 km away from Chatamput. Yet another compensation was the prospect of an employment in the new industrial undertaking.

The latter alternative was turned down by all of the Desia, the majority opting for the money and spending it without too much care about the future.[4] Others went away to settle on the new land.

---

3. Following Pfeffer (2002), I use the expression 'tribal society' to denote the indigenous population of highland Orissa, irrespective of their administrative classification as either Scheduled Tribe, Scheduled Caste or Other Backward Classes.

4 This case is similar to the one described by Parry concerning the construction of the Bhilai Steel Plant (BSP) in Madhya Pradesh. The local population, the Chattisgarhi, has been reluctant to join the BSP due to a

Being infected by malaria and facing severe economic hardships in due course, they returned to their native villages, thereby losing all rights of further compensation. Since the construction of the project, these Desia, formerly the owners of the now nationalized land, now inhabit the territory as coolies on the market[5] that has sprung up along with the hydro-electric project. Since the settlement was erected, the former villagers all reside on its outskirts in a small arrangement of some fifty houses. These tribal enclaves with their mud houses and their narrow paths appear as a stark contrast to the broad cemented streets built for trucks and lined by modern project quarters connected by an extensive net of electrical wires.

The labour force on the original construction site consisted of young unmarried men from the coastal plains of Orissa and Andhra who had been recruited by contractors, just as a good number of people from Kerala, Bengal, Gujarat, and Nepal joined the project. As a glaring contrast, the indigenous or tribal population of the region was completely excluded from the work force. During the time of construction, workmen lived in huge temporary quarters and were supplied with food in project canteens. Those not working on the construction site were occupied in those canteens and in the health office or they privately carried out the services of washermen, barbers, water-carriers, etc. in the newly erected township.

During this first decade, no temples, churches, or mosques existed. The site was unsuitable for families with children, and no

---

lack of industrial skills and experience and due to the conviction that the former way of earning a livelihood would still meet the consumption needs. In addition, most Chattisgarhi, have been suspecting human sacrifices to occur, as was the rule during the time of the *raja* whenever a major building was to be constructed. Although the authorities tried to convince them of the opposite, the suspicions were kept alive by the high mortality rate among construction workers (Parry 1999b,114).

[5] Only one Desia family has been able to keep the inherited fields and to obtain an even more substantial amount of land with the help of money given to them by the Government as compensation. The situation of this family was and still is a rather exceptional one, because of affinal ties to a politically powerful tax-collector (*mutadar*) of that region who provided information about the government's plans of nationalization. To the present day, this family is the only one to avoid daily wage-labour, being even able to send children to college.

schools were introduced. Similarly a market, nowadays the source of an increasing number of jobs, was initially conspicuous by its absence. Thus apart from the project itself, no other forms of employment were in sight. Everybody depended upon the new venture. It was a grand all-male expedition into the wilderness.

Some of the first generation settlers continue to live in Chatamput today. They deny that conflicts occurred between the different castes. No rifts have ever marred the atmosphere since the beginning. Similarly, they stress communal harmony. No tension has arisen between the followers of different religions, the speakers of different languages or the sons of different provinces. All have been equal—so they say—and as a result the social life of the settlement was distinguished by harmony. Equality prevailed, the settlers say, because all entered the Machkund Valley at the same time as isolated strangers and because all carried out the same kind of work. To prove their claims to equality, the informants made it a point to indicate the lack of commensal restrictions between the different social categories of settlers. While eating they all sat together in the canteen irrespective of their caste status, and after work they again joined together in groups composed of many different castes and religious communities to talk about their native villages and smoke the hookah together. Just a few informants added—once they knew me a little better—that on these occasions they would also drink *desi*-liquor, obtained from tribal villages in the neighbourhood.

Social life in the early days of the project—described by the oldest settlers—led me to the assumption that during its foundation period Chatamput had an identity based upon conviviality. Out of the huge mass of workmen smaller or larger groups composed of different castes emerged, groups of people eating together and sharing rounds of drinks along with the water pipe. Furthermore, only a single trade union existed in those days, uniting the workmen as such in their periodic struggles for higher wages and in their celebrations after the successful conclusion of the dispute.

For the settlers the patterns of social relations within Chatamput were regarded as being created temporary and secular. They were created by the project's authority. The new status order ignored caste to introduce engineers, foremen and ordinary workmen. The order was temporary, because it was limited to the length of time within the settlement and—as will be shown below—to the length of employment in the project. Thus we find all criteria of convivial groups according to Heidemann's definition.

Similarly, another important point of conviviality was given in Chatamput: spatial seclusion. None of the settlers had had earlier contacts with the region and the settlement was hundreds of miles away from their respective natal villages. We can thus visualize a small township sealed off from the world. The breaches of commensal rules—essential for convivial groups—took place with the general public being excluded.

Chatamput Today

Continuity and Change

Since the beginning of construction work and the creation of Chatamput, fifty years have passed and conditions have changed in many ways. Among these I will consider two as the most relevant for the present purpose. The first change occurred after the completion of the power plant and the settlement in the mid-1950s. At that time Chatamput adopted its present shape. The majority of workers left the Machkund Valley to return to their native villages or to find jobs elsewhere. In the settlement only those remained who had been able to secure permanent employment in the hydro-electric project, or those who saw a chance to build up small-scale businesses in the newly founded bazaar. (The latter formed only a marginal portion of Chatamput's population during that time.)

Those who had a permanent appointment were made government employees. Only after such guaranteed job security did they start to marry and found families. The vast majority of settlers returned to their native villages with the objective of finding a spouse according to the established socio-economic rules. A few of the new-comers, however, did engage in marital relations with the indigenous tribes or married women from Jeypore, the capital of the former *rajas* of this region, some 60 km away from the settlement.

In the course of this process the workers' mass accommodations were removed and most of the canteens stopped functioning. In Chatamput standardized types of project quarters were constructed, providing space just for a single family. These quarters—made of either tin or bricks—were graded according to the rank of the respective project employee and differed with regard to their comfort. Quarters of the same type were built next to each other so that they formed 'lines'. Lines of different types are situated in different parts of Chatamput. It is important to emphasize that generally people with high differences in caste status today occupy the same rank in the project. With the new residential grading, neighbourhood relationships almost came to be viewed as inter-caste relationships. To the present day, neighbours occupy similar positions in the secular hierarchy of the project, whereas they rarely share the same rank within the ritual hierarchy.

The major impact upon Chatamput was not caused by the new residential order, however, since within the mass accommodations too, 'neighbours' used to be of different caste affiliation. The major impact came with the arrival of the settler's wives. Along with them—so the elder settlers say—a sense of commensality entered the town. Apart from the love marriages between settlers and Desia women, all unions had been endogamous. From the arrival of the wives onwards, the canteens stopped providing food for the employees. From then on, the employees ate home-cooked meals most of the time, prepared by their wives, daughters or daughters-in-law. The local restaurants served 'tiffins', i.e. *pakaudi*, *samosa* and other snacks; but only in cases of emergency, when their wives left for their native villages, did workers eat there regularly. Since the arrival of the women even the food consumed during shifts would be prepared by the wives and brought to the power house in metal containers.

As I was told many times by all types of settlers, since this time a certain 'caste feeling' (*jati-fati*) emerged in Chatamput. The wives have been eager to see their husbands follow commensal rules. A married couple would regard the kitchen and the *puja* room of their quarters as out of bounds for anyone of lower ritual status. In spite of these changes, however, the sphere of commensality remained restricted. According to informants of all castes, commensal rules ceased to be valid once again during lunch breaks at the powerhouse. Workers on the same shift would freely exchange the food prepared by their wives irrespective of caste status[6]. Especially the brahmin employees, members of the lower castes liked to tell me with a grain of salt, had an interest in this exchange in order to get meat dishes unavailable at home.

---

[6] Parry (2000:147) mentions the same kind of conviviality taking place during lunch breaks at the Bhilai Steel Plant.

Thus, after the initial phase of construction, commensal and convivial spheres existed. Whereas commensality was confined to the privacy of homes, conviviality still ordered relationships within the hydro-electric project, the secular institution dominating all aspects of public life of the industrial settlement in the wilderness.

Another major change was initiated in the beginning of the 1980s, lasting five years with the mode of recruitment. The first descendants of the initial employees of the construction phase had become old enough to work in the project themselves. These descendants had mostly been appointed as government employees during the 1970s. For the younger sons, however, chances of obtaining employment in the project became increasingly dim, and dimmer still when the authority reduced the overall number of employees.

Some of those not employed by the project left the settlement to find work elsewhere, but the majority remained and tried to engage either in a trade or in a service. Those involved in trade mostly came from castes of high status such as Karana and Telega, two castes from Orissa and Andhra traditionally engaged in war and administration. The Kumuti, literally the trader's caste, also entered the bazaar. Muslims shopkeepers—known by the derogatory term 'Pathan'—had a south Indian background of petty trade and craft work. Members of the low castes, however, tended to work in the service sector which either implied a return to the kind of profession traditionally associated with their caste (washermen, carpenters and barbers), or the adoption of one of the new professions such as those of electricians and mechanics.

Along with this transformation in the mid-1980s, new settlers arrived in Chatamput, permanent settlers for a change. Earlier, single persons or families who arrived in the 1960s and 1970s had been—as a rule—engineers, teachers, and bank and postal staff, i.e. high cadre project employees or other government servants. The point was their impermanence. The well-known Indian 'transfer-raj' ruled their fate, and the length of their stay seldom exceeded a few years. This was—and still is—due to the fact that engineers, teachers, bank employees and the like can be transferred after a few years, a right which the lower cadre of project employees do not have. Most of the high-cadre professionals considered Chatamput as a location with an attraction resembling that of a penal colony and nobody was keen to spend prolonged periods of time in the wilderness.

Among the newcomers of the 1980s, however, a good number had an intention to stay. A permanent engagement in the market sector of the place was accepted as a career. These settlers were mostly of the high status Kumuti caste wearing the sacred thread. They had had virtually no former contact with the project but simply visualized profitable business. These changes—new kinds of settlers arriving with an eye for the market and the descendants of project employees engaging in private business—altered the spirit of settlement by adding a new quality of inhabitants. This new segment remains detached from the 'project-world' to this day.

For me, this continued distance between the market and the rest—seen together with the confinement of commensal rules to a mere private sphere—seems to indicate the persistence of Chatamput's basic character. Project employees continue to be guided by a concept of the old days, seeing themselves as temporary residents of an out-station. This concept rests upon much more than nostalgia. It has a realistic base. In fact, nobody will ever be allowed to acquire private property in town, and if a project employee is unfit for work, or dies without a primary relative on the job, the family must vacate the quarters and leave the place for good.

Furthermore, Chatamput remains a settlement created on a secular order. Houses are of different quality, and the reputation of a neighbourhood may be better or worse, but such standards depend entirely upon the settler's position in the project and never upon caste, region, or religion.

Commensality and Conviviality in Chatamput Today

Commensality

In Hindu religion matters related to the preparation, consumption and exchange of food is a precarious subject of the utmost importance. The relationship between givers and receivers of cooked food is at the core (Conzelmann 1996, 104), as indicated in the following quotation:

> L'aliment est un des véhicules privilégiés de la souillure, et c'est au moment on l'on mange que l'on est le plus vulnérable aux atteintes de l'impurité. Plus précisément, c'est dans l'aliment que se

> manifeste avec le plus de netteté l'opposition du pur et de l'impur et que se concentrent, par conséquent, les différenciations hiérarchiques dont cette opposition est le principe. (Malamoud 1989, 13)

Rules regulating the transfer of food are expressions of the hierarchical relationships between castes. As is demonstrated in countless ethnographies on caste relations, one can accept food only from those of one's own and higher castes.

As mentioned above, the settlers in Chatamput started to observe commensal rules only after the arrival of their wives. Commensality can be observed in two different contexts, first, in the context of formal feasting of groups, and secondly in the context of individual invitations. For the present purpose, I will confine my analysis to the formal context. The reasons for this choice are evident. First, I could observe, and was told many times by all types of settlers, that in Chatamput the decision to accept or not to accept food from someone is largely a personal one. I saw Brahmins and Karana dining in the houses of Muslims or Christians, just as I saw Dhoba and Mala, both Scheduled Castes, being served food inside a brahmins quarter. Others would reject food from anyone but their own caste people. Not refusing food does not imply sanctions of the traditional kind. A brahmin accepting food from a Muslim would not be avoided by other brahmins.

Second, in the course of formal feasting of groups, the commensal relationships between castes are observable 'on the ground'. Only in this context is hierarchy expressed both deliberately and publicly. The issue as to whether two castes are able to accept food from a third and sit in the same line, or whether they have to leave a space between themselves and members of another group (Mayer 1960: Plate IIIB; ibid., 1996, 35) cannot be ignored.

Feeding guests on formal occasions is called *bhoji*. I attended several of these *bhoji* in the sacred context of lifecycle rituals and during secular contexts, related to the hydro-electric project, so I initially enquired about those preparing the feasts. The question of caste arose. In Chatamput two Vadabalija, one of a Telugu peasant-fishermen caste and one Gudia, of Oriya sweet makers, serve as semi-professional cooks at both project functions and lifecycle rituals. Neither of these castes is in the Scheduled ones (still called Harijan in Chatamput), but they are of a rather low status. Ritually, no one of higher caste should consume the meals they prepare. Most of the settlers, however, with few exceptions, attended the *bhoji*. The absentees were some of the Oriya Brahmins and some of the Karana. In private they told me that they refuse to attend such *bhoji*, because they would be forced to sit next to people of lower or even Harijan caste status in the same line and would have to eat food prepared by low-caste cooks. Publicly, however, they certainly do not oppose the procedure of the *bhoji* attended by many of their caste members. The other settlers regard their refusal as a form of the silent resistance of a few unchangeable traditionalists. An exceptional position is granted to the few practising priestly Brahmins of the settlement: a Telugu Brahmin serving at the Rama temple and an Oriya Brahmin attached to the Shiva temple, as well as two other Oriya Brahmins, who work as school teachers and follow their priestly profession on request. These four would never eat at a *bhoji*, but take home the uncooked food as handed out to them by the hosts.

The features of project *bhoji* differ from those given in the course of lifecycle rituals in certain regards. Whereas the former are only attended by project employees, the latter include non-employees as well as outside guests. Another difference between the two contexts of a *bhoji* lies in the fact that the low-caste cooks do not appear in public whenever the feast is part of lifecycle rituals. They prepare and cook the food hidden in the backyards of the buildings where the *bhoji* is customarily held, i.e. the local Upper Primary School or one of the four trade union buildings. And while the Vadabalija or Gudia man is cooking, some of the settlement Brahmins stay inside the building that separates the cooking place from the dining location. Equipped with cooking utensils, they show themselves to the public regularly, representing themselves as the cooks of the *bhoji*.

Since all of the settlers in Chatamput are aware of who is actually cooking the food, this display is only meant to make the guests believe in a Brahmin cook. Such hypocrisies are unnecessary in the case of a project *bhoji*, where—in stark contrast—the food is openly prepared, giving public evidence of the cooks' identity and caste status.

Those fed first at a lifecycle ritual are the relatives of the ritual's officiant and other guests not residing in Chatamput. They are served their food first in order to avoid problems for them when they return to their respective villages. After them the so-called *bodo loko* (big people) are served, i.e. the important persons of the settlement. Generally, highest prestige is given to the engineers, the local chairmen of Congress and the BJP, and all those occupying official posts in the four trade unions. These distinguished guests come from different social categories. They are Telugu, Oriya and Nepali, Muslim, Christian and Hindu. The Hindu may be Brahmin, Karana, or Telega. However, among the engineers and trade union officials are also members of lower castes, e.g. Shakalalu or Dhoba, the Telugu and Oriya washermen castes respectively, and the christianized Dombo—they are all of Scheduled Castes. Without distinction, all of these VIPs sit together. The situation among the other guests is similar.

The male guests attend these feasts in the company of their colleagues, whereas the female guests attend with their neighbours. Both men and women sit down next to the people they came with. I observed the course of these feasts several times and it always followed the above mentioned pattern. I must add, however, that all the feasts I attended in Chatamput were conducted in the context of marriage or sacred thread ceremonies of only project employees. So far I was unable to attend a feast of a private businessman, so I could not say whether such feasts are at all conducted among them in Chatamput.

The sequence of serving attendants shows even more egalitarian features in the case of a project *bhoji*. At a vast feast, given in honour of a retiring Chief Engineer and attended by more than two hundred employees, only ten people, holding important positions within the project, where seated separately at a proper table. All other attendants, project employees without exception, sat in four different lines directly facing the table. Everybody sat down where s/he could find a seat and all castes, religious communities and language groups mixed in these lines. The female employees sat in the first line, but since not enough women attended to fill up the whole line, men, mostly those of middle-cadre rank, sat in the female line as well. No gap was left between the last woman and the first man. The two sat shoulder to shoulder just like everyone else. Furthermore, all attendants, men, women, and the 'big people' sitting at the table, were served almost simultaneously.

At the feasts I observed it was obvious that certain groups of inhabitants had not been invited at all. I never met any of the Desia or indigenous people living in and around the settlement, and I failed to come across any of the scavengers, called Haddi by the Oriya and Paki by the Telugu, when feasting with the project people. Furthermore, I never observed the attendance of those settlers of low-caste status who were not employed in the project. On other occasions these sweepers and washermen communicate freely with others, but at the feasts they are conspicuous by their absence.

The characteristics of formal group feasts in Chatamput reveal a certain analogy to those described by Conzelmann for the urban context in Mandi, Himachal Pradesh. There the asymmetry in the relations between the Scheduled Castes and the higher or clean castes does not come to the fore because the former are excluded from the feasts given by the latter who do not attend those of the Scheduled Castes (ibid., 1996, 106). In Chatamput, the asymmetry between the project employees and the Scheduled Castes members working in the private sector is hidden in the same way. At the same time, the attendance of Scheduled Caste project employees at the *bhoji* and the seating order that does not set them apart from high caste employees, indicates a qualitative difference between Mandi and Chatamput. Furthermore, whereas in Mandi the reciprocal attendance of all higher castes at each other's group feasts is only made possible by the fact that brahmins prepare the food (ibid.), in Chatamput the cooks' caste status would prevent the attendance of all clean castes, if, commensal rules were followed.

Conviviality

Convivial groups in Chatamput are established among mates at work or in school and college, among members of the same trade union and the same volleyball team. The atmosphere inside the settlement's numerous country liquor shops is also coloured by a certain conviviality.

In the whole region the settlers are notoriously heavy drinkers. Visitors describe are amazed by the openness of it. The consumption of liquor is not camouflaged. The only so-called 'Foreign Liquor Shop' of Chatamput, advertised by a loud signboard, is situated right at the centre of the main road. So, too, are five illegal country liquor shops situated on this road. As elsewhere in India public consumption of liquor is strictly prohibited, but especially in the late morning and early evening hours, drunkards staggering down the street are a regular feature of the settlement.

Every person is generally allowed to visit all types of liquor shops as long as s/he is able to pay. The only difference is made regarding the Paki, the Telugu scavenger caste. Although they are allowed to enter all shops, special glasses are reserved for them, which they must themselves rinse after drinking.

As I was insistently told several times, the visitors' caste status is of no importance inside the liquor den. All patrons drink together and eat *chakna*, small spicy dishes prepared in ghee, from the same plate or piece of paper irrespective of caste. Those who come later are offered seats next to those already on their way to intoxication. Newcomers must also be offered *chakna* and, as far as I could observe, they are obliged to eat it. While—as in any public place in Chatamput—it is regarded as highly offensive to talk about caste matters, the visitors frequently engage in discussions about trade union politics. Depending upon the union affiliation of the visitors, these discussions can easily turn into rather rough arguments.

Those meeting inside liquor shops cannot, however, be regarded as forming a convivial group. They meet more or less accidentally, since they frequent a single pub. Furthermore, neither in the liquor shop nor on other occasions do they act jointly. As mentioned above, convivial groups are mostly established among school and college friends, volleyball team mates and members of the same trade union. The procedures I could observe while attending gatherings, reveal the typical characteristics described by Heidemann. Convivials plan meetings whenever they learn about parents and/or wives of one of them leaving Chatamput for some time or of some other possibility to seclude themselves from the public.

On that occasion they share the cost and work necessary for arranging the meeting. Some provide liquor; others meat, and two to three people do the cooking. First a spicy and oily meat dish is served together with the first glass of liquor, when all are present. The convivials always sit in a circle on the floor or around a table. The meat is served on a single plate and is placed in the middle of the circle; and a glass of liquor is given to everybody. The meeting commences with all convivials present taking the first sip of liquor simultaneously. Subsequently, everybody eats from the plate at the centre. This phase of the meeting can last for up to one hour, but as far as I observed, it is normally terminated after half an hour, when the gathering runs out of liquor. Talks about local politics, business, and jokes about sexual matters, are the most convivial moment of every gathering. Commensal rules are demonstratively broken by all participants eating from the same plate.

Following this overture, a proper meal is served containing pilaw or white rice, dal, and another less spicy meat dish. In contrast to the dish served with the liquor, this meal is eaten off separate plates. Conversations continue in the same style while eating, but a short time after the meal is consumed, the group dissolves.

The four trade unions of the town regularly hold meetings, i.e. three to four times a year. These also are coloured by convivial elements. Not all union members will be able to attend every single meeting, because of the approximately 200 project employees residing in Chatamput, 28 are always on shift in the powerhouse and another 28 have to remain alert for the reserve shift to be sent to the powerhouse, in cases of emergency. In addition to those on shift, others are on leave and not present and some unionists refuse to attend the meetings. The latter are the same group of people who refuse to attend the *bhoji* in Chatamput, i.e. a handful of Oriya Brahmins and Karana.

The meetings take place in the respective union buildings. The office bearers and some other prominent union members are the first to come, and among this limited group the strongest convivial bonds exist. Before the other unionists arrive, they share a few snacks and alcoholic beverages and speak about the important issues that will be discussed later in the informal atmosphere of the union's *bhoji*.

When all other members are present, everybody sits down in no particular order and the food is served. Serious affairs such as union politics and complaints about delayed promotions as well as jokes and anecdotes are the characteristic topics of conversation. The gathering ends after about two hours. Such union get-togethers are given special importance by most employees. Without being a full-fledged member, and thus without becoming a convivial for other unionists—so they say—it is impossible to secure any type of promotion in Chatamput.

Conclusion

I conclude that social life in Chatamput is still coined by conviviality or by the breaking of commensal rules during all formal feasting conducted within the industrial settlement. The seating order ignores caste status. Furthermore, all attendants, irrespective of their ritual status, consume food prepared by low-caste cooks in the course of every *bhoji*.

As is compulsory for convivial get-togethers, the breaking of commensal rules takes place in seclusion. The settlement always was, and still is, a place sealed off from the rest of the world in the eyes of all settlers. This is explicitly so in the following statement given by a Vadabalija when asked about the intentional neglect of commensal rules at Chatamput: 'How can they know what we are doing out here? I even saw brahmins desperately trying to become employed as scavengers of the project, because of the high payment for all kinds of jobs. When they visit their native villages, however, these people will say "I work as a switch-board operator" or "I am a mechanic". How can they [the settlers' relatives] know?'.

As elaborated by Heidemann, not all rules of caste society lose their validity in the context of conviviality. The gender line appears to be the critical boundary, since the women do not partake in the secluded gatherings. Even though most male settlers consume all types of alcohol excessively, they never do so in front of women[7]. Few women of high caste participate in the *bhoji* at Chatamput, and most of them return to their native villages or those of their husbands whenever they can. Furthermore, the kitchen and *puja* room are strictly out of bounds for those who occupy a lower ritual status than the owner.

From the above-mentioned procedure of formal feasting, I conclude that a person's caste status plays a minor role as long as he is an employee of the project. I do not imply that—when eating at a public feast–it does not matter for a brahmin or a Karana whether his neighbour is a Dhoba or Christian Dombo. I mean that the ritual status of caste becomes secondary in relation to the secular status of a government servant. Once employment is lost, however, the ritual status once again becomes the primary criterion.

---

[7] The only exceptions to this rule are the women running the country liquor shops. Their position is highly ambivalent, but cannot be examined here.

Another feature of Chatamput could also be explained by conviviality. The workers are organized in four trade unions. The first was organized during construction time; the second, twenty years later. Thereafter, approximately every ten years a new one was founded. The impact of these is always explained in generational terms. Recent and young employees are in no position to oppose the older unionists and must, if they are eager to engage in labour politics, found a new union.

As described above, each union also constitutes a convivial group to some extent. In Heidemann's terms, the asymmetric relationship between fathers and sons or between elder and younger brothers should not dissolve in conviviality, not even temporarily so. The convivial character of union meetings is thus regularly responsible for the foundation of new trade unions in the small town.

In conclusion, I would see the secular order to be of higher value within the project settlement. Compared to the given ritual order of caste, the created order of job achievement takes precedence. For settlers, the main relations are those of the workers and unionists. The fact that the validity of commensal rules is limited to the most private sphere of kitchen and *puja* room, together with their open and unopposed neglect at public feasting, furthermore leads me to the conclusion that conviviality actually encompasses commensality in this isolated immigrant settlement in a tribal area.

Such encompassment is invalid outside the area. When an outsider attends the formal group feasts in Chatamput, brahmins represent themselves as cooks, clearly a compromise of conviviality, including the simultaneous breach of upholding of commensal rules. For the sake of the visitors, the settlers add a quality to the procedure without removing the convivial one.

In their native lowland villages the settlers once again reverse the relationship between conviviality and commensality. I could visit their original homes in the Ganjam and Srikakulam districts to observe how hierarchical relationships between castes persists. Almost all of the migrants have a strong orientation towards their home village to this day. They return 'home' in order to find the right spouses or to conduct lifecycle rituals. Above all, most of the settlers intend to retire in their natal villages. In their eyes Chatamput is not a real village, but a kind of camp, a place of temporary residence, as is the case with numerous colonies of inner-Indian migrant labourers. The equality of conviviality is in fact restricted to the length of employment and residence in the industrial settlement.

Equality is a temporal, not ontological, value. The process of industrialization did not result in the Western type of independent individual in India, one basically equal to the other, and it did not lead to a social transformation as envisaged in the early years after Independence.

References

Breman, Jan. 1994. *Wage Hunters and Gatherers: Search for Work in the Urban and Rural Economy of South Gujarat,* Delhi: Oxford University Press.

— 1999. 'The Study of Industrial Labour in Post-Colonial India—The Formal Sector: An Introductory Review', in Jonathan Parry, Jan Breman and Karin Kapadia (eds.), *The Worlds of Indian Industrial Labour*, Delhi: Sage, 1-42.

Béteille, André. 1991. *Society and Politics in India: Essays in a Comparative Perspective*, London: Athlone Press.

Chandarvarkar, Rajnarayan. 1998. *Imperial Power and Popular Politics: Class, Resistance and the State in India*, Cambridge: Cambridge University Press.

Conzelmann, Elisabeth. 1996. *Heirat, Gabe, Status, Kaste und Gesellschaft in Mandi,* Berlin: Das Arabische Buch.

Dumont, Louis. 1957. *For a Sociology of India. Contributions to Indian Sociology.* 1/1957, 7-22.

— 1980. *Homo Hierarchicus: The Caste System and its Implications*, Chicago: University of Chicago Press.

Heuzé, Gerard 1996. *Workers of Another World: Miners, the Countryside and Coalfields in Dhanbad*, Delhi: Oxford University Press.

Holmström, M. 1976. *South Indian Factory Workers: Their Life and their World*, Cambridge: Cambridge University Press.

—1984. *Industry and Inequality: The Social Anthropolgy of Indian Labour*, Cambridge: Cambridge University Press.

Malamoud, Charles. 1989. *Cuire le monde: rite et pensée dans l'Inde ancienne*. Paris: Éd. La Découverte.

Mayer, Adrian. 1960. *Caste and Kinship in Central India: A Village and its Region*, London: Routledge & Kegan Paul.

— 'Caste in an Indian Village: Change and Continuity 1954-1992' in C.J. Fuller (ed.), *Caste Today*, Delhi: Oxford University Press, 32-65.

Parry, Jonathan. 1999a. 'Introduction', in Jonathan Parry, Jan Breman and Karin Kapadia (eds.), *The Worlds of Indian Industrial Labour*, Delhi: Sage, pp. ix-xxxvi

— 1999b. 'Working and Shirking in Bhilai', in Jonathan Parry, Jan Breman and Karin Kapadia (eds.), *The Worlds of Indian Industrial Labour*, Delhi: Sage, pp. 107-40

— 2000. 'Two Cheers for Reservation: The Satnamis and the Steel Plant', in Ramachandra Guha (ed.), *Institutions and Inequalities. Essays in Honour of André Béteille*, Delhi: Oxford University Press, 128-69.

Pocock, David. 1960. 'Sociologies: Urban and Rural', *Contributions to Indian Sociology* 4: 63-81.

Pfeffer, Georg. 1997. 'The *Scheduled Tribes* of Middle India as a Unit: Problems of Internal and External Comparison', in Georg Pfeffer and Deepak K. Behera (eds.), *Contemporary Society: Tribal Studies*, Vol. I: *Structure and Process*, Delhi: Concept Publishing Company, pp. 3-27.

— 2004. 'Tribal Society of Highland Orissa, Highland Burma and Elsewhere', in Beltz, Frese and Malinar (eds.), *Text and Context*, Delhi: Manohar.

Ramaswamy, E.A. 1977. *The Worker and his Union: A Study in South India*, Bombay: Allied Publishers.

Ramaswamy, U. 1983. *Work, Union and Community: Industrial Man in South India*, Delhi: Oxford University Press.

16

The King's Two Kingdoms or How the Maharaja of Parlakimedi Finally Became the Ruler of Orissa

Georg Berkemer

Studies of the lives of 'Great Men' are not in fashion among academic historians. They may, however, serve purposes different from the traditional one of giving food to popular legends about national heroes. Heeding Biswamoy Pati's warning about popular perceptions,[1] their creation and dissemination, I shall nevertheless employ the quaint theme of the great man for arguments quite different from the usual.

Writing history being just one such endeavour, the creation of mental images of the past may be subsumed under society's many processes of constructing order out of chaos. A comparison of the different modes of shaping collective memory will clarify their dependence upon their respective cultural context, as Marshall Sahlins has demonstrated by contrasting Polynesian and European modes.[2] In India, I have already tried to illustrate the particular ways of preserving memories of the past,[3] such as those criticized by Pati. For him, the historiography of the Oriya National Movement, leading to the province of Orissa, was a one-sided affair of a Western style academic history without all the other modes of narration.[4] Apart from references to the voice of the subaltern or exotic 'other', I suggest that the question of the narrative mode must be taken into account. (Hi)stories can be more or less detailed or repetitive, more or less theoretical or reduced to narrative abbreviations.

The two parts of this paper carry the subtitles 'Process: The View from the Centre' and 'Structure: The View from the

---

[1] Pati 1993 and 2001.

[2] Sahlins 1985.

[3] Berkemer 2001.

[4] Both books of footnote no.1 criticize the style of attributing the success of the Orissa Movement to great men (politicians and intellectuals).

Periphery', respectively.[5] The theme of both is the role of the Parlakimedi kings, especially that of Maharaja Krushna Chandra Gajapati Narain Deo (1892-1974),[6] in the formation of the province of Orissa. While history books usually hail the importance of the maharaja as one of the leading figures of the Oriya Movement whose tireless struggle for unification was gratified with the integration of his native south Orissa, his role as the first chief minister of Orissa and founder of Utkal University is also well known. Other features are barely discussed or generally overlooked. One such instance is the unique role of the Parlakimedi zamindari itself, being the only zamindari which was divided into a smaller Oriya part and a larger area which remained with the Madras Presidency at the formation of Orissa. In all other cases the zamindari boundaries remained unchanged. Another issue refers to the maharaja's peculiar ways of officiating during his terms as chief minister of Orissa (1937 and 1940-2).[7] Both terms saw minority governments led by him as the president of the Orissa National Party ruling against a large Congress majority. In the case of the second chief ministry, the maharaja could stay in office only due to the fact that several Congress MLPs had been arrested on political charges.

As soon as the maharaja's principal political aim, the formation of a Oriya-speaking province within British India, had been achieved, his political actions were dominated by his fundamental pro-British and anti-modernist attitudes. In the same vein, his ritual and political rivalry with the rājā of Khallikota disclosed the

---

[5] The terms 'process' and 'structure' are adapted from C. Lévi-Strauss (cf. Hénaff 1991, 290-319) and M. Sahlins 1985, 136-56.

[6] The monarch assumed the throne in 1913 (Patro 1981, 46; http://www.alma-nach.be/search/i/indi_parlakimedi.html). His correct title was Raja-Saheb, an honour bestowed upon him in 1918 for his performance as Honorary Commissioner of the Land Forces of the Defence of India during the First World War. The title was made hereditary in 1922 (Rajaguru 1972, 268). S.N. Rajaguru, as the *rajaguru* of Parlakimedi and the most reliable source on such matters, uses the title Raja (for the British period) or no title at all for his predecessors in office. I use the traditional family title Maharaja throughout the paper when I want to refer to his role as a 'little king', otherwise I use his name, K.C. Gajapati.

[7] The office was actually called Prime Minister in British times.

personality of a rather conservative 'little king' and not a popular politician or benevolent supporter of the Oriya people.[8]

Process: The View from the Centre

The narrative on the political processes of the formation of Orissa fills the history books and the new anthologies of Oriya-ness, as produced around the fiftieth anniversary of the state (1986) and subsequently around the end of the millennium.[9] This new literature harps on the old themes such as the greatness of the Orissan empire[10] reconfirming the notion of a strong centre and a unified Oriya culture. These themes will be questioned in the following.

---

[8] The raja of Khallikota formed the Independent Party (Baral 1997, 258) and several times failed to obtain the post of premiership for himself (Baral 1997, 273). The rivalry was older: W.W. Georgeson (sub-collector of Chicacole) mentions in his diary a visit to Ganjam in 1934, conducted by the Governor of Madras, Sir George Stanley. The occasion caused what he called 'rival hospitality' between the raja of Parlakimedi and the raja of Khallikota (*Source*: University of Cambridge, Estates: Georgeson Papers).

[9] Cf. Mishra 1997, Patnaik 1990, and Tiwari 2000.

[10] It is one of the standard phrases in editorials and prefaces of books on Orissan history and culture that the empire or even the territories of Orissa have extended from the river Ganga in the north to the river Godavari in the south. The idea itself is old in the area that later became the state of Orissa; you find the notion of the empire between the rivers already in a Maṭhara inscription of the fourth or fifth century AD, and in the modern interpretations of that very scant evidence, of course. One of the *Sakaliṅgādhipati*s or rulers of Kaliṅga claims in a single inscription (the *Niṅgoṇḍi Grant* of Prabhañjanavarman (lines 2-3), edited by D.C. Sircar 1953 and S.N. Rajaguru 1958) to rule over subjects living '*from the Krishṇa as far as the Mahanadī*' (*Kṛṣṇaveṇā-Mahānadyāntara-sthā-prajā*). This is the sole argument for the hypothesis of an extended Maṭhara kingdom. Rajaguru claims this to be an empire, the two rivers demarcating 'the actual extent of Sakala-Kaliṅga at the moment when the Maṭharas changed their title to Sakala-Kaliṅgadhipati from Kaliṅgadhipati' (Rajaguru 1958, 65). Sircar more cautiously interprets this passage as a claim to rulership, saying that 'such claims do not point to the actual position of the rulers in question but to the political ideal of the period' (Sircar 1953, 114). A newer phenomenon it the putting of the label 'Orissa' to these constructs of or claims to imperial greatness. I know of no source of the time of the empire itself (before 1568) in which 'Orissa'

In accordance with our overall topic, the contribution of a peripheral area, that of Parlakimedi, will be discussed. The end of the old Parlakimedi zamindari in 1937, when Orissa was formed, is part of such a political process. Ironically the zamindar himself played the decisive part in both the formation of Orissa and the termination of his own zamindari. He was a leading figure in the Oriya movement which in fact included several political and cultural campaigns[11] for the creation of an Oriya language state. Integrating the various Oriya-speaking tracts of several British Presidencies and diverse Princely States into the separate province of British India was the declared aim of these campaigns, one of which included the maharaja's activities in the political decision-making process on the northern parts of the Madras Presidency. The Indian Statutory Commission—better known as 'Simon Commission'—had toured the area of future Orissa in a fact-finding mission (1927) and the maharaja had reacted. Since no recommendation for an inclusion of the Vishakhapatnam and Ganjam Agencies into the new province[12] was given by the commission, the proponents of Orissa were alarmed. As a result, the first Round Table Conference in London (1930), discussing the all-Indian findings of the Simon Commission, finally saw the maharaja of Parlakimedi as a participant in the political process at the highest political level.[13]

---

was actually used. There is just an Oḍḍāḍi or Oḍhra-vāḍi in southern Kaliṅga, whose little kings might have been of Orissan origin or copied the imperial style of rule. This anachronism, however, is obviously one of the core notions of contemporary Oriya identity.

[11] Mohanty 1982.

[12] Samal 1989, 147; in 1924, a previous committee, consisting of C.L. Philip, the Political Agent, Orissa State, and A.C. Duff, the Collector of Vishakhapatnam, had come to a different recommendation. They were of the opinion that Mandasa, Tarla, Tekkali, Budarasingi, Jalantra and Parlakhemundi should be a part of Orissa (Patro 1981, 69). In 1933 C.L. Philip said that the recommendation of the Philip-Duff-Committee 'was mostly guided by the views and wishes of the Maharaja of Parlakhemundi' (Philip 1933, 8, quoted in Patro 1981, 69).

[13] There were three Round Table Conferences in 1930, 31, and 32. Even though the Maharaja took the opportunity to emphasize the cultural and linguistic uniqueness of the Oriyas, the documents in London do not reveal him using the argument of 'race', as Samal 1989, 146f suggests.

The outcome of these conferences was a first Indian 'constitution' granting partial autonomy to the provinces, the Government of India Act of 1935. Orissa became the eleventh province in British India and was formed on 1 April 1936. The Act provided the legal background for elections to the provincial assembly and the political process was activated with the assembly elections of 1937 with a limited franchise depending on income.

The documents I have perused do not reveal exactly the manner in which the final decision for Orissa was conducted. It is clear that the decision was taken against the warnings of various administrative bodies regarding questions of budget. In a foreseeable future, the province would be dependent on financial support from outside. This concern was of obviously less importance than the rising popular pressure in favour of creating the province. One obstacle, seemingly insurmountable, remained, however: the question of the Oriya speaking areas in the extreme north of Madras Presidency. The region was inhabited by a mixed Oriya and Telugu population and the allegiance of the leaders, the zamindars of Jaipur and Parlakimedi, for a long time was not entirely clear. The final outcome depended on the fate of the Parlakimedi zamindari with its Oriya ruler and predominantly Telugu population. The long and tortuous process of decision-making came to an end only after the maharaja himself, in 1933, offered to divide the Parlakimedi zamindari. Against the recommendations of the Simon Commission, the hill tracts of the Vishakhapatnam agency (the Jaipur zamindari and the Oriya speaking parts of the Parlakimedi zamindari) were included in the new province of Orissa.

It is unlikely, however, that the vote of the southern zamindars for Orissa was exclusively motivated by nationalist zeal. In the case of Jaipur, such sentiments may have predominated: the new zamindar took a personal decision by supporting the case of Orissa in contrast to the convictions of his predecessor. In the case of Parlakimedi, the sources are not so easy to interpret. Apparently, the zamindar himself was more of a socialite and a benefactor than a political figure, whereas the young S.N. Rajaguru together with other intellectuals in Ganjam played a major political role.[14] The question remains how the zamindar became politically active and

[14] Patro 1981, 133.

how the crucial decision on the division of the zamindari came to pass during the Third Round Table Conference.

Clearly the extraordinary idea of dividing the zamindari was at the core of the decision to include parts of the Madras Presidency in Orissa, as mentioned above. No other zamindari has been divided in the process of the formation of Orissa, as can be seen from the Constitution of Orissa of 1936. The First Schedule (*see* Appendix), Part II of the Government of India (Constitution of Orissa) Order of 1936, delineates the land borders of the new state. Approximately two-thirds of this text are devoted to the division of Parlakimedi zamindari.

In the end, the maharaja of Parlakimedi became the first chief minister of Orissa for a period of three months. This and his longer second term in office (1940-42) saw minority governments without the approval of public opinion, opposed by the much stronger Provincial Congress Committee as well as all other independence movements. The maharaja to this day is seen as a national hero for Orissa, even though he was against Indian independence and an opponent of the long awaited land reform. Only few authors[15] criticize him for his pro-British attitude and his style of government. Thus, the centrist historical ideology lies at the core of the Oriya nation as a modern 'imagined community'. The procedure may be characterized by three specific features:

(a) the construction of a 'normal' state of affairs, in the present case the pre-existence of an Oriya nation;
(b) the view from within emphasizing the temporal and causal structure of the 'before' and 'after' of a particular event, in the present case the creation of Orissa;
(c) a view from the centre interpreting the event as a process in modern administrative terms. Thus the present cultural entity is spreading self-appraisal in the form of textbooks and newspapers, learned societies and universities to recreate itself.

[15] Bhatta 1990, Pati 1993.

Structure: The View from the Periphery

History writing creates a narrative that implies a certain bias or perspective. Inevitably, an author begins the process of writing when s/he is well aware of the end of the story to be told, the outcome of the historical process. This final phase, being closest to the here and now, may be the starting point from which a *post factum* view is being projected into a still undetermined past by teleological arguments in the form of historical ideology. This 'textbook perspective' is the narrative mode commonly shared by historians and their audience.

Writing on Orissa in this narrative mode presupposes the existence of the subject, Orissa, in a past form, the 'Orissa Empire'. Finally, the anachronistic treatment of historical time and the centrist point of view of historical space results in a form of historical narration which takes the status quo for granted and projects it into the past.

This means that an alternative approach must be proposed. It seems to me that it is at least as legitimate to interpret the events around 1936 as part of Orissa's historical structure rather than seeing them as a political process that began with the Oriya Movement and ended with the formation of the Orissa province. In order to use this alternative approach, a few theoretical premises will be used:[16]

(a) some societies tend to narrate events as myth, others as history. Myth is narrated structure, history is narrated cause-effect (or time);

(b) this opposition has been conceived in terms of 'hot' versus 'cold' societies by Lévi-Strauss;[17]

(c) both hot and cold narrative modes deal with the discrepancy between social norms and observed events, i.e. with contingency; this opposition can be explained in time as chains of cause and effect and thus temporalized, or narrated as a re-creation of the previous state, and thus structuralized;

---

[16] Derived from Hénaff 1991.

[17] Lévi-Strauss 1973.

(d) structure cannot be seen from the inside point of view; insiders are not aware whether they tell their tales in the form of myths or histories, containing values (*historia magistra vitae*) and their (re)creation in past and present; externals do not know the intricacies of such categories and their contexts, but they are able to recognize their structure.

Historical structure, as Marshall Sahlins has demonstrated in *Islands of History,*[18] can be deduced from historical narration when something happens that does not fit into everyday life or the annual ritual cycle. In this case, two sets of sources, Polynesian and European, seemingly clash and lead to contradictory statements about historical events. The Europeans report Captain Cook's discoveries and death. For the Hawaiians, 'cold' or mythic narration transforms Captain Cook into Lono, the god of fertility. At the same time, however, a 'hot' process is being initiated in which one member of the nobility, rather than becoming a traditional paramount chief, is elevated to the new position of King Kamehameha I, Polynesian myths and European histories leading a precarious co-existence.

In a similar way, traditional and colonial sources in Orissa use different narrative modes. Even in the rather narrow field of political history where narratives about the past are related for the sake of stating contemporary political claims, the texts are entirely different. Colonial sources focus on temporal sequences of cause and effect, presenting unilineal tales which lead to seemingly unambiguous results. Reports, statements, and letters are such texts. When traditional, they are more repetitive, using commonly known symbols and metaphors to make a single event meaningful in several political or ritual aspects of time and space.[19]

In previous papers I have described the maharaja of Parlakimedi as a 'little king'.[20] This term is used here in the context of a model of traditional Hindu kingship, the so-called 'little kingdom', as it has been developed by anthropologists and historians.[21] According

---

[18] Sahlins 1985.

[19] This has recently been demonstrated by Narayana Rao, Shulman and Subrahmanyam 2000.

[20] Berkemer 2001.

[21] Dirks 1987 speaks of the 'little king'. 'Little kingdom' as a technical term was introduced later (Berkemer 1993, Schnepel 1997); here

to this model the king has several functions and duties defining his relationship to his subjects, the neighbouring little kings, and his more powerful overlord. These functions are performed in his role as a just ruler and warrior king (*dharmarāja*), as patron of temples, festivals, and Brahmins, and as the highest sacrificer and devotee of the state deity. He is also traditionally a patron of the arts, a protector of the weak and a person whose successful rulership brings riches to his subjects. The latter is symbolized in his own conspicuous consumption, seen as a symbol of his sovereign command over the material goods of his state.

A little king of the twentieth century had to reconcile two worlds in his own person. Apart from the role of a modern prince of the British Empire and a state politician, K.C. Gajapati had to play the more traditional one of the Hindu king. These roles required him to fulfil functions within his zamindari which were quite difficult to reconcile with the image of the modern politician. He had to appear as the king of Parlakimedi protecting his subjects, Oriyas, and Telugus, being the heir of the title Gajapati and claiming to be the scion of the great medieval empire as well as the protector of Jagannath. This self-image would have easily become disruptive when propagated for the cause of the Oriya Movement outside the Parlakimedi zamindari, because this claim contested the claim of the rājā of Khurda, who was the Gajapati since 1590 and the official protector of Jagannath of Puri.

Taking these points into account, we can now see how our theoretical framework can be applied. In the case of Parlakimedi's role in the formation of the Orissa province, process is expressed in history books as a specific narrative mode, the voice of the centre, the 'textbook' perspective. Krishna Chandra Gajapati is thus presented as the political head of the southern Oriya Movement and as the first premier who ruled in Cuttack. Structure is used to forward a view from the periphery with particular reference to features of a process, seemingly odd at first glance, but tallying very well with the traditional attitudes of little kings. Historical structure may provide a way to explain some of the apparently strange details in the career of the maharaja.

We have to keep in mind here the relations of the traditional little kings of the Gajapati empire and its smaller successor states.

---

the term is defined more precisely when compared to earlier works on the history of the 'Dark Period' of Britain or that of the Old Testament.

We can interpret the maharaja's decision to divide his zamindari as a means to end the old antagonism between the Parlakimedi kings and some of the northern monarchs, primarily Khurda and, to a lesser extent, Khallikota. At least since the eighteenth century, Parlakimedi's claim to superiority was founded on the myth of the re-establishment of the true Jagannath at Parlakimedi, rather than at Puri, after the desecration by Kalapahar (1568). Through the twentieth century writings of S. N. Rajaguru (ignoring the implicit contradictions) Parlakimedi also claimed to be both of Gaṅga and of Gajapati origin. In the eighteenth century the older claims had lead to military actions, the direct cause of both the Maratha rule in Orissa and the short-lived ascent of the Pusapatis of Vizianagaram in the Northern Circars. In the nineteenth and twentieth centuries, military prowess was replaced by other dharmic features of royalty, such as the traditional role of the little king as the benefactor of mankind, manifested in the establishment of educational facilities[22] and conspicuous consumption.[23]

In this light, I would thus propose to re-interpret the role of the maharaja of Parlakimedi in the course of the decision-making processes of the years 1927 to 1937. In the context of traditional values, the role of the king as the ritual head of his state should be reconsidered. As elaborated by Kulke, the priests of Mukhalingam in Andhra Pradesh still use the *aṅka* years of the Parlakimedi kings as the basis of their ritual calendar. Even though the king of Parlakimedi may have lost the 'ownership' of the Telugu speaking parts of his zamindari and, nowadays, is in no position to give the traditional protection to his subjects his ritual importance lingered on at least until the 1970s due to his role as a patron of temples and

---

[22] Most important was the foundation of Utkal University during K.C. Gajapati's first chief-ministership. Others were a donation of Rs. one lakh in 1926 for the Indian Research Fund Association, a predecessor of the Indian Council of Medical Research (ICMR), and the foundation of colleges in Parlakimedi.

[23] There was a famous car, 'the magnificent Rolls-Royce Phantom II 1930, Ex H.H. The raja Sahib of Parlakemedi [*sic*]', which was exhibited at the 69th Geneva Salon d'Auto (internet); the raja's race horses and up to now the Parlakimedi Trophy at Bombay (oral information in Chennai, sports announcements on the internet), the struggle to be the host of the Madras governor in 1934).

rituals. Popular legends—or actual happenings deliberately recreating the structure of popular legends—are important here.[24]

The key to understanding may be conveyed by a story of P.S.N. Patro's biography of the maharaja,[25] the passage on K.C. Gajapati's reaction (in March 1933) to the official proposal for the boundaries of Orissa which did not include Parlakimedi:

> Krushna Chandra Gajapati felt very much disappointed at the publication of the White Paper of 17th March, 1933, as it excluded many Estates for the integration of which he had fought relentlessly. It pained him more as his own Estate was excluded from the proposed Orissa province. He went through much physical and mental strain. Only the persons who had seen him during those days in Parlakhemundi alone know what mental tension he has to undergo.[26] But he was not desperate and he drew his strength and inspiration from his domestic Deity 'Manikeswari'.[27] It is believed that the goddess Manikeswari appeared to him in his dream and blessed him by saying that: 'My dear boy! Go ahead and you will be successful.'[28]

I suppose that the maharaja's political strategy could be interpreted as follows. Political claims were to be cast in the form of traditional mythical narratives and symbols which were appropriate attempts to create traditional power networks within a modern political environment. K.C. Gajapati's disregard of democratic forms indicates that the traditional role of the little king was to be

---

[24] G.N. Dash (Berhampur University) in 2001 told me a popular legend: Right at the beginning of the maharaja's involvement in the Oriya Movement, he was still unsure whether to support the pro-Orissa side. During this phase he was invited by the Telugu king of Vizianagaram to discuss the matter. As the guest of honour he was supposed to sit on the right side of his host Pusapati Alankanarayana Gajapati Raju, but S.N. Rajaguru switched the place cards of the two kings, so that the Pusapati king came to sit on his right side. Thus infuriated, K.C. Gajapati immediately left Vizianagaram and decided to side with the supporters of the incorporation of Ganjam into Orissa.

[25] Patro 1981, 138.

[26] This is Patro's fn. 83: 'Digambar Rath, Karmayogi Sri Krushna Chandra Gajapati Narayan Deo', (an article), from *Samaj*, 9-10-74.

[27] This is Patro's fn. 84: 'Jugal Kishore Panigrahy, "Maharaja Mohanubhava" (Oriya), from *Our Homage to the Father of New Orissa*, 1969, 40.'

[28] Patro 1981, 138

continued at an all-Orissa level. In order to achieve this, however, a nationalist platform had to be created as well. This implied sacrifice of his kingdom; by doing so, he could effectuate his role as a respected fighter for the freedom of Orissa and thus become—against all odds and democratic procedures—the ruler of the new province.

Dividing the Parlakimedi zamindari was the last opportunity to achieve the great goal the Parlakimedi kings had been fighting for ever since the eighteenth century, the supreme rule in Orissa. The sacrificer king, I propose, saw the chance of becoming the ruler of modern Orissa by sacrificing his traditional little kingdom. This sacrifice was a kind of solicitory gift, as shown in the following passage from S.N. Rajaguru's *History of the Gangas*:

> After being assumed [*sic*] the *gādi* of the *Prime-Minister* (this designation was subsequently changed to *Chief-Minister*), the Maharaja visited, **for the first time** [my emphasis, GB], the Great temple of Jagannātha at Puri when the Gajapati Maharājā, Sri Ramachandradeva, as per the old custom, received him ceremonially at the out-skirts of the town and led him to the *Śrī-Mandīra.* This type of honour was never granted, as a rule, to any other Rāj-family except the Gaṅgavaṁśis of Pārlākhimuṇḍi, whose ancestors have constructed and maintained the great temple (*Śrī-Mandira*) in the good old days. The Mahārājā also received the royal honour from the *Paṇḍas* and *Sevakas* of the Temple whom he enriched, after *darśan*, by throwing gold coins on the *Ratansiṁhāsana* in accordance to the convention of the Gaṅgavaṁśi-Rājās.[29]

At first glance this is a rather curious statement, since Rajaguru himself states on page 271 of the same book that 'like his fore-fathers, he [the maharaja] started on pilgrimage to *Catur-dhāma* (four religious Centres of India): Jagannāth, Badrināth, Dwārakānātha and Rāmanātha'. This journey must have been in 1926 or 1927. How could he, after having visited Puri in 1926-7, visit it *for the first time* in 1937? The explanation of the apparent contradiction is probably best put in terms of historical structure by using a slightly altered image of the king's two bodies.[30] In our context, a 'modern' form of royalty is achieved only after the assumption of the *gadi* of the chief minister. Before that, the

---

[29] Rajaguru 1972, vol. II, 283-4.

[30] Kantorowicz 1966; Schnepel 1995.

maharaja was only the little king of his estate, and that function allowed him to visit Puri in 1926-7 as a private person who had left behind the insignia and status of his traditional office. He simply came to Puri as a pilgrim or tourist like many others. In 1937, however, after having achieved the 'conquest' of Orissa, he embodied a different kind of kingship. He symbolically reclaimed the status of the imperial ruler, thus reducing the rājā of Khurda to the status of a little king. This is very well described by Rajaguru when he uses the image of the Khurda rājā meekly waiting at the outskirts of Puri for the exalted visitor to arrive.

This motif, taken out of a historical structure, appears like a mythical tale come true, or—to put it as a historical rather than a structural myth—like the second coming of the Gangas from the south after Codaganga Ananatavarman some 800 years earlier. The motive also contains the plan for his political activities on a 'modern' stage which became the cause for the ultimate failure of K.C. Gajapati. He never anticipated that the Oriya movement for many did not—or not only—coincide with a recreation of the old 'Oriya' empire, but was a part of the Indian freedom struggle. He never overcame the idea of the benevolent authority of the Indian princes under a benevolent imperial umbrella, making him a regional ruler of a language based state. Therefore he never cared much about the election results (approaching 90 per cent of the votes cast against him) having no qualms about leading his governments against the majority in the State Assembly, against the will of the majority of voters, against Gandhi and the Congress, or even against the constitution of Orissa.

Conclusion

Akio Tanabe summarizes the ritual complex of the little king which came into existence in early modern times in the terms 'sacrificer king' and 'sacrificer state'.[31] Historical structure as a phenomenon of the *long durée* explains why its categories and values are still observable in the middle of the twentieth century or even later.[32] The role of the king as sacrificer is most clearly developed in the case of the politically impotent, but ritually very important rājā of

[31] Tanabe 1999, 1999a, 2000.

[32] Tanabe 1995.

Khurda. He had lost his kingdom, but became the leading figure in the Jagannath cult and thus a major figure in the formation of Oriya identity, even though he never played a major role in the Oriya movement.

In the end, the king, the paramount sacrificer in the traditional sacrificer state, had sacrificed his own kingdom in order to become a modern ruler. What does this act of seemingly self-denial denote? If seen in the flow of events one may wonder if this act has not achieved a goal implied by the historical structure of Orissa's south. On becoming the ruler of Orissa, has the king of Parlakimedi not finally accomplished what his ancestors had so persistently tried to achieve during the centuries of the old regime?

We find two contested centres and conflicting interests at work. The context of Orissa, the centre of which was obviously the main focus for the maharaja's political activities, gives us the well-known pattern of centre and periphery: Cuttack and Puri, the secular and the ritual centres, attracted the ruler of Parlakimedi making him even sacrifice the periphery of his own, subregional centre and his role as a little king which had become increasingly untenable in the light of the developments on both sides of the hotly debated Oriya-Telugu language divide.[33]

Appendix: The Definition of Orissa's Land Boundaries

The Government of India (Constitution of Orissa) Order, 1936, to this are attached three schedules for divisions of land, constituencies, debts and revenues; the first schedule, part II, 8-9, describes the land boundary of Orissa, of this about half goes to the divisional line through the Parlakimedi zamindari which had to be divided along village boundaries (the part concerning Parlakimedi is in italics):

FIRST SCHEDULE—PART II—

THE LAND BOUNDARY OF ORISSA

A. The Main Portion of Orissa

---

[33] This is in itself a fiction, since there was no clear language or cultural boundary and still nowadays is not (cf. Berkemer 1993). Its being politically established during the drawing up of the First Schedule of the Oriya Constitution did not change that fact, it simply helped the emerging centres on both sides to keep up the illusion of such a boundary and act accordingly with 'centralizing' attempts.

The boundary follows a line which starts at latitude 19°5' (approximate), at the point on the coast of the Bay of Bengal where the boundary of Patisonnapuram village, after following the coast from north to south, turns inland. From that point it runs along the existing village boundary (so as to include the village in Orissa) until it meets the boundary of the Berhampur taluk at a sharp re-entrant angle in that boundary; thence along the northern arm of that taluk boundary until it meets the south-eastern boundary of Chikati estate; thence along that estate boundary westwards and southwards until it again meets the boundary of the Berhampur taluk; thence along that taluk boundary south-westward until it meets the boundary of Jalantra estate; thence along that estate boundary westwards until it meets the boundary of the Ganjam Agency; *thence south-westwards along the boundary of that Agency until it meets the boundary of the Parlakimedi Estate; thence eastwards and southwards along that boundary to the point where the southern boundary of Peddahamsa village leaves the estate boundary; thence through the estate to the south-west of the village of Pedda /9/ Murangai along the existing village boundaries so as to include in Orissa the villages of Peddahamsa, Labonyogodo, Baduobada, Mamidipalle and Pedda Murangi (including Labonyogodo Reserved Forest); from the south-west corner of Pedda Murangi along the west boundary of the village of Mara, the north-western forest boundary of Banapuram Reserved Forest, the northern boundary of the village of Bagadalla and the northern boundary of the village of Surjani to the most northerly point (approximately) of the last-mentioned boundary; thence in a northerly direction for a distance of about half a mile across the saddle in the hills to the south-eastern corner of the village of Kosali; thence to the point where the south-west corner of the village of Omora meets the Mahendratanaya river along existing village boundaries so as to include in Orissa the villages of Kosali, Jangalapadu, Saradopuram, Agarakhandi, Bhinnola, Dhamidigam, and Omora; from the last-mentioned point into a westerly direction along the middle line of that river to the south-west corner of the village of Kaviti Khaspa; thence to the point where the western boundary of the village of Singupuram Agraharam meets the southern forest boundary of the Kurlanda Reserved Forest along existing village boundaries so as to include in Orissa the villages of Kaviti Khaspa, Cheruvidiguva, Venkatapuram, Paddakhinga (I), Mukkidipadu (I), Ranipeta, Siddamanugu (I), and Singupuram Agraharam; thence along the southern forest boundary of Kurlanda Reserved Forest until it meets the boundary of the village of Minigam; thence to the point where the eastern boundary of the village of Kinigam meets the Vamsadhara river along existing village boundaries so as to include in Orissa Kurlanda Reserved Forest, the villages of Minigam, Sitapuram, Kharada, Vistala, Hadobhangi, Jayapuram, Nilapuram and Kinigam; thence in a north-westerly direction along the middle of the river until it meets the boundary of the Ganjam district; thence along that district boundary, which is there the boundary of the Jeypore (Impartible) Estate, westwards and southwards until that estate boundary diverges from the district boundary; thence along that estate boundary (so as to include the estate in Orissa) until it meets the eastern boundary of the Pottangi taluk; thence along that taluk boundary (so as to include the taluk in Orissa) until it again meets the boundary of the Jeyepore (Impartible) estate;* thence along that estate boundary until it meets the boundary of the Madras Presidency; thence northwards, south-eastwards and again northwards along the Presidency boundary until it meets the boundary of the south-western portion of the Angul District; thence along the west, north and east boundaries of that portion of that district until it again meets the Presidency boundary at a point where that boundary is also the boundary of the Eastern States Agency; thence along the boundary of that Agency until it meets the boundary of the Bengal Presidency; and thence in a south-easterly direction along the Presidency boundary to the sea.

B. The detached portion of the Province formed by the part of the existing Angul district of the Province of Bihar and Orissa which is wholly surrounded by Indian States. The boundary follows the existing boundary.

C. The detached portion of the Province formed by the Sambalpur district of the province of Bihar and Orissa and the two areas transferred from the Central provinces. The boundary follows the existing boundaries.

Source:
British Library, Oriental and India Office Collections, Official Records, P&J (C) 6229, 41-8.

References

Baral, J.K. 1997. 'Government and Politics, 1937-1947', in P.K. Mishra, *Comprehensive History and Culture of Orissa*, Delhi: Kaveri Books, 257-82.

Bennett, C.J. 1980. 'The Morphology of Language Boundaries: Indo-Aryan and Dravidian in Peninsular India', in D.E. Sopher (ed.), *An Exploration of India. Geographical Perspectives on Society and Culture*, Ithaca: Cornell University Press, 234-51.

Berkemer, Georg. 1993. *Little Kingdoms in Kaliṅga: Ideologie, Legitimation und Politik regionaler Eliten*, Stuttgart: Steiner.

— 2001. *Banausia and Endo-history: European Conceptions of Indian Historical Consciousness.* Graduate School of Asian and African Studies, Kyoto University (ASAFAS special paper), Kyoto: ASAFAS.

— 2001a. 'Little Kingdoms: The Perspective from the South', in H. Kulke and B. Schnepel (eds.), *Jagannath Revisited: Studying Society, Religion and the State in Orissa*, Delhi: Manohar, 253-70.

Bhatta, Brajabandhu. 1990. 'The Election of 1937 in Orissa', *Orissa Past and Present* 4, 1990, 387-96.

Deo, Fanindam. 1997. 'Withdrawal: The Bhunjia and Paharia in Western Orissa', in Dev Nathan (ed.), *From Tribe to Caste*, Shimla: Indian Inst. of Advanced Study, 415-31.

Dirks, Nicholas B. 1987. *The Hollow Crown. Ethnohistory of a Little Kingdom*, Cambridge: Cambridge University Press.

Hénaff, Marcel. 1991. *Claude Lévi-Strauss*, Paris: Belfond.

Indian Delimitation Committee. *Reports and Proposals*, 3 vols., plus one sep. vol. for Burma, Delhi: Govt. Press 1936.

Kantorowicz, Ernst H. 1966. *The King's Two Bodies: A Study in Mediaeval Political Theology* (2nd rev. edn.), Princeton: Princeton University Press.

Lévi-Strauss, Claude. 1973. *Structural Anthropology* 2, Harmondsworth: Penguin.

Mishra, P.K. (ed.). 1997. *Comprehensive History and Culture of Orissa,* Delhi: Kaveri Books.

Mishra, P.K. 1997a. 'Language Agitation in the 19th Century', in P.K. Mishra 1997, 190-206.

— 1997b. 'Orissa's Search for Identity', in P.K. Mishra 1997, 237-56.

— 1997. 'Utkal Union Movement: 1903-1947', in P.K. Mishra 1997, 207-35.

Mohanty, Nivedity. 1982. *Oriya Nationalism. Quest for a United Orissa,* Delhi: Manohar.

Müller, Klaus E. 1997. 'Zeitkonzepte in traditionellen Kulturen', in Klaus E. Müller and Jörn Rüsen (eds.). *Historische Sinnbildung. Problemstellungen, Zeitkonzepte, Wahrnehmungshorizonte, Darstellungsstrategien,* Reinbek: Rowohlt, 221-39.

Narayana Rao, Velcheru, David Shulman and Sanjay Subrahmanyam. 2001. *Textures of Time: Writing History in South India 1600-1800,* Delhi: Permanent Black.

Pati, Biswamoy. 1984. 'Reviewing the Emergence of the Orissa Province', *The Quarterly Review of Historical Studies*, 24, 3, 47-55.

— 1993. *Resisting Domination. Peasants, Tribals and the National Movement in Orissa (1920-50),* Delhi: Manohar.

Patnaik, Gour Prasad (ed.). 1990. *Orissa Past and Present;* combined nos. 7 and 8 of vol. 4, 1990.

Patro, Kishori Mohan. 1985. 'Growth of National Consciousness and the Freedom Movement in Orissa', *Indian Historical Review*, 12, 317-27.

Patra, P.S.N. 1997. 'Makers of Modern Orissa: II', in P.K. Mishra 1997, 297-310.

Patro, P. Sanka Narayan. 1981. *Krushna Chandra Gajapati Narayan Deo—The Maharaja of Parlakhemundi*, Bhanjanagar: Gyana Prakashini.

Rajaguru, S.N. (ed.). 1960. *Inscriptions of Orissa* I.2, Bhubaneswar: Orissa State Museum.

Sahlins, Marshall. 1985. *Islands of History*, Chicago, London: Chicago University Press.

— 1999. 'Two or Three Things that I Know about Culture', in *Journal of the Royal Anthropological Institute (Man)*, 5, 399-421.

Samal, Bidyut Kumar. 1997. 'History of Freedom Struggle', in P.K. Mishra 1997, 311-57.

Schnepel, Burkhard. 1995. *Twinned Beings: Kings and Effigies in Southern Sudan, East India and Renaissance France*, Göteborg: Inst. for Advanced Studies in Social Anthropology.

— 1997. *Die Dschungelkönige. Ethnohistorische Aspekte von Politik und Ritual in Südorissa / Indien*, Stuttgart: Steiner.

Sircar, Dines Chandra. 1953. 'Niṅgoṇḍi Plates of Prabhañjanavarman', in *Epigraphia Indica* 30, 1953, 112-18.

Tanabe, Akio. 1995. 'Remaking Tradition: The State Government and Martial Arts Competition in Orissa, Indien', *Journal of Asian and African Studies*, 48/49, 1995, 221-41.

— 1999. 'Kingship, Community and Commerce in Late Pre-Colonial Khurda', in *Steering Committee of the Research Project ... : Rituals as Popular Culture. Towards Historico-Anthropological Understanding of Modern Indian Society*, Tokyo: Steering Committee of the Research Project, 129-200.

— 1999a. 'Kingship and Caste: the relationship between King/Dominant Caste and the Brahman Reconsidered', in *Steering Committee of the Research Project ... : Rituals as Popular Culture. Towards Historico-Anthropological Understanding of Modern Indian Society*, Tokyo: Steering Committee of the Research Project, 201-30.

— 2000. *Early Modern and Colonial Transformation: Rethinking the Role of the Little King in Eighteenth and Nineteenth Century Orissa, India*, Kyoto: ASAFAS.

Tiwari, A.N. (ed.). 2000. *Reference Orissa Millennium Edition*, Delhi: Enterprising Publishers.

17

Rebels, Rajas and the British Raj: The World According to Fakirmohan

Barbara Lotz

In Fakirmohan Senapati's fiction and autobiography texts, we find the presentation of a wide array of social groups in the outgoing nineteenth-century Orissa, the author himself having been a close witness to a crucial phase of change and transition. During his career, he was exposed to both rural and urban contexts and became a constructive member of a newly emerging public sphere from the 1860s onwards. Early orphaned and forced to earn a living, he rose from a modest background to a respected position as a teacher and educationist, before his administrative and communicative skills made him a much sought-after employee in the British administration.[1] In the second half of his autobiography, we find a detailed account of several postings in remote rural areas as Manager or Dewan, where he had to ensure a successful interaction between peasants, feudal lords, and tribal people in his function as the last executive link in the British administration.

In Fakirmohan we see the functioning and the mind-set of a new intermediate agency within the traditional social set-up in off-coastal Orissa. Secondly, we have a first-person narrator directly involved in the events, leaving a written record as part of his autobiography. The author's perspective is that of an insider as much as an outsider; it is from below as well as from above; it reacts and appeals to various loyalties; it thus shows distance and closeness, uncertain relations, and limited visions.

We can study Fakirmohan as an interpreter in a double sense. First, we have an author who puts a stream of events into a perspective, thereby shaping the past 'reality' according to his own

---

[1] Collector John Beames (1869-73 at Balasore and 1873-79 at Cuttack) offered Fakirmohan his first post as Dewan of Nilgiri State in 1871, when he was 27. F. worked as Dewan or Assistant Dewan in various other States and Estates, such as Dompada, Dhenkanal, Pallahada, Daspalla, Keonjhar, and Kendrapara, retiring in 1892 after more than 25 years in the administrative field.

ideas and needs. In short, he creates his story out of history, which is in turn not left unaffected by his own motives and manipulations. Besides, he qualifies for this through his lifelong role as a versatile interpreter between different languages and cultures. Perhaps it was his dilemma that he often remained a broker, mediating between two or more sides, being discarded by either side when there was no further need for his services.

In his autobiographical narration, we find the anonymity of groups breaking up into a series of interrelated actions and reactions of individuals. Positions are not presented in the focussed manner of historical records and sociological categories, but in a rather oscillating illumination changing with various angles at various times: in this light we find clichéd perceptions of the British, the tribes, and the Maharajas losing their contours: the relations between the groups become intertwined and entangled. It is curious that in spite of their feuding, all parts seem to confirm to Western values of enlightenment, at least as it appears from the author's perspective. All participants appear to be undoubtedly committed to the benefits of education, administration, social welfare, and, above all, justice. New concepts of citizenship, based on bourgeois values, have already been internalized by members of varied communities. Of course, what we also find is a rather pragmatic application of these ideas. The first to be discarded or distorted is always the one of equality: in the course of events, some turn out to be simply more equal than others, and the occupancy of the paramount position by the British is never to be questioned.

Autobiography, History, Fiction?

Fakirmohan wrote his autobiography towards the end of his life,[2] when he was living alone and ailing at Balasore. He could consider himself at that time to be a respected man, as is evident from certain acknowledgements in the last paragraph. Having himself become a historic figure in public life, he set out to compose a text that would serve posterity not only as a record of certain processes he had initiated or witnessed, thereby sharing individually remembered facts with a larger group before they would sink into oblivion; his

[2] Fakirmohan lived from 1843 to 1918. The autobiography was written from 1916 onwards and serially published in *Utkal Sāhitya* from July 1918.

text was also a means to ensure that his own fame was preserved, and that, too, in the way he wanted it to be. Therefore, the force of imagination at work in an autobiography is not so much a flaw as a prerequisite for the whole endeavour itself. As the author recreates his own existence, a fictitious image of his personality and life will certainly appear on his mental screen, to be corrected, shaped, and streamlined in the course of the text as per the message intended. The author knows the end of the story, and he can bestow a meaning on events or developments which may not have been evident at the time they occurred. At least he is now in the position to select one of several possible meanings, and the selection of what is narrated and what is left out is done accordingly. What we find transmitted in autobiographies is therefore a world view, and not an abstract recapitulation of the past. The autobiography itself becomes part of that meaning which an individual assigns to his or her life, the text serving as its summary and perfection.

For a historian, Fakirmohan's autobiography seems to offer a host of valuable information in the context of famous events and institutional history. Yet, probing the contents for informational veracity, critics have become increasingly doubtful about its veracity. When statements were proven to be misleading or outright false, a feeling arises of deceit and hence a disenchanted downgrading of the text as 'mere' fiction. This has happened especially in view of the chapters dealing with Fakirmohan's involvement in the Bhuyan revolt or *meli* of 1891-2 during his managership in Keonjhar.[3] It should be obvious, however, that an autobiography is created by an author with a certain background, motive, and intention. Even the most sober presentation of

---

[3] The question of whether F.'s autobiography should be considered 'a novel' was raised by Dasarathi Dasa in an essay published 1993 in *Jhaṁkār*: he found the text 'full of mistakes and lies'. His view was supported with more fault-findings by Ashok Kumar Das in *Jhaṁkār* in January 1999. The debate aroused considerable public response, a counterposition in defence of Fakirmohan's recordings being taken by Sachidananda Mishra in further articles in *Jhaṁkār* (1999). In the still ongoing debate, G.N. Dash's articles in *Jhaṁkār* (1994, 2000 and 2001) provide a host of historical facts gathered from official records that indeed differ with the 'facts' given by Fakirmohan. Dash however points out that it was inappropriate to speak of 'lies' in the context of a literary text, which should by no means be equated with a historical source.

historical data will inevitably bear the mark of its producer, and the compilation will continue to exist as a text in its own right: history itself could be described as a series of narratives. An autobiography, being the story of a life, is first and foremost a story. Even if, as in the present case, an objective faithfulness is proclaimed and pursued, or a certain historicity or authenticity ranks as one of the major motives of the author: the information here is not of the same quality as that found in a textbook, nor can the informational aspect alone be responsible for the tremendous popularity this text has enjoyed with its readership.

Especially considering Fakirmohan's background as an extremely successful prose writer, it can be expected that the entertainment aspect is not to be neglected in the autobiography either; and indeed, we have a narrative centred on the hero's adventures and achievements, following him through friendship and deceit. Ironical descriptions of society with vivid true-to-life dialogues, combined with a certain dosage of moralistic clichés in character construction, provide solid ethical guidelines; detailed landscape and journey images are peppered with bits of exotica, wildlife, and suspense. All these devices certainly were bound to be irresistible to a predominantly urban readership. It is interesting to note that the first serialized publication of the autobiography commenced exactly with the chapters on the adventurous Bhuyan-*meli*: their dramatic content contained all elements of narrative craft that would have the readership ask for more. In an autobiography, when dealing with personal errors and failures, the conscious or subconscious forces of remembering and forgetting have to be reckoned with very carefully. Contrary to hagiographic villain-turned-saint biographies, the autobiographical writer has to deal with the resurgence of bad habits once shed, the loss of control once gained, bitter failure after initial success, disillusionment after enthusiasm, and the betrayal of close friends. Thus, the mood and mental disposition in which an autobiography is written sets the tone and the light in which different events are presented: sometimes with a complacent feeling of having secured one's place in life, and sometimes out of a position still entangled in personal and political turmoil. Here the autobiography becomes a public platform to set things straight, as it is often evident in Fakirmohan's narration.

Contested Receptions

The Keonjhar-chapters do not render a historical account of the Bhuyan-*meli*. Even after a gap of about 25 years between event and narration, emotions such as resentment, disappointment, envy and glee would have tinted the author's perspective. With a certain public status attained at the time of writing, Fakirmohan's image was consolidated in a desirable way. The inevitably inflated 'ego' in this autobiography might easily lead to the impression that the author indeed was at the centre of activity, attraction and influence: something that is hardly ever questioned in the reception of Fakirmohan's autobiography. The hagiographic stock of texts that seek to present Fakirmohan as the 'Father' of Oriya nationalism, the language movement, and just about anything new and modern in Oriya literary history,[4] extends to school textbooks. In these the chapters of the Bhuyan-revolt are reprinted especially, presenting the author as a hero who mastered even the most complicated situation. In an attempt to 'de-mystify' Fakirmohan, Biswamoy Pati thus rightly points out the vital role the former's writing played in conditioning 'upper-class/caste perception' about this event. Pati criticizes F.'s account of the revolt, which 'served to disguise the structure of exploitation with which the creative writer was involved (as the manager of the state)'[5] and denounces Fakirmohan's remarks about the tribes as matching 'with the general upper caste and colonial construction of the tribespeople and lower castes and outcastes'.[6] Pati, however, seems to be deceived by Fakirmohan's self-assigned importance, when he epitomizes him as the person responsible for the quelling of the

[4] See the impressive list of 'firsts' in entries of literary histories of Orissa: first short story, first novel, first autobiography, first travelogue, etc. One of the greatest hagiographers of Senapati is surely Mayadhar Mansinha, who in his biography of Senapati religiously goes by the 'facts' of the author's autobiography, re-narrating it in a fairy-tale like manner. The Bhuyan-episode reads even more adventurous here, with Senapati being propagated as the brave hero throughout (Mansinha 1976: 35). By romanticizing ('the labour boy writes books') and using wild projections ('unconscious disciple of Machiavelli'), he fabricates a mythical success story out of his life.

[5] Biswamoy Pati 2001,144.

[6] Ibid., 46.

revolt: in Pati's words, the Bhuyan *meli* 'was crushed by Fakirmohana (aided by the colonial forces)'. Sticking to the popular perception of 'heroes', the old one is now deconstructed by Pati, but only to be reconstructed in the person of Dharnidhara, who is presented by him 'as a precursor of those who fought against the combined might of the colonial and feudal order in the 1930s and the 1940s in Orissa'.[7]

Both hagiographers and de-mystifiyers unfortunately seem to be little concerned with their use of the autobiography as a historical source, be it by checking on the facts (i.e. how far Senapati was actually involved or even responsible in the proceedings), or the author's perspective (of grossly exaggerating his own importance in the events), or the textual situation of the description of the Bhuyan (as dramatic effects by pointed dialogues, underscoring the wittiness and superiority of the author), etc. Although the text serves as the primary source on the event, very little attention has been given to textual or contextual matters.

In this context of hero-worship it is interesting to note that a kind of parallel history has developed in Keonjhar since the 1980s, when a booklet by Naba Krishna Mohanto (Kavi Kumkuma) appeared. This booklet aimed to bring into the limelight Dharnidhara's virtues as opposed to the ruling forces embodied by Fakirmohan[8] and glorified until then. After a period of neglect and contempt, a wave of appraisal for the tribal son-of-the soil turned Dharnidhara into a local hero. Even the Keonjhar College was after him in 1982. Dharnidhara's *Jayanti*-celebrations are held annually to commemorate his birthday believed to have been on 5 May 1864,[9] involving considerable participation of politicians and bureaucrats who have the huge tribal vote bank in mind. In the laudable efforts to rehabilitate the public image of the tribal leader, we find Fakirmohan again positioned against Dharnidhara as *the*

---

[7] Ibid., 45.

[8] Perhaps the first to turn the attention towards Dharnidhara was Godavarish Mishra of the Satyavadi-School who had earlier written a ballad entitled 'Dharanidhara', in which D. attains the image of a hero who suffered under the British. Fakirmohan is just mentioned in one line as the Chief Dewan.

[9] He is said to have died on 19 April 1944 at Ai near Puri, where he had led a saintly life after his release from prison; he never returned to Keonjhar.

counterplayer in the revolt, and Fakirmohan in turn reduced to the position of the elitist and the representative of an oppressive force. It seems hardly to be of interest whether he was indeed the main opponent of Dharnidhara, who fought in the first place against the Maharaja of Keonjharh and the oppressive Asst. Manager Bichitranandan Das, and there too, not against the feudal system as such, but in order to replace the Raja on the throne.[10]

Against this background of contested histories, it becomes difficult to promote an antagonistic construction of the elitist versus the subaltern: Dharnidhara himself could be easily regarded as an elitist within his group, and Senapati, although he seeks to portray himself as a winner,[11] could be seen as a tragic figure serving under several masters, isolated and completely cut-off from any traditional group membership. Both can be regarded as border cases within their own surroundings; both show a bundle of complex loyalties to which they are committed. Both function as strong role models not because they are so typical of a particular community, but because each transgressed the traditional borders set up for him. They have become mobile, tolerant in religious matters, multilingual, and adjustable to other modes of living, but are rendered extremely vulnerable at the same time. The common factor is that of 'not belonging', of being migrants in a larger sense, who have to search for new definitions as to what set of ideas, ideals, and values they would subscribe to.

Raja, Rebel and Dewan

Before referring to the events as described in the Keonjhar-chapters, the historic administrational background will be sketched briefly in order to contextualize Fakirmohan's post of Manager (also Mantri or Dewan) as a key position which required expertise and diplomatic skill when dealing with the affairs of the respective estates, as well as a determined stand to ensure peace wherever unrest brewed or had already flared up. As the British laws and

---

[10] This view (of Fakirmohan) is challenged, too, at Keonjhar: it is claimed that Dharnidhara only fought for justice and was never interested in taking the throne (Sahu 2001).

[11] Mansinha consolidates this impression by repeatedly praising F.'s capacitiy of 'solving' serious problems involving a Raja and his subjects 'with dignity and fairness to all concerned' (Mansinha 1976, 31).

regulations could not be enforced in the Tributary states due to their independent status stated in 1804, the feudatory chiefs were free to run their internal administration as they liked.[12] However, the British authorities had their own way of controlling administrative and judicial systems in these kingdoms. The establishment of schools, the construction of roads and canals, and the introduction of the postal system and other means of communication slowly worked towards a closer networking between the directly administered British Orissa and the indirectly controlled feudatory states.[13]

The British had thus managed to create a wide range of opportunities for intervention in the internal administration of the feudatory chiefs (and in Fakirmohan's account we can study how the British never failed in their duty to have all the complaints and disputes brought before them duly 'solved'). One of the most effective measures, however, was the appointment of (British or 'native') Managers as mediating or executive agents to ensure adequate administration of the estates. By cleverly placing their men on these posts, they managed to 'secure a partisan at every Raja's court', as Beames put it.[14] However, when a Commissioner/ Superintendent came to know of outright misrule or mis-administration, there remained considerable latitude as to how his

---

[12] By the end of 1805, fifteen tributary mahals (garjats) were brought under control; in 1812 the annual tribute of Mayurbhanj as the sixteenth state was fixed. In 1862 adoption sanads were granted to the chiefs by Lord Canning. In 1874 the hereditary title of 'Raja' was conferred on them all. In 1882 the Calcutta High Court ruled that the Tributary Mahals of Orissa did not form a part of British India. (Patra/Devi 1983, 146).

[13] Technically, the Commissionership of the Orissa division included the district Balsore, Puri and Cuttack under direct British rule, and seventeen Tributary States each ruled by its own Raja under the general supervision of the Commissioner, who was also entitled *ex-officio* Superintendent of the Tributary States, an office created in 1814 by Governor-General Moira (Patra/Devi 1983, 22).

[14] 'Ravenshaw and his predecessors had in a great number of cases induced the Rajas to appoint as Mantri persons of their own choosing, and by selecting men who were natives of British territory and had in many instances served in our courts and offices, they secured a partisan at every Raja's court, and one, moreover, who could be relied to keep his Raja straight' (Beames 1984, 261).

decisions should be enforced on the feudal chiefs, as the Commissioner was actually confronted with the problem of exercising power while not being entitled to it. In nearly all cases, however, control could be eventually secured by sheer military force or threats of annexion.[15]

In this intricate game of favouritism and control, however, the British had to motivate the Oriya rajas, chiefs and zamindars to cooperate with them when dealing with the tribal population, as they relied largely on the mediation of their traditional agencies. On the other hand, the rajas and their 'native authority' were despised by the British, who regarded them as 'devoid of all mental culture, an abjectly degraded class'.[16] The attitude of favouring the 'noble savage' against the 'cunning Hindu' (or educated native)[17] was part of the self-declared position of the British as social redeemers and saviours of the oppressed from their own countrymen, an attitude which is apparent in Superintendent Toynbee's reactions as

---

[15] Beames sarcastically described this dilemma: 'He [the Commissioner] was directed to keep them [the Chiefs] on the paths of virtue by his "moral influence". Here was a strange problem and it was wonderful how it was solved.... The system in force when I took over in 1877 was as follows. The Rajas were allowed the general administration of their territories, but any of their subjects who felt himself aggrieved by any act of his Raja might appeal to the Commissioner, who asked for an explanation of the Raja, and finally decided what ought to be done and communicated his decision to the Raja. If the Raja had refused to obey, no one knew exactly what would have happened. But it was tacitly understood that he would not refuse and, as a matter of fact, he knew better than to do so. This is what is called "moral influence". When backed by bayonets it is a great power' (Beames 1984, 261).

[16] In the view of Captain John Campbell, who served in the Kandh tracts from 1836-54 (Mojumdar 1998, 18).

[17] As Bailey observes: 'The motives which led the Government to protect the Konds are clear. First there were the difficulties of conquest and subsequently the fear of uprisings. Later this motive receded in importance and became replaced by a vague idea that the Konds were somehow more deserving than Oriyas. This attitude is found in any alien colonialist Government: It is the distinction drawn between the "educated native" and the "noble savage".... People like the Konds were admired by Europeans for their manliness, their lack of subtlety, and for their avoidance of the forms of servility' (Bailey 1963, 182).

narrated in the Keonjhar-episode.[18] The superior task of promoting humanism and justice legitimized all efforts that the British made in order to end the malpractices of a feudal age, at least when practised by others.[19]

Within the coordinates sketched above, we have to study the scenario of the Bhuyan-revolt of 1891-2 as narrated in Fakirmohan's autobiography.[20] The main agents include a Maharaja (Dhananjoy or Dhanurjay Narayan Bhanja at Keonjhar Fort), a tribal leader (the Bhuyan Dharnidhara at Keonjhar), a British Superintendent (Toynbee at Cuttack); a Manager (Fakirmohan Senapati at Anandpur) and an Assistant Manager (Bichitranandan Das[21] at Keonjhar).

In view of the complicated chain of events, a short summary of the Keonjhar-chapters is necessary. The narration starts in the third year of Fakirmohan's posting as Manager in one section of Keonjhar at Anandpur, when Fakirmohan has to come to the rescue of the Maharaja who has fled his palace after being threatened by a revolt of the Bhuyan. Their popular leader Dharnidhara has rallied several tribals in protest against the cruel practices of the Asst. Manager during canal constructions. Fakirmohan, sent by the Raja to seek military assistance from Toynbee in Cuttack, has to face the latter's stiff resistance in supporting an exploitative feudal lord

---

[18] Beames sees himself as a revolutionary when it comes to the uplift of the peasants exploited by illegal extortions: 'We did our best to protect them [the poorer classes of the rural population], but a mere handful of foreigners in so large a country cannot even hear of many of the things that are done behind their backs.... Had we been properly supported, the movement would have grown into a great revolution which would have been fruitful of unspeakable good for the down-trodden agricultural population' (Beames 1984, 212-14).

[19] During road constructions in tribal tracts, which was looked upon as a means of disseminating 'the civilizing influence of a benevolent administration', the British used the agency of the Oriya *patros*, *bissoyis* and *paiks* to get the works executed by *bethi* (unpaid labour) of the tribals. This practice took root as it proved far more economical than bringing coolies from the plains, although still in 1875 it was without any formal government sanction (Mojumdar 1998, 59-62).

[20] Senapati 1993, 154-84.

[21] Not to be confused with the better known Bichitranandan Das, one of the highest officers under Ravenshaw and co-founder of the Cuttack Printing Company with Gaurishankar Ray.

'who would not listen'. F. has to argue in favour of the Raja, depicting him as the victim of the cruel and excitable tribals, before support is reluctantly promised. Circumventing Toynbee's unsatisfactory arrangements, further help is asked directly from the government at Calcutta by telegram and granted soon after. In the meanwhile, Fakirmohan and the Maharaja recruit the latter's sepoys at Anandpur, F. having the doubtful honour of leading the ragged militia towards the beleaguered Keonjhar Fort. Yet all attempts to counter the rebellion prove fruitless, and F. is captured by the Bhunyans. Their leader Dharnidhara, employed earlier as state surveyor at the Maharaja's court and therefore known to F., turns out to be rather cooperative and willing to re-employ F. as Manager. Pretending to agree to that proposal, F. eventually outmanoeuvres the tribal people with a trick and manages to get help from the British; the tribal leaders are sentenced to long imprisonment by Toynbee. The British summon the Maharaja to Cuttack and order F. to temporarily replace him. Finally the British decide that the Maharaja be reinstated at Keonjhar, assisted by Manager Wylly. F. is dismissed by the Maharaja and has to return home.

Equally complex are the relations and varied commitments of the protagonists: as we learn at the beginning of the chapter, the Maharaja is an educated and learned man who develops the efficient management of his territory, has temples restored and elaborate irrigation plans executed for the benefit of his subjects, but has no qualms about recruiting *bethi* (unpaid forced labour) from the tribal inhabitants. The rebel leader Dharnidhara is one of the first tribal men to study at the Survey School at Cuttack;[22] that, too, with a scholarship from the Maharaja who promotes him. Upon his return to Keonjhar, he is employed as surveyor at the court, but, inspired by ideas of equality and justice, soon informs Toynbee of the malpractices in the state. Toynbee, the representative of impartial justice, follows up the case with unconcealed sympathy for the tribal's claim, and seeks to oust the Maharaja in vain because of the orders of his superiors. Fakirmohan for his part, as a member of the educated coastal society, enjoys the confidence of

---

[22] In 1872-3, the Survey class was introduced in the Normal School of Cuttack and Zilla Schools of Balasore, Puri and Cuttack. A Survey School was opened at Cuttack in January 1876 with 12 students (Swain 1999, 304).

the British, but is first and foremost devoted to the royal family. Though committed to the principles of law and order, he interprets them in his own way to secure the welfare of his King, by whom he is, however, eventually sacked. The supervisor Bichitranandan Das makes the tribespeople toil in inhuman conditions on the construction of the Machakandana canal, but is described himself as a hard working and committed officer who seeks to impart his strict work discipline to others.

In the Service of the British

In this paper, Fakirmohan's relation to, and his view of, the British, the Raja, and the tribes is treated in separate sections, starting with the several encounters with the British we find narrated in that episode. It will be necessary to follow the narration of Senapati to a certain extent for an insight into the situation of speech, the narrative position, the situation of the conversation, and the partners involved. This close review shall be continued in regard to his relation to his royal master and, lastly, his encounter with the tribals, but not with the aim of fragmentizing the episode further into 'positions'. I aim rather to re-enact its many facets by referring to the 'small drama and fine details of social existence'[23] visible not only in the real event, but also reflected in its narration.

The first meeting with Toynbee takes place when F. reaches Cuttack alone, having left the Maharaja and Bichitranandan Das at Anandpur. After a short talk with his friend and advisor, Toynbee's Asst. Superintendent, Ray Nandkishore Das,[24] he meets Toynbee. The paragraph describing their conversation is presented as a masterpiece of diplomatic but stubborn persistence on F's side. Toynbee first explodes after listening to his pledge, and to F.'s amazement ('a highly placed person like him, pacing up and down the room out of control with anger') he utters abuses, calling the Maharaja a tyrant who will reap what he had sown, and declares that no help whatever will be given by the British. F. plays the humble card, advising Toynbee to check the Maharaja's behaviour

---

[23] Sarkar 1997, 94.

[24] Ray Nandkishore Bahadur Das was a close associate and had provided F. with references when he applied for the post of Manager at Keonjhar, as F. faced a financial crisis after he gave up his post as Dewan at Palalhada and returned to Balasore (Senapati 1993, 154).

in the files. He describes the violence as initiated by the Bhuyan tribe, who were of a wicked nature, with a tendency to infighting. He assures Toynbee that the Maharaja would be very much able to quell the revolt himself, but has sent him, Fakirmohan, out of a feeling of duty, to obtain Toynbee's permission and support in order to avoid bloodshed. The sight of a hundred constables would be sufficient to keep these wild people in check, for they are extremely stupid, drink excessively and get upset by trivial matters. Toynbee doesn't seem very impressed, but promises to write to the Superintendent of Balasore to arrange the needful.

In the present context, Fakirmohan's description of the Bhuyan as ugly and wild is part of a strategy to divert Toynbee's wrath to another object. Within the text, the dialogue enhances the drama of the situation and highlights the author's quick-wittedness. The textual situation is different from the contemplative or observing passages, where Fakirmohan reflects on the nature of certain tribes, examples of which can also be found. In the dialogue with Toynbee, Fakirmohan will of course be harping on all the prejudices the colonial concept of the 'barbaric tribal' has in store in order to achieve the desired support from him. Restoring peace and order was one of the main duties of his post as Manager. He had to keep the centre informed about the events in the outposts and to avoid bloodshed by a timely initiation of deterrent measures. His own view of the nature of the tribals was of no concern, nor had he anything to gain personally by arranging for military support: nobody could have blamed him had the situation really escalated.

In a renewed attempt, the Maharaja and Fakirmohan, now both at Cuttack, work out a different strategy with Toynbee's assistant, who advises them to send a telegram to the Lt. Governor and to the Chief Secretary [Cotton] at Calcutta to inform them about the state of affairs and ask for military support. In this telegram, the case is to be described as ordinary, and no emergency suggested. The Maharaja, who will have to meet Toynbee personally, is advised by Fakirmohan not to produce himself as a miserable case 'in dhoti and kamiz', but instead should behave firmly and unimpressed by the revolt, to counter the Saheb's opinion that he was a coward who had fled the scene. He is advised to 'dress properly': a tailor is engaged on the spot to prepare a decent outfit by evening. By then, F's old friend and supporter, the great lawyer Madhusudhan Das, arrives on the scene. The Maharaja is further advised to employ this experienced lawyer in the Keonjhar case, as F. foresees legal procedures will develop. When the Maharaja and F. appear before Toynbee the next morning, the latter reacts as expected, rebuking the Maharaja straight away for having left his wife and children unprotected in the Fort and fleeing like a coward, whereupon F. corrects him and remarks that the Fort is safe, well guarded and surrounded by loyal villages. This intervention incites Toynbee even more, and the conversation seems to stagnate, when a telegram of the Chief Secretary arrives in reply to the one sent the day before. Toynbee's former arrangement is cancelled, and instead orders are given that 'Dawson Saheb' will approach Keonjhar Fort via Chaibasa with 200 soldiers. F. and the Maharaja then travel back to Anandpur, where they start recruiting 300 soldiers in a great hurry, since the Maharaja is in fact greatly worried about the fate of his Fort.

In the account of the second meeting, Fakirmohan projects an image of himself as an emancipated player who knows the rules of the British system so well that he is able to employ or circumvent them for his own purposes. In a reversal of the real situation, Fakirmohan presents himself not as a timid subordinate, but as the one in control. If necessary, he outplays one against the other, as demonstrated here in his triumph over Toynbee who is rendered a rather sorry figure in the end: instead of the Raja, *he* is cleverly paraded as the true tyrant. The whole scene including the dialogues is highly entertaining with its fusion of authentic and fictitious matter, mixing facts with fiction in a tongue-in-cheek presentation, employing a Panchatantra-like narrative wit. Passages like these are prone to become extremely popular, as they provide peep-holes into the secret chambers of politics, allowing the general public an amusing view of the Sahebs stripped of all their assumed dignity and grace, and enabling them to have at least an imaginary victory over them. F. presents himself further as a perfect networker within his peer group of competent and influential Oriya officials and lawyers.

What is most striking in this episode is Fakirmohan's competence as an interpreter with a perfect knowledge of the code that has to be observed when dealing with the British. The Raja's plan of demonstrating submissiveness by falling to the feet and pleading for mercy, appropriate in the feudal context of hierarchic behaviour, is wisely rejected by F. because he knows how perfectly that would match the British perception of the wretched figures of the feudal system who are ruthless towards their subordinates but crouch in front of their rulers. Instead, a poised and composed attitude that downplays the whole event and strictly sticks to the facts is advised, in order to expose the Saheb's behaviour as carried away by emotions, anger, and personal favouritism. A witty effect is achieved by reversing the standard images of the native guided by instinct as against the 'rational' European.

Towards the end of the Keonjhar-episode, another meeting with Toynbee takes place after Fakirmohan has been intercepted and caught by the rebels, and finally released after the arrival of the promised government soldiers under Dawson and Guise. (Fakirmohan, however, manages to present his release as a result of his own clever strikes, referred to later). Dharnidhara and four other leaders are arrested and the rebels subdued. Toynbee arrives at Keonjhar after a long office tour via Calcutta and Chakradharpur and brings charges against them: of insurgence against a partner princely state of the government, and of the imprisonment of the highest government officer posted in the region. To prepare the case, F. is appointed as peshkar (one who assembles and produces the files), to be assisted by a sirishtedar (to write the report). When the sirishtadar proudly produces his voluminous write-up to the Maharaja, F. discards it with satirical remarks and decides to write the report himself. Since the subordinate is furious, and since there is only one hour left, F. quickly composes the report on the spot, boiling down the contents to the assignment of all guilt to the 'crazy Dharnidhara and the nature of the Bhuyan'. The Maharaja signs the manuscript, but when it is read out before Toynbee, the latter immediately identifies Fakirmohan as the author, and, raging with anger, threatens him with imprisonment because of this deceit.

In this affair, Fakirmohan obviously overstepped his competence, acting high-handedly towards the subordinate in order to press through his own version of the incident favouring the King. By openly opposing Toynbee with his unauthorized interference, he reveals how indispensable he considered himself, overacting on several fronts in the service of his King. The author's retrospective view is of course tinted by the later fall-out with the Raja, and perhaps this paragraph was meant to underscore how much he was ready to sacrifice for the Raja's good and how badly he was rewarded. He notes with resignation that in his effort to prove the

Raja without fault, he had attracted the wrath of the Saheb. In parentheses it is added[25] that this possibly was a scheme of Toynbee to prove the Maharaja's incompetence and then replace F. with his own friend Wylly as Manager. But, as F. is eager to note, in spite of Toynbee's wish, all witnesses confirmed that the revolt had indeed been incited by the Bhuyan. Toynbee then leaves with F. and the convicts for Anandpur, where he stops for a day and announces the verdict. Dharnidhara receives five years imprisonment, the others two.[26]

When the party arrives at Bhadrakh, an order from 'Latt Saheb' (Lt. Governor Sir Charles Elliot) is read out to Fakirmohan: A letter should be written on Elliot's behalf to the Maharaja, that he should leave Keonjhar Fort immediately and report at Cuttack. F. is made to write this letter; it is signed by Toynbee, who arranges also that Fakirmohan should accept the responsibility for Keonjhar Fort during the Raja's absence until Wylly arrives there from Mayurbhanj. From Bhadrakh, Toynbee leaves for Cuttack, Wylly for Baripada in Mayurbhanj, and F. for Keonjhar to await the Raja. The latter, already enraged by the rude letter written by Fakirmohan, is even more insulted by the arrangement and suspects F. of having schemed behind his back; he leaves for Cuttack nonetheless. After two weeks, Wylly takes over Fakirmohan's charge, and the latter leaves for Anandpur. In the meanwhile, the Maharaja is proved innocent by the highest lawyer of Utkal, Madhusudan Das of the charge put up by Toynbee. The Lt. Governor, Sir Charles Alfred Elliot, was to personally investigate the case at Keonjhar, but finally the case is decided in Cuttack itself, and the Maharaja is allowed to return to Keonjhar.

---

[25] It is mentioned in the text, that the content in parentheses did not appear in the serialized version of *Utkal Sahitya*, but only in the first edition of Fakirmohan's autobiography: only one of several discrepancies between the serialized version and later editions. Fakirmohan's son, Mohini Mohan Senapati, was mainly responsible for the edition of the autobiography, and is thought to have added and deleted quite a bit, which is especially critical since he was not on good terms with his father and even filed a legal case concerning a property dispute against him in 1909.

[26] Here, too, official accounts differ with F.'s details concerning dates, durations, locations and even the duration of the sentences, showing clearly that this text should not be perceived as a historical source.

What could be viewed as a final triumph for Fakirmohan turns out to be an anti-climax in all respects. In a last meeting with the Lt. Governor, who just 'greets him briefly', F. is again interrogated for 'five, six minutes' about the Bhuyan case by Sir Henry Cotton, the Chief Secretary. After that everybody returns to their respective workplaces. F., however, seems to be responsible to clear up the mess: he is to return the nineteen elephants Wylly had used to bring down his luggage from Keonjhar to Cuttack, as Wylly is now returning to Mayurbhanj. After that, he is to return to Anandpur, but only to await the Raja's return from Cuttack. On his way from Bhadrakh to Anandpur on an elephant back, F.'s mind is, in his own words, 'tormented by all kinds of worries', and he gets the idea to write a compilation of all writers and great personalities of Utkal, which should not be a simple listing, but made up as a literary text appealing to all. On the elephant back itself he writes his famous *Utkaḷ Brahmaṇaṃ* ('Travels in Utkal') which is then hastily given for composing and printing at Anandpur, to be completed within two days before the Raja arrives and F. has to leave the place for good.[27]

At the end of the episode, in spite of the success claimed, rejoicing is conspicuous by its absence in the narrative. The last meeting with the British seems to have been amazingly brief, there is no mention of praise, no certain recognition of Fakirmohan's endeavours, nor is any pity shown for his imprisonment by the tribal people: the British officers seem to be quite busy with other matters and in a hurry to get rid of the lingering Keonjhar problem.[28] That the last meeting was so short is also a hint that in F's autobiography the differences he had with Toynbee were slightly exaggerated, as was F.'s general role in the affair, especially his self-assigned merit of having 'terminated' the revolt

---

[27] B. Pati, in his attempt to produce Fakirmohan as a 'winner', states that Fakirmohan wrote *Utkaḷ Brahmaṇ* 'to celebrate his victory during the elephant ride back from Keonjhar' (Pati 2001, 45), which seems a little far fetched given the explicit mention of F.'s tormented mind and the rather unceremonious circumstances.

[28] The Maharaja was finally allowed to resume control over his state again; Wylly was deputed to manage the affairs and redress some of the grievances of the tribal people. By 1894, the Bhuyan and other tribals were reconciled to the authority of Maharaja Dhananjoy Bhanja (Patra/Devi 1983, 154).

and tricked Dharnidhara into surrender. Toynbee after all had trusted him well enough to appoint him as a caretaker during the absence of the Maharaja unless one considers this as a mean attempt to drive a wedge between two friends. As far as F's posting is concerned, that, too, is terminated by the Raja, as we learn from the next paragraph, and obviously the British did not think it appropriate to come up with any alternative offer. Whereas on the surface the case was solved and decided, F. finds himself in a void: deserted by the British, and despised by the Maharaja. The only farewell is a clandestine one from the people of Anandpur with whom F. states to have had a close relationship due to several reform measures he introduced.

The Dewan and his Royals

Fakirmohan's relations with his feudal masters as described in his autobiography are in nearly all cases problematic, even when they had started with goodwill and optimism. Towards the end of the Keonjhar-chapter, too, a long paragraph explains the souring of his cordial friendship with the Raja whom in an earlier paragraph he had praised warmly as a man who was 'remarkable in every aspect': hardworking and with a progressive broadminded orientation towards the welfare of his state, who kept his own library and subscribed to several journals. At Anandpur, he supported the construction of proper school buildings, installed a printing press, and provided scholarships to his subjects. For his part, F. took care of the new office, and in his spare time created a vegetable garden and an orchard, as he often did at his postings, to propagate a wider range of cultivation among the rural population.[29] All seems well and prospering in those idyllic surroundings. The good relation of F. to the Raja and his family appears comfortably settled on a broad base of common values, interests and perspectives. The 'dirty' aspects of exploitation remained well

[29] This fancy for gardening and horticulture as well as the frequent description of 'idyllic' spots at rivers or under trees (where one gathered for socializing and drinking in the evening) can well serve as typical aspects of a 'bourgeois' lifestyle, as dirctly opposed to a 'peasant consciousness'. In fact F. once amusedly narrates how he tried to convince peasants to eat the cabbage he had grown, and how it was returned by them complaining of the 'stench' that emanated from the cooking pots.

covered under the clean surface of administrational tasks and the indisputable duties in the name of development and progress. Generosity, kindness and mutual respect could be expected in this working relationship. One has to keep in mind that F. never experienced feudal rule from the perspective of a subject, but was dealing with the rulers on nearly equal terms.[30] His secure employment with the British administration saved him from fears of losing favour to a large extent, although the immediate conditions obviously were decided by the Raja.

Fakirmohan's attitude towards royalty was generally positive, especially considering the background of their common engagement for the cause of Oriya nationalism, the spread of education, and the promotion of printing presses and journals. The more liberal and educated section of royalty was quite substantially involved in the public proceedings of the Oriya language movement and was expected to patronize it also financially, which was a significant aspect since most of the prominent leaders like Gaurishankar Ray and Fakirmohan, had no resources at all.[31] Madhusudhana Das' engagement to act as advocate for the Maharaja of Keonjhar has to be seen within this overall climate of patriotic solidarity within the upcoming Oriya elite.[32]

However, far from nurturing a general uncritical inclination towards feudal lords and kings, Fakirmohan appears to be sarcastic

---

[30] Fakirmohan's account provides interesting details of a Dewan's duties: a major task consisted of survey works, in order to sort out quarrels between two rulers or between villagers and the Forest Department, and above all to assess the amount of taxable land for the ruler. Irrigation work and the building of roads and schools were other central concerns (cf. Senapati 1993, 126-49).

[31] G.N. Dash points out that already during the mutiny, feudal rulers were prominent leaders of revolts against the British, and that way Fakirmohan's generation had good reason to realize the need of the support of the kingship for the eventual ouster of the British. In the context of Oriya nationalism, he cites F.'s contact with patriotic individuals like the Mayurbhanj King Shri Ramchandra Bhanja and many others as one reason to believe in their vital role as well-wishers of the nation (G.N. Dash 1994, 16).

[32] A highly educated man of public spirit, he actually belonged to the liberal section of the Oriya movement which firmly believed that only by loyalty to the government would the aspirations for an amalgamation of the Oriya speaking tracts be fulfilled.

about his immediate employers, some of whom in their royal grandeur he describes as quite dismissive towards a subordinate like him, or others who were completely dependent on the views of their entourage.[33] In fact, most of the descriptions of his encounters with the Rajas in his autobiography contain details about how they filled their coffers with money extracted from their subjects, while at the same time neglecting the affairs of the state, completely absorbed in disputed border and succession issues. F., however, nowhere calls for organized civil unrest, the dissonances he describes appear restricted to the personal level and nowhere do his critical observations lead to fundamental criticism. On the contrary, a largely unshaken confidence in the traditional set-up is apparent, failures being assigned to wrong individual decisions or the lack of co-ordination and far-sightedness, paired with the conviction that for every problem a rational solution can be found if it is tackled with persistence, discipline, and a sense of 'justice'. In spite of critical, even cynical remarks and descriptions of the feudal order, the time for large-scale *revolt* is far away, the field for *reforms* appearing vast and challenging enough.

It is interesting that a paragraph in the autobiography describing the origin of the revolt comes amazingly close to Toynbee's version: that the Maharaja's methods of exploiting the tribals had indeed been the main reason for the unrest. This ambiguity may be due to the author's disenchanted view of his erstwhile friend at the time of writing. He manages, however, to divert the blame to Bichitranandan Das, who had, in his view, allowed the situation to escalate by making the people slave without providing food, and had punished inadequate work with severe beatings.[34] Here,

---

[33] See for example the description of the Raja of Daspalla, who is ridiculed as the megalomaniac incarnate, full of quaint ideas and baseless pride, obsessed with his phantastic outfits, pompous jewellery and queer eating habits. At another posting at Dompada, F. describes the Raja as a cultured man with a knowledge of Sanskrit and English, who was however too simple-minded and so lazy that he left the administration completely to others. As in the former case, F.'s services were terminated, and here, too, he uses the autobiography to declare himself 'innocent', rectifying certain allegations made against him.

[34] This view comes close to the version of the local history at Keonjhar, according to which mainly Bichitranandan Das, a somewhat shady character with 'black spots' in his career, is blamed for having instigated the King against Dharnidhara and the Bhuyan, as B. Das was

Fakirmohan also seeks to prove his own innocence when mentioning that the Raja refused his initial cost plan of the canal work, calculated on the basis of paid labour, and instead opted for the cheaper version of forcibly recruiting tribal people. He also emphasizes that his responsibility rested with the Anandpur section, and that he had no control over the Keonjhar part. Typically, he expresses a certain concern for the hapless tribals and even justifies their anger, but the general system of forced and unpaid labour is not categorically questioned. It appears, in his view, that an escalation of the situation could have been surely avoided by a 'more human' treatment of the tribals.

Apart from that paragraph, Fakirmohan is eager to demonstrate his absolute loyalty to the King throughout the whole event. When captured by the Bhuyan, he states that he was never afraid for his own life and family, and only feared for the safety of the Maharaja's family. All the more amazing seems the decline of the friendship described towards the end of the Keonjhar chapter. Officials and subordinates are accused by Fakirmohan as the main culprits, who spread rumours and made the Raja in Cuttack believe that Fakirmohan was ultimately responsible for the Raja's removal from the throne. And so this episode ends as several others before: Fakirmohan's services are terminated by the Raja on somewhat disgraceful grounds, and he uses his autobiography to clear disputed facts in order to prove himself innocent and a victim of narrow-minded and scheming rivals.

Fakirmohan's postings as Manager in the Tributary Mahals almost regularly end with his more-or-less disillusioned retreat to his home town and family. But symptomatic for this episode of disintegrating traditional contexts, this last stronghold (however frail it might have been in his case) had given way in the meanwhile, too: Fakirmohan bemoans the fact that during his absence his joint family had split up, and the property had been divided into three parts.

---

facing tribal fury. According to the Keonjhar-version, the whole revolt to topple the King was an invention by B. Das, who biased the King with the rumour that Dharnidhara was claiming his throne, psychologically using the King's fear of impending revolt. On B. Das' accusation, Dharnidhara's brother was arrested and tortured, in order to intimidate the incited tribals, and only then the latter united in revolt under Dharnidhara (Sahu 2001).

Living with the Rebels

Fakirmohan's relation to the Bhuyan and to Dharnidhara is obviously marked by a considerable distance in his narration. The description of his encounter with the Bhuyan and of the days spent in their captivity seems to be the one most prone to fictitious embellishment and imaginative self-projection, tinted by an obviously still smouldering grievance. Generally there seems to be little or no space for the tribal inhabitants within F.'s concept of Oriya society, unless they were educated and integrated into the circle of useful and cooperative members, or function at the lowest level as readily available workforce. Other passages in the autobiography that mention contact with tribals are rare and are characterized by an almost 'Western' interest in the exotic.[35] Interestingly, the Keonjhar chapter itself opens with the quotation of a Santal song which describes the fun of drinking and when food is seasonally available, without caring too much for the rest of the year. The song is quoted by Fakirmohan since he considers this spendthrift and carefree nature as very appealing and akin to his own behaviour.[36]

In the Keonjhar episode, Fakirmohan's actual encounter with the Bhuyan starts on his way to Keonjhar Fort, when he reaches Ghatgram after an arduous night trek with his ragged army of aging and ailing sepoys. Betrayed by his spies, who turn out to be villagers collaborating with the Bhuyan, the army is ambushed by the rebels, and Fakirmohan is presented before Dharnidhara, the leader. Fakirmohan is asked to prostrate himself at the feet of the rebel leader, but he refuses to do so since 'Dharnidhara had been working under me'.[37] Fakirmohan narrates at this point how

---

[35] His description of a Kol settlement reminds one of a foreign anthropologist's report. The Kol are introduced to the readership with scientific details about their settlements, festivals, body features etc. A visit to their homes where F. questions them about all kind of religious habits ends in mutual amusement about the quaint behaviour of the other. (Senapati 1993, 34).

[36] The context here is that Fakirmohan had left on his own will his former job at Palalhada, but after spending all his financial resources in no time, had to apply for the post as Manager of Keonjhar.

[37] The fact that Dharnidhara was indeed junior to him and employed in a similar status to both the Managers Senapati and B. Das obviously

Dharnidhara had been educated at the Survey School at Cuttack[38] and, after working for a short time in his profession, started to accuse the Raja of atrocities and exploitation. He had returned from Cuttack with the self-assigned title 'The (adopted) son of the Queen',[39] with the aim of bringing justice to the region. Dharani, as opposed to the other tribal leaders and especially his elder brother,[40] is depicted as co-operative and forthcoming. Due to their earlier common background at work, he obviously behaves towards Fakirmohan as a colleague rather than a hostage, with no signs of hatred or brutality, at least in F.'s description. In fact, within the 'wild' world of the tribal leader's camp, Dharani appears to have been Fakirmohan's only guarantee for a rational, generous and civilized behaviour. His revolutionary concepts are explicitly not based on looting, dacoity and bloodshed, but are rooted in the same consensus on justice, equality and welfare Fakirmohan would

---

was the source of much resentment. Keonjhar history tells that Dharni was made to sit on a mat in the office by B. Das, since a tribal was not to occupy a chair (Sahu 2001).

[38] Dharnidhara studied not only on a scholarship of the Maharaja, but was also allowed to live in the Raja's city residence at Cuttack (Senapati 1993, 169). The need for trained survey workers is evident from the fact, that in 1872, a Survey Class was introduced in the Normal School of Cuttack and Zilla Schools of Balasore, Puri and Cuttack. A Survey School was opened at Cuttack in January 1876 with twelve students (Swain 1999, 304).

[39] This again is a much contested issue. Keonjhar history has it that Dharnidhara was in fact the adopted son of the Queen of Keonjhar, i.e. the wife of Dhananjoy Bhanja. He was brought up in the palace and is said to have been favoured since childhood on the basis of his intelligence, wisdom and handsome features ('tall and fair') (Sahu 2001). G.N. Dash however presents several sources to confirm that this title was used by Dharnidhara with reference to Queen Victoria (G.N. Dash 1994, 18). Fakirmohan too refers to the latter meaning when he makes fun of the Bhuyan who were 'naive enough to believe in Dharnidhara's tale of a Queen who ruled the whole world from Cuttack, and had adopted Dharnidhara, since she was angry with the Raja of Keonjhar' (Senapati 1993, 172).

[40] Dharnidhara's elder brother Gopal, who was the military leader of the rebels, is in fact depicted as the prototype of the barbaric tribal, with bloodshot eyes, 'as much cruel as stupid'. Fakirmohan mentions that he had seen him just six months before in jail, heavily chained and guarded (Senapati 1993, 168).

subscribe to. Here too, however, Fakirmohan puts it to his own credit that the dangerous situation could be converted into a sober work-relationship by presenting himself as a public servant with absolutely no designs in this whole confrontation, who would continue his services under the new 'regime' as before.

As the employee-to-be and hostage of Dharnidhara, Fakirmohan was of course not to question the legitimacy of the new incumbent. But for the readership, he inserts a paragraph presenting Dharnidhara's claim to the throne as part of the world order of the Bhuyan, who consider it their right to make or unmake their king, as they were the original inhabitants of Keonjhar. In Fakirmohan's view, this was a 'false belief', a 'misconcept' and a 'strange idea'. As he writes, the Bhuyan of Keonjhar had found it difficult to communicate with their then far-away capital in Mayurbhanj. So they abducted a child from the royal family of Mayurbhanj with the aim to install him on 'their' throne at Keonjhar. Having no horses or elephants for the crowning ceremony, two people had to serve as substitutes for the king to sit on, and one subject was symbolically killed by a strike of his sword. And, as F. concludes, 'this show is kept up until the present day'.[41]

By ridiculing the Bhuyan claim to the throne in this way, the origins of the revolt appear, in Fakirmohan's depiction, largely confined to the tribal uprising during the Machakandana canal construction. Considering the historical developments that anteceded the revolt, however, it becomes evident that the events of 1891-2 were a continuation of a long smouldering discontent of the Bhuyan, where all features of former uprisings seem to resurface—be it the capture of the Dewan by rebels, the Raja's appeal for help to the British, or the differences in government assessment of the situation. When rendering the Bhuyan 'tale' of the captured heir of

[41] There exists indeed a practice reaching back to the eleventh century when the Bhuyan abducted the brother of the Mayurbhanj heir from Jatipur and installed him as their king at Keonjhar because of the distance to Baripada. At the coronation ceremony the prince used to sit on the back of a Bhuyan, demonstrating the acceptance of the Bhanja-prince by the Bhuyan.

The traditional close relation of the Bhuyan to the Rajas of Keonjhar is evident, e.g. in their involvement with the major festivals of the state, such as the *Rath Yatra*, where they alone are entitled to supply the ropes and the wood for the chariot, etc.

Mayurbhanj, Fakirmohan only vaguely refers to a background of disputed secession to the throne of Keonjhar that had in fact led to widespread disturbances immediately after Dhananjoy had taken over the administration of Keonjhar in 1861.[42] After a provisional settlement between the rival parties mediated by Ravenshaw, the tribal sardars of the Bhuyan, Kol, and Juang headed by Ratna Naik rose in insurrection against Dhananjoy, and in 1868, attacked and plundered Keonjhar and even carried off the Dewan, whom they killed soon after. The Raja appealed to the government for help, and finally a police force under Dr. Hayes was sent to suppress the uprising.[43] As Hayes was not able to persuade the rebels to release their hostages, regular troops moved into the state. But the British had to suffer plundering and attacks on their camps. More troops were sent from Chaibasa. Finally Ravenshaw arrived at Keonjhar and assumed direct charge, quelling the revolt with military expeditions in all directions. There was a trial of the rebel leaders, and Ratna Naik and three of his associates were hanged at Cuttack;

---

[42] When the Maharaja of Keonjhar died childless in 1861, the two rival claimants to the throne were the Raja's concubine's son, Dhananjoy, and the grandson of the Maharaj of Mayurbhanj, Brundaban. It was claimed by the Dewan and his followers that the Raja had wanted Dhananjoy as his successor; the dowager queen on the other hand insisted that the Raja had adopted Brundaban before his death, and soon she was supported by the Bhuyan in her claim. After a thorough enquiry, Ravenshaw, however, decided in favour of Dhananjoy. The Rani filed petitions upto to the High Court and the Privy Court in London, but lost her case. Dhananjoy came of age in 1861 and was handed over the administration of Keonjhar (Patra/Devi 1983, 149). Interestingly, all of Fakirmohan's irrational loyalty to Dhananjoy and his disparaging remarks on the Bhuyan's claim fall in line with Ravenshaw's initial decision to install Dhananjoy as the 'right' successor on the throne.

[43] Ravenshaw's assessment, that the revolt was due to an instigation by the dowager Queen was not shared by the Commissioner of Chotanagpur, who attributed the rising to the oppression of the (later abducted and murdered) Dewan of Dhananjoy Bhanja. When finally Hayes, the deputy Commisioner of Singhbhum, was deputed to Keonjhar by the government, he indeed found widespread opposition against Dhananjoy, in which not only the tribal people but also caste Hindus had joined (Patra/Devi 1983, 150).

twenty-seven rebels were transported for life. Lt. Johnstone remained in Keonjhargarh to reorganize the administration of Dhananjoy. The Machakandana-dam revolt in 1891 thus appears as only the last spark to rekindle the Keonjhar People's Movement, now led by Dharnidhara, said to be the grandson of Ratna Naik.[44] This view, as mentioned above, is contested in local history where Dharnidhara is presented as a victim of the scheming Bichitranandan Das' instigation of the King, who, against the historical background, may have been all too ready to believe rumours about an impending revolt.

Although in one dialogue in Fakirmohan's text, Dharnidhara develops his ideas of people's rule, such as the officials working without salary in his state (which is of course immediately rejected by his employee Fakirmohan) and no rent to be levied on the subjects, he is presented as showing a strong inclination to keep up princely darbars and a god-like status. In F.'s description, he is worshipped by village women with elaborate pujas and feet-washing ceremonies, whereas F. himself, all enlightened citizen, strictly refuses to be venerated in a similar way. Also Dharni's self-assigned title 'Adopted Son of the Queen' provides a certain evidence that he was readily accepting the royal hierarchy (be it Queen Victoria or the Queen of Keonjhar) by suggesting a hereditary legitimization to the post. He seemed, however, to have firm faith in the British government, as he, before his revolt, had initially sought the way of legal assistance. It is evident from government documents[45] that Dharnidhara wrote to Superintendent Toynbee on 23 January 1891 in the name of the oppressed subjects, with a copy to the Mayurbhanj Manager Wylly and the Government of Bengal. Toynbee sent this letter to the Maharaja of Keonjhar on 3 February 1891 asking for an explanation. On 12 February 1891 the Maharaja sent a reply denying the charges. Instead, he accused Dharnidhara of inciting rebellion. The Maharaja therefore requested the approval of an arrest warrant he had issued. On 17 February

---

[44] As per a report in *Sambalpur Hitaishini* of 10 June 1891 (Dash 1994, 27). This belief, too, is discarded at Keonjhar as a malicious attempt to link Dharnidhara to rebel activities.

[45] G.N. Dash 1994, 27-8.

1891 Toynbee rejected the warrant and warned the Maharaja to be cautious in this matter.[46] By May 1891 the situation had escalated.

Dharnidhara's confidence in the British system is further demonstrated by his eventual voluntary surrender to Dawson. Dawson writes that when they encountered Dharni he was riding on an elephant he had taken from the Maharaja, but that he immediately dismounted and handed over his sword. Then he was surrounded by guards and captured[47] In Fakirmohan's narration, however, he himself had convinced Dharnidhara that the British troops 'had come to salute the new Raja' and he should welcome them. On Fakirmohan's advice, he dressed in fancy clothes and equipped with an old mare to enhance his royal status. Then he was 'sent off', in Fakirmohan's description a Don Quixote-like figure. A gleeful report of his arrest follows, which F. somehow managed to watch from far away. From the profusion of discrepancies between Fakirmohan's version and official records in this small example it can be estimated to what degree the author's perspective distorted and twisted the events in order to present himself as the hero in the whole affair.

---

[46] The Maharaja had perhaps not provided Fakirmohan with the full history of the case before sending him to Toynbee, otherwise Fakirmohan would not have been so surprised 'that Toynbee seemed to be somehow informed about the case'. In that case, Fakirmohan in all his self-proclaimed cleverness would appear himself a tragic figure, ridiculed by being sent straight into the lion's cage without being entrusted with all the relevant details. It seems however more probable that Fakirmohan was well aware of the state of affairs (given his close relation to the Assistant Superintendent), yet did not want to include these details in his autobiography.

[47] Report quoted in Dash 1994, 29-30. The fact that Dharni surrendered on his own is further confirmed by a report in *Utkal Dīpikā* on the trial of Dharnidhara, mentioning that Toynbee acknowledged Dharni's 'surrender without waging war' in his favour. *Utkal Dīpikā* also mentions Toynbee's acknowledgement of Dharni's restriction from dacoity, looting or torture, as well as his 'general good conduct'. Gaurishankar Ray suggests that had Dharni visited Toynbee personally after his letters got no response, perhaps nobody could have blamed him at all for what he did. *Sambalpur Hitaiṣinī* of 22.7.1891 refers to the judicial consideration, in which Dharni was found 'not morally guilty, but legally guilty' by the British, a rather artificial judicial construct (Dash 1994, 31).

In the paragraphs dealing with his imprisonment Fakirmohan describes how he managed to settle himself comfortably as the indispensable 'wise minister', who advises the tribes, presented as easy-to-convince hillbillies, in all state affairs and cunning war strategies. Here, too, Fakirmohan appears to be completely in control of the situation, as he even manages to delay the impending attack of the rebels on the fort with his clever rhetoric, successfully playing for time since he knows the British troops must be on their way. As the only educated man in the wilderness, he has to read out letters sent by the approaching British (which appears strange in view of Dharni's educational accomplishments, which were technically even higher than F.'s own!). A further proof of Fakirmohan's superior intelligence is provided with the often quoted story of the famous 'coded letter' that he sent home, asking for 'betel nuts and pan' in disguise for 'soldiers and weapons'. First, the 'code' seems to be rather bland and could have hardly deceived Dharnidhara. Second, if the story is true and not grossly inflated,[48] the letter would have done little to speed up the troops that eventually arrived from Chaibasa and captured Dharnidhara.

Given the apparently fair way he was treated by Dharnidhara, Fakirmohan himself turns out in his own depiction to be a shabby traitor who feels comfortable lying and deceiving, and making fun of the one who (as he writes) trusted him completely. Fakirmohan's resentful attitude towards Dharnidhara, which is based on moral accusations (he had proven unworthy of all the educational efforts that went into him, misused his good connections to the British, and schemed against the Maharaja who had been his erstwhile mentor),

[48] Also Biswamoy Pati takes the letter-story as a further proof in his endeavour to depict F. as the one responsible for the final 'triumph': 'Fakirmohana was the manager of the state at that time and led the anti-insurgency operations, under the aegis of the colonial government. He had sent a coded message asking for help...' (Pati 2001, 144). Mansinha's 'letter'-version of course is unsurpassed in exaggerating even F.'s own version: 'Fortunately for all, the authorities could correctly decipher Senapati's code-message ... and one fine morning, not long after, young pretender Dharnidhara with his cohorts was captured by the troops in a sudden swoop on his hideout. Sentenced to long years of imprisonment, young Bhuyan Dharnidhara's dream of being the Maharaja of Keonjhar was shattered for ever' (Mansinha 1976, 37).

thus loses credibility in view of his own rather flexible interpretation of values such as honesty, responsibility, or gratitude.

Conclusion

The conflict between the British, the Maharaja and the tribal people unfolds in the narration of Fakirmohan as a complex affair where multi-layered motives and commitments of each of the respective partners have to be considered. The players in the game themselves hold a contested position within their own group, where they are rather situated at the periphery, yet remain largely bound to their respective traditional group identities. Here the consensus on bourgeois values works as the major levelling and integrating force between and beyond. In Fakirmohan's description it appears that the process of a new orientation towards humanist values had caught on in more or less all sections of society, between the royals, the tribal leader, the British officer, and the Oriya administrator, notwithstanding the reality of exploitation, high-handedness and brutal control. Amongst those adopted, equality and justice seem to be the values most widely internalized. Even if doubted or severely criticized in singular decisions, the faith in these mobilized not only the Raja and his officer, making 'justice' appear as the biggest boon the British had eventually to offer—at least on the surface.[49] We have also seen how the Oriya elite, like the tribal leaders, had to some extent worked their way into the legal system of the British in order to effectively interfere with their supreme judicial control.

---

[49] In the fictional work of Fakirmohan, we find an outspoken concern for the discrepancy between 'the law' and what he considers to be 'justice'. Beames' satirical description of the law enforcement process reflect a similar scepticism: 'The difficulty lies not in the laws and rules that are promulgated but in getting them carried out.... The Act is printed and copies are sent to all the Collectors and other officers.... The native lawyers are as sharp as needles and very soon tear the heart out of it.... The rural masses, of course, neither know nor understand a word of it. So then cases are instituted in the courts and appealed and appealed till they reach the High Court.... These decisions are printed and published as 'rulings'. So that before long, there are two laws.... Then a new law has to be passed to rectify this error.... It *has* happened within my experience that the High Court has sat on the amended act and observed that 'the law as now amended implies that two and two make six'! (Beames 1984, 243-4).

In spite of his progressive outlook, Fakirmohan's view reveals a strong commitment to traditional hierarchies. Although his vision comprised path-breaking social, religious or educational reforms, he did not target either the colonial or the feudal system, and largely restricted his criticism to incongruities and malpractices. Though he propagated a strong belief in the power of the people's culture, he was still far away from a 'people's movement', that would have aimed at overturning existing patterns of power. His position towards the tribals in this particular episode shows him as an officer well aware of his rank and tasks towards his subordinates.

Last, it is interesting to note how far the autobiographical self-projection of having been an important player in the game matched with the self-esteem of an upcoming and rapidly extending bourgeoisie. His appropriation as a 'hero' in public memory (or in the subaltern perspective as the 'villain') seemed to have worked out exactly as intended in his own writings that propagated his importance not only during the quelling of the revolt, but within the whole social and administrational hierarchy. In public memory it is of little importance that he obviously played a rather insignificant role in the view of his royal and colonial masters. What renders him a prototype of the new citizen is the belief in his individual competence to bring about change, the belief that mankind could eventually gain control over the whims and odds of providence. With his ambivalent and wavering position, his dislocated, migratory and uprooted existence, his struggle for education, public recognition and influence, he mirrors a section of society which eventually became the leading force in shaping the Oriya consciousness in the twentieth century—a readership which appreciated its mirror image perhaps the most for the ironical glimpses that allowed an amused smile at itself.

References

Bailey, F.G. 1963. *Politics and Social Change: Orissa in 1959*, Berkeley, University of California Press.

Beames, J. 1984. *Memoirs of a Bengal Civilian*, Delhi: Manohar.

Boulton, J.V. 1993. *Phakirmohan Senapati: His Life and Prose Fiction*, Bhubaneswar: Orissa Sahitya Akademi.

Cobden-Ramsay, L.E.B. 1982 ([1]1910). *Feudatory States of Orissa*, Calcutta: Firma KLM Private Limited.

Dash, G.N. 1994. 'Phakirmohan o Dharnidhara', in *Gokarnika* October-December, 15-34.

Mansinha, M. 1962. *History of Oriya Literature*, Delhi: Sahitya Akademi.

— 1976. *Fakirmohan Senapati*, Delhi: Sahitya Akademi.

Mojumdar, K. 1998. *Changing Tribal Life in Orissa*, Delhi: Kaveri Books.

Mohanty, N. 1982. *Oriya Nationalism. Quest for a United Orissa: 1866-1936*, Delhi: Manohar.

Pati, B. 2001. *Situating Social History: Orissa (1800-1997)*, Delhi: Orient Longman.

Patra, K.M. and Bandita Devi. 1983. *An Advanced History of Orissa (Modern Period)*, Delhi: Kalyan Publishers.

Pradhan, S. (ed.). 1999. *Orissan History, Culture and Archaeology*. Reconstructing Indian History and Culture, no. 16, Delhi: D.K. Publishers.

Praharaj, D.M. 1988. *Tribal Movements and Political History in India: A Case Study from Orissa, 1803-1949* (Tribal Studies of India Series T 127), Delhi: InterIndia Publications.

Sahu, Janmjay. 2001. Interview with Historian Prof. Janamjay Sahu, Dharnidhara College Keonjhar, on 19 November 2001 at Keonjhar.

Sarkar, S. 1997. *Writing Social History*, Delhi: Oxford University Press.

Senapati, F. 1993. *Ātmajīvancarita*, Delhi: National Book Trust. [Fakirmohan]

Swain, A. 1999. 'British Impact on Orissa in the Nineteenth Century', in S. Pradhan (ed.), *Orissan History, Culture and Archaeology*, 299-314.

Two Bachelors of Arts. 1996 ([1]1919). *The Oriya Movement: Being a Demand for a United Orissa*, Bhubaneswar: Pentacle Printers.

18

Marginal Texts, Marginal Men: The Social Mobility Movement of the Kudmi-Mahantas of Orissa

Chandi Prasad Nanda*

The aim of this paper is to focus on the nature of 'consciousness' in a community. What one finds in this 'consciousness' is not only explicit defiance of authority but also a considerable degree of 'submissiveness and reverence' in the collective mentality of an oppressed and marginalized community.[1] This essay looks at these contradictory tendencies associated with popular consciousness by focussing on two texts, a biography of Niranjan Mahanta (1872-1957) and an autobiography of Siba Prasad Mahanta (1903-85) of Bhanjakia village in the Panchapidha subdivision, Mayurbhanj, Orissa. The reading of these non-official sources helps us overcome silences in the history of Mayurbhanj.[2] More importantly, a critical reading of these manuscripts points to the strategies adopted by a 'low caste' like the Kudmi–Mahantas in defining its social identity through community activism and the overall agrarian and

---

* I am grateful to the Charles Wallace (India) Trust and in particular F.H. Taylor for the award of fellowship which enabled me to consult materials pertaining to my ongoing research on nineteenth century Orissa in the India Office Library, London during 1999. Moreover, I have benefited from the valuable comments of Hermann Kulke, Georg Pfeffer, Biswamoy Pati and Georg Berkemer while finalizing this paper. I am also grateful to Bikash Barik and Murali Mahanta for their generous help during my field tour in Mayurbhanj.

[1] Work on similar themes can be seen in Sarkar 1989; Bhadra 1992.

[2] The present district of Mayurbhanj, formerly a princely state (finally merged with the Orissan province in January 1949) is bounded in the north by the Singhbhum district of Bihar and Midnapore of West Bengal, in the south by the districts of Balasore and Keonjhar of Orissa, in the east by the Midnapore and Balasore districts and in the west by the districts of Keonjhar and Singhbhum.

nationalist politics.[3] Being a Kudmi-Mahanta, Siba Prasad's autobiography in particular brings out his perceptions of society and religion. It reflects on his activities as a Gandhian nationalist and on the spread of Congress ideology in the princely state of Mayurbhanj. More significantly, it talks of his life and struggle to assert his community identity by challenging, overpowering, and disrupting the 'hegemonic symbolic order'.[4]

II

It is noteworthy that the Kudmi-Kshatriyas of Mayurbhanj, who were primarily enumerated as a tribe in the colonial census, migrated from Midnapur, Singhbhum, Keonjhar and Manbhum during the nineteenth century.[5] The reason was the 'attraction of the fertile valley in the inaccessible tracts of Simlipal forest zone'.[6] The Kudmis were often seen as *hatuas* (traders) by the original inhabitants of Mayurbhanj. The latter, however, primarily included Santhals, Bhumijas, Kols, and Hos, who were also called the *deshlog*. The *deshlog* considered the Hindu Sudras and the Kudmis to be usurpers who had acquired and settled the lands belonging to them. On the other hand, the Kudmis were treated as 'low castes', to be bracketed along with the other tribal people, in the perception of the Hindu upper castes. Thus being pushed to the margins of Hindu society, and socially distanced from the tribal people, the Kudmis sought to redefine their identity by claiming and asserting a Kshatriya status. This process assumed momentum in the early twentieth century, but grew more radical under the spell of nationalist politics and Gandhian ideological discourse.

We have ample references to the Mahanta-Santhal divide in the colonial records of 1851, 1866, and 1910 in the wake of successive

---

[3] Mahato 2000; Samaddar 1998. Samaddar treats 'community activism, agrarian politics and the nationalist movement in one single discourse to reconstruct the history of the region' (ibid., 163).

[4] Saurabh Dube 1993.

[5] Dalton 1973; Risley 1891. Dalton categorizes the Kurmis as an agricultural tribe and assigns to them a high status amongst the Hindu Sudras caste. Risley refers to the Kurmis as a very large cultivating caste of upper India, Behar, Chotanagpur and Orissa.

[6] Senapati, Sahu 1967 (Mayurbhanj *Gazetteer*), 101-2.

famines and droughts.[7] In fact, during the devastating famine of 1866-7, the *deshlog* of Bamanghaty in Mayurbhanj often raided and plundered the houses of the Kudmi-Mahantas. This was because the latter were agriculturists and traders who stored agricultural produce and lent paddy to the *deshlog,* However, what one also discerns is the solidarity between the *deshlog* and *hatuas* in the face of the oppressions of the survey and settlement staff.[8] In fact, the officiating superintendent of the Tributary Mahals of Orissa, T.E. Ravenshaw, did not talk about 'drought' and 'famine' as the cause of the 'disturbance' of 1866. Instead, he attributed it to 'the attempt to introduce a settlement and assessment of lands by measurement, which was largely characterized by misconduct and oppression of Raja's subordinate officials and lack of proper enquiry'.[9] This shows that both *deshlog* and *hatuas* found common cause to be united against the oppressive officials, perhaps along the lines of class.

Thus what one can witness is a Santhal-Mahanta solidarity co-existing with the recurring pattern of a Santhal-Mahanta divide. As the oppression of the survey and settlement officials had been going on for several years, it was quite likely that Ravenshaw located the cause of such 'disturbances' in the above-mentioned factors. The solution to the problem, from the colonial standpoint, was to blame the Maharaja of Mayurbhanj for his lack of good governance and control, and the subsequent handing over of Bamanghaty to the Deputy Commissioner of Singhbhum, an arrangement that lasted for twelve years. However, the rule of Maharaja Sriramchandra Bhanjadeo from 1890-1912 is often remembered by the populace as the phase when several measures for the social and economic development of the state took place. Sriramchandra's death in 1912

---

[7] Ibid., 75-6; Samaddar 1998. The following records and report pointedly bring out the issue of the Mahanta Santhal conflict. 'Hostility between the people of Bamanghaty and the Raja of Mayurbhanj, April 1866'; 'Deposition of Moochiram Mahato in the court of Deputy Commissioner of Singhbhum, 27 March, 1866'; 'T.E. Ravenshaw's (Officiating Superintendent of Tributary Mahals) report to the Secretary, Govt. of Bengal, 28.04.1866'; *Records on Government of Bengal (Political Deptt)*, April 1866, Orissa State Archives, Bhubaneswar.

[8] Senapati, Sahu, *op. cit.*

[9] *Report* of T.E. Ravenshaw, *op. cit.*

was followed by the rule of Purnachandra Bhanjadeo. As the king was a minor, the state was kept under the administration of the Court of Wards.[10]

It was during this administration that the Santhal-Mahanta solidarity witnessed a vigorous expression in the course of a peasant movement known as *medi* (*meli*, unity) which surfaced in Mayurbhanj during 1917.[11] The immediate context of this popular protest was the attempt by the Government to recruit tribal people to raise a labour corps for the army in France during World War I. The peasants, who had earlier allowed themselves to be recruited as coolies for tea gardens in Assam, now mistrusted the move to transport them across the seas. Furthermore, the Santhals of Mayurbhanj were inspired by a belief (based on rumours) that the *sahibs* (British) had been nearly finished by the German god and were now seeking help from the Santhal villages in the shape of men and money. It is important to point out in this context that popular resentment against the Mayurbhanj administration scaled new heights during this phase.[12] As the king was a minor, the administration was supervised by the Court of Wards. The British officials on the other hand, depended on the *sardars* (revenue collectors) and village heads to run the administration. These *sardars* turned out to be suppressive when collecting rent and

---

[10] Lenka 1999 ; Senapati Sahu, *op. cit.*

[11] Information regarding such often little emphasized peasant protests is culled from the following sources. Padma Lochan Mahanta (n.d.); Surendra Mahanta n.d.); Gopabandhu Mahanta 1997; Adikanda Mahanta, 1991; Pasupati Prasad Mahato 2000; Nilamani Senapati, Nabin Kumar Sahu *op. cit. Report on the Administration of Mayurbhanj for 1917-18*, 58-62, Orissa State Archives, Bhubaneswar; Ranbir Samaddar 1998.

[12] Padma Lochan Mahanta (n.d.); Adikanda Mahanta 2000a,b. Both authors assign the tensions building up in the region to the inherent conflict of interests between the society, i.e. *Khatikhia* (those who primarily labour and earn their wages) and *Lutikhia* (exploiters). Obviously, the anger of the *Khatikhia* section gained momentum during this phase and they targeted the state officials, labour supervisors, *sardars*, land revenue officials. However, what merits critical attention is that both the authors engaged in the re-writing of the history of the Mahantas within the overall ideological discourse of the contemporary Jharkhand politics tend to focus on the exploitation of the tribal people (including the Mahantas) by the non-tribal people in the given region.

recruiting coolies for the war. The rumour also spread in the region that the 'benevolent' king Sriramchandra Bhanjadeo had been murdered by British officials on a hunting expedition, and that the next move by the colonial authorities would be to send the able-bodied youths of the state to war. Other major grievances were the severe restrictions on the use of cattle-grazing lands, the ban on the cultivation of the princely lands by the landless peasants, auctions of the land when peasants failed to pay their rent, the inhuman obligation to carry the shoes of the land settlement *sardars* on the head, and the sexual exploitation of tribal women by the non-tribal labour supervisors in the iron mines.

The tribal people yearned for independence and a return to the 'golden age' when they had no overlords, and the Santhals and Kudmi-Mahantas joined together to proclaim a parallel government popularly known as 'Kanka-Kalia *Sarkar*' in the Betanti area of the *sadar* sub-division of Mayurbhanj. Kanka Majhi was declared King, supported by Kalia Mohanta as Minister and Nayan Singh Munda as the Commander-in-Chief. Peoples' councils were formed in several *parganas* where disputes were settled. It seems the rebels were supported by Gourachandra Bhanjadeo, a member of the Mayurbhanj royal family, whom they projected as the king in place of the minor Raja. A group of educated youths moved from village to village mobilizing the tribal people against the oppressive administration of the state. Thus, the desire to overcome excessive rent demands, excise rules, forest laws and the oppression of the *sardars*, along with the assertion of the dignity of the community, was expressed.

The resistance surfaced in the *sadar* sub-division under the youthful leadership of Bhima Mohanta, Anuraya Majhi, and Madhabananda Nayak. It culminated in the looting of a *bazaar* and the cutting of railway lines between Rupsa and Betanati in order to disrupt the transportation of iron ore.[13] The bridges between Balasore and Baisinga were destroyed to disturb the march of the British army. Later on, under the leadership of Chaitanya Majhi, a group of Santhals organized an attack on Bahalda, the headquarters

---

[13] The railway lines connecting Rairangpur-Baripada-Rupsa were targeted in order to disrupt the transportation of iron ore quarried in the mines of Badampahd, Suleipat, and Gorumahisani. Even dynamite used for blasting the mines was 'looted' to destroy the railway tracks at Rairangpur and the railway station at Aanlajodi.

of the Bamanghaty sub-division. Police officials left Bahalda upon their arrival. When the news reached Rairangpur, shops were closed and businessmen fled. The rebels looted the *bazaar* 'without any resistance'.

Finally, the colonial state had to use terror to curb the movement. Of the 1,118 persons tried in connection with this peasant movement, four were sentenced to death and hanged—Hridu Kolkamer, Kanka Mahanta, Katia Majhi and Rameshwar Singh Munda. While 977 persons were convicted, 33 were transported for life. This clearly points to the extent of mobilization.

III

Against this backdrop one can delve into Siba Prasad's autobiography.[14] The autobiography begins with the details of how the Mahanta community settled down in the village of Bhanjakia of the Panchapidha sub-division in Mayurbhanj during the second half of the nineteenth century. It shows the emerging social equations between the Mahantas and the other adivasis of the area. Siba Prasad then focuses on Niranjan Mahanta, who began his carrier as a primary school teacher in the village of Bhanjakia. It seems that Siba Prasad came to be considerably influenced by the ideas and vision of Niranjan Mahanta.

Niranjan Mahanta was a prosperous Kudmi resident of Bhanjakia village who organized and piloted the Kurmi-Kshatriya movement of the Mahantas in the first half of twentieth century with great determination. Hence, I shall briefly discuss the biography on Niranjan Mahanta[15] authored by his son before shifting my attention to Siba Prasad's autobiography.

Niranjan initially served as a teacher at the Bhanjakia village school, which was declared a government school in 1903. After serving for a few years, he became disillusioned and left to work with Siba Prasad's father, Nabina Chandra Mahanta. What really disturbed Niranjan then was the 'untouchable' status of his community despite the fact that the Kudmis were prosperous agriculturists and paid substantial revenues to the state of Mayurbhanj. He was shocked to realize that his people were barred

[14] Siba Prasad Mahanta (n. d.).

[15] Surendra Mahanta (n. d.).

from entering the Kichekeswari temple at Khiching, whereas other tribal people like Bhuyans and Bathudis enjoyed such a right. The brahmanical order as well as the Oriya-speaking tribal people and peasants treated the Kudmi-Mahantas as *achal jajman* (untouchables). It was in this context that Niranjan sought to mobilize and consolidate the Kudmi-Mahantas against the *varna-jati* system.

After leaving school, Niranjan became the disciple of the wandering Vaishnavite Baul Das and toured different parts of Mayurbhanj. These tours made him realize that Kudmi-Mahantas in Mayurbhanj were held in low esteem because of their lack of education and their 'unclean' habits. Thus began his campaign against illiteracy and drinking. He would exhort people to open schools for the education of their sons and daughters, give up drinking, child marriage, polygamy, and frequent divorces—practices predominant in his community. He propagated the following view: 'It is a crime against one's own self, one's caste, and one's nation to live without education and knowledge. It is dangerous to live with money and no education'. Under these circumstances, between 1908 and 1913, he consistently appealed to the Raja of Raruan under Panchapidha subdivision and the royal court of Mayurbhanj to accord the community the *sachal* or *jal-chal* status (from whom water can be accepted) and the right to enter the Kichekeswari temple at Khiching.

In order to defend the claims of his community before the royal court, Niranjan took the initiative of organizing a *pachisi patak sabha* (conference of the twenty-five ethnic groups of the Panchapidha sub-division) and secured its approval for the *sachal* status. However, the conservative brahmanical order and the authorities of the royal court condemned the move and turned down the appeal for *jal-chal* status.

It is interesting to note that a dejected Niranjan now realized the futility of receiving the sanction of the *dharmasabha* of the state for his community's claims and instead threatened the *dharmasabha* that the Kudmi-Mahantas would, *en masse,* embrace either Islam or Christianity.[16] In response to this threat, a 'nationalist Brahmin'

---

[16] The *dharmasabha* was a council of royal advisors consisting of the *rajguru* (teacher), *raj purohit* (priest), *raj jyotisa* (astrologer), *raj vaidya* (physician) and some other notable brahmins of the locality. The president of this council was called *routray sahab* and was a member of

volunteered to accept water from Niranjan, for which he was declared an outcaste by the *dharmasabha*.[17]

In the meanwhile, Niranjan got in touch with the leaders of several other religious sects. Nagendranath Banarjee, a Brahmaji, and Jogendranath Basu, an Arya Samajist, became his good friends. The Christian priest R.K. Elambi and a *maulavi* of Chaibasa also tried to persuade Niranjan to embrace Christianity and Islam respectively. Similarly, Narsingha Das the *balkaladhari babaji* (bark-clad monk) of the Mahima sect appealed to Niranjan to accept this religion. Moreover, Niranjan preferred to sharpen his understanding of these religions instead of accepting the idea of the conversion of his community. This made Niranjan shift to Calcutta in 1913. Here he contacted Dinabandhu Vedashastri in order to acquire a basic idea of *Vedic* and *Upanishadic* knowledge. In Calcutta he came to know about the organization of the All-India Kurmi Kshatriya Conference and immediately proceeded to attend its tenth session at Lucknow in 1915. Here, the realization dawned upon him that the Kudmis were not to be treated as low caste but as Kshatriyas. He impressed the audience in the conference 'through the sheer depth of his knowledge on the culture of Orissa and spoke extensively on the plight faced by his own community'. Deeply moved by his commitment to social reform and knowledge, the president of the conference awarded him the title *Maharaja* and he was made a life member of Kurmi Mahasabha. He attended the all-India Kurmi-Kshatriya conferences in 1916 at Agra and in 1917 at Farquabad. Moreover, he travelled through north, central and western India between 1915-17, visiting the sacred Hindu centres and collecting information about his community and society in these regions.

---

the royal family. In fact, the *dharmasabha* was the highest authority to decide on matters concerning caste and religion.

[17] It is interesting to note that Gopabandhu Das, one of the top nationalist leaders of Orissa, had served as a lawyer of Mayurbhanj state for two years during the reign of Sriramchandra Bhanjadeo. One of his followers, Radhakanta Acharya, subsequently came to support the demand of the Kudmis for Kshatriya status following the early nationalists' ideological battle against untouchability and illiteracy. It seems he became involved in the Kudmi movement for upward social mobility. Furthermore, he used to exhort the Kudmis 'to be educated so as to cleanse the evils which plagued their society'.

Finally, he was back in Balasore in 1917, where he published an Oriya tract entitled *Kurmi Vanshavali* in 1918.[18] The major thrust of the text was to popularize the idea that Kudmis were to be treated as kshatriyas and not to be equated with untouchables.

This was the backdrop against which the state of Mayurbhanj saw a massive peasant protest in 1917 which demonstrated solidarity between the Santhals and the Kudmi-Mahantas. Further, it was increasingly felt by the *durbar* and the colonial administration that a combination of Santhals and Mahantas would spark a 'violent rebellion'. Thus, the obvious strategy for the administration was to isolate the Kudmis from the Santhals. Perhaps it was in this context, that the *durbar* and the activists of *Utkala Sammilani* like Gopabandhu Das and Godavarisha Mishra relied on Niranjan to influence the Kudmi-Mahantas not to join the movement.[19] The publication of *Kurmi Vanshavali*, which was supposedly financed by the nationalist leaders of Orissa, was part of the strategy to popularize the idea that Kudmis were Kshatriyas and should hence distance themselves from the tribal people. The book was published in Oriya so as to acquaint the semi-literate Kudmis with the knowledge of their totemic clans and Sanskritized *gotra* as well as the linkage of their families with the Rajput lunar and solar dynasties, backed by a detailed mythological construction.[20] Besides, Niranjan who had tremendous clout in the Santhal villages, intervened decisively and explained to the people about the futility of their resistance to the government. He persuaded the people to

---

[18] Bhajji 1918. In fact, the text was translated into Oriya from Bengali. This vernacular tract is available in the India Office Library (OR.B. 66), London. Mahato 2000, 125. Mahato observes, 'The elites of the Orissa realized that Kudmi-Mahato and Santhals alongwith local artisans and 'medi' like movement can shook [*sic*] the entire administration. So according to the design of the Orissa Congress leaders, Shri Madhusudan Das and Sri Hare Krishna Mahatab, Naba Krishna Choudhury met Sri Niranjan Mahato again in the house of Satyananda Saraswati at Baleswar in December 1917 and suggested to him to write a book on Kurmi Kshatriya Vanshabali. The publication cost was financed by them.' This view of Mahato is based on his interview with Priyanath Singh, the eldest son of Niranjan Mahato.

[19] The major demands of *Utkal Sammilani* or Utkal Union Conference were the amalgamation of Oriya-speaking tracts into one administrative unit and the separate provincial status for Orissa.

[20] Mahato 1991, 125.

vent their grievances to the Maharaja of Mayurbhanj and to plead for reforms in the state administration. In return, the Maharaja fully endorsed both the caste conferences of the Kudmi-Mahantas and the demand for kshatriya status for the community. Niranjan was also offered the position of *deshpradhan* (the top-most head of the caste). It is worth noting that the Kurmi conference organized in Baripada town in 1917 was well attended. A representative of the Mayurbhanj royal household, a Christian missionary, a *maulavi,* and other notable worthies of the locality, participated. Besides, a mass sacred thread ceremony was organized during the conference, and many Kudmis shaved their heads and donned threads to the utter shock of the Brahmins. Such a conference lent tremendous boost and legitimacy to the claims of the community for upper-caste status. Niranjan had clearly achieved his objective.

What merits critical attention here is the fact that Niranjan, who had earlier threatened the brahmanical order with conversions to either Islam or Christianity, changed his position and emerged as a strong defender of Hindu religion in the post 1917 phase. On one occasion, he debated with a convert Christian Kudmi and convinced him that the Hindu theory of incarnation anticipated the Darwinian principle of evolution. Afterwards, Niranjan took up the drive to reconvert some of the young Kudmis and Kolhas to their original religion by asking them to shave their heads and wear the sacred thread. Drawing a comparison between the teachings of the Koran and Hinduism before a Muslim disciple of him, he observed:

> Hinduism represents a much superior philosophy than socialism, communism or what is conceived of in the Islamic symbolism of *Ajrakh.* Anyone who strictly adheres to the Hindu religious ethics is hardly left with excessive wealth. This is because the Hindu religion stipulates that from birth till death, a Hindu has to spend on several festivities and functions, and also to make provisions for gifts. Hence, a religion which entails so much of gifts and offerings, in such a religious land, should ideally not leave any room for poverty and deprivation. The latter would only be possible in such countries or religions where a section of the society lived in affluence and others sulked in poverty. *Ajrakh* in Islam basically symbolises the twin faces of happiness and sorrow as in the very religion we see a group of people living in luxury while others are a terribly deprived section.[21]

---

[21] Surendra Mahanta , 158.

Similarly, once Niranjan received a complaint that a Kudmi girl had sought shelter with a Muslim family and had thus been declared an outcaste from the community. He advised the community leaders to organize the marriage of the girl to save her from 'social stigma'. Such views point to the strong ideological impact on him of the Arya Samaj and *shuddhi*.

Despite his stout defence of Hindu religion and philosophy, Niranjan retained his critique of brahmanical orthodoxy. Around 1924, he laid the foundation of a Radha-Krishna temple at Dari Mouza by procuring the idols from Vrindavan. Moreover, he sought the permission of the sub-divisional officer of Panchapidha to take the idols to the *dola* festival (one of the important Oriya festivals centred around Krishna and Radha) of Karanjia, where the idols of various upper castes were brought for procession. The sub-divisional officer, who had been sympathetic to the cause of the Kudmi community all along, gave the necessary consent.

The brahmins loudly protested when they saw the idols being taken by the Mahantas to the procession. For them, the Kudmis were untouchables, their idols mere toys; they should not be allowed inside the *puja mandapa*. The officer, however, objected to such a view and explained that no god could be either Brahmin or Untouchable, and that the Hindu religion stood for liberalism and plurality. The very next day Niranjan sought to defend the Kshatriya status of his community in an open caste meeting wherein he debated with the local Brahmins on the issue of the sacred thread and the concept of Brahman (supreme self). Furthermore, he organized a mass sacred thread ceremony at the local temple by employing the services of a Marwari Brahmin instead of the local *Sasan* Brahmins.

Niranjan had a deep respect for the Mahima religion. On one occasion, when the local Brahmins refused to perform the rituals in connection with the foundation ceremony of the house of his son, he asked an Alekha disciple who was Pana by caste to perform the required rituals according to the Mahima Dharma tradition.

It is crucial to note here that Niranjan undertook to organize the regional Kudmi conference of Bengal, Bihar and Orissa in 1937 at Baripada. The conference was marked by the presence of a Christian missionary, Mr. Lehi, the local *maulavi,* and the *Brahmo* preacher, Nagendranath Banarjee. As usual, he appealed to the people at the conference to give up drinking, take up the programme of female education, and perform of rituals with the assistance of brahmins. Perhaps the opposition to Niranjan's programme of reform gathered momentum around this time, as a section of the Kudmis was not reconciled to the idea of Kshatriya status for the community.

At this conference, Niranjan remained critical of the attempt by a few 'less educated people' to oppose the campaign for reform. Opposition to reform increased over the years. In fact, the regional Kudmi conference of 1948 (supposedly the last caste conference which Niranjan attended) was marked by tremendous opposition and a disruption of the proceedings. Niranjan's answer to this opposition was that social service and reform could only be possible through love, and not through competition or opposition. He exhorted the Kudmis to behave like real kshatriyas and to fight against illiteracy, blind faith, alcoholism, and poverty. He was very critical of those Kudmi husbands who fathered many children and spent money on cosmetics instead of educating their offspring.

At the twenty-second session of All-India Kurmi Kshatriya Mahasabha organized at Jhargram, Midnapur, in 1939, Niranjan was awarded the epithet 'Swami Nirvayanandaji' for his lifetime commitment and his fearless and selfless services for the social uplift of the community. In response, Niranjan observed that 'as a mere sweeper he had utilized his limited strength to cleanse society for the last twenty-eight years'. Despite his efforts to promote social reforms, a group of Kudmis opposed them. They perhaps sensed a kind of cultural silencing in the efforts of Niranjan, who had emerged as an exponent of Sanskritization.[22] However, community activism seemed to have been capped with success when the colonial authorities started enumerating the Kudmis as a caste rather than a tribe in 1931. This new status of the Kudmis in the colonial census must have furthered the Santhal-Mahanta divide.

---

[22] Mahato 2000, 17-18. The efforts of Niranjan to Sanskritize the Kudmi-Mahantas evoked opposition from a section of the Kudmi-Mahantas. Niranjan's attempt at emulating the idioms, symbols, signs and rituals of the dominant Hindu caste order was perhaps sought to be questioned on the ground that such a model tended to silence (*nirbak*) the inherent cultural values of the Kudmi community. The reformatory strategy of Niranjan was increasingly seen as an attempt to isolate the Kudmis from the indigenous adivasi population of the region.

More so, it was around this time that some Santhals sought to Sanskritize.[23]

Apart from being a community activist, Niranjan was also involved in the nationalist activities of the period. During the phase of the Non-Cooperation movement, he used to wander in the villages of northern Orissa, southern Bihar and Bengal, playing the *ektara* and singing *bhajans* in praise of Rama and Krishna. On these tours, he used to mobilize his caste people and exhorted them to adopt reforms. His caste meetings were banned during this period in the states of Gangpur, Bonai, Keonjhar, and Sareikella.

Between 1928 and 1929, the nationalist leaders of Orissa sought the support of Niranjan to organize the Oriyas of the frontier region, Midnapur, so as to pressure the Simon Commission to make it a part of Orissa. In due course Niranjan, along with Godavarisha Mishra, came to be severely opposed by the Bengali nationalists.

Between 1930 and 1932, he seems to have been fairly active in the salt satyagraha. He led a group of peasants of the Thakurmunda area of the Panchapidha sub-division to meet the king in order to demand a reduction of the rent that had been hiked by 50 per cent in the previous settlement. In 1940, he attended the Congress session at Ramgarh.

It seems fairly clear that the nationalist leaders of Orissa in their political and ideological campaign sought to reach out to the princely state of Mayurbhanj by making use of the services of Niranjan. Niranjan's response to the call of the leadership was loud and clear, as his agenda of reform had been neatly spelt out by the Gandhian Congress leadership.[24]

IV

Quite clearly, Siba Prasad was considerably influenced by the ideas and vision of Niranjan Mahanta. The poems composed by Niranjan on the themes of 'nation and society' were often enthusiastically

---

[23] Samaddar 1998, 161.

[24] My argument here opposes the assessment '… local Mahato leaders like Niranjan Mahato had fought desperately against being "eaten up" by the hagemonic politics of Hare Krishna Mahatab, Naba Krishna Choudhury and Madhusudan Das' (Samaddar 1998, 150). What one rather notices is instead an increasing linkage of Niranjan Mahanta with the nationalist leadership.

sung by Siba Prasad. Under the ideological influence of Niranjan, Siba Prasad sought to question the rationale behind idolatory and also appreciated the ideologies of religious texts like the *Manu Samhita* and the *Satyartha Prakash.* Siba Prasad was impressed by the wisdom of Niranjan. In a moving passage, he observes:

> Once a *babaji* (saint) came to visit Niranjan riding a horse. He stayed with Niranjan for three days. After discussing with him several aspects of religion, the saint accepted Niranjan as his *guru* and left Niranjan's house. He also left behind his horse and other things. The *padris* (missionaries), *brahmos, satnamis* and the top officials also came to Niranjan for religious discussion. The political leaders also stayed in his house as guests. He had profound understanding about the contemporary politics religion and society. Moreover, he had an intimate relationship with the royal families of Mayurbhanj and other States. I used to consider him as a vast treasure of knowledge.

What is visible in the above description is the fact that Niranjan in his newly acquired *avatar* of Nirvayanandaji, or as the *Maharaja* of the community, could defeat and in fact be accepted by the *pandits* of other religions. The very fact that the saint came to Niranjan's house riding a horse signals the hegemonic dominance of the faith represented by the saint. But he had to leave the horse at Niranjan's house.

Similarly, we are told about Siba Prasad's debate with a Christian missionary called Lehi *Sahib* on the principles of Hinduism, monotheism, and rationalism which finally ended with Prasad's victory. This is equally suggestive of the disruption of the colonial power represented by Christianity. Niranjan was instrumental in tailoring Siba Prasad's ideological positioning as a social reformer and an ace nationalist in later years. In fact, Niranjan instilled in Siba Prasad the principle of Gandhian Swaraj as well as the objectives and activities of the Congress. In 1925, the latter had accompanied the former to Chaibasa in Bihar to attend a meeting addressed by Gandhi. Furthermore, Niranjan used to inspire people by his speeches and 'social meetings' organized with the avowed objective of social reforms.

Siba Prasad strove to champion the Gandhian ideas of Swaraj. He was convinced that exploitation by the Brahmin priests had to be resisted. An issue that disturbed him after he attended the meeting at Chaibasa was the fact that within the limits of

Panchapidha area, the adult Mahanta males of the village of Bandiraposhi could not marry the Mahanta girls of the village of Bargidiha, as the former lacked the sacred thread. The excessive fees claimed by Brahmin priests to conduct the thread rituals being beyond the means of Bandiraposhi villagers, they remained without the sacred thread even though ritually entitled to it. Siba Prasad took up the issue by organizing a common sacred thread ceremony for thirty-two villagers of Bandiraposhi who were issued certificates mentioning that Siba Prasad himself had conducted the thread ritual.

During the performance of these rituals at the fire-altar, under Siba's instructions, the participants vowed neither to drink liquor nor to eat chicken. This oath de-legitimized the authority of the brahmin priests significantly. Further, it hardened Siba's resolve to organize resistance against the oppression of the *deshpradhan*, *parganayat*, *parmanik*, *chariamahji* and *bhallbhai* in the name of religion.[25]

What we discern in the act of Siba Prasad is not only the appropriation of signs, symbols (thread, fire-altar and chanting of hymns) from the ritual hierarchy, but also the simultaneous abolition and rejection of the priests whose place and function are closely tied to the ritual hierarchy within caste society. All this not only questioned and disrupted the hegemonic symbolic order but at the same time helped create a transformed body and a new self within the Kudmi community. This new self can be located in the very act of Siba Prasad who assumed the authority of a priest and performed the rituals. It is equally suggestive of the transformation

[25] Interview with Arjuna Mahanta, Udala, Mayurbhanj, 9 November 2000. In fact, the Kudmis had their caste organizations at different levels. For instance, the Panchapidha, one of the Kudmi dominated sub-divisions of Mayurbhanj was divided into five distinct units such as Kerkera (Khiching area), Sarubali, Sananai, Bharadaposhi and Balisahi. Each unit had a *sabha* whose head was the *deshpradhan* or the head of the *jati*. The *deshpradhan* as the head of the community of a specified area looked into the overall social functioning of the community. Similarly, the *parganayat* was the head of the Kudmi *pargana*. The *bhallbhai* (which means a friend during the period of happiness and crisis) was the person who used to advise and guide a Kudmi at times of needs and crisis. The *padhan* was the head of the village. All these caste masters had a decisive say on the issues of marriage, divorce, birth, death rites and the overall social customs of the community.

of an oppressive world held in place by the dominant symbolic order and the consequent development of an oppositional symbolic order.[26]

Siba Prasad refers to community activism during the 1939-42 phase, and to the pattern of dissemination of Congress ideology in popular consciousness. It is worth noting that this phase was crucial from the standpoint of a peoples' movement and the overall nationalist mobilization which had grown since the formation of the Congress ministry in the province since 1937. In fact, massive peasant protests surfaced in states like Nilagiri, bordering Mayurbhanj. Similarly, the impact of neighbouring Bengal and Bihar had a considerable impact on the politics in the state.[27]

Against this backdrop Siba Prasad chose to take up a few issues in order to fight an oppressive social order. In fact, a significant portion of his autobiography focuses on his opposition to the subscription collected by the *mahantas* (temple priests) and the state officials on the occasion of the *dola* festival. This subscription was 'forcibly' collected from all classes of people of the Panchapidha sub-division in the form of cash or rice by the state officials and notably by the temple priests. It was neither an official tax nor a rent to be paid to the state, but a kind of feudal levy collected from the people in the name of the local god. Refusal to pay the subscription was seen as a serious offence by the temple authorities, and terror tactics were often resorted to by the officials to ensure regular collections. As Siba Prasad points out, the people of Panchapidha used to make voluntary contributions to the local god Raghunath during the *dola* festival; but after 1931, the subscription was raised, along with the land revenue. Failure to pay this levy was followed by the confiscation of house and property. Neither workers, the poor, nor beggars were spared. About 1200 maunds of rice and Rs. 1300 were collected annually under the respective heads of the *paika pancha* and the *dola* subscription.[28]

---

[26] Dube 1993, 134, 141-6.

[27] Pati 1993, 85-142; Nanda 1998, 80-100. These accounts provide elaborate discussions on the nature of popular protest in the princely states of Orissa, sharply critical of the scholarly works done on the same subject following the dominant nationalist historiographic tradition of Mahatab (cf. Mahatab 1957).

[28] Mahanta 1942. A peasant had to pay *paika* (which was more than a kilogram of rice or its equivalent). In fact, every peasant having one

In order to resist this terribly oppressive practice, Siba Prasad sought to mobilize the villagers of Bhanjakia in 1942. The other objective was to hasten the process of the Congress enrolment drive. The strategy adopted to highlight the issue was to preach to the people a simple logical message. The *mantra* was, as he puts it: 'Look brothers: we are taking our food daily and go to the latrine to relieve ourselves. But which latrine can take the load of 12/13 maunds of rice which god Raghunath consumes? Hence, you better ask the *padhan*, *choukidars* and *chattia* (the state officials who collect *paika pancha*) to show you the latrine which god Raghunath uses to relieve himself. If they can't show you the latrine, then you refuse to pay the subscription.'[29] This form of mobilization caught the popular imagination and evoked a massive response. In fact, it bred a crisis, and the *dola* subscription could not be collected until July 1942. The state *tahsildar* conducted an inquiry into the issue and a civil case was slapped against two persons of Bhanjakia village. However, the case was subsequently dismissed.

What needs to be investigated here is the strategy of defiance based on the rejection of the priestly status and the questioning of the relationship of power, shared by kingship and colonial state, in terms of a refusal to pay the subscriptions. However, the legal victory on the issue of *paika pancha* emboldened the resolve of Siba Prasad to take up the campaign more seriously in the whole of the Panchapidha sub-division. He issued a pamphlet to air his views on religion and his logic against the feudal levy. The pamphlet made a scathing attack on the priest of Jashipur *matha,* for his alleged use of force while collecting *dola* subscription.[30] It also noted with anguish that the worshippers/subjects of god Raghunath had started to evade the God because of the way the priests

---

plough for cultivation had to pay two *pai* or *duipai*. In case of joint families, where more than one plough was used for cultivation, the amount to be paid was doubled for every additional plough. For instance, if three ploughs were used for cultivation, a peasant family jointly paid three times the *duipai* which was equal to six *pai* (more than twelve *seers* of rice or its equivalent in cash). Even a very poor peasant whose rent for his tiny piece of cultivating land was one or half an *anna* was not spared the *pancha* (subscription). He was forced to pay the minimum of *paiea* (nearly half of the *duipai*) rice or its equivalent in cash, i.e. ten to twelve *annas*.

[29] Mahanta 1942 (i)70; (iii) 22.

[30] Ibid., (ii).

conducted themselves. Thus, Siba Prasad pointedly questioned: 'Have demons taken over God?'

The other notable feature of the pamphlet is its critique of the existing social hierarchy and the attendant discrimination of the Kudmi community. In a significant passage, we are told about the hierarchy that exists in the world of gods; the passage reads as follows:

> It is not only that discrimination exists in human society and race; the gods and goddesses are also not left out of the very scheme based on differences of social positioning. Gods or Goddesses who belong to the castes and sects of brahmanas, kshatriyas, Vaishnavas, etc., are brought to the *dola* festival. But in the festival, the god of Kudmis is given a separate place to be seated away from the Aryan gods and goddesses as the former are considered chicken-eaters and non-Aryan gods. The latter on the other hand, are known for eating sweets. But ironically god Raghunath of Panchapidha, who eats the *pahika* rice of all sections of population such as brahmana, Karana, Vaishnava, Mahanta, Bathudi, Bhuyan, Gond, Pana, Majhi and Kolha is given a seat in the middle.[31]

Thus, he goes on to ridicule Hindu religion by wondering: 'Oh! What a fantastic ideal the Hindus are following. Not a single egalitarian "nation" of the world can not but thank such an ideal. In a society where gods and goddesses are discriminated on the basis of dietary habits, in such a society sweet-eater Aryans equally indulge in gross discriminations against the non-Aryans. This is well known to the people of Panchapidha.'

Further the mentality of assertion and subversion is best reflected when he notes:

> Can those priests who consider their own gods and goddesses as supreme and more intelligent and who treat gods and goddesses of others to be inferior to dogs be really considered as the worshippers of divine beings? These selfish priests are virtually carrying on a trade in the name of religion to protect their vested interests and hence they have created such distinctions in society. ... In a society where morality and religion are highly valued, those who indulge in immoral practices and exploitation in the name of religion are sinners; and those who support such a system by paying their hard-earned money (in the shape of subscriptions) are also sinners.

[31] Ibid., 12.

> Therefore, we can not think of liberation unless and until we put an end to such illegalities which are carried on in the name of religion.[32]

However, the pamphlet also reflects the author's sense of reverence for royalty, the Maharaja of Mayurbhanj state. In the opening lines, the author sought to justify the Maharaja's rule by pointing out:

> As water vapours come back to us in the shape of rains similarly the kinds of tax or rent which our Maharaja *sahib* collects is given back to us in terms of schools, hospitals, orphanages, ponds, dams, wells, roads and gardens meant for peoples' welfare. In this manner, the kinds of payment such as rent, road tax, fruit tax, fish tax, *chaukidari* tax which we give to the Raja are repaid to us in one form or the other. That is why we do not have to speak anything against the Raja.[33]

This pamphlet of Siba Prasad needs to be read together with a poem authored by his father, Nabina Chandra Mahanta.[34] Claimed to have been composed in 1928, the poem attempts to portray the conflict between one Gouranga Mohapatra, the priest of Raghunath temple of Jashipur and the author, who worked as the clerk in Jashipur *matha*. The issue of the conflict centred around the opposition shown to Nabina Mahanta by Gouranga Mohapatra.

Once, Nabina Mahanta entered the inner chamber of the temple. This was severely resented by Gouranga Mohapatra, and a conflict began. The former argued that when tribals like Bhuyans and Bathudis entered the temple daily in large numbers, why should he be kept away, and how could the place of God be defiled by his entry, when he happened to be a kshatriya? He drew the attention of *mahanta* of Jashipur *matha* to this issue, but the *mahanta* defended the acts of the priest. This filled Nabina with anguish since he realized that the unholy brahmin-vaishnava combine sought to silence the Kudmi community's efforts to obtain a ritually elevated status. This anguish flowered into a world of poetry under the title *Nabina Padyabali*.

Beginning with a laudatory note on god Raghunath, the poem goes on to depict the specific event concerning Nabina and Gouranga and puts a poser to Raghunath: how can Nabina Mahanta

---

[32] Ibid., 13-15.

[33] Ibid., 1

[34] Mahanta 1939.

be less acceptable in the temple than persons (adivasis) who never wash after attending the calls of nature? There was no sign-board in the temple restricting the entry of certain categories of people. More so, the poem also asks the priest to furnish a list of castes who were allowed to enter the temple. It is emphatic on the point that God never exclusively belonged to the Brahmins, the proof of which could be obtained, it insists, if somebody visited *nilanchal* Puri, the abode of Jagannath. In another passage, the poem laments the emerging nexus between the Brahman and Vaishnava and their complicity to punish the Kudmis by removing Nabina Chandra from the Jashipur *matha*. Moreover, Nabina Chandra resolves to avenge the humiliation by fighting out the Brahmana–Vaishnava combine in the larger interests of caste and religion.

The poem is also emphatic about the glorious tradition and great ancestry of the Kudmi caste. It points out that the great Hindu kings like Vikramaditya, Bhoja, and Shivaji belonged to the Kudmi caste and that it was that caste that battled against the Mughals.

Critical readings of the pamphlet and the poem suggest that both question the relationships of power constituted by the ritual hierarchy of purity and pollution, a construct of the dominant caste, with cultural and ritual significance. As in other contexts of the autobiography, these pieces are aimed at subverting the 'hegemonic symbolic order'. This was sought to be done by engineering a displacement within the cosmic hierarchy: by lampooning the village gods or appropriating and repositioning the signs and practices of ritual hierarchy of purity and pollution. The final objective of such lower class or caste initiatives was to construct an oppositional symbolic order and to transform an 'oppressive world' represented by the dominant or hegemonic order.

V

My aim in this paper has been to focus on unpublished local level biographies and autobiographies in order to construct the history of the Kudmi Mahantas. This illustrates the possibilities of writing 'local' history based on non-official sources. What is significant in these narratives is the emphasis on peasant protests which displayed unprecedented solidarity amongst the adivasis of Mayurbhanj in 1917. This popular protest has received very little historiographic attention as far as the history of colonial Orissa is concerned.

Furthermore, it demonstrates the terror unleashed by the colonial administration when it sought to counter the large-scale struggle among the people of Mayurbhanj.[35]

The paper has mapped out the nature of the social mobility movement of the Kudmi community of Mayurbhanj. The upward social mobility of the Kudmi Mahantas which began as a popular protest challenging the Brahmanical order was ultimately incorporated into the very structure it had aimed to challenge. Perhaps this obliterated the community identity of the Kudmi Mahantas and ensured the triumph of the Brahmanical order. The social reform initiatives by Niranjan Mahanta and Siba Prasad Mahanta seriously criticized the Brahmanical order and at the same time betrayed the subaltern attempt by aspiring to, and finally getting co-opted into, the brahmanical hegemonic order. In other words, while challenging a specific hegemonic order, their reformatory politics aimed to be hegemonized by the very order. This phenomenon may show the limitations of the concept of 'subaltern autonomy'. Niranjan's agenda of social reform in the campaign for the Kshatriya status for the Kudmi community, its emphasis on education, the anti-liquor programme, and the mobilization of Kudmi peasants, highlights the process of Sanskritization. More importantly, it also points to the way such popular protest created space for the spread of Gandhian nationalist politics in the *garjats* (princely states). Niranjan's views on female education and family planning were remarkably radical given the broader social context of colonial Orissa and the *durbar* administration of the *garjats* which were often seen as an *andharua mulak* (dark zones) in popular perception. On the contrary, Niranjan's perception of Hinduism as superior to Islam and Christianity, and his ideas on the 're-conversion of Kudmis who had defiled themselves by coming in contact with Islam and Christianity and thus declared as outcastes'[36] showed the influence of the Arya Samaj and *shuddhi* on him, and complicated his reformatory tactics. Perhaps it imparted a retrograde element to the popular protest. Niranjan's community activism and his efforts to

---

35 Interview with Prasanna Kumar Das, 3 November 2000 Kendumundi, Mayurbhanj.

36 Niranjan's reference to *bidharmi* (heathen) as Muslims and Christians and his notion of Hinduism as the 'supreme' religion are significant.

Sanskritize the 'community identity' however, evoked opposition from a section of the Kudmi Mahantas in the 1940s, who raised the demand for tribal status for the community instead. This strand within the movement sought to arrest the trend of Sanskritization—seen as a process of 'culture silencing' (*nirbakization*)—by vigorously asserting the adivasi origin. The demand for tribal identity of the Kudmi community has gained momentum since Indian Independence. Systematic attempts have linked this movement with broader Jharkhand politics by a section of the Kudmi leadership.[37] This is however, a theme which is beyond the purview of the present paper.

References

Bhadra, G. 1989. 'The Mentality of Subalternity: *Kantanama* or *Rajdharma*', in Ranjit Guha (ed.), *Subaltern Studies* VI: *Writings on South Asian History and Society,* Delhi: Oxford University Press, 54-91.

---

[37] Mahato 2000; Mahanta 1991; 2001; 2000b; Interview with Padma Lochan Mahanta, Chitrada, 26 October 2000. The argument that the Kudmi Mahanta were a part of the broader *Had-Mitan* civilization in which human beings (*Had*) such as Santhals, Kolhas, Mundas Kudmis and their friends (*Mitan*), particularly artisans like blacksmiths, weavers, cobblers and the 'lower castes' (viz., Panas, Dombs, etc.) co-existed on a basis of mutual reciprocity and indigenous cultural symbols and values, strongly underscores the above accounts. Besides, there has been an organized attempt to re-write the history of the Kudmi Mahantas on the basis of Kudmi folk songs, tales and dances, etc. This emerging historiographic trend highlights the Kudmi peasant protests in the shape of anti-indigo plantation of the nineteenth century which symbolized forced labour (*belhi*), the 1917 popular protest leading to the establishment of 'Kanka-Kalia *Sarkar*' in Mayurbhanj and the movement opposing the merger of Mayurbhanj in Orissa which developed in 1948 under the leadership of Sonaram Soren, as aspects of the assertion of the *adivasis* for a 'community identity', challenging its incorporation into a hegemonic identity. Further, this historiographic framework dubs the Niranjan-led Kurmi-Kshatriya movement as 'elitist' and points out how the *durbar*, administration of Mayurbhanj awarded a fellowship to Niranjan to learn Sanskrit in Kashi so as to help him emerge as the top leader of the Kudmi-Kshatriya movement. This device of the *durbar,* it is alleged, was essentially meant to divide the Santhal-Mahanta solidarity of the region.

Dalton, E.T. 1973. *Tribal History of Eastern India*, Delhi: Cosmo Publications.

Das, J.N. 1990a. *Kurumali Bhasa Parichaya*, Karanjia: Kantharam Press.

— (ed.) 1990b. *Bamra* (journal), Karanjia: Kantharam Press.

— 1995. *Phalgu* (novel), Karanjia: Kantharam Press.

Das, P.K. 1996. *Karmeera Sadhana*, Cuttack: Rastrabhasha Press.

Dube, S. 1992. 'Myths, Symbols and Community: Satnampanth of Chhattisgarh', in Partha Chatterjee and Gyanendra Pandey (eds.), *Subaltern Studies* VII: *Writings on South Asian History and Society*, Delhi: Oxford University Press, 121-58.

Laeequddin, M. 1937. *Census of Mayurbhanj State,* Vol. I, Calcutta: Caledonian Printing Company Limited.

— 1938. *Village Directory of Mayurbhaj State*, Vol. II: *Peoples,* Baripada: Mayurbhanj State Press.

Lenka, S.P. 1997. *Mayurbhanja Itihasa: Eka Anudhyana: Bhanja Bhujanga Rajabansa*, Baripada: Rajashree Prakashan.

Mahanta, A. 1991. 'Mayurbhanjara Meli Bidroha: Eka Analochita Itiihasa', *Smaranika* (Silver Jubliee Journal of Ichinda U.P. School), Rairangpur: Sri Sri Jagannath Press, 16-19.

— 2000a. 'Jhumar Sangitare Mayurbhanj Sanskruti' in Rajendra Shadangi (ed.), *Loka Sanskruti Patrika*, Vol. IV, Jan-April, 1-12.

— 2000b. 'Adivasi Sanskrutira Eka Bibhaba', in *Esana,* Vol. 40, June, 160-7.

Mahanta, Arjuna. 1998-9. 'Niranjan Maharaja Ba' Swami Nirvayananda Maharaja Smruti Grantha', Vols. I, II, (unpublished).

— 'Odisabasi Kurmi Samajara Shikhita Sreniku Ahwana' (unpublished).

Mahanta, G. 1997. *Sankhipta Kudumi Itihasa*, Baripada.

Mahanta, M. 1997. *Kurmi Itihasa,* Betanati: Haragouri Press.

Mahanta, N.C. 1939. 'Nabina Padyabali' (unpublished).

Mahanta, P.L. 'Mayurbhanj Itihash' (unpublished).

— *Affidavit document of the President (Padma Lochan Mahanta) of Kurmi Kalyana Samiti*, Notary Public, Baripada, no date.

Mahanta, S.P. (no date). 'Mor Nija Jibanara Karyakalapa ba Samaja: Dharma O' Desa Andolana' (unpublished autobiography of Siba Prasad Mahanta).

— 1942. 'Deva Devi O' Parbaparbani: Pahika O' Dolachanda Sambadhare Pracharapatra' (unpublished pamphlet).

Mahanta, S. (no date). 'Niranjan Mahanta: Mayurbhanj Janajibanara Eka Smaraniya Alekhya' (unpublished biography of Niranjan Mahanta).

Mahanty, M. 1996. *Santhakabi Kantharam*, Karanjia: Kantharam Press.

Mahato Bhajji, N. 1918. *Kurmi Vanshavali*, Baleswar.

Mahato, P.P. 2000. *Sanskritisation Vs. Nirbakisation*, Calcutta: Sujan Publications.

Nanda, C.P. 1998. *Todards Swaraj*, Delhi: Kalyani Publishers.

Pati, B. 1993. *Resisting Domination,* Delhi: Manohar.

— *Report on the Administration of Mayurbhanj for 1917-1918*, (1919), Baripada: State Press.

Risley, H.H. 1891. *The Tribes and Castes of Benga: Ethonographic Glossary*, Vol. I., Calcutta: Bengal Secretariat Press.

Samaddar, R. 1998. *Memory Identity Power: Politics of the Jungle Mahals 1890-1950*, Delhi: Orient Longman.

Sarkar, S. 1984. 'The Conditions and Nature of Subaltern Militancy: Bengal from Swadeshi to Non-cooperation, 1905-22', in Ranjit Guha (ed.), *Subaltern Studies III: Writings on South Asian History and Society*, Delhi: Oxford University Press, 271-320.

Senapati, N. and N.K. Sahu (eds.). 1967. *Orissa District Gazetteers (Mayurbhanj)*, Cuttack: Orissa Government Press.

19

Identity, Hegemony, Resistance: Conversions in Orissa 1800-2000*

Biswamoy Pati

The idea of religious conversion tends to be associated with almost any religion but Hinduism. Although much has been written on the subject, it is almost impossible to get even the so-called 'thinking people' to accept that Hinduism also inspires conversion, or to ponder if adivasis and outcastes were ever Hindus.[1] This common perception has crystallized over the last fifteen years or so, but this process has its roots in the past. While colonialism and, with it, Christianity, have contributed to the emergence of this common perception, colonial and post-colonial communal politics and, more recently, Hindu fundamentalism have sustained it. Today a stereotype of Christian missionaries prevails, especially in urban and coastal Orissa. It was normal to encounter people who thought that padres were waiting to convert you in Orissa, especially after the criminal murder of the missionary Staines.[2]

In India, conversion has to be to Christianity or Islam or, on some occasions, to Buddhism, but very rarely to Hinduism. This notion co-exists with an understanding that Hindus can only be

---

*This forms part of an on-going project for which I am thankful to the Asia Research Centre, London School of Economics and Political Science for the Ratan Tata Fellowship. I thank Meghnad Desai, Gyanendra Pandey and K.N. Panikkar for their encouragement and the participants at the Orissa Research Programme Conference, 'Periphery and Centre: Groups, Categories, Values in Orissa', Salzau (Germany), 23-7 May 2001, for their suggestions and comments.

[1]Most of the material—especially the articles and some of the books—is of very poor quality. There is a very long list of books and articles that talk of conversions mostly to Christianity but also to Buddhism, and are centred on case studies of individuals. Two scholars who have studied adivasis as non-Hindus in the pre-colonial period are Bhairabi Prasad Sahu (1986; 1987) and Richard M. Eaton (2000).

[2] Cf. Pati 2000 for details.

born Hindus.[3] Yet re-conversion to Hinduism—or *shuddhi* as it is called since the nineteenth century—is easily acceptable to most scholars.[4] If re-conversion is widely accepted, why is the concept of conversion to Hinduism considered totally unacceptable? In contemporary India, we witness a lot of fanfare and media reports about adivasis who re-convert.[5] The fact that they may never have been Hindus to begin with seems to be forgotten. Their Hindu identity is taken for granted, which makes re-conversion perfectly possible, acceptable and, if need be, justifiable.[6]

One finds a set of contradictions in a view that homogenizes all sections of adivasis and outcastes as Hindus, and assumes their

[3] There are a few exceptions; e.g. Lamb and Bryant 1999. In the introduction, 'Conversion: Contours of Controversy and Commitment in a plural World', 1-19, the editors raise a question: 'Is there conversion to Hinduism?' This is resolved unsatisfactorily when they articulate that 'ethnic religions like Hinduism … seem less concerned with conversion except in so far as it is a negative force they have to confront'; 1, 3. See also Chapter 1 by Rambo and Farhadian, 'Converting: Stages of Religious Change', 23-34. They argue that on 14 October 1956 500,000 Mahars 'renounced their Hindu faith and embraced Buddhism, transforming them from being Untouchables to Buddhists'; 33, which implies that they were Hindus. Subsequently, in Chapter 2, 'Conversion: Inward, Outward and Awkward', 35-50, Donald Taylor argues that conversion is not a burning issue within Hinduism and becomes one only when Hindus come into contact with other religions. The traditional conservative Hindu—whom he identifies as a member of the RSS or the Arya Samaj—would not accept that a non-Hindu can convert to Hinduism. As he puts it: 'According to their way of thinking a person must be born a Hindu'; he finds this reasoning 'quite logical'; 43. This is perhaps the most illogical argument in the light of the present work, more so if one talks about the adivasis and outcastes.

[4] Oddie 1977. In fact, Jordens 1977 accepts this unquestioningly.

[5] Interestingly, although they are defined as Hindus, the entry of dalits into the temple of Jagannatha is not *actually* allowed. 'They are/they are not' is a logic that is invoked to explain many things in the strangest possible ways. Thus, as argued by the Puri Sankarachaya a few years ago, Harijans need not go into the temples since God himself will come to them; interview in the *Illustrated Weekly of India*, 24 July 1988.

[6] In Oddie 1977 the introduction refers to 'tribal' or 'primitive' religions within Hinduism, along with those influenced by beliefs and practices more characteristic of the 'Brahmanic tradition'. A rather crude homogenization results in such assertions.

'integration' into the varna order. But can a Hindu also simultaneously be the outcaste Other?[7]

More importantly, it needs to be emphasized that this process involves the establishment of power over, and the exploitation of, adivasis and outcastes.[8] While I am prepared to accept that Hinduism does not convert in the same way as, perhaps, some other religions, I take up its history over the last two hundred years in Orissa to illustrate the way it has indeed inspired the conversion of adivasis and outcastes. This process was marked by the interplay of a host of complex features which were rooted in shifting material conditions.

Existing Studies

As already pointed out, extant scholarship does not recognize conversion to Hinduism. A typical theme is the individualization of those who convert.[9] In other contexts, one comes across scholars who explore large-scale conversions. A study of coloured slaves who converted to Christianity in North America can be cited as an example. Here the stress is laid upon the religious encounters, with sudden disruptions that mark abrupt changes in their outlook.[10] A study of a community in Africa explores the 'generational' aspect associated with the converts to Christianity. It recognizes the importance of colonialism and argues that for the first generation, conversion was a decisive encounter with power that subsequently developed an anti-colonial and revivalist orientation This was then followed by an attempt to explore the Christian faith and give it a

---

[7] Cf. Ilaih 1996 to get an idea of this dimension.

[8] In fact, Max Weber (1967) mentions how power and control were established over these people by these means. He calls this 'discriminatory integration' in the social and economic sense, when it comes to the adivasis; 11-12; 16-17.

[9] Oddie 1977 is a classic example. Scholars like Meera Kosambi (1995), Uma Chakravarty (1998) and Gauri Vishwanathan (1998) are more nuanced and accept the pluralities/complexities associated with conversions to Christianity and Buddhism, etc., together with a shift to question Hindu patriarchy and caste oppression.

[10] 'God Struck Me Dead' 1945. This study is based on the evidence taken from one hundred individuals; i-iii.

firm African grounding.[11] Another work that examines conversions in contemporary North America talks about crisis points when colonial powers disrupt, in some cases even destroy, the existing socio-cultural reality of the indigenous people.[12] Nevertheless, both these attempts externalize the process of conversion and, by linking it to colonial expansion, overlook the internal dialectics of a colonial society. After all, religious conversions did not occur only after the advent of colonialism. Moreover, the latter work, although sensitive in accepting that conversion is a complex, multi-facted process involving personal, cultural, social and religious dimensions,[13] only hints at the economic world.

One should stress the importance of the concepts of Sanskritization and Hinduization when dealing with conversion. As has already been argued, Sanskritization was a route by which low castes were able to rise over a generation or two to a higher position in the hierarchy. They adopted vegetarianism and teetotalism and Sanskritized their rituals and pantheons. One can agree with this as long as one accepts that such shifts are linked to a certain degree of upward economic movement, and are not one-way processes.[14] Besides, this formulation separates caste from deeper economic processes and does not take into account the level of violence inflicted on the adivasis and on their ideas when negotiating this process. In fact, even sensitive socio-anthropological studies sometimes categorically assert that Hindu civilization did not generally seek to convert or displace tribals, although they agree that conflicts were frequent, and that tribes were forced to retreat to the 'remotest areas', the forests and mountains.[15] Taken together, these statements contradict the 'civilizational' claims of Hinduism.[16] In fact, if anything, the opposite seems to be the case.

---

[11] Okorocha 1987.

[12] Rambo 1993, 54.

[13] Ibid., 165.

[14] Srinivas 1952, 30-1. As he puts it, this was possible, especially for those in the middle regions of the hierarchy. This implies a degree of affluence that needs to be stressed. As for Weber (1967) and his 'diffusion model', its basic problem is that it sees this movement as a one-way process, involving the Hinduization of tribal beliefs.

[15] Padel 1995, 17.

[16] A major exponent of this 'civilizational' character of Hinduism is Ravinder Kumar. I am not aware of any serious work by him on the

One witnesses the process of hegemonization through which Brahmanical Hinduism actually operates. Its exploitation of those who are incorporated and hierarchized, yet 'Hinduized', cannot be overlooked.[17] Similarly, the process is marked by a high degree of exclusiveness, expressed in the very idea of keeping the order of varna 'clean' and 'pure'.

One also has to mention here that this process is not a one-way affair. It is not only contested and interrogated, but also altered. It is marked by a host of complexities which have to be taken into account by the social historian.

The Pre-colonial Background

Talking about pre-colonial, and especially early medieval, Orissa, scholars like Bhirabi Prasad Sahu highlight the dynamics of the feudalization of this region. The manifestations of this process included the intermediaries and superior landlords on the one hand, and the reduction of peasants and artisans to the position of semi-serfs on the other. He suggests that the evolution of the caste system in Orissa developed late, and when it did, it was marked by certain specificities and differences in comparison to the Indo-Ganjetic plain model. This was primarily because of the preponderant tribal population and the geographical variations in the region. The extension of agriculture and land grants to Brahmins implied the conversion of most of the tribes to Sudras, which in turn converged with the process of their peasantization. Alongside this, their chiefs were absorbed as Kshatriyas into the varna system. This implies the absence of any rigid polarization. The classic four-fold varna system continued to remain largely theoretical, whereas the two tier-structure with the numerous intermediary occupational castes constituted the functional reality. Consequently, two clearly identifiable varnas—the Brahmin and the Sudra—evolved. The Vaishyas surfaced only occasionally in times of trade, and the Kshatriyas never had any local roots but were created in this period.

---

subject, though he has published short newspaper pieces. This right-wing position veils the basic components of terror and violence directed at the adivasis and outcastes by Brahmianical Hinduism.

[17] While disagreeing with most of what Louis Dumount (Dumount 1980) says, I find his assertion that Brahmanical Hinduism incorporates and hierarchizes very valuable.

As delineated, the rise of the Kshatriyas/Karanas came with the emergence of feudalism.[18]

One can also refer to the research on the Bengal frontier by Richard M. Eaton for a slightly later period. He demonstrates the way in which agricultural expansion entailed the process of Islamization of the adivasis.[19] What is new about these two approaches is their openness and the way they engage with a shifting reality, Hinduization in pre-colonial Orissa but Islamization in the case of the Bengal frontier. In both cases, one sees the way the non-Hindu adivasis were integrated into the feudal systems

Colonialism and the Shifts and Changes

In the context of Orissa, colonialism reinforced the existing situation by various interventions, but most significantly by the land settlements and monetization that it created. An important point is a sharpening of the caste/class polarization, which had a clear association with the agrarian interventions, irrigation, commercialization of agriculture (albeit limited) and an increasing degree of monetization.[20] In fact, a very superficial survey of some of the available land settlement reports of the Temporarily Settled areas of Cuttack, Puri, and Balasore, the princely states and some of

---

[18] Sahu 1986. Kulke 1976 focuses on the issue of Kshatriyaization in medieval Orissa and extends its relevance to the seventeenth-eighteenth centuries AD. He emphasizes it as more useful/relevant than Brahmanization and the functional reality. Surajit Sinha, 'State Formation and the Rajput Myth in Central India', in Kulke 1995, feels that the diffusion of the Rajput model of the state and the indigenous developmental processes could gain ground only among those tribal groups who had attained the technological level of settled agriculture. Thus, as he puts it, we do not find shifting cultivating groups like the Juangs or the Hill Bhuiyas of Orissa developing a kingship supported mainly by their primitive technique of cultivation. Interestingly, Beverley (1872) mentions the absence of a 'pure' Kshatriya caste in Orissa and refers to the Khandaits (swordsmen) who formed the erstwhile militia and who took their caste from their profession (ibid., 193).

[19] Eaton 1993 and 2000.

[20] One has to be cautious about the variations between the erstwhile Mughalbandi—coastal tract—and the western interior. For details cf. Rout 1986, 136-50; Chaudhury 1991, 28-56; and, especially, Padhi 1999 for the variations between the coastal and the western tract.

the major zamindaris illustrates the rather serious fall-out of the agrarian interventions, and the polarization of social relations centred around caste.[21] Land settlement included a set of complex negotiations with the adivasis. The Ranas of Jeypore began to wear the 'sacred thread', believing that they had bought the right to do so from the maharaja of Jeypore.[22] The Gonds of Sambalpur invented new legends to re-locate themselves within the framework of Hinduism, and the Gond zamindars wore the 'sacred thread'.[23] This not only implied a degree of Hinduization, but also a strategy to cope with the agrarian interventions. Here one can also mention the Kandhas of the princely state of Ranpur who preferred to be identified as 'Oriya Kandhas'. This indicates an allied component of the process—Oriyaization.[24]

To this day, one witnesses the growing importance of the Kshatriyas. After all, the colonial power needed 'settlements' with 'rulers', princes and landed zamindars. The classic varna system was invoked to stake the legitimacy of alliances with the Kshatriya rulers. Starting with the Raja of Puri, who was 'a king without a kingdom',[25] this process of Orissa's colonization reinforced the pre-existing order of things we have already encountered. Another vital component related to the relatively affluent agriculturists, including a section of the adivasis. Many from this section emerged as 'rich' peasants during the nineteenth century. They are those who did well in producing for the market, and claimed 'khandayat'—the Oriya variant of Kshatriya—status. khanda means 'sword' and khandayat means 'sword wielding'. In fact, this caste accommodated a wide variety of the prosperous section of the adivasis. Thus Rajputization/Kshatriyaization converged with Hinduization, and

---

[21] For details, Pati 1993, Chapter 1.

[22] Senapati and Sahu 1966, 110.

[23] O'Malley 1932, 70. Senapati and Mohanty 1971, 117 refer to Gond zamindars wearing the 'sacred thread'.

[24] Singh 1963, 10.

[25] After all, the Raja of Puri was actually the Raja of Khurda, which was taken over by the British. The Khurda Raja was, in fact, re-invented as the Raja of Puri—and Orissa—and compensated by being made superintendent of the Jagannatha temple; for details cf. Kulke 1987, 345-57.

affected the affluent sections of the adivasis.[26] Some of the references in the Census Reports offer clues to understanding this process. For example the first Census 1871 mentions the presence of 'numerous' Savaras (adivasis) in the Cuttack and Puri tract.[27] At the same time, a very superficial survey of the tribal population shows a decline in some parts of Orissa between 1891 and 1941, and no explanation is available for this. One also sees a very large increase of the Khandayat population of 45.4% (the largest of any caste) between 1901 and 1931 in the Orissa Division and the Orissa States.[28] Consequently, the connection between the decline of the adivasi population and the phenomenal increase of the Khandayats should be borne in mind when discussing the question of conversions and Hinduization in Orissa.

Shifting identities marked the process of conversion. For example, there were some 'advanced' Binjhals—a tribe in the Sambalpur region—who claimed Rajput status and adopted the practice of burning their dead.[29] It hardly needs to be pointed out that such emulation was an attempt to join the Brahmanical order. Also, Hinduization and the complexities connected with it laid a stress on vegetarianism and led to a shift in the dietary habits. This has a special significance since it was not really easy for the

---

[26] Leading anthropologists like F.G. Bailey (1996) see the Oriyas as migrants to the Kandha hills. In the 1950s, Oriyas were about 3 in every 8 of the population, and Bailey feels that they were probably fewer at the beginning of the century (ibid., 3). Even though the question of Oriya migrants cannot be disputed, Bailey cannot conceptualize their emergence from among the Kandhas. Thus, the hillman/plainsman dichotomy haunts sensitive scholars. What also needs to be borne in mind is a complexity where 'Oriyas'—besides being migrants—emerged from among the adivasis in the pre-colonial and colonial period, as I have sought to demonstrate. Thus, castes like the warrior caste (Paikas or Khandayats) also emerged from among the Kandhas and other adivasi groups. This in fact illustrates the process of conversion of adivasis via Hinduization/Kshatriyaization/Oriyaization. Weber (1967) mentions how those who sought assimilation were integrated in the Hindu community. Thus, the 'barbarians' who formed the ruling stratum 'secured their superiority over the subject classes' (ibid., 16).

[27] Beverly *1872*, 191.

[28] Based on Lacey 1933, 267.

[29] Senapati and Mohanty 1971, 118; O'Malley 1933, 70 refers to 'rich' Binjhals being burnt.

unsettled pahariah adivasis engaged in shifting cultivation, to accept it.[30] It implied a certain degree of stability with regard to agricultural production and affluence. Besides being looked down upon by the Brahmanical order, relatively restricted access to the market (at least in the early years of the nineteenth century) meant that tribal people had no serious desire to convert. In fact, violent encounters with the colonial power in the hills, especially during the first half of the nineteenth century, created conditions under which it was no longer possible for the tribes to manage their livelihood, and many were either frightened into conversion to Hinduism, or else marginalized as outcastes.

It is quite usual to find innumerable references to a fractured adivasi reality that spoke of two chief categories—the plains people and the pahariah or dongariah (viz. *pahar* = hill; *dongar* = shifting cultivation)—with the colonial establishment clearly admiring the former.[31] Most adivasis who converted to Hinduism, at least in the initial years, retained their own social and religious customs. The Brahmanical order was comfortable with this. After all these were an 'ancient people' who had to maintain their customs. But they were integrated and at the same time hierarchized: it would, for example, be difficult to talk about adivasis who were accepted as Brahmins.[32] In fact, the Rajputization scheme, as well as categories like 'haliya' Brahmins, have to be borne in mind when explaining the limits up to which such transgressions could be accepted.[33] The most common routes by which the process of conversion seems to have been channelled was the linking of adivasi chiefs and affluent sections to the varna order. The Hinduized Kandhas of Puri had to employ Brahmin priests. More significantly—given their position in the hierarchy of caste—they had to employ 'low Brahmins' from

---

[30] This is where one has to keep in mind Sinha 1995.

[31] Lieutenant Elliot (Deputy Commissioner of Raipur) 'Report on Kalahandi State, 28 July, 1856' cited in Senapati and Kuanr 1980, 473; hereafter Elliot's Report.

[32] Some scholars tend to over-emphasize the 'openness' of the caste system in Orissa; cf. for example, Dash 1989, 16-17.

[33] Haliya Brahmans included those who took to agriculture (*hala* = plough) mostly in the coastal tract. Most probably it included some who desired upward social mobility, or sections of Brahmans who faced marginalization.

among low-caste Hindus, who were consequently elevated.[34] This was in striking contrast to affluent non-Brahmins, including Telis (oilmen) who aspired to upward social mobility and were accepted as patrons of the Utkala Brahmin Samiti (established 1899). 47 out of 217 who contributed to the Utkala Brahmin Samiti in 1906 were non-Brahmins.[35]

As has been mentioned, diet and social position are closely related features when it comes to the question of conversion among the adivasis. Inevitably the landless were excluded from this process. If anything, their position became marginalized with the polarization of the caste system. They were distinctly classified as the Other. This means that, whereas some adivasis were 'terrorized' into conversion, landless outcaste were a major threat not only to the 'purity' of the varna system, but also to the colonial system. So some 'animists' were 'civilized', others had to be 'tamed' and negotiated with as 'criminal classes'.[36]

Consequently, there appears to be a shift from pre-colonial times in the way the adivasis were re-positioned. This was the result of a very complex dialectical process. On the one hand it involved the varna system which seems to have opened up a space for 'integration', by incorporating a large section of the adivasis as Khandayats/Kshatriyas. On the other, it involved adivasi society itself, negotiating the new context and adopting conversion as a part of a broad survival strategy. Among many complex features, one can see that most of the big zamindars and princes—many of them colonial creations—were out to prove their association with the adivasis, in order to prove the ancient origin of their status. Many folk tales that were invented to establish this connection also served

---

[34] O'Malley, 1911, 235.

[35] *Utkala Brahmana Samitira Sastha Barsha Bibarani* 1906.

[36] Clarke 1985, appendix 324-9, indicates a classification strategy that incorporated this thrust. In fact, Clarke's idea was to rehabilitate them in Angul by giving them 'good' land and loans. Needless to say, the ideas related to the outcastes were most clearly influenced by the upper-caste tradition of Orissa. References to the Oriya proverb chora chandala (thief and outcaste are interchangeable) indicates the way the varna order located the outcaste.

the dual purpose of claiming legitimacy and of exercising power over the adivasis.[37]

Colonial officialdom was largely influenced by this 'integrative' component and found the Brahmanical order—especially the cult of Jagannatha—to be one of its greatest legitimizers. In fact, this was one of the most significant inventions associated with the princes and zamindars. There were pre-colonial efforts in this direction. Thus, the process of urbanization in most of the princely capitals and bigger zamindaris entailed the construction of both a Jagannatha temple with a *bada danda* (big street) in front of it, and the annual celebration of a *Ratha Jatra* modelled along the lines of Puri.[38] Orissa's colonization perfected this drive What is significant from the point of view of the present project is the emphasis on the oral tradition that highlighted the Savara (an adivasi community) origins of Jagannatha. Perhaps it formed the most vital component by which the colonial system and the internal ruling classes (princes and zamindars) negotiated with a region that had a very large adivasi population. The Pengo Parajas of Koraput began using Jagannatha's *mahaprasad* for 'purification' rites.[39] Although some form of purificatory rites did exist among adivasis, the entry of the mahaprasad into these cultures was new. Thus, if one talks about

---

[37] Even a cursory look at most of the Revenue Settlements reports illustrates this aspect. One can also cite here 'The Brief Histories of Each of the 24 States (1909)', R/2 (285/1). Elliot's Report mentions the coronation ceremony where a Khond Pat Majhi was dressed especially for the occasion. A rich cloth was thrown on his lap, on which the raja sat during the ceremony. This custom is said to have originated at the time of some ancestor whose name was unknown since 'the legend has been lost' (ibid., 478-9). Senapati and Sahu 1968 refer to a legend of the Binjhals (adivasis). According to it, the mother of the first Chauhan Raja of Patana had taken shelter in the hut of a Binjhal where she gave birth to Ramai who became the king of Patana and made the Binjhal the chief of Borasambar (ibid., 103). As can be seen, the theme of Kshatriyaization and the idea of securing legitimacy in the eyes of the adivasi population were a dominant theme in these customs and legends.

[38] Kulke 1976, 403-4, refers to the pre-colonial origins/spread of this cult and specifically to the building of Jagannatha temples in the second half of the nineteenth century, revealed by the Revenue Settlement Reports of the princely states or the big zamindaris, or studies the architectural pattern of the 'castle towns'.

[39] Thusu 1977, 15.

the specificities of Hinduization/peasantization associated with the process of conversion, one has to keep the Jagannatha cult in mind. Although one can detect parallels to the eighteenth century, the power of the cult was never felt as seriously as in the nineteenth century, when it co-operated with the colonial establishment and the internal ruling classes to extend and tap agricultural resources.

This co-existed with drives to build Hindu temples in some parts of western Orissa. Here one can especially refer to the temple-building project of the tahsildar Dinabandhu Patnaik. The scheme involved building a Sibamandira (temple for Shiva) in 1855 at Bisipara. This was Patnaik's headquarters. In fact, it was not built by the people of Bisipara alone, but by people of the Khondmals region by *bethi*.[40] In this way, Hinduization made deep inroads into western Orissa.

What one observes is the emergence of a system—however invisible it may have been—to direct conversions to Hinduism. This entailed mainly two methods. The first was a comparatively non-violent and long-drawn hegemonic process. Although it had pre-colonial roots, it was substantially altered during the nineteenth century.[41] The second included a set of terror campaigns by the colonizer and his privileged tenure holders in the hills.[42] These were marked by sudden disruptions.[43] The magnitude of this latter process is difficult to fathom unless one also keeps in mind the decimation of the adivasis. This decimation was caused by the conflicts with colonialists (and their feudal collaborators) in the nineteenth century. Thus the adivasis had to start from scratch and were forced to convert, or else be outcastes.

Significant is the way this process saw continuities as well as shifts and changes, as compared to the pre-colonial context. Thus,

---

[40] Bailey 1996, 18-19; *bethi* means forced labour. This co-exited with the drive to build Jagannatha temples.

[41] As long as one sees things in the perspective outlined in this paper, one can agree upto a point with Srinivas 1952, regarding the role of caste in enabling Hinduism to proselytise without the aid of a church (ibid., 31).

[42] As pointed out by Weber 1967, this process was marked by a certain degree of internalization of the caste hierarchies of the Hindu order by the underprivileged strata (ibid., 18). I have discovered this particular aspect in parts of coastal Orissa during my own field-work in the 1990s.

[43] Cf. Pati 1999, 345-59.

the Khsatriyization component seems to have continued on a much wider scale incorporating the non-pahariah adivasis into the 'order' of Hinduism, whereas most of them were sought to be 'integrated' as Shudras in the early medieval period. Later, the nineteenth century saw a toning down of this process Thus, what we see is a complex process that saw the co-existence of Hinduization, peasantization, Kshatriyaization, and Oriyaization, with the colonization of Orissa. This was in a context of major agrarian interventions that saw a significant shift towards monetization and the growth of a market for agricultural production. The landless section was mostly from among the outcastes and the pahariah adivasis. It constituted the mass of people who worked as landless labourers or those who migrated to far-off places in search of employment—a feature that seems to have begun before the colonial period, but which developed further during the nineteenth century.[44]

Questions of Identity and Resistance

In this section I will examine the complexities of the world of those who were converted. I shall also deal with the important questions of identity and resistance. After all, the changeover is never complete. The opposition/resistance to the conversion and the interrogation into one's own identity takes various forms. The most prominent are the adivasi rebellions in Orissa in the nineteenth century. The period up to the mid-nineteenth century saw major offensives against the hill people, and here the idea of 'civilizing' the 'barbarian' seems to have made the colonial machinery resort to brute terror. The price for being 'civilized' included unpaid labour that was extracted to build the communication links; links that were

---

[44] As can be seen, this process began in the coastal tract and spread into western Orissa during the nineteenth century. The issue of migration in Orissa is another area which has received little attention. It obviously had pre-colonial origins. We have a reference to a strike by the Oriya teeka bearers of Calcutta in May/June 1827 (Bengali newspapers, compiled and edited by Anil Chandra Dasgupta (1959, 214). This was a reaction to the government's move to licence them, and thereby convert them into company servants and requisition them for public duties. This is particularly significant since it shows a clear knowledge of the process of forced labour recruitment.

crucial to extend power and control the hills. A particular problem for the pahariah adivasis was the erosion of traditional forest rights.[45]

That the varna logic haunted the imagination of the colonial machinery is clear from the way it stereotyped the Kandhas as a tribe that resorted to meriah (human) sacrifice. Beside the fact that not all Kandhas were associated with it, the colonial offensive overlooked many aspects, including the fact that some of the princes and zamindars not only encouraged this practice, but were involved in it. Most importantly, it is necessary to emphasize that the idea of a human sacrifice itself was based on a survival strategy—to counter a set of conditions that marginalized the world of the adivasis and sought to terrorise them into submission.

Resistance is also visible in the development of popular cults like the Mahima Dharma that function as a counter to Hinduization and upper caste domination. This was especially triggered by the post-1866 famine context. Terror ensued for those who survived, because they were ex-communicated if they had accepted relief. The emergence of Chattra Khia as a new caste (outcaste) is directly connected with this period.[46] The Mahima cult not only resisted the varna order, but posed a serious challenge to it. It attracted the Kandhas as well. In fact, one of its leading exponents was Bhima Bhoi—a blind Kandha—who is associated with a host of fascinating *bolis* (compositions). People who became involved in this folk cult were expected to begin a new chapter of their life without any reference to their past. This aspect, related to the 'deletion' of one's memory with regard to one's past, implies transcending the varna boundary which had become rigid during the post-1866 phase. Its inclusive credentials and its rapid success in the Western tracts imply a mixed response. Whereas the varna order was terrified of it and regarded it as apocalyptic visions,[47] some of the feudal chiefs (like the chief of Dhenkanal) emerged as its champions. In a context of disruptions and changes which was reinforced by the famine of 1866 that severely undermined the process of Hinduization, the Mahima cult appealed to the adivasi and outcaste population. Thus the cult became particularly attractive to negotiate with the adivasis and the outcastes.

---

[45]For details cf *Resisting Domination*, Chapter 1.

[46] O'Malley 1933, 60.

[47] For details cf. Pati 2001, 44.

This socio-reformist movement that united the western and the coastal parts of Orissa was also marked by its ambiguity towards colonialism. This aspect is demonstrated in its followers' resistance to Christianity, which made its presence particularly felt in the coastal tracts during and after the Famine, as well as in the western tracts during the nineteenth century. Here one has to keep in mind the question of selectivity—Christianity was, after all, closely identified with colonialism and was thus seen as part of the process that had devastated the world of the adivasis and the outcastes. At the same time, its stress on the missionary character may reveal an attempt to draw from this component of Christianity. What we see in the cult is a co-existence that relates to a distanced existence from Christianity, a silence towards colonialism and an opposition that was directed against the varna order and the process of Hinduization.

Smallpox spelt doom for the Kandhas of Subarnaghurry in 1860. The disease was thought to be connected with the presence of the Paikas (an erstwhile martial caste which got increasingly involved in agriculture, and also included some converted adivasis) in Kanha country. The Kandhas felt that if the Paikas were expelled, they would be able to enjoy peace and comfort. About fifty Kandhas, led by Jagoo Pojaree and armed with battle axes, bows and arrows, went to Goomahgoodah village and 'shouted aloud to murder all the Paikas who hid in their houses'.[48]

We also witness the invention of the *Dharma Pinnu*—the smallpox goddess—by the Kuttia Kandhas to cope with the disease. *Dharma Pinnu* was seen as the source of smallpox and appeased at all agricultural festivals. Interestingly, she was identified as an Oriya (Hindu) goddess living in the lap of luxury. Ceremonies were performed in her honour just before sowing in the hill clearings. The invocations at her special ceremony were in Oriya, and the offerings were not the normal millet and rice beer but milk, *ghee*, rice and *mohwa* liquor.[49] This reflected part of a broader survival strategy of the indigenous people to negotiate with the process of Hinduization. They also invented their goddess *Mata*, who represents a close parallel to the *Dharma Pinnu* of the Kandhas.[50]

---

[48] Home Department (Public Branch), nos. 60-1 (A), 24 January 1861.

[49] Watts 1970.

[50] Guha, et al. 1968.

Thus we see the fusion of a number of highly complex strategies to resist conversion drives in the hill tracts as well as attempts at accommodation in the varna order. The Paikas were hated because they not only represented an exploitative order linked with colonialism, but also because they symbolized the process of Hinduization. Thus a link was established in popular cosmology between the colonialist and the non-tribals—including tribal converts—associated with exploitation and conversion.

The smallpox goddesses who emerged from the complex Hinduization process occupied a rather central position. The offering of *mohwa* (liquor) and *pana* (a ritualistic drink), the special invocations to the goddess in Oriya and the idea of abandoning her in a lonely place outside the village limits, illustrate two simultaneous processes. One is that of contesting Hinduization and those who were seen as its representatives in the hill tracts. The other is an attempt to negotiate and accommodate her or to be accommodated within the varna order.

Conversions to Christianity

Conversions to Christianity were not as simple as is made out either in the missionary tracts or the Oriya press.[51] Moreover, the number of conversions to Christianity was small. The association of Christianity with colonialism was a major reason why this religion was never seen as a serious alternative, although many outposts were created for the purpose.

After saying this, one should delineate certain complexities associated with the shift to Christianity. In a context of uncertainties and insecurities the Oraons, for example, felt that Christianity protected them from the witches and bhoots who were thought to be powerless against the new system.[52] Moreover, like the converts to the varna order who participated in the Hindu and tribal festivals,

---

[51] Talking about the missionary tracts, Anon 1858 is a typical example that refers to Gunga Dhor (one of the early converts) testing the divinity of Jagannatha by abusing 'him' and scratching 'his' back with a pointed iron, since he had not responded to his petition. Another example are the Oriya newspapers like *Utkala Dipika* 9/2/1867; 23/2/1867, which projected the activities of the Christian missionaries during the 1866 Famine.

[52] Dalton 1872, 247.

converts to Christianity observed certain customs and beliefs that were antithetical to the basic tenets of Christianity. They participated in tribal festivals and, when asked about their identity, mentioned their tribe, suppressing the Christian connection.[53]

The National Movement and Hinduization

The Indian national movement seems to have made a distinct mark on the process of conversion. In Orissa, Gandhian politics seem to have been very influential. Perhaps this would have not been possible if Hinduization and the process of conversion, along with other associated complexities, had not prepared the background. In fact, Gandhian politics saw the advent of a new phase in the history of conversion. A large number of adivasis and outcastes gave up meat and liquor.[54] Gandhian ideas of locating the outcastes as 'Harijans' had a strong impact in Orissa.[55] What is significant is that, although the issues affecting the outcastes were never taken up for any questioning or confrontation, its inclusive component brought this section into the movement. What happened was an extension of the process of Hinduization that co-existed with a socio-reformist current which sought to 'integrate' the adivasis and the outcastes, in the anti-colonial struggle, without confronting the Brahmanical order in any way.

It is very important to emphasize here that for the marginal sections—the adivasis and the outcastes—vegetarianism was a major sacrifice, since they were for a large part people who were not settled agriculturists and who did not have any stable source of income. After all, it meant giving up readily available food from the forests and rivers, or, from the occasional death of a cow in the village.[56] Gandhism provided space and scope for the outcastes and

[53]Senapati and Sahu 1966, 121-2.

[54] I am not for a moment discounting the pluralism associated with the perceptions of Gandhian calls for solidarity that *also* included drinking liquor or distributing opium after 'looting' them from shops.

[55] One can cite here the surname 'Harijan' adopted by dalits in western Orissa.

[56] Bailey 1996, 39 refers to the Panos and the idea of enjoying a meal when someone's cow died. Amin 1995 touches upon the issue of vegetarianism and abstinence from liquor, but what eludes him is the fact that this was a very major sacrifice for the marginalized adivasis and the

the adivasis to gain limited access to the Congress organization. They gained some self-respect in their immediate environment and, by this, a large number of them were incorporated in the struggle against colonialism. Thus, details about satyagrahies selected from Jeypur (1940-41) for the 'individual satyagraha' mention 'agricultural labourers', most of whom, besides spinning khadi, gave up eating beef and drinking liquor. We are told about adivasis who work in the Harijan *bastis* for 'their uplift', and about an adivasi aspirant stopping an early marriage.[57]

This resulted in a struggle between the national movement and the colonial establishment and the feudal landed sections in Orissa which centred around the process of Hinduization itself.[58] One can cite here the way some drunken *mehtars* (sweepers—outcastes) were deputed by the colonial administration to be on the roads in order to discourage people from attending a meeting in Khurda town during the Non-Cooperation Movement.[59] One could also mention the fact that common feasting was adopted as a strategy to unite the people and was regarded a serious matter by the Nilgiri durbar in 1937[60] and the attempts by the Dhenkanal durbar to divide people along lines of caste by mobilizing outcastes to cut away standing crops from the field of Prajamandal activists in 1947.[61] Even the limited electoral process in the 1937 elections saw elements of this.[62] Under pressure of the mass movements, the

---

outcastes. Besides animal flesh and fish, it meant giving up *salapa* and *tari* that could be tapped from the trees in the forests, or *handia* that could be made at home. It meant giving up major constituents of the diet.

[57] All India Congress Committee Papers, File no. P20/1940. This list was sent to the General Secretary of the All India Congress Committee by the Orissa Congress Committee.

[58] I am using the word 'feudal' to refer to the despotic chiefs and some of the oppressive zamindars.

[59] *Searchlight*, 22 February 1922.

[60] Nilgri Praja Andolana Compilation Committee 1982, 64; *Krushak* 3 January 1938.

[61] All India State Peoples' Conference, file no. 129 (hereafter AISPC).

[62] Mozumdar 1937, 14-6 refers to the Raja of Puri—Jagannatha's earthly incarnation—distributing mahaprasad at Kanika and seeking the pledges of the voters in support of the Kanika Raja. But as observed the voters bowed to the mahaprasad, dropped their ballot paper in the Congress Box, bowed again and walked out—adequate apologies were

colonial and feudal order tried to re-work the process of Hinduization by imposing the Brahmanical order. They wanted to retain control over something which they themselves had strongly supported during the nineteenth century. At the same time, one has to say that, given the nuances and the complexities of Gandhian nationalism in Orissa, it also reinforced both Hinduization and the conversion of the adivasis and outcastes by its inclusive and 'integrative' character. Hinduization thus became contested between the colonial and feudal order and Gandhian nationalism.

With the emergence of the Left in Orissa in the 1930s, Orissa was swept by powerful peasant movements and the state peoples' movement (in some the princely states). The Kisan Sangha and the Prajamandal operated on the idea of class-based struggles that not only challenged the colonial and feudal order, but also Gandhian politics. Although historians have highlighted the way the Left movement contested colonialism and the exploiting classes—who in the context of Orissa included the princes and the zamindars—the fact that class unity threatened Hinduization also needs to be stressed. This was a serious concern for both the colonial and feudal orders and the Orissa Congress and prompted serious action against the Communists.[63]

---

thus made to the Lord. Accepting the 'new' by apologizing to the old implied a structure of continuity that 'modern' democracy inherited. The Congress techniques of mass contact and electioneering included vote *geeti* sung by *sankirtan* parties. In some areas, Hindu sadhus held in high esteem campaigned for the Congress. In onc casc a Congrcss candidate was believed to have chosen blue as his colour at the insistence of Jagannatha whose Chakra was of the same colour. Yellow—the colour of the Congress—was seen as an auspicious colour given its association with Hinduism. Pictures of Hindu gods and goddesses also appeared on the election posters. Such complexities implied a transition that left the imprints of Hinduization on the electoral process itself.

[63]AISPC file no. 124; interview with Banamali Das May, 1982. What is clear is a level of collaboration between the Central Congress leadership, the Orissa Congress, the durbar and the colonial establishment when it came to 'containing' the Communists of Nilgiri. The fact that the militant class-based struggles of the Nilgiri Prajmandal threatened to obliterate the hierarchies of the Brahmanical order by uniting the state people—including the outcastes and the adivasis—needs to be borne in mind when explaining this anxiety.

The anti-imperialist struggle also demonstrates the way Christianity acquired new meanings among its converts. Thus, the Mundas of Gangpur—a princely state in which the Prajamandal movement was virtually non-existent—perceived it as a weapon to fight their oppressors, and as an instrument of solidarity. In January and February 1939, there was a no-rent movement led by Nathaniel Munda. The immediate issue centred on the sudden increase of rents by about 100 to 150 per cent in the 1910 Settlement. The people submitted a petition to the Rani and the officials at a meeting on 2 February 1939. This was attended by about 5,000 people from nearly 30 villages, and it reflected the anti-feudal aspirations of the people, which had been kindled by the Prajamandal movement and by the 'native' preachers. It included the abolition of *bethi*, customary levies and a host of oppressive features. The adivasis appealed to the Viceroy when the durbar failed to respond. However, even this did not solve their problems.

This created the basis for a no-rent movement in 1939 in the state. In a population of 60,000 Mundas there were 17,000 Lutherans, the rest Roman Catholics. The Lutheran Mundas rebelled, and it is possible that they translated into action the version of Christianity as preached by their own preachers (the Lutheran mission was initially indifferent to the movement). In contrast, the Roman Catholic Church found the rent hike to be reasonable and beneficial to the people in the long run, making people work harder, and this position was largely accepted by its followers.

While 5,000 Lutheran Mundas withheld their rent, the rest of the Lutherans and the Catholics continued to petition the durbar. As the movement gathered momentum, the position of the Lutheran establishment shifted from indifference to anxiety. Two Munda pleaders from Ranchi and the 'native' preachers influenced its followers. In its anxiety the durbar approached the Lutheran Church Council (Ranchi) to send a deputation to negotiate with the rebellious Mundas. The deputation reached Gangpur in early April, but failed in its efforts. In fact, after this the secretary of the Church advised the Diwan to take strong measures since he felt that only this would make the Mundas 'see reason'. This precipitated ruthless terror against the Mundas. Thirty-two people died and nineteen were injured in police gunfire.[64]

This rebellion shows the many aspects associated with Christianity in Orissa. Instead of being a legitimizing component of the durbar, it shows its subversive character in Gangpur. Thus, in the course of the rebellion, the Mundas not only rose against the durbar and its exploitative practices, but also refused to accept the codes of the Church and confronted colonialism. The way Christianity was transformed by some 'native' preachers and interpreted by the Munda converts for use as a weapon in their struggle, demonstrates its complexities and pluralities, given its association with popular aspirations and militancy.

Independence and After

Like so many others, the processes of conversion and Hinduization continued after India became a free country. The compulsions of the new state and its efforts to establish itself saw a renewed thrust towards Hinduization. The administration in Orissa stuck to symbols which, like the Jagannatha cult, had made deep inroads in the region. One is reminded here of the Bondas—an adivasi community of Koraput—who had to go through revenue settlements in the 1950s and 1960s. A method that clearly harked back to the colonial past saw the district administration select the oldest-looking man in the village as its maharajah. Through him, the settlement was apparently negotiated. He was given a rusty sword and a wooden chair as his throne. And, although he complained to me that he was among thc poorest people in the village, the administration managed to achieve its mission.[65] After this, the process of imposing new 'gods' and the Brahmanical order began

Afer Independence, perceptions of Christianity also changed. In the 1950s some Kandhas, for example, adopted Christianity, which was no longer identified with the government; it offered a defence against Hindu exploitation.[66]

---

[64]Home Political, 18/2/1939; 18/3/1939; All India Congress Committee, Private Papers G12/1937-39, 18 June 1939.

[65]I have seen both the sword and the 'throne' (wooden chair); interviews in the Bonda hills, Koraput: May-June 1980.

[66] Padel 1995,10.

Since the 1980s the situation has indeed changed. An unprecedented level of homogenization and a religious polarization has been reached.[67] Communalism and divisive politics have entered Orissa and have attained a high level of aggression. This has been legitimized not only by the political process, but also by the electronic and print-media, as well as by scholars and intellectuals.[68] Furthermore, the middle class has earned a degree of respectability. Communalized perceptions cloud the real world of poverty, hunger, and unemployment in a state where more than 55 per cent of the people and 89 per cent of the families live below the poverty line. Orissa in the present context seems to pose a serious set of problems for the very existence of 'civil society', and it is here that one needs to understand the deeper problems in historical perspective.

References

Archival Sources

'The Brief Histories of Each of the 24 States (1909)', R/2 (285/1), Crown Representative Papers, India Office Library, London.

All India Congress Committee Papers, file nos. P20/1940; G12/1937-39, Private Papers Section, Nehru Memorial Museum & Library, New Delhi.

All India State Peoples' Conference, file nos. 124; 129, Private Papers Section, Nehru Memorial Museum & Library, New Delhi.

Home Department (Public Branch), nos. 60-61 (A), 24 January 1861, National Archives of India, New Delhi.

Home Political, 18/2/1939; 18/3/1939, National Archives of India, New Delhi.

---

[67] There have been quite a few writings on this subject; see especially Panikkar 1999.

[68] I would like to point to the large number of studies that project the Jagannatha cult as 'Orissa's cult'. Here I should like to include Eschmann et al. 1978.

Microfilm
'God Struck Me Dead—Religious Conversion Experiences and Autobiographies of Negro Ex-Slaves, 1945', Social Science Source Documents, No. 2, Microfilm, British Library, London.

Newspapers
Krushak, 3 January1938.
National Front, 18 June 1939.
Searchlight, 22 February 1922.
Utkala Dipika, 9 February and 23 February 1867.

Reports, Books and Articles
Amin, S. 1995. *Event, Metaphor, Memory: Chauri Chaura, 1922-1992*, Berkeley and Los Angeles: University of California Press.

Anon. 1858. *A Brief Sketch of the Rise and Progress of the Baptist Church Orissa Mission*, Cuttack: Mission Press.

Anon. 1906. *Utkala Brahmana Samitira Sastha Barsha Bibarani* (Oriya: The Sixth Annual Report of the Utkala Brahmin Samiti), Puri: no publisher cited.

Bailey, F.G. 1996. *The Civility of Indifference: On Domesticating Ethnicity*, Ithaca and London: Cornell University Press.

Beverley, H. 1872. *Report on the Census of Bengal, 1872*, Calcutta: Bengal Secretariat Press.

Chakravarty, U. 1998. *Re-writing History: Life and Times of Pandita Ramabai*, Delhi: Kali for Women.

Chaudhury, P. 1991. 'Peasants and British Rule in Orissa', *Social Scientist*, vol. 19, no. 7, August-September, 28-56.

Clarke, R. 1985. 'Panas of Orissa', in M. Kennedy, *The Criminal Classes in India*, 1907 rptd. Delhi: Mittal Publications, appendix 324-29.

Dalton, E.T. 1872. *Descriptive Ethnology of Bengal*, Calcutta: Government Press.

Dasgupta, A.C. 1959. *The Days of John Company: Selections from Calcutta Gazette, 1824-1932*, Calcutta: Superintendent Government Printing.

Dumount, L. 1980. *Homo Hierarchicus: The Caste System and its Implications* (Translated by Mark Sainsbury, Louis Dumont and Basia M. Gulati), Chicago and London: Chicago University Press.

Eaton, R.M. 1993. *The Rise of Islam and the Bengal Frontier, 1204-1760*, Berkeley: California University Press.

— 2000. 'Who are the Bengali Muslims? Conversion and Islamization in Bengal', in *Essays on Islam and Indian History*, Delhi: Oxford University Press, Chap. 11, 259-75.

Guha, S. 1999. *Environment and Ethnicity in India, 1200-1991*, Cambridge: Cambridge University Press.

Guha, U. et al. 1968. *The Didayi: A Forgotten Tribe of Orissa*, Delhi: Anthropological Survey of India.

Ilaih, K. 1996. *Why I am not a Hindu: A Sudra Critique of Hindutva, Philosophy, Culture and Political Economy*, Calcutta: Samya.

Illustrated Weekly of India, 24 July 1988.

Jordens, J.T.F. 1977. 'Reconversion to Hinduism, the Shuddhi of the Arya Samaj', in G.A. Oddie (ed.), *Religion in South Asia: Religious Conversion and Revival Movements in South Asia in Medieval and Modern Times*, London: Curzon Press, 145-69.

Kosambi, M. 1995. *Pandita Ramabai's Feminist and Christian Conversions: Focus on Stree Dharma-Neeti*, Bombay: SNDT Women's University.

Kulke, H. 1976. 'Kshatriyaisation and Social Change: A Study in Orissa Setting', in S.D. Pillai (ed.), *Aspects of Change in India: Studies in Honour of Prof. G.S.Ghurye*, Bombay: Popular Prakashan, 398-409.

— 1987. 'The Struggle Between the Rajas of Khurda and the Muslim Subahdars of Cuttack for the Dominance of the Jagannatha Temple', in A. Eschmann, H. Kulke and G.C. Tripathi (eds.), *The Cult of Jagannath and the Regional Tradition of Orissa*, Delhi: Manohar, 321-57.

Lacey, W.G. 1933. *Census of India, 1931*, vol. VII, *Bihar and Orissa Part I: Report*, Patna: Superintendent Government Printing.

Lamb, C. and Bryant, M.D. (eds.) 1999. *Religious Conversion: Contemporary Practices and Controversies*, London: Cassel, Introduction, 'Conversion: Contours of Controversy and Commitment in a Plural World', 1-19.

Lieutenant Elliot (Deputy Commissioner of Raipur) 'Report on Kalahandi State, 28 July, 1856' cited in Nilamani Senapati and D.C. Kuanr. 1980. *Orissa District Gazetteers: Kalahandi*, Orissa Government Press, Cuttack, 457-82.

Nilgiri Praja Andolanara Itihasa (Oriya:'History of the Nilgiri Prajamandal'). 1982. Balasore: Nilgri Praja Andolana Compilation Committee.

Oddie, G.A. 1977. *Religion in South Asia: Religious Conversion and Revival Movements in South Asia in Medieval and Modern Times*, London: Curzon Press, 1977.

Okorocha, C.C. 1987. *The Meaning of Religious Conversion in Africa: The Case of the Igbo of Nigeria*, Vermount: Gower Publishing Company.

O'Malley, L.S.S. 1932. *District Gazetteers: Sambalpur*, Patna: Superintendent of Government Press.

— 1933. *Bihar and Orissa District Gazetteers: Cuttack*, Patna: Superintendent of Government Press.

Padel, F. 1995. *The Sacrifice of Human Being: British Rule and the Khonds of Orissa*, Delhi: Oxford University Press.

Padhi, S.P. 1999. *Land Relations and Agrarian Development in India: A Comparative Historical Study of Regional Variations*, Thiruvananthapuram: Centre for Development Studies.

Panikkar, K.N. (ed.) 1999. *Concerned Indian's Guide to Communalism*, Delhi: Viking Penguin.

Pati, B. 2001. 'The High:Low Dialectic in Fakirmohana's Chamana Athaguntha: Popular Culture, Literature and Society in Nineteenth Century Orissa', in *Situating Social History: Orissa (1800-1997)*, Hyderabad: Orient Longman, 26-49.

— 1993. *Resisting Domination: Peasants, Tribals and the National Movement in Orissa (1920-50)*, Delhi: Manohar.

— 1999. 'Environment and Social History: Kalahandi, 1800-1950', in *Environment and History*, vol. 5, no. 3, October, 345-59.

— 2000. 'Orissa Today: Fantasy and Reality', *Economic and Political Weekly*, vol. XXXV, no. 18, 29 April, 1516.

Rambo, L.R. and C.E. Farhadian. 1999. 'Converting: Stages of Religious Change'; in Christopher Lamb and M. Darrol Bryant (eds.), *Religious Conversion: Contemporary Practices and Controversies*, London: Cassel, 23-34.

— 1993. *Understanding Religious Conversion*, New Haven and London: Yale University Press.

Rout, S. 1986. 'Rural Stratification in Coastal Orissa, 1866-1900', in *Social Science Probings*, vol. 3, no. 1, 136-50.

Sahu, B.P. 1986. 'The Brahmanical model viewed as an instrument of socio-cultural change: An autopsy', in *Proceedings of the*

Indian History Congress 1985, Delhi: Indian History Congress, 180-92.

— 'Orissan Society: Past and Present Manifestations', paper presented at the Training for Development of Scholarship Society', Pune.

Senapati N. and Sahu, N.K. 1966. *Orissa District Gazetteers: Koraput*, Cuttack: Government Press.

— 1968. *Orissa District Gazetteers: Balangir*, Orissa Cuttack: Government Press.

Senapati, N. and Mohanty, B. 1971. *Orissa District Gazetteers: Sambalpur*, Cuttack: Orissa Government Press.

Singh G.N. 1963. *Final Report on the Original Survey and Settlement Operations of the Ranpur Ex-State Area in the District of Puri*, Berhampur: no publisher cited.

Sinha, S. 1995. 'State Formation and the Rajput Myth in Central India', in Hermann Kulke, *The State in India, 1000-1700*, Delhi: Oxford University Press, 304-42.

Srinivas, M.N. 1952. *Religion and Society among the Coorgs of South India*, Oxford: Clarendon Press.

Taylor, D. 1999. 'Conversion: Inward, Outward and Awkward', in Christopher Lamb and M. Darrol Bryant (eds.), *Religious Conversion: Contemporary Practices and Controversies*, London: Cassel, 35-50.

Thusu, K.N. 1977. *Pengo Parajas of Koraput*, Calcutta: Anthropological Survey of India.

Vishwanathan, G. 1998: *Outside the Fold: Conversion, Modernity and Belief*, Princeton: Princeton University Press.

Watts, N.A. 1970: *The Half Clad Tribes of Eastern India*, Bombay: Orient Longman.

Weber, Max. 1967. *The Religion of India: The Sociology of Hinduism and Buddhism* (Translated by Hans H. Gereth and Don Martindale, New York: Free Press 1958).

Interviews

Banamali Das, Nilgiri, May 1982.

Bonda hills, Koraput, May-June 1980.

20

When the Buffalo Becomes a Pumpkin: Animal Sacrifice Contested*

Cornelia Mallebrein

One stroke of the ceremonial sword, and a huge pumpkin placed on four small wooden legs falls into pieces.[1] The priest and his assistants immediately smear blood-coloured *kumkum* powder on each side of the two halves. 'The pumpkin represents the buffalo. We stopped the cruel buffalo sacrifice a year ago at our temple, as it violates the Prevention of Cruelty to Animals Act', says an onlooker.

This incident is symptomatic of the present sentiments towards animal sacrifice all over India, as expressed mainly by educated members of society. Fieldwork for the project on the 'Hinduization of tribal deities in Orissa' in the last few years revealed that this discussion about the legal right to perform animal sacrifice has reached nearly all major temples that have non-vegetarian deities, and it fills the newspapers.

There are many instances in Orissa where animal sacrifice—especially buffalo sacrifice—has been stopped in the recent years. The sacrifice of buffaloes is a characteristic element in rituals involving those deities who are of tribal origin and whose worship is still performed by a tribal or low-caste priest. It is the goddess, not a male god, who demands a buffalo. Although still rooted in their old tribal traditions, the deities are now on the verge of becoming absorbed into the realm of codified Hinduism, as such becoming assimilated to one of the pan-Indian Hindu deities. In the

---

* Research on this topic was carried out as part of a wider study on the tutelary deities of royal families in Orissa, their history and development, financed by the German Research Council (DFG) as part of the Orissa Research Programme (ORP). I would like to thank the DFG for making this research possible. I would also like to thank Dillip Sethi (M.A.) for his assistance during field work in Orissa.

[1] This offering is called *kūṣmāṇḍa-bali*. Kūṣmāṇḍa (*Benikasa cerifera*) is a kind of pumpkin gourd; see Monier Williams s.v.

case of the goddess, she is usually associated with Durgā.[2] Patronage of temples, worship, and the rituals linked with it are now a highly politicized, controversial issue among various groups, ritual specialists, as well as worshippers. Most of these contested deities are related to one of the many royal families of Orissa, who worship them as their family or tutelary deity (*iṣṭadevī*).[3] Until Independence and the formation of the state of Orissa, it was the local rulers, the many rājā who fostered and promoted their cult.[4] Regarded as *rāṣṭradevatā*, she was the protector of the land and the people. The rājā, as representative of the goddess on earth, played a prominent role in all the rituals, including animal sacrifice. Since Independence, the royal families have lost their influence over the *iṣṭadevatā* and local deities. With the loss of privy purses and special privileges (abolished by Indira Gandhi in 1971) they have reduced their patronage of, and participation in, the festivals of the various gods and goddesses of their former kingdoms. In most cases patronage has been taken over by the Religious Endowments Office and trustee committees.

In the present debate about animal sacrifice in Orissa, the deities most affected are those who trace their origins to an autochthonous deity of one of the various Kondh groups.[5] The traditional buffalo sacrifice (*kedu laka*) of the Kondh, in honour of the earth goddess, is the focus of the discussion on animal sacrifice, a point which will be discussed later.[6]

---

[2] See Mallebrein 2002.

[3] For example the goddesses Maṇināgeśvarī in Ranpur; Pāṭkhaṇḍā in Jarasinhga, Bāraḷī Devī in Balasgumpha, Kandhuṇī Devī in Sorada, Vyāghra Devī in Bhanjannagar, see Das 1999; Pradhan 1997. For the adoption of a tribal deity by the Chauhan ruler, see Pasayat 1997.

[4] Kulke 1978, 1992 discusses the role of tribal deities as tutelary deities and their role in the early State formation in Orissa.

[5] The Kondh are the largest tribal group in Orissa. They inhabit most of the Kondhmal district, but they are also prominent in the districts of Ganjam, Gajapati, Rayagada, Bolangir, Kalahandi and Dhenkanal. The Kondh call their area *Kui dina* (kui country). The Maliah Kondh are one of the five sub-groups of Kondhs (Maliah, Kuttia, Dongria, Kuvi, Desia). For further information: S. Banerjee 1999; Behera 1996; P.K. Nayak 1989; R. Nayak (et al.) 1990; R. Nayak & N. Soreng 1999; N. Patnaik 1982.

[6] It is mainly the buffalo sacrifice of the Maliah Kondh in the Kondhmal district which is contested.

I consider first the arguments of those who reject animal sacrifice, and then those in support of it. The information is based on interviews in Orissa on this topic during the past years, and on the lively discussions on animal sacrifice on the Internet, today the major communication forum for countless worldwide animal protection groups that are linked together.[7]

The arguments of the opponents of animal sacrifice, as they appear on the public scene, for example in different information and communication media like newspapers, journals, and of course the Internet, come through strongly. Conversely, the voices of the supporters of animal sacrifice, although a majority of the population, are barely represented in the public debate.

The Buffalo Sacrifice of the Maliah Kondh Contested

Let us begin with a short description of a situation that is quite common today in the Kondhmals district. In spring 2001 I had the opportunity to attend two buffalo sacrifices in two villages of the Maliah Kondh near Balliguda. In 1992, about ten years ago, I had documented the buffalo sacrifice in various villages of this area. At that time the mood of the participants was blithely boisterous, often quite ecstatic, whereas the situation last year seemed to be quite strained. The young boys of the village appeared at the site of the sacrifice neat and clean, dressed in freshly ironed shirts, while the girls were dressed in colourful new saris in the Oriya style. Large round badges in the form of rosettes were distributed—the same as those that are customary at political events—with the message: 'Peaceful buffalo sacrifice 2001'. Asked about the reason for this distribution, they informed me that the Collector of Phulbani had banned buffalo sacrifices. The two reasons he gave were, first, that the killing of buffaloes is illegal, as it violates the Prevention of Cruelty to Animals Act, and secondly, that buffalo sacrifice endangers the public order, due to its drunken participants carrying sharp knives to cut the flesh of the still living buffalo.

It was obvious that, with their call for a 'peaceful sacrifice', the young people were trying to weaken their opponents' argument that their traditional buffalo sacrifice is 'only a dangerous spectacle' and as such has nothing to do with religion. The 'peaceful sacrifice'

[7] For more information, see www.worldanimalnet.org

movement is supported by the Kui Samaj, a Kondh youth organization the president of which is a lawyer in Balliguda aiming to reform Kondh traditions and adapt them to modern times and customs.

A crucial point of the discussion on animal sacrifice is the District Collector's argument for its abolition, namely that buffalo sacrifice violates Constitution. The law is the main argument against animal sacrifice. It is therefore necessary to look more closely at the laws.

In comparison with other countries of the world, India has one of the most comprehensive set of animal protection laws enshrined in its Constitution. Concerning animal sacrifice, all over India, apart from Jammu and Kashmir, the Prevention of Cruelty to Animals Act (PCAA) of 1960, no. 59, is in force. This law is described as 'An Act to prevent the infliction of unnecessary pain or suffering on animals and for that purpose to amend the law relating to the prevention of cruelty to animals'. Section 28 of the Act gives details regarding the killing of animals and provides a crucial exception: 'Saving as respects manner of killing prescribed by religion. Nothing contained in this Act shall render it an offence to kill any animal in a manner required by the religion of any community'.[8] It is the last phrase that leads to strong controversy, and my paper circles around the various interpretations of this phrase.

There is another law that is even more important for the opponents of animal sacrifice. It forbids the performance of any animal sacrifice. It is called the 'Animal and Birds Sacrifices (Prevention) Act' and was passed in a few states of India, such as Andhra Pradesh, Karnataka, Gujarat, Tamil Nadu, Pondicherry, Orissa, Rajasthan and Himachal Pradesh.[9] The rules regarding animal sacrifice in all these states roughly contain the same provisions as Section 2(b) of the Andhra Pradesh Animals and

---

[8] See www.husbandrypunjab.org (see Act LIX of 1960)

[9] See www.indiatimes.com/pets/animalprotection under the section: 'Animal Laws in India as applicable to Animal Sacrifice'. They mention six states: 1. Karnataka, 2. Tamil Nadu, 3. Andhra Pradesh, 4. Orissa, 5. Gujarat, 6. Himachal Pradesh. This list differs from that in a booklet published by the Animal Welfare Board of India, called *How to Check Animal Sacrifices*, 4, in which Orissa is not included, though Rajasthan and Pondicherry are.

Birds Sacrifices (Prohibition) Act of 1950. This Act defines 'sacrifice' as the killing or maiming of any animal or bird for the purpose of any religious worship or adoration. This is illegal under Magic Remedies Act, which prohibits any person from officiating, performing, assisting, or participating in any sacrifice. The penalty for contravention is a fine or imprisonment. For opponents of animal sacrifice, this is a clear statement by the government against the performance of all types of animal sacrifice.[10]

The Animal Protection Organizations and Their Activities

Since the introduction of the Prevention of Cruelty to Animals Act eleven years after Independence, the numbers of those who actively support the implementation of the various laws in society have constantly grown in number. Among the leading activists in the animal welfare movement is Maneka Gandhi, daughter-in-law of Indira Gandhi, having been married to her late son Sanjay Gandhi. Since 1988, she has been actively involved in politics. As a member of the 13th Lok Sabha on 18 November 2001 she became Union Minister of State, Programme Implementation and Statistics, with the additional role of Animal Care (Independent Charge). She is the leading exponent of animal welfare as well as the founding chairperson of India's largest animal welfare organization, 'People for Animals', and chairperson of the Delhi SPCA (Society for the Prevention of Cruelty to Animals). She is also the patron of the Worldwide Fund for Nature (WWF). The organization 'People for Animals (PFA)' started its activities in Mumbai in 1994 and today has branches all over India and hundreds of thousands of active members. In Bhubaneswar there are two branches of this

---

[10] The aim of the booklet *How to Check Animal Sacrifices* is to provide the activist with guidelines on how to legally stop animal sacrifices with the help of laws. It mentions the laws which can be applied in those states which have not ratified the Animals and Birds Sacrifice (Prohibition) Act. In these cases one can refer to the Pollution Act. This comes under the Local Corporation Act and prohibits any act of animal sacrifice in a public place on the grounds that it will cause pollution. Further the Indian Penal Code (IPC), Section 268, 1860 enables a person to file a charge sheet to prohibit the sale of meat derived from sacrificed animals in any public place, other than those which are registered for this purpose.

organization, which is affiliated to the World Animal Net Directory, the world's largest database of animal protection societies. All the animal organizations of India are mentioned, together with their links.[11]

Central to the world view of the different organizations started by Maneka Gandhi and other activists is the concept of *ahimsā*.[12] For these activists, non-violence against all living creatures is the key to entering a new world. Respect for, and the protection of, animals are an indicator of moral standards. Animal protection becomes an important ethical and political question. According to Maneka Gandhi, '[i]t is only when nations recognise animals and provide them with certain constitutional guarantees that we can expect a more enlightened and equitable code of conduct towards other living beings. Animal protection is already an issue of public concern and morality'.[13] According to Maneka Gandhi, the media must be convinced that there is a direct nexus between animal rights and 'public health'.

The abolition of animal sacrifice forms only one part of the 'Peoples for Animals' programme. The different animal protection groups are influenced on the one hand by ideas of the early Western animal protection movements and on the other hand by the strong vote for animal rights of leading intellectuals such as Mahatma Gandhi and Jawaharlal Nehru. For Mahatma Gandhi, the greatness of a nation and its moral progress can be judged by the way its animals are treated.[14]

The different animal protection groups closely cooperate with the authorities, with politicians, and with priests, and seek their assistance to stop sacrifices.[15] In her campaigns for animal rights, Maneka Gandhi concentrates mainly on those states in India who

---

[11] For more information, see www.worldanimalnet.org. In Orissa there are two sections of 'People for Animals'. One section is run by students and is called the 'People for Animals' students group.

[12] See Schmidt 1968; Chapple 1993.

[13] Cited in an article on animal sacrifice published on the *World Animal Net*, see fn.13.

[14] Mahatma Gandhi is mainly concerned with the protection of the cow, see Gupta 2000; Doctor 1994.

[15] The brochure *How to Check Animal Sacrifices*, 7-8, gives clear instructions on how people should be addressed and convinced by activists to halt sacrifice.

have also passed the additional law, the Animal and Birds Sacrifices (Prevention) Act, which does not allow any type of animal sacrifice.

In February 2001 a severe fight between supporters of animal sacrifice and animal rights activists took place in Karnataka. The reason behind this was that H. Vishwanath, the state's Higher Education Minister, took part in a ram sacrifice in honour of the goddess Marikhamba, widely known for her thirst for blood. The writer and rationalist K. Ramdas raised the issue, and according to the *Times of India* of 25 February 2001, Maneka Gandhi called upon the Chief Minister to take action against the minister, as 'it is shameful that a minister of the State Government has deliberately violated the "Provisions of the prevention of cruelty to animals act of 1960" as well as the "Karnataka Prevention Act" from 1959, besides committing a serious offence in public view'. She called it an 'ugly incident at public functions'. In the *Times of India* online of 22 February 2001, the journalist Swami Anand put forward the view that the 'mere presence of a minister (at an animal sacrifice) amounts to violation of the Animal Sacrifice Act'.[16] In Baroda, in Gujarat, a severe clash occurred when activists of the Gujarat Society for the Prevention of Cruelty to Animals (GSPCA) launched a campaign against the traditional goat sacrifice of the 150,000 member strong Mali community. Together with the police they raided their houses to stop the sacrifice.[17]

The Muslim goat sacrifice at Bakri-Id has become a target for the opponents of animal sacrifice. The *Indian Express* of 28 March 1999 announced in a headline: 'Minister of Legislative Assembly beats up Shiv Sena Leader over Animal Sacrifice'. In that year the Jain festival of Mahavir Jayanti fell on the day of Bakri-Id.[18] To

---

[16] See www.timesofindia.com (22 February 2001).

[17] See www.indian-express.com (6 July 2000). There was a strong reaction against the activists, as the Mali felt that the campaign had brought disgrace upon them. Afterwards a police circular was issued directing that cases of animal sacrifice should not be registered. The Mali killed several goats to celebrate their victory against the ban of their animal sacrifice.

[18] There are also various animal welfare/environmental organizations set up by Islamic societies with the aim of preventing animal sacrifice. It is traditional to sacrifice goats at the end of Hajj at Id-ul-Azha, in India called Bakri-Id. According to the animal rights

stop this practice, the Shiv Sena, a Hindu Nationalist party put up posters containing an order not to sacrifice animals. This created a public nuisance and stimulated the anger of MLA (Member of Legislative Assembly) Matin Ahmed. He organized a group of friends, who all went to the private residence of the Shiv Sena leader and beat him up.

In Orissa the actions of the different animal welfare organizations against animal sacrifice are gaining strength, and these organizations announce their successes in the media: 'Orissa town gives up animal sacrifice', said the website Indiainfo.com on 5 October 2000. The target was the famous Bali Yatra of Subarnapur (Sonpur), a widely known festival with more than 50,000 participants every year. Among the big festivals in Orissa that are under strong attack from the activists surrounding Maneka Gandhi is the Sūlia festival in Bolangir district, a festival of the Kondh community. Every year more than 120 buffaloes and a great number of goats are sacrificed to their clan god Sūlia.[19]

These examples are symptomatic of the present situation. The discussion of animal sacrifice centres on the two laws mentioned above. One reason for the controversy lies in the PCAA law of 1960, as it leaves a wide range of interpretations. How is the phrase that the killing of animals is not an offence if performed in 'a manner required by the religion of any community', to be interpreted? According to Maneka Gandhi, this law only permits the killing of animals using the traditional slaughtering methods of the Muslim communities, which is prescribed by religion. It has no consequences for the religious practices of Hindus and tribes. Therefore it cannot be used to justify animal sacrifice, which is not prescribed by any religion. All animal sacrifice in India is propelled by commercial interests and is not a part of Indian culture. The activist groups deny that animal sacrifice has any religious content: it is no more than superstition and commerce.

To give an example: in the Mali controversy in Gujarat, mentioned above, a reformist leader is quoted saying that people indulge in a competitive show of devotion, and that they are

activists, sacrifice is not a pillar of Islam. Animal sacrifice is not required. In Islam, all that is required as a sacrifice is one's personal willingness to submit one's ego and individual will to Allah. See www.islamveg.com.

[19] On the Sūlia festival, see Mallebrein 2004.

frightened into sacrificing animals with threats like 'if you don't sacrifice animals, your family will be wiped out'. 'It is in fact a way to celebrate. People consume liquor, eat meat and have fun; sacrifice is only an excuse.'[20]

The Arguments Against Animal Sacrifice

Arguments branding animal sacrifice as non-religious go back to the British colonial period.[21] The colonial government characterized these rituals as 'savage', 'brutal', 'violent', 'unhygienic' and 'superstitious' and cited 'savage customs and culture' in India as a reason for their interventions. Theirs was a 'civilizing' mission.[22] For them, as for today's opponents, animal sacrifice was no more than blind superstition. Sacrifice as such was suppressed as being uncivilized.

After the Sepoy Mutiny of 1857, the British had introduced a policy of non-intervention in Indian people's religion. It therefore became a crucial question for the British government whether particular rituals were rooted in recognized religious literature and as such part and expression of the true religion, or whether they were mere spectacles put on for the people's enjoyment. This question had political implications. Rituals involving animal sacrifice were not considered part of religion, and were banned. The belief system of the popular masses was denigrated, the efficacy of their religious practices was denied, and the people were disempowered.

After Independence, the political and cultural elites took on the prejudices and attitudes. They instituted similar reforms and laws in the process of the development of the modern Indian State. According to Tanaka this caused a dilemma as, on the one hand, in

---

[20] See the *Indian Express*, 6 July 2000.

[21] In what follows I shall be referring to the article by Tanaka 1999. She discusses hook swinging, fire walking and animal sacrifice in south India (Madras Presidency) in the nineteenth century, and the situation in Sri Lanka shortly after Independence.

[22] Already Thomay Bowrey, who travelled in Orissa between 1669 and 1679, speaks with aversion about rituals like hook swinging: 'The promoters are the wicked Brachmans, the Sufferers the Ignorant Gentues and Orixas.... In India the Orixas are most ignorant...', see Temple 1905, 198-9.

claiming to be a modern state and a member of the international community, modern India has had to follow the ideology of the (Western) world powers and their concept of 'modernization and rationalization'. On the other hand, however, it had to re-establish its national culture as the symbol of its unity. This new culture and its traditions had to be situated within modern ethics and norms. 'The rejection of sacrifice can be interpreted as a sign of conflict between modern forms of disciplinary power (Foucault) and traditional forms of power based on "death and regeneration".'[23]

Since the roots of the ideas of the present activist movement go back to the colonial period, it is not surprising to find similar, if not the same, arguments against the sacred character of animal sacrifices:

- animal sacrifice within a yatra or ritual is no more than an open spectacle for the amusement of its spectators. The killing of the animals is only for enjoyment.
- animal sacrifice adds to the personal profit of meat-sellers, and also priests.
- animal sacrifice was invented by priests who form an unholy triumvirate with the moneylender and the butcher. It leads to rural bankruptcies. As most animal sacrifices are carried out in the dry season before the harvest, the sacrificer is short of funds and therefore has nothing to buy the animal with except his expected harvest, or else his land.
- the devotees and priests force the ritual specialists (Barua, Dehuri, etc.) to drink the blood of the decapitated animals against their will. They themselves become victims.
- animal sacrifice is not required by any religion. It is nothing more than a monetary exchange between man and god; one gives something and gets something back ... a meaningless exercise ... all civilized people have abandoned it.[24]

Background

One of the characteristic features of the religious landscape of Orissa is the co-existence of different religious movements such as

[23] Tanaka 1999, 127-8.

[24] For various arguments and examples, see: *How to Check Animal Sacrifices.*

Buddhism, Jainism, Shaivism, Vaishnavism and, of course the, many different tribal goddess cults, all flourishing in close proximity. Under the Somavāṃśis (700-1118) and the Imperial Gaṅgas (1038-1435), Vaisnavism acquired considerable influence, and with it, ideas of worshipping god with vegetarian offerings were introduced. According to these new beliefs, there was no need for animal sacrifice to reach god and attain salvation. During the rule of the Imperial Gaṅgas Jagannāth became the state deity, synthesizing the religious ideas of Shaivism, Shaktism and Vaishnavism. The Gaṅgas constructed the enormous Puruṣottama Jagannāth temple in Puri, now a major pilgrimage centre. In that era, the famous philosopher and Vaishnavite Reformer Rāmānuja (*c.* AD 1056-1137) promoted the worship of Lakṣmī-Nārāyaṇa, while the saint-poet Jayadeva, the compiler of the Gitāgovinda, elevated the erotic relationship between Rādhā and Kṛṣṇa. His *Gitāgovinda* is still one of the most famous books in Orissa.[25] This devotional form of religion, with the love of god at its centre, was the foundation of the movement of Prem Bhakti, which was started by Caitanya.[26] This movement spread all over Orissa and still shapes the religious landscape of the country.[27] It focuses on the relationship between Rādhā and Kṛṣṇa, with Rādhā being higher in the hierarchy. Caitanya's movement attracted everyone, irrespective of origin, social status or caste. Caitanya preached social equality and emphasized the meaninglessness of expensive offerings and animal sacrifices, thus angering the Brahmans. According to his teachings, ultimate salvation is only achieved by sincere and ardent love of god. His followers were meant to experience this true love by means of *nagara kīrtana*, a self-intoxicating technique of collective singing and dancing leading to the ecstatic experience of unification of the self with god.

In the following seventeenth and eighteenth centuries, Vaishnavism became dominant especially in the coastal region of Orissa, where it enjoyed tremendous patronage by the local rulers.[28]

---

[25] For the development of Vaishnavism in Orissa, see Patel 1997.

[26] Chaitanya was born 27.02.1484 at Nadia or Navadvia in Bengal. He spent the major part of his life at Puri (1516-33) worshipping god Jagannāth.

[27] For further information see also Mukherjee 1978.

[28] Due to the influence of Vaishnavism in Orissa, animal sacrifices were performed less often. Östör, 1991, 182 cites a similar

This continues to be a visible expression in the many Rādhā-Kṛṣṇa, Lakṣmī-Nārāyaṇa and Jagannāth temples that were constructed during this time. This development reached its climax under British rule, when local rulers who had become financially strong started to convert their seats of rule into centres of imperial power with impressive palaces and numerous temples.[29] The splendid Vaishnava temples were provided with valuable bronze figurines.[30]

The Influence of the Reform Movements

Socio-religious reform movements started in Bengal around 1800 and spread to Orissa. Rammohun Roy (1772-1833), called the 'Father of modern India',[31] formulated a new vision of 'rational monotheistic' Hinduism. He objected to idolatrous worship and superstition, and to the worship of gods with offerings like animal sacrifices. The first Brahmo Samaj in Orissa was founded in Cuttack in 1849. By the end of the nineteenth century, the movement had reached nearly all Orissa. It was not a mass movement but one supported by urban elites, who still had an important influence on the socio-religious situation in Orissa. Animal sacrifice was considered meaningless and inhuman.[32] In

---

incident for a town in Bengal where the kings converted. 'Since the kings were converted to the devotional Vaiṣṇava movement in the sixteenth century, there has been no [such] sacrifices' He refers to the human and animal sacrifice: 'when the kings stopped the human and animals sacrifices, the whole town followed their custom.... Later the blood sacrifices came back in a major way in the observance of Kālīpūjā. Even today there is no animal sacrifice to the Goddess Durgā.'

[29] On the construction of the new capitals and the importance of Jagannāth in the nineteenth century, see Kulke 1993.

[30] Besides the temple for Jagannāth, the shrines and temples for Rādhā and Kṛṣṇa were patronized by the rājā. Besides the temple in the village, they also constructed temples or shrines within the palace compound for the various forms of Kṛṣṇa. Mainly the female members of the royal household were fostering this form of worship, and many donations and constructions of temples and monasteries were given by them.

[31] He became famous for his fight against widow burning, child-marriage and caste restrictions.

[32] For the history of Brahmo Samaj in Orissa see N.R. Patnaik 1997, 624-7.

1875 Dayananda Sarasvati founded the Arya Samaj in Bengal that accepted only the Vedas as scripture and rejected temple cults, idol worship, and sacrifice. The Arya Samaj gained a huge following after 1875.

At the end of the nineteenth century, both progressive and conservative religious and social reform movements were becoming involved in the freedom struggle. In 1885, the Indian National Congress was founded. The ancient Indian cultural and religious heritage, based on the ancient scriptures like the Vedas and the Upanishads, was 'rediscovered', and the Brahmins were considered to be holders of traditional lore. The popular form of Hinduism, with its allegedly 'superstitious' practices like animal sacrifice, was rejected and condemned as morally reprehensible. This meant that the many local gods and goddesses had to be changed into Sanskritic deities, who could clearly only be given vegetarian offerings. Non-violence and vegetarianism became indicators of purity and superiority. This development had its repercussions in Orissa as well. The rājā of Nilgiri, Gobinda Chandra Mardhrāj, for instance, asked a famous tantric from Nepal to 'reform' his tutelary deity Progola—a goddess who had originally demanded human and animal sacrifices exclusively—into a vegetarian deity.

Today, nationalist Hindu groups like the Vishwa Hindu Parishad and the Rashtriya Swayamsevak Sangh) argue against animal sacrifice, which they condemn as a blind belief, and promote instead Dharma Jagran (religious awakening). 'The goddess does not need blood, she is already omnipresent and omnipotent.'[33]

The Influence of Christian Mission

Christian missionaries played an important role in social reform movements after the British occupied Orissa in 1803. They promoted their own Western ideas and values, and fought against the allegedly superstitious beliefs of popular and tribal religions, which they attempted to bring under the spell of 'civilization'. In their eyes, Western education was the only way to bring a sense of

[33] According to Mr Jena, the President of Vishwa Hindu Parishad, Bhubaneswar.

enlightenment into the mind of the natives. All types of sacrifice were condemned.[34]

Abolition of the Princely States

The abolition of the Princely States resulted in the break-up of the traditional Indian kingdoms.[35] Rituals linked with the gods were detached from the exercise of royal authority. Animal sacrifice lost its importance as the main ritual for the well-being of the state and the whole world. Until Independence, the welfare of a kingdom was dependent on the annual rituals and blood offerings made to goddesses, mainly to the tutelary deity (*iṣṭadevī*) of the king, who had the status of a state goddess (*rāṣṭrādevatā*). Important tutelary deities of neighbouring rājās were included, resulting in a system of mutual gift exchanges in the form of animals given for sacrifice. These goddesses were considered to be related as sisters.[36] The political authority of the rājā had a ritual character, the rituals contributed to the benefit and improvement of the world, the state and its subjects.[37] The exchange of goods between the deities was a mirror of the political relationships between rulers on earth. The power and importance of a goddess was a reflection of the status and hierarchy of one rājā versus his neighbour. The deities were ritually transformed into royalty as a visible legitimation of royal power and of the wealth of the divine king. According to Inden, '[t]he king as a microcosm of the Cosmic Man was treated as *axis mundi* and placed conceptually at the centre of his kingdom, the

---

[34] On the role of the Christian missions in Orissa, see N.R. Patnaik 1997; Pattanayak 1991.

[35] For information on the Princely States of Orissa (1905-47), see Samal 1988, Berkemer 1993 on the 'Little Kingdom in Kalinga', see Schnepel 1997 on the 'Jungle Kings'.

[36] Such a sister relationship exists between goddess Kālījāī, family goddess of the rājā of Parikud, Siddheśvarī, family goddess of the Zamindar rājā of Bhatapada (Banpur), Nārāyāṇī, family goddess of the rājā of Khallicot and Bhagavatī from Banpur, installed by the Gājāpati of Puri.

[37] In his excellent study, Hardenberg 2000 elaborately discusses the ritual character of the kingdom in India general with a special focus on the ideology of the Hindu kingdom of Puri, the structure and the meanings of rituals performed by the Gajapati kings.

microcosm of the world.... The king renews the gods, and they in turn renew the king.'[38]

The kingdom in many ways was a religious construction: the rituals were not performed to legitimate the power of the ruler, but in order to accommodate the present to the cosmic order. The offerings of animals play an important role, as the king is conceived as the first sacrificer and the main patron of the goddess.[39] Through his sacrifices, he maintains the human community and the cosmic order. There is a corresponding relationship between the king as sacrificer and the sacrificial animal. The sacrificer is identified with the sacrificial animal. The king sacrifices himself; he is like a warrior who sheds his own blood in fighting against his enemies in the attempt to restore order. He offers himself, his own blood, to the goddess.[40] Intoxicated by his blood, the goddess' fury increases, as does her strength to fight the evil that threatens the cosmos. Then, once satiated with blood, she becomes calm and peaceful. She needs blood to obtain the energy required in order to protect the land and its people.

Instead of the king, an ordinary human was formerly sacrificed to the goddess. Rituals continue to be performed in Orissa today which reflect this concept. In Nilgiri, Balasore district, the tradition of the Balināyak is performed.[41] During Durgā Pūjā, on the night of *āṣṭami* to *navami*, the Balināyak performs a 'game'. He is a man who belongs to a family that was formerly obliged to make an annual offering of a family member to the goddess.[42] What is nowadays considered a 'game' by the mainly young people who participate in it was formerly a deadly serious matter, a game of life and death. Within the palace compound, the movable metal image (the calanti pratimā) of Kanaka Durgā was placed on a throne in a

---

[38] Cited Inden 1998, 47-9.

[39] Schnepel 1977 (a), 231-42, very elaborately discusses the relationship between Durgā and the jungle kings.

[40] Self immolation for Durgā and Kālī to pacify or please them for the well-being of a village or community, was quite common in early India. For examples see Gurumurthy 1969.

[41] I would like to thank Bharat Chandra Mardhrāj of the Nilgiri royal framily and the present Balināyak for their kind permission to document this tradition.

[42] As a compensation they received land to cultivate from the king

mandapa.[43] All the priests gathered together with the members of the royal family. During the night the Balināyak approached the *mandapa* and fell into a trance in front of the goddess. After circling around the *mandapa* several times, he suddenly ran forward to catch one of the onlookers as an 'offering' for the goddess. These days, he will only offer a pumpkin. But according to the reports of the present Balināyak, formerly the person who had been touched would die within a few days, as the goddess consumed his blood. During the previous six days of the *śoḷa pūjā*, the priest had to catch one 'human sacrifice' every night. Finally, the Balināyak was offered to the goddess in the early morning of *navami*. Later, in British times, instead of a man a buffalo was sacrificed. This was also stopped, and now Kanaka Durgā receives only vegetarian offerings. When blood sacrifices were ended, the father of the present Balināyak suddenly died for no apparent reason. In the eyes of his son, in her fury over the abolition of animal sacrifices, the goddess had consumed his father's blood. According to the present Balināyak, the now reformed vegetarian goddess has lost all her power.

In Banpur, in Khurda district, too, the temple priests offer a 'human sacrifice' to the goddess Bhagavatī. This happens during Durgā Pūjā. The person called Balijenā also belongs to a family that traditionally had to offer one of its members for sacrifice. He is kept in a separate building about 700 m from the Bhagavatī temple called Sātabakharāghar, where the bronze image (*calanti pratimā*) of Kanaka Durgā and the wooden movable image of Bhagavatī, called Kāṭhi-Thākurāṇī, are worshipped. In the early morning, having sacrificed several hundred goats and a buffalo within the temple compound of Bhagavatī, the main priests proceed to the small house where the Balijenā waits. In front of the house they offer now a goat (as a substitute for Balijenā). The priests say that at this very moment the Balijenā 'dies', because the goddess takes his blood. They carry his 'dead body' in a procession to the main entrance of the Bhagavatī temple. There he is revived and brought

[43] The goddess Kanaka Durgā was always a much sought-after trophy. Kings tried to gain possession of her victorious power, see Schnepel 1997b.

into the temple compound.[44] So far no one has ever dared to raise objections to animal sacrifice in Banpur. Everyone is afraid of Bhagavatī's deadly revenge.[45]

In time, the buffalo became the prestigious substitute for human sacrifice and played an important role especially in the Durgā Pūjā. This was the central festival of the king, symbolizing not only the mythological or cosmic victory of Durgā, but also the worldly victory, the success of the king and his army over the enemies of his realm.[46] The expansiveness, the grandeur and elaboration of the Durgā Pūjā developed mainly in the nineteenth century, along with the remodelling of the capital, as a manifestation of power. The many animal sacrifices to Durgā were intended to strengthen her in the fight with Māhiṣa, the buffalo demon, who represents chaos and revolt against the cosmic order, which is ultimately restored by the goddess.[47]

With the abolition of the Princely States and the role of the King as first sacrificer, the situation has changed: animal sacrifice and the divine power of blood have lost their importance in a sacrifice that maintains the cosmic order, and can be substituted by vegetarian offerings. Fertility was another connotation of the blood sacrifice. One reason for this association was that many of the tutelary deities of the kings are of tribal, mostly Kondh origin. To the Kondh it was the earth goddess who had made life on earth possible, that is, by her self-sacrifice in offering her own flesh and blood for the well-being of the people. By offering blood and flesh to her, her regenerative powers are restored and preserved. She gives life and therefore she needs life, thus the king, in patronizing the animal sacrifice, takes care that the goddess will grant rich harvests and is satisfied so that she refrains from causing disease.

---

[44] The role of an ascetic called Yogi, mentioned also in connection with the Durgā Pūjā, is similar to that of the Balijenā, see Schnepel 1997a, 248 and Mallebrein 1998b.

[45] I thank the priests of the Bhagavatī temple and Manabendra Moharatha Dulal from Bhatapara Garh for their kind permission for, and their assistance in, documenting this ritual.

[46] Schnepel 1977a, 242-56, analysis the Durgā Pūjā in Jeypore and gives an excellent inside view into the role of the king.

[47] For the relation between Māhiṣa and the goddess in a Tamil version, see Shulman 1976, Berkson 1995.

With the abolition of the royal state organization, the above aspects lost their importance. Nowadays, others have become more significant. Today, the main attractions are the many colourful Durgā *mandals* of the various groups who fight for first place in the hierarchy.

With the abolition of the privy purses and privileges in 1971, there was a break in royal patronage of deities and festivals.[48] New patrons took over their administration. Whereas the former rājā depended on the labour of his subjects for cultivation and warfare and thus took a great interest in patronizing and promoting the cult of their autochthonous deities with blood sacrifice, the new patrons, the members of the Temple Trust, the officers in the Endowment Office, and representatives of the executive lack that kind of motivation.[49] They are administrators, in charge of the temple for a limited period of time. The abolition of animal sacrifices and the possible revenge of the goddess may have a personal effect, but this does not concern the power structure of the government they represent. The new power structure and the abolition of sacrifice by law find visible expression in new architectural forms of the temple. In the past thirty years, along with the changes in patronage, the idea of the temple has changed. The goddess was reformed, now Śiva accompanies the goddess, he enters her temple compound or even shrine, and both enjoy vegetarian offerings.[50]

The Arguments in Support of Animal Sacrifice

The arguments of those in favour of animal sacrifice are not found in the press media or on the world-wide web. Their voice is neither loud nor strong, but is reduced to a local area, a specific deity, its temple and its rituals. The supporters of animal sacrifice fear the consequences of the legislative power as embodied in the Collector and the police. As the majority of the population, why do they not resist the abolition of animal sacrifice?

---

[48] A striking example for a temple in Orissa that once enjoyed patronage by a king and its present situation is given by Preston 1980, who discusses the Chandi temple in Cuttack.

[49] Since Independence, more than twelve thousand temples and monastic institutions in Orissa are governed by the Hindu Religious Endowment Act of 1951.

[50] See also Eschmann 1978.

In the introduction I mentioned that the playing fields for activists in Orissa are rural and somewhat backward areas characterized by a mixed tribal and Hindu population. In these regions, the temples of the local goddesses, in which animal sacrifices are traditionally performed, are not in the hands of the Brahmins but in those of the members of tribal or low-caste communities who function as priests.

In the course of my research project, I had an opportunity to talk to priests and devotees, mainly in Bolangir, Sonepur, Kalahandi, Kondhmals and Ganjam districts, about animal sacrifice. Those devotees and priests who are educated and claim to be intellectuals are more in favour of abolition, but even they can hardly conceal their fear of the deities' revenge in consequence of abolition.

This transcendent, dangerous power of 'strong and unpredictable' deities is greatly feared by all those who believe in the effects of animal sacrifice. The great drought in Bolangir and Kalahandi districts in 2001 is interpreted as having been caused by angry, neglected gods. The Dr Ambedkar Dalit Forum reports on 3 January 2001 on the Internet: 'Animals sacrificed in drought-hit Orissa district to appease god.... People believe that the god's anger is the reason behind the acute drought the district is facing, therefore they offered more animals this year for killing during the festival.'

For those who believe in the power of animal sacrifice, its abolition creates a great fear. Abolition endangers the future. Among the most frequently uttered worries are those which affect their present existence. 'Without sacrifice there will be no rain, no crops, the women become barren, animals get diseases.' Many link the present situation with the Kaliyuga.

Why can't the supporters of animal sacrifice collectively express themselves more forcefully against abolition? Does not The Prevention of Cruelty to Animal Act (PCAA) clearly state that the killing of an animal is allowed if it is performed in 'a manner required by the religion of a community'? The crux of the matter is that the supporters of animal sacrifice have no arguments to prove that sacrifice is performed in 'a manner required by religion' and that it is as such a part of their religion. On the contrary, the opponents of animal sacrifice, who in most cases belong to the educated, intellectual, high-caste stratum of society, claim the right to interpret the law and to define when a sacrifice is religiously based and when it is not.

The Buffalo Sacrifice of the Maliah Kondh and the Concept of Blood

To illustrate this crisis, I would like to examine the buffalo sacrifice of the Maliah Kondh.[51] This is a striking example of the rootedness of the sacrifice of a buffalo in the religious ideas of a tribal community. For the Maliah Kondh, animal sacrifice is part of their religion, and as such there is no doubt that the killing is done in a 'manner required by the religion'. On the other hand, in many places in the Kondhmals Hills, for many reasons, today's performance of the buffalo sacrifice has lost much of its former religious aspect. Thus weakened, it gradually dissolves and therefore provides space for the arguments of its opponents.

Let us first look at the religious aspect of the buffalo sacrifice. For the Maliah Kondh it was Tārapenu, the earth goddess, who made the world habitable through her self-sacrifice. Formerly the earth was not stable; the ground shook, and life on earth was impossible. Tārapenu, in her human form as Sirseli, asked her sons to sacrifice her. She ordered her body to be cut into pieces and buried all over the world. Only then did the world become solid, and life was made possible. From her backbones the mountains arose, and from her hair the grass.[52] In memory of this sacrifice, the Kondh offered a human sacrifice every year. Creation requires death and dismemberment; life has been exchanged for life. Each

---

[51] The abolition of the buffalo sacrifice (*kedu laka*) is most prominently visible in the Kondhmal area within the Maliah Kondh. Other Kondh groups like the Kuttia Kondh and the Dongria Kondh are not affected by this trend. They still keep their old religion to this day and do not convert to Christianity like the Maliah Kondh. The buffalo sacrifice is a common practice in the whole of India. There are a lot of references on buffalo sacrifices in India, especially in south India, by Hiltebeitel 1980, on the performance, see Hiltebeitel 1985. For a discussion of the relation between the buffalo and the goddess, here Māriyāmman, see Beck 1981.

[52] There are different variations of this myth. I would like to thank Dr V.K. Nayak from Balliguda for translating this myth from Kui into English. For further information on this topic, see Boal 1982, 1999.

participant in the sacrifice was eager to obtain bits of the meat and bury them in his fields, as the whole world was considered to be the body of Tārapenu.

Under British influence, human sacrifice was replaced by a buffalo sacrifice. The annual buffalo sacrifice now forms the essential core of their religion; their lives centre on this sacrifice which links the different villages and clan groups and stabilizes social relations. The village and its surroundings become the sacred space for the collective performance of the month-long festival. Each and every part of this festival, the musical instruments, sounds and rhythms, dances, dresses, bronzes[53], has deep symbolic value and is part of the religious worldview and the concept of the cosmos.[54] Today, with the 'peaceful buffalo' movement, it is evident that the festival has lost its crucial religious, social, and symbolic value. For the opponents of the buffalo sacrifice, this is a clear sign that the sacrifice was never anything more than a mere spectacle for the personal enjoyment of some village folk.

Another argument used by the supporters of animal sacrifice is the importance of blood for the deity. One Kondh informant told me: 'As we eat food, so she needs blood and meat'. Without nourishment, the goddess withdraws her creative powers and fertility, and everything becomes barren and dry.

The concept of blood, animal or human, is essential for understanding animal sacrifice. All over Orissa, one can find the concept of the goddess as a hungry mother who needs food. Without this, she becomes angry and causes disaster and disease. In Orissa, there is an old tradition that the Baruā or Dehuri, who embodies the goddess in a state of trance, drinks the blood of the sacrificial animals on behalf of the deity. For the supporters, blood is nourishment containing the soul which animates the body. Blood

---

[53] On the various bronzes which are of essential importance within the buffalo sacrifice, see Mallebrein 1993, 1998a, 2001 and Boal 1982, 1999.

[54] Amongst the Gadaba and Sora the sacrifice of buffaloes is linked with ancestor rituals. Examples where buffaloes are associated with ancestors and represent them in this world are presented by Pfeffer 1991. The buffaloes also represent ancestors for the Sora. They sacrifice buffaloes to the deceased as food and as animals for ploughing the fields in the afterlife. For various examples within the Sora community, see Vitebsky 1993.

is a life-giving force, it is power, power against evil spirits, power to fulfil a wish, power to grant fertility, etc. If a deity does not receive blood, she loses her power. 'From now on you can take a photo of the deity. We have stopped the animal sacrifice this year, she has lost her power,' said the priest at the Hiṅgolā Devī temple, Gopalprasad, Talcher, in spring 2001.

But for the supporters of animal sacrifice, it is difficult to prove that this belief in the power of the blood forms an indispensable and essential part of their religion, even though animal sacrifice has a long history. For its opponents, this aspect of a hungry mother who needs blood as 'food' does not count, as food can easily be replaced by vegetarian offerings. By changing the deity's food into vegetarian offerings, they try to find a compromise: instead of the sacrificial animal, they offer a pumpkin.[55] The ritual remains the same, as does the act of killing: one stroke of the sword, and the pumpkin falls to pieces, the red *kumkum* marking the bleeding open wound.[56] Anxiously, the devotees await the coming month, whether the deity accepts the new offerings or not. If nothing serious happens, it means that she has accepted her new vegetarian offering. Whereas the supporters of animal sacrifice expect the worst in the form of the wrath of the deity, its opponents keep cool. In most cases they have been proved right.

Kālī: Animal Sacrifice Defended?

As already mentioned, in spite of the general reduction of animal sacrifices, the Śākta and various tribal communities still manage to

---

[55] For a discussion of different forms of *bali* and its relation to *pūjā,* see Fuller 1987. About offerings of vegetables or vegetarian food he writes 'two clearly distinct modes of offering need to be distinguished. First, a vegetable—typically a pumpkin or lime—can be offered as a surrogate animal, or the animal may be represented by cooked rice shaped into the form of an animal.... There is also a form of *bali* in which vegetarian food is not offered as a substitute for an animal, (ibid., 24).

[56] According to Heesterman, 1993, 9 who discusses the old Indian rituals, there is no difference between vegetal offerings and animal sacrifices. 'The pressing of soma stalks, the killing and cutting up of animal victim, and the grinding of the grain are all equally killings ... the text use the verb *hanti*, "to slay, kill".'

maintain their traditions. There is even an increasing tendency towards animal sacrifice dedicated to the goddess Kālī. The question arises as to why. In November 2001, on the occasion of the Kālī Pūjā on the night of Diwali, the darkest night of the year in Chandanpur, a very traditional Śāsan Brahmin village near Puri, more than 540 goats were offered to Dakṣiṇākālī, the 'South-facing' Kālī, covered with a garland of skulls and holding a sword and a demon head.[57] In its style, the face of the 20 ft. tall figure resembles strikingly the Jagannāth triad of Puri. A big crowd gathers in front of a huge statue of Kālī made out of mud and papier mache housed in a tall permanent cement *mandapa*. The priest's family is originally from Bengal, so the pūjā was performed in the Bengali Śākta manner. For her devotees, Kālī is the ideal mother who protects them from all dangers and kills all enemies. Every year, the priests very successfully perform this impressive tantric ritual which lasts an entire night. No one protests, no activist tries to stop this mass sacrifice by resort to the animal protection laws. And Chandanpur is not the only village around Puri where these extensive animal sacrifices are performed during Kālī Pūjā without opposition.[58]

One of the reasons is that the lobby of priests who perform Kālī Pūjā is very strong, and they do not allow outsiders to interfere. They take a great interest in the continuity of this sacrifice, which is profitable as they sell the goat meat as *prasād*.[59] Another reason may be that Kālī's revenge is dreaded. Politicians join in, out of fear of her wrath, and attend the sacrifice. It is said that on one occasion when the priests of Chandanpur thought of selling the goats instead of killing them in order to avoid bloodshed, Kālī appeared in the form of a fireball and burnt the whole village to ashes.

But the major reason for the continuity of animal sacrifice is the Śākta Tantra cult, in which great importance is attached to the act of

---

[57] On different forms of Kālī, see Mookerjee 1988.

[58] For a discussion of various interpretations of blood sacrifice in relation to Kālī and the imagery of fierce goddesses, see Kondos 1986.

[59] One informant told that the income of the sale will be more than Rs.1.5 lakh.

killing.[60] The sacrifice of the 540 goats began at 2.00 a.m. outside the *mandapa*, but in front of the goddess. The heads of the decapitated animals were then offered to Kālī in a bowl at her feet. The headless bodies were thrown into the hall on the floor in front of the deity, where they formed a growing heap of carcasses. Upon being sacrificed, the animal's body is transformed into the most sacred *mahāprasād*. 'She has licked the blood, she has blessed it', said an onlooker. Through this ritual, it is thought that both the devotees and the animals approach ultimate liberation.

Central to the Kālī Pūjā is the self in relation to the divine, the relationship between the sacrificer and the god.[61] Neither of these is a separate entity. There is a correspondence between the 'self' (*jīva*) of the sacrifier and the sacrificial animal (*paśu*).[62] The sacrifier gives his 'self' (*jīva*) as a gift to god. This self is conceived as being animal-like (*paśu*), crude, undigested. In totally offering itself, the animal self seeks salvation and union. Once 'devoured' by the deity, it is 'digested' by her over time. Finally its refined essence brings salvation. The sacrifier is animal-like in his lack of perception; he desires enlightenment. He invokes the perceptible goddess to 'devour' the flesh and 'drink' the blood of the deluded and bound self-animal, and thus assist in his enlightenment. The sacrifier offers his own 'animal quality' (*pāśubhāva*) or 'demonic quality' (*āsurikbhāva*).[63] The central logic is the self-transformation and spiritual progress of the *jīva-paśu* and its ultimate liberation within the cosmic scheme of lives and deaths.

The sacrificial animal is a substitute, an intermediary between the goddess and the human sacrifier. The best of all sacrificial victims is the human sacrificer. According to Fuller the 'Animal

---

[60] Bolle 1983, discusses blood and human sacrifices in India. He comes to the same conclusion, that the activity of sacrifice, or the act of killing *as such*, is important, see 59.

[61] The relationship is elaborately discussed by Samanta 1994. In the following I refer to her article.

[62] In accordance with Hubert and Mauss (1964) Samtanta (ibid.), fn. 3, uses the terms 'sacrifier' and 'sacrificer'. The 'sacrifier' commissions the sacrifice, and to whom its benefits accrue. The 'sacrificer' is the person actually performing the rites, such as the priest.

[63] It is of six basic types: six enemies: lust (*kāma*), anger (*krodha*), greed (*lobha*), delusion (*moha*), arrogance and egotism (*mātsarya*), and envy (*mada*).

sacrifice approximates that idea by merging the sacrificer with the deity–as puja does in a different way—but sacrifice also cuts the two parties apart when the victim dies, so that only the animal's life passes to the deity. The human sacrificer remains alive, able to reap the benefits of pleasing the deity by making a sacrifice.'[64] At the end of the Kālī Pūjā, the sacrifier invokes Kālī, who 'thirsts for blood', to accept this bali, so that his 'enemies' may be destroyed.[65] Through this sacrifice, both the sacrifier and the animal victim come closer to ultimate liberation. The aim is a refined faculty of perception and therefore a better rebirth. The head is of special importance and offered on a separate plate. It is a symbol of the self that the sacrifier offers to the goddess. She digests the sins contained in the animal, and refines it spiritually so that it may have a better rebirth.

Conclusion

In India, animal sacrifices were attested from the earliest times and are still performed by tribal groups and the Śāktas. Opposition to animal sacrifice is, however, at least as old as early Jainism and Buddhism and ever since, a growing tradition of non-violence has been rejecting and substituting animal sacrifice, usually in favour of vegetarian offerings.[66] Non-violence is traditionally favoured by religions that are based on scriptural traditions, especially Hinduism, Jainism, and Buddhism. In modern times, this tendency has been strengthened by influences from, (1) British rule and legislation and (2) modern, especially Western ideas concerning animal rights that have been incorporated into current Indian legislation. Under the influence of these powerful currents of contemporary thought, traditional animal sacrifice, such as the buffalo sacrifice of the Maliah Kondh, has been reinterpreted and transformed into vegetarian sacrifices. Animal protection groups,

---

[64] Fuller 1993, 84-5.

[65] For a description of the five phases of Kālī Pūjā according to the *Śriśri Kālī Pūjā Paddhati* 1984, 1985, see Samanta 788-9. In the first part, the goat desires that its blood is being transformed by death, the *bhāva*, or the emotional-intellectual essence represented by the blood of the 'animal' (*paśu*), wishes to achieve that of divinity. The animal expresses its desire to be born again as man in its next life.

[66] See Kapleau 1981, Chapple 1993.

represented mainly by the educated parts of society and closely associated with the Indian government, have come out most strongly in demanding that animal sacrifices be banned completely, since they have brought themselves into disrepute on account of their being 'primitive' and 'savage'.

The supporters of animal sacrifice, who are more or less withdrawing from the struggle and who in most cases lack the ability to reach a national or international audience, mostly refer to the dangerous power of the gods, who urgently require blood and might endanger the order of the entire human world if they are denied it. A most impressive exception to this development is the Kālī Pūjā, where animal sacrifices are even tolerated by the educated classes. Apart from the fact that Kālī has never failed to intimidate even cultural elites, this may very well be due to the circumstance that her cult is greatly influenced by philosophical Shaivaism, and thus, at least to a certain degree, by an important part of Sanskritic culture.

From a sociological point of view, it is the higher, educated classes who oppose animal sacrifice. It does not make a major difference whether this education is traditional and Sanskritic, or modern and 'Western'.

References

Anonymus (n.d.). *How to Check Animal Sacrifices*, New Delhi: Animal Welfare Board of India (Ministry of Social Justice & Empowerment).

Banerjee, S. 1968. *Ethnographic Study of the Kuvi-Kandha*, Calcutta: Anthropological Survey of India.

Beck, B. 1981. 'The Goddess and the Demon: A Local South Indian Festival in its Wider Context', in *Puruṣārtha* 5, 83-163.

Behera, B.K. 1996. *Tribal Culture, Modernisation and Development: A Study of Kondh Tribes,* New Delhi: Khama Publishers.

Berkemer, G. 1993. *Little Kingdoms in Kalinga. Ideologie, Legitimation und Politik Regionaler Eliten*, Stuttgart: Franz Steiner Verlag.

Berkson, C. 1995. *The Divine and the Demoniac: Mahisa's Heroic Struggle with Durga*, Oxford: Oxford University Press.

Boal, B. 1982. *The Konds. Human Sacrifice and Religious Change*, Warminster: Aris & Phillips.

— 1999. *Man, The Gods and the Search for Cosmic Well-being*, Bhubaneswar: NISWASS (National Institute of Social Work and Social Sciences).

Bolle, K.W. 1983. 'A World of Sacrifice', in *History of Religions* 23 (1), 37-63.

Chapple, Ch. 1993. *Nonviolence to Animals, Earth, and Self in Asian Traditions*, Albany: State University of New York Press.

Das, H.C. 1999. *Sākta Pithas: A Study*, Bhubaneswar: Bharati Prakashan.

Doctor, A.H. 1994. *Gandhiji's Ahimsa: Evaluation of Theory and Practice*, Dharwad: Karnataka University.

Eschmann, A. 1978. 'Hinduization of Tribal Deities in Orissa: The Śakta and Śaiva Typology', in A. Eschmann, H. Kulke and G.C. Tripathi (eds.), *The Cult of Jagannath and the Regional Tradition of Orissa*, Delhi: Manohar, 79-97.

Fuller, C.J. 1987. 'Sacrifice (Bali) in the South Indian Temple', in V. Sudarsen, G. Prakash Reddy, and M. Suryanarayana (eds.), *Religion and Society in South India (A Volume in Honour of Prof. N. Subba Reddy)*, Delhi: B.R. Publishing Corporation, 21-35.

— 1993. *The Camphor Flame: Popular Hinduism and Society in India*, Princeton: Princeton University Press.

Gurumurthy, S. 1969. 'Self-Immolation in Ancient South India', in *Bulletin of the Institute of Traditional Cultures Madras*, 44-9.

Hardenberg, R. 2000. *Ideologie eines Hindu-Königtums. Struktur und Bedeutung der Rituale des 'Königs von Puri' (Orissa/Indien)*, Berlin: Das Arabische Buch (Indus 7).

Heesterman, J.C. 1993. *The Broken World of Sacrifice: An Essay in Ancient Indian Ritual*, Chicago, London: University of Chicago Press.

Hiltebeitel, A. 1980. 'Rāma and Gilgamesh: The Sacrifices of the Water Buffalo and the Bull of Heaven', in *History of Religions* 19 (3), 187-223.

— 1985. 'On the Handling of the Meat, and Related Matters, in Two South Indian Buffalo Sacrifices', in *L'Uomo* 9, 171-99.

Hubert, H. and M. Mauss. 1964. *Sacrifice: Its Nature and Function*. Tansl. W.D. Halls, Chicago: University of Chicago Press.

Kapleau, P. and R.P. Kapleau. 1986. *To Cherish All Life: A Buddhist View of Animal Slaughter and Meat Eating*. Rochester,

NY: Zen Centre. Valuable links to sites on this topic are given under: http://online.sfsu.edu/~rone/Buddhism/BuddhismAnimals Vegetarian/BuddhistVegetarian.htm.

Kondos, V. 1986. 'Images of the Fierce Goddess and Portrayals of Hindu Women', in *Contributions to Indian Sociology (n.s.)* 20 (2), 173-97.

Kulke, H. 1978. 'Early State Formation and Royal Legitimation in Tribal Areas of Eastern India', in R. Moser and M.K. Gautam (eds.), *Aspects of Tribal Life in South Asia I: Strategy and Survival*, Studia Ethnologica Bernensia 1, Bern: The University of Berne Institute of Ethnology, 29-37.

— 1992. 'Tribal Deities at Princely Courts: The Feudatory Rājās of Central Orissa & their Tutelary Deities', in S. Mahapatra (ed.), *The Realm of the Sacred: Verbal Symbolism and Ritual Structures*, Calcutta: Oxford University Press, 56-78.

— 1993. 'Kṣatriyaization and Social Change: A Study in the Orissa Setting', in H. Kulke, *Kings and Cults*, Delhi: Manohar, 82-92.

Mallebrein, C. 1993. *Die anderen Götter—Volks- und Stammesbronzen aus Indien*, Heidelberg: Edition Braus.

— 1998a. *Darshan—Blickkontakte mit Indischen Göttern*, Berlin: State Museum for Ehtnography.

— 1998b. 'Daṇteśvarī and the family goddess (kulsvāminī) of the Rājā of Bastar, and the Daśahara festival of Jagdalpur', in A. Michaels, C. Vogelsanger and A. Wilke (eds.), *Wild Goddesses in India and Nepal*. Proceedings of an International Symposium Berne and Zurich, November 1994, Bern: Peter Lang Verlag. 483-511

— 2001. 'Tribal Art: Continuity and Change', in P. Pal (ed.), *Orissa Revisited*, Mumbai: Marg, 142-61.

— 2002. 'Entering the Realm of Durgā: Pāṭkhaṇḍā, a Hinduized Tribal Deity', in A. Malinar, J. Beltz and H. Frese (eds.), *Text and Context in the History, Literature and Religion of Orissa*, Delhi: Manohar, 273-305.

— 2004. 'Ruler, Protector and Healer; The Clan Gods Sulia, Patkhanda and Sikerpat of the Kondh Tribe', in C. Mallebrein; L. Guzy (ed.), *Facets of Orissa Studies*, *Journal of Social Sciences* (Spezial Issue) 8,2, 143-53.

Monier-Williams, M. 1899. *A Sanskrit-Englisch Dictionary,* Oxford: Clarendon Press (rpt. 1976).

Mookerjee, A. 1988. *Kali The Feminine Force*, London: Thames and Hudson.

Mukherjee, P. 1978. 'Caitanya in Orissa', in A. Eschmann, H. Kulke and G.C. Tripathi (eds.), *The Cult of Jagannath and the Regional Tradition of Orissa,* Delhi: Manohar. 309-19.

Nayak, P.K. 1989. *Blood, Women and Territory: An Analysis of Clan Feuds of Dongria Konds*, Delhi: Reliance Publishing House.

Nayak, R. et al. 1990. *The Kondhs—A Handbook for Development.* New Delhi: Indian Social Institute.

Nayak, R. and Nabor Soreng. 1999. *The Kuvi Kondhs—A Handbook for Development*, Bhubaneswar: NISWASS (National Institute of Social Work and Social Sciences).

Östör, A. 1991. 'Cyclical Time: Durgāpūjā in Bengal: Concepts, Actions, Objects', in T.N. Madan (ed.), *Religion in India*, Delhi: Oxford University Press, 176-98.

Pasayat, Ch. 1997. 'Tribal-Non-Tribal Interaction in Orissa: A Study of Samalei/Samaleswari Devi in Sambalpur', in G. Pfeffer and D.K. Behera (eds.), *Contemporary Society: Tribal Studies*, Vol. II, New Delhi: Concept Publishing Company, 304-16.

Patel, S.K. 1997. 'Vaiṣṇavism in Orissa', in P.K. Mishra (ed.), *Comprehensive History and Culture of Orissa*, Vol. 1, Delhi: Kaveri Books, 511-26.

Patnaik, N. R. 1997. 'Socio-Religious Reforms in the 19th Century', in P.K. Mishra (ed.), *Comprehensive History and Culture of Orissa*, Vol. 2, Delhi: Kaveri Books, 612-31.

Patnaik, N. and P.S. Das Patnaik. 1982. *The Kondh of Orissa*, Bhubaneswar: Tribal and Harijan Research-cum-Training Institute.

Pattnayak, S.K. 1991. 'Missionery activities and the up-lift of the Khonds in Orissa during the 19th century', in *The Journal of Orissan History* 11, 86-9.

Pfeffer, G. 1991. 'Der intra-agnatische 'Seelentausch' der Gadaba beim großen Lineageritual', in M.S. Laubscher (ed.), *Ganesha. Beiträge zur Ethnologie Mittel- und Süd-Indiens*, München: anacon-Verlag, 59-92.

Pradhan, B.C. 1997. 'Śāktism in Orissa', in P.K. Mishra (ed.), *Comprehensive History and Culture of Orissa*, Vol. 1, Delhi: Kaveri Books, 527-40.

Preston, J. 1980. *Cult of the Goddess: Social and Religious Change in a Hindu Temple*, Delhi: Vikas Publishing House.

Samanta, S. 1994. 'The "Self-Animal" and Divine Digestion: Goat Sacrifice to the Goddess Kālī in Bengal, in *Journal of Asian Studies* 53(3), 779-803.

Samal, J.K. 1988. *Princely States of Orissa (1905-1947)*, Allahabad: Vohra Publishers and Distributors.

Schmidt, H.P. 1968, 'The Origin of Ahiṃsā', in *Mélanges d'Indianisme R̲ la Mémoire de Louis Renou*, Paris, 625-55.

Schnepel, B. 1997a. *Die Dschungelkönige. Ethnohistorische Aspekte von Politik und Ritual in Südorissa/Indien,* Stuttgart: Franz Steiner Verlag.

— 1997b. 'Der Raub der Göttin. Rituelle Inszenierungen von Macht und Autorität in Orissa', in B.E. Schmidt and M. Münzel (eds.), *Ethnologie und Inszenierung. Ansätze zur Theaterethnologie*, Marburg: Reihe Curupira Band 5, 459-85.

Shulman, David. 1976. 'The Murderous Bride: Tamil Versions of the Myth of Devā and the Buffalo-Demon', in *History of Religions* 16(1), 120-46.

Tanaka, M. 1999. 'Sacrifice Lost and Found—Central India and Postcolonial Lanka', in ZINBUN (Kyoto University: Jimbun) 34(1), 127-46.

Temple, R.C. (ed.). 1905. *Thomas Bowrey: A Geographical Account of Countries Round the Bay of Bengal 1669-1679*, Delhi: Asian Educational Services.

Vitebsky, Piers. 1993. *Dialogues with the Dead: The Discussion of Mortality Among the Sora of Eastern India*, Cambridge: Cambridge University Press.

Index